World Regional Geography

Places, Peoples, and Cultures

Bassim Hamadeh, CEO and Publisher
Seidy Cruz, Acquisitions Editor
Sean Adams, Project Editor
Miguel Macias, Senior Graphic Designer
Alisa Munoz, Licensing Associate
Natalie Piccotti, Director of Marketing
Kassie Graves, Vice President of Editorial
Jamie Giganti, Director of Academic Publishing

Cover image copyright © Depositphotos/Pixelchaos; © Depositphotos/sdecore; © 2017 iStockphoto LP/Timothy Messick.

Printed in the United States of America.

ISBN: 978-1-63189-995-9 (pbk) / 978-1-63189-996-6 (br)

World Regional Geography

Places, Peoples, and Cultures

First Edition

Kazimierz J. Zaniewski

University of Wisconsin-Oshkosh

Heike C. Alberts

University of Wisconsin-Oshkosh

John T. Bowen

Central Washington University

BRIEF CONTENTS

DETAILED CONTENTS

1

GEOGRAPHIC PERSPECTIVES ON PLACES, PEOPLES AND CULTURE

GEOGRAPHY: WHAT, WHERE, AND WHY

The word *geography* is derived from two Greek words (*geo* = the Earth and *graphen* = to describe) and means the description of the Earth. Geography studies the Earth as the human habitat and is interested in answering three basic questions: what, where, and why. It is an integrating discipline that does not have its own subject matter but incorporates the findings of other disciplines, especially natural and social sciences, and looks at them from a geographic (spatial) perspective. The question where is of great importance to geographers. When geographers study a certain topic, they first want to know where it is found on the Earth's surface and why it can be found there. However, defining geography as the study of locations would not be a fair description of its scope. Early geographers utilized a descriptive approach to the study of the Earth's surface; contemporary scholars put much more emphasis on the systematic study of regional variations around the world, interactions between different places, and the relationship between humans and the natural environment.

Sub-disciplines of Geography

Geography, like any other discipline, is subdivided into a number of fields. The most common division of geography today is into physical geography, human geography, and geographic techniques (Fig. 1.1). Physical geography is interested in studying the patterns and processes in the natural environment or its selected components (landforms, climate, plants and animals, water, soil, or mineral resources) and their importance to humans. Physical geographers studying landforms (geomorphologists), vegetation (biogeographers), or weather and climate (climatologists) also utilize findings of related disciplines, in this case geology, biology, and meteorology, in their research. Human geography focuses on the study of people and their activities, how they survive in particular environmental settings, and how they interact with people in other places. Population geographers study the patterns of population distribution and change (fertility, mortality, and migration) around the world or in selected regions; economic geographers focus their attention on the production and distribution of goods and services; and political geographers are interested in the political organization of space (types of governments, administrative divisions of countries, international organizations, electoral systems, or conflicts). These geographers are familiar with research in the related disciplines of demography, economics, and political science. It is important to mention that the division of geography into the physical and the human does not indicate sharp boundaries between the two groups. On the contrary; there is some overlap between them. Physical geographers are interested in the human impact on the environment (e.g. global warming, environmental degradation, deforestation), and human geographers consider environmental conditions when studying agricultural activities or population movements.

Geographers use a variety of techniques in studying both the physical environment and human activities around the globe. Some may rely on field methods for collecting data; others may use satellite images and aerial photographs in their research. Still others may download information from Internet sites. All of them use various qualitative and quantitative methods to process the collected information and present the findings in oral, verbal, and/or graphic form. Geographic Information Systems (GIS) have become powerful tools for processing and presenting such information. In many cases, maps are the final products of geographers' research.

Five Basic Themes in Geography

In studying the world, geographers may arrange their inquiry around five basic themes: location, place, movement, human-environment interaction, and region (Fig. 1.2). The concept of **location** provides the answer to the basic question of where something is located on the surface of the Earth. There are two ways of expressing the position of an object on the globe. **Absolute location** is most often described as the distance north or south from the Equator and east or west from the Prime Meridian (an arbitrarily chosen line connecting the North and South Poles and running through Greenwich in the United Kingdom). A geographer can draw conclusions about a certain place knowing its absolute location. For example, a city located at 70°N latitude and 90°E longitude would very likely have a cold climate, and it would be 6 PM there when it is noon

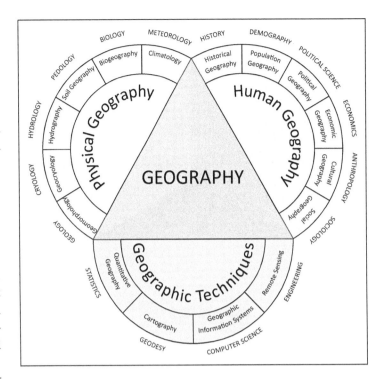

FIGURE 1.1 Sub-disciplines of geography—Geography is an integrating discipline that studies the physical and human features on the Earth's surface from a spatial perspective to provide answers to *where* and *why* questions. It utilizes a variety of techniques to analyze and present information.

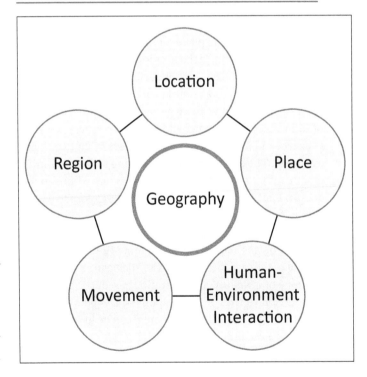

FIGURE 1.2 Five major themes in geography—First published 1984 in *Guidelines for Geographic Education: Elementary and Secondary* Schools by the Joint Committee on Geographic Education of the National Council for Geographic Education (NCGE) and the Association of American Geographers (AAG).

FIGURE 1.3 The city of Khorog in Tajikistan—This settlement of over 28,000 inhabitants, located in the Pamir Mountains, is an example of a place, one of five basic themes of geographic inquiry. What physical and human characteristics of Khorog do you see in this photo? *Source:* Pixabay.

in London. Most atlases have an index of many places and their absolute locations, and this information is very helpful in finding specific places on maps. **Relative location** (also called situation) is the location of an object (place) in relation to other objects on the surface of the Earth. Quite often, it is more important than absolute location since it can affect the area in many ways. For example, the city of Milwaukee is about 130 kilometers (80 miles) north of Chicago, and it is located along the western shore of Lake Michigan. The city has not been growing as fast as similar cities in other parts of the United States (e.g. Minneapolis and St. Paul in Minnesota or Denver in Colorado). One reason for this is Milwaukee's relative location; it is too close to Chicago and cannot successfully compete with its much bigger neighbor to the south. Milwaukee cannot expand to the east (because of Lake Michigan), so its potential zone of influence and attraction is reduced by half in comparison to that of Minneapolis or Denver. A city (or any other type of settlement or area) can be located in the center of a country or on its periphery; it can be well or poorly connected with the rest of the country by a network of highways or railroads; it can have a coastal location or be somewhere in the mountainous interior. Its relative location may make a big difference. While the absolute location of a place does not change, its relative location may change over time. For example, an important resource

(oil, gold, etc.) may be discovered in an area's vicinity or new highways may connect it with other places, and these developments would likely have significant impacts on the development of that area.

A **place** can be an area as small as a residential lot and as large as a country or continent (Fig. 1.3). Geographers describe places in terms of their physical (landforms, climate, vegetation, soil, etc.) and human (language, religion, agriculture, transportation, etc.) characteristics. The state of Wisconsin is an example of a place. One might describe it as a part of the Great Lakes region known for hilly terrain, a continental climate with warm summers and cold winters, dense forests, and numerous lakes in the northern part of the state. It has a population of over 5 million, mainly of European origin, that is English speaking and is concentrated in the southern half of the state. It is known for dairy farming, and it has a wide array of industries. The description could go on and on. Place features will change over time, especially in terms of its human characteristics. The Wisconsin of one hundred years ago is different from present-day Wisconsin, and it will undoubtedly be different a hundred years later.

By studying **human-environment interaction**, we learn how people make a living in different environments. Humans depend on the physical environment for meeting their basic needs (food, shelter, and clothing). They modify it by converting forests and grasslands to farmlands, building roads, railroads, and canals to connect distant places, or by opening up mines to extract mineral resources. Humans adapt to the surrounding environments by installing heating or cooling systems in their homes to feel comfortable in winter or summer months, by contour-plowing their land to reduce soil erosion, or by planting rows of trees to protect their crops from wind or other types of natural hazards. They can build dams to control flooding and irrigation or generate hydroelectricity. At the same time, humans impact the environment in many negative ways. For example, by burning **fossil fuels** to generate electricity, produce steel, drive cars, or heat residential structures, they generate greenhouse gases (e.g. carbon dioxide) which are responsible (at least partially) for global warming. Acid rain, which can damage natural ecosystems (forests and lakes) and some human-made structures, is another byproduct of our dependence on fossil fuels. The ozone layer depletion, which may expose people, animals, and crops to dangerous ultra-violet radiation, results mainly from production of chlorofluorocarbons (CFCs). The release of untreated sewage to rivers and ponds contaminates local water supplies and soils and endangers the health of many people.

Open-strip mining may lower local groundwater levels and adversely affect farming and may personally impact humans living in the surrounding areas. Large-scale deforestation, particularly of tropical rainforests, has numerous local (e.g. soil erosion and reduced biodiversity) and some global consequences (e.g. reduced absorption of carbon dioxide and limited generation of oxygen).

The movement of people, goods, and ideas between places is an example of spatial interaction. The uneven location of physical resources means that no place or country is self-sufficient in everything, so people must interact (trade) with each other to satisfy their needs. Transportation and communication networks and international trade provide evidence of spatial interaction. For example, a typical American breakfast consists of products from various parts of the United States and the world: bread made from wheat grown in Kansas; bacon from pigs raised in Iowa; eggs from Delaware; butter from Wisconsin; orange juice from Florida; and coffee from Colombia or tea from India. Different parts of the world are more connected with each other today than ever before. The quick global reaction to an event in one country or region (e.g. political instability

FIGURE 1.4 Major world culture realms.

in the Middle East and its impact on oil prices) is proof of that. Globalization, which will be discussed later in this chapter, provides another example of the growing global interdependence between places (countries).

Regions, areas characterized by certain shared characteristics, are basic units of geographical analysis. Geographers divide the world into a variety of regions to examine their physical and human features in greater detail. Regions, like places, can vary in size. They can be defined by a single feature (e.g. climate or religion) or several, often interrelated features (e.g. climate, landforms, agriculture, and technology level). Some regions may have clearly defined boundaries (e.g. countries as political regions); others may consist of core areas and zones of transition (e.g. the Corn Belt in the United States). Most natural regions (e.g. landform, climate, and soil) remain relatively stable over long periods of time; regions defined by human features, on the other hand, change their character and may expand or contract in size over time.

For the purpose of this textbook, the world has been divided into ten major regions known as world culture realms. A **world culture realm** is a large region characterized by organized rule, a coherent system of environmental use, and a similar culture. Some realms are large in area, others in population; some are characterized by high levels of development, others by low levels; some are more internally coherent than others. Each realm, consisting of a group of countries, is clearly defined by political boundaries and separated from the neighboring regions (Fig. 1.4). In reality, however, many regional differences, whether of a physical or human nature, do not always correlate with international boundaries. This division of the world into ten particular culture realms is by no means universally accepted. Some world regional geography textbooks may have slightly different groups of countries in each culture realm; others may have divided the world into a smaller or greater number of such realms.

Maps: Basic Tools in Geography (Reference and Thematic Maps)

Maps are basic tools in geography; most geographers use maps in their research and some (cartographers) make maps. **Maps** are graphic depictions of an area in which real-world features have been replaced by symbols in their correct spatial location at a reduced scale. They can be grouped into two major categories, reference and thematic maps (Fig. 1.5). **Reference maps**, like encyclopedias, dictionaries, or user manuals, are designed for many types of users and show the basic physical (e.g. landforms and hydrography) and human (e.g. transportation and settlement networks and political boundaries) features on the Earth's surface. Physical, political, road, and topographic maps belong in this category. **Thematic maps** display selected phenomena (themes or topics) and may be of greater interest to scholars and individuals curious to learn more about these topics. Maps showing types of climate, vegetation, soil, or other components of the natural environment are examples of thematic maps. Maps depicting farming practices, population change, or linguistic or religious diversity would also belong to this category. Thematic maps may be qualitative or quantitative. Qualitative maps show the distribution of various categories of physical (e.g. vegetation or climate types) or human (e.g. linguistic or religious groups) features. Quantitative maps show numerical information about phenomena (e.g. average annual precipitation in inches or millimeters or population size of countries or other territories in millions). There are several types of quantitative thematic maps (e.g. choropleth, proportional symbol, or dot density), each of which is appropriate for showing different types of numerical information. This textbook contains an extensive collection of thematic maps, and you will have a chance to study them while learning more about the different parts of the world.

PHYSICAL ENVIRONMENT

The physical environment surrounding us is essential to human survival. We cannot live without oxygen for more than a few minutes, without water for more than a few days, and without food for more than a few weeks. Each of seven major elements (landforms, climate, soil, plants, animals, water, and mineral resources) of the physical environment is utilized by people in various ways. Some outcomes of human-environment interaction have been positive, others (especially in recent times) negative.

There are four major types of landforms: plains, mountains, hills, and plateaus (Fig. 1.6). Plains have become the most densely populated areas in the world, especially if located in temperate regions. They offer many advantages to farmers and connect many places through dense transportation networks; however, their accessibility creates poor defensive qualities, and many have been sites of battles that changed the history of some countries or groups of people. Mountains, because of their rugged terrain, have

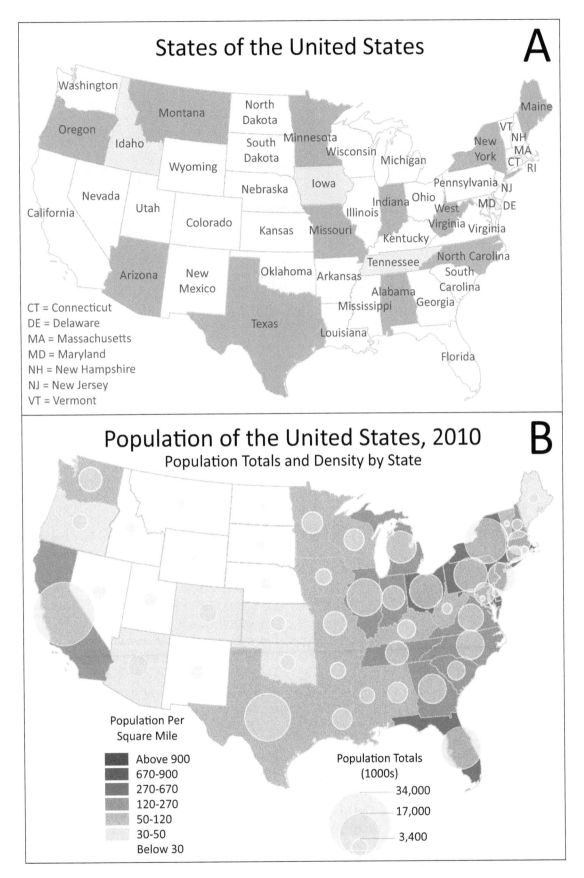

FIGURE 1.5 Types of maps: reference and thematic—Map A, showing the continental U.S. divided into states, is an example of a reference map. Map B is a quantitative thematic map showing the population in the U.S. at the state level. It is a combination of choropleth and proportional symbol maps. *Source:* U.S. Census Bureau.

FIGURE 1.6 Physical map of the world—Green areas are associated with low elevations (plains) and light brown colors show mountains and plateaus. Antarctica's and Greenland's glaciers are shown in white and light blue. *Source:* Natural Earth (www.naturalearthdata.com).

FIGURE 1.7 The Himalayas, Nepal—This prominent landform region has been an effective barrier to human interaction between East and South Asia and a home for various ethnic groups with distinctive cultures. *Source:* Pixabay.

been less attractive to humans, especially in colder regions (Fig. 1.7). Because of poor accessibility and isolation, they became refuge areas for minority groups and helped them preserve their folk culture. Most mountainous regions are associated with greater ethnic diversity than other types of landforms. Since rugged terrain can be an obstacle to farming, livestock herding is the dominant economic activity in these areas. Some mountains may also be major tourist destinations in summer (hiking) and winter (skiing). Mountains in tropical regions may also attract more people than neighboring coastal plains (elevation moderates climate), and some plantations crops (coffee and tea) do well at higher elevations. Hills in temperate regions are usually associated with lower population densities and livestock herding, and some may be densely forested. Many hills have been terraced and used for growing rice in parts of Asia, and they may also support coffee and tea cultivation in tropical regions. Plateaus (elevated plains), like hills, if located at lower latitudes, may be attractive to large-scale settlement and various types of farming activities (e.g. the *Altiplano* in Bolivia and Peru); very high plateaus or those found in cooler regions will be sparsely populated (e.g. the Plateau of Tibet in China).

Climate is the average weather condition over a long period of time (about 30 years), and is affected by latitude, land and water configuration, ocean currents, air pressure systems, and global wind patterns. Temperature and precipitation (shown in Fig. 1.8), precipitation seasonality, and native vegetation are the main determinants of climate types in the Köppen classification scheme, named after a German-Russian geographer. This most widely used typology identifies six major, and over two dozen minor, climate types around the globe; each major type is associated with a single letter (A through F) and minor types with a combination of two or three letters. The six major climate types are the following: tropical humid (A), dry (B), mid-latitude humid with mild winters (C), mid-latitude humid with cold winters (D), polar (E), and highland (F). They will be discussed in greater detail in subsequent chapters. Some climates have been attractive to humans; others have been associated with sparse populations and limited economic activities.

Most climatologists and other scientists strongly believe in and provide substantial evidence for the negative impact of human activities on global climate. They point to the thinning of the Arctic Sea ice, the melting of mountain glaciers, coral reef bleaching, increased precipitation, and more extreme weather patterns as proofs of global warming. Whether humans are responsible for it or not, the rising sea level may force many inhabitants of coastal plains (e.g. Bangladesh) to seek higher ground; several small island countries (the Maldives in the Indian Ocean or Kiribati in the Pacific Ocean) may completely disappear; and more violent storms and heavy rains may cause mudslides and enormous property damage in many urban areas.

The natural vegetation very closely reflects climate, soil, and landform types in most parts of the world. Forests, grasslands, and deserts are the dominant types of vegetation; each type is further divided into several categories. Forests occupy about one-third of the total land area, and they are found in two major zones. One is around the Equator (tropical evergreen forest), the other at mid and high latitudes in the northern hemisphere (deciduous and coniferous evergreen forests). Historically, many forests formed physical barriers to human settlement and restricted large-scale economic activities.[1] No major complex civilization, except perhaps the Mayan culture in Central America, originated in a forested area. On the other hand, forests (like mountains) provided refuge for minority groups and were used as grazing areas for some types of livestock (pigs) in the past. They have also been an important source of timber. Tropical forests provide high quality hardwoods (teak, mahogany, ebony, and rosewood), which are fairly resistant to rotting and cracking, sea water, and fire, and are used for making quality furniture and musical instruments; temperate forests provide timber used in construction and furniture making. Tropical forests are also the main producers of oxygen and the absorbents of carbon-dioxide, and their gradual shrinking (deforestation) is a major global concern.

Grasslands are found in semi-dry tropical (savanna), semi-dry temperate (prairie or steppe), and cold (tundra) regions. Many grassland areas have been major human migration routes (no tree barrier but limited water availability), zones of high mobility (nomadic way of life) and have provided a military advantage to their residents (e.g. the Mongolian Empire). Fertile soils of some grassland regions have attracted large-scale commercial grain (wheat) farming; other areas have become known for livestock herding (cattle and sheep).

Deserts are regions of very low and variable precipitation, high temperatures (at least in summer), low humidity, and scarce water and vegetation. Most deserts are found at mid-latitude locations and usually in the central and western parts of continents. They are usually sparsely populated, and pastoral nomadism (camels, sheep, and goats) has been the dominant activity among desert dwellers. Irrigated farming may be practiced in river valleys (e.g. the Nile River in Egypt) and such areas can be very densely populated. The dry and sunny climate is also considered very healthy, and settlements in some desert regions have been growing rapidly (e.g. Las Vegas in Nevada or Phoenix in Arizona) in recent decades.

Different types of soil are closely associated with specific climate and vegetation types. The most fertile soil is the black soil of temperate grasslands (Great Plains in the United States, Ukraine and southern Russia, and Argentina's Pampas region), volcanic soil of tropical regions (parts of Indonesia, the Philippines, and East Africa), alluvial soil (water-deposited silt) of river valleys (the Nile River and rivers in Southeast Asia), and loess soil (wind-deposited fine material susceptible to erosion) in some parts of Asia (north-central China), North America (the Great Plains), and South America (Argentina). Humans have been dependent on soil for growing food for thousands of years. Soil requires careful management to retain its fertility; farmers have practiced fallowing (allowing soil to rest between crops), crop rotation (each crop takes different nutrients and sometimes nutrients are added to the soil), contour plowing (slowing down erosion), and weeding to maintain soil quality. Irrigation, if not carefully managed, may lead to salt accumulation and serious soil degradation.

Water is the most crucial natural resource for humans and other living organisms. Freshwater comprises only 2.5 percent of all water in the world, and almost 80 percent of freshwater is in the form of ice (glaciers). It is

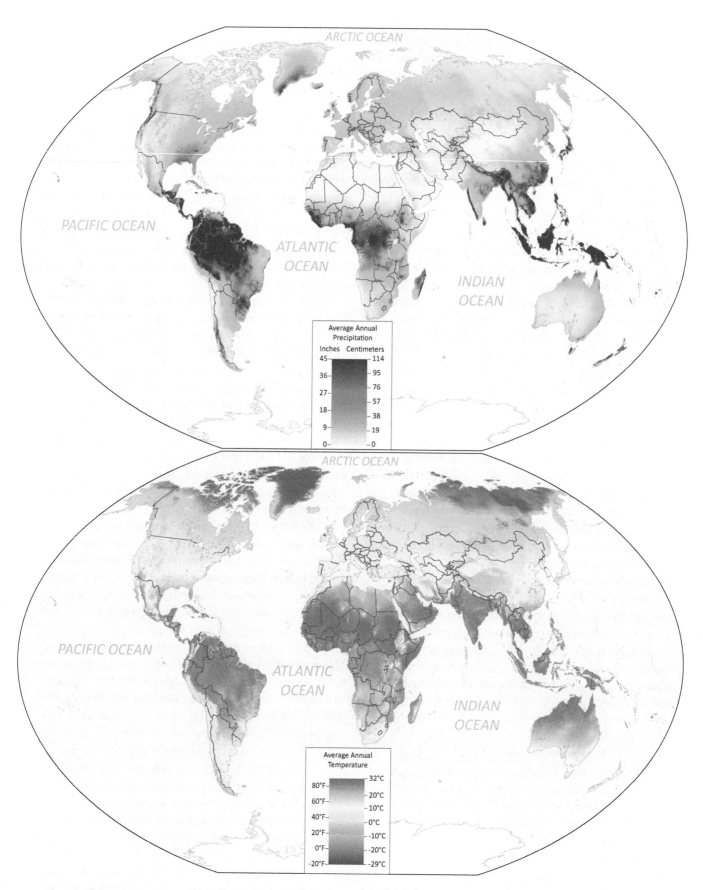

FIGURE 1.8 Global patterns of precipitation and temperature—Precipitation and temperature are the two major climatic variables. *Source:* WorldClim-Global Climate Data.

unevenly distributed around the globe, and there is a strong correlation between climate and water availability. Two-thirds of all freshwater used by humans is used for irrigation, which is very important in dry regions (e.g. the Middle East) and areas dependent on wet rice cultivation (e.g. Monsoon Asia). Water is also a major source of renewable energy, especially in humid and mountainous regions (e.g. Norway, Switzerland, and Japan). Rivers and canals were important transportation routes in the early-industrial era in Europe and North America, and the presence of lakes in some parts of Europe and other developed regions has led to the development of recreational tourism on a large scale.

Mineral resources, whether they are fossil fuels, metallic ores, or non-metallic ores, are essential for modern economies. Many regions rich in such resources attracted large numbers of migrants during the Industrial Revolution, and most of them remain densely populated and economically developed areas. Fossil fuels, especially oil, are critical energy sources for most developed countries, and they provide a lot of power to countries possessing large quantities of them (e.g. some Middle Eastern countries). Strategic minerals (e.g. uranium, chromium, and cobalt) are essential for the modern defense industry; countries rich in these commodities may also become major players in international affairs. Most Western countries maintained strong economic ties with the Republic of South Africa, widely criticized for its policy of racial segregation until the early 1990s, because of its control of large deposits of some strategic minerals.

WORLD POPULATION: PATTERNS AND TRENDS

Population geographers are interested in the size, distribution, composition, and change (including migration) of population around the globe or in smaller areas. The most common measure of population distribution is **arithmetic density**: the number of people per unit of land (square mile or kilometer). However, it can be a misleading measure of overcrowding (population pressure on the land), particularly for areas with unevenly distributed population (dry, cold, or mountainous regions). Many scholars consider **physiological density**, the number of people per unit of productive (agricultural) land, a more meaningful measure of human pressure on the land because it takes into consideration only areas that can produce food or support population. The physiological density is always higher than the arithmetic density for the same area; if it is only slightly higher, the area has a high proportion of productive land, and its population may be fairly evenly distributed; on the other hand, significant differences between arithmetic and physiological densities indicate a low proportion of productive land and an unevenly distributed population (e.g. dry or mountainous regions).

Population Distribution

The world is currently inhabited by about 7.6 billion people, and the population is very unevenly distributed around the globe. The majority live on a small land area (50 percent of the population occupies about 5 percent of the land area; some 50 to 60 percent of the land area contains only 5 percent of the world's population). Over 80 percent of the population lives in the Northern Hemisphere; population is concentrated on continental peripheries (some three-fourths of population live within 965 kilometers/ 600 miles of the coast and two-thirds within 483 kilometers/300 miles); and **population density** declines with altitude (about 56 percent of population occupies the areas up to 200 meters (650 feet) above the sea level, though these areas comprise only 28 percent of the total world land area).

Several factors influence population distribution, including the physical environment (climate, landforms, accessibility, water, and minerals), cultural characteristics (political organization, level of economic development, social customs and institutions, and duration of human settlement), and demographic factors (fertility, mortality, and migration). The significance of physical factors for human activities is quite often inversely related to the level of socioeconomic development of a particular area.

Major densely populated regions include East Asia, South Asia, and Europe (Fig. 1.9). East Asia has about 22 percent of the total world population; China alone has a population of 1.4 billion. Most people in this region are now urban residents. South Asia also has about 22 percent of the population, and India is the second largest country in the world (almost 1.3 billion). It is an agricultural cluster, that is, most of its population is rural and engaged in farming (rice cultivation). Europe is inhabited by 8 percent of the world's population, and it is an urban cluster (the majority of the population lives in cities, and the countryside is sparsely populated). Some of the smaller but very densely populated areas are the Nile Valley in Egypt, the coastal and some interior regions in West Africa, and the island of Java in Indonesia.

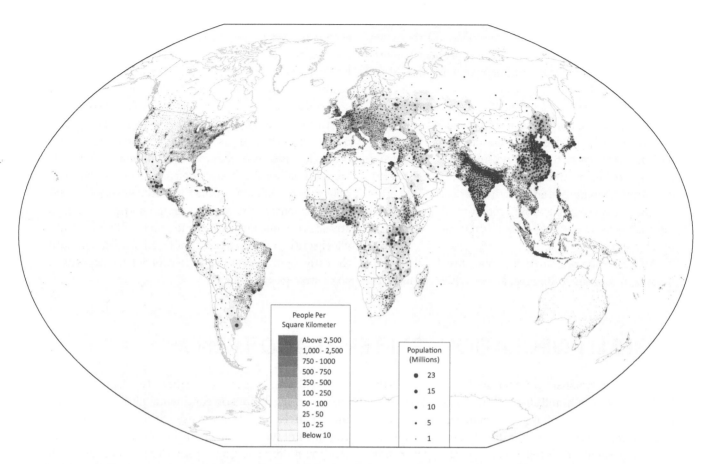

FIGURE 1.9 World population distribution, 2012—The map shows the arithmetic population density (people per square km) and population totals at the sub-country levels. Notice the two major population clusters in Asia and several types of sparsely populated areas. *Source:* websites of statistical agencies of individual countries.

Sparsely populated areas include cold (the Arctic and Antarctica), dry (the Sahara, Australia, and the Middle East), hot and humid regions (Central Africa and Amazon), and most mountainous or highly elevated areas (the Himalayas and Tibet, parts of the Rocky Mountains, and the Andes). The chief obstacle for large-scale settlement in cold regions is the very short growing season and poor soils; permanent settlement is limited to areas rich in minerals (mining) and the coastal regions and river valleys (fishing). Some population can also be found on military bases and scientific stations. Antarctica, the coldest continent, has no permanent population; Greenland, a cold island similar in area to India, has only 50,000 inhabitants. Northern Canada and Siberia, other cold regions, are also sparsely populated. The greatest obstacles to dense settlement in dry regions are the shortage of water and poor soils. However, if water is locally available, population densities may be high (e.g. the Nile Valley in Egypt). With the help of modern technology, prospects for settlement in some dry regions look promising, especially in developed countries (e.g. the southwestern part of the United States). Although humans are well adapted, from a biological point of view, to live

in hot and humid regions, these areas are rather sparsely populated; it is the excess of climatic energy (solar radiation, heat, and precipitation), poor soils, and dense natural vegetation that prevented the development of large-scale settlement in central Africa or the Amazon Basin in South America. However, like in the case of dry regions, there are exceptions to that rule (the island of Java in Indonesia). Although most mountainous regions are sparsely populated because of rugged terrain, poor soils, or cool climate, some mountains in tropical regions are associated with high population densities; since elevation moderates climate, high areas in the tropics attract people, especially if fertile volcanic soil is present (parts of the Andes, central Mexico, and parts of eastern Africa).

Population Composition

Age and sex are the two most important demographic determinants of population structure; they, in turn, influence fertility, mortality, and, to a lesser degree, migration rates. The sex ratio is the number of males

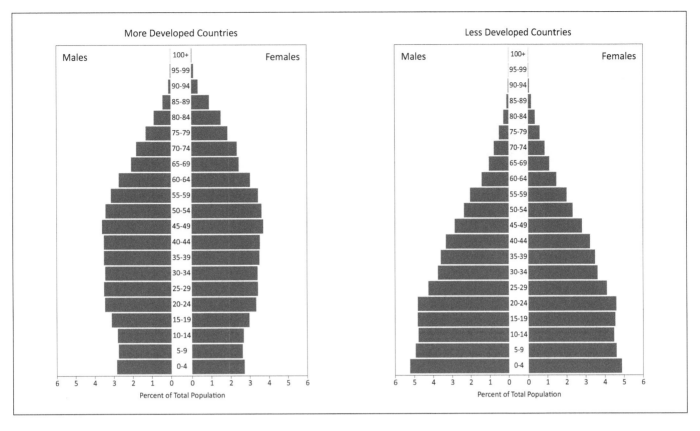

FIGURE 1.10 Population pyramids for more and less developed regions, 2010—These graphs are useful tools for studying the age and sex composition of a population. The shape of the pyramid can also reveal some information about population growth rates and the demographic history of the studied area. *Source:* United Nations. Population Division. World Population Prospects 2012.

per 100 females. For most societies, the sex ratio at birth is around 105 to 106. Because of higher male mortality, the sex ratio is closer to 100 for middle-aged people and below 100 for older populations. China and some Arab countries in the Middle East have some of the highest sex ratios in the world, while several countries that used to be part of the Soviet Union are characterized by the lowest sex ratios. The median age is the age that divides a population into two numerically equal groups with half the people younger and half older than this age. Some (mainly wealthy) countries are characterized by a high median age of their populations (35 years and more); while in some less developed countries the median age is less than 18 years. A high median age also indicates a large proportion of the elderly. In a few European countries and Japan this group comprises over 20 percent of the total population and presents a challenge to their governments in terms of health care provision and other age-related services. Different challenges exist in countries with a low median age where children may comprise up to 40 percent of the total population. The biggest challenge to governments of those countries is the provision of adequate

education and employment opportunities for this group of people.

A **population pyramid** is a graphic presentation of a population's age and sex structure (Fig. 1.10). The composition of the male population by age is shown on the left side of the graph, and the composition of the female population on the right side. Young-age cohorts are placed at the bottom, and old-age groups at the top of the graph. The shape of the pyramid can reveal some information about the demographic history of a specific population or of the entire country. Fast-growing populations (a high proportion of younger people and a low proportion of older people) are characterized by a pyramid-like shape of the graph with a wide bottom and narrow top. Demographically mature societies (a high proportion of the elderly and a low percentage of children) are associated with reversed pyramids that have narrow bottoms and wide tops (Fig. 1.11). Countries affected by wars or other calamities (periods of high mortality) are associated with pyramids of irregular shapes (one or more pinches and bulges). Population pyramids of selected countries will be discussed in subsequent chapters.

FIGURE 1.11 Elderly people in a park—As more countries become demographically mature, the growing number and proportion of the elderly and the shrinking size of economically active population cohorts may present serious challenges to many governments in the near future. *Source:* Pixabay.

Population Change and Demographic Transition

For the longest part of human history, world population size had virtually remained unchanged. Since around 1750, and particularly during the last fifty years, population has been growing rapidly, increasing from one billion around

1800 to 7.4 billion in recent years (Fig. 1.12 and Fig. 1.13). The **population growth rate** is the rate at which a population is increasing (or decreasing) in a given year expressed as a percentage of the total population at the beginning of the year. Population change has two components, natural increase and net migration. **Natural increase** is the difference between births (fertility) and deaths (mortality), and it can be positive (more births than deaths) or negative (more deaths than births). Fertility rates can be expressed in several ways, and the two most commonly used measures are crude birth rates and total fertility rates. The **crude birth rate** is the number of births per 1,000 population in one year. It has been popular among demographers and other social scientists because of good data availability. A more precise measure of fertility is the **total fertility rate**: the average number of children a woman has in her life. The **crude death rate**, the number of deaths per 1,000 population in one year, is the most commonly used measure of mortality. Negative natural increase does not always mean that a population will be declining. **Net migration**, the difference between in-migration (immigration) and out-migration (emigration), can also be positive or negative, and it is the combination of both components that explains population growth in some areas and decline in others.

The population has been growing at different rates throughout human history.[2] These rates reflect changing fertility and mortality levels which, in turn, reflect changing

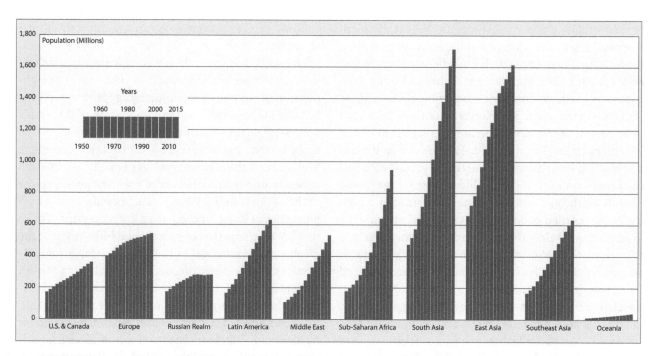

FIGURE 1.12 Population totals of major world regions, 1950–2015—Graphs show population totals at five-year intervals for the world culture realms discussed in this textbook. Notice the uneven growth rates among the major regions. *Source:* United Nations. Population Division. World Population Prospects 2012.

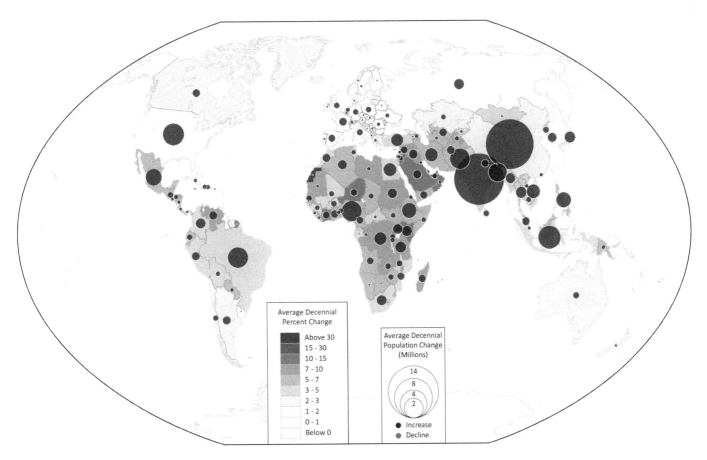

FIGURE 1.13 World population change, 1950–2010—Notice that India gained more people than China during the 60-year period, and the U.S. total population gain was similar to that of five other countries (Bangladesh, Brazil, Indonesia, Nigeria, and Pakistan). *Source:* United Nations. Population Division. World Population Prospects 2012.

levels of socioeconomic development. Scholars observed some time ago that as societies become more developed (less agricultural and more industrial), their fertility and mortality rates decline. This relationship between development and fertility/mortality became known as **demographic transition** theory (Fig. 1.14). According to this theory, most societies will go through several stages in their demographic development. Each stage will be associated with different fertility and mortality levels and, consequently, different rates of population growth. The high stationary stage, associated with pre-industrial societies, is characterized by high and fluctuating fertility and mortality rates and a low rate of population growth. Prior to industrialization, fertility was high because of the limited knowledge of birth control, religious beliefs, the demand for child labor (farming), and high levels of infant mortality. High mortality reflected poor medical knowledge, diet and hygiene, and frequent diseases and epidemics. Significant annual fluctuations in birth and death rates reflected changing agricultural productivity (dependent on weather conditions), political instability (wars), and outbreaks of

diseases and epidemics. As countries became more industrialized and urbanized, they entered the early expanding stage of the demographic transition when mortality rates started to decline in response to improvements in medical care, sanitation and water supplies, as well as the increased quantity and quality of food. Fertility rates declined a generation or so later and at a slower rate. Rapidly declining mortality and belated slower fertility decline resulted in an accelerating rate of population growth. The early expanding stage was associated with the European population explosion after the Industrial Revolution (around 1750) and the Third World population explosion after World War II. The late expanding stage was characterized by continued (albeit slower) mortality decline and accelerated fertility decline. Continued medical advances, the mechanization of production, urbanization, declining infant mortality, and reduced demand for child labor led to sharply declining fertility. The population continued to grow but at a slower rate.

Once a country reaches a high level of development or is in a post-industrial stage, both fertility and mortality levels will be low and the population will grow very slowly

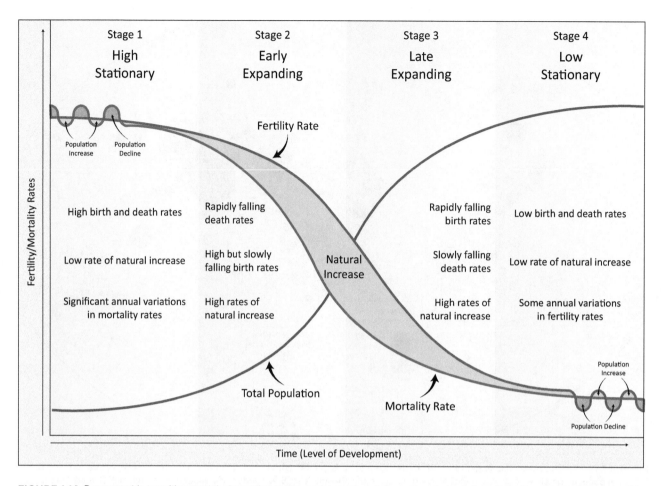

FIGURE 1.14 Demographic transition model—According to the model, most societies will go through four distinctive stages of demographic change, with each stage characterized by different fertility and mortality levels in response to changing levels of socioeconomic development. Notice periodic fluctuations in mortality and fertility rates in the first and fourth stage.

(if at all). Scholars point to the widespread access to contraception, a greater desire for material possessions than larger families, and women's emancipation (less pressure to have children) as major factors responsible for lower fertility in the low stationary stage of the demographic transition model. Some scholars identify a fifth stage in the demographic transition model associated with continued fertility and subsequent population decline, characteristic of many European and some Asian countries. The below-the-replacement fertility levels in these countries may reflect, among other things, the declining popularity of or postponement of marriage, rising divorce rates, and higher costs of having children. This stage is also called the second demographic transition.

Migration Patterns and Trends

Although humans have been on the move since the origin of our species, large-scale migrations of global proportions began after the European discovery and colonization of the Americas and other parts of the world.[3] During the past four centuries, millions of people relocated from one continent to another in several major migration waves. The largest of them was the European exodus to North America; it began in the early 17th century and ended before World War II, and it brought at least 45 million migrants from various parts of Europe to the United States and Canada. The European migration to Latin America began a century earlier, and it resulted in the relocation of some 20 million people, mainly from the southern parts of Europe. About 17 million Europeans moved to Australia, New Zealand, and parts of Africa and Asia during the past two centuries. The forced relocation of 10 to 12 million African slaves across the Atlantic between the 16th and mid-19th centuries had a tremendous demographic and economic impact on both regions. After the abolition of slavery, several million **indentured laborers** from South and East Asia relocated to Africa and the Americas. The Russian colonization of Siberia and the Far East contributed to the relocation of

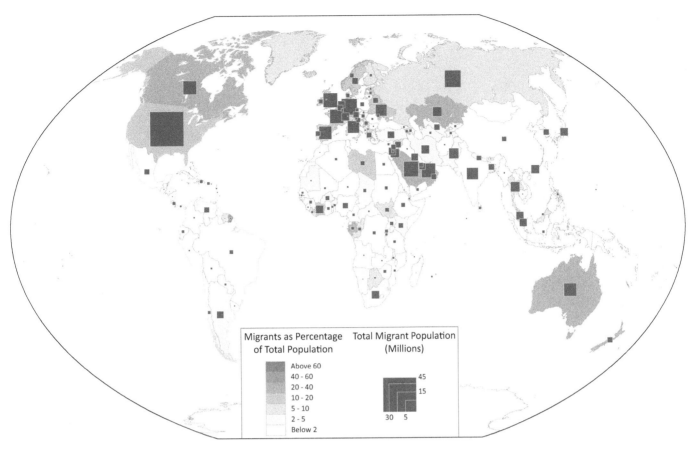

FIGURE 1.15 Distribution of migrants around the world, 2010—North America, Western Europe, and the oil rich countries around the Persian Gulf attract the largest numbers of migrants. The relatively large migrant populations in Russia, Ukraine, and Kazakhstan reflect population transfers after the collapse of the Soviet Union. *Source:* United Nations. Population Division. World Population Prospects 2012.

some 10 to 15 million people from the European to the Asian part of Russia. Finally, a migration of over 100 million people from the interior to coastal parts of China during the past forty years may be the largest mass migration in human history. All these migrations have left a permanent mark on the landscape and culture of the destination areas.

Most migrants have been moving for economic reasons through human history, mainly from less to more developed regions or from more developed to sparsely populated and less developed areas. There are four major migrant destinations in the world today (Fig. 1.15). The United States and Canada continue to attract millions of people, mainly from Latin America and Asia. Western Europe has become a destination for many Africans and Asians, and Australia and New Zealand for migrants from Asia. Finally, several oil-rich and sparsely populated Arab countries around the Persian Gulf have attracted millions of migrants from other Arab countries and, more recently, from parts of Asia. There is another category of migrants growing in importance: refugees. Political instability (mainly in Africa and the Middle East), natural hazards, and food shortages have displaced many individuals and families to other parts of their countries, where they are becoming internally displaced people, or to other countries, where they are considered refugees (Fig. 1.16 and Fig. 1.17).

Settlement Geography and Urbanization

When humans practiced hunting and gathering, they moved around in search of food and lived in caves or other types of temporary shelters. After the invention of farming, permanent settlements were established, usually near sources of water and fertile soils. When a surplus of food became available a few thousand years later, larger urban settlements appeared, first in the Middle East and later in other parts of the world. As time passed, and particularly after the Industrial Revolution of the 18th century, a network of cities developed, first in Europe and later in other parts of the globe. While only 3 percent of the world's population was urban around 1800, that number increased to 14 percent

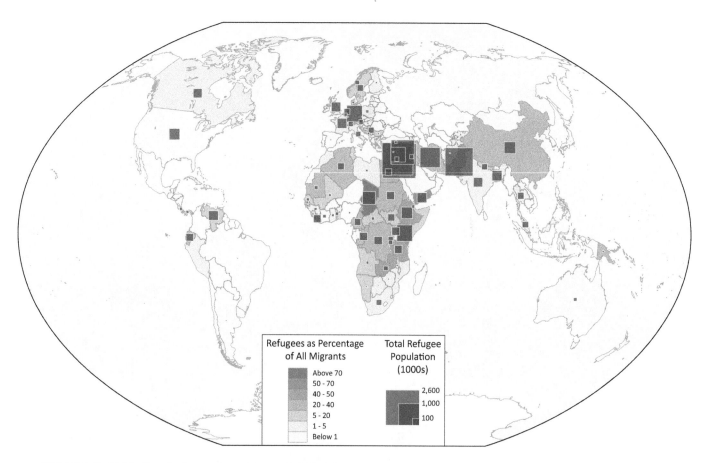

FIGURE 1.16 Distribution of refugees around the world, 2012—There is a strong correlation between political instability and the concentration of refugees. The conflicts in the Middle East and Afghanistan have generated the largest clusters of refugees. *Source:* United Nations High Commissioner for Refugees.

FIGURE 1.17 A refugee camp in Pakistan—Political instability in many parts of Africa and Asia has generated millions of refugees in recent years. Many of them became internally displaced people or fled to other countries and live in poor conditions in various types of temporary settlements. *Source:* Pixabay.

one hundred years later, and today over half of the world's population is urban (Fig. 1.18). Scholars estimate that urban residents will comprise two-thirds of the total population in 2050. Cities have been attracting rural people for a variety of reasons, including greater employment opportunities, cultural diversity, and anonymity. Large cities have been growing particularly fast. In 1950, there were only two mega-cities (cities with a metropolitan population of over 10 million): Tokyo and New York. Now, at least 28 cities can claim that status, and by 2030 there may be 41 cities of that size, over half of them in Asia. As Fig. 1.18 shows, urbanization levels vary from country to country and are usually associated with levels of economic development, but other factors may also play a role in determining what is considered urban or rural (e.g. settlement size). A large proportion of the urban population in many developing countries live in poor conditions, quite often without access to running water or even electricity, and they are exposed to various environmental (health) and social hazards.

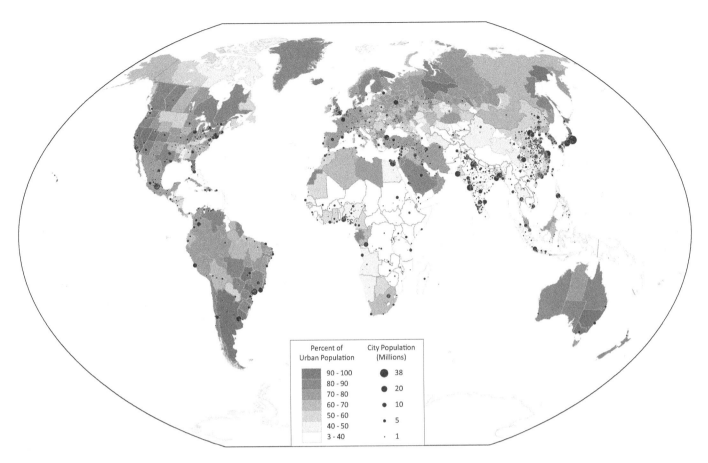

FIGURE 1.18 World urbanization patterns, 2012—Although there is a strong relationship between development and urbanization, some less developed and dry or cold areas have a high percentage of urban population. While East and South Asia have the largest number of cities over 1 million inhabitants, they are not highly urbanized regions. *Source:* United Nations. Population Division. World Urbanization Prospects 2014.

CULTURE AND CULTURAL CHANGE

Culture is a relatively broad concept, and there are many different definitions of this term. The Merriam-Webster Dictionary defines it as "the beliefs, customs, arts, etc. of a particular society, group, place or time." The Dictionary.com website states that **culture** is "the sum total of ways of living built up by a group of human beings and transmitted from one generation to another." For the purpose of this textbook, culture is a learned behavior that is shared by a group of people. It is simply their way of life. Culture is an acquired (not inherited), transmittable, adaptive, and cumulative trait. Some cultures are associated with large populations and are found in many parts of the world; others may be highly localized and practiced by very few people. Every culture changes over time, and cultural change occurs through four basic processes: discovery, invention, evolution and diffusion. Discovery is the act of finding something that is new to people, something that had existed in nature but was unknown to some groups of people before. The discovery of America by Columbus or oil in the Middle East has changed the world and people's lives forever. Invention is the process of creating new things that do not exist in nature but are products of human ingenuity. Transportation networks (roads and railroads), cities, farms, factories, and thousands of other things are examples of invention; modern life would be impossible without many of them. Evolution is the process of making minor or major changes (improvements) over time to things previously designed or produced. Examples of innovation would be making more efficient cars, developing more powerful computers, or amending a constitution. **Diffusion** is the spread of new things and ideas over space and time. The diffusion of farming practices from the Middle East and other centers of agricultural innovation to the rest of the world over a period of several thousand years is an example of cultural change. The spread of computer and cell phone technology during the last thirty years illustrates how much faster diffusion typically operates today.

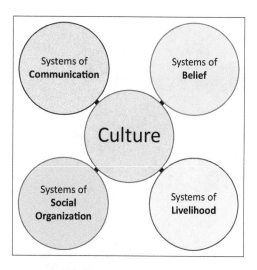

FIGURE 1.19 Culture and its components.

Components of Culture and Cultural Change

Every culture, no matter how complex or simple, has four major components: (1) systems of communication (language), (2) systems of beliefs (religion), (3) systems of social organization (institutions), and (4) systems of livelihood (skills and tools, material possessions, and economic activities) (Fig. 1.19 and Fig. 1.20). Communication is a process by which information is exchanged between individuals through a common system of symbols, signs, or behavior. Humans communicate with one another in a variety of ways. Originally, the spoken language was the main mode of communication; when writing systems were invented, they allowed people to accumulate large amounts of information and better preserve it for future generations. The printing press led to the widespread circulation and cheaper production of books and other printed material and the dissemination of knowledge and ideas among many social groups. Postal services could deliver letters from one continent to another in a matter of weeks. The invention of the telephone and telegraph allowed people located thousands of miles away from each other to stay in touch on a daily basis. Newspapers, radio, and television had an enormous impact on societies by providing them with news and other information from any part of the world in a timely fashion. The same communication media also became a major advertising tool for businesses and various organizations. The Internet and mobile phone technology have fundamentally changed the lives of many people in even the most remote areas of the globe.

FIGURE 1.20 Midsummer celebration in Sweden—This folk custom, celebrating the beginning of summer, is still very popular among Swedish people and is an example of the systems of social and political organization, one of the four components of culture. *Source:* Pixabay.

SYSTEMS OF COMMUNICATION (LANGUAGE)

Language is the main means of communication, no matter what technology is used. Quite often it is also a strong symbol of ethnic or national identity. It can unify or divide groups of people. Originally, early humans used a very small number of languages. As various groups migrated to different and more distant places and lost contact with one another, they added new words to their vocabularies, and eventually new languages emerged. This process continued for thousands of years and resulted in great linguistic diversity among humans. There are about 6,000 languages spoken in the world today, and they can be grouped into about one hundred linguistic families (Fig. 1.21). Most of these families are further divided into sub-families and branches. The Indo-European linguistic family has the largest number of speakers; about 45 percent of the world's population on several continents speaks one of over 400

languages belonging to this family (English is one of them). Some 450 languages of the Sino-Tibetan family (Chinese is a member of this family) are spoken by over 20 percent of the world's population, mainly in Eastern Asia. There is no strong correlation between the size of linguistic groups and their distribution. Although the Chinese and Hindi languages have over 900 and 300 million speakers respectively, they are localized languages, spoken mainly in China and India. On the other hand, English and Spanish are spoken and even serve as **official languages** in over sixty countries. The importance of language may change over time. Latin, the language of the Roman Empire, used to be the main means of communication in Europe for centuries; no one uses this language on a daily basis today. French later became popular among the upper classes in Europe. The technological (especially computer) revolution of the

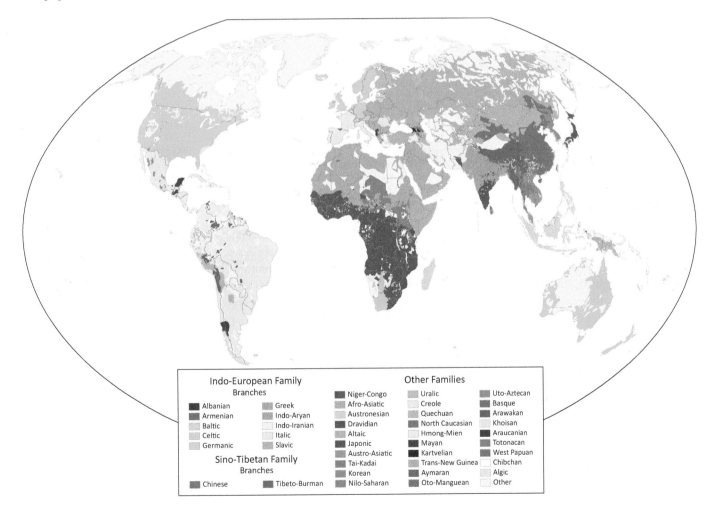

FIGURE 1.21 Distribution of major linguistic families around the world—Some 6000 languages spoken in the world today belong to about one hundred linguistic families. The Indo-European family is found on every continent; the Sino-Tibetan family mainly in East Asia. *Source:* World Language Mapping System.

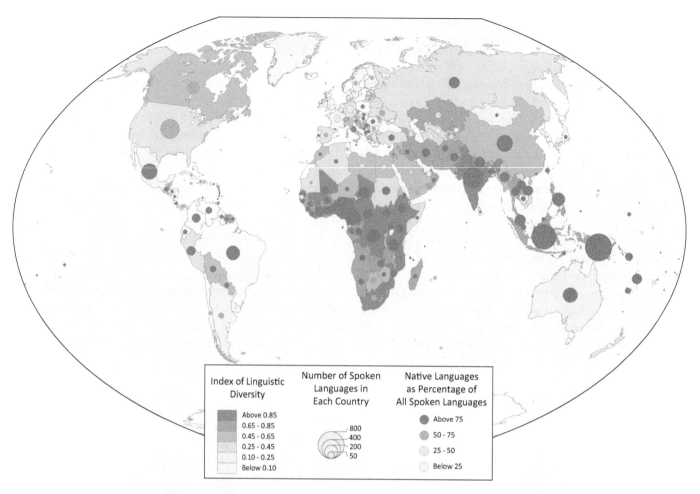

FIGURE 1.22 Linguistic diversity around the world—The index of linguistic diversity ranges from 0 to 1 and reflects the degree of linguistic diversity in each country. The greater the number, the greater the diversity. In extreme cases, 0 means that everybody speaks the same language, 1 means that every person speaks a different language (unrealistic). *Source:* Ethnologue-Languages of the World.

last fifty years, the spread of the British empire, American hegemony since World War II, and recent globalization made English the dominant language of the world today. The great linguistic diversity (shown in Fig. 1.22) is further magnified by the use of over twenty different writing systems. Most European languages (including English) use the Latin script; several languages in Eastern Europe and the Russian Realm are based on the Cyrillic script (invented by St. Cyril, a fifth century Greek missionary). Most languages in Asia and the Middle East are based on completely different scripts, and speakers of some languages (e.g. Arabic and Hebrew) write and read from right to left.

SYSTEMS OF BELIEF (RELIGION)

Religion can be defined as a set of beliefs and practices concerning the cause, nature, and purpose of the universe and our existence on Earth prevalent in a society or community. Like language, it can be an important symbol of ethnic or national identity. Religion can make a visible mark on the landscape and affect people's way of life. But unlike languages, which probably originated from one proto-language, major world religions originated independently in two parts of the world: Judaism, Christianity, and Islam, also called Western or Abrahamic religions, originated in the Middle East; Hinduism, Buddhism, and a few other Eastern religions were established in South Asia. These religions can also be divided into universalizing and ethnic religions. **Universalizing religions** (Buddhism, Christianity, and Islam) are considered applicable to all humans and seek converts, while **ethnic religions** (Judaism and

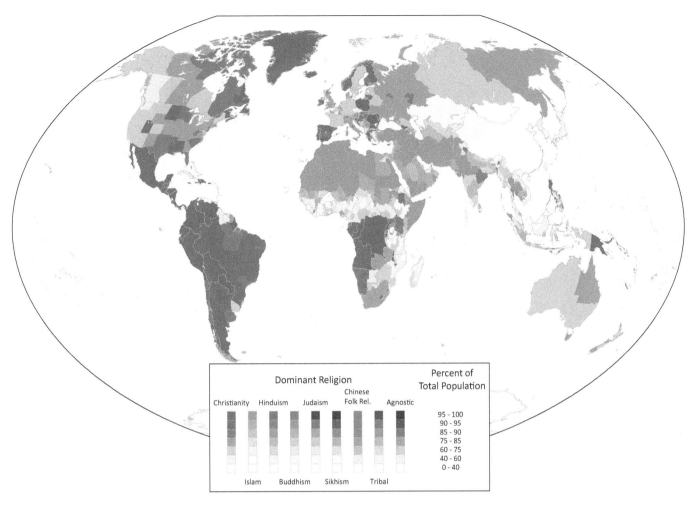

FIGURE 1.23 Distribution of major religions around the world—Christianity is the largest and most widespread religion while Islam is the fastest growing religion in the world. Hinduism and Buddhism are relatively localized religions. Notice the small proportion of the Chinese population adhering to any religion. *Source:* World Religion Database.

Hinduism) are associated with particular ethnic groups and generally do not spread their message outside the group. Most religions practiced today are monotheistic, (i.e., recognize only one god or deity). Hinduism, on the other hand, could be considered a polytheistic religion, but this is not a universally accepted classification. Some scholars do not consider Buddhism a religion since no divine being is worshiped.

About 86 percent of the world's population adheres to one of the major religions described above. Christianity, the world's largest faith, has over 2 billion adherents (33 percent of the total population), mainly in Europe, the Americas, and Sub-Saharan Africa (Fig. 1.23). Islam, the world's fastest growing religion, is dominant in the Middle East, Northern Africa, and parts of Asia and has over 1 billion followers (Fig. 1.24). Hinduism is found primarily in India, and the world's oldest living religion has over 900 million followers. Buddhism, an offshoot of Hinduism, is found in parts of East Asia and Southeast Asia where some

FIGURE 1.24 The Sheikh Zayed Mosque in Abu Dhabi, United Arab Emirates—It is the largest mosque, a Muslim house of worship, in the country. Religious structures are part of the systems of belief, one of the four components of culture. *Source:* Heike C. Alberts.

FIGURE 1.25 A Hindu procession in Kerala, India—Hinduism, a polytheistic and ethnic religion, is known for various ceremonies honoring numerous deities. *Source:* Wikimedia Commons.

400 million are considered followers of its founder Buddha (Fig. 1.25). Judaism, numerically the smallest of the major religions, is the official religion in Israel and has about 4 million followers in Israel, the United States, and Europe.

Linguistic and/or religious diversity has been responsible for political instability and violent conflicts in many parts of the world. Canada, Belgium, and Spain are good examples of countries divided by language, while people in Northern Ireland, Iraq, and Lebanon suffered because of religious differences. These and other case studies are discussed in subsequent chapters.

SYSTEMS OF SOCIAL ORGANIZATION (INSTITUTIONS)

Systems of social organization or institutions are of particular interest to geographers. The entire world, except Antarctica, is divided into 195 countries. A country or **state**, the basic unit of analysis in political geography, is an area that has a permanent population and an established government exercising full control over that area and its population, and it has sovereignty in international relations. The number of states has been steadily increasing since World War II. Countries are quite often classified as federal or unitary, republics or monarchies, and nation-states or multinational states (Fig. 1.26 and Fig. 1.27). In a **federal state**, there is a division of power between the central and local government. The United States is a good example of a federal country; each of fifty states has a constitution and can introduce laws (e.g. highway speed limit and income and gasoline tax) that are different from those introduced by the federal government in Washington, D.C. In a **unitary state**, the central government has much more power, and that power is usually uniformly imposed on local governments. France is a good example of a

FIGURE 1.26 Typology of countries by nature of government and internal organization—Most countries are classified as unitary states, although a few are unitary regionalized where the central government may grant (or take away) some powers to (from) sub-national areas. Relatively few countries are monarchies today, and even fewer have monarchs with absolute power. *Source:* CIA World Factbook.

unitary state. In some unitary states (unitary regional), a certain portion of central authority can be transferred to sub-national units (e.g. China and the United Kingdom). Countries can also be divided into republics and monarchies. In a republic, the leadership (president, prime minister, etc.) is either elected or appointed; some leaders may come to and stay in power by force. The United States is a republic, and its leader (president) is elected every four years. In a monarchy, the leadership is inherited and the monarch (e.g. king, queen, or sultan) usually stays in power until his or her death or abdication. The United Kingdom is probably the best known monarchy in the world today. Today, most countries with inherited leadership are constitutional monarchies where the monarch is just a figurehead with little executive power. A few countries (e.g. Saudi Arabia and Oman) are absolute monarchies; their rulers have much more legislative, judicial, and executive power. Finally, countries can be nation-states or multi-national states. A nation-state is a country with one dominant ethnic group (nation) that is united by religion, language, or historical experience. Poland or Iceland are good examples of such countries. A multi-national state has at least two dominant ethnic groups and quite often two or more official languages. India and Canada belong to this group.

FIGURE 1.27 The National Congress building in Brasilia, Brazil—The city became the national capital in 1960, and the relocation of government agencies from Rio de Janeiro to this interior city was supposed to lead to a more regionally balanced development of the country. Brazil, one of the largest countries in the world in terms of area and population, is a republic and a federal state. *Source:* Pixabay.

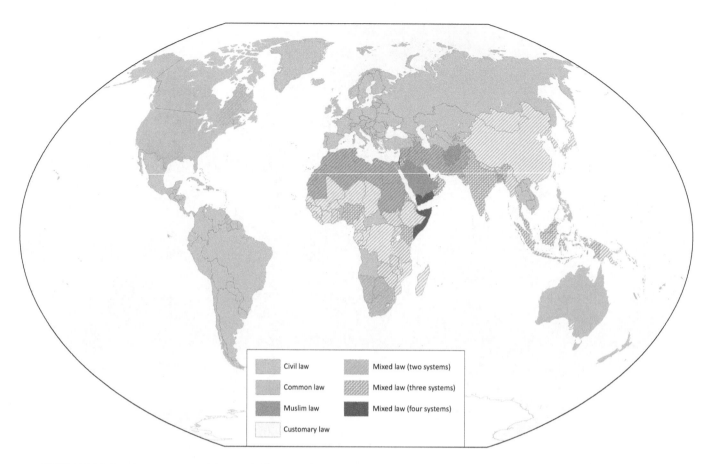

FIGURE 1.28 Legal systems around the world—The legal systems in most countries in Europe, the Russian Realm, and Latin America are based on civil law while the United Kingdom and most of its former colonies use common law. Mixed legal systems are dominant in Africa and Asia. Notice that the legal systems in Louisiana and Quebec have a mixture of common and civil laws. *Source:* JuriGlobe-World Legal Systems Research Group.

The general rule is that most countries with large populations and/or land will be federal and multinational, while small countries will be unitary and nation-states. However, there are many exceptions to this rule. For example, Switzerland, a small country in Europe, is a federal and multi-national state, while Japan, the tenth largest country (by population) in the world, is unitary and a nation-state.

There are five major types of legal systems around the world today (Fig. 1.28). Civil law, derived mainly from Roman and French law, gives precedence to written statutes

Features	Common Law	Civil Law
Origins	English common law (11th century)	Napoleonic Code (19th century)
Territorial extent	Most of the English speaking world	Majority of the non-English speaking world
Sources of law	Statues, precedents, administrative rules	Legislative statues
Presumption	Innocence (innocent until proven guilty)	Guilt (guilty until proven innocent)
Trial format	Adversarial (lawyers question witnesses, demand evidence and present arguments based on evidence collected by them)	Inquisitorial (judges question witnesses and demand evidence; lawyers present arguments based on evidence found by court)
Trial emphasis on	Procedural correctness	Factual certainty
Evidentiary rules	Formal and restrictive (exclusionary rule)	None (all evidence considered)
Role of lawyers in trial	Primary (debate and oppose)	Secondary (advise and inform)
Role of judges in trial	Referee (umpire)	Director (examiner)

FIGURE 1.29 Major characteristics of common and civil law—*Source:* JuriGlobe-World Legal Systems Research Group.

introduced by country legislatures and is the most widespread legal system in the world. Common law, based on decisions made by judges which may reflect the customs, culture, habits, or previous judicial decisions, is the law in the United States, the United Kingdom, and most former British colonies (Fig. 1.29). Customary law, based on local customs, traditions, and conduct, is no longer the dominant system in any country. Religious law used to be very common in the past; today it is the dominant legal system mainly in a few Muslim countries in the Middle East (e.g. Saudi Arabia and Iran). Finally, mixed law incorporates two or more legal systems and is most common in Africa and Asia.[4]

Some countries play a more active role in international relations because they have more economic power or political influence. Political geographers identify eight elements of national power; one or more of these elements determines the world or regional importance of each country (Fig. 1.30). In theory, a large country in area should be

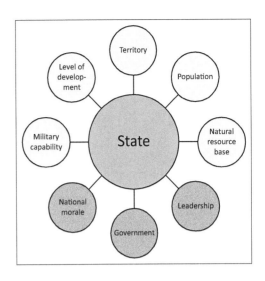

FIGURE 1.30 Elements of national power—The upper five elements are sometimes called tangible while the lower three are intangible elements of power.

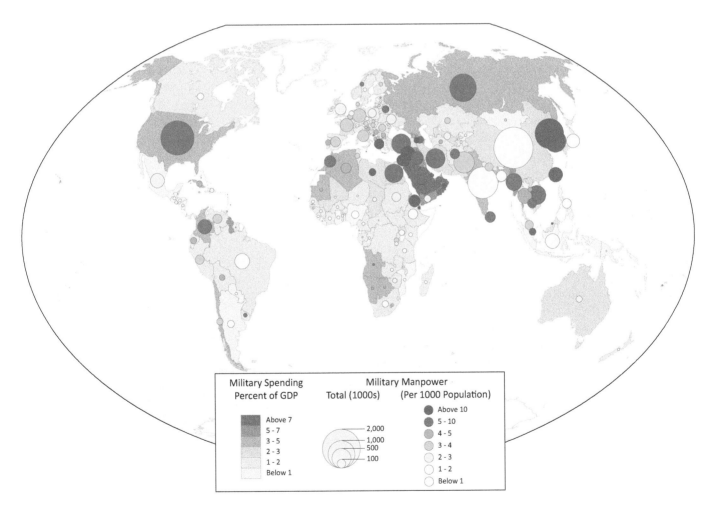

FIGURE 1.31 Military spending and manpower, 2010–2014—Military capability is a major element of national power. Notice the heavy militarization of the Middle East, especially the high proportion of GDP spent for military purposes in oil-rich countries on the Arabian Peninsula. Compare the military power of Pakistan and Bangladesh as well as North and South Korea. *Source:* Encyclopedia Britannica Book of the Year 2014.

FIGURE 1.32 The United Nations building in New York City—Established in 1945, it is the largest and best known organization in the world, and its objectives include promoting international cooperation and peaceful coexistence among all countries. It is an example of the systems of social and political organization as a major component of culture. *Source:* Pixabay.

larger the number of neighbors, and the greater the likelihood of a conflict with one of them. Different elements have contributed to the national power of various countries. Several elements have contributed to the global importance of the United States (e.g. territory, level of economic development, natural resource base, population, and military power), and it may be hard to determine which one has been the most important. In the case of China, the population size is likely the most important factor, although the level of development is becoming an increasingly important element as well. The former Soviet Union could credit its global superpower status mainly to its great military power (Fig. 1.31).

Country governments or other entities may form international organizations designed to deal with global or regional issues (e.g. trade, economic development, conflict, and global warming) or to promote cooperation among, or integration of, various countries. There are two major types of such organizations: intergovernmental and nongovernmental. The **United Nations** is the best known example of the first type at the global scale, while the International Committee of the Red Cross and Doctors Without Borders (Médecins Sans Frontières) are examples of the second (Fig. 1.32). There are also well known intergovernmental regional organizations such as the **European Union (EU)**, African Union, **North Atlantic Treaty Organization (NATO)**, and **North American Free Trade Agreement (NAFTA)**.

stronger than a small country. A large area may mean a greater quantity and variety of mineral resources as well as greater climatic diversity, allowing that country to produce a wider range of agricultural commodities. On the other hand, this can also be a liability; for example, the larger the area of a country, the longer its political boundary line, the

SYSTEMS OF LIVELIHOOD (ECONOMIC ACTIVITIES)

People's systems of livelihood vary from place to place and reflect many factors, including the natural environment, religious beliefs, political systems, and levels of economic development (Fig. 1.33 and Fig. 1.34). Economic activity is the most important element of this component of culture, and it is usually divided into three major categories. **Primary activities** involve the extraction of resources from the natural environment and include farming, fishing, hunting, forestry, and mining. The proportion of the population making a living from these types of activities has been decreasing over time, and today in some countries less than 1 percent of the labor force in engaged in this economic sector. **Secondary activities** focus on the processing of raw materials into finished products and include manufacturing and construction. The Industrial Revolution of the 18th century contributed to a steady increase in the importance of manufacturing in national economies, first in Europe and later in other parts of the world. Tertiary activities

FIGURE 1.33 A house on Lake Titicaca in Peru—This structure made of reeds and located on islands of living reeds represents an ancient and unique system of livelihood practiced by the Uros people who support themselves by fishing and selling reed handicrafts to tourists. *Source:* Heike C. Alberts.

FIGURE 1.34 Work on a rice farm in Myanmar—Rice cultivation supports more people than any other farming activity in the world, and most of the work is still done with traditional tools. It is the dominant system of livelihood in many parts of Asia. *Source:* Larissa Krüger.

are associated with the distribution of goods and services, and their importance has been quickly increasing in most parts of the world in recent decades. Trade, transportation, health care, and education belong to this group of activities (Fig. 1.35). An outcome of the growing importance of the **tertiary sector** was the emergence of a quaternary sector, which includes activities related to information-based services (news media, telecommunications and Internet, financial and legal services), and the importance of this sector is expected to increase as well.

People engage in various types of economic activities for two main reasons: to support themselves and their families or to make a profit. The first type is known as **subsistence economy** (Fig. 1.36). For most of human history, the great majority of the population practiced these types of activities, particularly subsistence farming. As indicated above, their most distinctive characteristic is the production of goods and services, particularly food, to meet

FIGURE 1.35 The Bremerhaven port facilities, Germany—Water transportation, an example of tertiary economic activities, has played an important role in global trade since the Industrial Revolution of the 18th century. *Source:* Heike C. Alberts.

Commercial	Subsistence
Purchase of goods and services	Exchange of goods and services
Production for market (profit)	Production for family needs
Division of labor based on skills (training)	Division of labor based on age/gender
Individual's occupation learned	Individual's occupation inherited
Large and mechanized production units	Small and unmechanized production units
High productivity	Low productivity

FIGURE 1.36 Major features of commercial and subsistence economies.

the needs of the immediate family. A typical production unit (farm, workshop, fishing boat, etc.) is very small and traditional tools are used in the production process. The division of labor is usually based on gender and age, and the individual's occupation is inherited (sons learn from their fathers and daughters from their mothers). In a pure subsistence economy, which is hard to find today except in some isolated and remote, sparsely populated areas, workers exchange some of their goods and services with others rather than buy them on the market. In a **commercial economy**, people produce various goods and services for the market, not their immediate family needs. Typical production units are large, highly mechanized, and fairly productive. Individuals involved in this type of activity acquire their skills through learning and training, and sons and daughters may have quite different occupations than their parents.

Finally, there are two major economic systems, free market economies and centrally planned economies (Fig. 1.37). A **free market economy**, the dominant economic system in the world today, is based on the private ownership of the means of production, a profit motivation behind most activities, and a supply-demand relationship in determining the price of goods and services. This system, at least in theory, provides numerous opportunities for individuals to succeed by establishing and running profitable enterprises (small or large) and quickly responding to consumers' needs. At the same time, stiff competition among similar businesses may lead to failures and even bankruptcies. Similarly, a free market economy can also lead to great disparities in income and wealth and temporal and structural employment fluctuations. A **centrally planned economy** was mainly found in the formerly Communist countries, although it is still the dominant economic system in a few

Characteristics	Free Market	Centrally Planned
Ownership of means of production Motivation for economic activity Price system Role of government Decision-making system	Private Profit Supply-demand relationship Limited Consumer-business interaction	State or collective People's needs Artificial and state controlled Very significant State-controlled and hierarchical
Advantages	Quick response to people's wants/needs Opportunity for innovation and efficiency (competition) Little or no red tape Opportunities for individual advancement	Can lead to more equal distribution of wealth and income Production for needs (not profit) Long-term planning (sustainable development) Greater employment opportunities
Disadvantages	Can lead to mis-allocation of resources and overproduction Can encourage consumption of harmful products Can lead to income/wealth inequality Can lead to employment fluctuations Not competent in providing some services	A lot of red tape (bureaucracy) Little motivation for hard work and innovation Delayed response to people's needs (shortage of consumer goods) Underproduction or overproduction

FIGURE 1.37 Major features of free market and centrally planned economies.

countries in Asia and Cuba. In this system, almost all the means of production are collectively or government (state) controlled, and the main purpose of economic activity is the fulfillment of people's needs (again, at least in theory). The price of goods and services quite often reflects decisions of government officials rather than the supply-demand relationship. Some goods that are considered luxuries may be very expensive, while others, considered daily necessities, may be very cheap (their price may even be below production costs). Individual production units (factories and farms) have very little (if any) freedom in determining what and how much is produced; they must meet production quotas determined by the central government. There is very little incentive for innovation or hard work since there is a policy of full employment, and consumer needs may be secondary in this system. While the free-market economy may lead to overproduction (and therefore to economic recessions) or encourage consumption of harmful products (e.g. sugary beverages), the planned economy has been associated with perennial shortages of consumer goods and services.

Some parts of the world are more economically developed than others, and the disparities between them have not decreased much over the past several decades. The most common measure of economic development is the **gross domestic product** (GDP) per capita (Fig. 1.38). The GDP is the total value of goods and services produced in a country (area) in a year. A similar measure, gross national income (GDP plus the value of foreign transactions) per capita, has also been popular in comparing countries' levels of development. However, both measures may be misleading in international comparisons since they do not reflect the differing costs of living around the world. Twenty dollars in India or Bangladesh have a greater purchasing power than the same amount in the United States or Switzerland. Hence, the GDP and GNI per capita expressed in terms of **purchasing power parity** (PPP) have been widely used in comparing countries' levels of economic development. There has been a lot of discussion whether GDP and GNI are the best indicators of development, particularly when it comes to measuring standards of living. Scholars proposed a variety of other indicators such as energy (electricity)

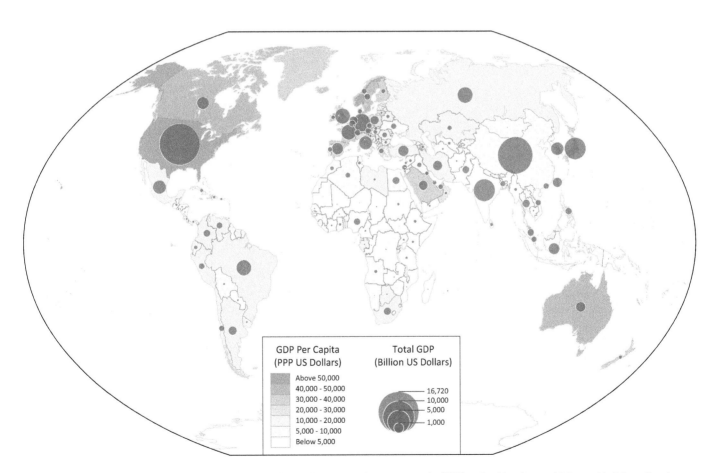

FIGURE 1.38 Gross domestic product by country, 2014—The purchasing power parity (PPP) method has been widely used in international comparisons of income levels. Notice that China has the second largest economy in the world, and the economies of Japan, Germany and India are similar in size. *Source:* CIA World Factbook.

Category	Characteristics	Developed Regions	Developing Regions
Demographic	Fertility levels Mortality levels Age structure of population Population growth rates Dominant family type	Low Relatively low High proportion of the elderly Low Nuclear	High Relatively high High proportion of children Moderate to high Extended
Economic	Income per capita Dominant economic system Dominant economic sector Globalization levels	High Commercial Tertiary and secondary High	Low (some exceptions) Subsistence Primary and secondary Low
Social	Literacy rates Health care access Major causes of death Cultural diversity	High Good Chronic diseases Low	Low Poor Infectious diseases High
Political	Dominant political system Human rights Political stability	Democracy Freedom of expression High	Dictatorship Control of expression Low

FIGURE 1.39 Major differences between more and less developed regions.

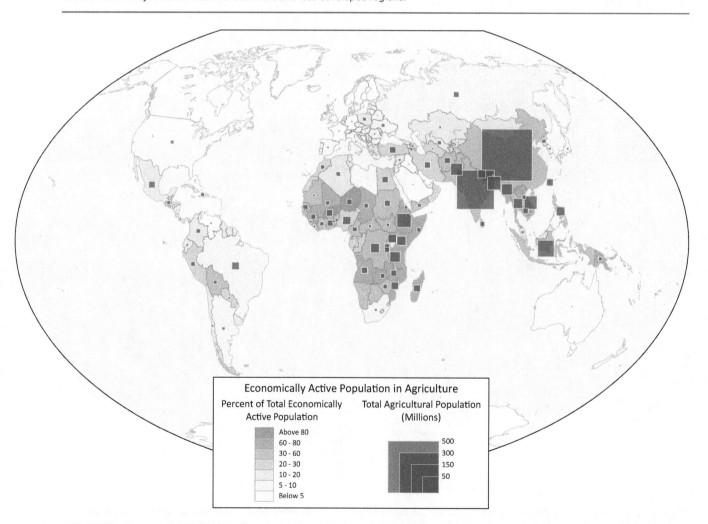

FIGURE 1.40 Economically active population in agriculture, 2014—Most people in less developed regions engage in agriculture or other primary activities. Sub-Saharan Africa and most of Asia have the highest percentages of agricultural population. Notice the small size of the agricultural population in the United States as opposed to that of China. *Source:* FAOSTAT.

consumption per capita, the infant mortality rate, the possession of selected consumer goods (e.g. cars and TVs), or even "gross national happiness" to show regional disparities in development around the world. Although none of them is a perfect measure, there is a fairly strong correlation between most of these indices and GDP or GNI per capita.

No matter what indicator is used to show differences in levels of development or standards of living on a map, similar patterns are seen around the world. Most countries in Europe, the United States, Canada, Japan, Australia, and New Zealand are at one end of the spectrum, while most of Sub-Saharan Africa, parts of Asia, and Latin America are at the opposite end. Although the world is often divided into developed (rich) and developing (poor) countries, it is important to mention that there is no clear separation of the countries into these two groups on the basis of any indicator. They form a continuum along the entire spectrum. Nevertheless, there are some important economic, demographic, social, and even political differences between the two groups of countries (Fig. 1.39). Most developed

countries have a high income per capita (over 40,000 dollars), and a very high proportion of their labor force is employed in the tertiary or service sector (Fig. 1.40). A typical production unit, whether a farm or a factory, is relatively large, highly mechanized, and characterized by high productivity. A commercial economy with strong global connections is the dominant system of production. A typical developed country has low fertility and low population growth rates, moderate levels of mortality (caused mainly by chronic (degenerative) diseases), low infant mortality rates, and a relatively high proportion of the elderly (as indicated earlier, in some countries this group comprises almost 20 percent of the total population) (Fig. 1.41). The nuclear family (parents and children) is the dominant type of household. Most people have access to medical care, education of children is compulsory, and adult literacy rates are high (Fig. 1.42). Because of almost universal access to some forms of information technology (newspapers, TV, radio) and well developed transportation and communication networks, the levels of cultural diversity within rich countries are relatively small as popular culture has

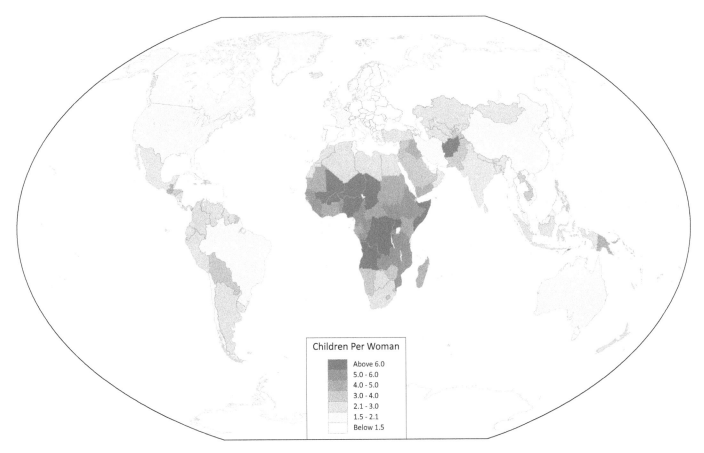

FIGURE 1.41 Total fertility rates, 2012—The total fertility rate is the average number of children a woman has in her life and is considered the best measure of fertility. Notice the difference between Sub-Saharan Africa and parts of Europe and the Russian Realm. *Source:* United Nations. Population Division. World Population Prospects 2012.

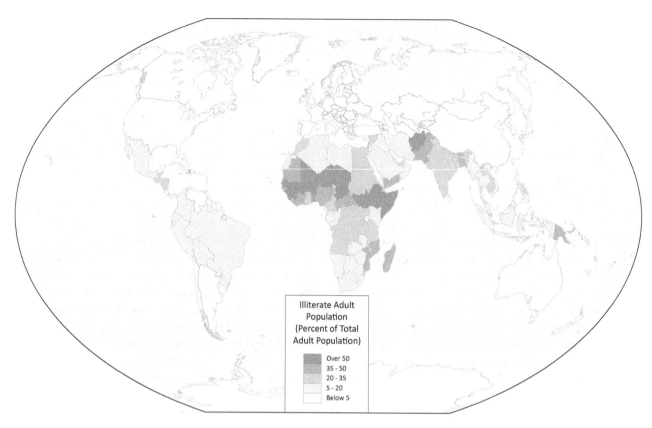

FIGURE 1.42 Illiteracy rates around the world, 2010–2014—Adult (il)literacy is a major social indicator of development. Notice the relatively high illiteracy rates in the Sahel region of Sub-Saharan Africa and parts of South Asia. *Source:* UNESCO.

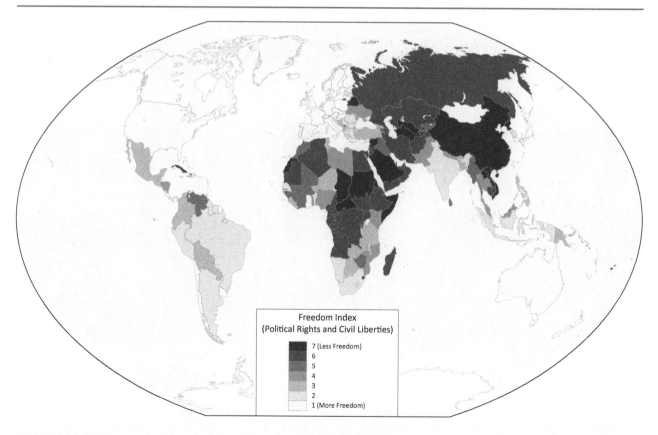

FIGURE 1.43 Freedom around the world, 2014—The freedom index is a comprehensive measure of civil liberties and political rights. Political rights include three components: electoral process, political pluralism and participation, and functioning of government. Civil liberties include four elements: freedom of expression and belief, association and organization rights, rule of law, and personal autonomy and individual rights. *Source:* Freedom House.

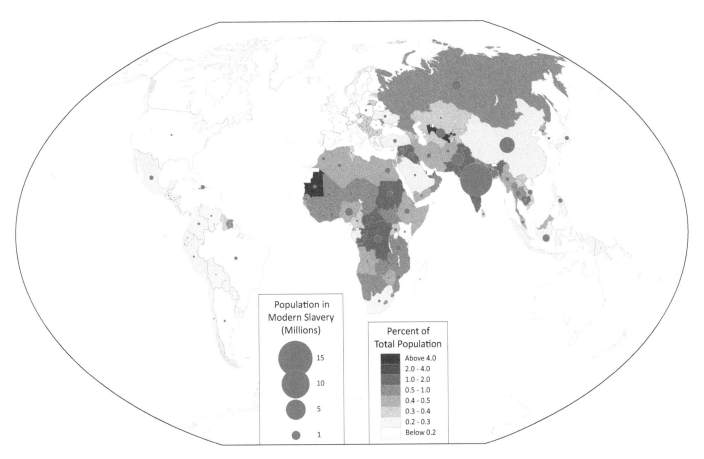

FIGURE 1.44 Modern slavery, 2014—The issue of human rights is a growing concern around the world. According to the Walk Free Foundation, a non-governmental organization dedicated to ending modern-day slavery, over 35 million people live in slavery-like conditions in the world today. *Source:* Global Slavery Index.

been expanding at the expense of ethnic culture. A typical, more developed country has a democratically elected government and a high level of political stability, and it protects the human rights of its citizens (Fig. 1.43 and Fig. 1.44). The concept of human rights may also vary across space and time. In many Western countries political rights (freedom of speech) are considered more important than social rights (right to basic needs: food, shelter, health care, and education). In the former Communist states, on the other hand, these priorities were reversed. The opposite characteristics, of course, would be associated with most developing countries, (i.e., low income per capita, a high proportion of their labor force in primary activities, high fertility and population growth rates, etc.).

GLOBALIZATION AND LOCALIZATION

If there were no physical and cultural differences from place to place, there would be no need for the discipline of geography. However, geographers can be assured that this will not happen. There will always be regional variations in environmental conditions. The great cultural diversity around the globe may be slightly reduced through the process of globalization, but there is no certainty about that either. **Globalization** is the increasing interaction and integration among people, businesses, and national governments through international trade and investment facilitated by information technology (Fig. 1.45). It has impacted the natural environment and culture in many ways. Some scholars see the origins of modern economic globalization at the Bretton Wood Conference (1944) and the establishment of the International Monetary Fund and the World Bank, as well as the General Agreement on Tariffs and Trade (1947) and its successor, the World Trade Organization (1995).[5] The internationalization of trade and finance through various neoliberal measures, the growing power of multi-national corporations, and the recent global

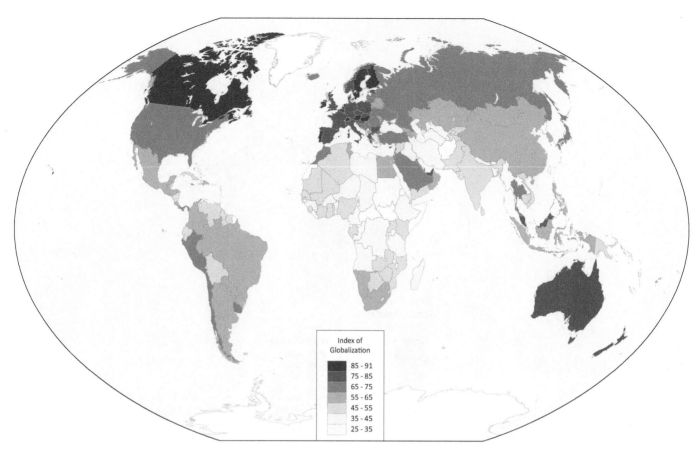

FIGURE 1.45 Globalization index by country, 2012—The index ranges from 0 (no globalization) to 100 (complete globalization) and measures three dimensions of globalization: economic, social, and political. *Source:* KOF Swiss Economic Institute.

FIGURE 1.46 A folk dance in Papua New Guinea—Some people are concerned that globalization may lead to the disappearance of many traditional cultures, and there has been a growing desire to preserve them. *Source:* Pixabay.

financial crisis are examples of economic globalization. The spread of democracy, formation of supra-national organizations (e.g. United Nations, European Union, and the Organization for Economic Cooperation and Development (OECD)), and the relaxation of border controls and establishment of various cross-border initiatives among many countries in recent decades represent political dimensions of globalization. Some scholars go as far as predicting the demise of nation-states. The development of the Internet and the collapse of Communism accelerated the spread of information within previously closed societies and between them and the rest of the world. Western music and dress codes, as well as some European languages, have been expanding in most regions. McDonald's fast food restaurants can be found today in most countries, and Skype, a free telecommunications software first developed in Estonia, allows people to stay in touch no matter where they live. Although globalization is seen as a positive development by many scholars, there is also a growing concern with regard to its ecological dimensions. Climate change, especially global warming, atmospheric ozone layer depletion, acid rain, tropical deforestation, worldwide loss of biodiversity, and many other outcomes of human activities pose a serious threat to the physical environment and future generations.

Every culture is characterized by a perpetual tug of war between forces of tradition and modernization. A similar tension is observed between forces of globalization and localization, the desire to preserve traditional culture and other local or unique characteristics (Fig. 1.46).

Almost every OECD or G7 (the Group of Seven) conference is associated with demonstrations against globalization and economic inequality between rich and poor countries. There has been strong opposition to Westernization in many societies, especially Muslim ones. The growth of nationalistic sentiments and/or separatist movements in some countries also means that the world is far from reaching consensus on the benefits of globalization.

CULTURE AND ENVIRONMENT

One of the major themes in geography is human-environment interaction. Two major schools of thought regarding culture-environment relations have developed during the past century. Environmental determinism was a popular school of thought among geographers and other social scientists in the early 20th century. Supporters of this theory believed that the physical environment, particularly climate and landforms, determined human activities, including people's culture. People living in temperate lands were believed to be more inventive and productive than those living in tropical regions. Residents of mountainous regions were believed to be more conservative and freedom-loving than those of the plains, and residents of the desert would adhere to monotheistic religions. Environmental determinism was discredited after World War II for two main reasons: First, it was used to justify territorial expansion by Nazi Germany; and second, the accumulated evidence indicated that complex cultures could originate in various physical settings. Environmental possibilism began gaining ground in the 1930s, and it emphasized that the physical environment offers a number of opportunities and limitations to humans, but it does not determine their culture. People make choices in interacting with the environment, and the number of choices is directly related to the technological level and complexity of the culture. Similar environments (climate regions) can be used differently (e.g. the southeastern parts of China and the United States), and different environments can be associated with similar cultures (e.g. Europe and Australia).

Some scholars consider seven events as "turning points" in the ever-growing human impact on the environment: (1) the use of fire, (2) the emergence of a spoken language, (3) the early human migration from Africa to other regions, (4) the invention of agriculture, (5) the emergence of the first cities, (6) the European colonization of the New World, and (7) the Industrial Revolution.[6] When our very early ancestors mastered the use of fire, they could clear vegetation and become more efficient hunters, protect themselves from carnivorous animals, warm their caves or other types of shelter and live in colder regions, and cook their food (improved nutrition, better health, and perhaps a larger brain). No other creatures could match humans in their impact on the environment.

When our ancestors began communicating via spoken language some 50,000 years ago, if not earlier, they could exchange and accumulate information about the environment (e.g. the location of good hunting areas and/or water), transmit it to the next generation, plan and conduct more efficient collective hunting, and engage in distant trading. Some 100,000 years ago, some of our ancestors left Africa and moved to other parts of the world, first to the present-day Middle East and Europe and finally to the southern parts of South America. Most of the Pacific islands were populated fairly recently, only about 2,000 years ago or even later. As people settled in new lands and hunted native species, many animals, especially big mammals, became extinct; some scholars also attribute this extinction to climate change (the end of the Ice Age).

The domestication of plants and animals and the invention of agriculture, first in the Fertile Crescent and later in several other regions, had an enormous impact on the human-environment relationship. The first agricultural revolution contributed to a significant population increase, permanent settlements, large-scale deforestation, and the conversion of deforested areas and some grasslands to farmland. This was also a time of growing importance of infectious diseases affecting both humans and domesticated animals. A new and controversial hypothesis states that the expanding agriculture (especially wet rice cultivation in Monsoon Asia) caused the rising methane levels in the atmosphere and triggered climate change about 5,000 years ago.

When the surplus of food became available, some people could engage in non-farming activities and live in new (usually larger) settlements called cities. The emergence of urban settlements was also associated with a new power structure (government and social stratification), monumental public architecture, the development of science (astronomy, horology, and mathematics) and long distance trade. Although most early cities were small in size (area and population), they had a significant and often negative impact on the local environment. Demand for firewood (cooking and heating) led to the deforestation of surrounding areas, and growing demand for water contributed to the lowering of the water table and the invasion of more drought-tolerant plant species. Some ancient cities contributed to the collapse of local ecosystems.[7] One of the outcomes of the European colonization of the Americas was the dispersal of plant and animal species from the New to the Old World and vice versa. Some plants previously unknown to Europeans and Native Americans (e.g. potatoes and wheat, respectively) became major sources of food for many people in both regions. The establishment of sugar cane, banana, coffee, and other plantations in the tropical regions of the Old and New World led to deforestation, soil degradation, and biodiversity loss. Several infectious diseases brought by the Europeans to the Americas decimated native populations and led to the importation of slave labor from Africa. The slave trade had a tremendous demographic, social, and economic impact on both regions. Finally, the Industrial Revolution of the 18th century resulted in the widespread and rapidly growing use of fossil fuels (coal, oil, and natural gas) and emission of greenhouse gases into the atmosphere, which has been blamed for global warming. The introduction of machines and the manufacturing process has had an ecological impact quite disproportionate to its duration; humans have transformed the environment during the last 250-year period to a much greater degree than during the entire pre-industrial era.

NOTES

1. Murphy, R. (1982). *The scope of geography.* New York, NY: Meuthen.

2. Livi-Bacci, M. (1989). *A concise history of world population.* Cambridge, MA: Blackwell.

3. Castles, S., de Haas, H., & Miller, M. J. (2014). *The age of migration: international population movements in the modern world* (5th ed.). New York, NY: Guilford Press.

4. University of Ottawa. (2017). JuriGlobe: World Legal Systems Research Group. Retrieved from http://www.juriglobe.ca/eng

5. Steger, M. B. (2013). *Globalization: a very short introduction.* Oxford, UK: Oxford University Press.

6. McNeill, J. R. (2010). The first hundred thousand years. In F. Uekoetter, *The turning points of environmental history* (pp.13-28). Pittsburgh, PA: University of Pittsburgh Press; Takacs-Santa, A. (2004). The major transitions in the history of human transformation of the biosphere. *Human Ecology Review* 11(1): 51–66.

7. Schultz, C. (2014). Urbanization has been destroying the environment since the very first cities. Retrieved from Smithsonian website: https://www.smithsonianmag.com/smart-news/urbanization-has-been-destroying-the-environment-since-the-very-first-cities-180948243

THE UNITED STATES AND CANADA

NORTH AMERICA

2

The United States and Canada occupy the northern third of the Western Hemisphere (also called the New World or The Americas) and most of the North American continent. Geologists consider the Isthmus of Tehuantepec (Mexico) to be the southern border of the North American continent, but culturally and politically North America ends at the United States-Mexico border. The region was sometimes called Anglo-America in the past, but because North America has indigenous populations as well as large non-English-speaking and non-Anglophone immigrant communities, the term North America is more widely used.

GEOGRAPHIC QUALITIES AND WORLD SIGNIFICANCE

The United States and Canada is a large region, similar in area to the Russian Realm, Sub-Saharan Africa, and Latin America, but geographically isolated from other regions and divided into only two countries (Fig. 2.1). It occupies most of the North American tectonic plate and is divided into several major landform regions characterized by a north-south orientation. It has a great variety and large amounts of mineral resources as well as large areas of productive farmland. It has relatively low population densities, and most of its inhabitants live in the warmer southern part of the region. Most of the population is of European origin, although indigenous groups and a growing number of immigrants from Latin America and Asia contribute to its increasing ethnic diversity. Both countries are federal states, have strong democratic traditions, and are members of NATO and NAFTA. The United States and Canada are among the most economically developed countries in the world. They have very productive agriculture and are

FIGURE 2.1 The United States and Canada—Both countries are federal states. The United States is divided into fifty states and the District of Columbia while Canada is divided into ten provinces and three territories.

among the world's major food exporters. Their industrial base is also very strong and they are important centers of scientific-technological innovation. The United States is the world's largest military power and is politically and militarily involved in several parts of the globe.

Although both countries share many similarities, there are also several differences between them. Most of Canada is cold and sparsely populated; most of the United States has a warmer climate and its population is more evenly distributed. While the United States has over 320 million people, its northern neighbor's population is only 36 million. Both countries can be divided into two parts in terms of selected physical and cultural features (climate, population density, or agricultural productivity); however, it is an east-west division in the United States and a north-south division in Canada. While English is the dominant language in both countries, Spanish has been gaining popularity in the United States, and French is the second official language of Canada. The United States is a republic, while Canada is a member of the British Commonwealth and the British monarch is its head of state. Finally, the United States still uses the imperial (British) system of measurement, but Canada switched to the metric system over three decades ago.

PHYSICAL ENVIRONMENT

Landforms

North America has a large longitudinal extent, from 52°W in Newfoundland to 172°E at the tip of the Aleutian Islands, as well as a large latitudinal range, from 83°N at Ellesmere Island to 19°N at the southern coast of Hawaii. The vast majority of North America, however, is located in the mid latitudes, with significant landmasses reaching into the high latitudes and only Hawaii located in the tropics.

The North American coastline is variable—some stretches are relatively smooth, but most of the coastline is irregular, with large bays indenting the coastline. In the north, Hudson Bay cuts about 1,200 kilometers (800 miles) into Canada's northern coast. The bay is frozen for several months every year. The Gulf of Alaska in the northwest and the Gulf of Mexico in the south may be less prominent, but are more important both climatically and economically. Smaller bays include Puget Sound and Cook Inlet in the west and the Gulf of St. Lawrence, the Bay of Fundy, and Chesapeake Bay in the east. There are also numerous islands—some 70,000. A significant part of Canada's land area consists of islands in the Canadian Arctic Archipelago

(Ellesmere and Baffin are the largest), and another cluster can be found in Canada in the St. Lawrence Gulf area (Newfoundland, Prince Edward Island, and Cape Breton and Anticosti Islands). With the exception of Long Island (New York) the islands off the eastern coast are quite small. The coasts of Alaska and British Columbia have many islands, and some of them are quite large. The Alexander Archipelago and Queen Charlotte islands off the coast of British Columbia are collections of smaller islands, but Vancouver Island farther south is 460 kilometers (290 miles) long.

North America is a region with great diversity in landscapes (Fig. 2.2). A sampling of the features in the eastern two-thirds of the continent can be observed by following a transect from the far north Atlantic shoreline moving counterclockwise through the continent and then back towards the Carolina coast. The most important features in the distant north are the Arctic Mountains on the larger islands of the Canadian Arctic Archipelago with their rocky slopes and extensive ice coverage; the Hudson Bay Lowland, a flat, coastal plain underlain by sedimentary deposits; and

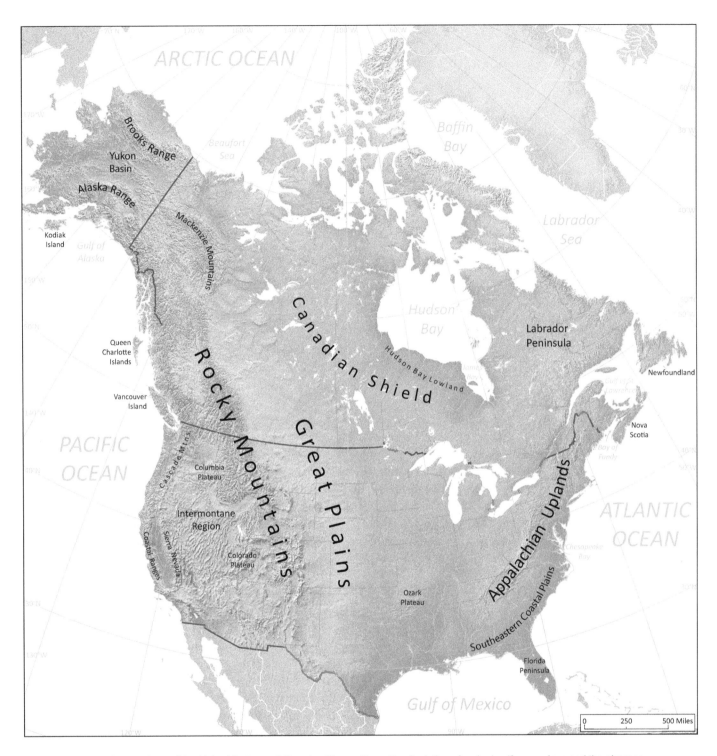

FIGURE 2.2 Landform regions of the United States and Canada—The north-south orientation of major landform regions and the absence of any east-west oriented landform barriers in the eastern part of North America has a great impact on the climate of the area as it allows cold air masses to reach the southern parts of the United States in winter and hot and humid air to penetrate northern parts of Canada in summer. *Source:* Natural Earth.

the Canadian Shield, a vast area of stable crystalline rocks. The landscape is gently rolling and covered in thousands of lakes connected by rivers. The interior of the continent is dominated by slightly undulating terrain (but some portions are almost completely flat). These Great Plains are mostly underlain by sedimentary rocks. Moving east the next prominent landform is the Appalachian Uplands, which begin on the island of Newfoundland. On the continental landmass, the Appalachians stretch from the Gulf of St. Lawrence south to Alabama. Much of the region consists

FIGURE 2.3 Canadian Rockies—The Rocky Mountains stretch from British Columbia in Canada to New Mexico in the United States. *Source:* Heike C. Alberts.

of low hills, but some parts have been folded into a sequence of parallel steep ridges separated by valleys. When the Appalachians were formed about 480 million years ago they were similar in height to the Rocky Mountains or Alps. By now they have been eroded, with the highest peak east of the Mississippi River barely exceeding 2,000 meters (6,700 feet). The Appalachians formed before the North American plate separated from Pangaea, and the Appalachians and the Atlas Mountains in Morocco were once part of the

FIGURE 2.4 California Coast—California's coast is known for the steep coastal ranges plunging abruptly into the Pacific Ocean. Highway 1 is one of the most scenic routes in the United States. *Source:* Heike C. Alberts.

same mountain chain. The Southeastern Coastal Plains is a flat landscape dropping gently seaward and continuing under water. In some places there are bluffs lining rivers or low ridges lining the coast. The actual coast is irregular, with numerous bays, lagoons, and islands made of sandbars.

West of the Interior Plains is North America's most dramatic landscape feature: the Rocky Mountains. Colloquially known as the Rockies, these mountains stretch over 4,800 kilometers (3,000 miles) from northern British Columbia in Canada to New Mexico in the United States (Fig. 2.3). The Rocky Mountains were formed 55–80 million years ago when several tectonic plates began sliding under the North American plate. Since then, the joint forces of tectonic activity and glacial erosion have sculpted rugged peaks and deep valleys. The Rocky Mountains are known for their spectacular scenery, abrupt rise out of the plains, and high elevations. In the Canadian Rockies, Mount Robson in British Columbia is the highest mountain at almost 4,000 meters (almost 13,000 feet), and in the United States Mount Elbert in Colorado reaches 4,400 meters (14,440 feet) and Denali (Mount McKinley) in Alaska 6,300 meters (20,320 feet). In Colorado, over fifty peaks exceed 4,200 meters (14,000 feet). The Rocky Mountains form the **Continental Divide** of the Americas. Triple Divide Peak in Glacier National Park even forms a three-fold divide between the waters flowing to the Atlantic, Pacific, and Hudson Bay.

To the west of the Rocky Mountains is the Intermontane Region. The Intermontane Region is very diverse and can be subdivided into three distinctive subregions: The Columbia Plateau in the north, basin and range topography in the middle, and the extensive Colorado Plateau in the south. The Columbia Plateau covers parts of Washington, Oregon, and Idaho. It is a wide basalt plateau dissected by the Columbia River. The Colorado Plateau covers a vast area in the Four Corners region (Colorado, Utah, New Mexico, and Arizona) of the southwestern United States. This dry area is drained mostly by the Colorado River (and small parts by the Rio Grande). Most of the Colorado Plateau consists of red rocks that have been shaped by dryness and erosion, forming spectacular features such as hoodoos (rock towers), natural arches and bridges, and slot canyons. The most prominent feature of the Colorado Plateau is the Grand Canyon. The Pacific Coast Region consists of a series of high and rugged mountains paralleling the coast such as the Alaska Range in the north, the Cascades in the Pacific Northwest, and the Sierra Nevada in California. The coastline itself is irregular in the north (bays, fjords, and peninsulas). In the southern parts, the steep coastal ranges plunge abruptly into the Pacific Ocean, forming some of North America's most famous coastal landscapes (Fig. 2.4).

Parts of Canada's Yukon Territory and the United States' Alaska comprise the vast Yukon Basin, which is actually a series of over a dozen individual basins, a variety of elevations, and different types of rocks (sedimentary, igneous, and metamorphic). **Permafrost** (permanently frozen ground) is dominant in this region. Finally, the Hawaiian Islands are an archipelago of eight major islands (e.g. Hawaii, Maui, and Oahu), and several small islands and seamounts in the North Pacific Ocean. The chain of islands developed when the Pacific Plate moved north-westward across a hotspot. As a result, the islands in the northwest are older and smaller (more eroded), while those in the southeast are larger and volcanically active. The Big Island, the largest island in the chain, consists of five volcanoes. Mauna Loa, which takes up about half of the island, is the largest shield volcano in the world by volume. Mauna Kea, its neighbor, is dormant, but slightly higher at 4,207 meters (13,802 feet). It is not only the high-est mountain on Hawaii, but also the tallest mountain in the world if measured from the seafloor (10,000 meters, or 33,000 feet). Lo'ihi to the southeast is currently still below sea level, but will eventually become Hawaii's youngest island.[1]

Climate Regions

In North America climate zones follow a north-south pattern in the west and form horizontal belts in the east. Starting in the northwest, the northern Pacific coast is characterized by marine west coast climate. This climate type has long (due to the northern location), mild (moder-ated by the ocean), and wet winters and short but pleasant summers. The western coast of Vancouver Island is the wettest place in North America with 660 centimeters (260 inches) of rain per year, and Mount Rainier further south on the Olympic Peninsula is the snowiest place with 1,760 centimeters (692 inches) of snow (Fig. 2.5). Further south (in California) the Mediterranean climate prevails. Summers are dry and warm, and in winter different fronts moving in from the west lead to alternating rainy and sunny periods. The major mountain areas have highland climates, where altitude is the most important determinant of temperatures. Vast areas in Alaska and Central Canada have subarctic climates. Due to the high latitude location, winters are long, dark, and bitterly cold. The coldest tem-perature was measured in the small settlement of Snag in Canada's Yukon Territory in 1947: –63°C (–84°F). Summers are short, but can be warm or even hot and are character-ized by long hours of daylight. There is little precipitation.

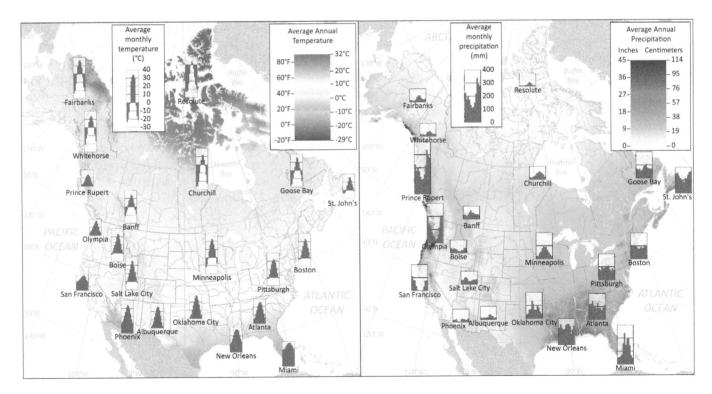

FIGURE 2.5 United States and Canada: patterns of temperature and precipitation—Latitude and landform configuration are the main determinants of temperature patterns in the eastern and western parts of the region respectively. The southeastern parts of the United States and most of the Pacific coastal region receive large amounts of precipitation while the southwestern United States and most of northern Canada are relatively dry regions. *Source:* WorldClim-Global Climate Data.

In the very north, the tundra region is dry and winters are very long.

The Intermontane Region and Great Plains have semi-arid steppe climates. Summers are hot and dry with occasional strong thunderstorms, and winters tend to be cold and windy. The Plains areas are prone to extreme weather events such as storms, hail, heat waves, and tornadoes. The southwestern interior has a desert climate, characterized by very little rain, clear skies, and high temperatures. Summers are long and can be scorching (the hottest temperature was measured in Death Valley in 1913 at 56.7°C or 134°F). Death Valley, due to its location in the mountains' rain shadow, is also North America's driest region with only about 3.8 centimeters (1.5 inches) of rain per year (even though there are some years with no rainfall at all).

In the eastern half of the continent, climate zones are arranged in horizontal belts. Much of the region south of the subarctic belt has a humid continental climate. The northern belt has short and cool summers and long and very cold winters, while the central belt has warmer summers and cold winters with significant snowfall. In this region, polar air masses from the north frequently clash with tropical air masses from the south, resulting in frequent weather changes, severe thunderstorms, and tornadoes. The southern belt is characterized by a humid subtropical climate. Winters are short and mild and summers are hot and humid. Hawaii's climate is described as tropical, but due to the varying topography Hawaii hosts a wide range of climate types. The Hawaiian Islands are influenced by trade winds, so that orographic rainfall produces wet conditions on the windward side (north/east) while the leeward side is drier. Due to their location relatively close to the Equator, there is little seasonal variation in temperatures.

Vegetation and Soils

North America's natural vegetation can be subdivided into three broad classes: forests, grasslands, and shrublands. However, it has to be remembered that in large parts the original vegetation has been destroyed by humans. North America has different types of forests: In the taiga, with its long and cold winters, coniferous trees are dominant. These boreal forests cover vast areas but have relatively low species diversity. South of this region, hardwoods, mixed forests, and pine forests dominate. In the Rocky Mountains, altitude determines the forest cover, with coniferous trees dominating (especially spruce, fir, and pine), but aspen (a deciduous species) is locally important. Along the Pacific Coast softwoods are most common. The largest trees on

Earth can be found there. In the north, fir, spruce, and hemlock are common, while redwoods dominate in Northern California. The title of the tallest tree in the world is currently held by a tree in Redwood National Park, which is 115 meters (379 feet) tall.

The second major vegetation region is grasslands, called **prairie** when tall grasses are dominant and steppe when they are shorter. The western part of the Great Plains was originally steppe and the eastern part prairie. Shrublands are most common in semi-arid and arid regions. Shrublands consist of bushes, stunted trees, and scant grasses. Parts of Texas are known for mesquite trees, while farther north sagebrush is the dominant species. In the southwestern United States, succulents and cacti are common. The most well known species in this region is probably the saguaro, a tree-like cactus that can reach 21 meters (70 feet) in height. Some species are protected by National Parks and National Monuments, such as Saguaro National Park near Tucson, Arizona and Organ Pipe Cactus National Monument at the Mexican border.

North America is blessed with a large share of the world's best soil.[2] In particular, the soil types best suited for agriculture are those that developed together with native forests (ultisols in the southeastern United States and alfisols in the Midwest and the northern prairies) or grasslands (mollisols in the Great Plains and parts of the Pacific Northwest). These soil types benefited from the addition of organic matter from leaves or roots. Most of the soil in the Midwest is also enriched by loess, wind-blown silt. During the ice age, glaciers pushed south from Canada, in the process scraping off soil and weathered rock. In Canada, the glaciers left behind exposed hard rock, but the meltwaters and wind distributed the material across the Midwest. Not all soil in North America is agriculturally productive, but the United States has large areas of excellent soil. It is therefore no surprise that the United States is one of the few net food-exporting countries in the world.

Water Resources

The Great Lakes of North America form the largest freshwater system on Earth by area and the second largest by volume; they contain 21 percent of the world's freshwater and 84 percent of the freshwater in North America.[3] The water of the Great Lakes could cover the entire land area of the United States to a depth of 1.5 meters (5 feet). The Great Lakes system stretches over 1,200 kilometers (750 miles) in the upper Midwest and along the Canada-United States border; from west to east the lakes are Superior, Michigan, Huron, Erie, and Ontario. They are connected to the Atlantic Ocean through the Saint Lawrence River. Lake Superior is the second largest lake in the world by area (the largest is the Caspian Sea). By volume, it has more water than the other four Great Lakes combined. Lake Michigan is the largest lake entirely within one country.

The Great Lakes were formed at the end of the last glacial period (14,000 years ago). Glaciers had carved out large basins that filled with meltwater. Lakes Superior, Huron, Michigan, and Erie are at about the same elevation, but Lake Ontario is significantly lower. Lake Erie and Lake Ontario are connected via the Niagara River, which forms the famous Niagara Falls to overcome the difference in elevation. The Niagara Falls are not particularly high (about 50 meters or 165 feet), but due to their width they have the highest flow rate of any waterfall in the world.

The Saint Lawrence and Great Lakes waterways, a series of locks and canals in Canada and the United States, allow ocean-going vessels to travel from the Atlantic Ocean as far west as Lake Superior. These ocean-going ships are called "salties," while the ships that operate primarily on the Great Lakes are called "lakers". While these ships can be quite large, the locks are too small to allow large container ships to pass. Much of the shipping on the Great Lakes is bulk material such as taconite (iron ore), limestone, grain, salt, coal, cement, and gypsum. The larger lakers are confined to the Great Lakes, and only small ships and barges can pass the Illinois Waterway to connect to the Mississippi River system. Despite their vast size, parts of the Great Lakes freeze over in winter. The Great Lakes also experience severe storms between October and December, posing a threat to even the largest lakers.

The Saint Lawrence River (Fleuve Saint-Laurent in French) connects the Great Lakes to the Atlantic Ocean and drains the entire Great Lakes region—the largest drainage in North America. The river flows roughly in a north-easterly direction and forms the border between Canada and the United States (between the province of Ontario and the state of New York). It is over 3,000 kilometers (1,900 miles) long and affected by tides eastward of Quebec. The river contains several island archipelagos and is home to thirteen different species of whale including sperm, beluga, blue, and bottlenose whales, several of which are endangered species.

The Mississippi River is the most important feature of the second largest drainage system in North America. The river begins in northern Minnesota and flows southward for over 3,700 kilometers (2,300 miles) towards the Gulf of Mexico, making it one of the longest rivers in the world (only the Amazon, Nile, and Yangtze are longer). The Mississippi drains thirty-one states in the United States and two Canadian provinces between the Rocky Mountains and Appalachians.

The Mississippi River is navigable from Saint Anthony Falls (the only true waterfalls on the entire river) in Minneapolis south to the Gulf of Mexico. Numerous dams line the Mississippi, and the river is an important commercial waterway. Like the Saint Lawrence Seaway, the Mississippi further enhances the considerable economic advantages North America enjoys through easy access to low cost waterborne transportation. During the steamboat era, cotton, timber, and other products were shipped downriver to New Orleans. The arrival of the railroad ended the era of steamboat shipping, and today pusher tugs are the most common transportation units on the Mississippi River. Several of the United States' largest ports are located in the Mississippi River Delta (e.g. Baton Rouge and New Orleans).

The Colorado River is the most important river in the southwestern United States.[4] It is over 2,300 kilometers (1,450 miles) long and drains seven U.S. and two Mexican states. The river originates in the Rocky Mountains and flows across the Colorado Plateau to Lake Mead. It forms a delta in Mexico, but the delta is now largely dry. The Colorado River is probably best known for the creation of and flowing through spectacular canyons such as the famous Grand Canyon as well as being part of several national parks (e.g. Arches and Canyonlands National Parks), but it is also of great economic importance as it provides water for about 40 million people in the Southwestern United States, irrigates a vast acreage, and generates hydroelectricity. Thanks to irrigation, California's Imperial Valley is now one of the most productive agricultural areas in the United States. In 1922 the Colorado River Compact, which divides the river's waters between the states, was signed, followed by a series of other treaties allocating the water to the various states in the Southwest and Mexico (today, more than a quarter of the Colorado River water is allocated to California, slightly less than a quarter to Colorado, 17 percent to Arizona, 10 percent to Utah, 6 percent to Wyoming, 5 percent to New Mexico, and 2 percent to Nevada; Mexico receives less than 10 percent of the water). In 1935 the gigantic Hoover Dam was completed, which collects the river's waters in Lake Mead, the largest artificial lake in the United States (Fig. 2.6). Apart from storing water and managing the Colorado River, Hoover Dam also generates huge amounts of hydroelectric power. (It was once the largest hydroelectric power station in the world but there are dozens of larger facilities today, and China's Three Gorges Dam alone has a rated capacity ten times greater than Hoover Dam). More dams and other projects followed, such as the Colorado River Aqueduct, which delivers water to Los Angeles, and the San Diego Aqueduct

FIGURE 2.6 Hoover Dam—Hoover Dam was built during the Great Depression. It provides over 1 million people with electricity, retains the water of Lake Mead, and has become a major tourist destination. *Source:* Heike C. Alberts.

(both completed in the 1940s), which supplies San Diego, as well as Glen Canyon Dam (completed in the 1960s), which created Lake Powell. Despite their importance for people, agriculture, and industrial development, these projects are highly controversial due to their environmental impact and the over-allocation of water. In some years the Colorado no longer reaches its delta in Mexico.

The other two major North American rivers are the Columbia River and the Rio Grande. The Columbia River is the most important river in the Pacific Northwest. It originates in the Rocky Mountains of British Columbia, Canada and then flows through Washington and Oregon before reaching the Pacific Ocean. The Columbia River is 2,000 kilometers (1,240 miles) long and the fourth largest river in North America by volume (and the largest emptying into the Pacific Ocean). The Columbia River is particularly known for its migrating salmon. Fourteen dams help navigation, provide water for irrigation, and generate hydroelectric power, but have gravely imperiled salmon populations and the Native American ways of life dependent on fishing. The Rio Grande is the second major river in the southwestern United States. It originates in Colorado and flows to the Gulf of Mexico. It forms a natural border between the United States and Mexico. Like the Colorado River, only a small amount of its waters reach the Gulf of Mexico because of the use of its waters for cities and agriculture. Water use on the United States side is regulated by the Rio Grande Compact, but, as with the Colorado River, more water is allocated to Colorado, New Mexico, and Texas than flows through the river.

HUMAN-ENVIRONMENT INTERACTION

Natural Disasters

North America, and especially the United States, experiences a wide range of natural disasters, such as hurricanes, earthquakes, and tornadoes (Fig. 2.7). The danger of being impacted by a natural disaster is highest in Texas and parts of the South, where all major hazards (except earthquakes) are present: floods, drought, hurricanes, hail, and tornadoes. Hurricanes and earthquakes are the deadliest and costliest natural disasters in North America.

The Galveston Hurricane was the deadliest one-day event in United States history. The hurricane was a category 4 storm with wind speeds of up to 233 km/h (145 mph). It made landfall in Galveston, Texas on September 8, 1900.

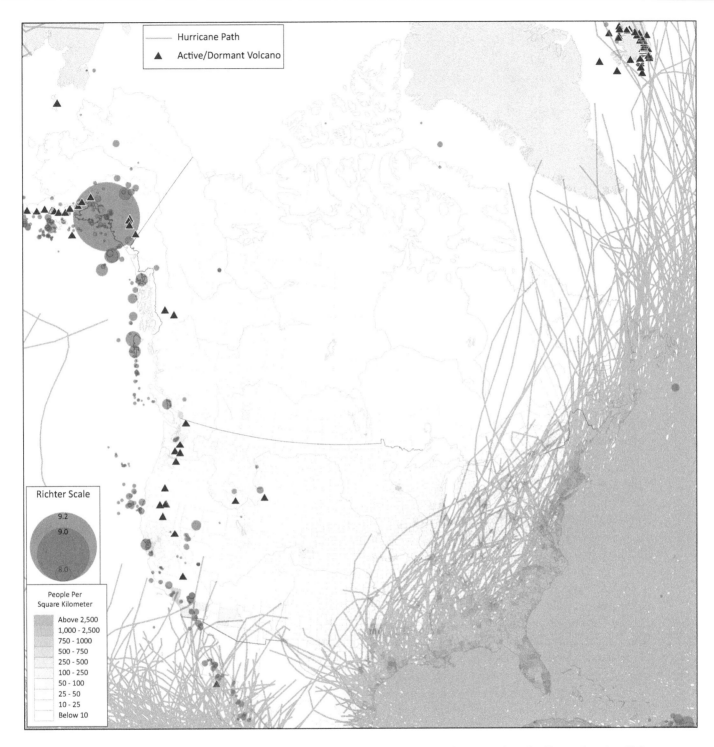

FIGURE 2.7 Selected natural hazards (20th century) and population distribution in the United States and Canada—The southeastern United States and coastal areas along the Atlantic Ocean are prone to hurricanes while the western periphery of both countries is a seismically active region which is part of the Pacific Ring of Fire. *Source:* NOAA National Climatic Data Center; Earthquake Hazards Program; GeoTech Center Data Library.

At the time the highest point in Galveston was less than 3 meters (9 feet) above sea level, but the **storm surge** reached a height of over 4.6 meters (15 feet), so that the storm surge washed over the entire island (Galveston Island is a barrier island off the Texas coast). Over 3,600 buildings were destroyed and between 8,000 and 12,000 lives lost (about a fifth of the island's population) as people drowned or were crushed by the debris. The Galveston Hurricane was the deadliest natural disaster ever to strike the United States, and more people were killed in this storm than in all other

FIGURE 2.8 Hurricane Katrina—The storm surge from Hurricane Katrina inundated large parts of New Orleans as several levees broke. *Source:* Wikimedia Commons.

hurricanes combined that have hit the United States since. It was also one of the costliest (after the Miami hurricane of 1926 and Katrina in 2005) natural disasters.[5]

In 2005, Hurricane Katrina became the most destructive hurricane in United States history (Fig. 2.8). When Hurricane Katrina hit Florida on August 25, it was only a Category 1 storm and caused minor damage. In the Gulf of Mexico Hurricane Katrina gained strength and became a Category 5 hurricane on August 28 with wind speeds of up to 280 km/h (175 mph). The storm weakened again before making landfall along the Louisiana-Mississippi border a day later, but the storm surge and heavy rains associated with the hurricane led to a rise in the water level of Lake Pontchartrain and major flooding along its shores. Several bridges were also destroyed. The most severe impact was on the city of New Orleans. The city essentially has a bowl shape, with much of the city below sea level. The storm surge led to the breaches of all major levees. Approximately 80 percent of the city flooded and remained inundated for several weeks after the hurricane. Despite warnings, numerous people had not evacuated, and the storm destroyed all major roads out of the city, leaving people trapped. Many of those who had not evacuated sought shelter at the Superdome, which, like many other buildings in New Orleans, sustained major damage as the roof membrane peeled off. Ultimately, over 1,800 people

died as a result of the hurricane and its aftermath, and more than 1 million people were displaced from the Gulf Coast. Hurricane Katrina also had a significant political and economic impact: The rescue and recovery efforts were heavily criticized as poorly managed, and the destruction of the transportation infrastructure as well as damage to thirty oil platforms in the Gulf of Mexico as well oil refineries led to a massive drop in oil production.[6]

The year 2012 was another very active hurricane season. Hurricane Sandy, the tenth hurricane of the season, became the largest hurricane on record with a diameter of 1,800 kilometers (1,100 miles). After hitting the Greater Antilles and the Bahamas, Hurricane Sandy moved north, ultimately affecting twenty-four states including the entire eastern seaboard from Florida to Maine and as far west as Wisconsin. It caused seventy-one deaths in nine states (most in New York and New Jersey). Hurricane Sandy's storm surge, amplified by particularly high tides (spring tides), led to serious flooding. In Manhattan, streets, tunnels, and subway stations were inundated. The waters also led to the breakdown of the electrical system, which left over 8 million people without electricity. Amtrak had to stop most of its rail services along the eastern seaboard, and almost 20,000 flights were cancelled. The New York Stock Exchange closed for two days, as did schools and university campuses.

While hurricanes are the deadliest and costliest disasters impacting the United States, the country is also prone to earthquakes. The strongest earthquake was the 1964 Prince William Sound Earthquake in Alaska. With a magnitude of 9.2 it was not only the most powerful earthquake in North America, but also one of the most powerful ones in the world. Landslides and soil **liquefaction** caused major damage to buildings, roads, water and sewer mains, and other infrastructure. All other North American earthquakes of a magnitude greater than 8 also occurred in Alaska. The 1812 New Madrid Earthquake (Missouri) reached a magnitude of 7.9. As opposed to the earthquakes in Alaska (usually connected to subduction) and those in California (often associated with strike-slip **faults**), the mechanism causing the New Madrid earthquakes is not well understood. It is believed that an ancient rift buried under the Mississippi River alluvial plan is reactivating faults that were formed when ancient supercontinents broke apart. Some scientists believe that the next "big one" may not occur in California, but in the New Madrid area.

The state of California is most associated with earthquakes in the popular mind. While the earthquakes in Alaska are usually stronger, many more people are impacted by earthquakes in California. The deadliest earthquake in the United States (approximately 3,000 deaths) was the 1906 San Francisco Earthquake (magnitude 7.8). The shaking of the earth resulted in substantial damage, but it has been estimated that 90 percent of the destruction was caused by fires (due to ruptured gas mains) that raged in the city for several days after the earthquake. Another major earthquake occurred in Northridge, northwest of Los Angeles, in 1994. The 6.9 magnitude earthquake occurred along a so-called blind-thrust fault (a blind fault is buried, so it is not visible on the surface). The earthquake's death toll was fifty-seven, with about 9,000 people injured. The earthquake caused extensive damage to parking structures and transportation infrastructure. For example, a section of the Antelope Valley freeway collapsed onto the Golden State Freeway. While liquefaction caused massive damage in the 1964 Alaska earthquake, the dry soil in Northridge reduced ground failures.

Tsunamis created by earthquakes have struck Hawaii, Alaska, and the United States' West Coast on various occasions. The most devastating was the 1946 tsunami in Hawaii, and the tsunamis generated by the 1964 Alaskan earthquake caused damage in all states bordering the Pacific Ocean. The United States is also prone to tsunamis created by landslides. In 1958 an earthquake triggered a landslide in Lituya Bay in Alaska, which resulted in a tsunami estimated to have exceeded 520 meters (1,710 feet) in height. The 1980 eruption of Mount St. Helens also created a massive landslide that pushed the water of Spirit Lake to a height of 260 meters (853 feet). Scientists fear that landslides from the Hawaiian volcanoes could trigger tsunamis in the future.

Tornadoes occur more frequently in the United States than in any other country in the world. More than 1,200 touch ground every year, the vast majority in the Great Plains, the Midwest, and the Mississippi Valley. Oklahoma and Kansas, the core of so-called **tornado alley**, are particularly prone to tornadoes (Fig. 2.9). Florida also experiences

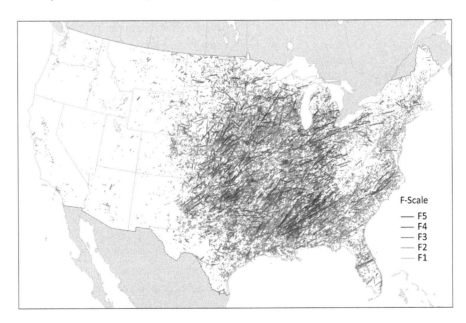

F-Scale

—— F5
—— F4
—— F3
—— F2
—— F1

FIGURE 2.9 Historical tornado tracks, 1950–2006—Most tornadoes occur in the central parts of the country (between the Rockies and the Appalachians) in the area known as "Tornado Alley." *Source:* National Weather Service.

a lot of tornadoes, but they tend to be much weaker and therefore less destructive than those in tornado alley. Tornadoes can occur at any time in the year (for example, a tornado in Illinois in winter blew railroad cars off their tracks, and in 2008 there was a major tornado outbreak in February), but are most common in spring when cold air from the north clashes with warm air from the south. The 2011 Super Outbreak resulted in 349 tornadoes in twenty-one states, covering a total length of 5,150 kilometers (3,200 miles). The current "tornado capital of the world" is Moore, Oklahoma, which has been hit by twelve tornadoes since 1950. The small city was devastated in 1999 by the Bridge Creek-Moore tornado (EF5) and the 2013 Moore tornado (EF4).

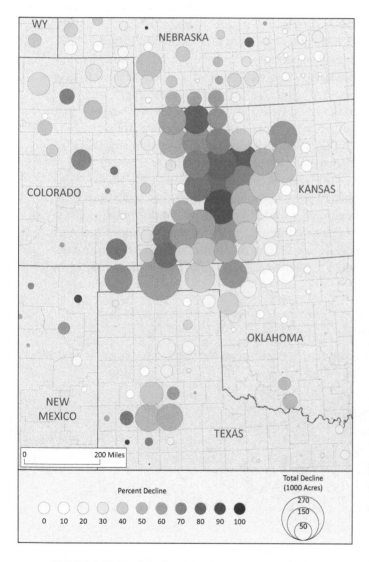

FIGURE 2.10 The Dust Bowl's impact on wheat cultivation, 1929–1934—The map shows the absolute and relative decline of areas devoted to wheat cultivation at the county level. Western Kansas and the Oklahoma Panhandle were particularly affected by the decline. *Source:* U.S. Census Bureau.

The United States is also prone to other disasters. For example, severe blizzards have resulted in major damage. The 1992 Storm of the Century resulted in 300 deaths. It affected the entire eastern half of the United States and Canada and covered areas that rarely see snow with several feet of it. Heatwaves can be even more deadly. For example, the Chicago heat wave of 1995 killed 739 over a period of five days. Most of the victims were poor and elderly residents who could not afford air conditioning. Furthermore, lack of preparation for the heat wave, power failures, and overwhelmed medical facilities aggravated the situation.[7]

Floods also result in massive devastation. The worst recent river flood occurred along the Mississippi and Missouri rivers and their tributaries in 1993. Some places along the Mississippi River were flooded for over 200 days. Over 100,000 homes were destroyed and 60,000 square kilometers (23,160 square miles) of farmland inundated.

Canada also experiences a wide range of natural disasters, but due to the low population densities in affected areas, the impact of these disasters is smaller than in the United States. Notable natural disasters include the 1873 Nova Scotia hurricane, which killed about 500 people, the 1903 Frank Rockslide, the 1910 Rogers Pass Avalanche, and the 2011 Slave Lake Wildfires. The 1998 Ice Storm resulted in a thick coat of ice that snapped power lines, brought down trees, and collapsed buildings. In 2013 the province of Alberta experienced serious flooding, the costliest disaster in Canadian history. Three years later, Alberta witnessed Canada's worst ever wildfires, prompting the largest evacuation in the country's history. In both Canada and the U.S., wildfire is a worsening issue. Decades of fire suppression have led to an accumulation of fuel while at the same time a growing number of people have moved into the wildland-urban interface, placing them in harm's way.

Environmental Issues

The **Dust Bowl** is one of the major events in North American history (Fig. 2.10). The term refers to a series of severe dust storms in the 1930s (1934, 1936, and 1939) that devastated the American and Canadian prairies. Due to a lack of ecological understanding and an unusually wet period, farmers had deep-plowed the top soil of the Great Plains in the 1920s (rather than practicing dry farming). This destroyed or damaged the deep roots of the native grasses that held the soil and moisture in place. During drought, the loose soil turned to dust and formed huge clouds that blackened the sky. The gigantic dust clouds, called black blizzards, reduced visibility in the Plains to 1 meter (3.3 feet) and travelled as far as the East Coast. The worst affected areas were parts of Texas and Oklahoma, as well as adjacent areas in Kansas, New Mexico, and California, and the dust storms reached an extent of 400,000 square kilometers (154,440 square miles). Because the Dust Bowl destroyed their livelihoods, tens of thousands of families were forced to abandon their farms and migrate to California and other western states. In total, over 3 million people moved out of the Plains states in the 1930s, the largest migration in American history.

The depletion of groundwater is another serious environmental concern in North America. In areas where surface water (lakes and rivers) is scarce, groundwater is the main water source for the needs of people, agriculture, and industry. In the United States, about half of the population (mostly in rural areas) depends on groundwater. Groundwater depletion refers to the practice of pumping out more groundwater than can be replenished through natural processes. As a result, the water table drops, wells dry up, lakes and rivers receive less groundwater input (leading to the drying up of wetlands), water quality declines (often through saltwater intrusion), and the land above the groundwater may subside. Groundwater depletion in the United States is a major concern in the Southwest and the Plains, and can occur at very local scales (the drying up of a single well) or impact large areas (when extensive aquifers shrink). The best known example of the latter is the Ogallala aquifer, a shallow aquifer beneath the Great Plains with an extent of 450,000 square kilometers (174,000 square miles). The large scale extraction of water from the Ogallala aquifer began after World War II to feed central pivot irrigation in the Plains (Fig. 2.11). Today, it produces almost a third of the groundwater used for irrigation and provides drinking water for the vast majority of people living in the Plains. In some areas the water level in the aquifer has dropped 90 meters (300 feet). Even though measures have been implemented to reduce the amount of water withdrawn for irrigation, the depletion of the aquifer in the last decade has been faster than before. The Ogallala aquifer is recharged by rainwater, but rainfall in this region is scarce and evaporation high, so it would take over 6,000 years to recharge it.

The United States is among the world's largest producers and consumers of fossil fuels. The United States is currently listed as the third largest producer of oil (after Saudi Arabia and Russia), the second largest producer of coal (after China), and the biggest producer of natural gas. The United States is also the second largest consumer of fossil fuels (after China), and responsible for over a quarter of global greenhouse emissions. (On a per capita basis both the U.S. and Canada are among the ten largest emitters). The production and consumption of fossil fuels has led

FIGURE 2.11 Ogallala aquifer—One of the largest sources of freshwater in the world, it has supported irrigated agriculture in the Great Plains since the 1940s. There is a serious concern that the continuation of this practice will lead to water depletion and a variety of negative consequences for residents and the economy of this region. *Source:* Qi, S. L. 2010. Digital Map of Aquifer Boundary for the High Plains Aquifer in Parts of Colorado, Kansas, Nebraska, New Mexico, Oklahoma, South Dakota, Texas, and Wyoming (https://pubs.usgs.gov/ds/543).

to serious environmental problems. The two main methods for extracting fossil fuels from the ground are mining (solid fossil fuels, such as coal) and drilling (liquid or gaseous fossil fuels, such as oil and gas). In the United States, most of the coal is now extracted through surface mining, a process that involves removing the soil to access the coal, which destroys the landscape. Even more destructive is mountaintop mining, where the entire top of a mountain is removed to access the coal layers below.

Oil and natural gas extraction also have severe environmental impacts. The relatively new method of hydraulic fracturing (fracking; the opening of existing gaps in the ground by injecting water at high pressure) has recently received the most attention, but other methods also harm the environment. For example, water trapped in the geologic formation that contains the oil or gas can be brought to the surface and carry heavy metals or other contaminants with it. Offshore drilling is even more risky than onshore drilling because of the complicated technology involved and the remote location of offshore drilling. This was demonstrated in 2010, when an explosion on the Deepwater Horizon oil rig in the Gulf of Mexico released massive amounts of oil for almost three months. Oil is now also produced from tar sand (especially in the Canadian province of Alberta) through a process that emits more greenhouse gases than conventional oil production.

The extraction of fossil fuels has a major environmental impact, but so has its transport. In the United States, most coal is transported via rail (the rest via river barge and truck), while natural gas is usually transported via pipeline and oil via tanker across the ocean and by pipeline, rail, or truck overland. The Trans-Alaska Pipeline transports oil from Prudhoe Bay in Alaska's north to the ice-free port of Valdez on the southern Alaska coast (Fig. 2.12). The 1,290 kilometers- (800 miles-) long pipeline was built in the 1970s (after the 1973 oil crisis caused oil prices to increase in the United States). It required advanced engineering to overcome the difficulties associated with permafrost (repeated freezing and thawing) and earthquakes. Leaks can be a

FIGURE 2.12 Trans-Alaska Pipeline—The Trans-Alaska Pipeline brings oil from Prudhoe Bay in the north to the ice-free port of Valdez. Much of the pipeline runs above ground in a zig-zag pattern so that it can expand and contract with changing temperatures. *Source:* Wikimedia Commons.

problem with any mode of oil transportation, and serious accidents have occurred. For example, in 1989, the Exxon Valdez oil spill in Alaska released 262,000 barrels of oil and devastated the ecosystem of Prince William Sound.

Another huge environmental impact is the burning of fossil fuels. In the United States, energy generation and transportation each contribute about a third of greenhouse gas emissions. Sulfur dioxide emissions lead to the formation of acid rain; acid rain can also be caused by nitrogen oxides, which also leads to smog. Coal-fired power plants also release mercury. All of these substances are not only harmful to the environment, but also to human health. Nuclear power produces much fewer emissions, but safely storing the nuclear waste generated by over 100 nuclear reactors in the United States poses a challenge. In 1987, Yucca Mountain (Nevada) was designated as the nuclear waste repository but was met with harsh criticism from the general public, the Shoshone tribe, and politicians because of the concerns of the site's location in an active seismic zone.

While North America, and especially the United States, faces a broad range of environmental challenges, many of which are related to the large-scale use of resources, the United States has been the leader in protecting areas through its National Park Service.[8] In 1872, Congress established Yellowstone as the first national park, and with this act laid the foundation for a worldwide national park movement (today, over half of all countries have together designated some 1,200 national parks). In the years after Yellowstone was designated, more national parks and monuments on federal lands in the West were created. In 1916 the National Park Service was formed to manage national parks and monuments. The National Park Service (an agency of the Department of the Interior) now oversees about sixty national parks and a total of 400 protected areas in all fifty states, the District of Columbia, Puerto Rico, Samoa, Guam, and the U.S. Virgin Islands.

Selection criteria for national parks include natural beauty, unusual ecosystems, and unique geological features. For example, a large number of national parks protect volcanic features (e.g. Hawaiian Volcanoes, Yellowstone, Lassen, and Crater Lake) or landscapes sculpted by erosion (e.g. Grand Canyon, Bryce, and Arches) (Fig. 2.13). National monuments are chosen for the historical or archaeological features such as Native American ruins (e.g. Canyon de Chelly, Montezuma Castle, Casa Grande, and Gila Cliff Dwellings) or natural features (e.g. Craters of the Moon, Devil's Tower, Dinosaur, and Mariana Trench). California has the largest number of national parks (nine), closely followed by Alaska (eight); Utah has five and Colorado four (Fig. 2.14). The largest national park is Wrangell-St-Elias

FIGURE 2.13 Crater Lake—Crater Lake was created by a violent volcanic eruption about 7,700 years ago. The lake is the deepest and most pristine lake in the United States. Crater Lake is one of numerous National Parks protecting volcanic features. *Source:* Heike C. Alberts.

FIGURE 2.14 National parks in Canada and the United States— Almost one hundred National Parks in both countries (thirty-nine in Canada and sixty in the United States) occupy about 2 percent of the total land area of both countries and are visited by millions of tourists every year. Most parks are located in the western parts of each country. *Source:* Earth Data Analysis Center; Government of Canada.

in Alaska, which covers over 32,000 square kilometers (12,300 square miles); it is larger than several U.S. states. The total area protected in national parks exceeds 211,000 square kilometers (81,450 square miles). The most visited U.S. national parks are the Great Smoky Mountains (which is near major East Coast population centers), Grand Canyon, and Yosemite. Canada has thirty-nine national parks and eight national park reserves administered by Parks Canada. National parks cover about 303,000 square kilometers (117,000 square miles) of Canadian territory. Canada's largest national parks are located in the remote Northwest Territories, Yukon Territories, and Nunavut, while the most known and popular ones are those in the Canadian Rockies (Banff, Jasper, Yoho, Mount Revelstoke).

POPULATION PATTERNS AND TRENDS

Settlement of the Americas

The early settlement of the Americas remains one of archeology's biggest puzzles.[9] The most widely accepted theory is that people migrated from Siberia across a land bridge in the Bering Sea that was exposed due to the lower sea levels during the last ice age (about 15,000 years ago). This migration is believed to have occurred in at least three different waves, as evidenced by DNA and linguistic proof. Once in northern America, people started moving south. There are two major theories how this migration occurred. Many scholars believe that people migrated through an ice-free corridor between two large ice sheets (one in the mountains paralleling the coast, one covering much of northern North America). These people were big-game hunters (mammoth, bison, etc.); the earliest example of a spear point was discovered in 1929 near Clovis, New Mexico. An alternative hypothesis is that people migrated down the western coast. Little archaeological evidence has been found in support of this theory, but it must be remembered that sea levels are much higher today, so any evidence of this migration would now be covered by water. Either way, the new arrivals quickly spread throughout the New World. Once the big game populations had shrunk, people increasingly turned to gathering, fishing, and hunting smaller animals, and some groups of people eventually developed into advanced civilizations.

FIGURE 2.15 Taos Pueblo—Pueblos such as Taos Pueblo in New Mexico are among the oldest continuously inhabited settlements in North America. Taos Pueblo is a UNESCO World Heritage Site. *Source:* Heike C. Alberts.

Some people, however, question that the Clovis people were the first settlers of North America. The most compelling evidence comes from Monte Verde in Chile (South America), where remains of settlements have been found that were dated to at least 12,000 BCE, a time when it was believed that the Clovis people were no farther south than in the Canadian Rockies. Therefore people must have crossed the Bering Strait much earlier than previously thought. A migration along the coastal route seems more likely in this case, as it would have allowed people to move more quickly and thus explain very early sites in South America. Other scholars, however, have forwarded a completely different hypothesis. Because more Clovis and even pre-Clovis sites have been found in eastern North America than the western part of the continent, these scholars believe that the Americas were first settled by Ice Age Europeans. Some South American archaeologists even believe that South America was settled first, citing the age of some South American sites as well as genetic similarities of South Americans to Pacific peoples as evidence. While the question of how the Americas were settled is still open to some debate, the Beringia hypothesis that people migrated across the land bridge from Siberia during the last Ice Age remains the most accepted theory.

Even though they probably never reached the sophistication of the great Mesoamerican (Aztec and Mayan) and South American (Inca) civilizations, several advanced cultures developed. One of the best known is the Hohokam culture along the Gila River in the Southwest. People grew corn, beans, and squash; developed polychrome pottery; and lived in walled compounds. One of the best known Hohokam sites is Casa Grande in Arizona. The Ancestral Puebloan culture occupied the areas now known as the Four Corners (Colorado, Utah, Arizona, and New Mexico). Pueblo people lived in large pueblos (clustered settlements) made of adobe or stone (such as Pueblo Bonito in Chaco Canyon or Taos Pueblo (Fig. 2.15), both in New Mexico) or cliff dwellings (such as those in Mesa Verde National Park in Colorado). The Mississippian culture, stretching through the Ohio and Mississippi valleys, is best known for large mounds and other earthworks, the most impressive of which are Cahokia Mounds in Illinois.

European Settlement

The Vikings (or Norse) were the first Europeans who reached North America in the 11th century. They established several settlements in Greenland, which survived for several centuries, as well as a short-lived settlement called Vinland in what is now Newfoundland. In 1492 Christopher Columbus reached the Americas, but never actually set foot on the North American continent. In 1494 the **Treaty of Tordesillas** (see Chapter 7) divided the New World between Spain and Portugal, but soon other European nations disputed the treaty and set up their own colonies in the Americas. Among the earliest colonies were the Spanish colonies in Florida (St. Augustine, 1565), the British colonies in Virginia (Jamestown, 1607), the French colonies in Canada (Quebec, 1608), and Dutch colonies in New York (New Amsterdam, 1625).

Many of the colonists came for economic reasons. Inspired by the gold the Spanish obtained from the Aztecs and Incas, British colonists also hoped to find gold. However, ultimately the riches the British exploited were agricultural products, such as the tobacco that was brought back to Europe. The French colonial economy was based on the fur trade with Native Americans. While economic considerations were an important motivator, other colonists came to North America in search of religious freedom. The Protestant Reformation in 16th century Europe had led to a variety of religious groups that faced persecution in Europe. For example, about 20,000 Puritans migrated to New England around the 1630s and founded multiple settlements. The Pennsylvania colony became a refuge for Quakers, but other religious groups also sought a new life free of persecution there.

The first slaves were brought to the British colony of Jamestown, Virginia in 1619. Soon after, slavery spread rapidly through the North American colonies as slaves were needed to work on the tobacco and rice **plantations**. After the

American Revolution (1775–83) northerners began to call for the abolition of slavery (slaves were less important to the economies of the northern colonies). Slavery, however, continued after the war, and the U.S. Constitution stated that people are allowed to own workers. A slave counted three-fifths of a person for the purposes of apportioning representatives in the U.S. Congress and votes in the Electoral College. In the later 18th century, demand for American cotton grew, and the invention of the cotton gin to remove the seeds made cotton production more efficient, so cotton plantations continued to rely on slave labor and became more widespread than tobacco plantations. Around the turn of the century all northern states abolished slavery, but the numbers of slaves increased in the South, reaching about 4 million by 1860. From the 1830s onward, more and more people called for the abolition of slavery. Free slaves, as well as northerners, helped slaves escape via the Underground Railroad, a system of safe houses. At the same time, the expansion of the United States towards the West also led to debates over whether slavery should be permitted in the new territory. The thirteenth Amendment to the U.S. Constitution finally abolished slavery after the Civil War (in 1865). In Canada, slavery had already been abolished in 1833, and slavery had never been widespread.

Westward Expansion

Manifest Destiny, the belief that Americans and their institutions are morally superior to others and that the U.S. was destined to spread these institutions to the Pacific, was a driving force behind the westward expansion of the United States. In 1803, the United States purchased the Louisiana Territory from France, thus gaining access to the Mississippi River as a transportation artery and doubling U.S. territory. President Jefferson asked Meriwether Lewis to mount an expedition to survey the natural resources in the Louisiana Territory and claim the Pacific Northwest for the United States. Accompanied by William Clark, the expedition (which became known as the Corps of Discovery Expedition) lasted over two years and returned with a wealth of knowledge about vast areas of land (Fig. 2.16).

In 1812 the United States fought a war against Britain, with most battles along the border between the U.S. and

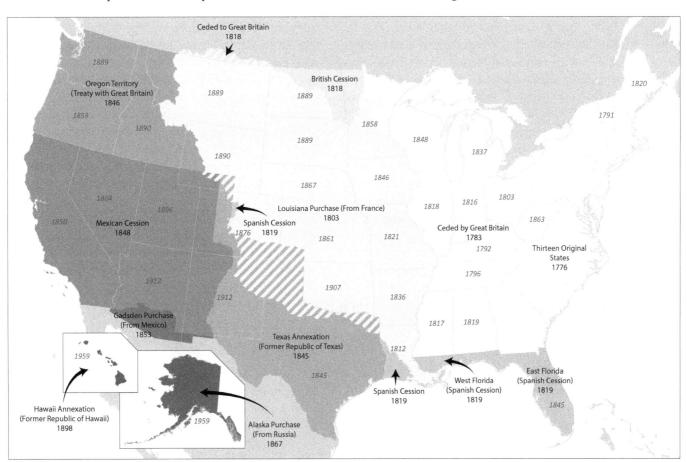

FIGURE 2.16 Territorial expansion of the United States since 1776. Purple dates (in italics) indicate admission to the union of particular states. *Source:* National Atlas (www.nationalatlas.gov).

what was still British-controlled Canada. The war did not end with a clear winner, but it pushed Native American tribes (many of which had sided with Britain in the conflict) farther west, thus opening new territories for the United States. In 1823 the United States adopted the **Monroe Doctrine**, which declared any attempt by European powers to further colonize areas in the Western Hemisphere as an act of aggression. At the same time, it made it clear that the United States would continue to expand westward to bring any un-colonized areas under their control.

Meanwhile the United States began a systematic effort to move Native Americans from the Southeast to what is now Oklahoma. President Jefferson had wanted to allow the tribes to remain east of the Mississippi if they acculturated to colonial society, but President Jackson signed the Indian Removal Act in 1830 to move them westward. Due to poor planning, the removal of the Choctaws did not go well. Food shortages and lack of shelter made it a deadly undertaking. The removal of the Cherokee was even worse, as about a quarter of the 16,000 Cherokees perished, earning the event the name Trail of Tears. The Seminoles resisted their removal, resulting in the Seminole Wars, the most extensive war between Native Americans and the U.S. Army.

In the 1840s Americans colonized the lands west of the Mississippi River. While for most the trek West was motivated by finding riches, the Mormons travelled in search of religious freedom. Four trails—the Santa Fe Trail to the Southwest, the Overland Trail to California, the Mormon Trail to the Great Salt Lake, and the Oregon Trail to the Northwest—brought tens of thousands of people westward.

In 1845 the United States annexed the Republic of Texas (encompassing present-day Texas, Oklahoma, Kansas, Colorado, Wyoming, and New Mexico). Tensions with Mexico led to the Mexican-American War. The war ended with the signing of the Treaty of Guadalupe Hidalgo in 1848, in which Mexico gave up all rights to Texas and accepted the Rio Grande as the border between the two countries. In 1853 the remaining parts of southern Arizona and New Mexico became part of the United States.

In 1863 construction on the Transcontinental Railroad began. Due to labor shortages caused by the Civil War, over 80 percent of the workers on the Central Pacific railroad were Chinese, and many of the workers on the Union Pacific railroad were Irish immigrants. The railroad ended the era of the great overland trails and allowed the rapid settlement of the Western United States (often at the expense of Native Americans). The construction of the Transcontinental Railroad also coincided with the 1862 Homestead Act, which provided settlers with 160 acres of land for free if they improved the land and built a shelter on it for at least five years. By the end of the century, almost 500,000 homesteaders had been granted land, and about one tenth of U.S. territory was settled through the Homestead Act. In 1867 the United States purchased Alaska from the Russian Empire; Alaska became the forty-ninth state of the United States in 1959. Hawaii was annexed late in the 19th century and became the fiftieth state of the United States in 1959.

Canada, an even larger country than the U.S., has a broadly similar story of westward expansion, though its territorial growth involved no great wars and was somewhat fairer (and certainly less violent) to the indigenous peoples displaced by white settlement. Until the 1860s, a huge swath of central and northern Canada was controlled by the Hudson Bay Company, which had been given a charter by the king of England in 1670 to explore and exploit the resources of the entire Hudson Bay drainage. The company focused on the fur trade and a small population of white fur traders and settlers mixed with the native population already in the territory. By the 19th century, Canada was anxious to gain possession of the territory, known as Rupert's Land, to prevent the U.S. (which had just purchased Alaska) from gaining control of the vast area separating the Canadian provinces in the east (e.g. Ontario, Quebec) from the province of British Columbia in the west. Britain too wanted to stop the U.S. from acquiring the territory and pressured the company to sell. So, in 1869 just two years after Canada gained its independence from the United Kingdom, the Hudson Bay Company sold 3.9 million square kilometers (1.5 million square miles) (more than twice as large as the Alaska purchase completed two years earlier) for $1.5 million (Alaska had cost the U.S. $7.2 million). The purchase went forward without the consent of the people living in the region, including **First Nations** peoples and the Métis, a group of mixed European-First Nations ancestry people. The Métis in particular resisted the sale to Canada in an uprising called the Red River Resistance in present-day Manitoba, but ultimately the takeover was completed with virtually no loss of life. In 1885, Canada finished its own transcontinental railroad further accelerating the integration of the country and the development of the west.

Migration

Immigration to the United States and Canada is closely tied to each country's westward expansion. Already at the time of the United States' independence, most of the population was foreign born, and the numbers picked up early in the 19th century. The period of mass migration began in 1820 (Fig. 2.17). Most of the people migrating at this time came from north-western European countries such as England,

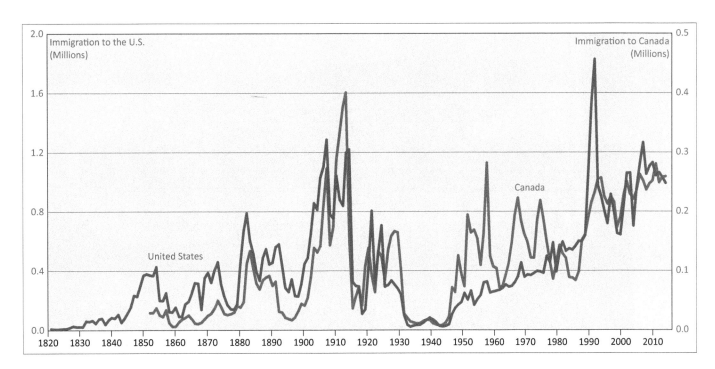

FIGURE 2.17 Immigration to the United States and Canada, 1820–2013—Notice the similarities in immigration trends in both countries prior to World War II and the greater relative importance of immigration to Canada during the 1950–1980 period. *Source:* 2013 Yearbook of Immigration Statistics; Statistics Canada.

Ireland, Germany, and Sweden. The construction of the Transcontinental Railroad and the Homestead Act made the Midwest and the Great Plains even more attractive to European immigrants in search for farm land. In contrast to most immigrant groups, however, the Irish (who had fled from Ireland primarily because of the potato famine) stayed in cities on the East Coast such as New York and Boston. The Irish also differed from the other groups in their religious affiliations—because they were Catholic, they encountered more prejudice and discrimination. The Chinese, who had come to the United States to work on the Transcontinental Railroad, faced even more discrimination (Fig. 2.18). In 1882 Congress passed the Chinese Exclusion Act, which excluded almost all Chinese from immigration to the United States until 1943. In 1892 the first comprehensive immigration law was passed, which excluded the migrants who could become a public burden such as criminals and people with contagious diseases. In 1917 a new immigration law prevented almost all Asians from migrating to the United States. In the meantime, the composition of the immigrant flow had also changed. Northwestern Europeans kept on arriving in large numbers, but after the 1880s they were joined by increasing numbers of southern and eastern Europeans, especially Italians, Russians, and Hungarians. As opposed to the "old migrants" from northern Europe, the "new migrants" from the south and east were largely Catholic, Orthodox, or

Jewish. They encountered prejudice due to their religion and darker skin and hair color and were seen as a threat to American society. They tended to stay in the large cities on the East Coast where they formed visible ethnic neighborhoods, which further increased some Americans' opinion that this group of newcomers would not integrate to the same degree as the "old immigrants." Nevertheless, migration flows continued to climb. During the peak time from 1905 until 1914, about 1 million immigrants arrived in the United States every year, and about 5,000 people entered through Ellis Island every day. Ellis Island, situated in New York City's harbor, remained a gateway for migrants from 1892 to 1954, and today over 100 million Americans can trace their ancestry to migrants who came through Ellis Island (Fig. 2.19).[10]

Restricted immigration officially began with the 1924 National Origins Act, which limited immigration to 2 percent of those of any nationality already in the United States in 1890. This policy was obviously aimed at limiting the numbers of Southern and Eastern Europeans. First, much smaller numbers of them were in the United States at that time than Germans or Brits, and the cut-off date of 1890 further favored "old migrants" as the "new immigration" was only beginning at that time. In practice this meant that roughly four-fifths of people allowed in from then on were Northwestern Europeans, about 15 percent Southeastern Europeans, and about 2 percent Asians who were not

FIGURE 2.18 Chinatown in Victoria, British Columbia—The Chinatown in Victoria, British Columbia, is Canada's oldest Chinatown. It was founded in the mid-19th century. *Source:* Heike C. Alberts.

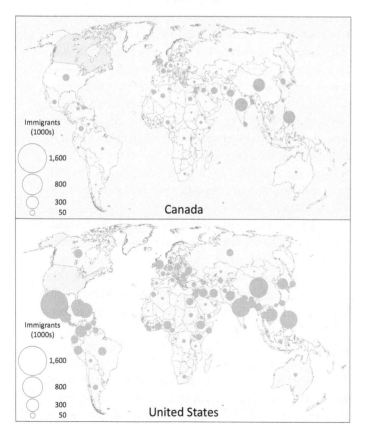

excluded by any other legislation. There were no restrictions on people migrating from the Americas, as Mexicans were needed as low-wage laborers and most other migrants at this time came from Canada.

During the 1930s immigration declined due to the Great Depression and then increased through World War II and the postwar period. World War II changed Americans' world view. Military needs meant cooperating with some countries whose people so far had been barred from entering the United States, and American servicemen married women abroad that they wanted to bring to the United States. In 1945 the War Brides Act made provisions for the wives to enter the United States, and the restrictions on countries such as India and the Philippines were lifted. World War II also resulted in some labor shortages that were filled by recruiting laborers from Latin America.

FIGURE 2.19 Origin of immigrants to Canada and the United States since 2010—Both countries are the world's major migration magnets and attract over 1.25 million newcomers each year. Most of Canada's legal immigrants (about 250,000 a year) originate in Asia (India, China, and the Philippines) while immigrants to the United States are mainly from Latin America (Mexico and the Caribbean Islands) and Asia. *Source:* U.S. Census Bureau; Statistics of Canada.

The largest program was the **Bracero Program** (in effect until 1964) that brought agricultural labor from Mexico, but workers for factories were also brought in from Central America and the Caribbean. Other legislation was passed that further relaxed immigration restrictions. The biggest change was brought about by the Civil Rights era, when the 1965 Immigration and Nationality Act finally eliminated national origin as a criterion for immigration. The 1965 changes in immigration law coincided with economic and political crises in several Latin American countries, bringing more Latin Americans to the United States. By the 1970s the composition of the immigration flows had changed significantly, and by the 1990s Asians had become the largest immigrant group ahead of Latin Americans.

Illegal immigration, which accelerated after the 1964 termination of the Bracero Program, became an even bigger problem over time. The 1986 Immigration Reform and Control Act (IRCA) tried to address this issue through multiple approaches. It allowed illegal migrants who had worked in the United States for a certain number of years to regularize their status (amnesty) but also imposed sanctions on employers who knowingly hired illegal workers. The Immigration Act of 1990 once again addressed regular immigration by increasing the "ceiling" (number) of people admitted as legal immigrants and creating so-called diversity visas that allowed people from a predetermined list of countries to enter the United States if they won the visa lottery.

In 1996 legislation once again turned to the issue of illegal immigration. The Illegal Immigration Reform and Immigrant Responsibility Act (IIRIRA) focused on preventing illegal immigration by strengthening the Border Patrol and imposing harsher punishments for those who enter the United States illegally. In the 1990s, a series of walls and fences was built along the U.S.-Mexican border to prevent drug smuggling and illegal immigration as part of Operation Gatekeeper in California, Operation Safeguard in Arizona, and Operation Hold-the-Line in Texas (Fig. 2.20). As a result of the border fortifications, more people tried to cross in inhospitable (desert) areas, which increased the number of deaths. In 2016, one of the principal promises of presidential candidate Donald Trump was to build a wall along the entire length of the border and to make Mexico pay for it.

The terrorist attacks of September 11, 2001 were a shock to the American immigration system as some hijackers had valid visas and others entered via the little-protected Canadian border. To address the security concerns brought to light by the terrorist attacks, immigration issues were moved to the newly created Department of Homeland Security, and stricter policies, including strict limitations on

FIGURE 2.20 Border Fence between Mexico and the United States—Segments of border fences and border walls between Mexico and the United States have been built since the 1990s; there are now proposals to build a continuous wall along the border. *Source:* Wikimedia Commons.

migrants from some (Muslim) countries, more extensive screening of migrants, and requirements to report undocumented migrants, were implemented. These policies and migrations generally remain highly controversial.

Immigration has been just as important to Canada's history but less contentious. Immigration to Canada occurred in five waves. The first wave began with the French migration to Quebec and Acadia, peaked with the influx of British loyalists fleeing the American Revolution, and ended with the migration of Scots to Canada. The second wave in the early and mid-1800s brought British and Irish immigrants who were encouraged to settle in Upper Canada (present-day Ontario) to counter the French influence in Quebec. The 1872 Dominion Lands Act essentially copied the U.S. Homestead Act to attract more settlers, but Canada distinguished itself from the United States by not excluding certain nationalities as the United States had done. The third wave (before World War I) and fourth wave (after World War II) brought more Europeans, with Ukrainians being one of the largest groups. The fifth wave started in the 1970s and overwhelmingly brought migrants from developing countries. As opposed to the United States, Canada today selects its migrants based on a point system. Would-be migrants get points for characteristics such as their level of education (at least completion of high school, with more points awarded for advanced university degrees), English and French proficiency, previous work experience in approved occupations, age (with preference for those between 21 and 49 years of age), already arranged work, and adaptability to Canada (such as previous experience or family in Canada).

Population Trends and Patterns

With over 320 million people, the United States is the third largest country in the world by population. Canada is home to about 36 million people and is currently ranked thirty-eighth. The most populous state in the United States is California with almost 40 million people, followed by Texas (almost 38 million), Florida and New York (both about 20 million), and Pennsylvania and Illinois (about 12 million each). The least populated states are North Dakota, Alaska, Vermont, and Wyoming. Generally speaking, most of the population in the United States is located in the

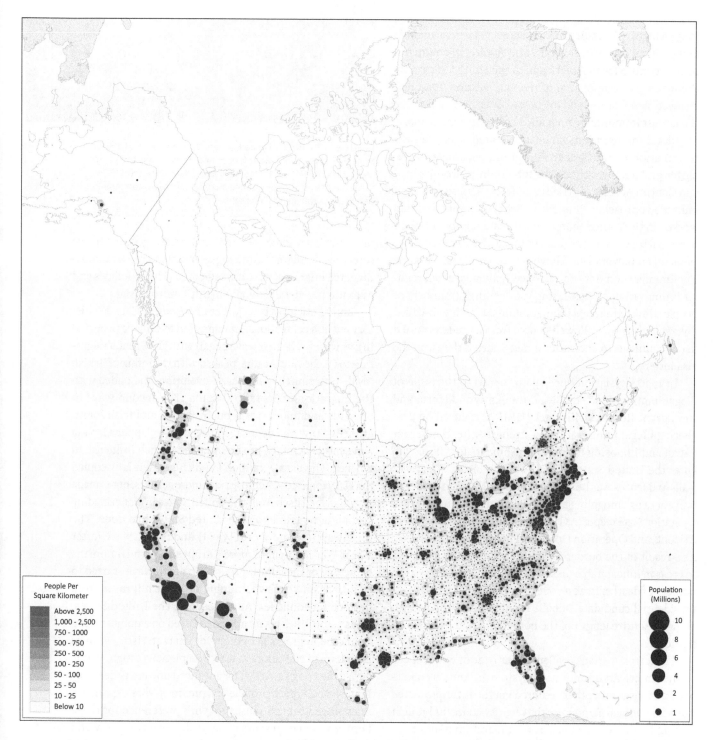

FIGURE 2.21 Population distribution in the United States and Canada—Notice the major east-west differences in distribution patterns in the United States and north-south differences in Canada. *Source:* U.S. Census Bureau; Statistics Canada.

eastern half of the country (especially in the Northeast, Midwest, Florida, and Eastern Texas) as well as along the West Coast (especially in California) (Fig. 2.21). Over time, the U.S. population has shifted from east to west (since the westward expansion of the country) and north to south (migration towards the **Sun Belt**). The highest population gains are now in the South (especially Florida) and the West (especially Nevada and Arizona) (Fig. 2.22). In Canada, the most populous province by far is Ontario (13.5 million), followed by Quebec (8 million). British Columbia and Alberta both have populations of over 4 million. By contrast, the Northwest Territories, Nunavut, and the Yukon Territories are home to fewer than 50,000 people each.

The total fertility rate has declined to 1.84 in the United States, and so lies below the replacement level of 2.1. However, the population growth rate in the United States is higher than that of most other industrialized countries due to the high immigration rates. It is also important to note that there are differences in fertility rates among different ethnic/racial groups. The fertility rate is below the U.S. average for Whites and Asians, slightly above for Blacks and Native Americans, and substantially above (at 2.5) for Hispanics. Canada's total fertility rate is lower than the United States' at 1.67. Its fertility rates are highest among immigrant women and indigenous Canadians in Nunavut and the Northwest Territories.

North American Cities

The United States and Canada are both highly urbanized countries, with about four-fifths of their population living in cities (Fig. 2.23). In the United States, the largest metropolitan areas are New York (21 million), Los Angeles (13.5 million), Chicago (9.5 million), Dallas-Fort Worth (7.5 million), and Houston (6.5 million). In Canada, Toronto is by far the largest city with a population of almost 6 million, followed by Montreal (4 million), Vancouver (2.5 million), and Calgary, Ottawa, and Edmonton (all at about 1.3 million).

Even though the various groups of people who settled North America each brought their own urban traditions, early settlements shared some characteristics. They were very small in area and population, were settled by people with a similar heritage, had irregular streets patterns (except for Philadelphia, which was built on the grid pattern that later became the dominant urban form in North

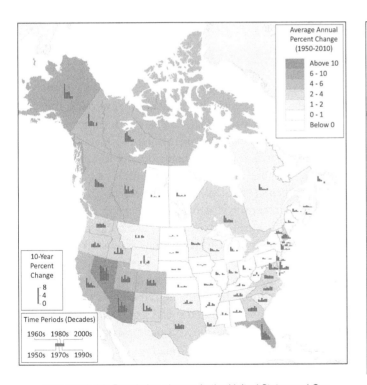

FIGURE 2.22 Population change in the United States and Canada, 1950-2010—The southwestern and southeastern parts of the United States and western and northern parts of Canada recorded the highest rates of population growth while most of the interior areas of both countries and the Maritime provinces in Canada were characterized by the slowest rates of growth. *Source:* U.S. Census Bureau; Statistics Canada.

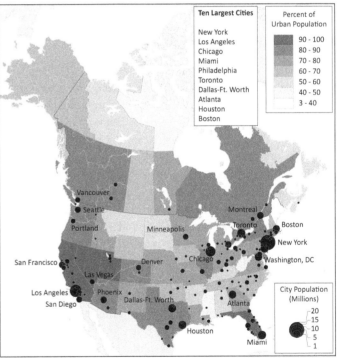

FIGURE 2.23 Urbanization levels in the United States and Canada—Just over 80 percent of both countries' population is urban. California and New Jersey are the most (95 percent) and Maine and Vermont the least (less than 40 percent) urbanized states. *Source:* U.S. Census Bureau; Statistics Canada.

FIGURE 2.24 Chicago's Central Business District—Chicago exemplifies the contemporary North American city, with a business district with high-rise buildings forming the center of the city. *Source:* Heike C. Alberts.

America), and played an important role in the trade with Europe. As cities flourished over time, they attracted a more diverse population. Shortly before independence, the thirteen American colonies had at least a dozen major cities. After independence, New York became the capital city of the United States in 1789 and was quickly replaced by Philadelphia in 1790 and then Washington, DC in 1800.

While New York lost the government capital function, it emerged as the most important business center in the new country, partly because of its advantageous geographic situation. The Hudson River and the Mohawk River provided a lowland route through the Appalachian Mountains. New York City therefore had easy access to the resources of the vast continental interior. From other cities along the Atlantic, getting through the Appalachians was a more formidable challenge. Later the Erie Canal from near Albany to near Buffalo (completed in 1825) linked the city to the Great Lakes, and then early railroads further cemented New York City's transportation advantages.

Throughout the 19th century, first expanding canal networks and then railroads promoted urbanization generally and favored individual cities in particular. Cities in the East grew quickly, cities farther West developed,

and the South increasingly lagged behind the North in urban development as industrialization developed and spread from the Northeast. In the late 19th century the era of the great metropolises began, fueled by technological advances and migration. Technological innovations, such as the elevator and steel construction, allowed buildings to grow skyward (Fig. 2.24), and by the early 20th century New York's famous skyline began to develop. However, cities did not just grow vertically, but also horizontally, as transportation innovations (e.g. horse-drawn streetcars, electric streetcars, and later the car) made it possible for people to live even farther away from downtown. Suburbanization became one of the characteristics of North American cities and promoted social segregation. During the late 19th century, urban populations grew rapidly, partly from migrants coming from rural areas and partly from new immigrants arriving from Europe. New immigrants often formed ethnic clusters, making cities overall much more diverse but also promoting the segregation of people into different neighborhoods (Fig. 2.25). Industrialization brought tremendous wealth to some people in the cities, but the increasing demand for housing resulted in many poorer people living in overcrowded tenements, being exposed to

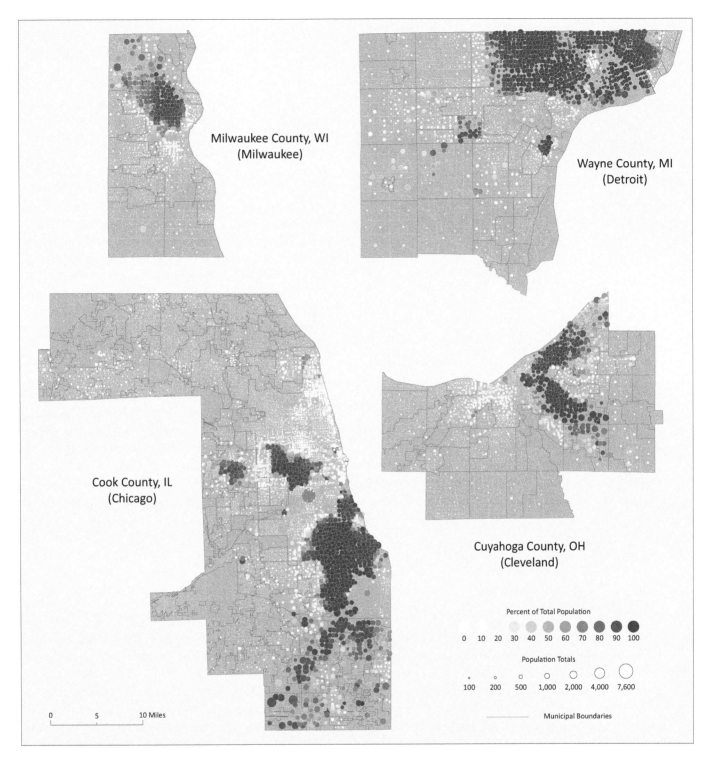

FIGURE 2.25 Examples of racial segregation in American cities, 2010—These maps show the African American population which is characterized by a higher degree of spatial concentration than any other major racial or ethnic minority group. *Source:* U.S. Census Bureau.

industrial and household pollution. By 1920, more people in the United States lived in cities than in rural areas.

Since the 1950s, North American cities have been characterized by several major trends: suburbanization, decline of inner cities, continuing segregation, and economic shifts.[11]

Suburbanization accelerated after World War II as widespread car ownership allowed more and more people to live in the suburbs, and suburbs developed ever farther away from the cities. By now, more people live in the suburbs of North American cities than the cities themselves.

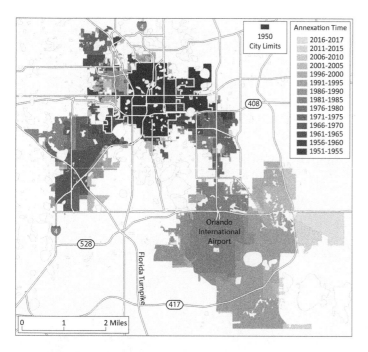

FIGURE 2.26 Urban sprawl in America: the city of Orlando, Florida—The city increased its area almost seven times during the past six decades, from 17 to 118 square miles between 1950 and 2016. Its population increased from 52,000 to 277,000 during the same period. *Source:* City of Orlando.

segregation. Suburbanization also has significant environmental impacts as cities gobble up more and more rural land at the fringes. This urban sprawl is more pronounced in North America than anywhere else in the world (Fig. 2.26). Furthermore, suburbs typically consist of single-family dwellings and rely on personal transportation by car (as public transportation only rarely extends into the suburbs), so that they are also responsible for a significant amount of greenhouse gas emissions. As people moved outwards to the suburbs, jobs and retail went with them. Shopping malls sprang up in suburban locations and especially in **edge cities.**[12] Tysons Corners near Washington, DC, Hoffman Estates near Chicago, and Bellevue outside Seattle are examples of edge cities, a phrase that refers to large suburbs with significant concentrations of jobs; they are places that workers commute *to* rather than the traditional bedroom community suburb that people commute *from*. Edge cities are located at the intersection of urban highways and beltways surrounding cities. Many companies moved their workforces into these edge cities as well and only kept their front offices at prestigious downtown addresses. For instance, in the 1990s, Sears began moving its headquarters from Sears Tower (once the tallest building in the world) in downtown Chicago to Hoffman Estates. As people, jobs, and shopping opportunities moved to the suburbs, inner cities (the area surrounding downtown) declined. Some cities have tried to address this through gentrification to bring back people and businesses, but the problem persists.

Suburbanization has led to homogeneous neighborhoods as individual suburbs house people with similar socio-economic characteristics and can be seen as a form of voluntary

LANGUAGE AND RELIGION

Language

At the time of European contact, over 300 Native American languages were spoken in North America. Today that number is halved, with about 110 languages being spoken in the United States and 60 in Canada. Many of these languages are endangered; two-thirds no longer have any native speakers, and many have only a few. Native American languages are very diverse; they belong to fifty-seven different linguistic families, some of which only have a single language. Scholars have attempted to group these families into larger groups, such as Eskimo-Aleut and Hokan-Siouan, or even a single Amerind language family based on grammatical similarities, but these classifications are controversial.[13] At the time of European contact, none of the Native American languages in North America had a writing system (as opposed to, for example, the Maya in Mesoamerica). However, after contact, missionaries, teachers, and linguists developed writing systems such as the Cree syllabics for Cree and Ojibwa or the Great Lakes syllabary for Fox, Sauk, and Potawatomi.

From about 1790 to 1920 the United States implemented an Americanization policy intended to integrate Native Americans with mainstream American culture. For example, the government forbade many traditional religious ceremonies and required Native American children to attend boarding schools where they were forced to give up their tribal traditions in favor of attending church and speaking English. The policies regarding eradicating Native American languages were finally repudiated in 1990 with the Native American Languages Act, in which the United States committed to preserve, protect, and promote the use of Native American languages. Since then, bilingual and immersion programs have been implemented on Native American reservations.

American English is now the most widely spoken language in North America. American English clearly reflects the influence of the different peoples who settled in North America and had contact with Native American languages. Since British settlers outnumbered French and German settlers in the early colonial period, English was the obvious choice for a common language. American English borrowed from Native American languages, adopting words like *caribou*, *moccasin*, *moose*, *raccoon*, *skunk*, *squash*, and *totem* from Algonquian languages and *igloo* and *kayak* from Eskimoan languages. Over time, as more settlers arrived from non-English-speaking countries in Europe, words from their native languages were incorporated into American English too. Examples include *bayou* from French and *cookie* and *waffle* from Dutch. As the United States expanded to the west, northern European settlers came in contact with Spanish-speaking settlers, and American English absorbed words from Spanish like *tortilla*, *plaza*, and *ranch*. The diversification of immigrants brought more foreign words to English such as *sauna* from Finnish and *spaghetti* and *pizza* from Italian.

Today, American English is considered clearly distinct from British or Australian English as there are differences in pronunciation, words, spelling, and grammar. For example, while British English speakers pronounce the word *specialty* in five syllables (spe-ci-al-i-ty), Americans say only three (spe-cial-ty). For British speakers the word *schedule* begins with a "sh" sound, while Americans pronounce it "sk." Sometimes the two varieties of English use different words, such as British *crisps* and American *chips* or the *boot* vs. the *trunk* of the car, *sidewalk* vs. *pavement*, etc. The differences also extend to spelling, which was formalized by American lexicographer Noah Webster. For example, Webster removed the "u" from words such as *honour* and *labour*, replaced "c" with "s" in words such as *defense* and *license*, and shortened *programme* to *program*. While Canadian and American English are quite similar, Canadian English remains closer to British English due to Canada's longer and closer association with Britain.[14] Furthermore, regional variations have developed in both the United States and Canada. For example, Southern American English is quite different from the varieties spoken in the North or Midwest. African American English (sometimes called Ebonics) is also clearly distinct from standard American English but shares many characteristics with Southern American English.

The United States is a multilingual country. Unlike many other countries it does not have an official language, but English is the primary language used by government, the court system, and in schools. Laws, however, require important documents, such as election ballots, to be printed in multiple languages. While English is not the official language of the country, thirty individual states have declared English as their official language. In Hawaii, both English and Hawaiian have official status, and in Alaska English, as well as a variety of native languages, enjoy this status.

Spanish is the second most important language in the United States. It is spoken by about 38 million people, making the United States one of the largest Spanish-speaking countries in the world. It is important to remember that in the course of its territorial expansion, the United States acquired Spanish-speaking territories in the Southwest, and large numbers of Spanish-speaking immigrants continue to migrate to the United States. In many states with large Spanish-speaking populations, Spanish is also frequently taught to native English-speakers in schools. Many of the bilingual communities in the Southwest, Florida, and New York also use Spanglish, a non-standard language that blends Spanish and English (Fig. 2.27).

Descendants of immigrants still speak a variety of languages such as German, Italian, Polish, and French. Asian languages such as Tagalog, Chinese, Hindi, Korean, and Vietnamese are spoken in recent immigrant communities. It is currently estimated that over 60 million people, a fifth of the population, speak a language other than English at home. The biggest recent increases were in Spanish, Chinese, Arabic, and Urdu, and the languages with the largest number of speakers are Spanish (38 million), Chinese (3 million), Tagalog (1.6 million), and Vietnamese, French, Korean, and Arabic (all over 1 million speakers). The states with the largest percentages of foreign language speakers include California (45 percent), New Mexico, Texas, New Jersey, Nevada and New York (all over 30 percent).

Canada is officially a bilingual country (English and French). In practice, however, most Canadians speak only one of the two official languages, and for the vast majority that language is English. Roughly half of the Canadian population speaks only English and about 90 percent of the population (both native and second language speakers) is fluent in English. By contrast, French-speaking Canadians are much less numerous, and 90 percent of them live in Quebec, the only province where French is the dominant language (Fig. 2.28). In New Brunswick less than a third of the population speaks French, and in all other provinces the number drops to below 2.5 percent. As mentioned above, Canadian English is distinctive from British English, but is more closely related to it than American English. Similarly, Canadian French is different from the French spoken in France. French Canadians tend to use archaisms (old-fashioned terms, pronunciations, and grammar that are no longer used in modern France).

Originally Canada was an English-speaking country, but since the Quiet Revolution in the 1960s Quebecers have demanded official status for their language (French).

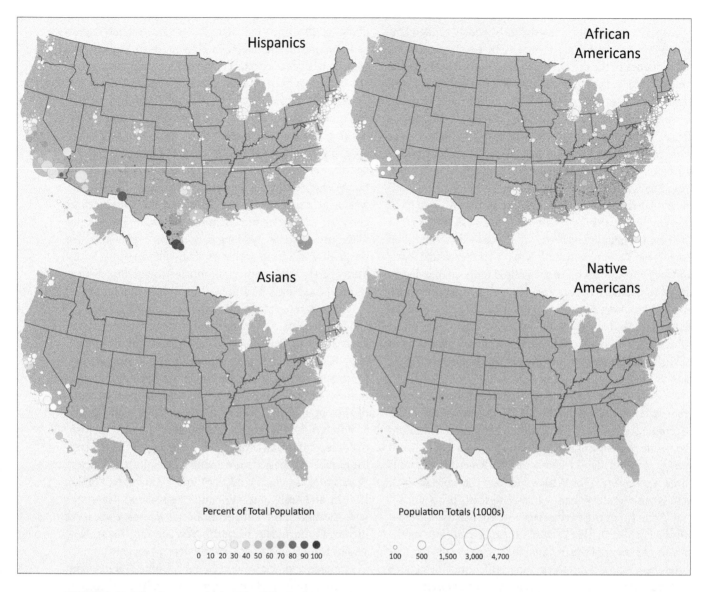

FIGURE 2.27 Minority groups in the U.S., 2010—Racial and ethnic minorities comprise about 23 percent of the U.S. total population. Hispanics are concentrated along the U.S.-Mexican border and in Florida, African Americans in urban areas of the northeast and across the southeast part of the country, Asians in California, and Native Americans in several parts of western regions and Alaska. *Source:* U.S. Census Bureau.

Since the Official Languages Act of 1969, English and French have equal status. In practice, any service provided by the federal government must be available in both languages, from government affairs to post offices. The Canadian government promotes the learning of English in Quebec and French in the rest of the country, but still less than a fifth of the population speaks both languages. In addition to English and French, the most commonly spoken languages in Canada are Chinese, Punjabi, and Spanish. Native American languages in Canada were almost entirely wiped out during colonial times. More recently, however, the Canadian government has protected and promoted the surviving native languages. Only about 120,000 Canadians speak a Native American language at home, with the vast majority of them speaking Cree (in Quebec, Manitoba, and Saskatchewan) and Inuktitut (in the north). In Nunavut, Inuktitut is an official language alongside French and English, and eleven Native American languages are official in the Northwest Territories.

Religion

Religion has always played an important role in the United States. Many of the early English and German settlers came to the United States in search of religious freedom, and

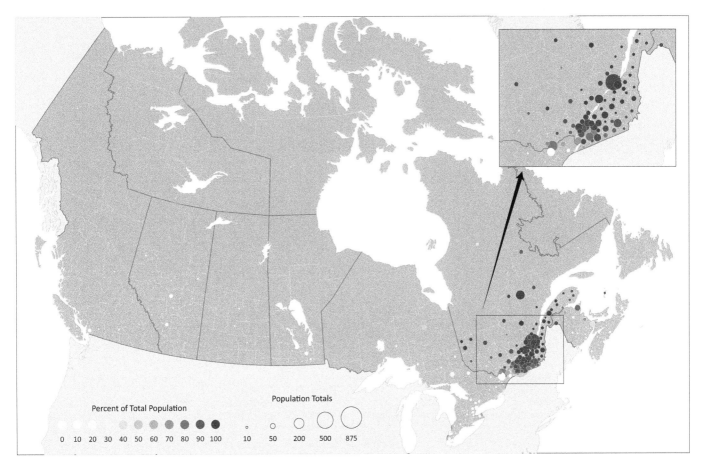

FIGURE 2.28 French Canadians, 2011—While French speakers comprise one-fifth of Canada's population, French Canadians comprise almost 80 percent of Quebec's and 28 percent of New Brunswick's populations. *Source:* Statistics Canada.

many of them formed communities of co-religionists such as the Massachusetts Bay Colony established by Puritans or the Pennsylvania Colony by Quakers. The First Amendment to the United States Constitution guarantees people the freedom to practice their religion, while at the same time disallowing the declaration of a state religion. Even today, religion plays a more important role in the United States than in any other highly developed country. For example, while over a half of Americans state that religion plays an important role in their lives, only a third say so in the United Kingdom and even fewer in Italy and Germany. More than two-thirds of Americans claim to be Christian. Roughly 46 percent of Americans are Protestant and 21 percent Catholic (Fig. 2.29). Protestants are split into a number of different denominations. With over 16 million adherents, Southern Baptists are the largest group. About 1.6 percent belong to the Mormon faith (The Church of Jesus Christ of Latter-Day Saints) (Fig. 2.30). Other religions are followed by about 6 percent of the population.

Distinctive religious regions can be identified in the United States. Catholics outnumber people with other religious traditions in nearly twenty states across the Northeast,

Midwest, and Southwest. Utah and parts of Idaho constitute the Mormon core area, the western states are more secular, and the Bible Belt in the southern states is known for socially conservative evangelical Protestantism. Church attendance is much higher in the Bible Belt than anywhere else in the United States. Mississippi is labeled the most religious state in the United States, with almost two-thirds of its population considering religion as very important to their lives and attending religious services every week.

Mormonism emerged in the 1820s in New York during the Second Great Awakening. Joseph Smith had a vision that told him that the existing churches were wrong and that he should found a true Christian church. The Book of Mormon would provide the foundation. According to Joseph Smith, who is seen as a modern prophet, the Book of Mormon was revealed in golden plates that an angel showed him, and, after writing down the contents, the plates were returned to the angel. Early Mormons were persecuted by other Americans, and they fled first to the Midwest and eventually to Utah Territory. The Mormon Church, which has a strong missionary tradition, now has a worldwide membership of about 15 million and over 70,000 missionaries. The focus of

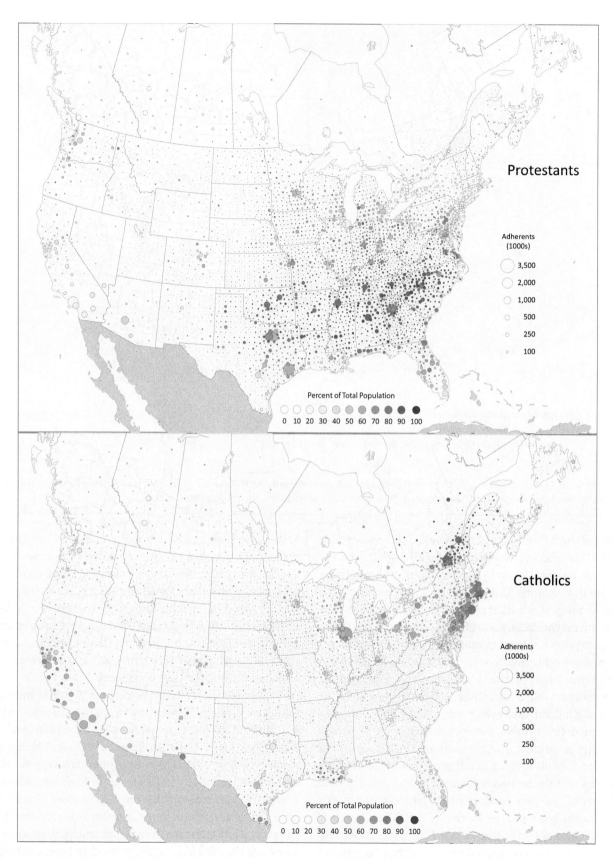

FIGURE 2.29 Protestant and Catholic population in Canada and the United States, 2001-2010—Protestants form the dominant religious group in the United States where over 46 percent of the total population adheres to various denominations while Catholics account for almost 40 percent of Canada's population. Notice the differences in patterns of distribution of both religious groups. *Source:* Association of Religion Data Archives; Statistics Canada.

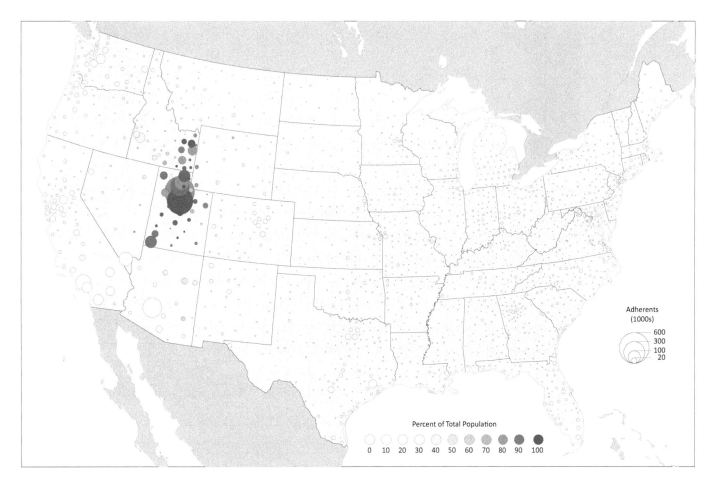

Adherents
(1000s)

600
300
100
20

Percent of Total Population

0   10   20   30   40   50   60   70   80   90   100

FIGURE 2.30 Mormon population in the United States, 2010—The adherents to the Church of Jesus Christ of the Latter-day Saints, also known as Mormons, are heavily concentrated in Utah and a few surrounding states, particularly Idaho, where they comprise 55 and 20 percent of the total population respectively. *Source:* Association of Religion Data Archives.

the Mormon Church is Utah. Over 60 percent of the people in Utah are Mormons, mostly in rural areas, but about 40 percent of the population of Salt Lake City is Mormon as well (Fig. 2.31). The high percentage of Mormons in Utah has a strong impact on the demographic characteristics of the state. For example, the birth rate among Mormons is significantly higher than among other groups, and the average age is lower.

According to projections, Christianity will remain the most important faith in North America in the near future. However, while in absolute numbers the Christian population will continue to grow, other religious groups are expected to increase at much faster rates, thus decreasing the proportion of Christians.[15] The non-religious population is expected to double, and the number of Muslims will likely triple to about 10 million by 2050. Currently, Muslims account for about 1 percent of the United States population, but high fertility rates (about 2.7) and migration will propel the growth of this group. By contrast, while close to 2 percent of Americans are Jewish, their population is

projected to decrease slightly due to low fertility rates and the high average age of this group.

In Canada, Christianity is the dominant religion (two-thirds of the population, mostly Catholics). Almost a quarter of Canadians do not claim any religion, and rates of religious adherence are decreasing. Canadians, on average, are less religious than Americans (the vast majority of Christians only infrequently attend church), but more religious than most Europeans. Canada does not have any official religion and views religious pluralism and freedom of religion as important Canadian values. Islam is the second most important religion in Canada, with about 3.2 percent of Canadians adhering to this faith. About 1.5 percent of the population is Hindu, 1.4 Sikh, 1.1 Buddhist, and 1 percent Jewish. However, Canada is becoming religiously more diverse through immigration, especially in large cities such as Toronto, Vancouver, and Montreal. In summary, the most important trends in Canada are the increasing secularization of Christians as well as an overall diversification of religious affiliation.

FIGURE 2.31 Mormon Temple in Salt Lake City—The temple in Salt Lake City, Utah is the largest Mormon temple and the focus of the Mormon cultural area. *Source:* Heike C. Alberts.

POLITICAL ORGANIZATION OF SPACE

The United States of America is a federal republic. Formed in 1789, the United States (the more commonly used short version of the country's name) was the world's first modern constitutional republic. As a federal republic, the power is shared between the federal government and the state governments of the fifty states (Fig. 2.32). The degree to which power should be delegated from the federal government to the state level has been debated ever since the U.S. Constitution was adopted. Today, due to the wide range of powers delegated from the federal level to the state level and below, state, county, and municipal governments have the greatest influence over people's lives. For example, as issues such as health and education are handled at the level of individual states, there are often great differences in policies and procedures from state to state. Each state has its own constitution and laws and a governor as the elected head of state. The United States of America currently consist of fifty states, a federal district (the District of Columbia, the location of Washington, the seat of government), five territories (American Samoa, Guam, Northern Marianas, Puerto Rico, and the U.S. Virgin Islands), and several possessions (mostly in the Pacific Ocean).

Puerto Rico is by far the most populous territory over which the U.S. has sovereignty that has not been incorporated into the union as a state. The U.S. acquired the island in 1898 after the Spanish-American War. Since 1917 Puerto Ricans have been U.S. citizens, and since 1952 Puerto Rico has been a Commonwealth, freely associated with the United States (*Estado Libre Asociado*). The big question is therefore whether Puerto Rico should remain a Commonwealth, become the fifty-first state of the United States, or become an independent country. Five referenda have been held regarding this question. In the first three, Puerto Ricans clearly preferred maintaining their current status. The two most recent, in 2012 and 2017, resulted in statehood as the favored option but both votes were marred by high numbers of voters sitting out the election.[16] In 2017, only 23 percent of eligible voters cast a ballot and 97 percent of those who did so chose statehood. In both 2012 and 2017, many Puerto Ricans objected to the wording of the ballot believing it was biased to favor a particular outcome. If Puerto Rico became independent, Puerto Ricans would no longer be U.S. citizens, and the United States would not be obligated to support Puerto Rico. If Puerto Rico

FIGURE 2.32 The Capitol, Washington, DC—The Capitol in Washington, DC is the seat of the United States' Congress. The capital cities of U.S. states also have capitols. *Source:* Heike C. Alberts.

became a state, Puerto Rico would have all the rights and responsibilities that the current fifty states have, including representation in the Senate and the House of Representatives and the right to vote for the U.S. President. A key obstacle to Puerto Rican statehood is that there is no other potential new state to balance Puerto Rico politically. In 1959, Hawaii and Alaska were admitted almost simultaneously with the former expected to be a reliably Democrat-voting state and the latter expected to be a Republican stronghold, which has turned out to be right. Given its ethnic makeup and poverty, Puerto Rico probably would be a reliably Democratic state. Republicans therefore are unlikely to support its statehood. In the meantime, millions of Puerto Ricans have left the island for the brighter economic prospects on the mainland. If Puerto Rico were a U.S. state it would be by far the poorest. Another group associated with concentrated poverty in the U.S. is the Native American population on reservations, which are mainly located in the rural west far from the main economic centers of the country (Fig. 2.33).

Native Americans are considered domestic dependent nations that operate as sovereign units. While tribal governments are subordinated to federal authority, they are outside the jurisdiction of state governments. The term **reservation** is the legal designation for land managed by Native American tribes rather than the state governments in the states where they are located. This structure can lead to conflict. For example, Native Americans believe that treaties between their ancestors and the United States government grant them fishing rights, while others believe that states are responsible for regulating fishing. A similar situation arises with casinos and other forms of gaming, which individual states cannot forbid as the tribes have sovereignty over their territories. Tribes can establish their own membership criteria, and those accepted as citizens of that tribe then hold voting rights within that tribal government. There are currently over 300 reservations (and over 500 tribes) mostly west of the Mississippi River. Most reservations are small, but the Navajo Nation Reservation is similar in size to West Virginia.

Canada is dotted with reserves, which are akin to reservations in the U.S. In 2011, the total indigenous population of Canada (called **First Nations**) was about 700,000 of which about 45 percent lived on reserves. By comparison, in the U.S. in 2010, there were 5.2 million people who claimed at least partial American Indian or Alaskan Native ancestry and about 21 percent lived on reservations or similar entities. Among the 2.9 million people who claimed only American Indian/Alaskan Native ancestry, 31 percent lived on reservations. As in the U.S., the indigenous population in Canada is found mainly in the western part of the country; British Columbia, Alberta, Manitoba, and Saskatchewan are home to about 60 percent of native people. Two of the territories in Canada's north have majority indigenous

FIGURE 2.33 Native American and First Nation reservations—Reservations occupy just over 3 percent of the total area, over 5 percent in the U.S. and less than 1 percent in Canada and are inhabited by about one-third and one-half of all indigenous populations of both countries respectively. *Source:* U.S. Census Bureau; Statistics Canada.

populations. Nearly 90 percent of Nunavut's small population is native (mainly Inuit) as are more than half of the people in the Northwest Territories.

In fact, Nunavut was created to provide a separate territory for the Inuit. The major difference between provinces and territories are that provinces received their power from the British North American Act and can act largely independently from the federal government, while territories are granted specific limited powers from the federal government. The Northwest Territories (population 42,000) and Yukon (36,000) were formed in 1870 and 1898 respectively, but Nunavut was only created in 1999 (it was formerly part of the Northwest Territories). Nunavut is the fifth-largest country subdivision (in North America only Greenland is larger) and covers most of northern Canada and the Canadian Arctic Archipelago.[17] If it was an independent country, Nunavut would be the fifteenth largest one. The settlement of Alert (population sixty-two) is the northernmost permanently inhabited place in the world (located just 800 kilometers/500 miles south of the North Pole).

Among the ten provinces, Quebec is the most distinct in many ways. As previously discussed, Quebec is Canada's second most populous province (and the largest by area) and the core area of French-speaking Canadians. Because of its distinctive heritage and French language, Quebec has considered leaving Canada and becoming an independent country. In the 1970s outright independence was considered, but since there was a lack of support, a sovereignty-association, a status where Quebec would be largely independent but share some things (like the currency) with Canada, was proposed. In the 1980 referendum the majority of voters rejected the idea. The margins narrowed significantly in the 1995 referendum, where 50.6 percent voted against the proposal. Since then, voices demanding a separation of Quebec from Canada have become much more muted, partly because the one in eight people in Quebec who are immigrants have little interest in seeing the province break away. In 2006, however, the Canadian government passed a symbolic motion that grants *statut particulier* (special status) to Quebec to recognize its distinctive heritage, but it remains unclear what exactly this status means.

Foreign and Domestic Policy

The United States and Canada have many commonalities. Both are former British colonies (but reached independence at different times and in different ways), both receive a lot of immigrants and are multicultural countries but are pre-dominantly English-speaking, and both have similar federal, democratic, and legal systems. Both are large, highly developed and highly urbanized countries, people use the same brands and shop at the same stores, and U.S. and Canadian cities look similar. However, there are also some major differences between the two. Most importantly for international politics, the United States is a military and economic superpower.

The United States pursues its economic and strategic military interests much more aggressively than Canada as evidenced by its military spending, maintenance of military bases abroad (mostly in Europe, East Asia, and the Middle East), and military involvements abroad (Fig. 2.34). For example, in the past, the United States frequently intervened in Latin America, and in recent years, the wars in Iraq and Afghanistan clearly show American military power. By contrast, Canada follows a softer approach (more like the European Union's), and while it sometimes supports the United States militarily, it has much more limited strategic military interests.

While the differences between the United States and Canada are probably most visible in their global political and economic power, there are also some domestic policy differences. The most important one is probably their attitude towards social programs. Canada has developed a generous social safety net that encompasses health care, unemployment benefits, and a welfare system that benefits all Canadians and prevents extreme poverty. The social safety net in the United States is much more limited, and it is much more contentious among the population. As a result of the differences in access to health care, Canada ranks better than the United States on health indicators such as life expectancy (82 in Canada versus 79 in the U.S. in 2015) and infant and maternal mortality.

Political Polarization in the United States

Recent presidential, congressional, and many state elections in the United States have been hotly contested and sometimes led to skirmishes between the supporters and opponents of both major political parties. Political polarization, or the growing disparity between people (both politicians and the electorate) adhering to opposing views (i.e., liberal or conservative), on many issues such as the government's role in society, abortion, same-sex marriage, health-care policies, gun control, immigration policies, or income inequality has been increasing for the past two decades. The number of Republicans and Democrats with negative opinions of the opposite party has more than doubled since the 1990s, and more of them claim that the policies of the opposite party are harmful to the national interests of the United States. People with strong political views are more likely to associate with like-minded individuals and live in similar neighborhoods. Research on geographic political polarization has confirmed that Americans began clustering into communities with similar values and lifestyle preferences in the early 1970s. Increased residential clustering has been observed in terms of levels of education, income, and marital status but, interestingly, not in terms of race or ethnicity. This polarization has been observed at various territorial levels, from the nine census regions to the over 3,000 counties. Remarkably, Donald Trump won more than 70 percent of the vote in 1,559 counties in 2016 and Hillary Clinton cleared the same

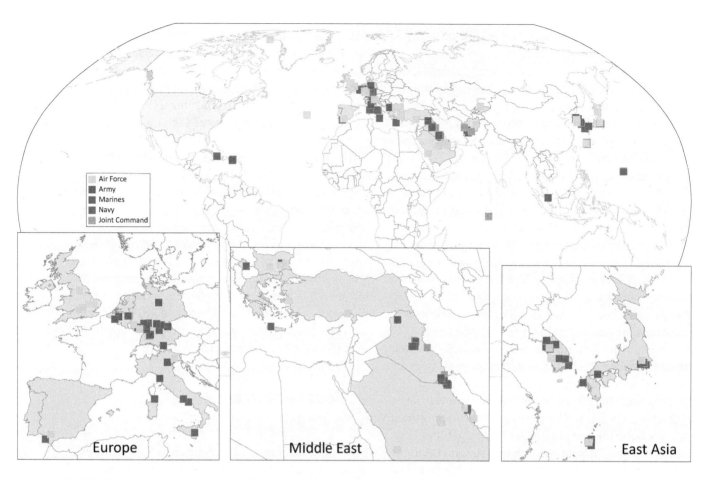

Air Force
Army
Marines
Navy
Joint Command

Europe

Middle East

East Asia

FIGURE 2.34 United States overseas military bases—Over one hundred bases are clustered in Europe, the Middle East (including Afghanistan) and East Asia. Almost half of them are army bases while the remaining half is relatively evenly divided between air and naval bases. *Source:* U.S. Department of Defense.

threshold in 99 counties. By comparison, in 2000 (another very close election nationally), George W. Bush and Al Gore won more than 70 percent of the vote in just 546 and 70 counties, respectively.[18]

While certain parts of the United States have been Republican or Democratic strongholds for decades, as evidenced in the popular vote in presidential elections, the gap between them has been increasing (Fig. 2.35). Traditional Republican strongholds such as Utah or the Great Plains region, and Democratic ones such as New England or coastal areas of California, seem to be further apart than ever before. Some researchers have blamed gerrymandering, the manipulation of the redistricting process to benefit a particular political party in subsequent elections, as one of the main reasons for political polarization. Others claim that place of residence seems to have a greater impact on polarization. Regardless of its causes, the declining number of swing districts (districts with approximately the same number of supporters of both major political parties) is further proof of the growing Republican-Democratic polarization. When political polarization

happens in countries with two-party systems, such as the United States, moderate politicians and opinions are often marginalized and have less impact on policy making. Recent congressional gridlocks (which prevented laws from being passed), filibusters (a tactic to delay legislative actions), delays in appointing judges and other officials or blocking their nominations, likely reflect the growing political polarization in this country. However, some scholars say that political polarization can also affect countries with multi-party systems of government or that it is not necessarily a negative phenomenon.

Canada has its own political geography with four significant parties in play. The Liberals are dominant in the Atlantic provinces, the territories, and the major cities, especially Toronto and Montreal. The Conservative Party leads in the Prairie provinces and some suburban areas elsewhere in the country. The moderately socialist National Democratic Party is strongest in British Columbia, and the Bloc Quebecois—which has favored independence for Quebec—seems to be a political party in decline but still has some support in Quebec.

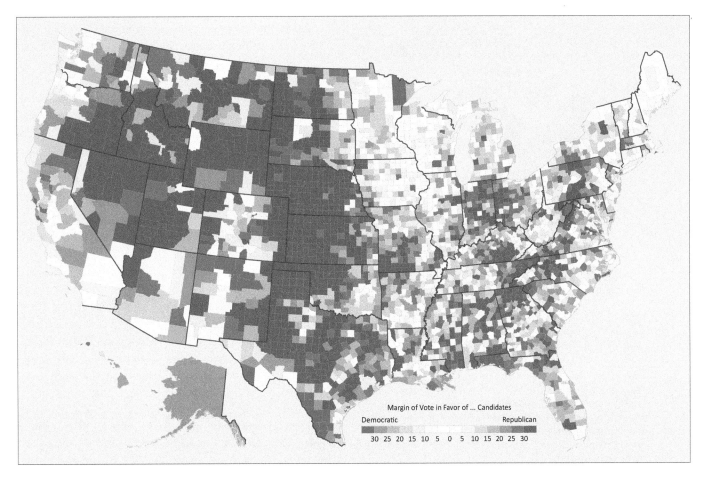

FIGURE 2.35 Presidential elections, 1980-2016: average margin of vote for Republican and Democratic candidates at the county level—The map clearly shows several Republican and Democratic strongholds. The rural areas of the Great Plains and the predominantly Mormon region of Utah and Idaho are the best examples of the former type and New England and most of the Western coastal region of the latter type. *Source:* U.S. Census Bureau; Dave Leip's Atlas of U.S. Presidential Elections.

ECONOMIC ACTIVITIES

The United States and Canada have played the dominant role in the global economy for over one century, and their economic development has been supported by the rich and diverse natural resource base as well as entrepreneurial, well-educated populations and favorable institutions. Together the two countries comprise about 5 percent of the world's population but account for over a quarter of global economic output. Their GDP per capita amounts to over $57,000 and $45,000, respectively (Fig. 2.36).

Agriculture

The United States and Canada have large amounts of land suitable for farming and have been major producers and exporters of various agricultural commodities. One of the most important trends in American farming is the continuing decline of small family farms (and the loss of a way of life) and the expansion of large farms (Fig. 2.37).[19] In 1935, there were almost 7 million farms in the United States, but that number has dropped to about 2 million. There are several reasons for the disappearance of small family farms. First, small farms do not generate enough income. Farmers today are often forced to work additional jobs to make ends meet. Furthermore, most young people do not want to pursue work that requires substantial investments and requires hard work for little money, so most farmers are older. Second, farms have been consolidated for decades, forming even larger farms that smaller farms cannot compete with. For example, between 1970 and today almost 90 percent of the dairy farms in the United States were lost, and the average number of cows per farm rose from 19 to 170. Hundreds of "mega-dairies" now have more than 2,000 cows each. Additionally, more regulations and

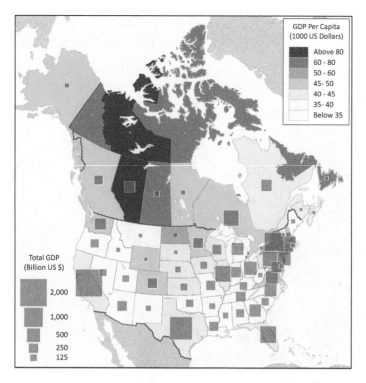

FIGURE 2.36 Gross domestic product in the United States and Canada—The United States' economy is over ten times bigger and its GDP per capita over 20 percent higher than those of its northern neighbor. However, notice the high levels of GDP per capita in parts of Canada, particularly resource rich Alberta and the Northwest Territories.

stable in the recent past and now amounts to 915 million acres (370 million hectares) or just over 40 percent of the land area. Average farm size continues to increase and is now at about 434 acres (175 hectares). However, there are large variations in farm size across the United States. Farm sizes in the entire eastern half of the country, the Pacific Northwest, and California are significantly smaller than those in the Plains, West, and South (Fig. 2.38).

The second major trend is the increasing productivity of U.S. agriculture. On average, a single American farmer now produces enough food for ninety-six people, and the agricultural output continues to increase at a rate of about 5 percent per year. The increase in productivity is partially an outcome of the consolidation of farms and partially of the development of new farming methods. While in the past agricultural innovations were often improvements in irrigation or fertilization, contemporary innovations in agriculture include **precision farming** and **genetically modified organisms** (GMOs). Precision farming is based on satellite or aerial imagery, scientific crop analysis, and advanced forecasting methods to observe, measure, and respond to variations between and within fields. For example, these techniques, coupled with advanced machinery, allow the application of just the right amount of water and fertilizers to small parts of the field (or even individual plants). This has multiple benefits, as it reduces the amount of input (e.g. water, fertilizer) to protect the environment while at the same time increasing the output (e.g. higher yields). Geographic Information Systems (GIS), remote sensing, and other technologies associated with geography have been instrumental in these developments. Genetic engineering or genetically modifying organisms refers to a technique where an organism's genetic makeup has been altered to produce a specific outcome (e.g. resistance to disease). This approach is highly controversial. Opponents raise objections on ethical grounds (e.g. Is it acceptable to implant a fish gene into a tomato?),

pressure by big companies like Monsanto that force farmers to buy their seeds put great strain on family farms. Urbanization, urban areas encroaching on rural lands, also contributes to the disappearance of small family farms. Since 1979, 300,000 small farms have disappeared in the United States, the number of farmers is declining, and large farms (which make up just 9 percent of farms) produce more than half of the country's agricultural output. The amount of land in farms, however, has remained relatively

FIGURE 2.37 Dairy Farm—This is a fairly large dairy farm in Wisconsin. Notice that the dairy cattle are kept inside. *Source:* John A. Cross.

the environmental impact (e.g. contamination of neighboring fields and decline in species diversity), and human health (e.g. long-term studies that show the impact of GMO crops on human bodies are still lacking). Proponents point to the increase in yield and other desirable characteristics (e.g. longer shelf-life and disease-resistance), the possibility to use land that could otherwise not be farmed (e.g. some GMO crops are resistant to salt, flooding, or drought), a less invasive farming technique (e.g. some GMO crops do not require tilling fields, so the soil is better protected), and reduced space needs. Because U.S. agriculture is so productive, Americans spend only about 10 percent of their income on food, one of the lowest rates in the world.

The third trend is a change in farm subsidies. While the farm bills that led to these subsidies predate the Great Depression, the beneficiaries have changed over time. Originally designed to support small farmers, the vast majority of subsidies now go to a small number of large farms. The most heavily subsidized agricultural product is corn. However, only a small percentage of corn is used for human consumption—roughly 40 percent is used for ethanol and only slightly less (36 percent) for animal feed. Some corn is exported and only a small fraction is used for food, and much of that is in the form of high-fructose corn syrup.

The fourth trend is the increase in both exports and imports of agricultural products, but there was a recent decline in exports. The United States produces about half of the world's corn and 10 percent of its wheat. Its most important export products are grains (also for animal feed), soybeans, and livestock products, mostly to China, Mexico, and Canada. Its most important import crops are fruits, vegetables, tree nuts, wine, essential oils, and hops. Sugar and other tropical crops (such as coffee and cocoa) now account for about a fifth of agricultural imports. Canada and Mexico provide most of the food imports, followed by the European Union and parts of South America (especially Brazil, Chile, and Colombia).

Agriculture is practiced in all fifty states of the United States, with California the leading producer of crops and livestock, accounting for almost 11 percent of the total, followed by Iowa, Texas, Nebraska, and Minnesota. Those five together produce about a third of the entire agricultural output as measured by value. There are pronounced regional patterns in where specific agricultural activities take place. California produces a wide variety of crops; it grows almost all of the country's apricots, dates, figs, nectarines, prunes, and walnuts and is the largest producer of avocados, grapes, melons, peaches, plums, and strawberries as well as the second largest producer of oranges (after Florida). California also grows lettuce, tomatoes, broccoli, cauliflower, garlic, mushrooms, onions, and peppers, and

FIGURE 2.38 Average farm size in the United States and Canada—Notice the significant differences in farm size between the eastern and western parts of both countries. *Source:* U.S. Department of Agriculture; Statistics of Canada.

produces wine, milk, eggs, turkey, hogs, and beef cattle. Florida is most known for oranges and other citrus fruits such as limes and grapefruit as well as tomatoes, but it also produces a variety of vegetables and is the leading producer of sugar cane. Washington State is the major producer of apples, but it also grows raspberries, grapes, and cherries.

While the production of fruits and vegetables is concentrated in the coastal regions, the Midwest is particularly known for corn (with Iowa, Nebraska, Minnesota, and Illinois being the major producers) and soybeans (produced in the same region, with Illinois and Iowa leading) (Fig. 2.39). Most hogs are raised in the Midwest as well, with North Carolina (second in production) being the major exception to the concentration in the Midwest. The United States has the fifth largest livestock population by head of cattle, and is the largest producer of beef. Texas has roughly 13 percent of the cattle in the United States (11.8 million heads), followed by Nebraska and Kansas. By contrast, the most important states for dairy are California, Wisconsin, Idaho, New York, and Pennsylvania. The poultry industry is focused in North Carolina and Georgia.

Despite the fact that only a relatively small portion of Canada's land is suitable for farming (7 percent), Canada is also one of the largest agricultural producers and exporters in the world and practices a wide range of types of

FIGURE 2.39 Production of corn and wheat in the United States and Canada, 2010–2014—Most of American corn is produced in the Midwestern states known as the Corn Belt while the Great Plains region, from northern Texas through the Prairie provinces of Canada, is one of the leading producers of wheat in the world. *Source:* U.S. Department of Agriculture; Statistics Canada.

agriculture. Most of the farming is concentrated in the western prairies states of Alberta, Saskatchewan, and Manitoba. The most important agricultural crops are grains (wheat, oats, barley, rye, flaxseed, and corn) and oilseeds (mainly canola), red meats (beef, hogs, veal, and lamb), and dairy. Grain production is concentrated in Canada's Prairie provinces, while fruits are mostly grown in the eastern provinces of Nova Scotia and New Brunswick as well as British Columbia's Okanagan Valley. Potatoes are grown in the Maritime Provinces, and maple syrup is primarily harvested in the Saint Lawrence River region. Despite the northerly location, grapes can be grown in the Maritime Provinces, southern British Columbia, and the Niagara Peninsula. Canada exports more agricultural products than it imports. The United States is Canada's largest export market, especially for pork, beef, and other animal products. Most grain and oilseeds, however, are exported to Japan, China, the European Union, and Mexico.

In many ways agricultural developments in Canada mirror those in the United States. The average size of farms has increased over time (as has the capital value of these farms), and the number of farms and people working them has declined. There are now about 205,000 farms in Canada, with an average size of 315 hectares (779 acres).

However, despite the trend, Canada still has many small farms (21 percent of all farms) with annual sales of $10,000 or less. The output of the largest farms (5 percent of farms) accounts for half of Canadian farm revenue. Forestry is another important economic activity in Canada. About 42 percent of Canada's land area is forested, which equals about 10 percent of the world's forested land. Even though only a very small percentage is logged each year (about 1 percent), Canada is the world's second most important exporter of forest products (especially wood and paper products).

From the Manufacturing Belt to the Sun Belt

The term **Manufacturing Belt** refers to the industrial heartland of America centered in the American Midwest. The region benefited greatly from its excellent transportation infrastructure. The Great Lakes waterways, canals, and railroads linked the iron ore, originating in northern Minnesota, Wisconsin, and Upper Michigan, with the coal mined in the Appalachian Mountains, allowing steel industries to develop (the region was called the Steel Belt at this time). Over time, the region more generally became known for manufacturing. Coal, steel, and the automobile industry were the most important industrial sectors. Around the turn of the 19th century, migrants from Europe and the southern states flooded into the region in search of work. Later, World War II fueled demand for steel and manufactured goods. Chicago, Cleveland, Detroit, Buffalo, Baltimore, and Pittsburgh were the major industrial cities in the Manufacturing Belt.

Chicago (Illinois) became a major transportation center. It was easily accessible via Lake Michigan and is connected to the Mississippi River via canals. It also boasted an extensive rail network. Chicago was particularly known for processing and wholesaling wheat, cattle, and lumber. Baltimore (Maryland) was a major center of metal industries and transportation equipment (especially ships), and Pittsburgh (Pennsylvania) had large steel mills and weapons factories, so it played a major role in supplying the United States during World War II. Buffalo (New York) was the gateway to the West for wheat and grain (much of the grain produced in the Midwest was milled here), but also had significant steel industries. Cleveland (Ohio) benefited from nearby coal and iron deposits, making steel a major industry in the city, but it also refined large amounts of oil. Detroit (Michigan) was the heart of the American automobile industry. After World War II there was a large demand for automobiles,

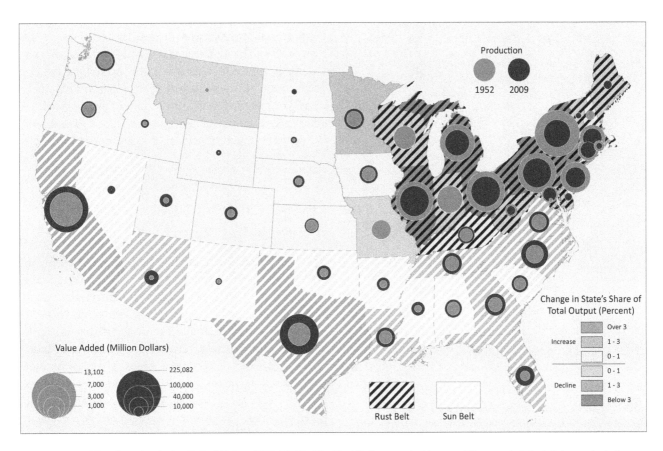

FIGURE 2.40 Manufacturing in the United States, 1952–2009—The Rust Belt accounted for over 70 percent of the total manufacturing production in 1952 but only 40 percent in 2009. The relative decline of industrial production in this region was accompanied by its increase in the Sun Belt states, particularly Texas and California. Their share of production increased from 9 to over 20 percent during that time. *Source:* U.S. Census Bureau.

and Detroit became home to Ford, General Motors, and Chrysler.

In the 1960s and 1970s, however, economic shifts, such as the decline of the iron and steel industries, the relocation of manufacturing to regions with cheaper labor, the increasing automation that lowered the demand for labor, and growing competition from abroad, led to a decline and the formation of what is now known as the **Rust Belt**. The core states of the Rust Belt are Pennsylvania, Ohio, Michigan, Illinois, and Indiana, but parts of Wisconsin, New York, Kentucky, and West Virginia, as well as the Canadian province of Ontario, are also considered to be part of the Rust Belt (Fig. 2.40). The cities in the Rust Belt struggled with adapting to the new situation. Cities lost population, unemployment and crime rates rose, tax revenues fell while dependence on welfare increased, and poverty became widespread. Nevertheless, this region remains vitally important in manufacturing but its many plants employ far fewer people than a few generations ago.

While the population in the Rust Belt has been declining, the **Sun Belt** in the Southern and Southwestern United States has experienced substantial growth. The region attracts people because of its pleasant climate (mild winters, sunny weather) and growing economic opportunities. This growth was made possible by the spread of air conditioning, which made the hot summers bearable. California and oil-rich Texas first attracted people to the South, followed by the West and now the "New South" in the Southeastern United States. The Sun Belt attracted both domestic and international businesses through lower energy costs, cheap wages (no unions), and a business-friendly political climate. Such advantages have helped the South attract most of the new auto assembly plants, for instance, built since 1980. Examples include Toyota plants in Kentucky, Mississippi, and Texas, a BMW plant in South Carolina, and Mercedes-Benz and Hyundai plants in Alabama. The emphasis on developing fuel sources also resulted in economic growth, and in the West the increasing trade with Pacific Rim nations provided a further boost.

The North American economy is now based primarily on service activities (tertiary sector); in both countries, about four-fifths of jobs are in this sector. While the tertiary sector encompasses both low-end service jobs (e.g. cleaning and retail) as well as high-end jobs (e.g. finance, insurance,

FIGURE 2.41 California's Silicon Valley—It is one of the largest clusters of high tech industries in the world located in close proximity to several major research centers and universities (e.g. Stanford), international airports (San Francisco and San Jose), and various recreational and cultural amenities. *Source:* U.S. Census Bureau; Wikipedia.

real estate, medical services, and education), North America is now a **knowledge economy** (also called post-industrial economy) focused on the creation, processing, and communication of knowledge. Knowledge industries are not dependent on natural resources like the steel industry was, so they can be anywhere where a highly skilled workforce is available as much of it is done via the Internet, but are most often located in proximity to research centers or universities. Highly skilled workers demand amenities such as a pleasant climate, nice neighborhoods, and recreational facilities. A prime example of this is Silicon Valley around San Jose in the southern part of the San Francisco Bay area.

Originally silicon chips were made in the area, but now the many well known high tech giants and innumerable start-ups in the area focus on designing and marketing products, with much of the manufacturing done in lower-cost locations. For instance, many products sold by Apple, whose giant spaceship-shaped headquarters is located in Silicon Valley, are stamped "Designed in California Assembled in China" (Fig. 2.41).

Globalization and the North American Economy

The United States and Canada are both major economic players, and their joint economy is similar in size to the European Union's. To be globally competitive, the United States has changed its economic relationships with the rest of the world. Originally, the United States was fairly isolationist in economic terms. For example, after independence, the U.S. government imposed barriers to trade with other countries in order to protect its economy. Now, however, there are more advantages to trading freely with other countries. The most important free trade agreement is the **North American Free Trade Agreement** (NAFTA), which has connected the United States, Canada, and Mexico since 1994. NAFTA has been controversial from the beginning. Trade among the three member states has increased substantially by opening up new markets. However, from the United States' point of view, NAFTA has also led to a trade deficit, with the United States spending more money on imports from Mexico than what it earns from exports to Mexico. NAFTA is also blamed for job losses in the United States. From the Mexican point of view, NAFTA has been blamed for having a negative impact on work conditions in Mexico as well as on environmental problems. Concerns like these were among the reasons President Donald Trump withdrew the U.S. from negotiations to establish the Trans-Pacific Partnership (TPP) in 2017. TPP would have linked eleven economies in Asia, North America, and Latin America.

FUTURE PROBLEMS AND PROSPECTS

The United States and Canada, like the rest of the developed world, face a series of challenges that their governments and people will have to deal with in the foreseeable future. One of them is the demographic maturity of their societies: a growing number of retired people and a shrinking pool of economically-active individuals. This demographic trend has been increasing pressure on limited Social Security or other retirement resources and created an imbalance between growing demand for benefits and the decreasing contributions to such funds. The greying of the American and Canadian societies has also led to the increased pressure on their healthcare systems, magnified by rapidly rising costs of medical services and drugs, at least in the United States.

The transition to a post-industrial economy and globalization have significantly decreased the number of relatively well-paid manufacturing jobs. Although employment opportunities in some segments of the tertiary sector have increased, most of these jobs are low-paid positions and often without any fringe benefits. The rising costs of living make life for many individuals and families with such low-paying jobs much harder. On the other hand, a small segment of the population has benefitted from the economic transformation and increased its share of the total wealth significantly during the past few decades. The richest 1 percent of Americans now controls 40 percent of all wealth. The growing income inequality in the United States concerns many economists and others, and these concerns were expressed during the 2016 presidential election.

Immigration is a very controversial issue, and the presence of about 10 million undocumented migrants is a great concern for many Americans. It was also one of the top issues of the 2016 presidential campaign. Various proposals to solve this problem, such as mass deportations, the wall along the U.S.-Mexican border, and attempts to help undocumented migrants through legalization proposals or sanctuary city resolutions, are equally controversial. The immigration issue has recently been connected to the spread of global terrorism.

The American political and military involvement in many parts of the globe, particularly the War on Terror in the Middle East and growing tensions in East Asia, whether with North Korea over its nuclear weapons program or with China over its territorial claim in the South China Sea, has been a major challenge for recent U.S. administrations. Growing political and economic tensions with Russia and sometimes with European allies may also impact foreign policy and national power.

Despite many problems facing the United States and Canada, the region remains a global economic and political powerhouse. It continues to attract people from the rest of the world who still see it as the land of opportunity and the supporter of freedom and democracy around the globe. It is hard to imagine another country replacing the United States as a global power in the near future.

NOTES

1. McKnight, T. (2004). *Regional geography of the United States and Canada* (4th ed.). Upper Saddle River, NJ: Prentice Hall.

2. Montgomery, D. (2012). Soil wealth. Why North America feeds the world. Retrieved from http://www.cornandsoybeandigest.com/issues/soil-wealth-why-north-america-feeds-world

3. U.S. Environmental Protection Agency. (2017). Great Lakes facts and figures. Retrieved from https://www.epa.gov/greatlakes/great-lakes-facts-and-figures

4. Reisner, M. (1993). *Cadillac desert: The American West and its disappearing water.* New York, NY: Penguin.

5. National Oceanic and Atmospheric Administration. (2018). U.S. billion-dollar weather and climate disasters. Retrieved from https://www.ncdc.noaa.gov/billions/events/US/1980-2017

6. McQuiad, J., & Schleifstein, M. (2006). *Path of destruction. The devastation of New Orleans and the coming age of superstorms.* New York, NY: Little, Brown and Company.

7. Klinenberg, E. (2015). *Heat wave: A social autopsy of disaster in Chicago.* Chicago, IL: University of Chicago Press.

8. National Park Service. (2018). History. Retrieved from https://www.nps.gov/aboutus/history.htm

9. Adovasio, J., & Page, J. (2009). *The first Americans: In pursuit of archaeology's greatest mystery.* New York, NY: Random House.

10. Miyares, I. (2016). Creating contemporary ethnic geographies: A review of immigration law. In C. Airriess (Ed.), *Contemporary ethnic geographies in America* (pp. 31–55). Lanham, MA: Rowman and Littlefield.

11. Wyly, E., Glickman, G., & Lahr, M. (1998). A top 10 list of things to know about American cities. *Cityscape, 3*(3), 7–32.

12. Garreau, J. (2011). *Edge city: Life on the new frontier.* New York, NY: Random House.

13. Greenberg. J. (1987). *Language in the Americas.* Stanford, CA: Stanford University Press.

14. Kretzschmar, W. (2000). American English. In *Microsoft Encarta Online Encyclopedia 2000.* Retrieved from http://autocww.colorado.edu/~toldy3/E64ContentFiles/LinguisticsAndLanguages/AmericanEnglish.html

15. Pew Research Center. (2015). The future of world religions: Population growth projections, 2010-2050. Retrieved from http://www.pewforum.org/2015/04/02/religious-projections-2010-2050

16. Newkirk, V. (2017). Puerto Rico's plebiscite to nowhere. Retrieved from https://www.theatlantic.com/politics/archive/2017/06/puerto-rico-statehood-plebiscite-congress/530136

17. Kikkert, P. (2007). Nunavut. *In Canadian Encyclopedia.* Retrieved from http://www.thecanadianencyclopedia.ca/en/article/nunavut

18. Dave Leip's Atlas of U.S. Presidential Elections. Retrieved from https://uselectionatlas.org

19. Halweil, B. (2000). Where have all the farmers gone? *World Watch Magazine,* September/October 2000, 13(5). Retrieved from http://www.worldwatch.org/node/490

3

EUROPE

GEOGRAPHIC QUALITIES AND WORLD SIGNIFICANCE

Europe is a relatively small region occupying the westernmost part of the Eurasian continent. It comprises only about 3 percent of the total land area (smaller than the continental United States), but is inhabited by 7 percent of the world's population. For a long time, Europe was considered a separate continent. The concept of Europe as a separate continent, popular in ancient Greece and Rome, proved to be false several hundred years ago, and the Ural Mountains in Russia have been widely accepted as the border between Europe and Asia on the Eurasian continent. However, one may still hear and see references to Europe as a distinctive physical region. For the purpose of this book, Europe is the land west of the former Soviet Union (except for the three Baltic states of Estonia, Latvia, and Lithuania which are now part of Europe). It is a distinctive world culture realm that is characterized by organized rule, a coherent system of environmental use, and a similar culture. This region is characterized by great natural diversity and a favorable physical environment, a rich history full of human achievements and inventions (but also the source of some global problems), religious and linguistic diversity, past political fragmentation, and recent attempts of economic and political unification (Fig. 3.1).

For several centuries, Europe played the leading role in world political and economic affairs. Millions of Europeans migrated to other parts of the world, and several European powers imposed their control on Latin America, most of Africa, and many parts of Asia and the Pacific in the form of large colonial empires. European culture has also penetrated other regions, and many of its traits are popular or even dominant in other parts of the world today (e.g. classical music, the English language, Christianity).

FIGURE 3.1 Political map of Europe—No other part of the world of similar size is divided into so many states as Europe is: 41 independent countries (including 5 mini states) and 4 dependent territories.

However, the region is no longer the economic and political center of the world. One reason behind Europe's relative decline in the 20th century was the effect of the two World Wars that were started and mainly fought here. Some 65 to 80 million people were killed and large amounts of infrastructure were destroyed in both conflicts. The emergence of two military superpowers, the United States and the Soviet Union, and their leading role during the Cold War was also a factor in Europe's diminished political importance after World War II. The decolonization process of the 1950s and 1960s led to the loss of some raw material sources and markets for European goods. Industrial dispersion (part of the globalization process) and demographic stagnation have reduced the region's share of the world economy and population between 1900 and 2015 by half (Fig. 3.2). Nevertheless, Europe continues to be an important global player and will undoubtedly remain one of the main power centers in the foreseeable future (in addition to North America and East Asia).

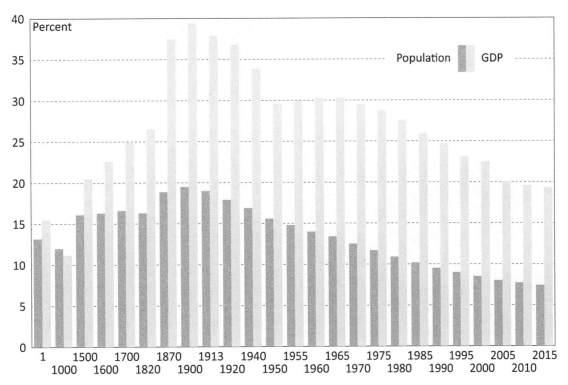

FIGURE 3.2 Europe's world importance—The peak of European importance, at least in terms of its share of the world population and economic power, was at the turn of the 19th and 20th centuries. Since then, the region's demographic and economic significance has been steadily declining. *Source:* Groningen Growth & Development Centre.

PHYSICAL ENVIRONMENT

Irregular Outline and Northern Location

Europe, a large peninsula of Eurasia, is characterized by an irregular outline, northern and central location, diverse topography, mild climate, and a radial pattern of river systems.[1] It is a land of numerous islands and peninsulas surrounded by large bodies of water on three sides: the Arctic Ocean, the Atlantic Ocean, and the Mediterranean Sea (Fig. 3.3) in the north, west, and south, respectively. Its coastline of about 80,000 kilometers (50,000 miles) is longer than that of Africa, although the latter is a much bigger region. About 80 percent of Europe's population lives within 160 kilometers (100 miles) of the coast. Its favorable coastline configuration contributed to the development of trade and naval power in the past. In the north, the Scandinavian Peninsula stretches for over 1,600 kilometers (1,000 miles) and is divided between Norway and Sweden. Denmark is located on the smaller Jutland Peninsula. Three large peninsulas are found in southern Europe: the Iberian Peninsula (Portugal and Spain) in the west, the Italian Peninsula (Italy, San Marino, and Vatican City) in the center, and the Balkan Peninsula (Greece, Albania, and Macedonia) in the southeast. The United Kingdom, Ireland, and Iceland are insular countries occupying three large islands in the western and northwestern parts of Europe. There are numerous smaller islands in the Mediterranean and Baltic Seas. Jared Diamond claims that the fragmented physical geography of Europe (many peninsulas, large islands, great mountain chains cutting across the region) favored fragmented political power (many states), which, in turn, was conducive to the emergence of capitalism and competitive geopolitics (such as the quest for colonies) and these factors helped foster the centuries-long dominance of the world by Europe.[2]

Europe's northern location means that most of its land is at high latitudes, north of the 36°N parallel (north of Atlanta and Memphis in the United States). The east-west mid-line has about the same latitude as the U.S.-Canadian border. Areas located at high latitudes have very long summer days and winter nights. The phenomenon of "white nights" is well known in Europe and is a summer tourist attraction in most Scandinavian countries. The nights are very short at high latitudes in the northern hemisphere in June and July, and the sun may be above the horizon for several days in the northern parts of the region. On the other hand, some visitors from southern regions have difficulties in adjusting their body clocks to long winter nights. There are even suggestions that the high per capita coffee consumption in Scandinavia might have some connections to this phenomenon.

Diverse Topography

Europe is usually divided into four major landform regions, each associated with a different geologic era: coastal and interior lowlands, central uplands and plateaus, northwest highlands, and southern mountain ranges.[3] The North European Plain, the largest part of the coastal and interior lowlands, stretches from southwestern France through Belgium, the Netherlands, northern Germany and Poland, Denmark, and the southern parts of Sweden and Finland to the Baltic states of Estonia, Latvia, and Lithuania. It widens to the east and also occupies most of the western part of the Russian Realm. It was formed by the accumulation of various materials from the adjacent areas by melting ice at the end of the last glacial period. The northern part of the region contains deposits of clay, sand, and gravel, and there are numerous lakes and some marshes. The southern zone of windblown loess deposits has pockets of fertile soil. There are also large deposits of fossil fuels (formed during the earlier geologic periods) in parts of the region (e.g. natural gas in the Netherlands, coal in Poland).

FIGURE 3.3 Mediterranean Coast—Europe has a very long coastline. The Amalafi Coast in Italy is one of the best known in Europe. *Source:* Heike C. Alberts.

FIGURE 3.4 Landform regions of Europe—Each of the four major landform regions consists of several smaller parts, some of them well known such as the Alps and others less familiar (e.g. Rhodopes in Bulgaria) to most people outside the countries they are located in. *Source:* Natural Earth.

Fertile soils, mineral wealth, and good accessibility result in high population densities in this part of the lowlands region (Fig. 3.4).

The zone of the southern mountain ranges is a geologically young area that occupies most of southern Europe and was formed about 50 million years ago. It

FIGURE 3.5 Alps—The Alps are Europe's most significant mountain chain. Wooden houses are common throughout the Alpine region. *Source:* Heike C. Alberts.

is a seismically active region known for sporadic strong earthquakes and several active volcanoes. The Alps are the longest (about 1,200 kilometers/750 miles) and highest (Mt. Blanc: 4,810 meters/15,781 feet above sea level) mountain range in Europe, an arc-shaped area extending from the French Riviera to Slovenia and the Danube River in Austria (Fig. 3.5). Their central part is composed of erosion-resistant crystalline rocks forming high peaks and very steep slopes; to the north and south of the higher Central Alps lie the Limestone Alps known for their high cliffs and canyons. Great differences in the height between peaks and the adjacent U-shaped valleys are the products of glacial erosion. There are several glaciers in the highest parts of the Alps, and together they cover an area of over 2,590 square kilometers (1,000 square miles). The northern and southern parts of the mountain chain also have many lakes including Lake Geneva along the Swiss-French border, Lake Garda in Italy, and the Bodensee (Lake Constance) bordered by Switzerland, Austria, and Germany. Some of the other mountain chains in this zone include the Pyrenees along the French-Spanish border, the Apennines in Italy, the Carpathians in Eastern Europe, and the Dinaric Alps in the former Yugoslavia. The Pyrenees, a 435 by up to 160 kilometers (270 by up to 100 miles) range, are a major transportation barrier between the Iberian Peninsula and the rest of Europe, although they are not very high in comparison to the Alps. The Apennines are one of the youngest mountain ranges in Europe and are characterized by frequent earthquakes and periodic volcanic activity (Vesuvius, Etna, and Stromboli), especially in the central and southern parts. The Carpathians form a

crescent-shaped range about 1,450 kilometers (900 miles) long, running from Slovakia through southern Poland to Romania; they are not very high (maximum elevation is 2,655 meters/8,711 feet above sea level) and do not form a transportation barrier. The Dinaric Alps are a relatively low but rugged and difficult-to-cross mountain range best known for **karst** topography. The Kras Plateau in Slovenia and Croatia, a part of this range, is known for dry, barren, and deeply eroded limestone with numerous sinkholes, underground corridors and caves, and many streams disappearing into the ground and appearing again some distance away. There are also three large plain regions in this zone. The Hungarian Plain, located between the Alps, Carpathians and Dinaric Alps, is filled with river-deposited and wind-blown material and ranges in elevation from 76 to 198 meters (250 to 650 feet) above sea level. Some parts are grasslands with poor soils unsuited for commercial crops. The Po River Plain in northern Italy was formed by the accumulation of eroded material from the Alps. It has a mixture of good soil in the river valleys and poor soil in the out-wash plains. The Wallachian Plain in southern Romania was a part of the Black Sea that was filled with river deposits from the Carpathian Mountains.

The central uplands and plateaus are located north and west of the Alpine system of mountains and were formed about 200 million years ago. They are smaller in area and lower in elevation, have less rugged topography, and are more isolated from one another. Many parts are densely forested, others rich in some mineral resources, and a few have pockets of fertile soil. Some of the best known regions are the Massif Central in southern France, the Jura Mountains along the Swiss-French border, the Black Forest (Schwarzwald) in southwestern Germany, the Ardennes in Belgium, and several ranges along the Czech-German (Ore Mountains and Bohemian Forest) and Czech-Polish (Sudeten Mountains) border.

The northwestern highlands, extending from Ireland and Scotland to the Scandinavian Peninsula, are the oldest part of Europe, formed about 450 million years ago. They are lower in elevation than most of the southern mountains, but higher than the central uplands and plateaus. Their topography has been affected by prolonged erosion and glaciation and includes, among other features, many U-shaped valleys (**fjords**) along the coast of Norway that were flooded by the rising ocean after the last glacial period (Fig. 3.6). There are numerous good harbors (excellent sites for seaports such as Bergen, Trondheim, and Narvik) and short rivers that supply hydroelectric power and water to urban areas. The lower areas are also summer pastures for cattle and sheep.

FIGURE 3.6 Geiranger Fjord, Norway—Fjords have very steep sides and are a popular destination for cruise ships travelling along Norway's western coast. *Source:* Wikimedia Commons.

Mild Climate

Considering Europe's northern location, its climate is exceptionally mild. For example, the average January temperature of Copenhagen is 0°C (32°F), the same as Lexington, Kentucky even though Copenhagen is nearly 20 degrees latitude farther north. One major factor responsible is the warm ocean current (Gulf Stream) along the Atlantic coast; warm waters moderate temperatures, especially in winter, and keep seaports open year round as far north as northern Norway and Iceland. The east-west orientation of major mountain chains allows moist Atlantic air masses to reach most of Europe and the western parts of the Russian Realm and keep them mild, both in summer and winter. The relatively short distances to large bodies of water from all parts of Europe are another moderating climatic factor. Temperatures decline from west to east in winter and south to north in summer. The distance from the ocean and latitude explain these patterns (Fig. 3.7).

There are three major types of climate in Europe.[4] Marine west coast climate is dominant in most of Western Europe. It is characterized by mild temperatures year round (even the coldest month has temperatures above the freezing point), cool summers (heat waves are only sporadic),

adequate precipitation throughout the year (most of it is in the form of gentle showers), a high degree of cloudiness (fog may be quite common), and the absence of violent weather (although strong storms over the North Sea may occur). Most of Southern Europe, especially coastal areas, is in the Mediterranean climate zone, which is characterized by two distinctive seasons: hot-dry summers (with a low degree of cloudiness) and mild-wet winters (with temperatures well above the freezing point). The eastern parts of Europe from the Balkan Peninsula in the south to the Baltic States in the north lie in the zone of humid continental climate, which is characterized by sharp contrasts between winter and summer. Winters can be very cold, and snow stays on the ground for a few months (especially in the northern part of this zone). Summers are rather warm, and thunderstorms may be common. Precipitation is adequately distributed throughout the year, although more of it comes in summer. The marine west coast, Mediterranean, and humid continental climates of Europe are similar to the climates of New England, southern California, and the Midwest in the United States, respectively. Parts of Northern Scandinavia and Iceland are located in the zone of Sub-Arctic climate, characterized by cool and short summers and long and cold (Scandinavia) or mild (Iceland) winters.

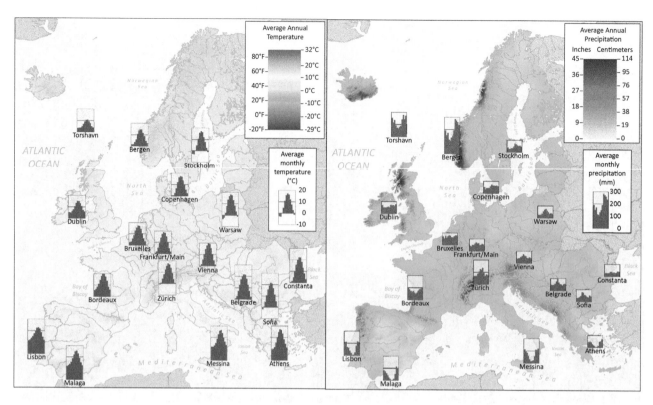

FIGURE 3.7 Europe: patterns of temperature and precipitation—Average annual temperatures decline from southwest to northeast. Notice the growing temperature differences between summer and winter months as one moves away from the Atlantic Ocean. The wettest parts of Europe are the western parts of Norway and Scotland. Also notice the significant differences in precipitation amounts between summer and winter months in southern Europe. *Source:* WorldClim-Global Climate Data.

Radial Pattern of River Systems

Most European rivers originate in the Alps and run in various directions, forming a star-like pattern and connecting the interior areas with the surrounding ocean and seas. Rivers in Western, Central and Eastern Europe are mature streams with well-graded valleys and are navigable; those in the northern and southern regions are more youthful and not navigable because of mountainous terrain and winter freeze (north) or summer drought (south). However, some of them have good hydroelectric potential. The mouths of rivers flowing to the Atlantic Ocean form estuaries and are good sites for seaports; rivers flowing to the internal seas (Mediterranean, Baltic, and Black Seas) created broad, flat deltas, and their mouths are less favorable seaport sites. Flooding is a problem in many parts of Europe; rivers in Eastern Europe most often flood in spring (melting snow); those flowing to the Atlantic may flood after heavy or prolonged rain over the entire catchment area.

FIGURE 3.8 Europe's river system—Most major European rivers originate in the Alps and run in different directions, forming a star-like pattern of waterways. Some rivers in the North European Plain are connected by canals.

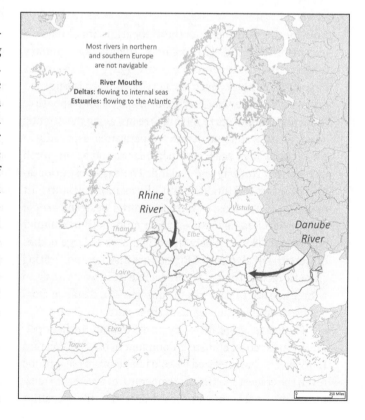

Summer drought and high evaporation as well as porous limestone beds in Southern Europe may be responsible for the low water level and poor navigability of many rivers (Fig. 3.8).

The Rhine is the most important water transportation route in Europe. It originates in Switzerland and runs through densely populated and economically developed parts of Germany and the Netherlands. There are many large cities along its course including Basel in Switzerland; Strasbourg in France; Mannheim, Mainz, Koblenz, Bonn, Cologne, Düsseldorf, and Duisburg in Germany; and Rotterdam (one of the largest seaports in the world) in the Netherlands. The Danube is the longest river in Europe; it originates in southern Germany and runs through several countries before reaching the Black Sea in Romania. There are also several large cities along its course, among them Vienna (Austria), Budapest (Hungary), and Belgrade (Serbia). However, it is a less important transportation route than the Rhine for at least three reasons: (1) it runs through less populated and developed parts of Europe, (2) it forms an international border along parts of its course and is therefore peripheral in importance to some countries, and (3) its delta region is not a suitable site for a large seaport.

Freshwater lakes occupy only 2 percent of Europe's area, and most of them were formed at the end of the Ice Age. One cluster is found in northern Europe, particularly in Finland, Norway, and Sweden; in Finland, lakes occupy 10 percent of the total area. Northern Germany, Poland, and the Baltic states also have many lakes. These lake regions are major summer tourist destinations. The periphery of the Alps is the other cluster of lakes in Europe; although not as numerous as those in the first cluster, some lakes here are quite large and deep.

HUMAN-ENVIRONMENT INTERACTION

Europeans have been interacting with and changing their natural environment for thousands of years through deforestation and the conversion of grasslands to farmlands, extraction of mineral resources through mining, land reclamation and drainage of marshes and other types of wetlands, introduction of new plant species, and industrial development. Some of their actions have led to serious environmental problems in many parts of the region.

Land Reclamation in the Netherlands

Land reclamation and flood protection projects in the Netherlands provide good examples of human-environment interaction. The Netherlands are flat and low and one of the most densely populated countries in the world. About a quarter of its area, inhabited by 20 percent of the population, is below sea level. This part of Europe has sunk about 18 meters (60 feet) since the end of Ice Age (20 centimeters or 8 inches per century) despite the fact that silt deposition by three major rivers partially offsets the sinking process. The phrase "God created the Earth, but the Dutch created the Netherlands" reflects a long history of people's struggle to survive on the land prone to flooding and other water- and weather-related disasters. Hundreds of *terpen*, artificial dwelling mounds offering protection during high tide or river floods, were built over 1,000 years ago. Windmills have been used to drain marshes and other wet areas since the 15th century and are still part of the Dutch landscape.

Land reclamation and flood protection were the main objectives of the Zuider Zee Project that started in 1920 (it was approved in 1918 after a flood two years earlier). The major step was the construction of the 25 mile (40 kilometer) long and 82 meters (270 feet) wide Afsluitdijk (the work began in 1927 and was completed in 1932). It divided a shallow inlet of the North Sea into two parts, one of which eventually became the freshwater lake Ijsselmeer. The next major step was land reclamation and the creation of four **polders** from portions of the Ijsselmeer: Wieringermeer (16,180 hectares/40,000 acres) in 1930, Noordoostpolder (38,850 hectares/96,000 acres) in 1942, Eastern Flevoland (43,700 hectares/108,000 acres) in 1957, and Southern Flevoland (34,000 hectares/86,000 acres) in 1968 (Fig. 3.9). Plans for creating another polder (Markerwaard) were abandoned in 1986. The four polders increased the country's land area by 18 percent; most of the reclaimed land (73 percent) is used for agricultural purposes.[5] The purpose of another project, the Delta Works, was to protect the southwestern parts of the country from flooding. It was in response to a severe North Sea flood in 1953 that affected 150,000 hectares (375,000 acres) of land and killed 1,800 people. An elaborate water-diversion system consisting of a series of flood barriers, storm surge barriers, dams, and locks was built to direct the flow of Rhine, Meuse, and Scheldt rivers into an adjacent lake in case of a storm. The lake can absorb water for several days;

FIGURE 3.9 Polders in the Netherlands—Polders are areas of flat land reclaimed from the sea. *Source:* Heike C. Alberts.

the excess water can be released to the sea. The American Society of Civil Engineers considers the Zuider Zee and the Delta Works projects as one of the Seven Wonders of the Modern World (Fig. 3.10).

Environmental Degradation

The **Black Triangle** is a crescent-shaped border region about 56 to 61 kilometers (35 to 38 miles) wide and 200 kilometers (125 miles) long in the Czech Republic, Germany (former East Germany), and Poland, known for severe environmental degradation due to a high concentration of polluting industries developed during the communist era. A relatively rich mineral resource base (coal, cobalt, copper, lead, nickel, uranium, and zinc) attracted various industrial activities even before the communist governments came to power. However, the industrial base was greatly

FIGURE 3.10 Land reclamation and flood protection projects in the Netherlands—The Dutch have been reclaiming land from the North Sea for centuries, and today about one-third of the country is reclaimed land, most of which is below sea level. *Source:* Natural Earth.

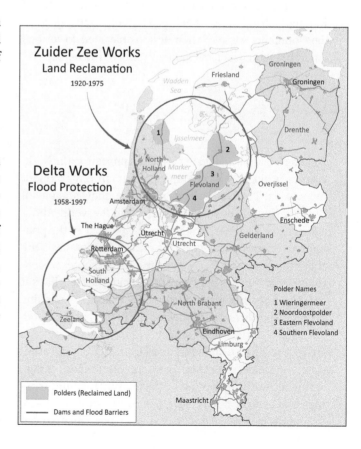

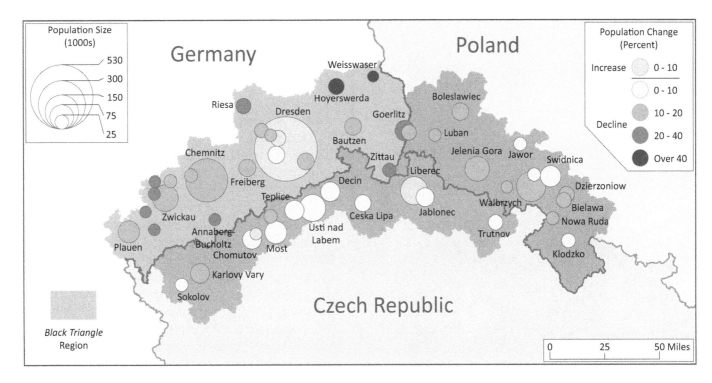

FIGURE 3.11 The Black Triangle: population change in major cities between 1991 and 2015—Only four cities shown on the map gained population during the examined period. Several small cities in the German part of the region recorded the fastest population decline. *Source:* City Population (citypopulation.de).

expanded after World War II when the three countries (on directives from the Soviet government) decided to industrialize the area on a large scale and built chemical, steel, and uranium-processing plants, oil refineries, and coal-fired power plants. Several decades of almost uncontrolled emission of various pollutants to the air, ground, and water have been responsible for acid rain and forest destruction as well as serious health problems and high mortality rates among local residents. Things have changed for the better after the collapse of communism; the region has undergone a major environmental cleanup. However, it continues to be a producer of many industrial goods and energy resources. After the closure of many polluting industries that led to higher unemployment, the Black Triangle has also been losing population, especially in smaller cities (Fig. 3.11).

POPULATION PATTERNS AND TRENDS

Europe is one of the three most densely populated regions in the world. Its total population of about 545 million accounts for over 7 percent of the global population. The four largest countries, Germany (82 million), France (64 million), the United Kingdom (63 million), and Italy (61 million), have almost half of the region's total population.

Population Distribution and Change

Europe's unevenly distributed population reflects environmental conditions and the history and levels of economic development. There are two densely populated belts, one of east-west orientation, extending from England through the Low Countries (Belgium, the Netherlands, and Luxembourg), Northern France, Central Germany, and Southern Poland. This area is a part of the coastal/central lowlands and central uplands/plateaus. Due to its good accessibility (flat terrain and numerous rivers) and deposits of mineral resources (coal and iron ore in particular), it attracted various industries (and migrants) to a rapidly growing number of industrial cities during the 19th century. Pockets of fertile soils (wind-deposited loess) have also made farming a profitable activity here. The other densely populated belt has a northwest-southeast orientation and runs

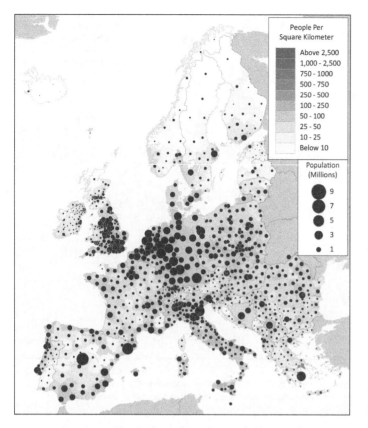

People Per
Square Kilometer

Above 2,500
1,000 - 2,500
750 - 1000
500 - 750
250 - 500
100 - 250
50 - 100
25 - 50
10 - 25
Below 10

Population
(Millions)

9
7
5
3
1

FIGURE 3.12 Population distribution in Europe—The map shows the population density and population totals for sub-national territorial units. Notice the large population clusters in England, the Low Countries, the western parts of Germany, and northern Italy as well as small populations in northern Scandinavia, the interior of the Iberian Peninsula, and northern Scotland. *Source:* GeoHive (www.geohive.com) and statistical agencies of individual countries.

through Italy and Switzerland (interrupted by the Alps) and merges with the first belt along the French-German border. Historical factors may have contributed to higher population densities here. Present-day Italy is the center of the ancient Roman Empire, and it already had a relatively large population 2,000 years ago (estimates range from 6 to 14 million). Rome was a city of over 1 million inhabitants by the second century CE. The population of that area remained relatively stable (with periodic ups and downs) until about 200 years ago when it reached 18 million and began to increase rapidly.[6]

The lowest population densities are found in northern Europe where cool climate, dense forests, poor soil, and mountainous terrain prevent large-scale settlement. Iceland, similar in area to Belgium and the Netherlands (two of the most densely populated countries in Europe), has a population of just over 300,000, while the two Low Countries have a combined population of 28 million. The northern parts of Norway, Sweden, and Finland (similar in area to Germany) have a population of about 2 million.

Mountainous regions and most of the dry interior in the Iberian Peninsula also have low population densities (Fig. 3.12).

Europe has been well known for very low fertility and population growth rates during the past several decades. Since 1950, its population has increased by only 36 percent; that is the slowest growth among all major world regions. All European countries have now below replacement fertility levels (2.1 children per woman). In the absence of migration, the region would already be losing population. An interesting fact is that the lowest fertility is now found in the less developed countries of Eastern (mainly former communist states) and Southern Europe, while most of Western and Northern Europe has fertility rates 30 to 40 percent higher. For example, in Lithuania, Romania, Poland, and Slovenia, the average woman has only 1.3 children; in Ireland and Iceland, that number is close to 2.0. Why are Europeans not interested in having more children? Numerous studies offer a variety of answers. First, many couples and individual women postpone having their first child for several reasons including (1) increased emphasis on individual reproductive rights, rejection of traditional norms regarding women's family role, importance of "higher order needs" (i.e., material goods and/or education and career), and greater gender equity; (2) rise in women's educational attainment and labor force participation; and (3) uncertainty during young adult years in terms of employment and economic stability.[7] Second, a high level of secularization and growing marital instability and/or changing concept of marriage (e.g. lower marriage and higher divorce rate, single parenthood, cohabitation and same sex unions, marriages at a later age) have been observed in most European societies for the past four to five decades. Third, the introduction of oral contraceptives in the 1960s and later improvements in access to other forms of contraception allowed many women to control their fertility.[8] Fourth, the growing importance of the costs of children, direct maintenance costs and opportunity costs (lost employment and educational, recreational, and other opportunities due to raising children), and the declining importance of children's benefits means that raising a child is considered too expensive by many couples (Fig. 3.13).

In response to low fertility, many European countries introduced a set of measures designed to reverse this trend perceived by some governments as a serious demographic threat. With the exception of a few former Communist countries (Romania in particular), governments in Western Europe did not introduce any strong pro-natalist polices (e.g. prohibition of abortions or taxation of unmarried adults) because they would be seen as violations of basic human rights. Instead, they provided a variety of financial

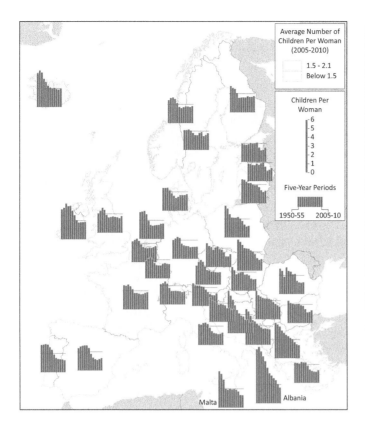

FIGURE 3.13 Total fertility rates in Europe, 1950-2010—Currently, countries in Western and Northern Europe have the highest fertility rates in the region. These rates sharply declined in most European countries in the 1960s and have remained relatively stable since then or began going up in recent years. The red line in each graph indicates the replacement level fertility of 2.1 children per woman. Notice that currently every country has below the replacement level fertility. *Source:* United Nations. Population Division. World Population Prospects 2012.

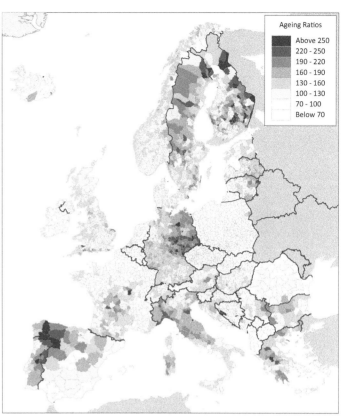

FIGURE 3.14 The graying of Europe—The ageing ratio is the number of people over 65 years of age (retired) per 100 people under 15 years of age (children). Notice the particularly unfavorable demographic conditions in the former East Germany and northwestern Spain. *Source:* EUROSTAT.

incentives and family- and work-related initiatives to encourage childbearing and parenting such as generous maternity (and paternity) leaves, birth payments, and subsidies for child care.

One major outcome of Europe's current population trends is demographic ageing: the shrinking proportion of children and increasing proportion of the elderly. The ageing or greying of Europe, described as an unprecedented, pervasive, and enduring process with profound implications, has received a lot of attention among researchers, economists, and politicians. Nineteen out of twenty of the demographically oldest countries in the world are in Europe. In Germany and Italy over 21 percent of the total population is 65 years of age and older. Even in the demographically youngest societies (Albania and Ireland), over 10 percent of the population is in that age category (for comparison, 15 percent of the U.S. population is in the same age category). The ageing process will lead to, among other things, increased pressure on the health care and pension

systems. It will also affect many European economies already challenged by high unemployment rates. Although Europe is the first region to be challenged by population ageing, this phenomenon seems to have global dimensions. Therefore, there are recommendations of developing policies and cultures that accept older societies instead of those that reverse fertility decline. Examples of the former would be increasing the retirement age, increasing social security and pension contributions of the current economically active population, and changing the pay structure by determining wages/salaries on the basis of performance rather than seniority (Fig. 3.14).

Migration

Migration has been an important component of population change in Europe for several centuries, and its significance has increased in recent decades. While Europe was the origin of millions of migrants going to the Americas, Australia, and New Zealand before World War I, it has been the

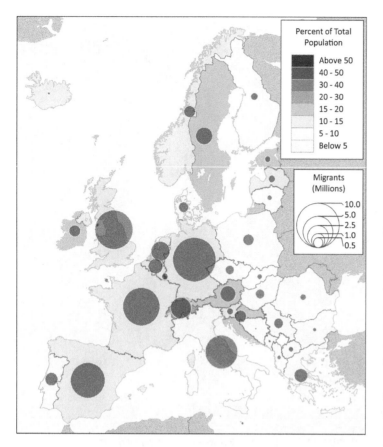

FIGURE 3.15 Foreign-born population in Europe—Notice the difference between most countries in Western Europe and former communist states in Eastern Europe. *Source:* United Nations. Population Division. World Population Prospects 2012.

destination for a large number of labor migrants and refugees from Africa and Asia since World War II. High demand for labor (mainly in Western Europe) was the result of postwar economic recovery, U.S. financial help (Marshall Plan), and war-related population loss. Originally, most migrants were recruited from countries in southern Europe (Italy, Spain, Greece, and Portugal). These countries were less developed and had labor surpluses (Spain and Portugal did not participate in World War II). After economic conditions improved and labor surpluses disappeared there, Western Europe became an attractive destination for migrants from the Middle East and Northern Africa. French-speaking countries became the major destination for North African migrants, while German-speaking states began attracting migrants mainly from Turkey and the former Yugoslavia. Most migrants from South Asian countries (Bangladesh, India, and Pakistan) came to the United Kingdom. The political instability in the Middle East and sharp increase in oil prices in 1973 led to economic recession in Western Europe and other developed countries. As a result, there was a sharp decline in the demand for migrant labor as

well. Some migrants went home but most stayed in their host countries. After the collapse of communism, Eastern Europe became the main supplier of labor migrants. There are over 54 million migrants in Europe now, and Germany has one-fifth of them. Other countries with large numbers of foreigners are the United Kingdom (7.8 million), France (7.4 million), Spain (6.5 million), and Italy (5.7 million). Most of the migrants come from Romania (2.8 million), Poland (2.7 million), Turkey (2.6 million), and Morocco (2.5 million) (Fig. 3.15).

Refugees, including asylum seekers, comprise another group of migrants that has increased in size in recent years because of political instability and conflict in several Middle Eastern and African countries. Smugglers transport many of them by boat across the Mediterranean Sea and drop them off the coast of Italy, Spain, and Greece. Some of these refugees later apply for political asylum in other European countries. There were over 1 million refugees in Europe in 2014, most of them (over 50 percent) in France, Germany, and Sweden (Fig. 3.16).

The presence of foreign-born people (labor migrants and refugees) and their children born in the host countries has been a controversial issue in many European countries for some time. The fact that many of them are of a different race or religion, speak another language, and may be dependent on government help in the initial phase of resettlement, has led to increased anti-immigrant sentiments, violence against foreigners, and culture clash in several countries. Some far-right and/or anti-immigrant political parties have won enough votes to be represented in national parliaments (e.g. the Freedom Party in Austria, National Front in France, Progress Party in Norway, and the Party for Freedom in the Netherlands). French secular culture has been challenged by tensions regarding the display of religious symbols in public schools when several Muslim girls refused to remove their head scarfs in class.

While labor migrants and refugees came to Europe recently, the Roma people, popularly known as the Gypsies, have lived there for centuries. The Roma people left northern India about 1,500 years ago and reached Europe via the Balkan Peninsula about 900 years ago. They faced heavy persecution in the past, most catastrophically during World War II when 1 million of them perished in Nazi concentration camps. Roma culture is very rich and in many ways different from that of other local residents, and some groups practiced a nomadic way of life until recent times. There are about 12 million Roma people in the world, and over 7 million of them live in Europe, mainly in the southeastern part. Most Roma people are bilingual; they are fluent in Romani and the language of their home country. They have been engaged in such occupations as horse traders, metal

FIGURE 3.16 Syrian Refugees—Millions of Syrians have left their home and sought refuge in Europe, the vast majority in Germany. *Source:* Wikimedia Commons.

workers, tinkers and scrap dealers, violin makers, as well itinerant circus entertainers, musicians, and fortune tellers. The Roma have been stereotyped as petty criminals and often live on the margins of mainstream societies.[9] Periodic tensions between the Roma people and local residents have been occurring in some countries (Fig. 3.17).

Urbanization Levels

Although the first urban revolution originated in the Middle East over 5,000 years ago, Europe was the first world region to establish a true urban system and experience large-scale urbanization. Ancient Greece was a collection of city-states. Some cities (e.g. Athens, Sparta) were quite large in population and had two distinctive parts, the *acropolis* (center of power and religion) and the *agora* (place for public meetings

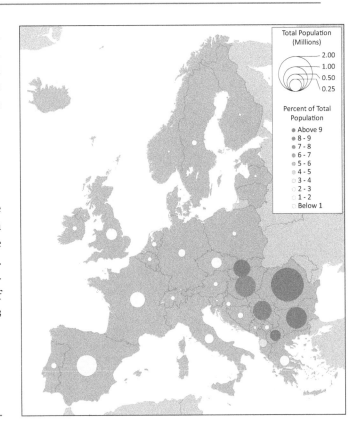

FIGURE 3.17 Distribution of the Roma people in Europe—In Bulgaria, Macedonia, and Slovakia the Roma comprise over 9 percent of the total population while Romania, Bulgaria, Hungary, and Spain have the largest numbers of them. *Source:* Wikipedia.

FIGURE 3.18 Roman Ruins—These Roman ruins in Ostia (the port of Rome) show how sophisticated cities in the Roman Empire were. *Source:* Heike C. Alberts.

and commercial activities). Living conditions in residential quarters were quite low by modern standards. Many Roman cities were established at former military camp

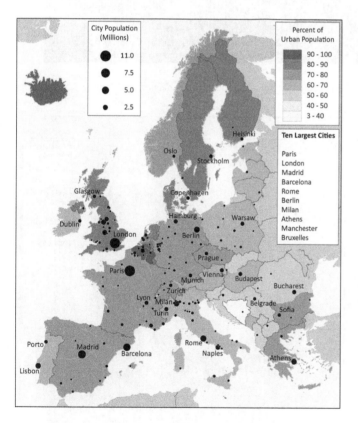

FIGURE 3.19 Urbanization levels in Europe—Belgium and Iceland have the highest percentage of urban population (over 95 percent) while Bosnia and Herzegovina has the lowest (40 percent). Paris and London are clearly the largest urban agglomerations in the region. *Source:* United Nations. Population Division. World Urbanization Prospects 2014.

sites and were better planned settlements (grid-iron street patterns) than the Greeks'. The *forum* was the major functional zone of a typical large Roman city; centrally located, it combined the functions of the Greek acropolis and agora (Fig. 3.18). The arena or Colosseum (an equivalent of a modern sports stadium) and public baths were two new features in the urban landscape. The largest arena in Rome could seat 80,000 spectators, and the city had hundreds of public baths; some of them could be compared to present-day urban parks and combined shopping and culture centers.

Europe experienced an urban decline during the **Dark Ages**. Many cities lost population and economic importance; however, some Christian centers survived and even expanded during the latter part of this era. Large-scale urban renewal took place during the medieval period, and most contemporary European cities were established at that time. Five symbols reflected the major functions of a typical medieval city: fortress (defense), charter (political autonomy), wall (defense and legal urban boundary), market (trade and other economic activities), and cathedral (religion).[10] Medieval cities have impacted (to various degrees in different parts of Europe) the layout, institutions, and culture of many contemporary urban settlements. Prague in the Czech Republic, Rothenburg in Germany, Carcassonne in France, Edinburgh in Scotland, and Sienna in Italy are good examples of such cities. The urbanization process was associated with the centralization of political power, formation of nation-states, and increased interest in urban planning during the Renaissance and Baroque periods. Many European cities, especially national capitals and those located along the coast, significantly increased their population size.

The Industrial Revolution and capitalism led to a major transformation of many urban settlements. Factories, railroads, and slums became new features of the urban landscape. Growing income inequality, speculation, and land transactions resulted in mixed and chaotic land-use patterns. Industrial pollution caused higher mortality rates. Major changes have occurred in European cities since that time, including urban decentralization (development of public transportation), an increase of housing and environmental standards, the gentrification of older neighborhoods, the development of suburban residential and commercial outlets, and many others.

Europe is a highly urbanized region today; over 70 percent of its population is urban, although that number ranges from over 90 percent in the United Kingdom and Belgium to about 50 percent in the southeastern parts of the region (Fig. 3.19). Although Europe, the U.S., and Canada are developed regions and similar in many ways, there are major differences between their cities.[11] First, European cities are much older; most of them were established in medieval times or earlier, and the medieval urban core is still part of the modern urban landscape in most of them. Second, a typical European city is much smaller in area and more densely populated than its American counterpart of similar population size. Land has been a more precious resource in Europe, and this fact prevented the horizontal expansion of most urban areas; and, the automobile, with its city-sprawling effects, has been less influential (e.g. there are about 40 percent fewer cars per 1,000 people in Denmark than in the U.S.). A much higher proportion of urban residents live in high-rise apartment blocks. Third, most European cities have irregular street patterns. This feature has its origin in the medieval period associated with little if any urban planning. Fourth, low skylines are another feature of many cities in Europe. The absence of high-rise office structures in the city center is particularly visible in Southern Europe, the Scandinavian countries, and cities such as Paris, Brussels, Amsterdam, Prague, and Budapest. Many city centers are historically important areas, and there are height limits on construction of new buildings. Fifth, medieval plazas and market squares have been preserved in many cities. They may perform different functions today, but they are also tourist attractions and many have been closed to traffic. Sixth, greater neighborhood stability is another feature of European cities. Urban families usually stay in the same place for generations. Housing has been more expensive and, in many places, in short supply. Once a family obtains an apartment or single family dwelling, it is less likely to look for something else. Seventh, symbolism also plays an important role in urban life. Many cities have distinctive architectural features from the past, famous libraries, museums, sacred structures, and monuments commemorating major historic events and figures. Finally, there is a greater mixture of commercial and residential activities in the downtown or the historic core area. Europeans have been less dependent on private transportation and value proximity to various retail services and cultural amenities, many of which are found in the city center.

Despite these differences, there are a number of common features shared by European cities. For instance, cities in Eastern Europe used to be similar to those in Western Europe prior to World War II but were significantly transformed during forty years of Communist rule. A typical large city under Communist rule had a high proportion of public (government-owned) housing composed of high- and medium-rise apartment blocks made from pre-fabricated elements. There was little residential segregation and poverty, a high dependence on public transportation, almost no advertising and competing businesses, and a very low level of services. Some of the post-Communist changes include a growing number of tourist amenities (hotels and restaurants) and the construction of high-rise office and residential structures and shopping malls either in the city center or on the periphery.

Although Europe has a well-developed and dense network of urban settlements of various sizes, it does not have many large cities. Only London and Paris are **megacities** with more than 10 million people in their respective metropolitan areas. Two other large cities, Madrid and Barcelona, have a population of at least 5 million each. Some countries have a poorly-balanced urban system with one large city (**primate city**) that is several times larger than the next largest settlement. Paris in France, Vienna in Austria, Athens in Greece, Copenhagen in Denmark, and Budapest in Hungary are good examples of such cities. On the other hand, Germany, the United Kingdom, Italy, Poland, and a few smaller countries have much better balanced urban networks. In comparison to the rest of the world, European cities have been growing slowly due to low rates of natural increase and counter-urbanization (migration from urban to rural areas).

LANGUAGE AND RELIGION

Linguistic Diversity

Compared to the United States and Canada, Europe is a linguistic mosaic. However, European languages belong to a very small number of linguistic families, smaller than in any other major world region. Despite the low genetic diversity of European languages, several countries have had to deal with various linguistic problems and political stability and national unity have been at risk in some of them. Language is quite often a major symbol of cultural and group identity.

Over 95 percent of Europeans speak a language that belongs to the Indo-European family. As indicated in Chapter 1, it is the largest and most widely dispersed family of languages in the world. There are three major and five minor branches of that family in Europe. The Italic (Romance)

FIGURE 3.20 Linguistic diversity of Europe—Most languages spoken in Europe belong to the Indo-European family. The Finnish, Hungarian, and Estonian languages are members of the Uralic family while the Basque language forms its own family. *Source:* World Language Mapping System.

branch or sub-family includes languages that originated from Latin, the language of the ancient Roman Empire. Some languages, such as Italian, French, Spanish, Romanian, and Portuguese, have at least 10 million speakers and are the national languages in their respective countries while Catalan and Galician, two other large languages in this group, are confined to parts of Spain.

Germanic languages are dominant in the countries of Western and Northern Europe. They originated from a language spoken by residents of Northern Europe (Southern Scandinavia and present-day Northern Germany) at least 2,000 years ago. German has the largest number of speakers in Europe and is the language of Germany, Austria, Liechtenstein, and parts of Switzerland, Belgium, and Italy. The second most important language in this group, English, is used in the United Kingdom and Ireland. Many other Europeans have good English proficiency as well. Dutch is spoken in the Netherlands and Northern Belgium where it is known as Flemish. The four largest Scandinavian languages, Swedish, Danish, Norwegian, and Icelandic, have relatively small numbers of speakers but

are official languages in Sweden, Denmark, Norway, and Iceland, respectively. Swedish is also one of two official languages in Finland.

The Slavic languages, divided into three branches, have a large number of speakers, but most of them live in the Russian Realm. The western branch includes Polish, Czech, and Slovak languages. The major languages of the southern branch are Serbo-Croatian, Bulgarian, Slovene, and Macedonian. Russian and Ukrainian are members of the eastern branch (the largest one), but they have few speakers in the European region (Fig. 3.20).

Speakers of two less important linguistic sub-families, Baltic and Celtic, are found in Lithuania and Latvia, as well as on the western fringes of the British Isles and France, respectively. The Celtic languages used to be more widespread; today, their speakers are mainly confined to the western peripheral parts of the United Kingdom, Ireland, and France. Welsh, Scottish Gaelic, Irish Gaelic, and Breton are known to only a small fraction of the population in these countries despite the attempts by some governments to keep these languages alive. Two Indo-European languages, Greek and Albanian, are less related to other languages and form their own branches. Finally, the Romani language belongs to the Indo-Iranian branch and is used by the Roma people who are found mainly in countries of Southeastern Europe, Spain, and France.

The remaining 5 percent of Europeans speak a language that belongs to the Uralic, Altaic, Afro-Asiatic, or Basque families. The Hungarian language has the largest number of speakers among the Uralic languages; in addition to Hungary, it is also spoken in parts of Romania and Slovakia. Finnish and Estonian, very similar to one another, are also members of this family. Another Uralic language, Saami, is used by the Saami people (also known as the Lapps) living in northern Scandinavia who are best known for reindeer herding. Maltese, spoken by about 300,000 people and one of the two official languages of Malta, is the only Afro-Asiatic language native to Europe. The Basque language is used by about 1 million people occupying the western parts of the Pyrenees (along the border of Spain and France) who traditionally have been engaged in sheep herding. It is a language of unknown origin and is not associated with any other linguistic family (Fig. 3.21).

Considering Europe's great linguistic diversity, it should be no surprise that over half of the adults claim to know at least one other language. In most countries, students in primary schools have to study at least one foreign language, and in secondary schools two languages. English is the most popular foreign language in all the countries except Luxembourg, where French is the most popular tongue, and the Baltic States, where Russian is the most important second language. The Netherlands, Malta, Denmark, and Sweden have the highest percentages of people who know English as a foreign language.[12]

All but two European countries (Finland and Luxembourg) have official languages. Belgium and Switzerland have three official languages; Ireland and Malta have two. Bosnia and Herzegovina also has three official languages (Bosnian, Croatian, and Serbian), but in reality all three are variations of the same language known as Serbo-Croatian. German is the official language in five countries (Austria, parts of Belgium, Germany, Liechtenstein, and Switzerland); French in four (Belgium, France, Monaco, and Switzerland); English in three (Ireland, Malta, and the United Kingdom), and Dutch in two (Belgium and the Netherlands). The European Union (EU) has twenty-four official languages, and all documents have to be published in each language so that citizens of individual countries can read them in their native tongue. To accomplish this, the EU has a permanent staff of 1,750 linguists and 600 support staff in addition to 600 full-time and 3,000 freelance interpreters.

Some European societies have been very concerned about the purity of their language and have tried to protect it from foreign influence, especially in the era of globalization. In France, for example, the French Academy (established in 1635) is the official authority on the usage, vocabulary, and grammar of the French language. In recent years, it has tried to shelter it (without much success) from the influence of English by recommending French terms for such global words as "software" (*logiciel*) and "e-mail" (*courriel*). Iceland established a Language Institute in 1985 and later merged it with other institutions to form the Institute for Icelandic Studies to protect the Icelandic language from foreign influence and maintain its purity as much as possible. For example, the word "telephone" is *telefon* in Danish, Norwegian, and Swedish, but *síma* in Icelandic. There used to be a law that an individual acquiring Icelandic citizenship had to adopt an Icelandic name by dropping

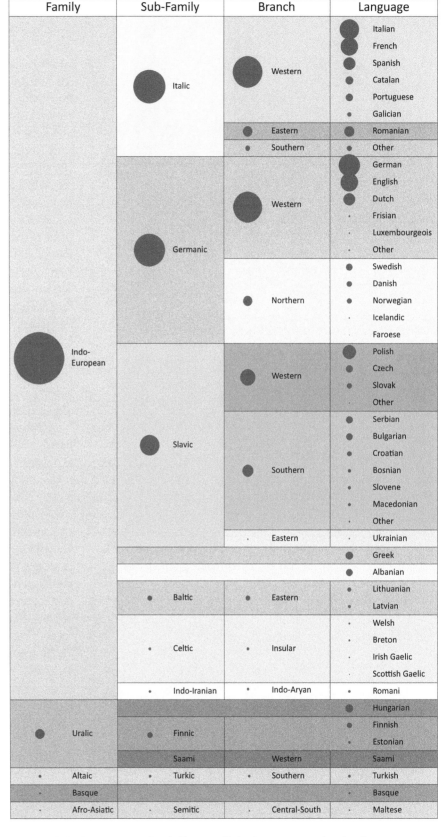

FIGURE 3.21 Languages spoken in Europe—Circle sizes are proportional to the number of speakers of each language (or linguistic branch). *Source:* World Language Mapping System.

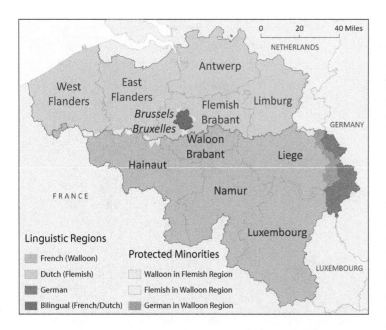

FIGURE 3.22 Linguistic regions in Belgium—The country is divided into the Walloon (French), Flemish (Dutch), and Brussels-Capital (bilingual) regions. The German language area is part of the French-speaking Liege Province. The Walloon, Flemish, and Brussel-Capital regions have a population of 3.5 million, 6.4 million, and 1.2 million respectively. *Source:* StatBel-Belgium in Figures.

his or her native name completely or by modifying it to become Icelandic.

Linguistic diversity has been a source of tension in some countries.[13] Belgium is an example of a country divided along linguistic lines. It became independent in 1830 and included Dutch-speaking areas in the north (Flanders) and French-speaking regions in the south (Wallonia). A small German-speaking area in the east was added to Belgium after World War I. Originally, Belgium was a highly

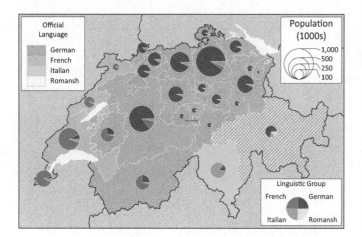

FIGURE 3.23 Linguistic diversity in Switzerland—Shaded areas indicate official languages in each canton and pie charts show the number of speakers of the four major languages. *Source:* Swiss Statistical Office.

centralized state, and French was the language of government, business, and higher education. The Dutch-speaking population, numerically and later economically dominant, had been calling for more linguistic rights and eventually for cultural autonomy. In response, the French-speaking population began supporting a similar movement for their cultural autonomy. The outcome of that was the partition of Belgium into four linguistic or cultural regions in the early 1960s: the French-speaking area of Wallonia, the Dutch (Flemish)-speaking region of Flanders, the German-speaking region in the eastern part of Liege province, and the bilingual region of Brussels, the capital city. Many things in the country, even the Parliament, are divided along these linguistic lines. If the United States were Belgium, there would be four major political parties, the French- and Dutch-speaking Democratic and Republican ones. Candidates for public service positions are expected to be bilingual and have to take a language test. There are even claims that Belgium is an artificial country that was created to separate France from Germany in hopes of minimizing political instability in Western Europe at that time (Fig. 3.22).

Switzerland is a multi-lingual country with three official languages (German, French, and Italian). However, it may also be the best example of a successful multi-lingual country in the world. Its population of over 8 million is divided into German, French, Italian, and Romansh speakers (65, 18, 12, and 1 percent of the total population, respectively; the remaining 4 percent includes speakers of other languages). Switzerland, one of the oldest countries in Europe, has been a federal state from its formation, and the federal government allowed each canton (as individual states are known in Switzerland) to make its own decisions about language. For example, in 1978 the new canton of Jura was established to satisfy the demands of the French-speaking population in the predominantly German-speaking canton of Bern. Each canton has an official language, and, until recently, the entire country had four official languages. The Romansh language is now official in only one canton. Swiss children are required to learn at least one other major language starting in elementary school (Fig. 3.23).

The Baltic states of Estonia, Latvia, and Lithuania had some linguistic issues after their independence in 1991. All three countries restored their national languages as the only official language in each country. Additionally, Estonia and Latvia required non-native residents to pass a language test for citizenship. This policy created tensions between Russia and the Baltic states as there is a sizable Russian population, especially in Estonia and Latvia, which feared being degraded to second-class status. Some of these issues have been resolved through the relaxation of requirements for citizenship, and the number of individuals without citizenship has dropped by more than half since their independence over twenty years ago.

Linguistic diversity in Spain has also been associated with political instability and even violence in recent years. As mentioned earlier, the Basque language, spoken by about 1 million residents in Northern Spain and Southwestern France, is the oldest language in Europe, very different from the other languages used in Spain. The Basque Country is a relatively well developed part of the country, and economic prosperity has attracted migrants from other regions. Consequently, Basque speakers comprise only one-third of the entire population. Their language and culture had been frequently suppressed, most recently during the dictatorship of General Francisco Franco (1936–75). More radical elements in the Basque community formed a militant organization that resorted to violence and terrorism in the late 1960s and 70s. The region was granted autonomy in 1978, and things have been relatively peaceful since, although the debate about how much power should be transferred from the central to regional government continues (Fig. 3.24).

Catalonia is another Spanish region that has been at odds with the central government. Like the Basque region, it is one of the richest parts of the country, and it has been a magnet for migrants. The Catalans, who comprise about 50 percent of the total population, also experienced linguistic and cultural discrimination before 1975. The region received limited autonomy in 1979. A recent non-binding referendum in Catalonia on the region's future was overwhelmingly in favor of independence, but the Spanish Court declared it illegal even before it took place.

Religious Diversity

It may be pure coincidence that there are a few similarities between linguistic and religious patterns across Europe. First, a great majority of people speak one of many Indo-European languages, and a great majority of Europeans claim Christian roots. Second, there are three major branches of the Indo-European linguistic family in Europe (Italic, Germanic, and Slavic), and there are three major Christian denominations (Catholic, Protestant, and Eastern Orthodox). Third, there is some spatial correlation between linguistic and religious patterns in Europe; the Italic-speaking regions are predominantly Catholic (Romania is an exception), the Germanic-speaking regions predominantly Protestant (Austria is an exception), and the Slavic-speaking regions predominantly Eastern Orthodox (Poland and the former Czechoslovakia are exceptions). Fourth, linguistic differences have played a role in political instability and conflicts in some countries, and similarly

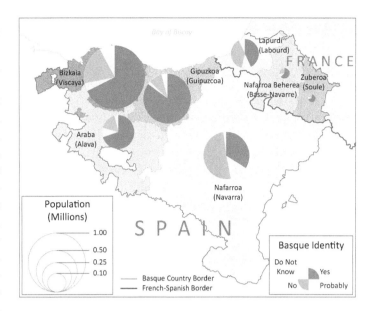

FIGURE 3.24 The Basque region—There are about 2 million Basques in the region, and over 90 percent of them live in Spain. *Source:* Wikipedia.

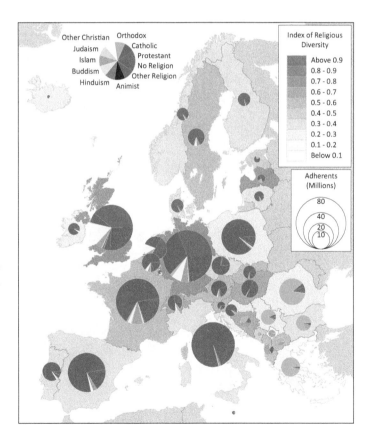

FIGURE 3.25 Religious diversity in Europe—A low value of the index of religious diversity means that there is one dominant religious group (e.g. Eastern Orthodox in Greece); a high value indicates the opposite situation--the presence of two or more groups (e.g. the Netherlands). *Source:* Association of Religious Data Archives.

religious differences have caused numerous tensions and wars (Fig. 3.25).

Religion, like language, is a very important symbol of cultural identity, and Christianity and European culture used to be almost synonymous. Numerous works of architecture, art, literature, music, and philosophy were inspired by Christianity. This religion, in the past, also had a major impact on the natural environment, political organization of space, and economic activities. Although its role in the daily life of many Europeans has significantly declined in recent decades, other religions, particularly Islam, have been growing in importance.

Christianity replaced the polytheistic religions of the ancient Greeks and Romans by the early fourth century when it was legalized by the Emperor Constantine (313 CE) and later (380 CE) became the official religion of the Roman Empire. It spread to the British Isles (first to Ireland and later to Britain) in the fifth and sixth centuries, the Germanic lands in the seventh and eighth centuries, and the Slavic areas and Scandinavia in the tenth and eleventh centuries. Present-day Lithuania was the last part of Europe to convert to Christianity in the second part of the 14th century. Two major events contributed to the split of Christianity into three major branches. First, the Great Schism of 1054 led to the establishment of the Eastern Orthodox Church, centered in Constantinople (present-day Istanbul in Turkey) through separation from the Roman Catholic Church centered in Rome. Second, the Reformation of the early 16th century, led by Martin Luther (1517) in Germany, Ulrich Zwingli (1520) and John Calvin (1530) in Switzerland, and King Henry VIII (1534) in England, among others (e.g. John Knox), resulted in the establishment of several Protestant denominations, including the Lutheran and Anabaptist in Germany, the Reformed in Switzerland and France, Presbyterian in Scotland, and Anglican in England. There have been more divisions within the Protestant movement since that time.

The Roman Catholic Church is the largest Christian denomination in Europe (Fig. 3.26). About 47 percent

FIGURE 3.26 Catholic Procession in Bavaria—Religious processions such as this one for Corpus Christi (sixty days after Easter) in southern Germany are common in Catholic areas of Europe. *Source:* Heike C. Alberts.

FIGURE 3.27 St. Peter's Basilica in Rome—St. Peter's Basilica is the focal point of the Vatican, the papal enclave in the city of Rome that is technically an independent country. *Source:* Heike C. Alberts.

of the region's population adheres to this faith. It is the dominant religion in several larger countries of Southern, Western, and Central Europe, including Italy, France, Spain, and Poland. The smaller countries of Portugal, Austria, Belgium, Ireland, Slovenia, Croatia, Slovakia, Lithuania, Luxembourg, and Malta, as well as four ministates (Andorra, Liechtenstein, Monaco, and San Marino) are also predominantly Catholic. Vatican City, technically an independent country, is the religious center of Roman Catholicism (Fig. 3.27). The Protestant denominations, accounting for about 18 percent of the total population, are dominant in all five Scandinavian countries. The Eastern Orthodox Church, whose followers comprise 14 percent of Europe's population, is the majority religion in the southeastern countries, especially Greece, Romania, Bulgaria, Serbia, and Macedonia. The Christian population in Germany, the Netherlands, and Switzerland is fairly evenly split between Catholics and Protestants.

Islam is the second largest and fastest growing religion in Europe. Muslims comprise less than 5 percent of the total population and are largely found in two parts of

Europe. The first region with a sizable Muslim population is Southeastern Europe, including Albania, Kosovo, and Bosnia and Herzegovina. This area was part of the Ottoman Empire until 1918, and some residents converted to Islam under Turkish rule. Their descendants comprise most of the Muslims in this part of Europe today. The second concentration of Muslims, bigger in size than the first one, is associated with the post-World War II labor migration from the Middle East, North Africa, and parts of Asia to countries of Western, and more recently, Southern Europe. France, Germany, and the United Kingdom have the largest number of Muslims in Europe (Fig. 3.28).

Prior to World War II, Europe had a large Jewish population amounting to over 9 million, and three-fourths of them lived in Eastern Europe, particularly in Poland and the Soviet Union. The Jews had been there since the 14th century when they were expelled from Western Europe after being falsely accused of causing the **Black Death**, which killed one-third of Europe's population. The systematic and large-scale persecution of Jews began again after Hitler came to power in Nazi Germany. Between 1941 and

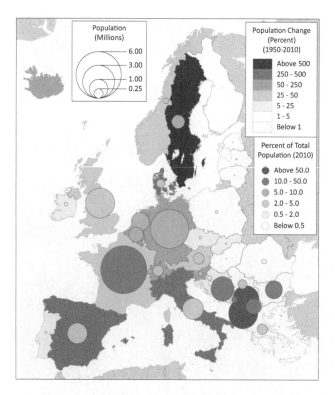

FIGURE 3.28 The Muslim population in Europe—The total Muslim population is over 27 million. Sweden, Spain, and Italy have recorded the fastest rate of growth of this population. *Source:* Kettani, H. (2010) "Muslim Population in Europe: 1950–2020" in *International Journal of Environmental Science and Development* 1 (2): 154–164.

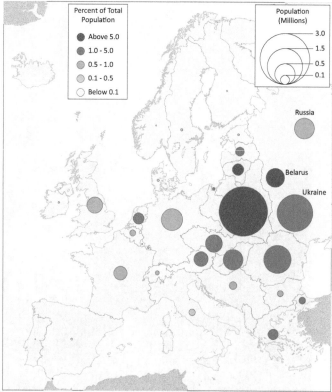

FIGURE 3.29 The Jewish population of pre-World War II Europe—There were over 9 million Jews in Europe before World War II; 42 percent of them lived in Poland where they comprised over 9 percent of the country's population. *Source:* American Jewish Yearbook.

1945, some 6 million Jews were killed, over half of them in extermination camps. Many of those who survived the Nazi **genocide** (Holocaust) migrated to Palestine and the newly formed state of Israel. As a consequence, the number of Jews in Europe declined significantly. Today, there are just over 1 million, and almost half of European Jews live in France. The United Kingdom and Germany also have sizable Jewish populations (Fig. 3.29).

A significant and growing segment of the European population is characterized by a high degree of secularization. Regular church attendance is very low in some countries; only about 3 to 5 percent of the population in Scandinavian countries and Estonia attend church services regularly. A quarter of the population in Germany, the United Kingdom, and France, and three-quarters in the Czech Republic and Estonia have no religious affiliation. For over 80 percent of people in Sweden, Denmark, and Estonia, religion plays no role in their lives, according to a recent (2009) Gallup poll (Fig. 3.30).[14]

Despite the high secularization levels in many countries, Europeans seem to be less concerned about the separation of church and state than Americans are. In Denmark, Iceland, and Norway, some of the most secularized countries in Europe, Lutheranism is the official state religion. The Anglican and Presbyterian churches are official in England and Scotland, respectively. The British monarch is the supreme governor of the Church of England. Eastern Orthodoxy is the state religion in Greece and Roman Catholicism in Malta, Monaco, and Vatican City.

Religious pilgrimages to numerous sacred sites have been popular in some parts of Europe. Millions of Catholics visit Lourdes in Southern France, Fatima in Portugal, or Czestochowa in Southern Poland. These and many other sites have been associated with religious apparitions and miracles, and many pilgrims go there with the hope for physical healing and spiritual renewal (Fig. 3.31). Religion has made an important architectural imprint on the landscape in many parts of Europe. Romanesque, Gothic, and Byzantine churches are part of the cultural landscape in the Catholic, Protestant, and Eastern Orthodox areas, respectively. Some Roman Catholic structures are very prominent (e.g. St. Peter's Basilica in Rome or Cologne Cathedral in Germany).

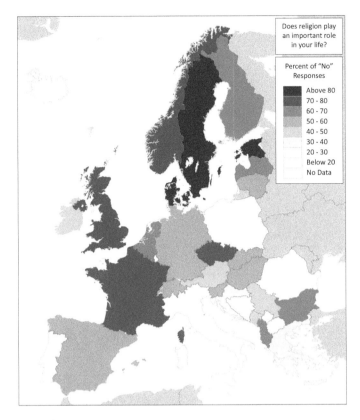

FIGURE 3.30 Secularization in Europe—Notice the high percentage of negative responses to a question on religion's role in personal life in some West European (four Scandinavian countries, France, and the United Kingdom) and East European (Estonia, the Czech Republic, Bulgaria, and Albania) countries. *Source:* Gallup Poll.

FIGURE 3.31 Major religious pilgrimage sites in Europe—The most important sites are labeled, and they are visited by millions of pilgrims every year.

Linguistic and Religious Tensions

Religious differences played a role in numerous internal and international conflicts in Europe in the past. Several conflicts followed the Reformation movement in Germany and Switzerland in the 16th century (e.g. the German Peasants' War). The Eighty Years' War in the Low Countries and the Thirty Years' War in the Holy Roman Empire of the 17th century are other examples of such conflicts.

Although the recent struggle between Catholics and Protestants in Northern Ireland had more cultural, social, and historical causes than religious motivations, it became a popular example of a religious conflict as well. The island of Ireland, a predominantly Catholic area, had been under British control for several centuries. Many Protestant settlers from England and Scotland moved to the northern part of the island (known as Ulster) and by the early 18th century controlled most of the land there. Ireland became a part of the United Kingdom in 1801, but the Irish Catholics were discriminated against in many ways. Periodic Irish uprisings were quickly suppressed by the British. The present-day Republic of Ireland became independent in 1921. However,

the northern part of the island with a Protestant majority opted for union with the United Kingdom. The Irish Republican Army, a Catholic paramilitary organization, formed in 1919, reverted to violence to reach its goal of uniting both parts of Ireland, and was responsible for over 1,700 deaths during the 1969–93 period known as "The Troubles." Protestant paramilitary organizations responded in kind, and both sides used terrorist methods to redress their grievances. Over 3,500 people were killed in this conflict. The Good Friday Agreement of 1998 started the peace process which has been interrupted by periodic tensions and even terrorist attacks. Most of the Catholic-Protestant tensions had taken place in two major cities, Belfast and Londonderry. Although the situation in Northern Ireland has been relatively peaceful in recent years, both cities, but especially Belfast, remain segregated. Many Protestant and Catholic neighborhoods remain physically divided by a wall, and social interaction between them is limited (Fig. 3.32).

The early 1990s conflict in the former Yugoslavia, especially Bosnia and Herzegovina, also had many dimensions, and religious differences were of major importance. This conflict is discussed later in this chapter.

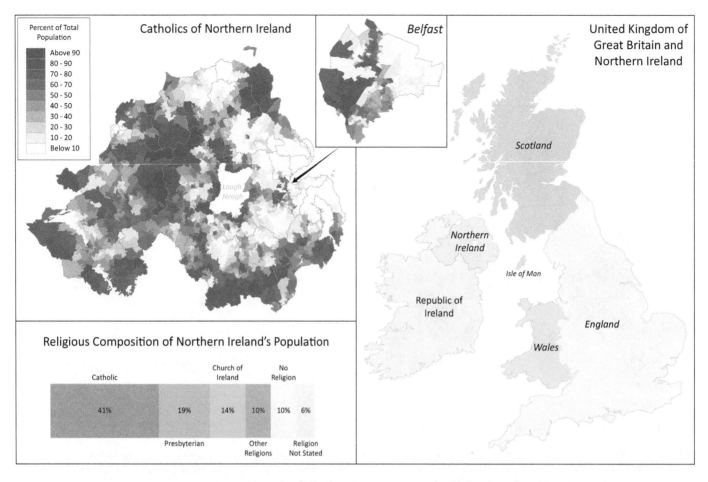

FIGURE 3.32 Religious divisions in Northern Ireland, 2011—Notice the high degree of residential segregation in the city of Belfast and other parts of the region. Data are shown at the ward level. *Source:* Census Office for Northern Ireland.

POLITICAL ORGANIZATION OF SPACE

Political Fragmentation

Europe has been a politically fragmented region for most of its written history. Ancient Greece was a collection of city-states characterized by periodic internal and external conflicts. The ascent of the Roman Empire was a centuries-long departure from the fragmentation of the region as Rome gained control of vast territories in Southern, Western, and Eastern Europe and beyond, but its dominance was dependent on massive military force to maintain law and order in this culturally and economically diverse region. The fragmentation (including the divergence of Latin into the myriad Romance languages) that ensued with the collapse of the Roman Empire returned Europe to its seemingly inherent tendency toward division. The Dark Ages were a time of great political fragmentation, economic regress, and limited interaction between various parts of the region. Similarly, medieval Europe was a period

of empires and monarchies, some quite large in size and composed of culturally diverse groups of people; in the 17th century, for instance, the Holy Roman Empire encompassed about 300 small, largely self-governing "free" territories. The late 18th century (especially the French Revolution) marked the birth of nation-states that co-existed with several empires until the early 20th century.

Political fragmentation and conflicting interests and ambitions of several powers resulted in two World Wars that brought enormous destruction to the region. Some 15 million people were killed in World War I and 45 million in World War II, in addition to the catastrophic destruction of industrial and transportation infrastructure. The interwar Great Depression contributed to economic misery in many parts of the region. The first part of the post-World War II era (the Cold War) was characterized by political and

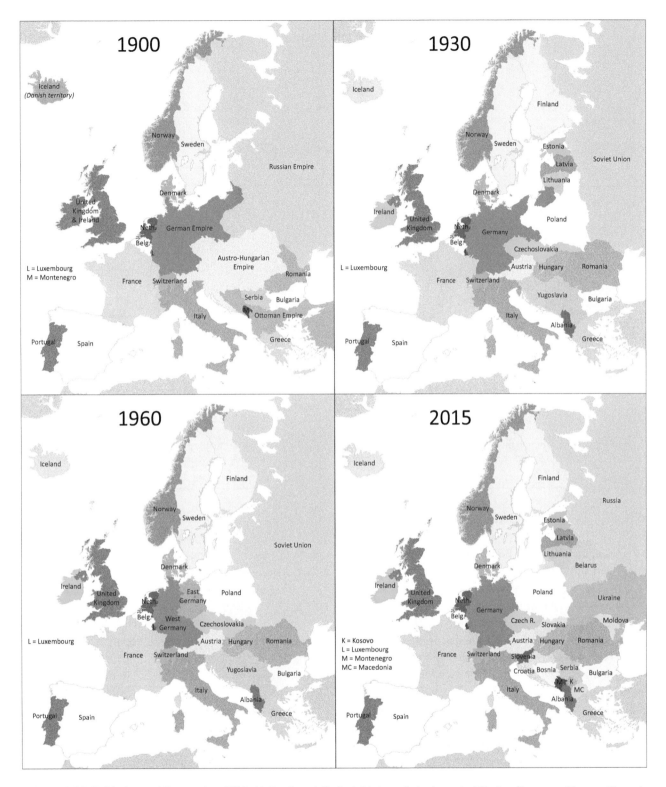

FIGURE 3.33 Political map of Europe since 1900—Notice the relatively stable boundaries in most of Western Europe and frequent boundary changes in Eastern Europe. *Source:* MPIDR Population History GIS Collection.

military tensions between Western Europe and the Communist countries of Eastern Europe and, more recently, after the collapse of Communism, by attempts to bring most European countries together (Fig. 3.33 and Fig. 3.34).

The Cold War began in the late 1940s after the Soviet Union established full control over several countries in Eastern Europe, from Poland in the north to Bulgaria in the south. The United States offered military and economic aid

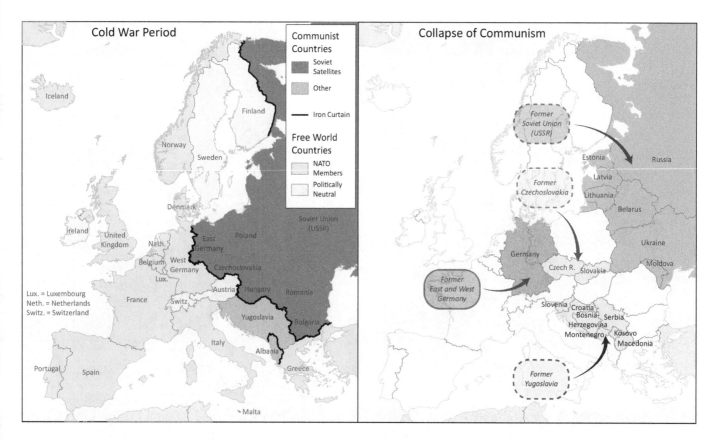

FIGURE 3.34 Europe during the Cold War and after the collapse of communism—The Iron Curtain separated the Soviet satellite countries of Eastern Europe from the democracies of Western Europe. Although Yugoslavia and Albania were communist states, they were outside Soviet political influence.

to Western Europe through the Marshall Plan to counterbalance Soviet expansion. Several crisis situations around the region, including the Berlin Blockade (1948–49), the Hungarian Uprising (1956), the Berlin Wall Crisis (1961), and the Soviet invasion of Czechoslovakia (1968), were associated with increased tensions and the possibility of a nuclear war between the two superpowers. The fear of mutual destruction prevented the use of nuclear weapons by both sides. Europe was divided into two opposing camps along the **Iron Curtain** for over forty years. Different political, military, and economic conditions existed on both sides of the line. Western European countries had democratically elected governments (with a few exceptions in the early part of the Cold War); most were members of the North Atlantic Treaty Organization (NATO), a military alliance with the United States and Canada, and the European Economic Community (EEC), later renamed the European Union. On the other side of the Iron Curtain, one-party Communist dictatorships ruled with an iron fist in most countries; formed the Council for Mutual Economic Assistance (COMECON), the Soviet-controlled economic counterpart of the EEC; and were members of the Warsaw Pact, the military counterpart of NATO.

A handful of countries in the region—e.g. Switzerland, Sweden, Yugoslavia, and Albania—maintained a degree of political neutrality during this time (Fig. 3.35).

The break-up of the Soviet Union and the collapse of Communism in the early 1990s significantly redrew the political map of Europe. First, several new countries were established after the fall of the Soviet Union (Estonia, Latvia, and Lithuania); the Czech Republic and Slovakia emerged from the "velvet divorce" of the former Czechoslovakia; Slovenia, Croatia, Bosnia and Herzegovina, Serbia, Montenegro, Macedonia, and Kosovo from the violent collapse of former Yugoslavia; and Germany from the merger of East and West Germany. Second, the COMECON and Warsaw Pact were dissolved, and some countries that were once members of these organizations later joined the European Union and NATO. Third, competitive parliamentary elections were held in every country between 1989 (Poland) and 1991 (Albania), and democratic systems of government were introduced. Fourth, democratization also brought less political stability and a rise in ethnic tensions in some countries, particularly the former Yugoslavia. Other major changes began taking place gradually as well, including the privatization of economic activities and the closure or downsizing of many industrial enterprises, production decline and higher unemployment, expansion of trade with Western Europe and other developed countries, better supply of consumer goods through the expanding network of domestic and foreign-owned shopping malls, temporary and permanent large-scale migration of workers and younger people to developed countries, and a gradual increase in income inequalities among social groups.

Despite many changes in the former Communist states of Eastern Europe during the past twenty-five years, the old political divisions are still apparent in some ways. Significant differences in levels of economic development and personal income (purchasing power) between former East and West Germany are one example of such divisions. Regional disparities in demographic conditions between East and West European countries provide another example.

The breakup of Yugoslavia was the bloodiest event in Europe since World War II and profoundly affected the region's political geography as it caused a medium-sized country created in the 1920s to break into seven smaller ones. A popular refrain (it rhymed when said in Serbo-Croatian) stated that Yugoslavia had seven neighbors, six republics, five nationalities, four languages, three religions, two alphabets, and one currency. This group of culturally diverse people was kept together under the tight rule of Communist leader Joseph Tito. After his death in 1980, the country's new leadership was unable to prevent the emergence of ethnic tensions; in fact, some of the most influential leaders actively cultivated nationalism among the different groups in the country. Most famously, on June 28, 1989, Slobodan Milosevic, the president of Serbia—then still part of Yugoslavia—gave a vividly nationalistic speech in front of approximately 1 million people. The speech was given at the same site and on the 600th anniversary of a great battle between Christian and Muslim forces at a site in Kosovo called the Field of the Blackbirds. For Milosevic, as for many other Serbs, the losing battle the Serbs had fought in 1389 had stemmed the advance of Islam in Europe and was a great point of pride. Milosevic's speech invoking that pride stirred nationalist fervor among many Serbs. For other Yugoslavs—especially Muslims—it was met with dismay and in retrospect may have signaled the beginning of the end for the country.

Many other factors also contributed to the break-up of Yugoslavia.[15] In addition to linguistic and religious diversity, regional inequalities in development played a role. The northwestern parts, like Slovenia and Croatia, were more developed than the southeastern areas like Macedonia and Kosovo, and the transfer of wealth from the former to the latter caused periodic friction. Different historic

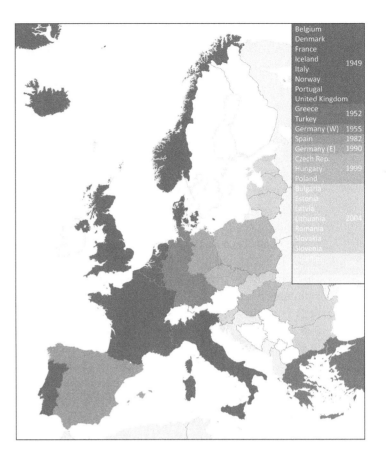

FIGURE 3.35 The expansion of NATO in Europe—Originally NATO membership was limited to some West European countries and the United States and Canada. The major expansion took place after the collapse of communism when most former Soviet satellites in Eastern Europe joined this military alliance. Notice that several West European countries are not NATO members. *Source:* Wikipedia.

experiences were also important. Most of the area was under control of the Austro-Hungarian (northwestern parts) and the Ottoman Empires (southeastern parts) until World War I, and both powers created different social and economic conditions in the occupied areas that had not been completely erased by the time of the break-up. Hostilities between Serbs and Croats, going back to World War II, surfaced again. The poor correlation between ethnic and internal political boundaries meant that parts of some groups found themselves on the wrong side of the border after the break-up. The numerically and politically dominant Serb population was particularly affected by this, and their desire for a greater Serbia was a very important factor in **ethnic cleansing** and prolonging the conflict. Finally, mountainous terrain contributed to the isolation of some areas and to the preservation of regional cultural differences.

Events elsewhere, especially the break-up of the Soviet Union and collapse of Communism in Eastern Europe, served as catalysts for the disintegration of Yugoslavia.

Less than a year after Lithuania became the first republic to declare its independence from the Soviet Union, Slovenia and Croatia proclaimed their independence from Yugoslavia following overwhelming support in referendums. Slovenia, which was ethnically homogeneous (overwhelmingly Slovene), was permitted to go with little violence, but Croatia had to fight a war that killed nearly 20,000 people.

But even that death toll pales in comparison to the catastrophe that befell Bosnia and Herzegovina. The most ethnically diverse republic of the old Yugoslavia, Bosnia and Herzegovina too declared its independence following a popular vote. Yet independence was strongly opposed by the significant Bosnian Serb minority and by Serbia itself. The crisis rapidly devolved into civil war on multiple fronts. Bosnian Serb forces received significant help from the Serbian-controlled government in Belgrade and began expelling or killing the Muslim population, and the Serbs imposed a three-year siege on Bosnia's capital, Sarajevo, which just a few years earlier had hosted the 1984 Winter Olympics. Over 100,000 people were killed during the three-year long conflict, and the international community considered the Serb-supported policy of ethnic cleansing as genocide (Fig. 3.36). The 1995 Dayton Peace Agreement divided Bosnia and Herzegovina into two major self-governing parts, the Bosnian Serb Republic and the Muslim-Croat Federation, and a self-governing District of Brcko. Somewhat remarkably, the peace agreed to at Dayton has largely held, though Bosnia and Herzegovina remains deeply troubled.

FIGURE 3.36 Old Bridge in Mostar, Bosnia—The 16th-century Old bridge in Mostar, Bosnia, was destroyed in 1993 during the country's civil war and has now been rebuilt. *Source:* Heike C. Alberts.

The newest state in Europe also resulted from the fragmentation of Yugoslavia. Kosovo broke away from Serbia in a violent conflict in 1997–1998. As with Bosnia and Herzegovina, there was widespread ethnic cleansing. For Serbia, letting Kosovo, whose population was mainly Albanian and Muslim, gain independence was an anathema because the region was important to Serb identity (it contains the Field of the Blackbirds previously mentioned), had a significant ethnic Serb minority, and was part of Serbia rather than a separate Yugoslav republic like Croatia or Macedonia. As in Bosnia and Herzegovina, intervention by NATO forces ultimately compelled the Serb forces to back down. However, nearly two decades after the end of the war, the status of Kosovo remains somewhat in doubt as Serbia and its important ally Russia refuse to recognize Kosovo's sovereignty; it also has not been accepted as a United Nations member.

European Union

Political instability and frequent wars in European history inspired some leaders and scholars to propose various solutions to bring peace and prosperity to the region. Englishman William Penn in his *Essay on the Peace of Europe* (1693) proposed creating a pan-national European Parliament with a weighted voting system based on the economic power of each country, with French and Latin as official languages, and a three-quarter majority requirement to reach binding decisions. Italian politician Giuseppe Mazzini (1843) supported the principle of democracy and national self-determination in establishing the federation of European republics composed of eleven countries. French writer Victor Hugo (1849) and many other prominent individuals dreamed of the United States of Europe. Proposals for a Pan-European Federation gained some support during the 1920s. The first meaningful and successful proposal for European unity led to the establishment of the European Coal and Steel Community (ECSC) in 1951. This organization gradually evolved into the European Economic Community (1958) and later the European Union (1993). It has grown from the six original members of the EEC to the twenty-eight member EU today (Fig. 3.37).

France and Germany had fought several wars over control of two adjacent regions, the Saarland in Germany and Lorraine in France, and the French-German border moved back and forth on several occasions. The Saarland had large deposits of coal while Lorraine was rich in iron ore, and since both resources are necessary to produce steel, each country wanted to control both areas. In 1950, French foreign minister Robert Schuman proposed

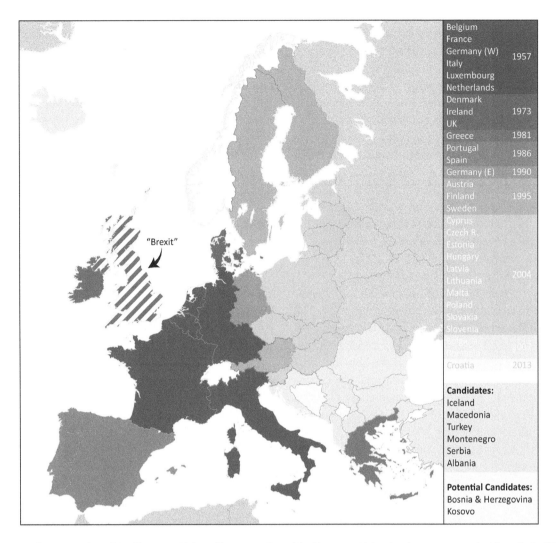

Belgium
France
Germany (W)   1957
Italy
Luxembourg
Netherlands
Denmark
Ireland   1973
UK
Greece   1981
Portugal
Spain   1986
Germany (E)   1990
Austria
Finland   1995
Sweden
Cyprus
Czech R.
Estonia
Hungary
Latvia
Lithuania   2004
Malta
Poland
Slovakia
Slovenia
  2007
Croatia   2013

Candidates:
Iceland
Macedonia
Turkey
Montenegro
Serbia
Albania

Potential Candidates:
Bosnia & Herzegovina
Kosovo

"Brexit"

FIGURE 3.37 The expansion of the European Union—The expansion of the European Union has been more gradual than that of NATO. The United Kingdom is the first member state to leave the union. Notice that Switzerland does not belong to NATO or the European Union.

creating a common market for coal and iron ore to eliminate competition for these resources among neighboring countries. Steel production would be cheaper through cooperation rather than confrontation. The ECSC, by removing trade barriers in coal, coke, steel, pig iron, and scrap iron among its six member states (Belgium, France, West Germany, Italy, Luxembourg, and the Netherlands), became a successful customs union. Six years later, the same countries formed the European Economic Community (EEC), an economic union designed to remove trade barriers among member states, establish a single commercial policy toward other countries, coordinate various economic policies (e.g. transportation and agriculture), remove various measures restricting free competition, and allow free mobility of labor, capital, and goods. The Treaty of Rome, which formed the EEC, also established the European Atomic Energy Community (EAEC), an organization sponsoring the development and peaceful use

of nuclear energy in Europe. In 1967, the Merger Treaty combined the ECSC, EEC, and EAEC into the European Community (EC).

The successful integration of six national economies encouraged other countries to join the organization; in particular, new members wanted in because their firms would then gain preferential access (i.e., lower **tariffs** and other trade barriers) in selling to the millions of consumers located within the group. In 1961, the United Kingdom (UK), Ireland, Denmark, and Norway applied for membership; when France vetoed UK membership two years later, other countries withdrew their applications. In 1966, the UK applied again, but France vetoed the British application for the second time. The third British attempt to join the EC in 1973 was successful. Ireland and Denmark were also admitted that year, but voters in Norway rejected membership. The years 1950–1973 are considered the first period of European integration.[16]

The second period of integration lasted through the mid-1980s. Greece was admitted in 1981, and Portugal and Spain joined in 1986. Morocco and Turkey applied for membership a year later; Morocco's application was rejected (it was not considered a European country as it is located in Africa) while Turkey's was postponed.

The next period of integration (mid-1980s–1993) was associated with a major expansion of administrative powers of the EC and of further economic integration. The Single European Act of 1986 led to the elimination of all trade barriers and stronger political integration. The **Schengen Agreement** of 1985 went into effect ten years later. It eliminated border checks among most member states. East Germany, after the unification with West Germany, was admitted to the EC during this period (in 1990).

The **Maastricht Treaty** of 1993 marked the beginning of the fourth stage of European integration. The treaty established the European Union (EU); its principal objectives were to establish European citizenship; ensure freedom, security, and justice; promote economic and social progress; and assert Europe's role in the world. The EU was based on three pillars: (1) the single market and freedom of movement across international borders; (2) a common foreign and security policy; and (3) cooperation in the field of justice and internal affairs. The monetary union establishing the common currency (Euro) in 1999 was another major accomplishment during that period. The organization was enlarged in 1995 when Austria, Finland, and Sweden were admitted. Norway, once again, rejected the opportunity to join partly because the country's great wealth and more narrowly specialized economy (oil and natural gas account for two-thirds of the country's exports) reduced the advantages in becoming a member.

The fifth period of integration began in 2004 when ten countries (mainly former Communist states in Eastern Europe) joined the EU: Cyprus, the Czech Republic, Estonia, Hungary, Latvia, Lithuania, Malta, Poland, Slovakia, and Slovenia. Bulgaria and Romania became members in 2007 and Croatia in 2013. This was the single greatest expansion of the group, increasing the population of the EU countries from a combined 383 million in 2004 to 507 million in 2014. The new states were generally poorer—some, like Romania, were markedly poorer—than the existing members, but their addition made the EU the largest trade bloc in the world, by far. The expansion made the group more unwieldy (e.g. adding eleven new official languages) and exacerbated some long-standing tensions, including those over the freedom of people in member states to migrate to other member states for work.

Partly because of these tensions, the EU moved for the first time towards disintegration instead of integration in 2016 when the voters in the United Kingdom approved, by a slight majority (51.9 percent), most of them in England and Wales, a proposal to leave the EU. Under the plan, popularly known as Brexit (i.e. "British exit"), the UK will leave the EU by April 2019. Supporters of the proposal raised several economic and immigration concerns, including high membership fees, cumbersome regulations on business activities, and no control of who was coming into the country. The opponents pointed to various economic benefits from British membership in the EU which, in their opinion, outweighed the immigration concerns. Brexit will undoubtedly have a number of economic and political consequences for both sides, and it is hard to predict them now as no other country has left the EU before. Similar calls for leaving the EU have been heard in other member states, however, particularly in France and the Netherlands. Some political parties in favor of leaving the EU have gained a lot of support in these countries in recent years.

What began in 1951 as a customs union of six countries had expanded into an economic and political union of twenty-eight states by 2013. Five other countries would like to join the EU and two more are potential candidates. New entrants might offset the loss of the UK and shift the EU's center farther east.

Despite its recent travails, the European Union has been successful at stemming Europe's long history of division and bloodshed and it has enormous clout in the world. In 2017, its twenty-eight member states had a combined population of 507 million (versus 324 million in the U.S.) and a gross domestic product of over $16 trillion (in comparison, the gross domestic product in the United States is over $18 trillion). The Euro, which has been adopted as the sole official currency of nineteen EU member states, is the second most widely traded currency after the U.S. dollar. Furthermore, the EU has engaged in joint efforts to suppress piracy, maintain peace, and strengthen democracy in more than a dozen countries beyond EU borders in Europe, Africa, and Asia.

The EU operates through a system of supranational institutions, including two executive ones, the European Council and the European Commission; two legislative ones, the European Parliament and the Council of Ministers; and a judiciary one, the European Court of Justice. The European Commission, for example, based in Brussels (Belgium), initiates proposals for legislation as well as implements approved legislation and the budget; it also negotiates international agreements and represents the EU internationally. The European Parliament, based in Strasbourg (France) and elected every five years by EU citizens, is the legislative body, has power over the budget (citizens

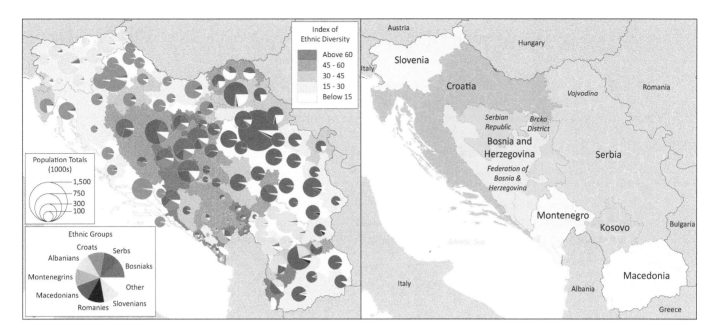

FIGURE 3.38 Ethnic diversity and the break-up of former Yugoslavia—The map on the left shows the ethnic composition according to the most recent census of each country; the map on the right shows independent countries and their administrative divisions. *Source:* Bosnia and Herzegovina Agency for Statistics; Croatian Bureau of Statistics; Kosovo Agency of Statistics; Macedonia State Statistical Office; Statistical Office of Montenegro; Statistical Office of the Republic of Serbia; and Republic of Slovenia Statistical Office.

of member states pay taxes to the EU), and supervises the executive branch of the EU. It has 751 members who are grouped by political affiliation, not national origin. Several other institutions, such as the European Central Bank or the European Court of Auditors, implement monetary policies and are responsible for fiscal discipline.

Political Organization of Space

Most European countries are unitary states, but at least five have a federal system of government where there is a division of power between the central and local governments. Austria and Germany are examples of such countries. Austria is divided into nine states (Bundesländer), although currently they have a limited amount of legislative power, while Germany is divided into sixteen states (Länder) with considerably more legislative authority. Federalism in both countries has historical roots. Linguistic and/or religious diversity have also led to federal structures in Belgium and Switzerland as previously described. Bosnia and Herzegovina is perhaps the best example of federalism in Europe. Its two main components, the Serbian Republic (Republika Srpska) and the Federation of Bosnia and Herzegovina (dominated by the Muslim-Croat Federation), are largely self-governing with a very weak central government in Sarajevo. The presidency comprises three people representing the Bosnian Serb, Croat, and Muslim

Bosniak communities, with the chair of the presidency rotating every eight months (Fig. 3.38).

Another interesting feature of the political geography of Europe is the existence of several mini-states: Andorra, Liechtenstein, Monaco, San Marino, and Vatican City. Most of them are remnants of the political fragmentation that had characterized medieval Europe. They occupy very small areas, have small populations, and have developed unique economic activities (in addition to tourism) to be fiscally viable entities. For instance, Liechtenstein, a remnant of the Holy Roman Empire and independent since 1806, is a principality located between Austria and Switzerland. Its population is about 35,000. It has attracted thousands of companies (known as "letter-box companies") to establish registered offices due to the low business tax. The principality of Monaco, located on the French Riviera, occupies an area of less than 1 square mile (2.6 square kilometers) and is inhabited by over 35,000 people. It has existed since 1297 but gained full independence in 1861. It is the richest country in the world in terms of income per capita (over $132,000). It has been well known for the gambling industry (as featured in two James Bond films) for over 150 years. Vatican City is a unique state, established in 1929 and occupying an area of only 44 hectares (110 acres) within the city of Rome. It is a theocracy, and the Pope is the head of state. Its population of about 700-800 consists mainly of the Roman Catholic clergy and members of the Swiss Guard. Tourism and the sale of stamps and coins are some of the major sources of revenue.

ECONOMIC ACTIVITIES

Although Europe's share of the global economy has declined from almost 40 percent around 1900 to less than 20 percent currently, the region is one of three major centers of economic power; the others are the United States/Canada and East Asia. It is the origin of several peaceful revolutions, including the second agricultural and the first industrial revolution. Both revolutions made Europe an innovative and productive area, although some of these accomplishments were attained at the expense of other regions and peoples in the form of colonialism and the slave trade.

Agriculture: Trends and Patterns

With its mainly mild climates and extensive areas of flat, well-watered land, Europe is rich in arable land, which occupies over 23 percent of its area; countries located

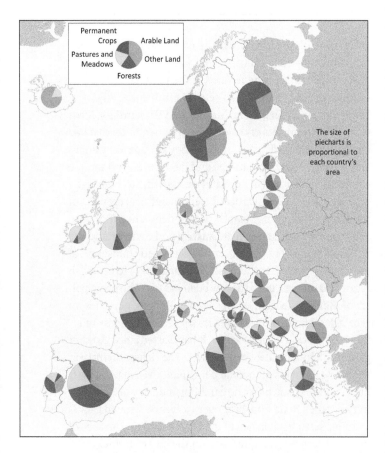

FIGURE 3.39 Land use patterns in Europe, 2013—Arable land comprises over 23 percent of Europe's area, permanent crops account for 2.5 percent, pastures and meadows for 15 percent, forests occupy over 36 percent of the land, and the remaining 23 percent is other land. *Source:* CIA World Factbook.

within the European Lowlands region having the highest proportions (Fig. 3.39). With the passage of time and technological improvements, European agriculture has become more diverse and intensive. The introduction of new crops (e.g. citrus fruits, potatoes, and corn), expansion of irrigation, and changes in land use systems have led to the greater commercialization and specialization of farming. One of the most important changes associated with the second agricultural revolution of the 17th to 18th centuries was a switch from the three-field to the four-field system of crop rotation (also known as the Norfolk four-course system). In the three-field system developed in the Middle Ages, land was rotated among one field planted with wheat, barley, or rye in autumn; one planted with oats, peas, or beans in spring (the peas and beans fix nitrogen in the soil, helping to restore its fertility); and a third field left fallow. The four-field system eliminated fallowing and increased the importance of fodder crops such as turnips, which ultimately yielded not only well-fed animals and their numerous direct products (e.g. milk and wool) but also the valuable byproduct of manure to enrich soil. European innovation and the transformation of farming into a profit-oriented business eventually led to the emergence of specialized agriculture such as dairy farming, commercial grain cultivation, and market gardening (truck farming).

Large-scale dairy farming developed in Northwestern Europe and the Alpine region in response to urbanization and the rapidly growing urban population's demand for milk and its products. The mountainous terrain and/or cool and moist climate also favored this activity. Europe gave the world several major breeds of dairy cattle (e.g. Brown Swiss and Holstein). Regional specialization within the northwestern dairy belt developed over time and reflected the distance to the major market (England). The surrounding areas emphasized the production of fresh milk; areas farther away processed more milk into cheese (the Netherlands) and butter (Denmark). Some of the most popular brands of cheese (Munster, Cheddar, and Swiss) also originated in Europe. As other parts of the world became more industrialized and urbanized, Europe's share of milk production has declined from 13 percent in 1960 to 7 percent today. However, the region continues to be the largest producer of cheese, accounting for almost half of global production.

The Mediterranean climate of Southern Europe favors the cultivation of specialty crops such as olives, citrus fruits, and grapes. The region supplies two-thirds of the olives in the world, and Spain, Italy, and Greece are the major producers. These countries are also the largest producers of citrus fruits. The cultivation of grapes and the production of wine is another specialty of the Mediterranean region, although viticulture has also expanded to other parts of Europe, which today accounts for over half of the wine made in the world (Fig. 3.40). Greenhouse farming emphasizing the production of vegetables is also well developed in Southern Europe, especially in the coastal areas of Southern Spain and Italy. It is an important activity in other countries such as the Netherlands and Poland as well as around major cities in other parts of Europe; vegetables and fresh cut flowers are major crops there. Many farms in Central and Western Europe raise livestock, especially hogs, for meat. Some of the best known meat products (ham and sausages) have names associated with places of origin (e.g. Polish sausage, Bologna, and Danish ham). Commercial grain farming is found in many regions of Europe. Wheat is the dominant crop and is especially important in the warmer and more fertile parts of Western and Southern Europe (France, Germany, and Spain). Barley, oats, and rye are other grains grown in the cooler and less fertile regions of Western, Central, and Northern Europe (Fig. 3.41).

A typical European farm is much smaller than its American counterpart. However, there are regional differences in farm size that reflect environmental, historical, and political conditions. In general, farms increase in size from southeast to northwest. Europe has a higher proportion of the labor force in farming as well, and family farms are still the dominant production unit in most countries. European farming has been greatly affected by the **Common Agricultural Policy** (CAP) of the European Union, introduced in 1962. It has had three main objectives: (1) providing farmers with an adequate standard of living, (2) making available quality food at fair prices to all EU residents, and (3) preserving the rural heritage of agricultural areas. Farmers receive subsidies for crops and cultivated land and are guaranteed a minimum price for agricultural products. Import quotas and tariffs on selected goods from non-member states may be imposed. About 70 percent of the CAP budget is spent on income subsidies for farmers, 20 percent on rural development incentives (mainly farm modernization), and 10 percent on market-support measures (e.g. when bad weather destabilizes the market for agricultural products).

This policy has been controversial for years.[17] Its opponents claim that it is a waste of funds as it ignores the law of supply and demand and leads to overproduction and a disproportionate allocation of funds to a small segment of society (farmers comprise 4.5 percent of population).

FIGURE 3.40 Vineyards—Vineyards are common in many parts of Europe. This one overlooks Lake Constance, a large lake bordered by Germany, Austria, and Switzerland. *Source:* Heike C. Alberts.

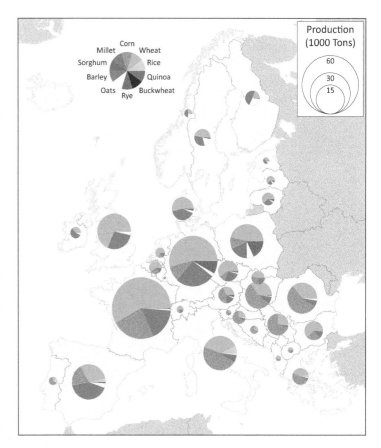

FIGURE 3.41 Production of cereals in Europe, 2000-2013—Although wheat is the dominant crop, corn has been gaining popularity in recent decades, and it is now the dominant crop in southeastern Europe and Italy. *Source:* FAOSTAT.

Industry: Trends and Patterns

The Industrial Revolution of the 18th century transformed Europe from a land of farmers and local markets into an industrial society with global connections. Prior to that time, manufacturing activities were organized in guild and cottage production systems, and all the work was done manually. The Industrial Revolution brought about two major changes in the manufacturing process: machines replaced human hands, and inanimate power was used to run the machinery. A series of inventions in textile manufacturing, coal mining, and iron and steel production originally revolutionized five European industries: cotton textiles, wool textiles, iron and steel, shipbuilding, and coal mining. These changes first happened in the British Isles and were later dispersed to other parts of the region. By the end of the 19th century, Europe had become the global economic power; it accounted for 90 percent of the world's total industrial production. Several industrial clusters, usually in close proximity to coal and/or iron ore deposits, were established in a belt extending from England through Northern France and Belgium, Central and Southern Germany, to the present-day Czech Republic and Southern Poland. Some areas outside this belt also attracted industrial activities. In fact, Northern Italy became the second largest industrial cluster in Europe after the Ruhr region in Germany.

Although large deposits of coal stimulated industrial development in Europe 200 years ago, the region is dependent on imported energy resources today, particularly oil and natural gas (Fig. 3.42). Only Norway, the United Kingdom, the Netherlands, Germany, and Poland are significant producers of fossil fuels these days, but production in these countries has been declining in recent years. To compensate for the shortage of traditional fossil fuels, some countries have emphasized development of nuclear energy (Fig. 3.43 and Fig. 3.44). Over time, some industries, especially those dependent on imported bulky raw materials (iron/steel and petrochemicals), moved to coastal locations.

After World War II, European industries, particularly iron and steel, shipbuilding, and textiles, began facing serious competition from rapidly growing Asian industries. At the same time, the region developed various high-tech (computer, defense, electronics, and medical technology) and consumer goods industries. Today, the tertiary sector (service economy) is the dominant activity in every European country. Manufacturing generates only a quarter (or less) of the gross domestic product in many countries (Fig. 3.45).

The European automobile industry is one of the strongest in the world. It employs over 12 million people (3 million in production, 4.3 million in sales and maintenance, and 4.8 million in transportation) and accounts for 4 percent of the GDP.[18] Although the production of passenger cars has slightly declined during the past fifteen years, the industry remains highly competitive on the world market. Europe produces a variety of models, from small-sized and relatively cheap to high-end luxury and race cars. Germany has been the clear leader in automobile production, and its vehicles can be found around the

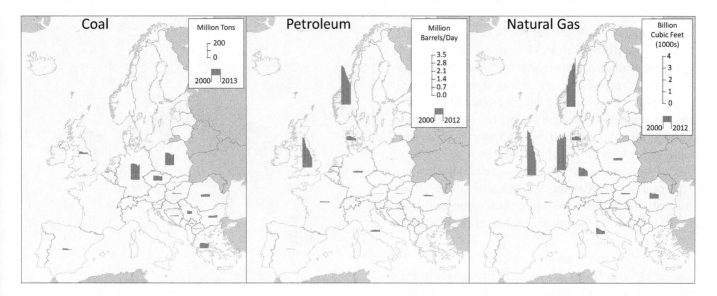

FIGURE 3.42 Production of fossil fuels in Europe, 2000-2013—Only Germany and Poland are major producers of coal today, Norway and the United Kingdom of oil, and the Netherlands, Norway, and the United Kingdom of natural gas. Most of Europe is therefore dependent on imported fossil fuels, mainly from Russia and Middle Eastern countries. *Source:* U.S. Energy Information Administration.

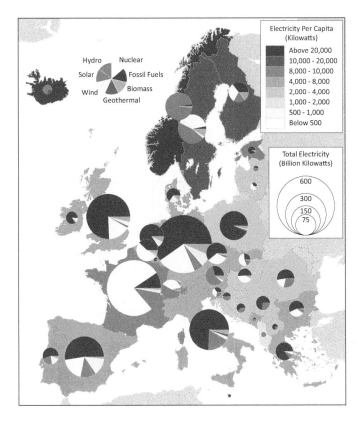

FIGURE 3.43 Electricity production in Europe, 2012—Most countries depend on domestic or imported fossil fuels to meet their electricity needs; some generate most of it from nuclear or hydroelectric power plants. *Source:* U.S. Energy Information Administration.

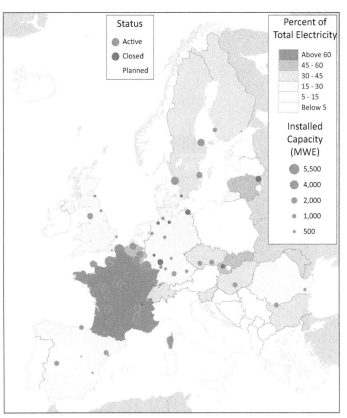

FIGURE 3.44 Nuclear energy production in Europe, 2012—France is more dependent on this source of energy than any other European country. Notice the number of closed power plants in Germany. *Source:* International Nuclear Energy Agency.

world (Fig. 3.46). Volkswagen, Opel, Audi, BMW, and Mercedes are symbols of quality and reliability. French Renault and Peugeot-Citroen, Italian Fiat, and Swedish Volvo and Saab are other well known cars of European design. Some countries are also important producers of luxury cars such as Ferrari and Lamborghini (Italy), Rolls-Royce and Jaguar (the United Kingdom), and Porsche (Germany). While the production of cars has been declining in Western European countries (except Germany) in recent years, it has been increasing in Eastern Europe mainly through the construction of assembly plants by major American, Asian, and European automakers, especially in the Czech Republic, Poland, and Slovakia (Fig. 3.47).

Like the United States, Europe also has a number of high-tech clusters. Although none of them can be compared in size to California's Silicon Valley, some clusters are important centers of innovation and production of

FIGURE 3.45 Gross Domestic Product per capita and by sector—Norway and Switzerland have the highest GDP per capita. Notice the very small contribution of the primary sector to the total GDP. *Source:* CIA World Factbook.

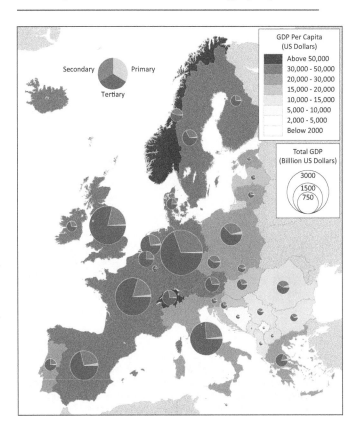

FIGURE 3.46 Volkswagen factory—Europe has many car producers. This factory in Dresden, Germany produces high-end Volkswagen cars. *Source:* Heike C. Alberts.

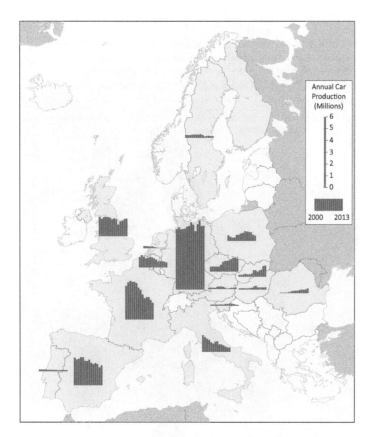

FIGURE 3.47 Car production in Europe, 2000-2013—Bar graphs show the annual car production by country between 2000 and 2013. Notice the significant production decline in France and Italy and the growing importance of the former Czechoslovakia as a car-producing region. *Source:* U.S. Bureau of Transportation Statistics.

sophisticated military and civilian equipment. For example, the Aerospace Valley in Southwestern France around the city of Toulouse is a cluster of some 500 companies, including Airbus and Dassault Aviation, specializing in the production of passenger and military planes. The M4 Corridor (Silicon Corridor) between London and South Wales in the United Kingdom may be the largest concentration of computer, telecommunications, software, and electronics companies in Europe.

The Fortune Global 500 annual list of the largest global corporations includes many European companies such as Royal Dutch Shell, British Petroleum (BP), Total (a French oil company), BASF and Siemens (German chemical and engineering companies), Philips and Ericsson (Dutch and Swedish electronics companies), Maersk (Danish shipping company), and Nestle (Swiss food company), just to name a few. These and many other global corporations maintain production facilities in other parts of the world, and economic prosperity in many European countries has been dependent on foreign trade (Fig. 3.48). Although Germany is the most important trading nation in Europe, the economies of Belgium and the Netherlands are particularly dependent on foreign trade.

Despite the high levels of industrialization and urbanization in Europe, regional differences in levels of economic development still exist and reflect the early patterns of industrial expansion. In general, the early industrial core region of England and the Low Countries of Belgium and

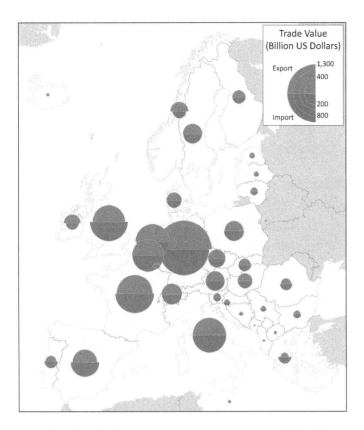

FIGURE 3.48 Foreign trade of European countries, 2005–2013—The map shows the average annual value of exports and imports by country during the eight-year period. Notice the importance of trade in the economies of Belgium and the Netherlands. *Source:* 2013 International Trade Statistics Yearbook.

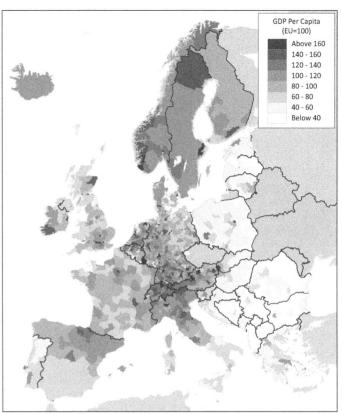

FIGURE 3.49 Regional inequalities in gross domestic product per capita in Europe—Notice the significant disparities between most of the former communist states of Eastern Europe and the rest of the region. *Source:* EUROSTAT.

the Netherlands are the most densely populated and urbanized part of Europe. Away from the core region development levels decline. For example, the northern parts of France, Spain, and Italy are more developed than their southern parts. Similar disparities can be observed between western and eastern regions of Germany, Poland or the former Czechoslovakia, and the southern and northern parts of Scandinavian countries. These disparities can even be observed in Southeastern Europe. As indicated earlier, Slovenia and Croatia, located in the northwestern parts of former Yugoslavia, have higher levels of development than Macedonia, Montenegro, and Kosovo. Similar patterns can be observed in Hungary, Romania, and Bulgaria. Another general observation is that levels of development decline from west to east and north to south (Fig. 3.49 and Fig. 3.50).

Transportation Networks

Europe, a densely populated and early industrialized region, has the densest transportation network in the world.

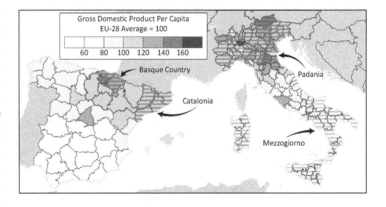

FIGURE 3.50 Regional disparities in Italy and Spain—The north-south disparities in economic development are well visible in these two countries of southern Europe. The much less developed southern Italy is known as the Mezzogiorno. The Basque Country and Catalonia are the two best developed parts of Spain. *Source:* EUROSTAT.

The first railroads and limited access highways were built there. England pioneered railroad construction and passenger and freight service in the early 19th century.

FIGURE 3.51 Channel Tunnel Car Shuttle—The Channel Tunnel links the U.K. and France. Cars and trucks travel through the tunnel on specially designed railroad cars. *Source:* Wikimedia Commons.

Italy constructed the first high-speed highway (autostrada) between Milan and Venice in 1924, and Germany built a relatively dense network of expressways (Autobahnen) in the 1930s. Europe has been ahead of the United States in the development of high-speed rail service. The French TGV network began operations in 1981 between Paris and Lyon and today serves about 120 million passengers a year. Germany's Intercity Express (ICE) connects the country's major cities and those of neighboring countries and has been in service since 1991. Spain and Italy also have high-speed lines. One of the biggest construction projects in recent decades was the Eurotunnel between France and the United Kingdom, built underneath the English Channel and open for service since 1994. It consists of two railway tunnels and a service tunnel (Fig. 3.51). Over 10 million passengers use it each year.

Europe does not have as dense a network of airports as the United States due to the shorter distances between the major cities and greater reliance on rail transportation, but London's Heathrow, Paris' Charles de Gaulle, and Frankfurt airport are among the ten largest in the world. Amsterdam's Schiphol and Madrid's Barajas airport are among the next ten largest. Germany's Lufthansa and a low-cost Irish carrier, Ryanair, are the two largest European airlines in terms of passengers served. Budget airlines like Ryanair have been instrumental in fostering closer ties within the European Union, even facilitating long-distance commuting by people who live in Central and Eastern Europe and work in the more lucrative markets to the west. Other major airlines are the Air France-KLM and the British Airways-Iberia groups. Rotterdam used to be the busiest seaport in the world, but it was displaced from its leading position some time ago by several East Asian (especially Chinese) ports (Fig. 3.52 and Fig. 3.53).

As European national transportation networks are relatively small due to the small size of most countries, there are few competing lines (and often government ownership of transportation facilities), and poor connections in border

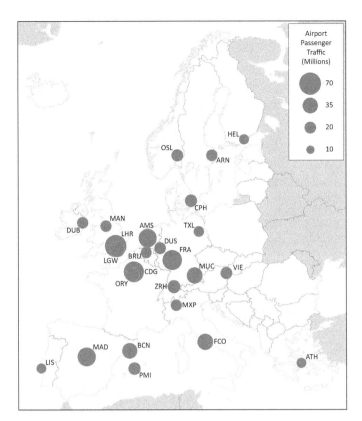

FIGURE 3.52 Largest airports in Europe by passenger traffic, 2010–2011—The four largest airports in Europe are Heathrow (London), Charles de Gaulle (Paris), Frankfurt Airport, and Schiphol (Amsterdam). London and Paris are served by more than one airport. Notice that Berlin is not an important airline hub. *Source:* The Guardian.

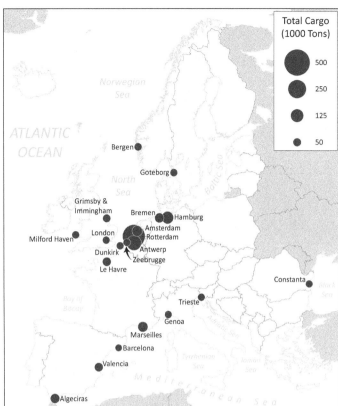

FIGURE 3.53 Largest seaports in Europe by total cargo, 2011—Rotterdam used to be the largest seaport in the world. Today it is the 4th largest, displaced from the top rank by three Asian ports. *Source:* American Association of Port Authorities.

regions. To improve transportation services and standardize the existing network of roads, railways, airports, and seaports in different countries, the European Union introduced a new transportation infrastructure policy to establish the Trans-European Transportation Network (TEN-T). The goal is to complete the project by 2030 for the core connections (e.g. from Scandinavia to Italy via a new immersed (underwater) tunnel—the longest of its kind in the world—linking Denmark and Germany and a massive new tunnel under the Alps) and by 2050 for the remaining connections.[19]

Tourism

Europe accounts for almost one-third of all tourist arrivals in the world. Its rich history, sunny and warm climate in the southern part of the region, diverse cuisine, good hotel infrastructure, and dense transportation network make it an attractive place to visit. Large-scale tourism is a post-World War II phenomenon and most tourists are residents of other European countries. The coastal areas along the Mediterranean Sea from Spain to Greece attract the largest number of tourists, most of them from northern and western parts of Europe. The beautiful scenery of mountainous regions, especially of the Alps, brings many hikers in summer and skiers in winter. Numerous historical sites (e.g. castles and palaces, churches, and ancient ruins) and museums are visited by millions of people. The growing number of amusement parks (e.g. Disneyland Park near Paris and Tivoli Gardens in Copenhagen) also attracts millions of visitors. Health tourism is another fairly popular form of recreation, especially in areas known for spas. Many Europeans believe in the curative qualities of mineral waters and may spend a week or two in such health resorts. France and Spain are the major tourist destinations in Europe visited by about 79 and 56 million people a year, respectively. In France, the Paris region and the Mediterranean coast (Côte d'Azur) are prime destinations. The beaches of Catalonia (Costa Brava) and the Balearic Islands are the most popular tourist destinations in Spain (Fig. 3.54 and Fig. 3.55).

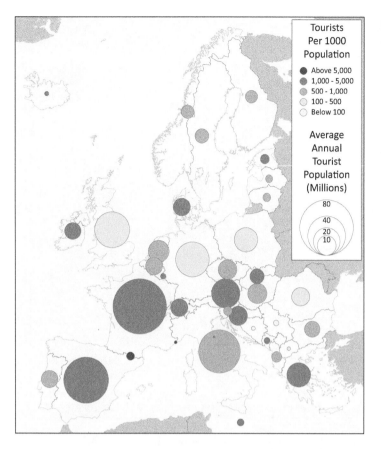

FIGURE 3.54 Tourism in Europe (tourist arrivals), 2005–2012—France, Spain, and Italy are major tourist destinations in Europe. Notice the small number of tourists visiting the former Yugoslavia. *Source:* World Bank.

FIGURE 3.55 Visitors to major amusement parks in Europe—Disneyland near Paris, Europa Park in southwestern Germany, Efteling in the Netherlands, and Tivoli Gardens near Copenhagen are the most popular amusement parks in Europe. Tivoli Gardens was opened in 1843 and is the second oldest theme park in the world. *Source:* Wikipedia.

FUTURE PROBLEMS AND PROSPECTS

Although the establishment and subsequent expansion of what is now the European Union, as well as the collapse of the Communist governments and break-up of the Soviet Union, offered many hopes of a better future for Europe, recent developments within and outside the region have exposed several challenges that may impact the stability and prosperity of this area. An apparently successful economic and political integration of most European states was questioned after the 2016 vote in the United Kingdom to leave the European Union. The "Brexit" vote was a shock across the entire region, and it may have serious implications for the future of European economic and political integration. Some politicians and segments of the population began expressing concerns about further expansion of the EU, especially the admission of several culturally distinct countries of the Caucasus region (e.g. Georgia) and Turkey. The increased influence or rise to power of anti-EU and Eurosceptic political parties in several countries

(Denmark, Finland, France, Hungary, the Netherlands, and Poland) may lead to a slowdown or even a reversal of the integration process among the member states.

Migration has been an important component of population growth in many European countries for the past several decades and generally has been perceived as a positive phenomenon. However, a recent large-scale influx of refugees from the Middle East (mainly Syria, Iraq, and Afghanistan) and North Africa, amounting to over 1 million in 2015, has revealed the lack of coherent and effective migration and asylum policies across the region. While Germany and Sweden welcomed many migrants, some countries (Hungary, the Czech Republic, Slovakia, and Romania) expressed concerns that the predominantly Muslim newcomers would influence the predominantly Christian identity of their societies and the rest of Europe. In response to increased migration flows, several EU members of the Schengen group (Austria, Germany, Denmark, and Sweden) introduced temporary border controls which, in the opinion of some people, may become permanent, further complicating the integration process.

The Russian annexation of Crimea in 2014 and support for separatist forces in Eastern Ukraine have raised concerns about European security and managing relations with a resurgent Russia. Although the EU imposed economic sanctions on Russia in response to its aggressive policy of interfering in internal affairs of neighboring countries, there has been some difference of opinion among European leaders regarding their duration. Some countries (e.g. Germany and Italy) consider Russia an important economic partner and prolonged sanctions, in their opinion, might have an adverse impact on their economies. Other countries (e.g. Sweden) are concerned about increased Russian military activities in the Baltic Sea region or a proposed new gas pipeline which could increase European dependence on Russian energy sources. There is also a growing anxiety about Russia's attempts to influence public opinion or election outcomes in some European countries through the spread of disinformation over the Internet and through cyberattacks on government and political parties' websites.

Countering terrorism has become an urgent task for several West European countries. A series of recent religion-inspired terrorist attacks in France, Belgium, and other countries, some of them committed by citizens of the European Union and others by asylum-seekers, has not only endangered the security of ordinary citizens but also brought into question the policies designed to integrate migrants of different cultural backgrounds. The attacks have revealed some weaknesses in intelligence sharing among member states and made it difficult to assure a proper balance between maintaining national security and protecting the civil liberties and human rights of all EU residents.

Yet while Europe faces daunting challenges, it is first and foremost a peaceful, prosperous, and democratic region that serves in important ways as a model for the world. In surveys assessing how happy people are around the world, European countries typically dominate the top of the rankings; in the 2017 report, for instance, European countries occupied seven of the top ten rankings (led by Norway) and thirteen of the top twenty. The factors that support such a high quality of life, which have developed over centuries of European ingenuity and struggle, are likely to remain in place.

NOTES

1. Hobbs, J. J. (2013). *Fundamentals of World Regional Geography* (3rd ed.). Belmont, CA: Brooks/Cole.

2. Diamond, J. (2017). *Guns, germs, and steel: The fates of human societies*. New York, NY: W.W. Norton.

3. Nijman, J., Muller, P. O., & de Blij, H. J. (2016). *The World Today: Concepts and Regions in Geography* (7th ed.). New York, NY: John Wiley & Sons.

4. Jordan-Bychov, T. G., & Bychkova Jordan, B. (2002). *The European Culture Area: A Systemaic Geography* (4th ed.). Boston, MA: Rowman & Littlefield.

5. Hoeksema, R. (2007). Three stages in the history of land reclamation in the Netherlands. *Irrigation and Drainage, 56*, 113–126.

6. Cascio, E., & Malanima, P. (2005). Cycles and stability. Italian population before the demographic transition 225 BC-AD 1900. *Rivista di Storia Economica, 21*(3), 5–40.

7. Billari, F. (2008). Lowest-low fertility in Europe: Exploring the causes and finding some surprises. *Japanese Journal of Population 6*(1), 2–18.

8. Aggarwal, A., Purushotham, A., & Sullivan, R. (2013). The state of Europe's fertility: Causes, consequences and future policies. *European Journal of Social Sciences 40*(2), 217–230.

9. Rogers, A., (Ed.) (1992). *Peoples and cultures*. Oxford, UK: Oxford University Press.

10. Morris, A. (1994). *History of urban form before the industrial revolutions*. (3rd ed.). New York, NY: Routledge.

11. McCarthy, L., & Danta. D. (2003). *Cities of Europe*. In S. Brunn, J. Williams, & D. Zeigler (Eds.), *Cities of the World* (pp. 169–22). Lanham, MD: Rowman & Littlefield.

12. European Commission. (2012). Europeans and their languages. Special Eurobarometer Report. Retrieved from http://ec.europa.eu/commfrontoffice/publicopinion/archives/ebs/ebs_243_en.pdf

13. Esperson, M. (2014). *Multilingualism in Belgium and Switzerland: A comparative analysis of the two countries' linguistic conflicts and the significance of language to national identity*. Saarbrücken, Germany: Lambert Academic Publishing.

14. Crabtree, S. (2010). Religiosity highest in world's poorest nations. Retrieved from Gallup website: http://news.gallup.com/poll/142727/religiosity-highest-world-poorest-nations.aspx

15. Global Security. (2011). War and ethnic cleansing in Yugoslavia. Retrieved from https://www.globalsecurity.org/military/world/war/yugo-hist4.htm

16. Murphy, A., Jordan-Bychov, T., & Bychkova-Jordan, B. (2014). *The European culture area*. (6th ed.). Lanham, MD: Rowman & Littlefield.

17. Debating Europe. (2018). Arguments for and against the Common Agricultural Policy. Retrieved from http://www.debatingeurope.eu/focus/arguments-for-and-against-the-common-agricultural-policy/#.VYTaikarHSg

18. European Commission. (2018). Automotive industry. Retrieved from http://ec.europa.eu/growth/sectors/automotive/index_en.htm

19. European Union. (2018). EU transport policy. Retrieved http://www.euintheus.org/what-we-do/policy-areas/transportation/trans-european-transport-network

4

RUSSIAN REALM

The Russian Realm is the area of the former Soviet Union with the exception of the three Baltic States that are now considered part of Europe. This region stretches from Belarus, Ukraine, and Moldova in the west to the Pacific Ocean in the east and from the Arctic Ocean in the north to Turkmenistan and Tajikistan in the south (Fig. 4.1). The Soviet Union used to be, and now Russia is, the largest country in the world. The enormous territorial extent has been both an asset and a liability to governments controlling this area. This region is very rich in mineral resources, especially fossil fuels and metallic ores; it contains large areas of forests and fertile farmland and ample (albeit unevenly distributed) freshwater resources. Its large size protected many parts from foreign control during World War II. On the other hand, large territorial extent also means greater likelihood of political instability due to the enormous ethnic diversity of the population and the common land border with many countries. One indication of the region's large size is its division into eleven time zones; when it is noon in Kaliningrad (a Russian exclave between Poland and Lithuania), it is 10 PM in the easternmost region of Kamchatka. It takes nine hours to fly from one end of Russia to the other, as much time as to fly from Europe to Chicago. One needs almost a week to travel by train from Saint Petersburg to Vladivostok on the Sea of Japan.

GEOGRAPHIC QUALITIES AND WORLD SIGNIFICANCE

The Russian Realm is known for its harsh physical environment, especially climate. The eastern part of the region, Siberia, is associated with very cold winters and dense forests, and it used to be the place of exile for many outlaws and opponents of the Tsarist and Communist governments. While most of the population is found in the western parts of

FIGURE 4.1 The Russian Realm—The former Soviet Union is now divided into 15 independent countries. The three Baltic States are part of the European region. Nine of the remaining countries belong to the Commonwealth of Independent States (CIS), two countries (Turkmenistan and Ukraine) are associate members of CIS, and one (Georgia) left the organization in 2009.

the Russian Realm, most natural resources are located in Siberia and other less hospitable parts of the region. This weak population-natural resource correlation has been an obstacle to economic development. Various governments have used incentives and forced labor to correct this problem, but with uneven success.

A lackluster economy and Russian control of this ethnically diverse region have been responsible for political instability and periodic uprisings against the strong central government. These forces eventually led to the rather unexpected and quick collapse of the Soviet Union in the early 1990s. The area has experienced even more turmoil since that time, including attacks carried out by Islamist terrorists and war in the region of Chechnya and, more recently, Ukraine.

Even though the Russian Realm is hard pressed by natural, economic, and political challenges, it will nevertheless remain a vitally important part of the world for several reasons. First, it is a major supplier of energy resources for other parts of the globe, particularly Europe. It contains 40 percent of the world's natural gas reserves, 20 percent of coal, and 10 percent of petroleum. Second, Russia (like

the former Soviet Union) is one of two nuclear superpowers (the United States is the other one), and its military capability seems to be on the rise again. Russian intercontinental ballistic missiles with nuclear warheads can reach any part of the world in twenty minutes. Third, the region is also a major source of some strategic minerals such as chromium (18 percent of global production) and vanadium (20 percent). These minerals are essential for modern defensive industries and are found in limited amounts in just a few countries in the world. Fourth, Russia alone has 20 percent of global forests (important for many reasons, including their capacity to naturally cleanse the atmosphere and offset greenhouse gas production) and freshwater supplies, and the state of its natural environment is of great importance to the rest of the world. Fifth, Russia's large territorial extent means that it borders many politically unstable areas (countries) and has a lot of influence on them. Political and economic conditions in some of these areas (e.g. Central Asia, the Caucasus region, and Ukraine) are critical for the stability of neighboring regions (e.g. Afghanistan, Georgia, and the European Union) which, in turn, is very important to American strategic interests.

Sixth, Russia has veto power in the United Nations as a permanent member of the Security Council, and it can be a swing vote in the international arena, especially when dealing with matters of interest to Iran, North Korea, or Syria. Seventh, although Russia is only the world's twelfth largest economy, it is a large market for Western goods and investment opportunities. Finally, Russia can be an ally in the war on terror and a peacemaker if it chooses to do so.[1]

PHYSICAL ENVIRONMENT

Landform Configuration

Considering landform configuration, the Russian Realm can be compared to a huge amphitheater. It is semi-circular in shape with a relatively low and flat center and increasing elevations toward the periphery, except in the west where the North Russian Plain (eastern extension of the North European Plain) provides easy access to Eastern, Central, and Western Europe. It is surrounded by ranges of high mountains in the southwest, south, and southeast. The North Russian Plain occupies the western part of the region; it is the eastern extension of the North European Plain, and it widens eastward (Fig. 4.2). The northern and central parts of the plain were covered with a thick layer of ice during the last glacial period and are today composed of moraines, eskers, outwash plains, and other glacial features. They also contain numerous lakes, especially in the northwestern part of the region adjacent to Finland; some parts of that area are also poorly drained and form swamps. The southern part of the North Russian Plain has better soil and is more densely populated.

The Ural Mountains are a narrow and elongated mountain range of north-south orientation running from the Russian-Kazakh border in the south to the Arctic Ocean

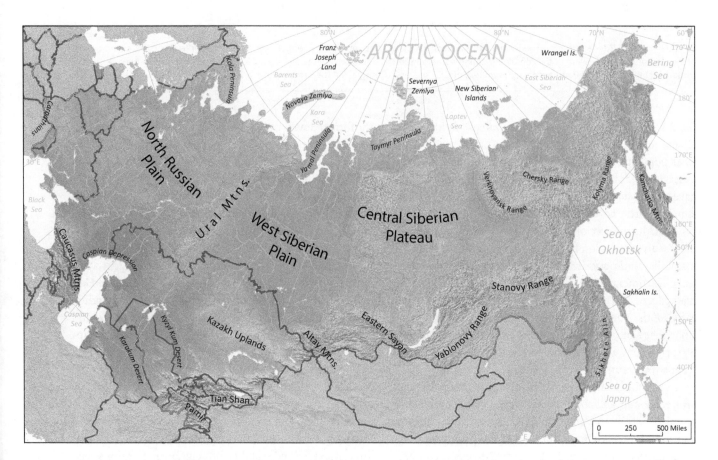

FIGURE 4.2 Landform regions of the Russian Realm—Low areas occupy a large part of the realm while very high mountains are found in a few peripheral regions. *Source:* Natural Earth.

in the north (Fig. 4.3). The island Novaya Zemlya is an extension of this relatively low mountain chain. Most geographers consider the Ural Mountains the border line between Europe and Asia. The region is very rich in mineral resources, especially iron and other metallic ores, and its southern part is an important and strategically located industrial region of Russia. Because of relatively low elevations, it is not a transportation barrier and is bisected by several major railroad lines connecting cities in Siberia and Central Asia with those in the North Russian Plain.

Siberia is a very large region east of the Ural Mountains and is frequently divided into three parts: the West Siberian Plain, the Central Siberian Plateau, and the East Siberian Uplands. Siberia's average elevation increases when moving toward the east. The West Siberian Plain is one of the largest plains in the world. Although it is very rich in petroleum and natural gas, it is also poorly drained, densely forested, and sparsely populated. The Central Siberian Plateau is a region of relatively undisturbed crystalline rock formations of an average elevation between 488 and 700 meters (1,600 and 2,300 feet) above sea level. It is located between the Yenisey and Lena Rivers and rich in mineral resources including fossil fuels and metallic ores. The Eastern Siberian Uplands are a collection of several mountain ranges, some of them reaching elevations of 4,572 meters (15,000 feet) above sea level, and plains in the central part. The Verkhoyansk and Chersky Ranges are the most prominent mountain chains of Eastern Siberia. At the far eastern end of Siberia lies the Kamchatka Peninsula. As part of the **Pacific Ring of Fire**, the peninsula contains twenty-nine active volcanoes, including the Kluchevskaya Sopka (4,750 meters/15,584 feet), the highest active volcano in the Northern Hemisphere.

Most of Central Asia is an area of internal drainage composed of two major plateaus (Kazakh and Ustyurt) with alluvial plains located between them. Most of the area is very dry, and the Kyzylkum and Karakum Deserts occupy the southwestern part of the region. The zone of southern mountains on the periphery of the Russian Realm extends from the Caucasus Mountains in the southwest through several mountain ranges towards the Pacific coast. The Caucasus Mountains are a high and rugged range between the Black and Caspian Seas and are considered, by most geographers, a border line between Europe and Asia (like the Ural Mountains) (Fig. 4.4). The Pamir and Tian Shan Ranges are among the highest mountains in the world, part of the "Roof of the World" which includes the Himalayas, with elevations over 7,620 meters (25,000 feet) above sea level. The entire belt of southern mountains is a seismically active area, and some of the deadliest earthquakes in the world occurred there, including a 7.3

FIGURE 4.3 The Ural Mountains—The northern part of this low mountain range and the adjacent North Russian Plain are densely forested areas with numerous lakes created by the melting glaciers. *Source:* Pixabay.

magnitude event in Ashgabat (Turkmenistan) in 1948 that killed 110,000 people, and a 6.8 magnitude earthquake that destroyed the city of Spitak in Armenia in 1998 and resulted in 25,000 deaths.

Harsh Climate

Most of the Russian Realm, and especially Siberia, is well known for its harsh climate, particularly its very cold winters. Several factors are responsible for the climatic conditions in this area including the high latitude,

FIGURE 4.4 The Caucasus Mountains—This relatively short but high mountain range, located between the Black and Caspian Seas, is considered the border between Europe and Asia. Mt. Elbrus (5,642 meters/18,510 feet), shown in this photo, is its highest peak. *Source:* Pixabay.

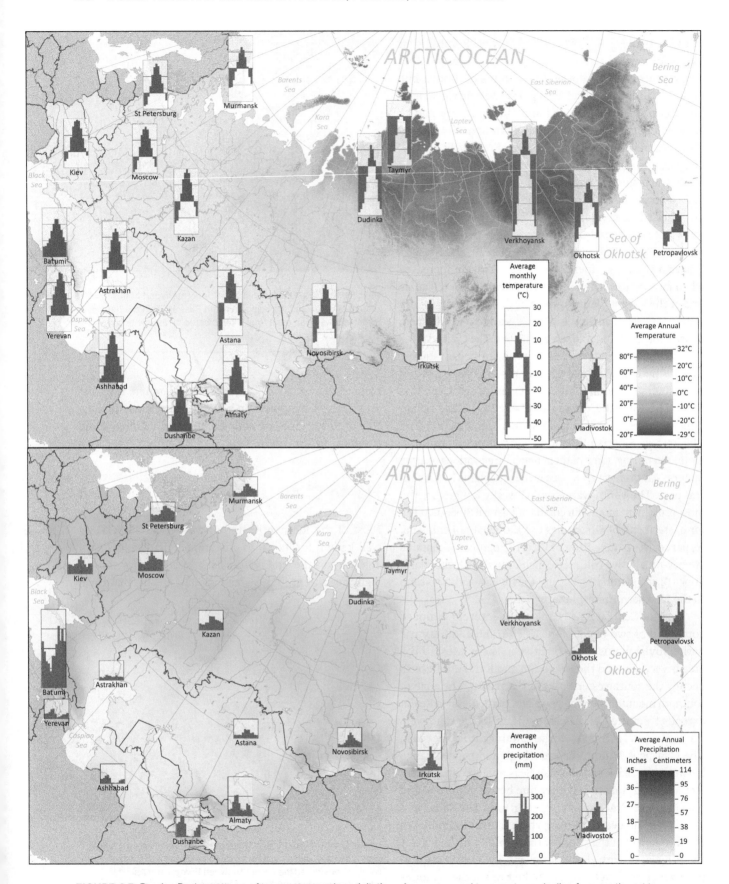

FIGURE 4.5 Russian Realm: patterns of temperature and precipitation—Average annual temperatures decline from southwest to northeast and mainly reflect the distance from the Atlantic Ocean and latitude. Notice the great differences between summer and winter temperatures in northeastern Siberia. Precipitation is more evenly distributed over time in most parts of the region. Notice the relatively low precipitation in northeastern Siberia and the very high precipitation in coastal parts of Georgia. *Source:* WorldClim-Global Climate Data.

great distances from large bodies of water (oceans), and landform configuration. In general, average annual temperatures decline from southwest to northeast; Southern Russia and Ukraine, parts of the Caucasus region, and the southern parts of Central Asia are the warmest places in the Russian Realm, while Northeastern Siberia is the coldest place on Earth, after Antarctica and Greenland (Fig. 4.5).

There are significant differences in temperature patterns between winter and summer months. In winter, distance from the Atlantic Ocean is the major factor behind the declining temperatures from west to east; in summer, latitude is mainly responsible for higher temperatures in the south and lower temperatures in the north. Regardless of the region, the winter-summer temperature differences are among the largest in the world. The landform configuration is mainly responsible for the harsh climate in most parts of the Russian Realm. The belt of high southern mountains prevents the flow of warmer air masses from the south. On the other hand, there is no barrier to cold air masses from the Arctic Ocean.

Although precipitation is more evenly distributed throughout the region than temperature, there are significant differences in the amount of rain and snow various parts of the Russian Realm receive. The European part and the Russian Far East have higher precipitation than Central Asia and northeastern Siberia. The small coastal plain along the Black Sea in Georgia is the wettest part in the entire region. Sheltered by the Caucasus Mountains in the north, it has a fairly warm and humid climate that is able to support the cultivation of subtropical crops such as citrus fruits and tea. As mentioned earlier, most of Central Asia is a very dry area, and most of it is a desert. Summers can be very hot with temperatures over 38°C (100°F) while snow can be on the ground for a short time during some winters (Fig. 4.6).

Another relatively dry region is northeastern Siberia. Although winters are very cold here, low humidity makes life bearable (with proper clothing). The seasonality of precipitation increases as one travels from northwest to southeast; European Russia and Northern Siberia have fairly evenly distributed precipitation throughout the year while the southern periphery and the Pacific coast are characterized by much greater winter-summer differences in precipitation. The Russian Realm is characterized by less climatic diversity than other areas of similar size, partly because of its landform configuration and high latitude location.

FIGURE 4.6 The city of Batumi, Georgia—Its location on the Black Sea coast and humid subtropical climate with an average winter temperature of 7°C (45°F) and annual precipitation of 2,400 mm (95 in) makes it one of the warmest and wettest parts of the Russian Realm. *Source:* Wikimedia Commons.

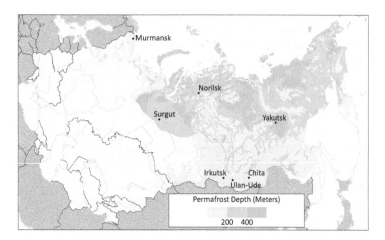

The top layer, known as the active layer, thaws out down to 3 meters (9 feet) in summer. This phenomenon is a major obstacle to construction and transportation activities. Building foundations can tilt, crack, and sink if improperly constructed (e.g. not built on piles above the ground); oil and natural gas pipelines have to be insulated or above the ground to avoid similar problems; railroad tracks and paved roads need frequent repairs; and many permafrost areas become muddy and inaccessible in summer months.

FIGURE 4.7 The extent of permafrost in the Russian Realm—Most of Siberia and the northern part of European Russia are regions of permanently frozen ground. It is a serious obstacle to construction and transportation. *Source:* National Snow and Ice Data Center.

Water Resources

The Russian Realm has ample (just over 9 percent of the world's total) but unevenly distributed freshwater resources. Most of the water is in sparsely populated Siberia, although there are a few sizable lakes in Central Asia. The Caspian Sea is the largest lake in the world by area; its average depth is 210 meters (690 feet) and its surface water is 28 meters (92 feet) below the mean sea level (Fig. 4.8). It is an important source of fish, especially several species of sturgeon known for their caviar, and fossil fuels (oil and natural gas).

The northern parts of European Russia and two-thirds of Siberia are the land of permafrost. The thickness of permafrost varies from place to place, and it can exceed 500 meters (1,500 feet) in some parts of Siberia (Fig. 4.7).

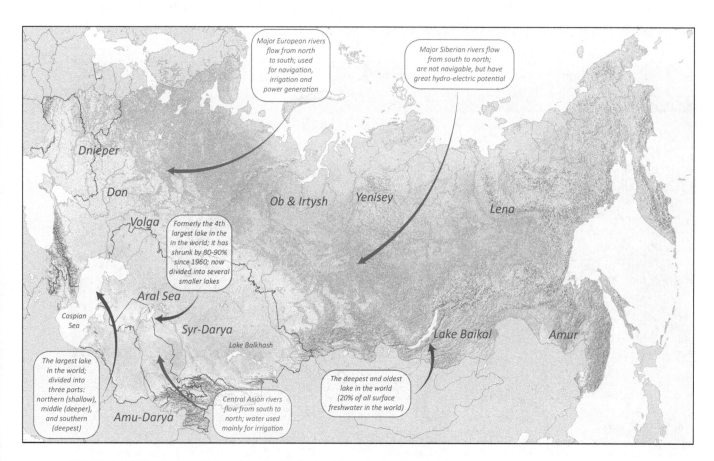

FIGURE 4.8 Major rivers and lakes of the Russian Realm—The map identifies three large rivers in the European part of the region, three in Siberia, two in Central Asia, and one in the Russian Far East. *Source:* Natural Earth.

The Aral Sea used to be the fourth largest lake in the world, but it has been shrinking for the past fifty years and today occupies only a fraction of its original size. The desiccation of the lake is considered the largest human-induced environmental disaster in history and is discussed later in this chapter. Lake Baikal, located in Southern Siberia, is the oldest and deepest lake in the world; it contains one-fifth of all surface freshwater in the world, more than the five Great Lakes in the United States and Canada together, and is a home to over 1,700 species of plants and animals, most of them endemic. Its pristine waters and biology have been threatened by human activities, mainly pulp and paper industries. Lake Baikal is an ancient **rift lake** formed by a deep fissure in the Earth's crust (Fig. 4.9).

Some of the largest river systems on Earth are found in Siberia, including the Yenisey-Angara-Selenge, Ob-Irtysh, and Lena Rivers. Almost all of them flow north to the Arctic Ocean and are not very important for navigational purposes as they are frozen for many months and run through sparsely populated areas. However, some of them have great hydroelectric potential. The Sayano-Shushenskaya and Krasnoyarsk dams on the Yenisey River are among the ten largest hydroelectric projects in the world.

Most rivers in the European part of the Russian Realm run south and empty their waters into the Black or Caspian Seas. Their waters are used for navigation, irrigation, and power generation. The Volga is the best known and most important river in Russia; it runs through relatively densely populated and economically developed areas, and several large industrial centers are located along its course, including Nizhny Novgorod (former Gorky), Kazan, Togliatti, Saratov, and Volgograd (Fig. 4.10). The Volga River is connected with the Don River and the Black Sea by the Volga-Don Canal, completed in 1952. A series of canals on the Volga tributaries and other rivers in the northern part of European Russia connects the capital city of Moscow with the Azov, Baltic, Black, Caspian, and White Seas; the city is sometimes called "the port of the five seas." The Dnieper River is another important waterway in the western part of the Russian Realm, especially in Ukraine. It runs through the western fringes of a highly industrialized region of Donbass. Several hydropower stations were built along its course, and they provide about 10 percent of Ukraine's energy needs.

Vegetation and Soil

Natural vegetation and soil are closely related to climatic conditions, water availability, and landform types. There are several fairly well-defined vegetation-soil regions, determined mainly by latitude and modified by terrain

FIGURE 4.9 Lake Baikal—It is the world's deepest lake containing over 20 percent of the global surface freshwater. The paper and other industries along the lake shore pose enormous danger to its marine life which includes many endemic species of plants and animals. *Source:* Wikimedia Commons.

configuration, across the Russian Realm (Fig. 4.11). The belt of tundra is dominant along the Arctic Ocean and the Bering Sea. This cold climate grassland and treeless landscape is associated with infertile soil, a short growing season, low population density, and localized reindeer herding. A much wider belt of boreal or evergreen coniferous forests (taiga) extends from the Russian-Finnish border in the west to the Pacific Ocean in the Far East. This is the largest forested area in the world and is an important carbon dioxide sink and source of oxygen for the entire world. Pine and spruce

FIGURE 4.10 The Volga River—It is the longest (3,690 km/2,293 mi) and economically most important river in the European part of the Russian Realm. It is also of great historical and cultural importance to the Russian people. *Source:* Pixabay.

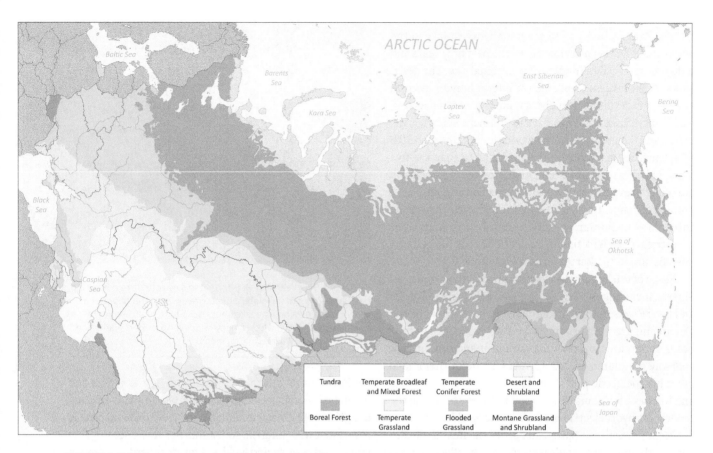

FIGURE 4.11 Major ecosystems in the Russian Realm—Forest ecosystems occupy the largest part of the Russian Realm. Notice the influence of latitude and landforms on the distribution of various ecosystems. *Source:* Terrestrial Ecoregions of the World.

are the dominant species in the European parts of taiga, but larch is more common in most of the Siberian forest. Poor soils and the cool climate prevent any large-scale farming activities in this area; the harvesting of lumber, on the other hand, particularly in Siberia, has been growing in importance in recent years. The belt of mixed forest, located south of the taiga zone mainly in European Russia, is composed of several species of coniferous (pine and fir) and deciduous (birch) trees, and soil is more fertile there than that in the zone north of it. Many parts of the mixed forest zone have been cleared and converted to agricultural land where dairy farming and the cultivation of potatoes and small grains are dominant activities. The temperate grassland (steppe), the next natural vegetation zone moving south, is associated with fertile soil (black earth) and sufficient moisture

to practice large-scale commercial grain (wheat) cultivation. It extends from Western Ukraine through Southern European Russia and Northern Kazakhstan. This relatively densely populated area is the breadbasket of the Russian Realm. However, drought and soil erosion are two major environmental challenges here. Most of Central Asia is a dry climate zone, as described earlier, and the desert and shrub landscape is characteristic of this region. Most soil has high mineral but low organic content and is not good for agriculture. However, the southern parts of this dry region have fertile loess (wind-blown) soil and became major centers of irrigated agriculture emphasizing the cultivation of cotton, fruits, and vegetables. These farming practices have led to disastrous environmental consequences that are discussed later in this chapter.

HUMAN-ENVIRONMENT INTERACTION

Not much information had been published about the state of the natural environment in the former Soviet Union. Environmental protection was not a high priority for

the Communist government for several reasons. First, state control of all means of production meant that any environmental problem was the result of state activities, and the government would not admit any wrongdoing. Second, the Soviet Union's natural resource base was considered almost limitless, and there was no concern about using it sustainably. Third, environmental protection was considered detrimental to economic growth; meeting production targets was far more important than limiting the emission of greenhouse gases or other pollutants. Fourth, there was an ideological belief in the subordination of nature to humans; the natural environment should be utilized and transformed rather than protected. Fifth, environmental protection quite often required purchasing expensive Western technology; limited funds allocated for environmental protection were often used for other purposes.

The desiccation of the Aral Sea in Central Asia is one example of the large-scale environmental degradation in the former Soviet Union (Fig. 4.12). The Aral Sea is just a small fraction of its original size. The water volume decreased from 1,080 to 98 cubic kilometers between 1960 and 2010, and the lake's water salinity increased thirteen times during the same period. Two rivers originating in the Pamir and Tian Shan Mountains, the Amu Darya and Syr Darya, used to provide 80 percent of all water to the lake; the remaining 20 percent was supplied by rainfall. In the late 1950s, the Soviet government decided to divert water from these two rivers to irrigate land devoted mainly to cotton cultivation in the five Central Asian republics, particularly Uzbekistan and Turkmenistan. Some 32,000 kilometers (20,000 miles) of canals, including the Karakum Canal (1,368 kilometers/850 miles long), and dozens of dams and reservoirs were built for that purpose. Unfortunately, a large part of the diverted water was wasted (between 25 percent and 75 percent) before reaching the cotton fields due to low canal construction standards and evaporation. This grandiose project has negatively impacted the environment in many ways. First, the rapidly declining water volume increased differences in the lake's surface water temperature between summer and winter months (higher temperatures in summer and lower in winter) and subsequently changed the local climate so that summers were shorter and hotter, winters were longer and colder, precipitation was lower, and winds were stronger. Second, increased **salinization** and evaporation of water resulted in thinner and/or smaller ice cover of the lake in winter, soil degradation (salt accumulation), and lowering of ground water level in the surrounding areas. Third, stronger winds led to more frequent dust storms carrying large amounts of salt that were deposited on the surrounding settlements and farmland. Fourth, the lowering of the ground water table and salt accumulation in the soil were responsible for the thinning

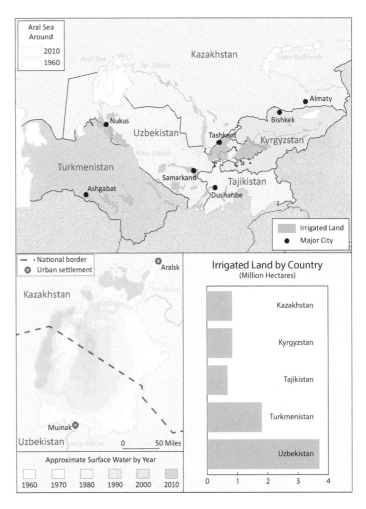

FIGURE 4.12 The Aral Sea problem—The Aral Sea has been shrinking for the past fifty years, and only a small portion of the original lake remains today. Too much water has been used for irrigating cotton farms in Central Asia, particularly in Uzbekistan and Turkmenistan. *Source:* Mappery. Aral Sea Historic Coastline; FAOSTAT.

of the protective vegetation cover, which, in turn, led to **desertification** of the adjacent areas. Fifth, the shrinking lake is no longer a modifier to cold Siberian winds and does not provide much moisture for the snowfall in the mountains to the south and southeast and, consequently, is indirectly responsible for the retreat of glaciers that are sources of water to the rivers flowing to the lake. Sixth, the shrinking lake has killed or severely reduced the fishing industry and led to higher unemployment rates in several surrounding settlements (e.g. Muinak and Aralsk). In some cases, frozen fish from other places are brought here for processing to keep the previously important industry alive. Finally, soil degradation and consequent increased use of fertilizers and pesticides, as well as frequent dust storms, contributed to increased health risks among local

FIGURE 4.13 Abandoned fishing boats in the former Aral Sea—Over 80 percent of this at one time fourth largest lake in the world is now a dry land; numerous rusting fishing boats are just one example of the economic collapse in the surrounding areas. *Source:* Wikimedia Commons.

residents, including respiratory diseases and high infant mortality (Fig. 4.13).

Although the Soviet Union created this disaster, now independent Kazakhstan and Uzbekistan have to deal with the problem and find solutions to remedy it (with international help). An improved system of irrigation canals increased the flow of water from Syr Darya to the northern (now separate) part of the former Aral Sea known as the Small Aral Sea. At the same time, a dam financed by the World Bank was completed in 2005 to control water levels in that part of the lake. There is some hope that this project will bring life back to coastal communities such as the city of Aralsk.

The Chernobyl nuclear accident of 1986 is another example of a limited Soviet concern about the natural environment and even human health. The April 26 explosion at one of the four reactors of the nuclear power plant near the city of Pripyat (145 kilometers/90 miles north of the capital city of Kiev) was the result of engineering deficiencies and human error. Large amounts of radioactive materials were released into the environment, and a radioactive cloud spread across many parts of Europe.

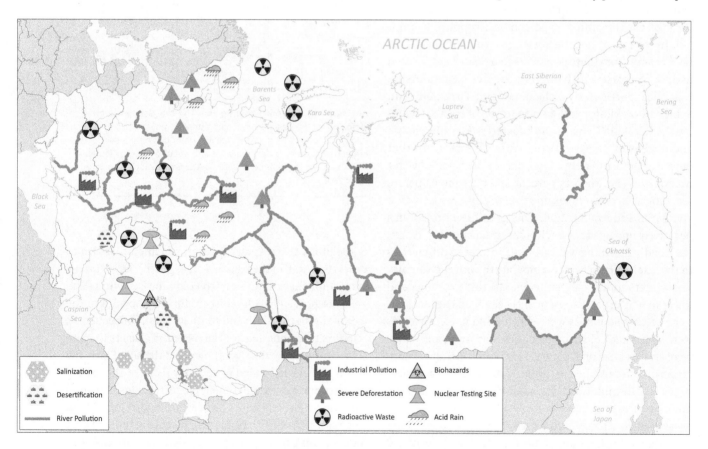

FIGURE 4.14 Environmental degradation in the Russian Realm—Most information about environmental degradation during the communist era was revealed after the break-up of the Soviet Union. Many parts of the region have suffered from various forms of pollution, and large areas in Siberia and northwestern Russia have been affected by deforestation. Drawn after a similar image in White, G. et al. (2014). *Essentials of world regional geography* (3rd ed.). New York: McGraw-Hill.

The problem was first reported in Sweden, but the Soviet government tried to hide the calamity for several days. In fact, residents of Kiev, a city of over 2 million people, completely unaware of what was going on to the north of them, were encouraged to participate in the May 1 (a major Communist holiday) outdoor activities. Meanwhile, some 116,000 residents of the city of Pripyat were ordered to evacuate, and thousands of individuals were involved in managing the crisis and its outcomes. At least 4,000 deaths related to radiation contamination were reported, although some claim the toll has been much higher. As with the Aral Sea disaster, new infrastructure, built partly with foreign funds, has helped to ameliorate this problem. In this case, the European Bank for Reconstruction and Development and other international donors funded the construction of a giant sarcophagus. The massive arch, which is the world's largest moveable structure, was rolled over the destroyed reactor in 2016 and will safely entomb the radioactive site for at least one hundred years.

Not all of the Russian Realm's environmental problems are disasters stemming from the Soviet era (Fig. 4.14). One of the most momentous challenges is the likely retreat of sea ice in the Arctic Ocean as a consequence of global climate change. Russia has the longest Arctic coastline and will be the most affected by predicted changes. On the positive side of the ledger, an ice-free Arctic would facilitate transportation from Europe to Asia via the Northern Sea Route and would make it easier to access Arctic mineral resources. The costs of these changes could be severe, however, as many species might be lost forever, the livelihoods of Arctic communities will be undermined, and flooding will be more likely in many areas.

POPULATION PATTERNS AND TRENDS

The Russian Realm is inhabited by over 285 million people. Considering its large territorial extent, we can say that it is a relatively sparsely populated region. Russia has half of the total population (142 million); if we add Ukraine (44 million) and Uzbekistan (29 million), their combined population accounts for over 75 percent of the region's total population. The population geography of the Russian Realm is characterized by at least four major issues: (1) the uneven distribution of people throughout the region, (2) regional differences in population growth rates, (3) high mortality among the middle-aged male population, and (4) a very diverse ethnic structure. Each issue has been a serious concern for the Soviet and Russian governments for decades.

Uneven Population Distribution

A great majority of the population resides in the European part of the Russian Realm. It occupies a quarter of the territory but houses over 60 percent of the total population. Siberia and the Russian Far East, on the other hand, comprise half of the total area but have only 35 million residents. The unevenly distributed population reflects environmental conditions. More densely populated central and southern parts of the North Russian Plain have a milder climate and better soil, while cold Siberia and large parts of dry Central Asia are sparsely populated (Fig. 4.15). Yet, Siberia needs more people and investment to fully develop its rich mineral and forest resource base. Low population densities along the lengthy Russian-Chinese border, plus past political tensions between the two countries and Chinese territorial claims to parts of the Far East and Siberia, were a source of major concern for the Soviet government. Various economic incentives and/or force were used to transfer people from other parts of the country to this sparsely populated but economically and strategically important region. Some of these efforts are discussed later in this chapter.

Unfavorable Demographic Trends

The population in the Russian Realm has been growing very slowly, and sometimes declining, since the collapse of Communism due to low fertility, relatively high mortality, and emigration. However, there have been strong regional differences in population growth rates for quite a long time. While most parts of Russia, Ukraine, and Belarus have been losing population, Central Asia and the Caucasus region have been gaining population at a fairly fast rate (Fig. 4.16). The population-losing regions are predominantly Slavic (mainly Russian) in ethnic composition, the areas of population growth are inhabited by various non-Slavic speaking groups, and most of them are Muslim. The Soviet government (1922–91) was concerned about the slowly shrinking proportion of the Russian population from 54.6 percent in 1939 to 50.2 percent in 1989. There was a fear that Russians would become a minority in this Communist country controlled by Russians. More and more soldiers drafted into the Red Army were non-Russians, and their understanding of the Russian language and loyalty to Communist

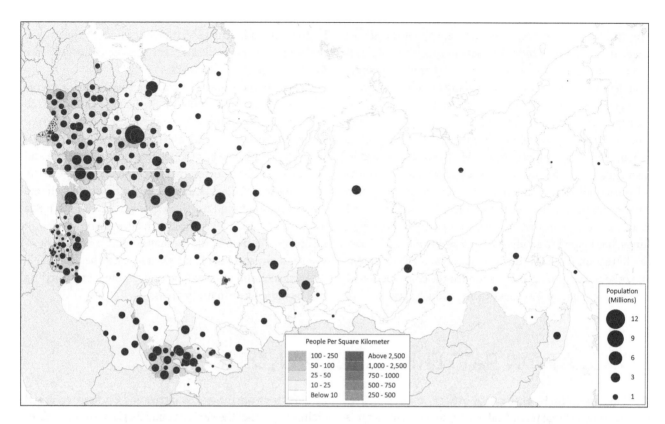

FIGURE 4.15 Population distribution in the Russian Realm—The east-west and, to a lesser extent, north-south disparities in population distribution reflect environmental conditions, particularly climate and landform configuration. Notice the relatively high population densities in parts of Central Asia and the Caucasus region. *Source:* GeoHive (www.geohive.com) and statistical agencies of individual countries.

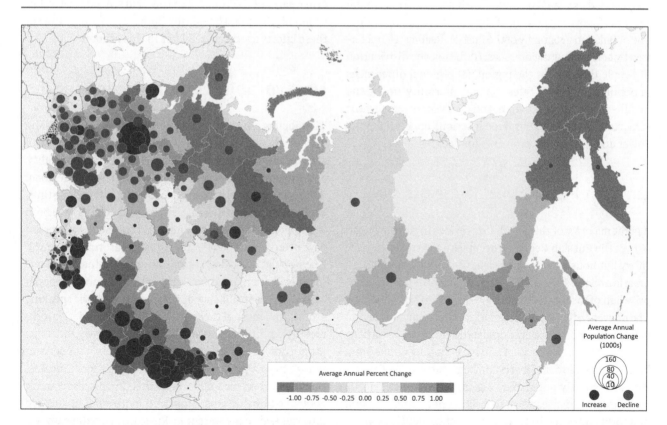

FIGURE 4.16 Population change in the Russian Realm, 2000–2012—Most parts of Russia, Belarus, and Ukraine have been losing population in recent decades. Only major urban agglomerations and parts of western Siberia (oil and natural gas mining areas) have been gaining population. Notice the significant population growth in Central Asia and eastern parts of the Caucasus region. *Source:* statistical and demographic yearbooks of individual countries.

FIGURE 4.17 Total fertility rates in the Russian Realm, 1950–2010—Notice the declining fertility rates in all countries of the Russian Realm and below the replacement level rates (2.1) in Russia and other countries except those in Central Asia. *Source:* United Nations. Population Division. World Population Prospects 2012.

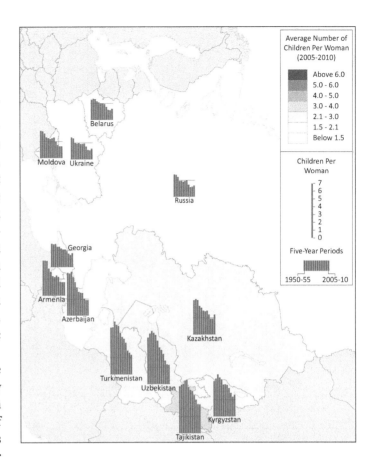

principles were not always assured. The Communist government introduced various policy measures to encourage higher fertility among the Russians without much success. Regional disparities in population growth rates have not diminished since the break-up of the Soviet Union. Only the largest urban agglomerations (Moscow, St. Petersburg, Kiev, and Minsk) in the European part of the realm, fossil fuel-producing regions of Western Siberia, and some areas north of the Caucasus Mountains have been gaining population in recent years. Like during the Soviet era, most of Central Asia and Azerbaijan have also been gaining population, in many cases at the rate of over 1 percent per year (Fig. 4.17). The depopulation of Siberia will be a major demographic and economic challenge to the Russian government.

Sharp increases in mortality, especially among the middle-aged male population, and a simultaneous fertility decline shortly after the collapse of Communism, known as the **Russian demographic cross**, have received a lot of attention among demographers and other social scientists (Fig. 4.18). Most point to factors such as stress, economic insecurity (unemployment), poor quality of health care,

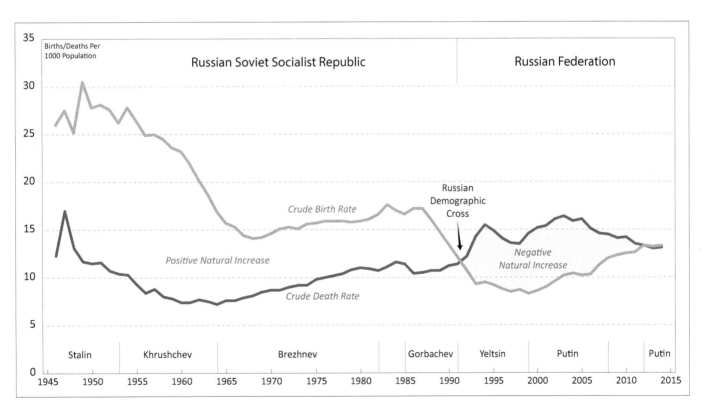

FIGURE 4.18 Demographic trends in Russia, 1945–2014—Crude birth and death rates had been declining for about two decades after World War II but began to increase around the mid-1960s. A sharp decline in birth and simultaneous increase in death rates shortly before and after the collapse of the Soviet Union became known as the "Russian demographic cross." Russia's demographic conditions have been slowly improving since that time, and a modest population increase is possible in the near future. *Source:* Russian Federal State Statistics Service.

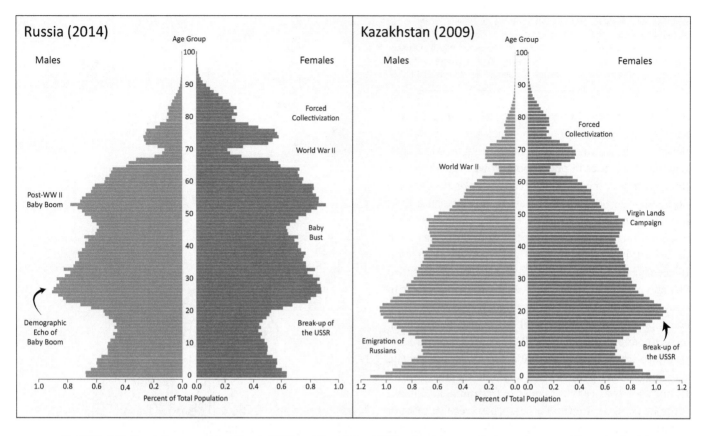

FIGURE 4.19 Population pyramids of Russia (2014) and Kazakhstan (2009) —Russia's pyramid shows the scars of forced collectivization of the 1930s and World War II while Kazakhstan's also shows the Virgin Lands Campaign of the 1950s. Both pyramids show demographic changes associated with the collapse of communism. *Source:* State Committee of the Russian Federation on Statistics; Ministry of National Economy of the Republic of Kazakhstan. Committee on Statistics.

unsafe working conditions, and, perhaps most importantly, alcoholism as major causes of death. A typical Russian man is expected to live about sixty-five years today and a woman over ten years longer. These are levels comparable to the U.S. in the early 1940s and early 1970s, respectively. The male-female gap in life expectancy in Russia today is the largest in the world.[2]

Population pyramids are useful demographic tools as they can reflect some economic, political, and other events that took place in a given society during the past three or four generations. The population pyramid for Russia still shows the scars of forced **collectivization** (transfer of agricultural land from private to state and/or collective ownership) of the 1930s (briefly discussed later in this chapter), World War II, and the collapse of Communism twenty-five years ago (Fig. 4.19).

Urban Trends and Patterns

Some 64 percent of the Russian Realm's population is urban today, but there are significant regional differences in urbanization levels, ranging from 73 and 76 percent in Russia and Belarus to 26 and 45 percent in Tajikistan and Moldova, respectively. In general, most of Central Asia, the Caucasus region, and the southern part of European Russia are the least urbanized areas. In industrial centers of Eastern Ukraine, the Moscow area, the Volga River Basin, and the Urals region, as well as some mining regions in Siberia and the Russian Far East, over 80 percent of population is urban (Fig. 4.20). The capital city of Moscow, with a metropolitan population of about 12 million, is the largest urban center in the entire region. The city's central location, accessibility by various modes of transportation, and its historical and political importance contributed to its dominant position in the Soviet and Russian urban hierarchy (Fig. 4.21). Despite its size and regional importance, Moscow is not a city of world importance like London, Paris, New York, or Tokyo. Other major urban centers include St. Petersburg (5 million people) on the Baltic Sea (the capital of the pre-Soviet Russian Empire), Kiev (3 million) on the Dnieper River (now the capital of Ukraine), and the capital cities of Tashkent (2 million) in Uzbekistan and Baku (2 million) in Azerbaijan (Fig. 4.22).

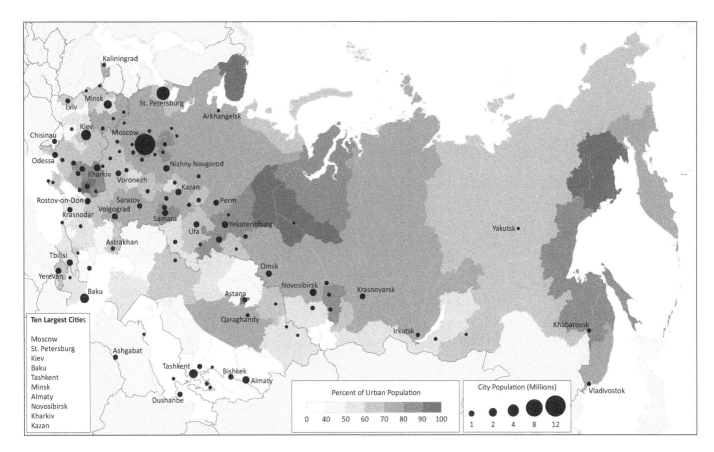

FIGURE 4.20 Urbanization levels in the Russian Realm, 2010—Relatively high urbanization levels are found in several industrial regions (e.g. Donbas in eastern Ukraine or the Ural region), some mining areas of western and eastern Siberia, and the Kola Peninsula in northwestern Russia. Most of Central Asia and some agricultural regions of Ukraine, Kazakhstan, and southern Russia are the least urbanized parts of the Russian Realm. Notice the absence of large urban agglomerations (except Moscow and St. Petersburg) in this part of the world, an outcome of communist restrictions on migration to large cities. *Source:* United Nations. Population Division. World Urbanization Prospects 2014; statistical agencies of individual countries.

FIGURE 4.21 Moscow, the capital of Russia—This urban agglomeration of over 12 million people is the political, cultural, and economic center of the country. Although Soviet style architecture is still dominant in most parts of the city, new residential and commercial developments have emerged since the collapse of communism. *Source:* Wikimedia Commons.

FIGURE 4.22 The Palace Square in St. Petersburg, Russia—This second largest Russian city was built by Peter the Great at the beginning of the 18th century and was the capital of tsarist Russia until 1917. Its rich history and numerous neoclassical structures attract many visitors from Russia and abroad. *Source:* Pixabay.

The history of urbanization in the Russian Realm can be divided into three major periods, each associated with different principles of urban planning and/or the role of the urban sector in the national economy. Most of the present cities were established during the pre-Soviet era as trading, military, or political centers of various regions. Some of them are over 1,200 years old (Novgorod, Pskov, and Kiev in the European part of the region); others are even older (Tbilisi and Yerevan in the Caucasus region, Samarkand and Bukhara in Central Asia). Moscow (originally established as a fort in the 12th century) and other cities in central Russia were built or expanded around military posts or monasteries in the 15th century. Several major cities were built by Peter I and Catherine II in the 18th century as new centers of political power (St. Petersburg) or military posts in Siberia and the Far East (Yekaterinburg, Tomsk, Irkutsk, and Yakutsk). The Industrial Revolution, which came to Russia in the second part of the 19th century, was associated with urban growth around Moscow and areas rich in fossil fuels and iron ore, especially the Volga and Urals regions.

The second (Soviet) period of urbanization was characterized by reconstruction of older cities, according to the Communist principles of urban design as well as the establishment of new cities, many of them in remote and/or environmentally challenging areas rich in mineral resources (e.g. Norilsk, Vorkuta, and Magadan). Soviet cities had several unique features and were different in many ways from their Western (including European) counterparts. First, there were limits on population size in most major cities. Residence permits obtained through the internal passport system were required for outsiders to move into these urban centers. People were not eligible for housing or employment opportunities in the city without such a permit. Second, the great majority of residents lived in publicly (state) controlled housing units where living space was allocated on a per capita basis. These units were in high- or medium-rise apartment-type structures made of prefabricated (usually low quality) materials. Third, there was a great dependence on public transportation for commuting to work and for other purposes. A fairly dense network of bus and street car lines in most cities and subway lines in the largest agglomerations served the urban population fairly well. The Moscow subway network has long been one of the largest and best run systems in the world. Limited private car ownership also forced most residents to rely on

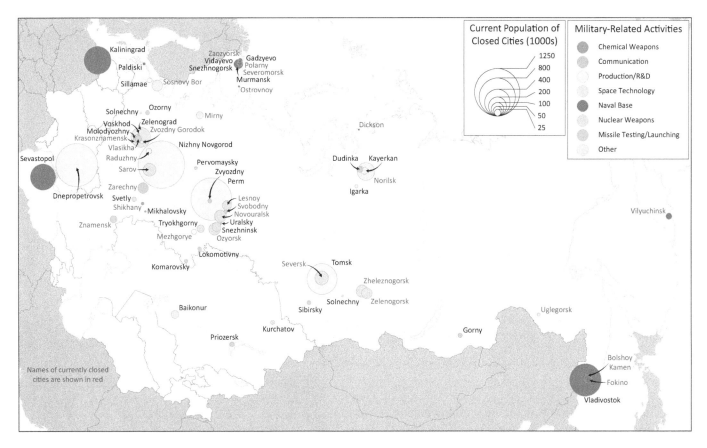

FIGURE 4.23 Secret cities in the former Soviet Union—Some cities still remain closed, particularly to Western visitors, as they continue to house various military-related research and development activities. Notice that several cities with a population of over half a million were affected by travel and residency restrictions. *Source:* Wikipedia; Pensando el Territorio (www.pensandoelterritorio.com).

inter-city bus, train, or air service to travel further away. Fourth, there was a low level of retail services, even in the largest cities. Most stores had generic names (bakery, grocery store, etc.) and were poorly supplied with consumer goods. There were one or two department stores in larger cities but no shopping malls similar to those in the West. Fifth, the Communist government put a lot of emphasis on visual symbolism, especially in large cities. Extensive public squares used for military parades and other gatherings, monumental architecture (museums, government buildings, and statues of Lenin), and large billboards full of Communist slogans were part of the urban landscape throughout the Soviet Union. Finally, two features found in many large American agglomerations, inner-city decay and urban sprawl, were absent in Soviet cities.

There were a few dozen cities of various sizes in the Russian and Kazakh Socialist Republics that were not shown on most maps published in the former Soviet Union. These **closed cities**, established in the 1940s, were settlements with travel and residency restriction for their inhabitants and visitors (Fig. 4.23). Almost all of them were centers of military-related research and/or development or production

and testing sites of various types of weapons. Residents of these cities enjoyed better living conditions (e.g. higher salaries and larger housing units) in exchange for various travel restrictions. Some closed cities were quite large in population size such as Gorky (now Nizhny Novgorod), Perm, Vladivostok, Dnepropetrovsk, and Kaliningrad. Most cities, however, were of medium or small size, located on the periphery of, or a short distance from, larger urban agglomerations and surrounded by forested areas or deserts. Many of them were also known by other names such as Tomsk-7 (Seversk) or Sverdlovsk-44 (Novouralsk). After the collapse of the Soviet Union, all large cities became open to all Russians and foreigners. However, there are still about forty settlements that have closed city status. Some of them are open to Russian visitors, but closed to foreign visitors.

Many cities in the Russian Realm have changed significantly since the collapse of Communism, the third period of urban development.[3] The removal of restrictions on migration to large urban centers has led to the influx of newcomers from other places in Russia and former Soviet republics in search of better economic opportunities.

FIGURE 4.24 The Moscow International Business Center—This prime example of post-communist development occupies an area of 60 hectares (150 acres) and is a collection of skyscrapers (many still under construction) and other structures designed for attracting 250,000 to 300,000 people (employees and visitors) each day. *Source:* Pixabay.

FIGURE 4.25 The capital city of Astana, Kazakhstan—This planned city has a population of over 1 million and has been the capital of the country since 1997. *Source:* Pixabay.

Urban sprawl has become a new phenomenon as some richer residents moved to single family dwellings on the urban periphery. The emergence of Western-style shopping malls has greatly improved shopping opportunities for many residents. However, the increased number of automobiles has also led to greater pollution and traffic congestion. The free market economy has increased socioeconomic inequalities and led to homelessness among some urban residents. The rise in urban crime rates was another outcome of the collapse of Communism (Fig. 4.24 and Fig. 4.25).

LANGUAGE AND RELIGION

The Soviet Union used to be, and Russia still is, one of the most linguistically diverse countries in the world. Perhaps only India, Indonesia, Nigeria, and a few other countries in Asia and Africa are characterized by greater diversity. The linguistic diversity was probably the most important factor behind the break-up of the Soviet Union in 1991 (Fig. 4.26). The last Soviet population census of 1989 provided information on the size of the 130 largest ethnic groups. Since that time, all twelve now independent countries in the Russian Realm, except Uzbekistan, conducted at least one population census. However, any comparative study of ethnic diversity in the entire region is much harder now than twenty-five years ago because there is no official data on ethnicity for the same year for the entire region. Nevertheless, the available information can be used to describe the current complex ethnic patterns fairly well. Russians are numerically dominant; they account for over half of the total population. Most of them live in Russia (111 million) where they account for over 80 percent of the total population. Other countries with sizable Russian populations are Ukraine (8 million) and Kazakhstan (over 3.5 million). Some 23 million Russians used to live in other parts of the Realm before the break-up of the Soviet Union, but many of them have moved to Russia since that time. Ukrainians comprise the second largest ethnic group (44 million) in this region, and most of them are in Ukraine (37 million)

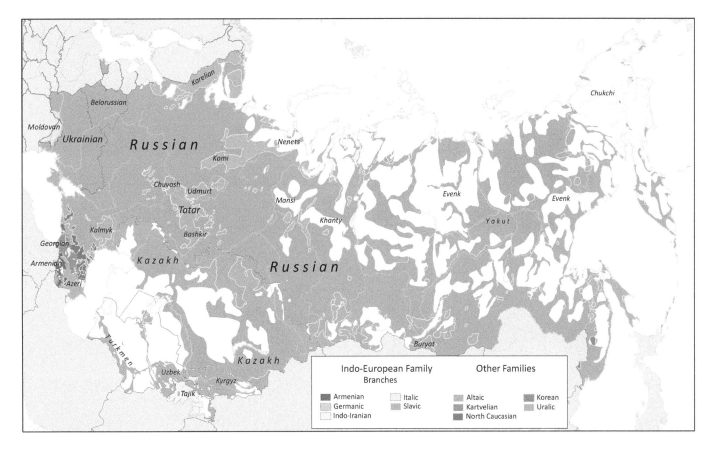

FIGURE 4.26 Distribution of major linguistic groups in the Russian Realm—The Soviet Union was and Russia is today one of the most ethnically diverse countries in the world. There were over one hundred ethnic groups and many had official recognition in the form of ethnic territories of various political status. Russians comprise about a half of the total population, followed by Ukrainians and Uzbeks. The Caucasus region is the most linguistically diverse part of the Russian Realm. *Source:* World Language Mapping System.

and Russia (2 million). Most of the Belorussian population (10 million) lives in Belarus (8 million) and Russia. These three Slavic groups have many things in common, including mutually intelligible languages written in Cyrillic script, Eastern Orthodox Christianity, and a common history. Together, they account for over 70 percent of the Russian Realm's population, although their share of the total population has been slowly declining due to higher rates of growth among other ethnic groups.

Other major Indo-European languages spoken in the Russian Realm are Moldovan, Armenian, and Tajik. The Moldovan language, used by over 2.5 million people in Moldova, which used to be a part of Romania until World War II, belongs to the Romance (Italic) branch of languages and is very similar to Romanian. After Moldova became one of the Soviet republics in 1945, the Soviet authorities replaced the Latin script with the Cyrillic one to emphasize differences between the two languages and justify their annexation of the area to the Soviet Union. After independence, the Moldovan government switched back to using the Latin script. The Armenian language, an independent

branch of the Indo-European family, is spoken by about 3 million residents of Armenia and Nagorno-Karabakh (a part of Azerbaijan claimed by Armenia). It uses a unique writing system introduced around 405 CE. About 80 percent of Tajikistan's residents (over 6 million) speak Tajik, a language closely related to Iranian (Persian). It was based on the Persian-Arabic script until 1928 when the Cyrillic system of writing was introduced. The government is considering switching back to the previous writing system.

The second largest group is comprised of people speaking various Altaic (mainly Turkic) languages and is found in three major regions: Central Asia and Azerbaijan, east-central parts of European Russia, and central and eastern regions of Siberia. Over 25 million Uzbeks, 13 million Kazakhs, over 4 million Turkmen and Kyrgyz, as well as 9 million Azeris inhabit the first region. More than 5 million Tatars, 4 million each Chuvash and Bashkirs, and some 180,000 Kalmyks are found in the second area. Much smaller groups of Yakuts, Tuvans, and others reside in the third area. Together, some thirty Altaic languages are spoken by over 36 million inhabitants, making it the

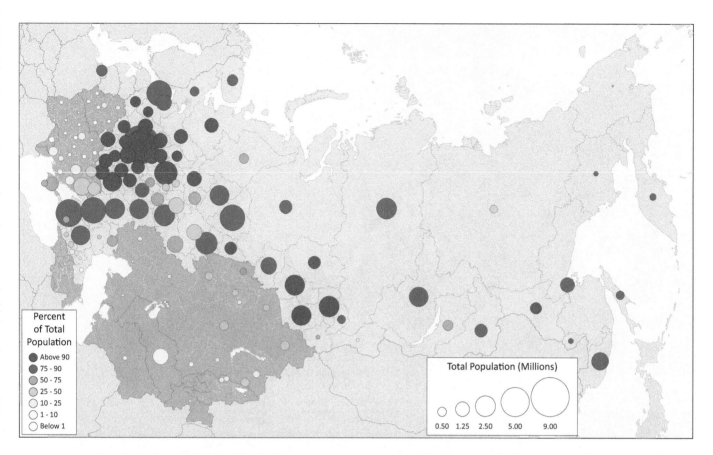

FIGURE 4.27 Distribution of the Russian population—Although the majority of Russians live in Russia today, some 25 million used to inhabit other parts of the Soviet Union. Many of them migrated to Russia after 1991, but there are still millions of them living in Ukraine, Kazakhstan, and other former Soviet republics. The Russian presence in these countries has been a source of tension between the Russians and their governments. The conflict in Ukraine is the best example of such tensions. *Source:* statistical agencies of individual countries.

second largest linguistic group in the Russian Realm. The Soviet authorities imposed the Cyrillic alphabet on most of these languages, but several groups switched to or added the Latin script to their language after the collapse of communism. The Caucasus region is the most linguistically diverse part of the Russian Realm. The mountainous terrain became a refuge area for several linguistic minorities; at the same time, it isolated various groups from each other and allowed them to retain their original languages. In addition to the Azeri and Armenian people, over 4 million Georgians inhabit the western and central parts of the region. The Georgian language belongs to the Kartvelian family and also has a unique writing script (like Armenian). The rest of the population is divided into several groups including the Chechens (the largest group), Ingush, Avars, Abkhaz, and other people. The great linguistic diversity in this region has contributed to political instability and conflict since the break-up of the Soviet Union.

While the declining share of the Russian population was a concern to the Soviet government prior to 1991, the status of some 25 million Russians living in the fourteen

newly independent countries (also known as the **Near Abroad**) after the break-up of the Soviet Union became a new concern for the Russian government. During the Soviet period, many Russians were sent to other parts of the country to provide skilled labor to less developed regions (Central Asia), reduce labor shortages in demographically stagnating parts of the country (the Baltic republics), or simply to help the Soviet authorities better control the non-Russian areas (Fig. 4.27). Since the Russian language was used in the entire country, these migrants had no need to learn the local language. After the collapse of the Soviet Union, however, the Russians became foreigners in the newly independent countries. They were required to learn the local language in order to receive citizenship and own property in some countries. Many also feared that they would become second-class residents with an uncertain future. The Russian government began encouraging them to immigrate to Russia and threatened to intervene in case the Russian minority was mistreated in any country. The annexation of Crimea in 2014 and the support for anti-government activities in the Russian-dominated

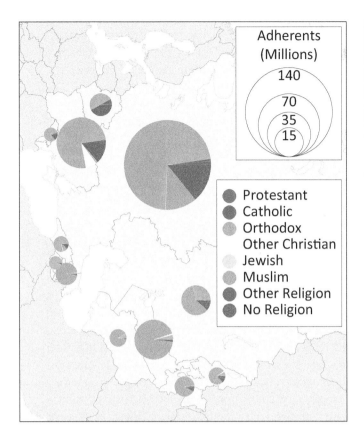

FIGURE 4.28 Religious affiliation of people in the Russian Realm—Eastern Orthodox Christianity is the dominant faith in Russia, Ukraine, Belarus, Moldova, and the two Caucasian republics of Armenia and Georgia, while Islam is the majority religion in the remaining countries of the region. Notice the relatively high proportion of people without any religious affiliation, particularly in Belarus. *Source:* Association of Religious Data Archives.

FIGURE 4.29 The Cathedral of Christ the Savior, Moscow—Built in 1883, destroyed by the Soviet authorities in 1931 and rebuilt in 1995–2000, it is the tallest Eastern Orthodox church in the world. *Source:* Wikimedia Commons.

parts of Eastern Ukraine were justified by Russia in this way.

Eastern Orthodox Christianity is the dominant religion in Russia, Ukraine, Belarus, Moldova, Armenia and Georgia (Fig. 4.28). Christianity was introduced to Georgia and Armenia in the fourth century and to Russia in 988 CE. From a theological point of view, Eastern Orthodox Christianity is much closer to Roman Catholicism than Protestantism. Although most Eastern Orthodox churches are not as large as Catholic ones, they are known for their characteristic architecture, especially the onion-shaped domes. A typical church has five domes but some may have thirteen (or any other odd number between five and thirteen). There are no carved statues and pews inside the church (people stand during the service), but there are numerous paintings (icons) depicting biblical events and various saints and lots of burning candles and incense (Fig. 4.29). The Eastern Orthodox Church is more traditional than other Christian faiths with regard to dress code, gender roles, fasting, and liturgy. For example, women are

expected to wear skirts or long dresses while attending church services and are not allowed to enter the sanctuary. No musical instruments are used during the service but *a cappella* singing is common.[4]

The Uniate (Byzantine) Church is a branch of the Eastern Orthodox Church that is under the Pope's authority. The union with the Roman Catholic Church came in 1596; in exchange for accepting the Roman pontiff's authority, the church was allowed to retain its Orthodox practices, including married clergy. Uniate or Byzantine Catholics are mainly found in Western Ukraine and parts of Belarus and Moldova.

Islam is the second largest religion in the region. **Sunni Muslims** are dominant in Central Asia and parts of European Russia (the Volga region and northern Caucasus) while **Shia Muslims** are found in Azerbaijan. Islam was introduced to various parts of the Russian Realm between the 12th and 18th centuries. The highest proportion of Muslims among the local population is found in Azerbaijan (over 90 percent) and the Central Asian countries of Turkmenistan (89 percent), Uzbekistan (88 percent), Kyrgyzstan (75 percent), and Kazakhstan (47 percent). Sizable Muslim majorities also exist in the northern Caucasus region of Russia in the republics of Dagestan, Chechnya, Ingushetiya, Karachay-Cherkessiya, and Kabardino-Balkaria as well as in the Volga Region in the republics of Tatarstan and

FIGURE 4.30 The Bibi-Khanym Mosque in Samarkand, Uzbekistan—This historic structure, one of the largest mosques in the world, was built in the 15th century but fell into disrepair during the Soviet era. Its reconstruction began in 1974. *Source:* Larissa Krüger.

fasting, and pilgrimage). Islam has gained more followers since that time, especially among young and more educated urban people rather than economically disadvantaged rural dwellers (Fig. 4.30).

The Russian Realm is also one of the most secularized parts of the world, an outcome of seventy years of Communist rule and its opposition to any form of religion. Many churches were demolished or closed and religious practices discouraged or prohibited, especially under Stalin's rule (1928–53). There has been some religious revival since 1991; new churches, mosques, and temples have been built, and new religious groups registered. Although the Russian government recognizes six traditional religions (Eastern Orthodoxy, Roman Catholicism, Lutheranism, Islam, Judaism, and Buddhism) and tolerates their existence, it is suspicious of other religious movements (often seen as representatives of foreign interests) and creates roadblocks to their official recognition or closes the existing religious centers for various reasons. Despite greater religious tolerance since the collapse of communism, most inhabitants of Russia and other countries in the region are not very religious. A Pew Research Center survey in 2008 found out that 56 percent of Russians believe in God and 72 percent associate themselves with the Eastern Orthodox Church, but only 7 percent attend religious services at least once a month.[5] This low level of religiosity is similar to that in Western Europe.

Bashkortostan. Most of these people may be Muslims in name only and do not practice their religion on a regular basis. This was the case under the Soviet rule; surveys conducted after the break-up of the Soviet Union revealed that a majority of Muslims could not even identify the five basic pillars of their faith (confession of faith, prayer, charity,

POLITICAL ORGANIZATION OF SPACE

Territorial Expansion of Tsarist Russia and the Soviet Union

Even after the break-up of the Soviet Union, Russia remains the largest country in the world. How did Russia become such a large country? The short answer is because it expanded its territory through the incorporation of neighboring areas for over 700 years between the 12th and 19th centuries. The cumulative incorporation of different regions and peoples had led to the creation of a huge political entity that became one of the two superpowers in the world after World War II. Some political geographers believed that the Soviet Union (even before it became a superpower) was destined to control the world. The collapse of communism and the break-up of the Soviet Union twenty-five years ago put those fears to rest; nevertheless, because of its large area and rich natural resource base (among other things), Russia will remain a major player in world affairs in the foreseeable future.

The history of Russian expansion from its core area around the city of Moscow can be divided into four major periods (Fig. 4.31). The first period (prior to the 16th century) was associated with the incorporation of the lands to the northwest, north and northeast of the Russian core area. Some of them (e.g. Novgorod and Tver) were well organized and strong competitors for power and influence to the Grand Duchy of Moscow. Most of the areas, however, were cold and sparsely populated, and native inhabitants engaged in hunting and gathering, fishing or nomadic herding, and were not sufficiently organized to offer any resistance to Russian encroachments. Although early Russian expansion was partially checked by the Tatar-Mongol Empire, several major Russian victories of the 14th and 15th centuries broke the Tatar-Mongol yoke forever and cleared the road to Russian colonization of Siberia and the Far East region along the Pacific Ocean.

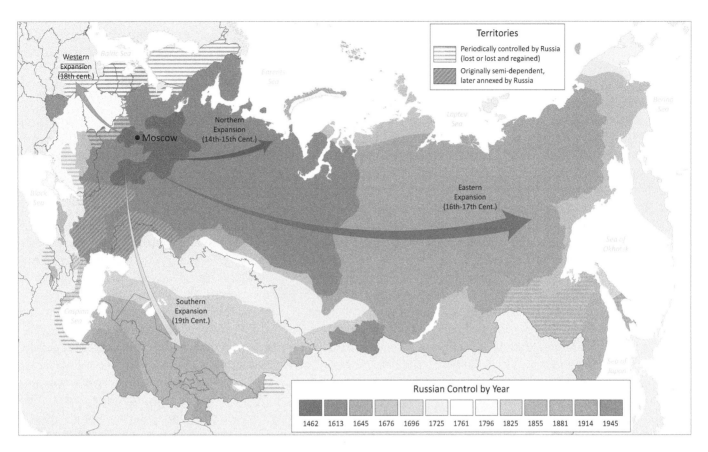

FIGURE 4.31 Territorial expansion of the Russian state—Each of the four major stages of Russian territorial expansion was associated with movement in a different direction. The expansion to Siberia and later Alaska was the greatest period in Russian colonization history. Notice that some parts of eastern and northern Europe used to be under Russian control but are now independent countries.

The colonization of these areas in the 16th and 17th centuries was the second and most important period of Russian territorial expansion. The expansion to the east was very fast, and its main objective was to gain wealth from trade in fur animals. Siberia, a densely forested and sparsely populated area, had large numbers of sables, foxes, weasels, and other fur animals. The furs were obtained in several ways, including the payment of tribute in furs by the natives (known as *yasak*), confiscation, hunting expeditions, and farming of fur animals (a much later activity). The fur trade became unsustainable and led to a large-scale reduction in the number of many species throughout the region. The colonization and settlement of Siberia was originally along the major rivers; they were fairly reliable transportation routes both in summer (when land transportation was almost impossible due to muddy surfaces resulting from upper layer permafrost thaw) and winter (frozen rivers facilitated sleigh transportation). Russian explorers and traders reached the Pacific Ocean in less than a century.

The third stage of Russian expansion (the 18th and early 19th centuries) was directed mainly toward more densely populated and economically developed areas west of the Moscow core region. The territorial gains here were less impressive, but economic benefits from incorporation of relatively well industrialized parts of present-day Poland, the Baltic States, and Finland were quite significant. Peter the Great moved the capital functions from Moscow to the newly built city port of St. Petersburg, which became Russia's window to Europe. He hoped to modernize the less economically developed and predominantly rural Russia through the influx of modern Western European ideas and culture. Catherine the Great extended Russian control over central parts of Europe through Poland and pushed the Russian border toward the Black Sea by defeating the Crimean Tatars in 1783. Alexander the Great annexed Finland from Sweden in 1809 and Bessarabia (present-day Moldova) from the Ottoman Empire in 1812. This period was also associated with the exploration of Alaska and establishment of Russian settlements as far down along the Pacific Coast as Fort Ross in Northern California. The United States bought Alaska from Russia in 1867 for $7.2 million (two cents per acre). It was one of best bargains in American history but the first major contraction of Russian territory.

The fourth and final major Russian expansion during the pre-Soviet era was the incorporation of the Caucasus region in the early part, and Central Asia in the second part of the 19th century. Most of the Caucasus region, which included present-day Armenia, Azerbaijan, Georgia, and several autonomous republics (e.g. Chechnya and Dagestan) on the north side of the mountain range, became Russian possessions after the two wars with Persia (now Iran). Most of Central Asia was acquired after 1867 and was known as Russian Turkestan. The growing demand for cotton on the world market prompted the Russian government to build two railways and increased the area devoted to cotton cultivation. The new transportation links also facilitated Russian migration to the region.

After the Bolshevik Revolution of 1917, the new Russian government lost control of Finland, Poland, and the three Baltic States, which became independent countries in 1918. However, by the 1940s, the border had shifted west again to reincorporate Estonia, Latvia, and Lithuania as well as eastern parts of Poland, Karelia from Finland, and the northern part of East Prussia (now the Kaliningrad Oblast) in 1945.

Communist Leaders and Their Programs

The tsarist Russia of the early 20th century was a relatively poor country facing numerous economic and political problems, including high prices, food shortages, and a weak and unpopular government. Its involvement in World War I, for which it was not well prepared, only worsened economic conditions and other problems. Most Russians wanted a change and the Communist activists took advantage of the widespread popular discontent and staged an uprising which allowed them to seize the power. The Bolshevik Revolution of 1917 marked the beginning of the seventy-four-year long Communist rule in Russia (later renamed the Union of the Soviet Socialist Republics or the Soviet Union). The founders of Communist ideology (Karl Marx and Friedrich Engels) predicted that the capitalistic system of production would collapse and be replaced by a Communist system based on the formula "from each according to his abilities and to each according to his needs." Shortly after coming to power, Vladimir Lenin (the leader of the Bolshevik Revolution) realized that such a utopian ideal was unachievable in Russia in the immediate future. However, the new government introduced a series of radical changes to consolidate its power and eliminate its opponents. The nationalization of banks and the confiscation of private bank accounts, seizure of church property, repudiation of all foreign debt, confiscation of farmland and forcible take-over of food surpluses from the peasants to feed the urban population, control of factories by the workers' committees (soviets), as well as fixed wages and a shorter working day were examples of such changes.

After Lenin's death in 1924, a personal and ideological battle for power between Joseph Stalin and Leon Trotsky took place. Stalin's ideological victory over his rival marked the beginning of a quarter-of-a-century-long rule characterized by the collectivization of agriculture, industrial expansion, establishment of forced labor camps, relocation of entire ethnic groups, ruthless suppression of his opponents, and victory in World War II. His first two five-year plans of economic development (1928–32 and 1933–38) had two major objectives: the collectivization of agriculture and rapid industrialization. The collectivization of agriculture was a violent and bloody process, especially in Ukraine, the breadbasket of the Soviet Union. After declaring that the peasants were petty capitalists and enemies of the people, a large-scale campaign to force them into collective farms began in 1929. The peasants resisted this program by slaughtering their livestock and burning crops. The outcome was a significant drop in agricultural output and a widespread famine that killed over 10 million people. Many richer farmers (kulaks) were either killed or sent to labor camps.

In the end, Soviet agriculture was collectivized and two types of rural production units were established: collective (**kolkhoz**) and state (**sovkhoz**) farms. Collective farms were dominant in the European part of the country; the land and farm machinery were collectively owned by the farmers who could decide (at least in theory) what to grow and how to dispose the surplus. They received a share of the farm's output and profit in accordance with the amount of their labor input. The state farms were more common in the eastern, less fertile, part of the Soviet Union, and were even larger in area than the collective farms. They were owned and operated by the state, and farmers worked for wages (like factory workers) and had no decision-making power. Both collective and state farmers (and their children) were bound to their place of work and had little freedom of movement to urban areas.

The program of industrialization resulted in the expansion of heavy industries in the existing regions and to new areas. It focused on the extraction of natural resources, mainly coal and iron ore, and increased production of iron and steel, heavy machinery (e.g. mining and transportation equipment), and military hardware. A series of industrial complexes were built, including the Magnitogorsk (the Urals region) and Kuznetsk (southern Siberia) iron and steel plants, the Moscow and Gorky (the Volga River region) automobile plants, the Urals and Kramatorsk (Eastern

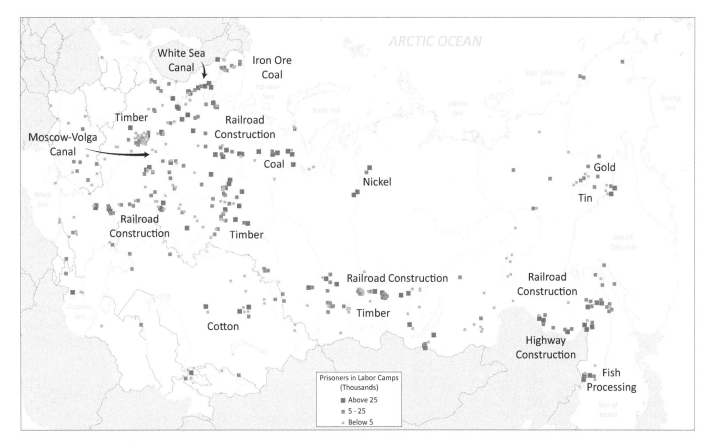

FIGURE 4.32 Labor camps in the former Soviet Union—Hundreds of labor camps were established under Stalin's rule where millions of Soviet citizens were coerced to perform various types of work, including mining mineral resources, building canals and railroads, cutting trees, or harvesting cotton. *Source:* GULAG (www.gulag.memorial.de).

Ukraine) heavy machinery plants, and the Stalingrad and Chelyabinsk (the Urals region) tractor plants.

The program of forced labor, modeled after Tsarist Russia's katorga system, was greatly expanded and organized into the gulag system. It consisted of hundreds of camps, many of them located in remote and environmentally harsh areas where they housed various types of convicts (from petty criminals to political prisoners) forced to work in mines, at railroad and canal construction sites, or at industrial project sites (Fig. 4.32). The number of gulag prisoners had increased from about half a million in 1934 to over 1.4 million in the early 1940s. Harsh working conditions, sub-standard housing, and poor diets killed thousands of inmates every year. The gulag system was an important part of the Soviet economy at that time. It accounted for over 75 percent of the country's tin, 60 percent of its gold, 45 percent of its nickel, and 25 percent of its timber production.

Prior to and during the Nazi invasion of the Soviet Union (1941–44), Stalin deported several ethnic groups as well as other groups, mainly from the European part of the country, to Central Asia and Siberia, among them Poles

and Germans from Ukraine and the Volga region, Finns from Karelia, Chechens and Ingush from the Caucasus region, and Crimean Tatars from Crimea. Most of them were accused of anti-Soviet and/or pro-Nazi sympathies and activities.

The Soviet Union paid a heavy price for winning World War II together with its European and American allies. It lost over 8 million soldiers and about 20 million civilians. Some scholars claim that the total human loss in the Soviet Union exceeded 40 million. About 1,700 cities and 70,000 villages were destroyed. Despite Stalin's rule of absolute terror and the killing of millions of Soviet citizens, some Russians consider him a national hero who transformed the country from a feudal economy into an industrial power and was instrumental in defeating Nazi Germany.

Stalin was harshly criticized by one of his successors, Nikita Khrushchev, at a closed Communist Party meeting in 1956. The new Soviet leader accused Stalin of fostering a personality cult, breaking the rules of Communist collective leadership, repressing many Communist party activists, and several other offenses. The major economic project during the Khrushchev rule (1953–64) was the

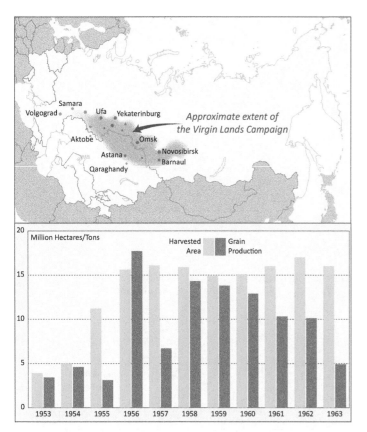

FIGURE 4.33 The Virgin Lands Campaign—The program was designed to increase the production of wheat and other grains in order to increase the production of meat and other animal products in the Soviet Union. The campaign did not bring about any major improvements in agricultural productivity and eventually led to the dismissal of its founder, Khrushchev, in 1963. *Source:* Open Society Archives.

Virgin Lands Campaign, an expansion of agricultural land into the semi-dry regions of Russia and Kazakhstan to increase agricultural production and eliminate perennial food shortages (Fig. 4.33). Some 300,000 square kilometers (115,000 square miles) of idle land (an area similar in size to the states of Arizona or New Mexico) were plowed and cultivated with wheat. Despite its initial success, this large-scale agricultural scheme was a fiasco and the main reason for removing Khrushchev from power in 1963. Major challenges included manpower shortages and the poor living conditions of farm workers (many of them brought from Ukraine and the European part of Russia), machinery and repair shop shortages, improper climate for wheat monoculture, and inadequate grain storage facilities. During the Khrushchev rule, the Soviet Union used military force to suppress the Hungarian uprising of 1956, supported building the Berlin Wall in 1961, and was very close to nuclear war with the United States because of the Cuban Missile Crisis.

By the 1970s and 1980s, the Soviet Union was mired in an era of stagnation. The country began falling behind the West in terms of economic and technological development.

The expensive arms race between the two Cold War superpowers, lack of any meaningful reforms, and widespread corruption significantly slowed down the Soviet economy in the 1970s. Political and cultural repression was widespread and living standards of ordinary citizens fell as well; Soviet-Chinese tensions, caused by ideological differences resulting from different interpretations of the communist philosophies, remained high. The Soviet invasion of Afghanistan in 1979 was a costly disaster. The country's leaders were ineffective in responding to the Soviet Union's mounting challenges.

However, the last general secretary of the Communist Party, Mikhail Gorbachev, was different from his post-World War II predecessors in at least two ways. First, he was relatively young (fifty-four years of age) and energetic; and second, he was bold enough to publicly admit that the Soviet system did not function well and needed serious political, social, and economic reforms. His policies and their outcomes are discussed later in this chapter.

Administrative Structure Under Communism and After the Collapse of the Soviet Union

Five years after coming to power, the Bolshevik government of Soviet Russia changed the name and administrative structure of the country. The Treaty on the Creation of the Union of Soviet Socialist Republics (USSR) of 1922 made the Soviet Union a federal state. A federal state, as described in Chapter 1, is a political entity characterized by the division of power between the central and local government. It is a federation (union) of self-governing administrative units (called states, republics, territories, provinces, etc. in various countries) under the central or federal government. In case of the Soviet Union, the first level of self-governing units was based on ethnic criteria and included union republics (Soviet Socialist Republic or SSR). The number of union republics varied during the early decades of the USSR but by 1956 had stabilized at fifteen, where it would remain until the break-up of the Soviet Union in 1991. Three conditions had to be met for establishing a union republic: (1) the area had to have over 1 million people of the titular nationality; (2) the titular nationality had to comprise at least 50 percent of the area's total population; and (3) the territorial unit had to have a border with another country. In theory, each union republic had the right to proclaim independence or join another country (hence, the condition of a common border with another country). However, no mechanism for accomplishing this objective

FIGURE 4.34 Administrative divisions of countries in the Russian Realm—There are five types of sub-national territorial units in the countries of the former Soviet Union. Some of them, mainly in Russia, are based on ethnic criteria (republics, autonomous okrugs, and oblasts). *Source:* Global Administrative Areas.

was proposed until 1990, just before the collapse of the country. In reality, the Soviet government did not expect, or would not allow, this to happen.

Despite the ethnic basis of the various union republics, the Russians were in control of the entire country, and the policy of **Russification** began in the 1930s. The most visible aspects of that policy included the compulsory study of the Russian language in all schools after 1938, the introduction of the Cyrillic script to most non-Russian languages, and mandatory two- to three-year military service for all young men (usually far away from home) where Russian was the only language of instruction.[6]

When the Soviet Union collapsed, the former fifteen republics became independent countries. While Russia, Armenia, Azerbaijan, and Moldova introduced major administrative reforms after 1991, the remaining countries, particularly those in Central Asia and Belarus, kept their administrative structures almost intact (Fig. 4.34). Russia remains a federal state and is now divided into eighty-five administrative units. Most provincial boundaries have not changed since 1991. However, all former autonomous oblasts, except one, are now republics. They were created for selected

ethnic groups and enjoy (at least in theory) a certain degree of autonomy in internal affairs. The Russian government is in charge of their foreign and military interests. Some of them are quite large in area and rich in mineral resources (e.g. Sakha in Eastern Siberia). Territories (*krays*) are similar to provinces in terms of administrative status but are located in peripheral (frontier) areas and/or have one or more lower-level autonomous territorial units (*oblasts* or *okrugs*) inside them. Autonomous districts (*okrugs*) were created for smaller ethnic groups living in the northern part of Russia. The Jewish autonomous province, located in the Russian Far East, is the only former autonomous *oblast* not elevated to the status of republic after 1991. It was established in 1934 for the Jewish population, most of which was concentrated in the European part of the Soviet Union. Jews never comprised more than a quarter of the area's total population, and today only 1 percent of the total population living there is Jewish. The Crimean province (*oblast*), a predominantly Russian-speaking part of Ukraine, transferred from Russia in 1956, was annexed by Russia in 2014, and is discussed later in this chapter. The United States and many other countries consider its annexation illegal.

Break-up of the Soviet Union

When Gorbachev came to power in 1985, the Soviet Union had a highly centralized, inefficient, and stagnant economy falling behind the West on many fronts, and its Communist ideology suppressed any form of criticism and political innovation. Some Soviet politicians, economists, and managers may have seen the necessity of reforms but were afraid or unwilling to even propose them. Gorbachev was convinced that major economic and political changes were necessary to stop economic decline and deterioration of living conditions of Soviet citizens. He did not want to abolish the Communist system but reform it. However, his five-year long rule ended with the break-up of the country and proclamation of independence by all fifteen republics within a relatively short time, starting with Lithuania in August of 1990 and ending with Kazakhstan in December of 1991. The Soviet collapse, which surprised most Western countries, including the United States, had many causes associated with Gorbachev's and his predecessors' policies, the nature of the centrally planned economy, and the ethnic structure of the country's population.

First, economic stagnation, the result of inefficient management, outdated technology, lack of incentives, corruption, high military spending, and many other factors, had been pushing the Soviet Union far behind its Western counterparts with respect to standards of living and economic productivity. In 1975, Russia's gross national income per capita, adjusted for purchasing power parity, was about 36 percent lower than that of the U.S.; by 1990, the gap had widened to 52 percent. Second, Gorbachev was aware of these developments and tried to correct them through his policies of **perestroika** (restructuring) and **glasnost** (openness). These policies, however, accelerated the process of economic, political, and social deterioration of the country. Limited free-market policies contributed to failed businesses and unemployment, which, in turn, increased resistance to further changes. The decentralization of the decision-making system encouraged some republics to demand more autonomy. Greater political openness brought corruption or mismanagement secrets to the surface and reduced public confidence in the government. Third, the ten-year long, very costly, fruitless, and humiliating military campaign in Afghanistan (1979–89) discredited the Red Army as an invincible force, encouraged many non-Russians who saw this conflict as a Russian war against the Afghan people to demand more freedom or even independence, and created a large army of politically active war veterans.[7] Fourth, the Chernobyl nuclear disaster of 1986 and the initial government cover-up of this accident revealed the lack of concern among many central and local government officials about people's health and led to popular dissatisfaction and increased interest in alternative sources of information. According to Gorbachev, this disaster, not *perestroika* or *glasnost*, was the main cause of the break-up of the Soviet Union. Fifth, the policy of Russification imposed on the ethnically diverse population and the tight control of any form of ethnic nationalism created a lot of hidden resentment to Communist rule among many non-Russian groups. Once the government began tolerating some freedom of speech through the policy of *glasnost*, ethnic nationalism, especially in the Baltic States, Ukraine, and the Caucasus region, surfaced and soon got out of control. In the opinion of many scholars, ethnic discord was the most important contributor to the collapse of the Soviet Union.

Political Instability After the Break-up of the Soviet Union

The collapse of Communism and independence of the former Soviet republics was greeted with great enthusiasm in many parts of the globe. Suddenly, there was a lot of hope for a better future and a less politically and economically polarized world. The Cold War was over and opportunities for closer cooperation between former adversaries seemed to mark a new beginning. However, as soon as the Soviet Union collapsed (in a few cases even earlier), tensions among several newly independent countries began to rise and sometimes led to military action. Instead of peaceful coexistence and cooperation, increased instability became a new feature of the political landscape in the Russian Realm. Some tensions resulted from the presence of Russian populations in the newly independent states, especially in Estonia, Latvia, Moldova, and Ukraine. Instability in the Caucasus region reflected the great ethnic diversity of southern Russia, Georgia, and Azerbaijan, as well as past political boundary manipulation in this region.

The Russian Realm is home to four so-called **frozen conflict** zones. The first of these concerns a region along the Dniester River called Transdniestra. Two years before the break-up, the government of the Moldovan SSR declared that Russian was no longer the official language in the republic and that Moldovan, now the only official language in the republic, would again be based on the Latin script. It also confirmed the shared Moldovan-Romanian linguistic identity and did not exclude the possibility of a future reunification with Romania. In response to that, the eastern part of Moldova known as Transdniestra, where Russians comprised 60 percent of the population, proclaimed itself a Soviet republic and later an independent country.

A war broke out between the two parts of Moldova in 1992. Although the brief war ended with a ceasefire, the status of Transdniestra remains unresolved.

A second frozen conflict involves Armenia and Azerbaijan. A dispute between these two republics over the Nagorno-Karabakh region began in 1989. It changed into a full-scale war after this Armenian-populated enclave inside Azerbaijan (created according to the divide-and-rule policy of Stalin in 1923) first voted to unify with Armenia and later proclaimed independence. Although a ceasefire between the warring factions was reached in 1994, sporadic clashes have been occurring since that time. This conflict resulted in 28,000 to 38,000 deaths and the displacement of thousands of residents on both sides (Fig. 4.35).

A third conflict concerns Abkhazia and South Ossetia, two autonomous regions located inside Georgia. Prior to the break-up of the Soviet Union, Abkhazia was against Georgian independence and preferred to become a Soviet republic for fear of cultural repression from Georgia. However, after Georgia became independent in 1991, Abkhazia also proclaimed independence a year later. This move led to the Georgian-Abkhaz war of 1992. Russia offered military support to the break-away republic and recognized its independence in 2008. South Ossetia declared independence from Georgia in 1990. In response, the Georgian government abolished its autonomous status and moved in to restore full control over the area. This led to the Georgian-South Ossetian war and the Russian occupation, as well as the subsequent recognition of South Ossetia's independence.

Finally, the conflict between Russia and Ukraine has focused on two areas. One of them is Crimea, a predominantly Russian-inhabited region that was transferred from Russia to Ukraine in 1954 and then taken back by Russia in 2014. The other area is Eastern Ukraine, also a Russian-dominated and heavily industrialized region that has been seeking closer political and economic ties with Russia. The 1954 administrative transfer of Crimea was Khruschev's symbolic and personal gesture to commemorate the 300th anniversary of Ukraine's unification with the Russian Empire. Some economic reasons may have also been behind this decision. The region became an autonomous republic with extensive home rule within independent Ukraine after the collapse of the Soviet Union. A political crisis in Ukraine caused by tensions between pro-European and pro-Russian elements within the government and the population prompted Russia to send unmarked military forces to take control of the area. After a controversial referendum approving the merger of the self-proclaimed independent Republic of Crimea with Russia, the Russian President signed the treaty of accession and Crimea became part of Russia again. Most countries, including Western nations, consider this annexation illegal.

FIGURE 4.35 The Caucasus region: an administrative map. *Source:* Global Administrative Areas.

After Ukrainian President Yanukovich refused to sign an agreement with the European Union and opted for a closer union with Russia in 2013, the country became divided and street demonstrations opposing or supporting this action took place in several cities. The strongest support for closer ties with Russia was found in the Donetsk and Luhansk regions of Eastern Ukraine (Fig. 4.36). This support quickly turned into an open rebellion against the new government in Kiev after the ouster of Yanukovich, and it received strong diplomatic and military backing from Russia. The pro-Russian rebels demanded a referendum on

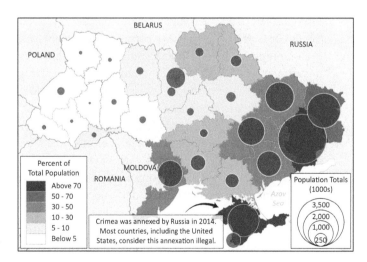

FIGURE 4.36 The Russian population in Ukraine, 2010—There are over 8 million Russians accounting for over 17 percent of the country's total population. Most of them live in eastern and southern Ukraine. *Source:* Ukraine. State Committee of Statistics.

the status of the eastern and southern parts of Ukraine, making Ukraine a federal state and establishing Russian as the second official language in the country. Some even demanded a union of these areas with Russia. The government counteroffensive led to a war in some parts of Eastern Ukraine. Although a ceasefire between the warring factions was reached in 2015, the differences have not been resolved and the future for this area is unclear.

ECONOMIC ACTIVITIES

Major Characteristics of the Soviet Economy

In the centrally planned economy of the Soviet Union, the state (government) owned all means of production. Factories, farms, transportation, retail trade, and almost everything else to produce and distribute goods and services was state or collectively owned. Industrial enterprises were nationalized shortly after the Bolshevik Revolution of 1917, and the farms were collectivized about ten to fifteen years later. A hierarchical decision-making system was another feature of the Soviet economy. All major, and most minor, decisions related to production and distribution of goods and services were made by the central government in Moscow. Individual production units had to follow orders from the top. As the name indicates, the **centrally planned economy** was based on pervasive economic planning. Thirteen five-year plans were introduced (first in 1928) and carried out (except for the last one due to the break-up of the Soviet Union) during the Communist era. Each plan specified production goals for the entire economy; some of them put more emphasis on industrial development, others on agriculture, but each one had specific annual and five-year production targets in each area. A strong emphasis on meeting the production targets at almost any cost also characterized the centrally planned economy. Each factory or farm manager's major concern was to meet, and preferably exceed, these targets. "Storming the plan" was a common phenomenon in many industrial enterprises during the last quarter of each year when many employees worked overtime to produce the assigned amount of output.

There was a strict control of prices in the Soviet economic system. As discussed in Chapter 1, most prices were artificial, did not reflect the supply-demand relationship, and remained unchanged for long periods of time. The price of many items considered daily necessities (e.g. food, housing, and utilities) was very low, quite often below production costs. On the other hand, some goods considered luxury items were very expensive, beyond the means of ordinary citizens. Most prices remained unchanged for quite a long period; for example, the Moscow subway fare remained unchanged for thirty years (1961–1991).

The Soviet leaders also put emphasis on large projects. They were very proud to have the largest steel mill, hydroelectric dam, or tallest smokestack in the world. Some of these largest production units were the only enterprises of this kind in the country, and problems could occur if production had to be stopped for whatever reason. Preference was given to heavy manufacturing (i.e., production of iron and steel and other metals, mining equipment, military hardware, chemicals, etc.). The production of consumer goods was less important to Soviet planners; they were produced in limited quantities and of inferior quality, mainly for domestic and other Communist markets. There was a perennial shortage of many goods in the limited network of state-owned retail stores.

Gorbachev's Economic and Political Reforms

As indicated earlier, Gorbachev wanted to introduce significant economic and political reforms to keep the Communist system in better health after coming to power in 1985. Some of the major objectives of *perestroika* were decentralizing the decision-making system, putting greater emphasis on profitability as an economic indicator, encouraging limited private initiative, implementing agricultural reform (mainly the expansion of personal agricultural plots), closing the gap between production and consumption, establishing joint ventures with foreign companies, and discouraging alcohol consumption. The policy of *glasnost* aimed at granting Soviet citizens more personal freedom, relaxing the censorship of news media, and allowing more room for criticism of corruption and inefficiency.

These, and other limited reforms, did not bring about any major improvements, however, but created more problems as the government continued to control prices and owned almost all the means of production; additionally, the Soviet currency, the ruble, remained unconvertible. Such constraints made it difficult for people to take advantage of the new freedoms introduced by Gorbachev. The economy remained stagnant.

Farming: Characteristics and Problems

The pre-1917 Russian Empire was an agricultural society where peasants comprised the majority of the population. The agricultural sector was completely reorganized during the Communist era. The forced program of collectivization, discussed earlier in this chapter, did not bring about any major improvements in agricultural productivity in terms of meeting the demand for food. In fact, it was associated with a large-scale famine in Ukraine, the breadbasket of the Soviet Union, and other parts of the country. Soviet farming after World War II could periodically claim some achievements, but it had been unable to keep up with the growing demand for food, particularly grains and meat. This shortfall has been described as the Soviet Union's permanent crisis. The country became the largest importer of grain in the world during the 1960s and 1970s despite large-scale investments in the agricultural sector.

Some of the major problems were the central government's inability to properly manage this large and diverse economic sector as well as their slow response to modernization and innovation. Frequent breakdowns of farm equipment and lack of spare parts resulted in work stoppages and delayed harvesting of many crops. The lack of

a properly trained and motivated labor force also slowed down agricultural productivity. Many young people saw more opportunities in the cities than on collective or state farms; the older generation left behind was less productive. The shortage of storage facilities and transportation bottlenecks led to a tremendous waste of harvested grain and perishable crops. According to some estimates, about a quarter of agricultural output perished that way. The weather also frequently affected agricultural productivity, particularly in the semi-dry regions emphasizing cultivation of grain crops.[8]

Personal plots (sometimes also called household plots) comprised an interesting component of Soviet farming. Each collective and state farmer was allowed to cultivate a small piece of land (half an acre or less) to produce food for his or her family needs. The land in these household plots was state owned but leased rent-free to the farmer. Any surplus could be sold on the local market. These plots occupied only 2 to 3 percent of the total farmland but produced over a quarter of the agricultural output in the country. They were particularly important producers of potatoes, vegetables, milk, and meat. Although government support for personal plots changed periodically, they had always been a major source of food for Soviet farmers. The importance of household plots has increased after the break-up of the Soviet Union; their share of agricultural land went up from 2 percent in 1990 to about 10 percent in 2005, and their share of the agricultural production from a quarter to over half during the same period (Fig. 4.37 and Fig. 4.38).

FIGURE 4.37 The Russian countryside—Although many cities in the Russian Realm have experienced major socioeconomic changes during the past 25 years, the countryside has been less affected by the new developments as many roads remain unpaved and old wooden houses are still very common. *Source:* Wikimedia Commons.

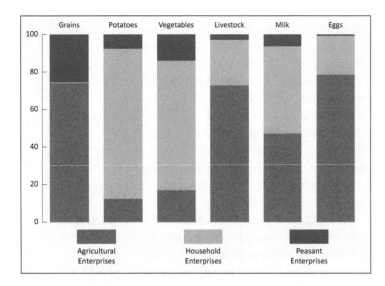

FIGURE 4.38 Agricultural production in Russia by type of farms, 2014—Former collective and state farms, now called agricultural enterprises, account for over three-fourths of the country's grain production. Household enterprises (former personal plots) produce the great majority of potatoes and vegetables. Peasant enterprises, relatively new types of farms, emphasize the production of grain and vegetables. *Source:* Russian Federal State Statistics Service.

The transition from collective to market-oriented farming after the break-up of the Soviet Union hit many roadblocks. For private farmers, it meant less assured access to state supplied fertilizers, machinery, and other resources. This led to a significant decline in livestock and grain production during the first decade of the transition. Although many state and collective farms were transformed into corporate farms, their production system has not changed much. About 80 percent of agricultural land in Russia belongs to such farms, but they generate only 40 percent of agricultural output. The most favorable conditions for agricultural activity are found in the **Fertile Triangle** region extending from the western borders of the Russian Realm through Ukraine and Southern Russia to Northern Kazakhstan and Southern Siberia. The northern part of this region has a cooler climate and less fertile soil, so the cultivation of potatoes, barley, rye, oats, and flax, as well as dairy farming, are important activities here. The southern parts of the Fertile Triangle, which are warmer and more fertile, emphasize the cultivation of wheat, corn, sugar beets, sunflowers, and vegetables. Some parts of Central Asia and the Caucasus region are also important producers of vegetables, grapes, and cotton. The only part of the Russian Realm with favorable conditions for growing subtropical crops is Georgia. Tea plantations and citrus fruit orchards are found in coastal areas. Livestock herding is also an important activity in the Russian Realm (Fig. 4.39). Cattle ranching is relatively important in the semi-dry

regions of Central Asia and Russia; pigs are raised on a larger scale in Western Russia, Ukraine, and Belarus, and sheep in Central Asia.

Mineral Resources and Industrial Regions of the Russian Realm

The Russian Realm is one of the richest parts of the world with regard to mineral resources, particularly fossil fuels and some strategic metals. The most important fossil fuel produced is natural gas. The region accounts for a quarter of global production, and Russia is the second largest producer in the world (after the United States). About 90 percent of natural gas comes from West Siberia, most of it from the Yamal-Nenets region where harsh environmental conditions make production very difficult and expensive. Several gas pipelines, some built during the Soviet era, others more recently, connect the West Siberian fields with Europe and Turkey. Some European countries are completely dependent on Russian gas. This dependency is a great concern to those and other countries (including the United States) as Russia could use gas as a political and economic weapon in times of tension. Revenues from export of gas amount to 14 percent of Russia's total export revenues.

The Russian Realm also has ample petroleum reserves, and it produces 12 to 13 percent of all oil in the world. Russia, Kazakhstan, and Azerbaijan account for most of the production. In Russia, production is concentrated in West Siberia and the Volga-Urals region. The Volga-Urals fields were discovered shortly before World War II, and the oil deposits of Western Siberia were discovered in the 1960s. Despite large quantities of oil in this region, production costs are very high and the oil quality relatively low. Most of the petroleum is exported to Europe, mainly to Germany, the Netherlands, and Poland; the rest goes to Asia, especially to Japan and China. Petroleum exports account for 54 percent of Russia's total exports. Several pipelines connect the major oil fields with Europe, including the oldest and longest pipeline, the Friendship Line, completed in 1964. Two Baltic Pipeline System lines to Primorsk and Ust-Luga on the Gulf of Finland were completed in recent years.

Most of Kazakhstan's oil comes from two Caspian Sea oil fields in the northwestern part of the country and is exported to Europe. And, on the other side of the Caspian, the Baku oil fields of Azerbaijan used to provide most of the Soviet oil needs before World War II. Nazi Germany wanted to control the Caspian Sea oil fields, which was the principal reason for its disastrous incursion deep into the Soviet Union in 1942; the crushing defeat of the Germans

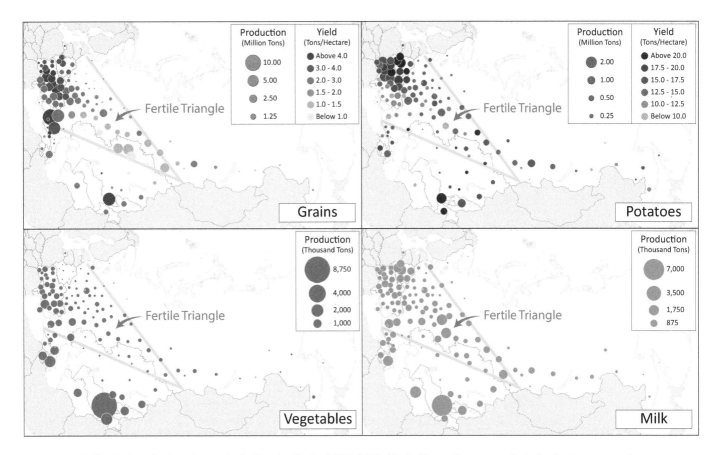

FIGURE 4.39 Production of selected crops in the Russian Realm, 2000–2013—Most of the grain crops, particularly wheat, are grown in the southern belt of the Fertile Triangle, extending from Ukraine through southern Russia and northern Kazakhstan. Potatoes prefer cooler and less fertile soils and are a dominant crop in the northern part of the Fertile Triangle. The cultivation of vegetables is also concentrated in the warmer regions of southern Ukraine, the Caucasus, and Central Asia. Milk production is closely correlated with population distribution and levels of urbanization. *Source:* statistical agencies of individual countries.

at Stalingrad in early 1943 was a pivotal turning point in the war.

For Azerbaijan, Kazakhstan, and Turkmenistan (a major gas exporter), fossil fuel exports have brought significant economic gains but also great corruption. For instance, the 2006 completion of the Baku-Tbilisi-Ceyhan pipeline linking Azerbaijan to a Turkish port on the Mediterranean has permitted the small country to export up to a million barrels of oil per day. The influx of money in return has transformed the capital Baku much like cities in the Persian Gulf with artificial offshore islands, new skyscrapers, and luxury retailers. However, the new developments have not fostered much political liberalization.

Meanwhile, the importance of coal as an energy source has been declining in the Russian Realm in recent decades. The region currently produces only 7 percent of the world's total output, down from 13 percent a decade ago. Russia, Kazakhstan, and Ukraine are the largest producers. The Kuzbas region of southern Siberia accounts for over half of the Russian coal production; most coal in Ukraine comes

from the Donbas region and in Kazakhstan from the Karaganda and Ekibastuz fields. The Kuzbas and Donbas coal comes from underground mines while most of Kazakhstan's coal comes from open-pit mines. Both types of mining pose serious safety and environmental concerns.

A great variety of metallic ores is also found on the territory of the former Soviet Union, particularly in Russia and Kazakhstan. These countries are among the top ten world producers of iron ore, nickel, copper, gold, chromium, titanium, and others. The Kursk Magnetic Anomaly in Western Russia is one of the largest iron ore deposits in the world and contains 65 percent of Russia's reserves of this ore. The largest center of nickel production is around the city of Norilsk in Northern Siberia. Developed in the 1920s and greatly expanded in the 1930s, the mining and smelting operations originally depended on forced labor. This region also has large deposits of copper, platinum, and many other ores. Unfortunately, its mineral wealth has helped to make it one of the most polluted areas in the world. Kazakhstan is rich in a variety of metallic ores, including chromium

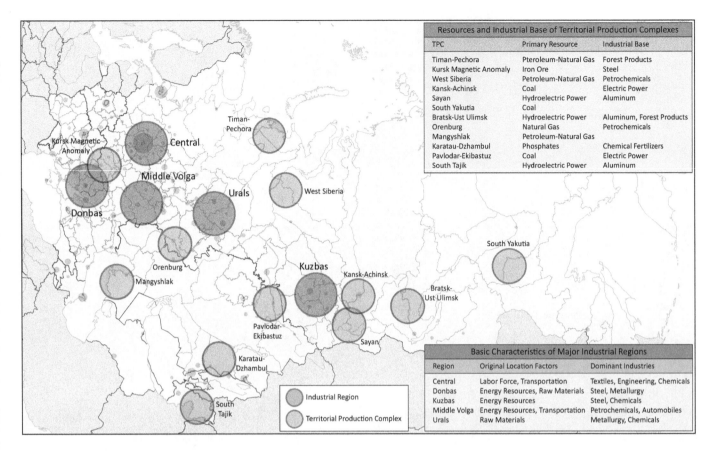

Resources and Industrial Base of Territorial Production Complexes		
TPC	Primary Resource	Industrial Base
Timan-Pechora	Pteroleum-Natural Gas	Forest Products
Kursk Magnetic Anomaly	Iron Ore	Steel
West Siberia	Petroleum-Natural Gas	Petrochemicals
Kansk-Achinsk	Coal	Electric Power
Sayan	Hydroelectric Power	Aluminum
South Yakutia	Coal	
Bratsk-Ust Ulimsk	Hydroelectric Power	Aluminum, Forest Products
Orenburg	Natural Gas	Petrochemicals
Mangyshlak	Petroleum-Natural Gas	
Karatau-Dzhambul	Phosphates	Chemical Fertilizers
Pavlodar-Ekibastuz	Coal	Electric Power
South Tajik	Hydroelectric Power	Aluminum

Basic Characteristics of Major Industrial Regions		
Region	Original Location Factors	Dominant Industries
Central	Labor Force, Transportation	Textiles, Engineering, Chemicals
Donbas	Energy Resources, Raw Materials	Steel, Metallurgy
Kuzbas	Energy Resources	Steel, Chemicals
Middle Volga	Energy Resources, Transportation	Petrochemicals, Automobiles
Urals	Raw Materials	Metallurgy, Chemicals

Industrial Region

Territorial Production Complex

FIGURE 4.40 Major industrial regions of the Russian Realm—The five major industrial regions were established before 1917 but were significantly expanded during the Soviet period. The territorial production complexes are smaller centers of industrial and/or mining activities established during communist rule.

(it is the third largest world producer), and uranium (the world's largest producer, accounting for about 40 percent of the global market). The mining industry accounted for one-third of the gross domestic product and employed over 190,000 workers in the mid-2000s. The intensive exploitation of Kazakhstan's mineral resources during the Soviet era led to the critical depletion of several metallic and non-metallic ores.

The program of industrialization introduced by Stalin in the 1930s and continued by his successors led to the expansion of manufacturing in the existing industrial clusters such as the Donbas Region in Ukraine and the Central Industrial Region around Moscow, as well as the establishment of new industrial centers in Southern Siberia and Central Asia. The location of various industries was affected by economic and political factors.[9] The distribution of fossil fuels (especially coal) and metallic ores strongly influenced the location of the iron and steel industry in the Donbas and Kuzbas Regions (Fig. 4.40). Large deposits of petroleum in the Middle Volga region attracted petrochemical and automobile industries to this area. The concentration of heavy manufacturing in the Ural Region reflected both the abundance of local raw

materials (metallic ores) as well as strategic factors, including low vulnerability to foreign (German) attack during World War II. Ideological commitment to eliminating or reducing regional inequalities in levels of development was at least partially responsible for establishing industrial centers in Central Asia and parts of Siberia.

The Donbas Industrial Region, located in Eastern Ukraine and adjacent parts of Russia (an area of recent conflict as previously noted), is the largest industrial cluster in the Russian Realm and one of the largest in the world. Large deposits of local coal and nearby ferrous ores (iron and manganese) around Krivyy Rog and Nikopol attracted heavy manufacturing to this area relatively early (before the Bolshevik Revolution). This region is now an important center of iron and steel, metallurgy, automotive, agricultural machinery, military hardware, and chemical industries. The major industrial centers are the cities of Donetsk, Luhansk, Dnepropetrovsk, Krivyy Rog, Rostov-on-Don, and Mariupol.

The Central Industrial Region around the capital city of Moscow is the oldest industrial cluster in the Russian Realm. The first textile mills, ceramic, glass, and gun factories were built in the 18th century. This area has a diverse cluster of industries, including textiles, food processing, metallurgy, machine buildings, chemical, and military hardware. In addition to Moscow, Ivanovo, Tula, Ryazan, Tver, Vladimir, and Bryansk are among the largest centers of manufacturing.

The Middle Volga Industrial Region stretches from Saratov in the south through Samara and Kazan in the center to Nizhny Novgorod in the northwest and Perm in the northeast. This elongated industrial cluster attracted petrochemical, automotive, and aerospace industries, among many others. Until recently, it was the main center of car production in Russia. Some of the largest car and truck assembly plants in the world are found in Togliatti, Nizhnyy Novgorod, and Neberezhnye Chelny. The aerospace industry is located in Samara (airplanes, satellites, and spacecraft), Ulyanovsk, Nizhnyy Novgorod, and Saratov (airplanes and fighter jets).

The Ural Industrial Region has a well-developed iron and steel industry. Some of the largest steel mills in the world are found here, including those in Magnitogorsk, Nizhnyy Tagil, Chelyabinsk, and Novotroitsk. Non-ferrous metallurgy (copper, nickel, aluminum, titanium, and magnesium) is also a fairly important industrial activity here. This region also has a large concentration of military research and production centers (particularly nuclear weapons). The greatest disadvantage to iron and steel industries in this area is the absence of local coal, which is a necessary ingredient in the steel production process. This resource had to be delivered from the Kuzbas region in Southern Siberia. The Kuzbas region, however, does not have any iron ore reserves, so the two regions became complementary to each other: coal was transported by train from the Kuzbas to the Urals region, and on the way back iron ore was delivered to steel mills in the Kuzbas region. This mutual dependency is less critical today than it was several decades ago, partly because of greater diversity of raw material suppliers to both regions.[10]

The Kuzbas Industrial Region, located in southern Siberia near the Kazakhstan and Mongolian borders, also has fairly well developed iron and steel, metallurgical, chemical, and non-ferrous metal industries, and it played a major role in the Soviet economy during World War II due to its distant location from the frontline in Western Russia. The major industrial cities here are Novokuznetsk, Kemerovo, Barnaul, and Tomsk.

Over ten smaller industrial clusters, known as territorial production complexes, were also expanded or developed from scratch during Communist rule. Most of them were located in areas rich in energy resources or metallic ores and became important producers of steel, aluminum, petrochemicals, and electricity.

Transportation and Trade

Transportation played a very important role in the centrally planned economy of the Soviet Union. The long distances between various parts of the country and the necessity to haul large amounts of raw materials to industrial regions favored railroad traffic as the major mode of transportation. Railroads carried over 80 percent of the freight and 90 percent of the passenger traffic during the 1970s and the 1980s.[11] However, the railroad density was much lower than in other more developed countries. Until the 1990s, there was only one railroad connection between the western and eastern parts of the country. The Trans-Siberian Railroad, built between 1891 and 1916, mainly by soldiers and convicts, is the longest railway line in the world (Fig. 4.41). It connects Moscow with the city-port of Vladivostok on the Sea of Japan. It runs through seven time zones, and it takes about eight days for a train to go from one end to the other. Most of the American supplies to the Red Army during World War II were also delivered this way. The Trans-Siberian Railway has continued to be an important transportation link after the break-up of the Soviet Union for Russia and other countries. About 30 percent of all Russian exports are transported this way, and it is a major land link between China, Japan, and some European countries. A typical shipment from Europe to East Asia (or vice versa) takes from twelve to twenty-five days today (Fig. 4.42).

The Trans-Siberian Railway is very close to the Russian-Chinese border in some areas, and this proximity was a major concern to the Soviet government during the 1960s and 1970s when Soviet-Chinese relations were sometimes very tense. The possibility of a Chinese disruption of traffic along this route prompted the Soviet government to build an alternative railway route farther away from the border line. The construction of the Baykal-Amur Mainline from the city of Tayshet in the Irkutsk region to Sovetskaya Gavan on the Pacific coast began in 1974 and was completed in 1991. This new line, located several hundred miles north of the Trans-Siberian Railway and connecting several mining centers with the rest of the country, is of great economic and strategic importance to Russia today. Russia has the second longest rail network in the world (after the United States), and over half of it has been electrified. About 45 percent of total freight and a quarter of passenger traffic are moved by railroads.

Water transportation did not play a major role in the Soviet economy; it is also peripheral in importance in the Russian economy today, accounting only for 2 percent of the total freight and a tiny fraction of the passenger traffic. There are serious environmental obstacles to expanding this mode of transportation. Many rivers are frozen for several months each year and run through sparsely populated

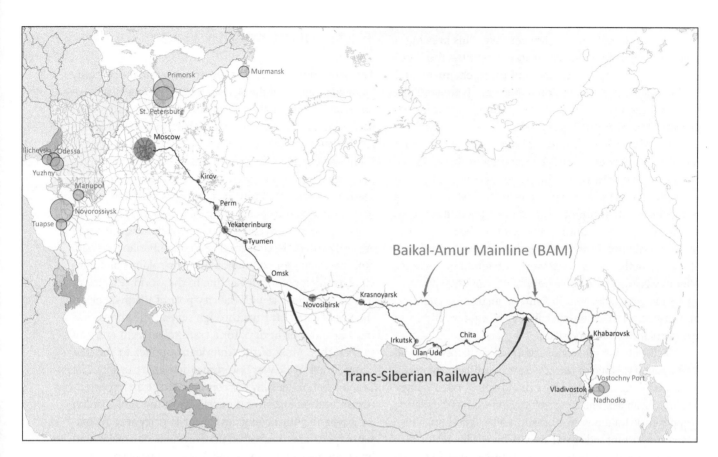

FIGURE 4.41 Railroad network and seaports in the Russian Realm—The railroad network is much more dense in the western parts of the region. Notice that most of Siberia has no railroads, a serious impediment to the development of that region. *Source:* Natural Earth.

FIGURE 4.42 The Trans-Siberian Railway—Completed shortly before the Bolshevik Revolution, it was the only line connecting the Russian Far East with the European part of the country until 1991. It is of great economic importance to Russia as one-third of its exports and millions of passengers are moved this way every year. *Source:* Pixabay.

regions. Yet, some of them are connected by canals, and several large interior cities are also important "seaports." The Volga-Don Canal, completed in 1952, has been heavily used for transporting coal, grain, and minerals from the Don to the Volga region and lumber, minerals, and petroleum products in the opposite direction. The White Sea-Baltic Sea Canal, built by prison labor (like many other projects of the Soviet era) and completed in 1933, has been mainly used for delivering petroleum products to the city of Murmansk and for export. The capital city of Moscow is also known as the "port of five seas" thanks to the Moscow Canal which connects the city via the Volga River and other canals and rivers with the Baltic, White, Black, Azov, and Caspian Seas.

There are a few suitable sites for seaports despite Russia's long coastline, and only a few of them are open all year round. St. Petersburg and Kaliningrad on the Baltic Sea, Murmansk and Archangelsk on the White Sea, Novorossiysk and Sevastopol (annexed from Ukraine in 2014) on the Black Sea, and Vladivostok and Nakhodka on the Sea of Japan are the largest Russian ports. As noted above, a warming Arctic might make the Northern Sea Route more attractive and change the importance and distribution of maritime traffic in this region.

Road transportation in the Soviet Union was not well developed not only in comparison with Western nations but even with some Asian or Latin American countries. The total length of roads in relation to the country's area and their quality were quite low. There were no limited access highways (expressways) in the entire country, and car ownership was also very low. Some major cities in Siberia were not connected by road at all (e.g. Irkutsk and Chita). A rapid increase in private car ownership has been the most important change in road transportation since the collapse of the Soviet Union. Although road quality has been slowly improving, it lags far behind the rapidly growing demand. Consequently, the roads in the Russian Realm are more crowded today, and traffic congestion in major cities is a serious problem. Inter-city bus service is relatively well developed and usually a cheaper mode of transportation than railroad or airline.

The state-owned Aeroflot used to be the largest airline in the world and the only airline in the former Soviet Union. Its fleet consisted of domestically made propeller and jet planes that were of lower quality and less fuel efficient than their Western counterparts. After the collapse of the Soviet Union, several regional airlines were created, and some of them added Western-made planes to their fleet. Most of these planes, however, had been in service in other countries before their purchase by the newly established airlines in the Russian Realm. Russia has been slowly rebuilding its passenger plane industry, which nearly collapsed in the early 1990s, with new models and hopes to compete for customers around the globe. Nevertheless, air transportation is a relatively unimportant mode of travel in this part of the world; it accounts for less than 1 percent of the total passenger traffic.

FUTURE PROBLEMS AND PROSPECTS

The break-up of the Soviet Union and the end of Cold War in 1991 generated a lot of hope for peace, economic prosperity, and a better future among most people in the Russian Realm and around the world. The end of arms race between the two superpowers, the collapse of totalitarian governments, and the introduction of free market economies in most of the former Soviet republics were supposed to be the keys to achieving these objectives. The initial euphoria associated with these changes began to decline as new economic and political realties set in. A quarter century later, Russia and most other parts of the former Soviet Union are still facing numerous challenges, and responses to them have varied across space and time.

Although Russia has a large and modern military and advanced space technology, its civilian economy is still much too dependent on revenues from exporting mineral resources, mainly fossil fuels, which account for over 70 percent all exports. A high dependence on income from mineral (energy) resources is also characteristic of Kazakhstan, Turkmenistan, and Azerbaijan. Such dependence can be beneficial if prices of these commodities are very high. A marked increase of standards of living in Russia and impressive construction projects in Kazakhstan (e.g. the development of its new capital Astana) during the first decade of the 21st century were associated with high oil prices and high popularity of Russian (Vladimir Putin) and Kazakh (Nursultan Nazarbayev) political leaders at that time. The recent petroleum price decline has been associated with economic stagnation in these countries, particularly in Russia.

Several frozen and active conflicts on the periphery of the Russian Realm threaten regional security in parts of Asia and Europe. The 2014 Russian annexation of Crimea and Russia's support for separatist movements in Eastern Ukraine, has strained its relations with Europe and the United States and led to the imposition of economic sanctions by Western countries. These sanctions, in addition to low oil prices, have been responsible, among other things, for Russia's recent economic stagnation. Political instability in the Caucasus region, including the wars in Chechnya and Ingushetia, the Nagorno-Karabakh conflict, the Georgian civil wars, and the Georgian-Russian war, is particularly of great concern to many countries as this region borders the war-torn Middle East and may be a fertile ground for Islamist ideologies. Conflicts in Moldova (Transdniestra) and Central Asia (Tajikistan and Kyrgyzstan) may also have adverse impacts on regional security in Europe and Asia.

The Russian military buildup and growing influence in the peripheral parts of the region (the "Near Abroad"), as well as the presumed interference in the democratic process (elections) of some European countries and the United States, has caused a lot of concern among European Union and NATO members. Putin's desire to strengthen Russia's military power and expand its global influence as well as curtailment of internal opposition to his increasingly dictatorial rule, further exacerbate tensions with Western states and within the Russian Realm.

Although Russia's population began to grow again in recent years, its demographic crisis (and that of Ukraine and Belarus) is far from over. High mortality among middle-aged men, low fertility rates, a growing proportion of the elderly, a declining number of working-age people, an increasing number of migrants from other parts of the former Soviet Union, a large army of drug addicts and alcoholics, an HIV/AIDS epidemic, and limited government spending on public health may lead to a "perfect demographic storm," according to some UN demographers.[12]

Environmental degradation, inherited from the Soviet era, has not been significantly reduced in many parts of the region. Although some inefficient and outdated factories have been modernized or closed, many are still in operation and continue polluting the environment. A sharp increase in car ownership during the past two decades, most of them using leaded gas, has contributed to increased levels of air pollution in large cities. Restrictions on, and even hostility to, activities of environmental groups, some of them labelled as "anti-Russian" by the Putin administration, corruption, and poor enforcement of the existing environmental regulations do not look promising for cleaning up the already severely degraded natural environment.[13]

Despite these many challenges, however, progress in the Russian Realm from the tense decades of the Cold War has been an enormously positive development for Russia, its neighbors, and the world. The number of nuclear weapons in the Soviet Union's arsenal reached a maximum of about 40,000 in the mid-1980s. Today, Russia has about 7,000 such weapons. U.S. nuclear forces are also much smaller in number, and the likelihood of a cataclysmic conflict between these two powers has been reduced dramatically. The political, economic, social, and demographic changes in the Russian Realm that accompanied the end of the Cold War were similarly large in scale and scope. It is unsurprising, perhaps, that the region is still struggling to steady itself after such dramatic shifts.

NOTES

1. Collins, J. F., & Rojansky, M. (2010). Why Russia matters: Ten reasons why Washington must engage Moscow. *Foreign Policy*. Retrieved from http://foreignpolicy.com/2010/08/18/why-russia-matters/

2. DaVanzo, J., & Adamson, D. (1997). Russia's demographic crisis: How real is it? Retrieved from https://www.rand.org/pubs/issue_papers/IP162/index2.html

3. Shaw, D. J. B. (1995). Urban development. In D. J. B. Shaw (Ed.), *The post-Soviet republics: a systematic geography* (pp. 117–131). Essex, UK: Longman.

4. Blinnikov, M. S. (2011). *A Geography of Russia and its neighbors* (pp. 202–205). New York, NY: Guilford Press.

5. Pew Research Center. (2014). Russians return to religion, but not to church. Retrieved from http://assets.pewresearch.org/wp-content/uploads/sites/11/2014/02/religion-in-Russia-full-report-rev.pdf

6. Shaw, D. J. B. (1995). Ethnic relations and federalism in the Soviet era. In D. J. B. Shaw (Ed.), *The post-Soviet republics: a systematic geography* (pp. 23–33). Essex, UK: Longman; Smith, G. (1995). Ethnic relations in the new states. In D. J. B. Shaw (Ed.), *The post-Soviet republics: a systematic geography* (pp. 34–45). Essex, UK: Longman.

7. Reuveny, R. and A. Prakash. (1999). The Afghan War and the breakdown of the Soviet Union. *Review of International Studies* 25: 693–708.

8. Pallot, J. (1995). Agriculture and rural development. In D. J. B. Shaw (Ed.), *The post-Soviet republics: a systematic geography* (pp. 101–116). Essex, UK: Longman.

9. North, R. N., & Shaw, D. J. B. (1995). Industrial policy and location. In D. J. B. Shaw (Ed.), *The post-Soviet republics: a systematic geography* (pp. 46–65). Essex, UK: Longman.

10. Symons, L., Dewdney, J. C., Hooson, D. J. M., & Mellor, R. E. H. (1990). *The Soviet Union: A systematic geography*. London, UK: Hodder & Stoughton.

11. Lydolph, P. (1987). *Geography of the U.S.S.R.* (4th ed.) (p. 372). Random Lake, WI: Misty Valley Publishing.

12. Baer, D. (2015). A 'perfect demographic storm' is crippling Russia. Retrieved from http://www.businessinsider.com/a-perfect-demographic-storm-is-crippling-russia-2015-9

13. Newell, J. P. & Henry, L. A. (2017). The state of environmental protection in the Russian Federation: A review of the post-Soviet era. *Eurasian Geography and Economics* 57(6): 779–801. DOI: 10.1080/15387216.2017.1289851

SOUTHWESTERN ASIA AND NORTHERN AFRICA

5

THE MIDDLE EAST

The Middle East, made up of Southwestern Asia and Northern Africa, is one of two major world realms located on two continents (the other one is Latin America). If you consider Europe a separate continent, then the Middle Eastern region spreads across three continents, as a small northwestern part of Turkey is located in Europe. Although the North African part of this realm is larger in area than the Southwest Asian one, it is only divided into six countries and one disputed territory (Western Sahara), whereas there are fourteen independent countries and several disputed political entities (the Palestinian territories of the West Bank and Gaza, the Golan Heights, and the northern part of Cyprus) in the Southwest Asian region (Fig. 5.1). The Middle East is almost twice as large as the continental United States, and its territorial dimensions are over 7,240 kilometers (4,500 miles) from east to west and about 3,540 kilometers (2,200 miles) from south to north.

GEOGRAPHIC QUALITIES AND WORLD SIGNIFICANCE

The dry climate, Islamic religion, and Arabic language are the three most characteristic features of this region. The Sahara is the largest desert in the world and covers approximately 90 percent of Northern Africa. Another large desert known as the Empty Quarter (Rub al-Khali) occupies the southern part of the Arabian Peninsula. Only some coastal and mountainous regions have a wetter climate, but even these areas are considered dry in comparison to most of Europe or the Eastern United States. Islam, the second largest and most rapidly growing major world religion, originated in present-day Saudi Arabia and is dominant in all but two countries (Cyprus and Israel) of the Middle East. In most it is the religion (and a way of life) for over 90 percent of their populations. Although

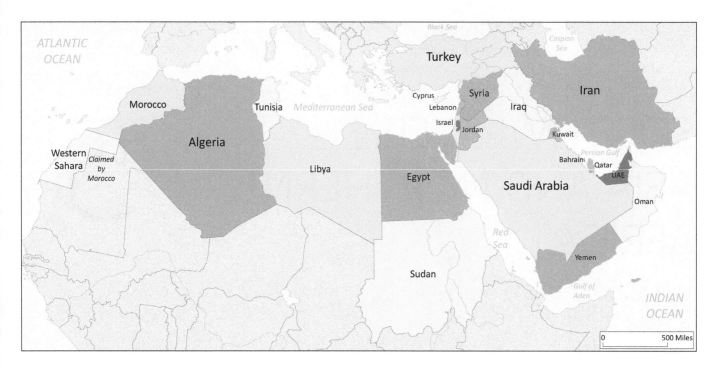

FIGURE 5.1 Countries of Southwestern Asia and Northern Africa—The region is divided into twenty-one independent countries, fifteen in Southwestern Asia and six in Northern Africa. Western Sahara is a disputed territory claimed by Morocco. Cyprus is a divided island, and the West Bank and Gaza (not labeled on the map) are Palestinian territories under Israeli control.

the Arabic language is a native tongue for only half of the region's population, it is the language of Islam and therefore has a relatively high political status in the non-Arabic Muslim countries of Africa and Asia. The Arabic script also influenced the writing systems of some other major languages of this region such as Persian, Kurdish, and Turkish (until 1928). Arabic is also one of six official languages of the United Nations. A fast growing population is another geographic quality of the Middle East. This population, amounting to over 540 million, has more than quadrupled since 1950. Only Sub-Saharan Africa has higher population growth rates among the major world regions today. Almost one-third of that population (in some countries 40 percent) is below fifteen years of age. Providing education and employment for such a large number of young people has been a major challenge for many Middle Eastern governments. Regional inequalities in wealth, particularly those between oil-rich states along the Arab/Persian Gulf and some other Arab countries, have also been characteristic of this region for several decades and have contributed to social tensions and political instability in this part of the world.

The Middle East has dominated the news headlines for decades but its global significance is hardly new. The domestication of some plants (wheat and barley) and animals (sheep and goats), collectively called the agricultural revolution, took place in parts of present-day Iraq, Iran,

Syria, Lebanon, Israel, and Turkey around 8000 BCE. In this area, known as the Fertile Crescent, some groups of people switched from a nomadic to a sedentary lifestyle and established permanent settlements in river valleys. The invention of the plow, the wheel, and other simple tools, as well as irrigation, eventually led to a surplus of food. This, in turn, allowed some people to engage in non-farming activities and congregate in cities. The urban revolution, which began around 3500 BCE, had led to the establishment of a relatively dense network of cities, particularly in the southern part of the Tigris-Euphrates Rivers Valley by 2000 BCE. Some of them may have had populations of 50,000 to 100,000. The establishment of cities was subsequently associated with the development of writing and sciences, social stratification, the centralization of power, and the emergence of the first empires and civilizations. The Middle East is also the birthplace of three monotheistic religions: Judaism, Christianity, and Islam. Although Judaism is a relatively small religion in terms of the number of adherents, about half of the world's population is either Christian or Muslim.

The world importance of the Middle East is perhaps best evidenced today by large deposits of fossil fuels (petroleum and natural gas). Over half of the currently known global petroleum reserves are found there, and this resource has given the region vast political power. The prosperity of many developed countries is closely tied to Middle

Eastern oil. Natural gas, the cleanest burning fossil fuel, is also disproportionately concentrated in the Middle East. The location of several internationally significant waterways (**chokepoints**) in this part of the world further increases the strategic importance of this region.

Finally, political instability, evidenced by numerous internal and several international conflicts, has made the Middle East a global battle ground of conflicting ideas and a focal point for repeated humanitarian crises.

PHYSICAL ENVIRONMENT

The Middle East can be divided into three parts with respect to the physical environment, particularly landform configuration and climate patterns: (1) the Northern Highlands, (2) the Middle River Valleys, Plains, and Hills, and (3) the Southern Desert Zone.[1]

Landform Regions

The Northern Highlands zone is a seismically active region composed of mountains and plateaus located in Turkey and Iran as well as the Maghreb region (Northern Morocco, Algeria, and Tunisia). The Zagros and Elburz Mountains in Iran, the Anatolian Plateau, the Pontic Range to the north and Taurus Range to the south of the plateau in Turkey, and the Atlas Mountains in the Maghreb are the dominant features of this region (Fig. 5.2). The possibility of a strong

earthquake, especially in Turkey and Iran, is the major natural challenge to many inhabitants of this region. For example, the Izmit earthquake in 1999 near Istanbul in Northwestern Turkey killed over 17,000 and injured nearly 44,000 people. The Bam earthquake of 2003 in Southeastern Iran left at least 30,000 people dead. Although volcanic activity is not a common natural hazard in this region today, there were a number of eruptions in ancient and more recent times. One example of such activity is Mt. Ararat (elevation of 5,137 meters/16,854 feet) in Turkey; its last eruption occurred in 1840.

Most of the Middle River Valleys, Plains, and Hills region is located in the Southwest Asian part of the Middle East, just south of the Northern Highlands. The Tigris-Euphrates Rivers Plain (the historic region of Mesopotamia, whose name means "a country between two rivers") and the Eastern Mediterranean region of Levant (Israel,

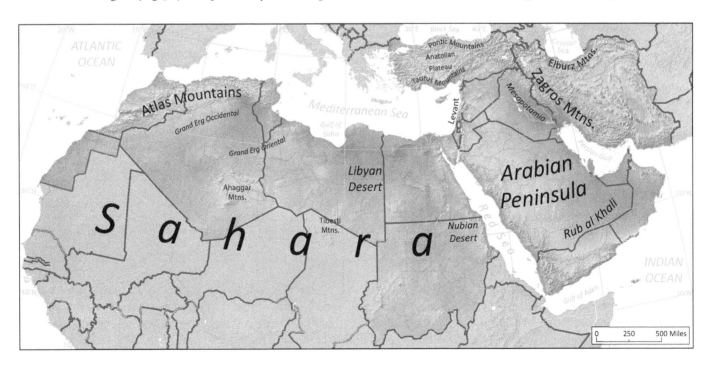

FIGURE 5.2 Landform regions of the Middle East—The Northern Highlands occupy Turkey, most of Iran, and the Atlas Mountains. Mesopotamia, the Levant, and the Nile River Valley are the major parts of the Middle River Valley, Plains, and Hills. The Southern Desert zone includes the Sahara and most of the Arabian Peninsula. *Source:* Natural Earth.

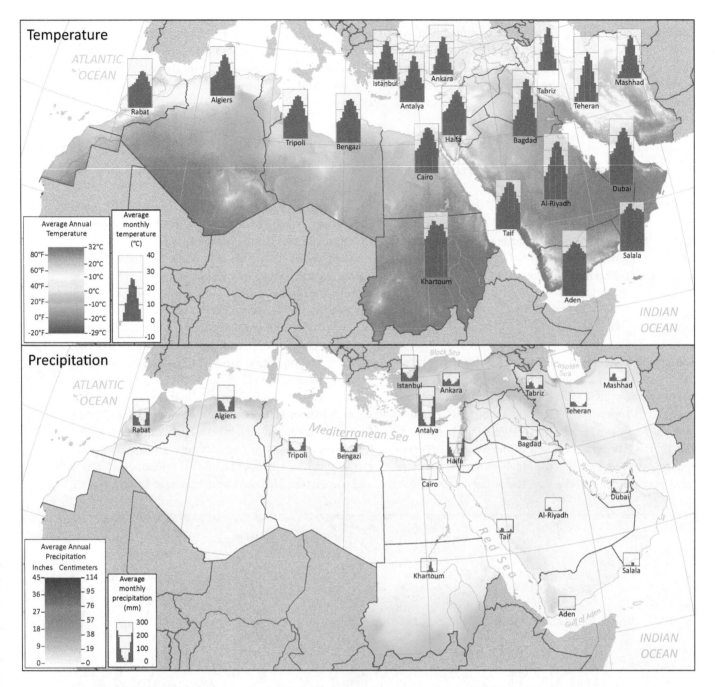

FIGURE 5.3 Middle East: patterns of temperature and precipitation—There is some correlation between landform configuration and temperature and precipitation patterns. Mountainous areas in Turkey, Iran, northern Africa, and southwestern parts of the Arabian Peninsula are cooler and more humid than the rest of the region. The coastal parts of the eastern Mediterranean region (Levant) and southern part of Sudan are relatively humid too. *Source:* WorldClim-Global Climate Data.

Lebanon, and the coastal areas of Syria) form its backbone. These two parts comprise the Fertile Crescent, which is, as previously mentioned, the birthplace of civilization. Two parts of Northern Africa, the Nile River Valley and Delta, and the northeastern part of Libya, known as Cyrenaica, also belong to this region. Periodic river flooding used to be a major challenge (but also a blessing) to inhabitants of Mesopotamia and Egypt. The availability of freshwater

and fertile soils has attracted settlers to the region's alluvial plains (formed by accumulation of water-deposited silt), which are among the most densely populated areas in the world.

The Southern Desert region occupies the rest of the Middle East and is composed of two parts: the Sahara in northern Africa and the Arabian Peninsula in Southwestern Asia. Although the Sahara is delineated on the basis of climate, this large area, similar in size to the United States or China, is composed of several areas of mountains (sometimes also called plateaus) and sand dunes. The Ahaggar Mountains in Southeastern Algeria, the Tibesti Mountains in Southern Libya (and neighboring Chad), and the Red Sea Hills in Eastern Egypt are examples of desert rocky mountain or plateau landscapes. The areas of sand dunes occupy a relatively small portion of the Sahara. The Grand Western Erg and the Grand Eastern Erg of North-central Algeria, as well as the Libyan Desert in Eastern Libya and Western Egypt, are representatives of the sandy desert landscape. Gravel plains, dry valleys, dry lakes, and salt plains can also be found in parts of the Sahara.

The western part of the Arabian Peninsula has two major mountain ranges parallel to the Red Sea: the Hejaz in the northwest and the Asir in the southeast. Both are composed of sedimentary rocks (limestone and sandstone) and have diverse topography with the highest elevations above 3,048 meters (10,000 feet). Some parts receive sufficient moisture to support certain types of dry farming (farming without irrigation). The Najd region, a rocky plateau sloping eastward, occupies the central part of the peninsula and is sparsely populated. The Empty Quarter or Rub al-Khali in the southeastern part of the Arabian Peninsula is the largest sandy desert in the world. Virtually uninhabited, it occupies an area similar in size to Texas and has been an effective natural barrier to interaction between Saudi Arabia and its two southern neighbors, Yemen and Oman.

Dominance of Dry Climate

The dry climate of the desert type is undoubtedly the most important physical feature of the Middle East. Some 80 to 90 percent of the region lies in this climatic zone where evaporation exceeds precipitation. The limited precipitation (below 18 centimeters or 7 inches a year on the average) is erratic in its distribution over time, local in nature, and irregular in amount (Fig. 5.3). There is no rainy or dry season in the desert; some parts of the Eastern Sahara may not record any rain for up to five years. Then when the rains do come, they take the form of local, short convectional downpours (Fig. 5.4). Periodic sand storms may also affect any part of this region (Fig. 5.5).

The desert regions of the Middle East are also characterized by great daily temperature ranges. The afternoon temperatures may reach 49°C (120°F) and twelve hours later the same place may record only 10°C (50°F). Clear skies at night are responsible for this phenomenon. El Aziziya, a small settlement in Northwestern Libya, recorded a temperature of 58°C (136.4°F) in 1922. It was officially

FIGURE 5.4 The Negev Desert, Israel—Most of the Middle East is very dry and desert is the dominant type of landscape. There are two major types of deserts, sandy and rocky. The Negev Desert is an example of the rocky type. *Source:* Pixabay.

considered the highest temperature on record until 2012. Interestingly, the disqualification of the 1922 record was decided by a committee led by a geographer. The committee considered factors like the imprecise instruments used in Libya a century ago, the observer's lack of experience, the incompatibility between the reading at El Aziziya and other nearby readings the same day. The highest temperature

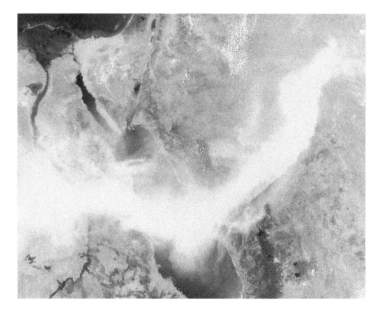

FIGURE 5.5 A satellite image of a sand storm—Sand or dust storms are caused by strong winds, can affect large areas, and cause significant damage to plants, animals, and humans. *Source:* Pixabay.

FIGURE 5.6 The Maghreb region, Algeria—This is one of the "wettest" parts of the Middle East where the Mediterranean climate is dominant. *Source:* Pixabay.

record now (as of 2017) belongs to a 1913 reading in California's Death Valley, but the Middle East is unquestionably a very hot region.

A very small part of the region—most coastal areas along the Mediterranean Sea, particularly those in southern Turkey, the Levant, and the Maghreb regions—has a Mediterranean climate (Fig. 5.6). It is characterized by two distinctive seasons: mild, wet winters and hot, dry summers. The sunny weather in summer attracts many tourists to sea resorts, while sufficient winter moisture supports certain forms of dry farming like small grain (wheat) cultivation and **horticulture** (nuts and fruits). The hilly and mountainous interior areas of Turkey and Northwestern Iran lie in the zone of continental temperate climate.

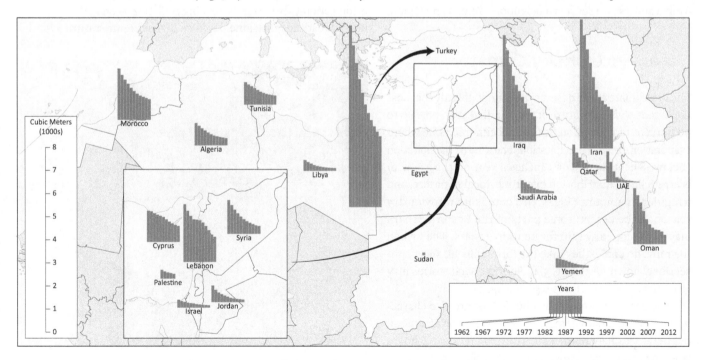

FIGURE 5.7 The Middle East: renewable internal freshwater resources (river flow and rainfall) per capita, 1962–2012—Due to rapidly growing populations per capita water resources have been declining in most countries. Notice the small amount of water in Egypt which has the largest population in the region. Information for Sudan is incomplete and it is unavailable for Kuwait and Western Sahara. *Source:* World Bank.

The precipitation, although not very high, is more evenly distributed throughout the year than in the rest of the Middle East. The winter-summer temperature differences are more pronounced here, but even the coldest months have average temperatures above 0°C (32°F) in most low-lying places, and certain types of farming (livestock herding) can be practiced year around. The northeastern coastal parts of Turkey along the Black Sea are quite humid and densely forested, and some subtropical crops, such as tea, can be grown here.

Limited Water Resources

The shortage of freshwater is the most challenging physical geography feature of this region. The Middle East occupies 10 percent of the total land area and is inhabited by over 7 percent of the world's population, but it has only 1 percent of the global freshwater supply. The water shortage is further magnified by its uneven distribution. Turkey controls half, and Iran one-quarter, of the region's total water supply. According to the World Resources Institute, all but two countries (Sudan and Egypt) are characterized by high or extremely high water stress.[2] The water shortage has become more severe over past decades due to fast population growth, economic development (irrigation and industrial use), and increased household demand (growing affluence). The amount of water per capita has been rapidly decreasing in the last five decades (Fig. 5.7).

Two major river systems, a few freshwater lakes, and several aquifers are the major suppliers of water in most parts of this region. The Nile River, the longest river in the world, satisfies almost all water needs of Egypt and Sudan. It originates in the Lake Plateau of East Africa and Ethiopian Highlands as the White Nile, Blue Nile, and Atbara streams (Fig. 5.8). The first two streams converge at Khartoum in Sudan, and the third one joins the Nile about 320 kilometers (200 miles) northeast of the Sudanese capital. From Khartoum to its mouth at the Mediterranean Sea, the Nile River is about 2,090 kilometers (1,300 miles) long and can be divided into three parts. The first part from Khartoum to Lake Nasser, about 1,290 kilometers (800 miles) long, has five major waterfalls called cataracts and is not navigable. The second part, from Lake Nasser to the delta region north of Cairo, runs smoothly and is navigable. The third part forms the delta region, a triangle-shaped flat area, where the Nile used to split into several streams. Some of these streams have been redirected since ancient times and now the Nile River empties its waters into the sea through the Rosetta and Damietta streams. The Nile is well known for its annual floods that sustained the Egyptian

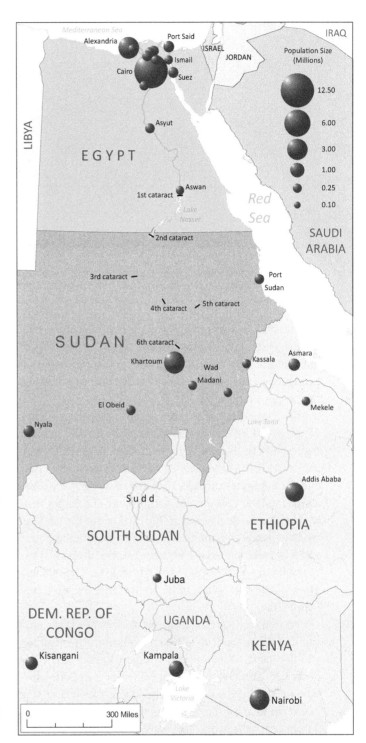

FIGURE 5.8 The Nile river system. *Source:* Natural Earth (www.naturalearthdata.com); United Nations. Population Division. World Urbanization Prospects 2014.

civilization from antiquity until the middle of the 12th century. The high (August–October) and low (March–May) water levels corresponded to rainy and dry seasons in East Africa and determined the agricultural cycle of the entire region. Almost everything in ancient Egypt depended on

FIGURE 5.9 The Nile River, Egypt—Most of the country's population and agriculture is found in the narrow river plain. Notice the desert landscape a short distance from the river bank. *Source:* Heike C. Alberts.

the river flood; years of low or high flood brought about poor harvest, famine, and disease (Fig. 5.9). The importance of the Nile River to Egyptian civilization was best expressed by ancient Greek historian Herodotus for whom Egypt was *the gift of the Nile.*

The Tigris-Euphrates River system has been an important source of water for inhabitants of the Fertile Crescent region since the beginning of civilization. Both rivers originate in Eastern Turkey; the Tigris River runs through Iraq, and the Euphrates through Syria and Iraq (Fig. 5.10). They merge into Shatt al-Arab in Southern Iraq and empty their waters into the Arab/Persian Gulf. The water flow in both rivers depends on winter rain and snowmelt in the Pontic and Zagros Mountains. They have two flood periods, one of smaller magnitude caused by winter rains (November–March) and the other, more important, by snowmelt (April–May).

There is a limited number of freshwater lakes, and some of them are critical sources of water for irrigation and domestic consumption. The best known is the Sea of Galilee, also known as Lake Gennesaret or Lake Tiberias, in Northern Israel. It is the lowest freshwater lake in the world and a major supplier of water to Central and Southern Israel via the National Water Carrier, a network of canals completed in the 1960s. Water from several lakes in Western Turkey, especially Lake Beysehir, is used for irrigation and aquaculture. Lake Arth-Therthar in Iraq was artificially created in 1956 to collect excess water from the Tigris River during the wet season and release it during the dry period. A number of other lakes, some of them fairly large, are found in Iran, Turkey, Tunisia, Algeria, and other countries, but their saline water cannot be used for irrigation or human consumption. The Dead Sea is the most interesting in this group of lakes. It is almost 305

meters (1,000 feet) deep at the lowest place and its water surface is 425 meters (1,407 feet) below sea level. A very high salt content (34 percent) makes any plant or animal life impossible. It is also a tourist attraction, and there are many hotels on the Israeli and Jordanian sides of the lake. The high water salinity prevents swimmers from drowning. Unfortunately, the lake has been shrinking and its water level has fallen by 18 meters (60 feet) since 1930. The lake has separated into two parts, and the southern

FIGURE 5.10 The Tigris-Euphrates river system. *Source:* Natural Earth (www.naturalearthdata.com); United Nations. Population Division. World Urbanization Prospects 2014.

part is now used for the extraction of salt and other minerals.

Freshwater is also found in aquifers, underground layers of water-bearing permeable and porous rocks, in many parts of the region. The amount and quality of water and its recharging rate varies from aquifer to aquifer. Some have non-renewable groundwater, and parts of others have contaminated (saline) water. The Nubian Sandstone Aquifer system of Eastern Sahara, occupying most of Egypt and parts of Libya and Sudan, is the world's largest fossil water deposit and contains about 150,000 cubic kilometers (36,000 cubic miles) of groundwater. The Northwest Sahara Aquifer system, spanning parts of Algeria, Libya, and Tunisia, is a reservoir of over 29,000 cubic kilometers (7,000 cubic miles) of groundwater. The aquifers of the Arabian Peninsula contain at least 2,000 cubic kilometers (500 cubic miles) of water, but most of it is a non-renewable resource. Waters of these and other aquifers in the region have been used at a high rate, mainly for irrigation, and the groundwater depletion will be a serious challenge for many, especially densely populated areas.

Vegetation

The shortage of wood is another physical quality of the Middle East. Since most of this region is dry, forests occupy a small proportion of the land, less than 3 percent. The most "densely forested" countries are Cyprus, Turkey, Lebanon, and Morocco, but even in these countries only 10 to 18 percent of the land is forest-covered. The famous cedar forests of Lebanon (whose flag is dominated by an image of a cedar) have been depleted over the centuries, and now there are only twelve fragmented patches left at higher elevations in the Lebanese Mountains, accounting for about 5 percent of the country's territory. Patches of fairly dense temperate broadleaf deciduous and mixed forests are found in Northern Iran and Turkey along the Black and Caspian Seas, respectively. Some reforestation attempts, especially those in Israel, have been successful. The Biriya Forest in the northern part of the country, about twenty-one square kilometers (8 square miles) in area, is the largest planted forest in this part of the region.

HUMAN-ENVIRONMENT INTERACTION

As indicated earlier, the Fertile Crescent is the birthplace of agriculture and urban settlements. These developments began at a time when the Middle East was wetter and more environmentally resilient than today. Furthermore, the small number of people meant that even as their relationship with the surrounding landscapes changed, their impact was slight. The thousands of years since have shown a progressively increasing environmental impact. Deforestation, desertification, and salinization are the three major environmental issues facing the Middle East today.

Forests covered most humid parts of the region several thousand years ago. Pine and cedar forests were found in Lebanon and other hilly and mountainous areas of present-day Turkey, Iran, and the Maghreb region as late as 3000 BCE. However, many of them disappeared in ancient times as timber was needed for construction. The first Jewish temple in Jerusalem, built during King Solomon's reign, was made of cedar wood from Lebanon. The Phoenicians living along the Eastern Mediterranean coast needed timber for shipbuilding. Livestock herding (sheep and goats) has also contributed to deforestation as these animals destroyed many young trees. The shortage of wood had a major impact on the construction sector and furnishing of a typical Middle Eastern house. Most traditional buildings were made of clay, adobe, or brick, and there was some wooden furniture inside them (but plenty of carpets as wool and cotton were easily available).

Desertification threatens most dry regions in the world today, and it is particularly widespread in the Middle East. Some experts blame human activities (overgrazing) and others climate change (global warming). Regardless of its cause, desertification threatens large parts of the entire region, especially in the Fertile Crescent (Iraq, Syria, Jordan, Lebanon, and Israel), the Nile Valley, Northern Africa, and the Arabian Peninsula.

Salinization, the accumulation of salt and other minerals in the soil which can be dangerous to plants, can have very negative consequences for farmers. It is the outcome of improper irrigation practices (e.g. providing insufficient amounts of water to irrigated fields) and high evaporation rates. A steady increase of the salt content will lead to soil degradation and its inability to support cultivation of most plants. Over 5 percent of the region's soils are saline, and a quarter of irrigated land suffers from this problem. Salinization can also affect drinking water supplies and accelerate corrosion of underground metal pipes and cables, and it can indirectly contribute to soil erosion. Many scholars claim that salinization was partially responsible for the collapse of some Middle Eastern ancient cultures. It is the most serious environmental problem in the southern part of the Tigris-Euphrates River Valley and the Nile River Delta today.

Although the Middle East was and is known for freshwater shortages, the Mesopotamian Marshes, located in Southern Iraq and parts of Iran, provided a habitat for a variety of plant and bird species and supported fishing and farming activities of the Ma'dan people (Marsh Arabs) for centuries. However, parts of this 18,000 square km (7,000 square miles) area were drained for land reclamation, eradication of mosquito-breeding grounds, and oil exploration purposes by the Iraqi government from the 1950s through the 1970s. These actions led to serious environmental consequences, including the loss of biodiversity, salinization of soil and reduced agricultural productivity, desertification, and saltwater contamination of freshwater aquifers. The marshes were drained again during the First Gulf War (discussed later in this chapter), this time for political purposes, to deprive resistance forces of hiding grounds during this conflict. Another purpose was to drive out the Marsh Arabs, accused of anti-government sympathies, from this area. Their number has declined from half a million in the 1950s to about 20,000 today (many people fled to Iran). The new Iraqi government began re-flooding parts of the marshes after 2003, and the region became a UNESCO World Heritage Site in 2016.

Finally, the richest states in this region have used some of their wealth to transform their environments. Before 1950, it is estimated that fewer than 500,000 people lived along the entire southern rim of the Arab/Persian Gulf where summertime humidity and temperatures both soar to uncomfortable levels. But the diffusion of air conditioning has permitted the emergence of new soaring skylines from Kuwait City to Dubai. Incredibly, Dubai also has an indoor ski resort. Ski Dubai consists of five ski slopes and a snow park area with live penguins. And Dubai, like several other cities in the area, has reclaimed land from the sea. One famous development off Dubai comprises little artificial islands meant to resemble the world. Another is shaped like a giant palm tree and hosts luxury residences. The contrast between those who live in such artificial environments and those elsewhere in the region who still live very much at the mercy of the environment is jarring.

POPULATION PATTERNS AND TRENDS

Population Distribution and Growth

The region's population of about 540 million accounts for over 7 percent of the world's total population. Like most dry areas, the Middle East is characterized by an uneven population distribution, and there is a very strong relationship between population density and the distribution of freshwater resources. Middle Eastern countries can be divided into three groups with respect to the number of their inhabitants. The first group includes Egypt, Iran, and Turkey; these three large countries, ranging in population from 78 to 90 million, have over 45 percent of the region's total population. The next seven countries' populations range from 20 to 40 million (Sudan, Algeria, Iraq, Morocco, Saudi Arabia, Yemen, and Syria) and account for a slightly smaller share (42 percent) of the total population. Twelve percent of the population lives in the remaining countries or territories.

The unevenly distributed population means great differences in population densities among various countries (Fig. 5.11). The small (both in area and population) country of Bahrain has over 2,000 people per square kilometer (5150 people per square mile). Israel, Lebanon, and the Palestinian territory are also fairly densely populated areas with densities varying from 380 to 720 persons per square kilometer (980 to 1860 persons per square mile). Western Sahara and Libya, on the other hand, are almost empty areas; population densities here are 2 and 4 inhabitants per square kilometer (10 and 20 inhabitants per square mile), respectively. Physiological density, or the number of people per unit of productive land (farmland), is a much more meaningful measure than simple arithmetic density in this region. The difference between these two measures can tell us something more about real population pressure on the limited natural resource base in most parts of the Middle East. For example, Egypt's physiological density is about twenty-eight times higher than its arithmetic density (2,520 versus 90 persons per square km or 6,630 versus 240 persons per square mile). Some 95 percent of Egypt's population occupies only 5 percent of the territory, the fertile Nile River Valley and Delta, and population densities here are among the highest in the world. In the 1990s, Egypt's government embarked on the massive undertaking to divert water from Lake Nasser behind the Aswan High Dam in the far south of the country to irrigate a vast new area of desert near the border with Sudan. However, technical problems, including the high salinity of the soil in the area, and political turbulence in the

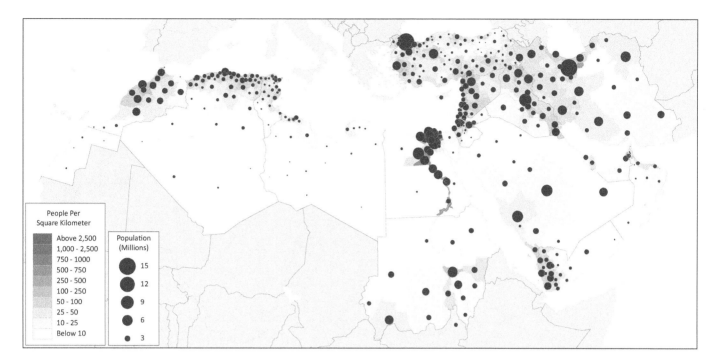

FIGURE 5.11 Population distribution in the Middle East—Notice the strong correlation between population distribution and freshwater availability. Most humid regions, including mountains and some hilly coastal areas and major river valleys are densely populated while dry regions (deserts) are virtually empty. *Source:* GeoHive (www.geohive.com) and statistical agencies of individual countries.

country have so far prevented the New Valley Project from coming to fruition. Meanwhile, physiological densities are also very high in some desert countries of the Arabian Peninsula (Oman, Kuwait, and Bahrain), Libya, and Western Sahara.

The Middle East had a population of just over 100 million in 1950, almost four times smaller than the population of Europe at that time. Today, the region's population is similar in size to that of Europe, and only Sub-Saharan Africa has a faster rate of population growth today. The population of some Middle Eastern countries has multiplied during the past sixty years. The United Arab Emirates has over 130 times more people today (9 million) than in 1950. Qatar's population (2.2 million) is now over eighty times larger than that of six decades ago. Kuwait and Jordan have also recorded impressive population gains during the same time period. Most large countries have increased their populations mainly through natural increase, while for the smaller, richer ones net migration has been the main driver. Although fertility rates have been declining in all Middle Eastern countries for some time, they are still above the replacement level of 2.1 children per woman in most states (Fig. 5.12). In response to high population growth rates, many governments introduced various measures to lower fertility rates, including support for family planning programs.

Labor Migrations to Oil-rich States

Parts of the Middle East have become globally significant migration magnets in recent decades. Although labor migration to this region began in the 1930s after the discovery of oil in the Arab/Persian Gulf countries, it only emerged as a large-scale movement after the 1973 oil boom. Originally considered a short-term solution to the sudden increase in labor demand in six Gulf states (Bahrain, Kuwait, Oman, Qatar, Saudi Arabia, and the United Arab Emirates), this migration flow has shown little sign of abating. The number of foreign workers increased to over 4 million by 1985, 7 million by the end of the 1990s, and over 10 million a decade later. Most of the migrants have found employment in the private sector, especially construction, commerce, and domestic services. The original preference for Arab workers has been replaced by favoritism for Asian migrants as they are cheaper, easier to lay off and control, and more productive and manageable. Most come from India, Bangladesh, Pakistan, the Philippines, Sri Lanka, and Indonesia. The over 17 million foreign workers comprise a very large segment of each country's labor force today, including over 88 percent in the United Arab Emirates, 85 percent in Qatar, 69 percent in Kuwait, 52 percent in Bahrain, 44 percent in Oman, and 32 percent in Saudi Arabia.

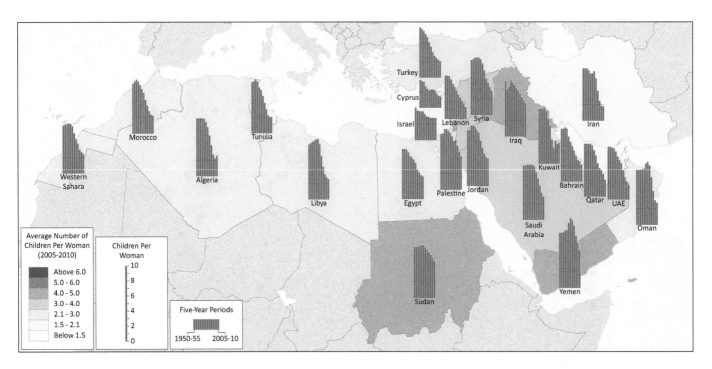

FIGURE 5.12 Total fertility rates in the Middle East, 1950–2010—Fertility rates have been declining in every part of the region but they are still above the replacement level of 2.1 (shown as a red horizontal line) in most countries. Notice the high rates in Sudan, Yemen, and the Palestinian territories. *Source:* United Nations. Population Division. World Population Prospects 2012.

A dual labor market now exists in these countries; most foreigners are employed in the private sector and nationals in the government sector. The policy of reducing the dependence on foreign workers in the private sector has been largely unsuccessful due to a tremendous wage gap between both groups of workers (foreign workers' wages are much lower than those of local citizens), as well as too liberal immigration policies and lax enforcement of labor regulations.[3]

Urbanization: Past and Present (Islamic Cities)

As indicated earlier, the Middle East is the birthplace of the urban revolution. The first cities were established in the Fertile Crescent region at least 5,000 years ago. Some of the cities became centers of innovation and political, religious, and economic power and extended their influence over the surrounding areas and eventually over more distant places. The cities of Uruk, Mari, Babylon, and Girsu may have had more than 40,000 inhabitants (some probably much more) by 2000 BCE. They were known for their monumental public architecture best exemplified by ziggurats, pyramid-shaped massive structures and seats of political and religious power. Many of these early cities were later abandoned and today only their ruins remain. The landscape of Southern Iraq, for instance, is dotted by tells, hill-like mounds of the accumulated debris left by millennia of human occupation.

The spread of Islamic culture after the seventh century CE was also associated with the transformation of existing, and the rise of new, cities throughout the region. Their location and layout were influenced by several factors, including the physical environment (climate, topography, and water), economy (trade), and religion (Islam). Several distinctive features were found in a typical Islamic city (Fig. 5.13). The main mosque, a house of Friday public prayer, occupied the central part of the city. A religious school (***madrassa***) was quite often part of the mosque complex. A market place (*suq* in Arabic, *bazaar* in Persian, and *carsi* in Turkish) usually surrounded the central mosque; it was a trading place where various vendors sold their merchandise. This space could also be used for other public activities (Fig. 5.14). A fortress or citadel, a center of power, often surrounded by its own walls with its own mosque, occupied a hilly or other defensible part of the city. The street network consisted of narrow and twisting public and private streets and dead-end alleys. Residential quarters, occupying the largest part of the city, were divided along ethnic and religious lines (Fig. 5.15 and Fig. 5.16). These were high density areas with local mosques

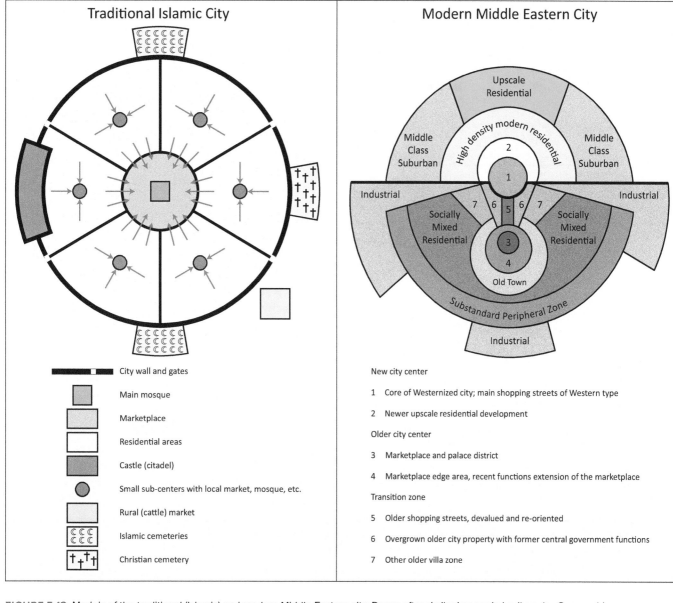

Traditional Islamic City

City wall and gates

Main mosque

Marketplace

Residential areas

Castle (citadel)

Small sub-centers with local market, mosque, etc.

Rural (cattle) market

Islamic cemeteries

Christian cemetery

Modern Middle Eastern City

Upscale Residential

Middle Class Suburban

High density modern residential

Middle Class Suburban

Industrial

Industrial

Socially Mixed Residential

Socially Mixed Residential

Old Town

Substandard Peripheral Zone

Industrial

New city center

1 Core of Westernized city; main shopping streets of Western type

2 Newer upscale residential development

Older city center

3 Marketplace and palace district

4 Marketplace edge area, recent functions extension of the marketplace

Transition zone

5 Older shopping streets, devalued and re-oriented

6 Overgrown older city property with former central government functions

7 Other older villa zone

FIGURE 5.13 Models of the traditional (Islamic) and modern Middle Eastern city. Drawn after similar images in Lexikon der Geographie: islamisch-orientalische Stadt (www.spektrum.de).

and basic retail facilities.[4] Most building structures were designed to delay the entry of heat into the living quarters during the day and release it at night by using high heat capacity materials (mud, stones, and adobe), compact geometry (dome-shaped roofs) and highly reflective colors to minimize surface area exposed to sunlight. Residential structures had flat roofs used for various activities during the cooler part of the day and at night. Walls with several

FIGURE 5.14 A marketplace, Morocco—It was an important feature of the traditional Islamic city, and it still plays a major role in the daily life of many urban residents. *Source:* Heike C. Alberts.

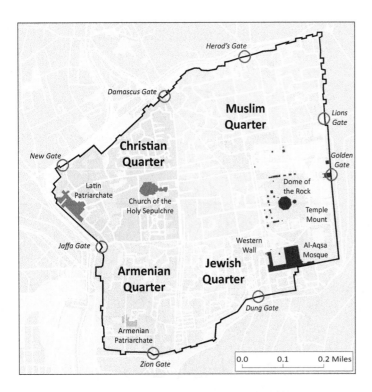

FIGURE 5.15 The old city of Jerusalem—The walled city occupies only 0.35 square miles and is divided into four ethnic/religious neighborhoods. The Western Wall, once part of Solomon's Temple, is a sacred place for Jews. The Church of the Holy Sepulchre (Church of Resurrection) is the center of the Christian Quarter. The Temple Mount and the Dome of the Rock are sacred places for Muslims. Drawn after a similar image in Diercke International Atlas.

gates surrounded the cities. Cemeteries, weekly animal markets, private plots, and gardens were found outside the city walls. Some Islamic cities became quite large by the end of the 10th century. For example, the city of Baghdad in Iraq had over 1 million residents by that time, and Cairo in Egypt half a million by the mid-14th century. Many Middle Eastern cities, especially the larger ones, have changed considerably during the last fifty years. Population growth, migration, economic development, and wealth accumulation from oil after the 1970s have impacted the urban sector in several ways. First, there has been an unprecedented increase in the population of many cities, particularly those in the Arab/Persian Gulf region. Dubai, a city of 2.4 million people today, had only 73,000 residents in 1970, and its average annual population rate growth of 8 percent since that time has been among the highest in the world. Riyadh, the capital of Saudi Arabia and a city of 4.8 million residents, had a population eleven times smaller in 1970. Jeddah and Mecca in Saudi Arabia and Tripoli in Libya are other examples of rapidly growing Middle Eastern cities. Even the slowest growing, major urban agglomerations such as Beirut in Lebanon, Cairo and Alexandria in Egypt, Casablanca in Morocco, and Oran in Algeria, have at least doubled their populations during the past forty-five years. Second, urban sprawl has paralleled the rapid population growth in many places. For example, Cairo and Riyadh have doubled, and Istanbul tripled, their territorial size since the early 1970s. New

FIGURE 5.16 The old part of Jerusalem—This sacred city for Jews, Christians, and Muslims retains its ancient character of narrow and irregular streets, numerous sacred structures, and ethnically and religiously segregated neighborhoods. *Source:* Pixabay.

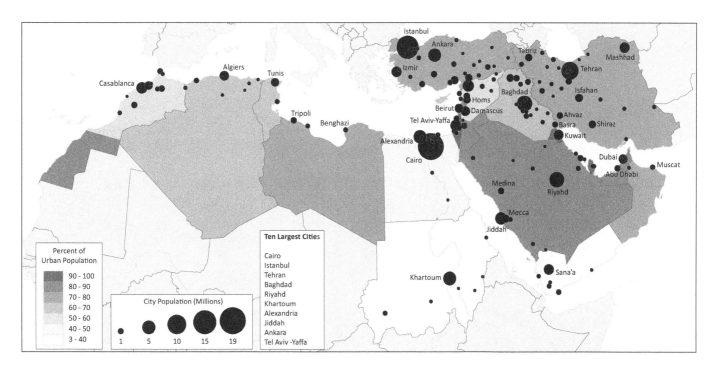

FIGURE 5.17 Urbanization levels in the Middle East—Notice that most urban settlements are located inside a triangle connecting the three largest cities, Istanbul, Cairo, and Tehran. *Source:* United Nations. Population Division. World Urbanization Prospects 2014.

Western-style city centers with shopping malls, usually located outside the historic urban core, and middle and upscale residential areas have appeared in many larger cities. Istanbul, Tel Aviv, and cities in the Arab/Persian Gulf region are good examples of such developments. Third, the urban sprawl has been associated with the expansion of transportation infrastructure, including wider streets and limited access highways (to accommodate the growing number of motor vehicles) as well as subway systems. Istanbul, in 1989, was the first Middle Eastern city to open a subway. Today at least thirteen other cities have such systems (e.g. Cairo, Teheran, Algiers, Dubai, Mecca, and Ankara), and several more are under construction.

The Middle East today, with 62 percent of its population living in cities, is the second most urbanized developing part of the world (after Latin America). In only three countries (Sudan, Yemen, and Egypt) does the majority still live in rural areas (Fig. 5.17 and Fig. 5.18). The small Arab/Persian Gulf states (Bahrain, Kuwait, and Qatar) and Israel are the most urbanized parts of the region, where over 90 percent of the population is urban. The region's urban population has almost doubled since 1990 and is expected to continue increasing in the foreseeable future (Fig. 5.19). Cairo, Istanbul, and Teheran are the three largest Middle Eastern cities; the first two are considered mega-cities since their populations are over 10 million each.

The rapid urban growth will very likely be associated with several challenges, including water scarcity, shortage of land for development, unplanned growth, health risks, climate change, and seismic activities (in some parts of the region).

FIGURE 5.18 A desert settlement, Morocco—Adobe and clay are major building materials in most desert regions of the Middle East. Notice the high walls, small windows, and compact form of a typical desert settlement. *Source:* Heike C. Alberts.

FIGURE 5.19 The city of Doha, Qatar—These ultramodern structures, characteristic of larger cities in several Arab/Persian Gulf countries, reflect the power of oil and gas money and its investment into construction and other projects. *Source:* Pixabay.

LANGUAGE AND RELIGION

Linguistic Diversity

Many people in Southwest Asia and North Africa share two important cultural characteristics: they speak Arabic and they are Muslim; but there are many exceptions to both patterns. Although Arabic is the native tongue for over half of the Middle East's population and has an important political status as the language of Islam, there are several other languages spoken by millions of people in this region. Most of these languages belong to three major linguistic families. The Arabic, Hebrew, and Berber languages are members of the Semitic branch of the Afro-Asiatic family (Fig. 5.20). Arabic is the official language in all but three Middle Eastern countries. There are three forms of this language: colloquial, standard, and classical, and most people may only be familiar with the first two types. Due to its wide territorial spread, several dialects of spoken Arabic can be identified, including the Western dialect used in the Maghreb region; the Central dialect in Egypt and Sudan; the Northern dialect in Syria, Lebanon, Jordan, and Iraq;

and the Peninsular dialect spoken in the Arabian Peninsula. Arabic is the native language for about 290 million people. Egypt is the largest Arabic-speaking country in the world.

Hebrew, the ancient language of the Jews, is now one of two official languages in Israel (Arabic is the other official language). It became extinct by the fourth century CE and was not used in daily life during the **Jewish diaspora** (except for liturgical purposes). It was revived by the end of the 19th century and became a unifying force among Jewish migrants travelling to Palestine in the 20th century. Today about 90 percent of Israeli Jews and 60 percent of Israeli Arabs are proficient in it, but it is the native tongue for only about half of the Israeli adult population. When Israel proclaimed independence in 1948 and Hebrew became its official language, there was some opposition to using it for non-religious purposes (i.e., in daily life). There has also been some support for protecting it from foreign (mainly

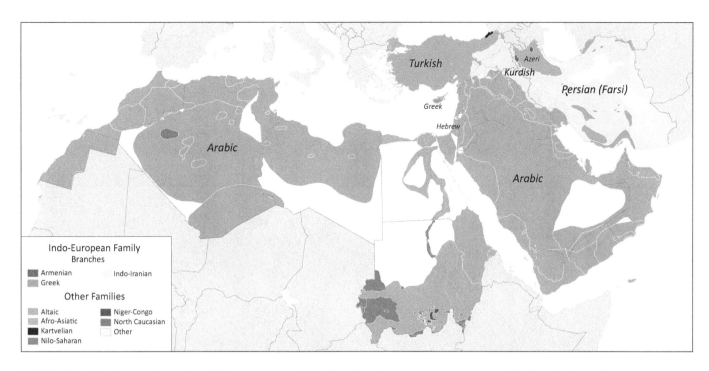

FIGURE 5.20 Distribution of major linguistic families in the Middle East—The Arabic language, a member of the Afro-Asiatic family, is dominant in Northern Africa and the central and southern parts of Southwestern Asia. Turkey and Iran are inhabited by people speaking Altaic (mainly Turkish) and Indo-European (mainly Persian and Kurdish) languages. *Source:* World Language Mapping System.

English) influence. Both the Arabic and Hebrew scripts are written and read from right to left.

The Berber language is spoken in the Maghreb region, mainly in Morocco and Algeria. It used to have a low status but has been recently recognized as a national language in both countries (along with Arabic). There are some 16 million Berber speakers, including 10 million in Morocco and over 4 million in Algeria.

The Altaic family, to which the Turkish and Azeri languages belong, is the second largest group of languages spoken in the Middle East. Turkish was brought from Central Asia to present-day Turkey between the 10th and 13th centuries CE. It originally used the Arabic script, but the Latin alphabet was introduced in 1928 to cleanse the language of Arabic and Persian influences. The switch to the Latin script also symbolized post-World War I Turkish attempts toward achieving close integration with Europe. There are some 60 million speakers of this language in Turkey and much smaller numbers of speakers in Cyprus and Syria. The Azeri language, closely related to Turkish, is spoken in parts of Northwestern Iran and Eastern Turkey by over 11 million people. The Indo-European family is represented by several languages spoken in Iran and parts of Iraq, Turkey, Syria, and Cyprus. The Persian (Farsi) language has some 30 million speakers mainly in Iran. Kurdish is the mother tongue for some 20

million people inhabiting parts of Turkey (7.5 million), Iran (6 million), Iraq (4.6 million), and Syria (1.5 million). Greek is the native language for about two-thirds of the residents of Cyprus (over 650,000). It was also spoken in parts of Western Turkey in ancient times, including the period described in the New Testament of the Christian Bible.

Religious Diversity and the Dominance of Islam

The Middle East is the birthplace of three monotheistic religions with common roots: Judaism, Christianity, and Islam. The first two faiths originated in present-day Israel and the surrounding areas, while Islam began in the western part of the Arabian Peninsula. Judaism, the oldest monotheistic religion in the world, traces its roots to Abraham who is also recognized as a founding figure in Christianity and Islam, so all three are considered Abrahamic faiths. Jerusalem, one of the oldest continuously inhabited cities in the world, became the Jewish religious and political capital around 1000 BCE. A millennium later, the city and surrounding hinterland were incorporated into the Roman Empire as the province of Judea. After challenging the Roman occupation and interference in their religious affairs, the Jews

FIGURE 5.21 The Wailing Wall in Jerusalem—The only remaining part of the ancient Solomon Temple, it is the most sacred site for Jews. It is adjacent to the Dome of the Rock, a sacred place for Muslims. *Source:* Pixabay.

were forced to leave their homeland in the first century CE—one of the most famous instances of ethnic cleansing in world history—and were scattered throughout the Middle East and Europe for the next 2,000 years. This scattering, known as the **Jewish Diaspora**, resulted in almost 90 percent of the world's Jews living in Europe by the middle of the 19th century ce. But persecution of Jews there, culminating in the catastrophe of the Holocaust, generated several migration waves of European Jews to what was, by then, called Palestine during the first part of the 12th century and after World War II. The new state of Israel, discussed more fully later in this chapter, became the official Jewish homeland and Judaism its official religion. Since it is the state religion, government offices, stores, and public transportation are closed on Saturdays in most of Israel to observe the Sabbath (Fig. 5.21). Jews today comprise about 75 percent of Israel's total population, and they represent about half of the world's Jewish population; the other half is dispersed mainly throughout Europe and the Americas.

Christianity, the largest monotheistic religion in the world, was born 2,000 years ago in the Jewish region of Palestine. Though early Christians were persecuted by the Romans, the roads and sea routes of the Roman Empire facilitated the rapid diffusion of the new faith. In the Middle East, Christianity was the dominant religion (except for in present-day Iran and the Arabian Peninsula) by the fourth century CE. Some theological differences among early Christians resulted in the establishment of several denominations, and some of them have survived in the region to present time. The Coptic Orthodox Church is an example of such an early branch separated from the mainstream Christianity in the fifth century CE. Although theologically close to Roman Catholic and Eastern Orthodox Churches, its rejection of belief in dual nature of Christ (human and divine) classifies it as a monophysitic Christian denomination. Coptic Christians puts emphasis on fasting and frequent prayer, and their Church has a clearly defined organizational structure, including its own pope (the patriarch of Alexandria). There are some 10 to 15 million Coptic Christians in Egypt today, and they comprise about 15 percent of the country's total population. The Maronite Church was also established in the fifth century CE in present-day Syria. It united with the Roman Catholic Church during the era of the Crusades (12th century) and recognizes the Roman pontiff as its spiritual leader but has its own religious traditions (e.g. liturgical services in Aramaic, no kneeling but standing during such services). Today there are about 900,000 Maronite Christians in Lebanon (22 percent of the total population) and 50,000 in Syria. The Greek Orthodox Church is dominant in Cyprus where it has over 600,000 adherents. Much smaller groups

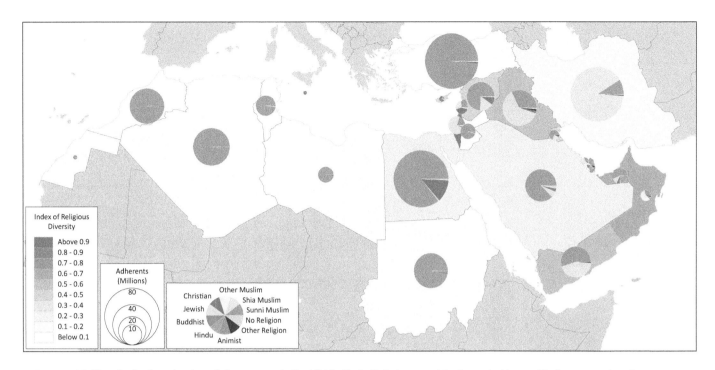

FIGURE 5.22 The distribution of major religious groups in the Middle East—Only four countries have sizable non-Muslim groups: Israel (Jews), and Cyprus, Lebanon, and Egypt (Christians). Shia Muslims are dominant in Iran, Iraq, and Bahrain, and Sunni Muslims in the rest of the region except Oman where Ibadhi Muslims comprise the majority of population. *Source:* Association of Religious Data Archives.

are also found in Turkey, Syria, Egypt, Iraq, and Israel. Several other Christian denominations also exist in these countries. However, recent political instability in Iraq and Syria has led to an exodus of many Christians from both countries.

Islam is by far the most important religion in the Middle East (Fig. 5.22). For most people living there it is also a way of life. It is hard to understand this culture realm without knowing some basic facts about this religion, which originated in the seventh century CE. Mohammad, a resident of the city of Mecca in the western part of the Arabian Peninsula and the founder of Islam, received a series of divine revelations that were later written down by his followers and compiled into the **Koran** (Quran), the holy scripture for all Muslims. This religion, established on the Judeo-Christian foundation, has many similarities with the two other monotheistic religions (Fig. 5.23). For example, all three religions believe in the same God, although each one has a different concept of this deity. Muslims recognize Abraham, Moses, and Jesus as prophets to whom God revealed a certain amount of truth. However, there are also several major differences between these religions. Muslims believe that Mohammad was the last and only prophet to whom God revealed the entire truth; Jews and Christians reject this belief. Muslims reject the Jewish concept of a chosen nation. They also reject the Christian belief in the divine nature of Jesus and the Holy Trinity.

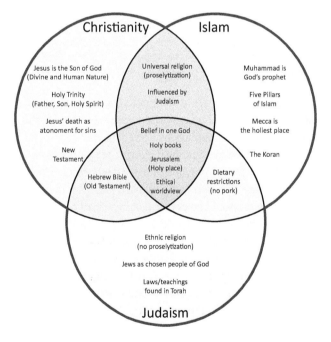

FIGURE 5.23 Similarities and differences between Judaism, Christianity, and Islam. *Source:* Drawn after a similar image at www.cpschools.org/cms/lib2/MI01001578/Centricity/Domain/344/Venn%20of%20monotheistic%20religions.pdf.

The basic Muslim beliefs and practices can be best summarized as the **five pillars of Islam**: confession of faith, frequent prayer, almsgiving, fasting, and pilgrimage. First,

FIGURE 5.24 A mosque in Cairo, Egypt—Cairo has been known as "the city of a thousand minarets" as numerous mosques, like the Sultan Hassan mosque shown in this image, dot the city skyline. *Source:* Pixabay.

the confession of faith is a statement that there is no God but Allah and Mohammad is His messenger. This profession must be made publicly by each believer at least once in his or her lifetime. Second, frequent prayer means that each Muslim should pray five times a day: before sunrise, at midday, late afternoon, after sunset, and after nightfall. These prayers should be performed in a clean place (mats are often used for that purpose) and the faithful should face Mecca, the holiest place for Muslims, during each prayer. The Friday congregational noon prayer in a mosque is obligatory for men (Fig. 5.24). Third, almsgiving is a charitable act of giving a portion of one's personal wealth to help those in need and to support the Muslim community. Fourth, fasting requires abstaining from eating, drinking, smoking, and sexual relations during the daylight during Ramadan, the ninth month of the Muslim calendar. This pillar can be a real challenge when it occurs in summer when days are long and hot in many parts of the Middle East. Many Muslims see this pillar as an opportunity to practice self-discipline. Fifth, the pilgrimage (*hajj*) is a journey to Mecca, the birthplace of Islam. It should be done at least once in a lifetime and can only be excused by physical disability or poverty. The pilgrimage should take place

during the first ten days of the last month of the Islamic calendar. Several million Muslims visit Mecca each year during these days, and it is a significant financial commitment for most travelers. The Saudi Arabian government is in charge of the logistics of this annual event (Fig. 5.25 and Fig. 5.26).

There is a series of other rules guiding the daily life of Muslims, although they are not part of the five pillars of faith. Sharia regulates all human actions pertaining to worship, civil matters, criminal activities, and business transactions. It is based on the Muslim holy scripture (Koran), teachings of Mohammad and his followers (*sunna* in Arabic), consensus among Muslim legal experts, and analogical reasoning or legal precedent. It is considered divinely inspired (unlike the human-inspired law in Western societies) with no separation of church and state and strongly influences official law in Saudi Arabia and some other Muslim states. Regarding the civil matters and criminal activities, for example, Sharia states that a man can have up to four wives and a husband can divorce his wife, but a wife needs her husband's consent for divorce. It prescribes the death penalty (in some countries carried out by stoning) for adultery, murder, and apostasy from Islam and

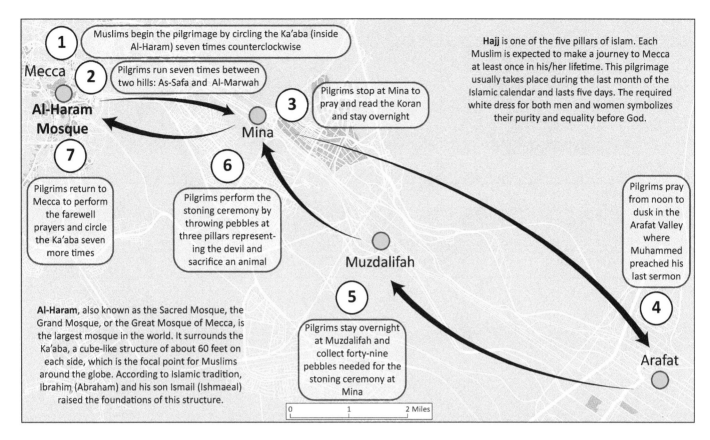

1 Muslims begin the pilgrimage by circling the Ka'aba (inside Al-Haram) seven times counterclockwise

2 Pilgrims run seven times between two hills: As-Safa and Al-Marwah

Mecca

Al-Haram Mosque

Mina

3 Pilgrims stop at Mina to pray and read the Koran and stay overnight

Hajj is one of the five pillars of islam. Each Muslim is expected to make a journey to Mecca at least once in his/her lifetime. This pilgrimage usually takes place during the last month of the Islamic calendar and lasts five days. The required white dress for both men and women symbolizes their purity and equality before God.

7 Pilgrims return to Mecca to perform the farewell prayers and circle the Ka'aba seven more times

6 Pilgrims perform the stoning ceremony by throwing pebbles at three pillars representing the devil and sacrifice an animal

Muzdalifah

Pilgrims pray from noon to dusk in the Arafat Valley where Muhammed preached his last sermon

4

Al-Haram, also known as the Sacred Mosque, the Grand Mosque, or the Great Mosque of Mecca, is the largest mosque in the world. It surrounds the Ka'aba, a cube-like structure of about 60 feet on each side, which is the focal point for Muslims around the globe. According to Islamic tradition, Ibrahim (Abraham) and his son Ismail (Ishmaeal) raised the foundations of this structure.

5 Pilgrims stay overnight at Muzdalifah and collect forty-nine pebbles needed for the stoning ceremony at Mina

Arafat

0   1   2 Miles

FIGURE 5.25 The pilgrimage to Mecca—The pilgrimage to Mecca is one of the five pillars of Islam. Before entering the Grand Mosque, pilgrims wash themselves (*wudu*) and put on white garment (*ihram*) symbolizing purity and equality before God. While inside the Grand Mosque, pilgrims walk around the Ka'aba (*tawaf*) seven times, then quickly walk seven times between two hills, Safa and Marwa (*sa'y*). At Arafat, they ask God for forgiveness (*waquf*). At Mina, pilgrims throw pebbles at three pillars representing temptation (*ramy*). After that, they offer an animal to remember Ibrahim (Abraham) and his son Ishmael (*qurbani*). Finally, they cut their hair, nails, shave and circle the Ka'aba seven times again. Drawn after a similar image in Huffington Post.

FIGURE 5.26 The Grand (Al-Haram) Mosque in Mecca, Saudi Arabia—The Ka'aba, a cube-like structure covered with black silk cloth, is the most important part of this sacred mosque. A pilgrimage to Mecca is one of the five pillars of Islam, and walking around the Ka'aba seven times is one part of that pilgrimage. *Source:* Pixabay.

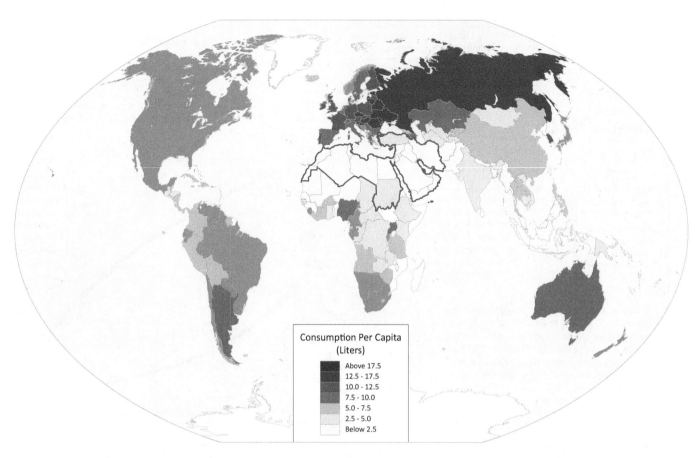

FIGURE 5.27 Consumption of alcohol around the world, 2003–2005. *Source:* World Health Organization.

hand amputation for theft. Women are supposed to dress modestly, but they do not have to completely cover their faces. However, the interpretation of this and many other rules regarding the status of women varies from country to country. In Saudi Arabia, for example, women have to wear *niqab*, a veil that only exposes eyes but covers the rest of the body. On the other hand, in Lebanon or Turkey many women do not cover their heads at all. No business transaction can be based on interest, uncertainty, gambling, or trade in prohibited products and industries (alcohol, pork, prostitution, pornography, and tobacco). The sale and consumption of alcohol is strictly forbidden in most Muslim countries; as a result, the Middle East records the lowest alcohol consumption per capita in the world (Fig. 5.27).

To enforce certain elements of Sharia, especially those regarding behavior in public places (e.g. dress code and interaction between sexes), some countries have created morality police forces including undercover agents, who have the power to reprimand, fine, and arrest people suspected of breaking the law. For example, the Committee for the Promotion of Virtue and the Prevention of Vice in Saudi Arabia has been enforcing the code of behavior forbidding socializing between unrelated males and females

since 1940. The Guidance Patrols in Iran have been enforcing the dress code for women since 1979. Similar agencies were also established in Sudan in 1993 and the Gaza Strip (part of the Palestinian Territories) in 2009.

The concept of *jihad*, part of the sharia law, has not always been correctly interpreted or used both in the Middle East and the Western world. It means an internal and external struggle, to make an effort to be a good Muslim (internal) and to defend the religion from outside danger (external). Military external *jihad* is permitted if other means have been unsuccessful to protect the Muslim religion and its followers. Many Muslims consider early wars against the Byzantine and Persian empires and against the Crusaders in the 11th and 12th centuries as examples of justified *jihad* activities. Unfortunately, the concept has been hijacked by some Islamist groups in the Middle East as an excuse for horrific violence against innocent people, including many fellow Muslims. Islamist groups fuse a radical political ideology, often violent, with a fundamentalist religious outlook.

The Islamic calendar, which is official only in Saudi Arabia, is very different from the Western one. It is a lunar calendar and its months are determined by the phases of

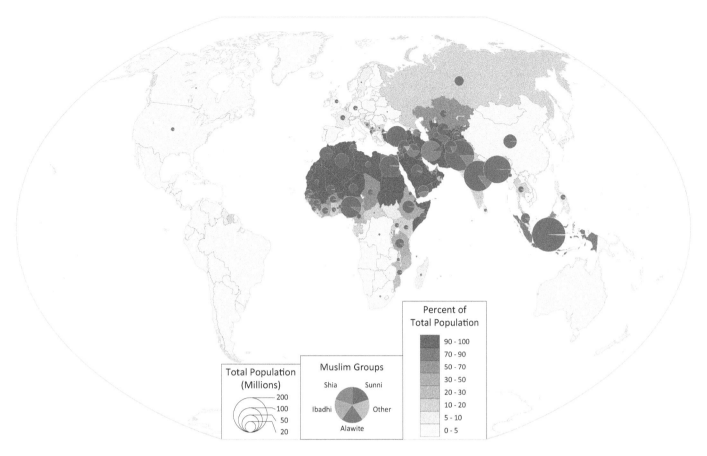

FIGURE 5.28 The world of Islam—Notice that the four largest Muslim countries in the world (Indonesia, Pakistan, India, and Bangladesh) are outside the Middle East. *Source:* Association of Religious Data Archives.

the moon. The Muslim year is divided into twelve months that are twenty-nine or thirty days long, and it is about eleven days shorter than the solar (Western) year. Consequently, Islamic months are not tied to seasons, and the same month can occur in any season over the span of about thirty years. The Islamic calendar begins on July 16, 622 CE of the Western calendar; this beginning marks Muhammad's migration from Mecca to Medina. The latter city, which is the second holiest site in Islam, is 340 kilometers (210 miles) north of Mecca and is the place to which Muhammad fled after being persecuted when he first began preaching what would become Islam in Mecca. The year 2018 of the Western calendar is 1439/1440 in the Islamic calendar. Fridays are holy days for Muslims, and government offices and many private businesses are closed for Friday–Saturday weekends in most countries in the Middle East. Lebanon, Morocco, Tunisia, and Turkey have Saturday–Sunday weekends, but longer Friday breaks are given for the mid-day prayer in these countries.

Islam, like every other major religion, is divided into branches (denominations or sects). There are two major Muslim groups, and the main difference between them—the

belief who is the rightful successor of Mohammad—is more political than theological. After Mohammad's death in 632 CE, one group of followers claimed that Mohammad, prior to his death, appointed his son-in-law Imam Ali as the leader of Islam. The other group rejected that claim and insisted that the leader should be appointed through consultation and election. The members of the former group became known as Shias and the latter as Sunnis. Shia Muslims comprise about 15 percent of the total Muslim population and are found mainly in Iran and Iraq. Smaller groups also live in Lebanon, Yemen, Syria, Bahrain, and other countries around the Arab/Persian Gulf. The Sunnis comprise a great majority (85 percent) of the Muslim population (Fig. 5.28). A third main school of Islam, called Ibadi, is dominant only in Oman. It is one of the oldest surviving denominations of Islam and predates the development of the Sunni and Shia schools.

Within these two main denominations, there are further branches. Wahhabism, for instance, is an especially rigid and austere form of Sunni Islam that is the dominant creed in Saudi Arabia. It stems from the teachings of a Muslim preacher who lived in the Najd region in the 17th century. Saudi Arabia's oil wealth in the last century

FIGURE 5.29 The major sacred places in Islam—Notice that five out of seven holy places for Shia Muslims are in Iraq.

and Indonesia. The leaders of Al Qaeda and the Taliban in Afghanistan have been influenced by Wahhabism.

Islam, like other religions, has several sacred places associated with various events in the life of its founder Mohammad or his successors. Mecca, Medina, and Jerusalem are the holiest places in Islam (Fig. 5.29). The city of Mecca is the birthplace of Mohammad and the place where he began to preach at the age of forty. The most important part of the city is the Grand Mosque and Kaaba, a cube-shaped structure covered with black silk fabric. Muslims believe that the Kaaba was built by Abraham. Only Muslims are allowed to enter this city, and highways leading to the city are clearly marked with signs indicating that all non-Muslims must exit before getting too close. The second holiest place in Islam is the city of Medina. It is the place of Mohammad's burial and the site of his last revelation. The three oldest mosques in the world are also located here. Only the sacred part of the city is closed to non-Muslims. Jerusalem is the third holy city for Muslims. According to Islamic beliefs, Mohammad journeyed to heaven one night, and this event took place in Jerusalem; the last judgement will also take place in this city. The Dome of the Rock on the Temple Mount is the main Muslim structure in Jerusalem. There are several additional holy places for Shia Muslims, including the city of Karbala in Iraq. It is a martyrdom site of one of the early Shia leaders, Hussein ibn Ali. Millions of pilgrims visit this city every year.

has enabled it to spread this severe form of Islam to communities around the world, especially through madrassas sponsored by the Saudi government in places like Pakistan

POLITICAL ORGANIZATION OF SPACE

The written human history began in the Middle East over 5,000 years ago, and two major ancient civilizations emerged over time, one in Mesopotamia and the other in Egypt. Both civilizations were river-based cultures and achieved a high degree of sophistication. Writing (*cuneiform* in Mesopotamia and *hieroglyphics* in Egypt), urban life, political organization, social stratification, and arts and sciences were present in both centers by 3000 BCE. The classical period of Middle Eastern history was associated with the unification of most of the region as the Persian Empire in the sixth century BCE, the Hellenistic Empire in the fourth century BCE, and the Roman Empire in the second century BCE. The medieval period gave birth to Islam, and the Islamic Empire made several important contributions to human history, including preserving the knowledge of ancient civilizations and making advances in agriculture, medicine, mathematics, and social sciences, including geography. The rise of the Ottoman Empire in

the 15th century, based in the strategically situated city of Constantinople (now Istanbul), was the beginning of modern Middle Eastern history. After achieving its peak by the middle of the 16th century, the empire entered a period of gradual decline, and by the end of the 19th century it became "the sick man of Europe."

The growing European influence in the region eventually led to the British, French, and Italian control of many parts of the Middle East. The French took control of Algeria (1830), Tunisia (1881), and Morocco (1906), and Italy took control of Libya (1911). Morocco was later divided into a French and a Spanish part. After unsuccessful French attempts (led by Napoleon Bonaparte) to control Egypt, the British eventually gained control of this ancient land by 1882. The British also took control of Sudan in 1896. As Western powers expanded their presence in the region, the Ottoman Empire's domain continued to contract. In the early 20th century, the crumbling empire joined Germany and the Austro-Hungarian Empire in World War I, a war for which it was poorly prepared. When the war ended, the empire fragmented; France took control of Lebanon and Syria, Great Britain of Iraq and Palestine; other smaller parts were given to Italy and Greece; other areas gained independence; and the remnant at the empire's core became the modern country of Turkey a few years later.

Independence came to most Arab countries in the 1950s and 1960s. Although the region was fragmented into numerous pieces politically, the strong linguistic and religious similarities across much of the Middle East inspired the popular ideology of Pan-Arabism. Its major objective was to unify Arab countries into a single political entity. President Gamal Abdel Nasser of Egypt was a strong proponent of this philosophy. A few efforts at unification briefly changed the map of the Middle East. Egypt and Syria formed the United Arab Republic in 1958 until they broke apart in 1961. Jordan and Iraq were united for six months as the Arab Federation in 1958. Libyan leader Qaddafi tried to promote the Pan-Arabic ideology in the 1970s by supporting the Federation of Arab Republics, composed of Libya, Egypt, and Syria. This union, formed in 1972, lasted five years. There have only been two enduring unification attempts in the Arab world so far. The United Arab Emirates, a federation of seven emirates, was formed in 1971, and North and South Yemen merged in 1990.

Another example of developing closer relations between the Arab states was the establishment of what is now known as the Arab League (1945). It originally consisted of six states: Egypt, Iraq, Jordan (formerly called Transjordan), Lebanon, Saudi Arabia, and Syria. This supra-national organization now has twenty-two members (Syria was suspended in 2011). The main objective of the Arab League, headquartered in Cairo, is to have closer relations and cooperation among member states, to protect member independence and sovereignty, and to consider the affairs and interests of Arab states.

The Gulf Cooperation Council, a narrower organization, is a political and economic organization of six Arab/Persian Gulf countries formed in 1981 to strengthen relations and promote cooperation (economic and military) among member states based on similar cultural (religious) identities.

The Jewish-Arab Conflict

The ethnic and religious confrontation between Jews and Arabs has been the major source of political instability in the Middle East for almost a century. It has resulted in many deaths and much suffering on both sides, extensive physical and economic destruction, stunted economic development, and waste of the region's human and physical resources. Several issues are at stake in this multi-dimensional confrontation, including Israel's right to exist, Israel's control of occupied territories, Palestinians' rights in the occupied territories, the status of Jerusalem, and access to water from the Jordan River.[5]

The origins of this conflict can be traced to an increased sense of nationalism among the Jews in Europe and Arabs in the Middle East. Jewish nationalism was expressed in a desire for a secular Jewish state in Palestine (the ancient Jewish Promised Land and by then a part of the Ottoman Empire). Frequent persecution of the Jews in Eastern Europe (and the Russian Empire) at the end of the 19th century resulted in a movement supporting the Jewish migration to Palestine. This movement, led by Hungarian Jew Theodor Herzl, who believed that the Jewish self-determination was possible only by establishing their own independent country, became known as **Zionism**. It encouraged a large-scale migration of "people without a land" (Jews) to "a land without people" (Palestine). Many Jews in Europe responded to this call and began moving to Palestine starting in the 1880s. Five major migration waves (*Aliyah*) occurred before World War II, totaling 410,000 people. The migrants began outnumbering the native Arabs in many parts of Palestine (which was not a "land without people") within the first three decades of this movement. In response, Arab resistance grew, leading to more frequent and violent clashes between the two groups.

After World War I and the dissolution of the Ottoman Empire, Palestine became a British mandate, meaning a British-administered territory. Near the end of the war, the British government had issued a one-paragraph letter known as the Balfour Declaration (1917) in which Britain promised to support the establishment of a Jewish state in Palestine while also protecting non-Jewish communities in the area. The declaration fostered increased Jewish immigration and laid part of the groundwork for what would ultimately become Israel.

After World War II, Great Britain gave up the control of Palestine and transferred its mandate to the newly formed United Nations in 1947. Hoping to please both sides, the United Nations partitioned Palestine into three parts, the Jewish part comprising 56 percent of the area, the Arab part (43 percent), and the International Zone of Jerusalem (1 percent). The Jewish parts included about 400,000 Arab residents while the Arab parts had 10,000 Jews. The Jews accepted this partition and the Arabs rejected it on the grounds that over half of the territory was granted to one-third of the population who owned only 7 percent of the land (Fig. 5.30 and Fig. 5.31).

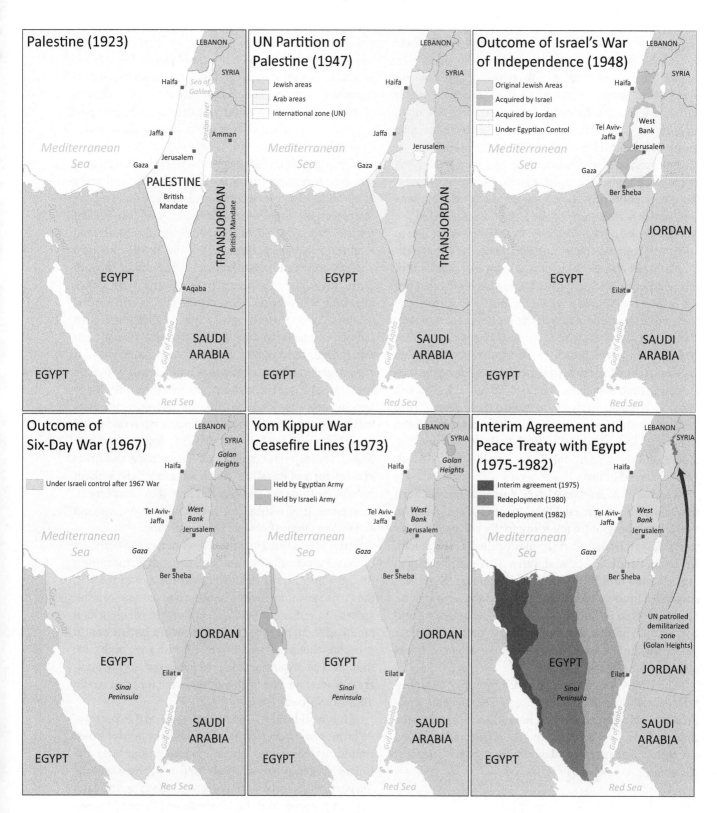

FIGURE 5.30 The Jewish-Arab conflict in maps—Drawn after similar maps found at the Israel Ministry of Foreign Affairs website.

After the Jewish parts proclaimed independence in 1948, the neighboring Arab countries (Egypt, Jordan, Lebanon, and Syria) and Iraq invaded the newly formed state of Israel. The War of Independence (1948–49), as it is known in Israel, lasted several months and ended in a Jewish victory and in the incorporation of about half of the Arab-controlled parts of Palestine into Israel. Jordan took control of the West Bank and Egypt of the Gaza Strip. The next

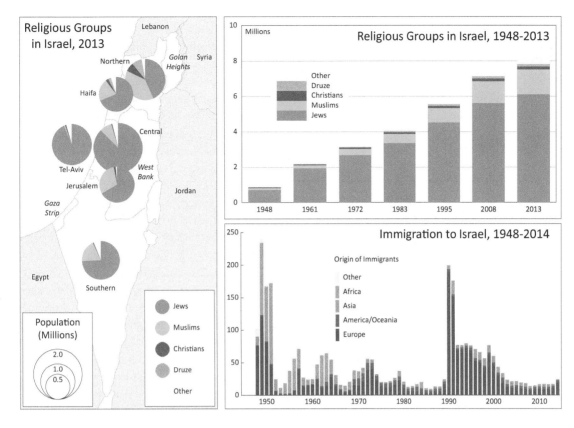

FIGURE 5.31 Israel: population composition by religion and immigration—Notice the growing proportion of Arabs since the establishment of the country and a sharp increase in Jewish immigration after the break-up of the Soviet Union in 1990. *Source:* Israel's Central Bureau of Statistics.

major Jewish-Arab conflict became known as the Six Day War (June 5–10, 1967), a war between Israel and its three neighbors, Egypt, Jordan, and Syria. In response to the growing Jewish-Arab tensions and Egyptian mobilization along the Israeli border, the Jewish state, in a series of surprise pre-emptive air strikes, destroyed most of the Egyptian air force and invaded the Gaza Strip and the Sinai Peninsula. After Syria and Jordan entered the war, Israeli counterattacks led to the occupation of the West Bank and East Jerusalem (taking those territories from Jordan) and the Golan Heights (seizing the highlands from Syria). The quick Israeli victory on multiple fronts reflected the element of surprise and well-executed military strategy on the part of Israel and the low quality of the Arab military leadership.

The tables were turned somewhat during the Yom Kippur War (1973), which began as a surprise attack by Egypt and Syria on the very important Jewish holiday of Yom Kippur and during Ramadan, a time of Muslim fasting. The Arab forces made some territorial advances in the first three days of the conflict, but the Israeli army was able to stop the advances, regain the briefly lost territories, make inroads toward Damascus, and cross the Suez Canal. A ceasefire was reached less than three weeks

later. In response to American military help for Israel in this conflict, the Arab members of the Organization of Petroleum Exporting Countries (OPEC) imposed an oil embargo on the United States that lasted for about five months.

One major indirect outcome of the 1973 war was the beginning of negotiations between Egypt and Israel, which culminated in the Camp David Accords of 1978. After thirteen days of talks (sponsored by the United States) known as the "Framework for Peace in the Middle East," both sides accepted an agenda for a peace treaty between Israel and Egypt as well as plans for Palestinian self-government in the West Bank and Gaza. The Egypt-Israel Peace Treaty of 1979, also sponsored by the United States, ended the state of war between the two countries. Israel withdrew from the Sinai Peninsula, and Egypt recognized Israel's right to exist and opened the Suez Canal for Israeli ships. In return for becoming the first Arab state to recognize Israel's sovereignty, Egypt gained significant U.S. support and has received many billions of dollars in U.S. aid since. However, the agreement cost the Egyptian president his life as Anwar Sadat, who had signed the treaty and shared the Nobel Peace Prize with Israel's leader in 1978, was assassinated in 1981.

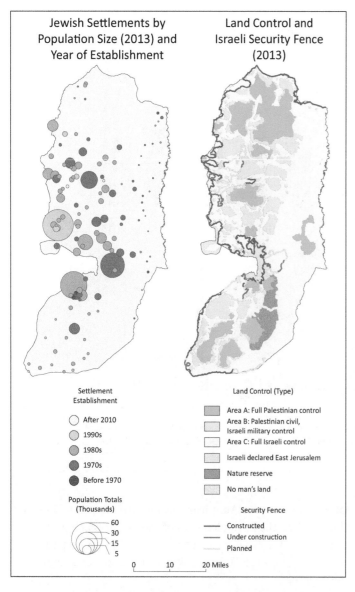

Jewish Settlements by Population Size (2013) and Year of Establishment

Land Control and Israeli Security Fence (2013)

Settlement Establishment

○ After 2010
○ 1990s
○ 1980s
● 1970s
● Before 1970

Population Totals (Thousands)

60
30
15
5

0   10   20 Miles

Land Control (Type)

Area A: Full Palestinian control
Area B: Palestinian civil, Israeli military control
Area C: Full Israeli control
Israeli declared East Jerusalem
Nature reserve
No man's land

Security Fence

Constructed
Under construction
Planned

FIGURE 5.32 The West Bank under Israeli occupation—The area has been under Israeli occupation since the Six Day War of 1967. Although some autonomy has since been given to the Palestinian residents, most of the West Bank is still under full Israeli control. *Source:* Humanitarian Response.

The U.S. was also the driving force behind negotiations that culminated in the Oslo Accords of 1993. Negotiated after several Arab states sided with the U.S. in the first Gulf War (which expelled Iraqi invaders from Kuwait), the accords included the mutual recognition of Israel and the Palestinian Liberation Organization (PLO) as well as plans for creating the Palestinian Authority with limited self-governing powers in the Israeli-occupied West Bank and Gaza. Hardliners on both sides rejected this agreement and, in 1995, Israeli Prime Minister Yitzak Rabin was assassinated by a radical opposed to the Oslo agreement.

Despite these and other hard-won agreements, the relationship between Israel and its neighbors remains tense and volatile, especially in the Occupied Territories. Several decades of Israeli occupation of the West Bank and Gaza and the displacement of many Arab residents from, and construction of Jewish settlements in, these territories have fueled deep enmity between these two groups (Fig. 5.32).

These tensions have been released in the form of popular uprisings among the Palestinians. The First Intifada (1987–1993) was caused by several factors, including the accelerated expropriation of the Palestinian land and construction of Israeli settlements in occupied areas and the dissatisfaction with the PLO leadership among younger Palestinian activists. The intifada, which means "shaking," often took the form of Palestinian youths throwing rocks at Israeli tanks and the Israelis firing back with live rounds and later with plastic bullets. This uprising resulted in some 2,000 deaths, overwhelmingly among the Palestinians. The Second Intifada (2000–2005) or Al-Aksa Intifada was more violent and led to over 4,000 deaths on both sides. Its direct cause was the Israeli Prime Minister's visit to the Temple Mount in Jerusalem (a sacred place for Muslims); the breakdown of a new round of Camp David talks also coincided with this uprising. During this intifada, militant Islamists among the Palestinians carried out numerous suicide bombings in Israel at restaurants, aboard buses, in train stations, and in dancing clubs. In response, Israeli forces destroyed whole neighborhoods in the Occupied Territories where the bomb-making was believed to be centered. Ultimately, Israel constructed a high wall separating the Jewish and Palestinian settlements in the West Bank to stop the suicide bombers, but the wall also separated many Palestinians from the jobs in Israel (Fig. 5.33).

A Conflict-Prone Region

Although the Jewish-Arab conflict has been the main source of political instability in the Middle East, it is hardly the only challenge. Israel's neighbor Lebanon, for instance, experienced decades of turbulence.

Religious, political, and economic inequalities were responsible for a disastrous civil war in Lebanon (1975–1990). The problem was magnified by the presence of many Palestinian refugees in that country, an outcome of the 1967 Six Day War and internal conflict in Jordan in 1970. Although the Lebanese are Arabs, they are divided along religious lines. The 1932 census, conducted by the French colonial authorities, revealed that about 60 percent of the population was Christian and 40 percent Muslim. Each group was divided into several denominations. When Lebanon

FIGURE 5.33 The wall separating the Jewish and Palestinian settlements in the West Bank—The construction of this controversial Israeli project began in 2000 and has not yet been completed. Israel considers it necessary for protecting the Jewish settlements against Palestinian terrorist attacks while the Palestinians see it as an attempt to annex parts of their land by Israel and legalize residential segregation of their people. *Source:* Wikimedia Commons.

proclaimed independence from France, the National Pact of 1943, an unwritten compromise between both groups, allocated political power in the parliament on the basis of religion: six to five in favor of Christians. Furthermore, the country's president would always be a Maronite Christian, its prime minister a Sunni Muslim, the speaker of the parliament a Shia Muslim, and the deputy prime minister a Greek Orthodox Christian. This type of fixed distribution of power plan was supposed to prevent any future problems caused by religious diversity. However, the Muslim population had been growing at a faster rate, comprising about 60 percent of the total population by the early 1970s. Despite its numerical majority, it still had less political and economic power than the Christian minority. Tensions between both groups began to increase and developed into a civil war after a series of tit-for-tat killings. The fifteen-year conflict went through several phases characterized by fighting between various religious and political groups (sometimes switching sides), as well as the involvement of Syrian and Israeli troops. The Taif Agreement of 1989, by changing the power-sharing formula to fifty-fifty, eventually ended this conflict that had caused about 120,000 deaths and the displacement of 1 million people.

The Iraq-Iran War (1980–88) was the outcome of a long animosity between the two countries that intensified after the 1979 Iranian Revolution. The Iraqi secular government feared that the Iranian Revolution, which established a theocratic government in Tehran strongly influenced by Shia Muslim ideology, might inspire the suppressed Iraqi Shias to attempt the same in Baghdad. Iraq also hoped to take advantage of the chaotic situation in Iran during the early stages of the Revolution. A border dispute along the 120-mile (193-kilometer) long Shatt-al-Arab waterway was one of major reasons for the Iraqi invasion of Iran in 1980. Iraqi hopes of quick victory did not materialize, however, and the conflict became an eight-year long stalemate. War casualties exceeded 1 million and were especially heavy among young Iranians. Economic impacts, on the other hand, were more severe in Iraq. The war calamity was worsened by the fact that most population and economic resources in both countries were found near the common border. The Iraq-Iran war was the longest conventional conflict in the 20th century; it favored Iraq due to its more advanced military technology (acquired with financial help from Saudi Arabia, Kuwait, and other Arab states); and it was characterized by the implementation of new military strategies, including indiscriminate missile attacks on populated places, widespread use of chemical weapons, and attacks on oil tankers of neutral countries.

Two years after the end of the Iraq-Iran war, Iraq again invaded a neighboring country—this time the small country of Kuwait. Kuwaiti refusal to cancel Iraq war debts was one of the reasons, but Iraq always considered Kuwait a part of its territory that was made an independent country by the British. Additionally, by invading Kuwait, Iraq also hoped to gain access to more oil and expand its power in the region. The United Nations condemned the invasion, imposed trade sanctions, and demanded Iraq's withdrawal. In response, Iraq annexed Kuwait. These developments alarmed the United States. Fear of losing access to a significant portion of world oil reserves prompted the United States to form a military coalition of NATO and some Arab states to liberate Kuwait. The First Gulf War (1990–91) consisted of two stages. Operation Desert Shield was a military buildup to protect Saudi Arabia from possible Iraqi invasion, and the purpose of Desert Storm was to liberate Kuwait and destroy the Iraqi military and selected civilian infrastructure. The first objective of Desert Storm was accomplished in less than four days. A ceasefire between Iraq and the coalition forces called for Iraqi recognition of Kuwait's independence and destruction of all weapons of mass destruction (that Iraq was believed to possess or be developing) and short-range missiles.

Tensions between the U.S. and Iraq remained high throughout the 1990s. The United States and its allies imposed a no-fly zone over Northern Iraq to protect the Kurds and Southern Iraq to protect the Shia population. The United Nations implemented economic sanctions to prevent the development of any weapons of mass destruction, and the UN inspectors were in charge of monitoring Iraqi compliance. In the wake of the September 11, 2001

attacks in the U.S., and the subsequent American-led invasion of Afghanistan, the U.S. and several of its allies raised concerns that Iraq was close to possessing nuclear weapons technology. In early 2003, the United States issued an ultimatum to Hussein to step down and leave the country within forty-eight hours. When he refused to do so, American and allied forces invaded Iraq, and the Second Gulf War began. The capital city of Baghdad was taken in less than three weeks and the entire country within five weeks. Chaos and looting of government and public property characterized the first few weeks of the U.S. occupation of Iraq. Various paramilitary groups were formed and sectarian violence, which erupted in many parts of the country, marked the beginning of the Iraqi civil war. Violence against the U.S. troops had also increased, and restoring law and order was a difficult task for the occupying forces. Nevertheless, an election to form a transitional assembly to write a new constitution was held in 2005. These developments were followed by a general election (also in 2005) to elect members of a permanent parliament. In 2008, the Iraqi government reached an agreement with the United States to withdraw the U.S. troops from that country by the end of 2010. The last American troops left Iraq in 2011. However, the country remains divided along sectarian lines and is among the most violent places on Earth. After the Second Gulf War, some outsiders, including then-U.S. senator and later vice president Joe Biden, advocated dividing the country into a Kurdish northeast, Shia south, and Sunni west; but that idea never advanced far, partly because the Sunni-dominated regions lack oil and would not be economically viable if separated.

One country in the region that has been divided is Sudan. Before 2011 Sudan was the largest country in Africa and an example of a country deeply divided by language and religion. A long-running civil war in which millions died culminated in the predominantly Christian and non-Arabic-speaking South Sudan gaining independence that year, the new (Northern) Sudan became a more ethnically and religiously uniform country than the former Sudan, yet the remnant Sudan is still divided. In particular, tensions between pastoral nomads of Arabic origin and sedentary farmers of African descent led to the conflict in Darfur (in the western part of the country) in 2003 (Fig. 5.34). Desertification and drought had pushed the pastoral nomads in their quest for water and grazing lands into the non-Arab areas. The Muslim nomadic rebel groups, known as **Janjaweed**, were supported by the Sudanese government in their fight against the African farmers (who were also Muslims). The rebels were accused of ethnic cleansing and genocide, and the Sudanese president was indicted for war

FIGURE 5.34 Sudan: the Darfur region.

crimes and crimes against humanity by the International Criminal Court. However, as of 2018 Omar al-Bashir is still in charge of Sudan, and several attempts to arrest him have been unsuccessful.

Unfortunately, the conflicts described above do not exhaust the list of recent and current violent disputes in the region.[6] Turkey has been engaged in a decades-long struggle with Kurdish groups in the country's southeast. Affiliates of Al Qaeda have carried out terrorist attacks since the 1990s in Algeria, Tunisia, Saudi Arabia, and other countries. Morocco has been at war with secessionists in lightly populated Western Sahara. The list goes on. While conflict has been an unhappy commonality across the Middle East for a long time, the level of instability has risen since the 2011 Arab Spring, a popular uprising that was initially hailed across the world as signaling a turn toward democracy in the region.

The Arab Spring and Its Aftermath

The **Arab Spring** was a revolutionary wave of demonstrations and protests against authoritarian rule, government corruption, human rights violations, sectarianism, and economic problems, such as inflation and unemployment, across the Arab world. The protesters called for democracy, free and fair elections, respect of human rights, and new governments and leaders. This movement took various forms, from demonstrations, Internet activism, and civil disobedience to riots, urban warfare, and uprisings. It began in Tunisia at the end of 2010, after a young man set himself on fire in protest against corruption among the police and other local government branches, and rapidly spread throughout the region. In Tunisia, the protests led to President Ben Ali's resignation (after twenty-three years in power) and his exile in Saudi Arabia. He was later sentenced to life in prison in absentia. The country held its first democratic election in 2011 and a moderate Islamic party won 41 percent of votes. Although democracy has been introduced to Tunisia, tensions between various secular and religious groups continue.[7]

Similarly, but on a much larger scale, street protests in Egypt forced President Hosni Mubarak to step down after thirty years in power. He was also later convicted of abuse of power, but the sentence was overturned on appeal. After his resignation, a military council assumed power. The subsequent elections brought to power an Islamic party, the Muslim Brotherhood. Its leader became the president in 2012, and he quickly revoked a military decree limiting his power, dissolved the parliament, and changed the military leadership. Public opposition to President Mohamed Morsi's

rule began to grow after he issued a decree granting himself far-reaching powers and proposed a new constitution that was strongly influenced by Islamic interests. In a violent response, many leaders and supporters of the Muslim Brotherhood were jailed or killed in street protests. A new constitution was introduced in 2014, and the new elections brought to power the former head of the country's armed forces, General Abdel Fattah Al-Sisi. So, Egypt returned to where it had been before the Arab Spring: with a former general in charge of a totalitarian government.

In neighboring Libya, President Muammar Qaddafi, who ruled the country for forty years, used force against street protesters. A particularly harsh response against the protesters sparked a civil war, and the country fell into chaos as violence among various paramilitary groups intensified. Unfortunately, the removal from power and death of Qaddafi in 2011 have not brought peace and stability to this country. Libya is now controlled by two major opposing groups, one (Islamist) based in Tripoli in the western part of the country and the other (democratically elected and internationally recognized) in Tobruk in the eastern part.

Yemen is another example of a country in which the Arab Spring events led to the removal of a leader from power; a leader who, as in the three previous cases, had ruled the country for quite a long time. Unlike in Libya, anti-government protests were fairly well organized and relatively peaceful at the beginning. President Ali Abdullah Saleh, who had ruled the country for over thirty years, made some concessions and promised not to run for office again, but the protesters were not persuaded by those moves. Continued protests eventually led to violence, and the president hardened his position. An explosion in the presidential palace wounded Saleh, and he was taken to Saudi Arabia for treatment. He later resigned and his successor proposed to make Yemen a looser federation with more regional autonomy for minority groups. In response, the Houthis, a Shia Muslim group living in the northern part of the country and comprising about a third of the total population, rebelled and took control of some military bases and eventually moved to the capital city of Sana. The Houthis had enjoyed self-rule before 1962 and were now fighting for protection of their religious and cultural rights. After their challenge to the Sunni government, Saudi Arabia became involved in this conflict by offering help to the besieged president (who later resigned). It formed a coalition of Gulf States and launched an air campaign and later sent ground troops against the Houthis. The Saudi involvement was also prompted by fears that Iran was supporting the Houthi rebellion. Several other insurgent groups, including Al-Qaeda on the Arabian Peninsula, are also active in Yemen.

The conflict in Syria has been the most tragic out-come of the Arab Spring to date. It has led to the death of at least 250,000 people, 4 million refugees, and 10 million internally displaced persons. It began in 2011 after fifteen children were arrested and some tortured for anti-government graffiti. This action generated public protests followed by violence. The Syrian conflict is perhaps the most complex case as there are many key players in this civil war. The country has been ruled by the Assad family for over thirty-five years; Hafez Assad was in charge of the country from 1971 to 2000 and his son Bashir since that time. Both rulers, members of the Alawite group (a Shia branch of Islam), were accused of numerous atrocities against the Syrian civilians. In the civil war, the Assad government has received strong support from Iran (a predominantly Shia country), Hezbollah (a Shia military group in Lebanon), and Russia (Assad's long-time supporter). The anti-government camp is composed of the Free Syrian Army, a military force under the leadership of defected officers from the government forces, and the Syrian Democratic Forces, an alliance of the Kurdish and other ethnic groups of Eastern Syria. The Islamic State of Iraq and Syria (ISIS) and the Al-Nusra Front are Sunni-inspired terrorist groups controlling mainly central parts of Syria. The Syrian Democratic Forces have been more engaged in conflict with ISIS than the government forces. Turkey, the United States, and some other countries have also been helping the anti-government forces, although this help has sometimes been inconsistent.

The origins of the **Islamic State (IS)**, also known as the **Islamic State in Iraq and Syria (ISIS)**, the **Islamic State in Iraq and the Levant (ISIL)**, or *Daesh* in Arabic, go back to 2004 when a Jordanian national Abu Musab Al-Zarqawi formed Al-Qaeda in Iraq, a military opposition group to the Iraqi government and foreign control of the country. After the death of its founder in 2006, the group merged with several smaller groups and renamed itself as the Islamic State of Iraq. It quickly expanded its control over parts of Iraq and Eastern Syria, established headquarters in Al-Raqqah (Syria), and renamed itself as the Islamic State of Iraq and Syria. This Sunni (mainly Wahhabi) inspired group wanted to return to a pure form of Islam, imposed strict Sharia law on the controlled territory, established religious police to eliminate any kind of vice, imposed mandatory attendance at Friday prayers, brutally treated its opponents and many other innocent people (frequent use of capital punishment), and used social media (videos) to spread its message. It declared a caliphate (religious state) on its territory and began performing some basic government functions such as the collection of taxes and the provision of basic services and education. For a time, it generated millions of dollars

per day from oil wells in territory it controlled. ISIS unrelenting and brutal persecution of other religious groups (Christians, Shia Muslims, and Yazidis) and destruction of sacred sites alarmed the international community, and there was a growing pressure to take action against it. The United States, and later other countries, began targeting the group in 2014. By the end of 2017, it had lost almost all of its territory. However, the provocative social media presence and notoriety of ISIS has inspired many deadly terrorist attacks in other parts of the world from San Bernardino, California to Manchester, England to the southern Philippines. The conflict in Syria and other parts of the Middle East has led to an exodus of millions of civilians who became refugees or internally displaced persons. Syria has gained the unfortunate distinction as the world's top source of refugees. Many have made it to an uncertain future in Europe, but most have fled to neighboring countries in the Middle East, imposing a heavy burden on the region's weak governments.

Geostrategic Location: Chokepoints

The geostrategic importance of the Middle East is further increased by the presence of several chokepoints. These are internationally significant waterways; they tend to be narrow and shallow and are located close to or in politically unstable areas. Their closure (even temporary) to maritime transportation would have great economic impact on the entire world as it would disrupt trade flows, particularly of energy resources, and increase transportation costs. There are several major chokepoints in this region (Fig. 5.35).

The Suez Canal, a 305-kilometer (190-mile) long canal completed in 1869 by Great Britain and France, connects the Mediterranean and Red Seas. It shortens the travel between Europe and the Arab/Persian Gulf region by more than half. The canal has been widened a few times since its reopening, and it can now handle traffic in both directions at the same time. About fifty-five ships pass through it every day. Northbound traffic is mainly Middle Eastern oil destined for Western Europe while southbound traffic is a more diverse mixture of manufactured goods and grain from Europe and North America to East and South Asia (Fig. 5.36). The Strait of Hormuz connects the Arab/Persian Gulf with the Indian Ocean between Iran and Oman. It is approximately 53 kilometers (33 miles) wide in its narrowest part and considered the most important chokepoint in the world. Navigation is difficult and limited to two one-way channels (each less than 3.2 kilometers or 2 miles wide). A "tanker war" between Iraq and Iran took place during

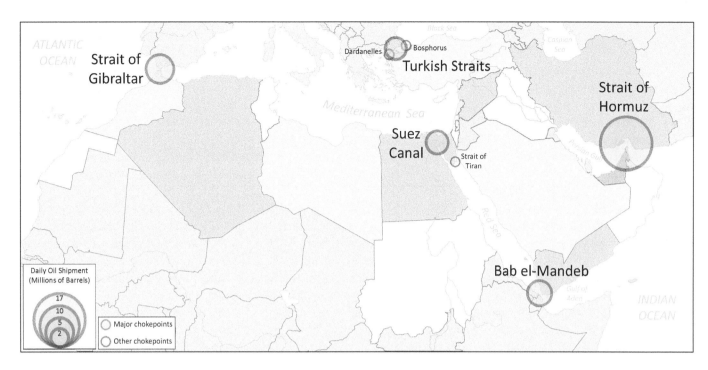

FIGURE 5.35 Major choke points in the Middle East. *Source:* U.S. Energy Information Administration.

FIGURE 5.36 The Suez Canal, Egypt—Completed by the British and French in 1869, it greatly shortens the shipping distance between Europe and parts of Asia and Africa. It was closed to navigation for about eight years after the Six Day War of 1967. *Source:* Pixabay.

the 1980–88 conflict between the two countries—each country tried to prevent shipment of oil from its adversary by attacking oil tankers belonging to other countries. Iran also threatened to close the strait by mining it. Today about 85 percent of all Arab/Persian Gulf oil, most of it destined for Asia, is shipped through the strait. The Turkish Straits consist of two waterways, the Bosporus and Dardanelles, connecting the Black and Mediterranean Seas. The Bosporus Strait is 29 kilometers (18 miles) long but only one kilometer (0.6 miles) wide in its narrowest part, and the Dardanelles is about 60 kilometers (37 miles) long and over 4.8 kilometers (3 miles) wide. Both straits separate the European and Asian parts of Turkey, and they are the only maritime route to the rest of the world for several countries on the Black Sea. The Turkish Straits were very important for the Soviet Union during the Cold War. By admitting Turkey to NATO in 1952, the United States could monitor the movement of the Soviet navy through these channels. The Strait of Bab el-Mandeb connects the Red Sea with the Indian Ocean. It is 32 kilometers (20 miles) wide, but navigation is limited to two over three-kilometer (two-mile) wide channels. The strategic importance of this waterway for the United States has significantly increased in recent years as some aircraft carriers were stationed in the Red Sea during the Gulf wars. The Strait of Gibraltar is one of the best known chokepoints. It connects the Mediterranean Sea with the Atlantic Ocean and separates Europe from Africa.

Water Conflicts

Since freshwater is a scarce resource in the Middle East and demand for it has been growing in this dry part of the world, concerns about a possible conflict over access to it have been on the minds of many individuals in the region and beyond.[8] The ingredients for a conflict over water are present in the hostile relations among many Middle Eastern countries and the multiple cases where two or more countries are dependent on the same water source (rivers in particular). As discussed earlier in this chapter, the two major river systems, the Nile and the Tigris-Euphrates, are principal sources of water for several countries (Egypt, Sudan in the case of the former; Iraq, and parts of Syria and Turkey in the latter), and these countries have no choice but to cooperate in utilizing this water. Agreements governing the Nile River's water have generally favored Egypt. The 1929 agreement between Egypt and Sudan called for providing 48 and 4 billion cubic meters (12.6 and 1 trillion gallons), or 92 and 8 percent, of water for both areas respectively. The flow of the river in dry seasons was reserved

for Egypt, which also had the right to monitor the flow in upstream countries. It could develop projects without consent of other countries but had the right to veto any project that negatively affected its interests. A more equitable agreement signed in 1959 gave 34 percent of the water to Sudan. Egypt's right to build the Aswan High Dam and store the flow water for the entire year was affirmed, while Sudan could build the Rosaries Dam on the Blue Nile and other irrigation or hydroelectric projects to utilize its share of water.

The waters of the Tigris-Euphrates Rivers system are shared by Turkey, Syria, and Iraq. The Turkish control of both rivers' headwaters and its ambitious plan of utilizing them for irrigation and electricity generation had caused some tensions between the three neighbors. The Southeastern Anatolian Project (known by the acronym GAP in Turkish) has been in development since the 1980s and calls for building twenty-two dams and nineteen hydroelectric power stations on both rivers and their tributaries to expand irrigation and electricity generation. It will double the area of irrigated land in Turkey and provide a fifth of the country's energy needs. It is also supposed to lead to economic development of Southeastern Turkey, one of the least developed parts of the country. However, its critics say that the project may further increase tensions with the two neighbors as well as displace many people (mainly Kurds) and worsen the already tense relations between the government in Ankara and the Kurdish population.

The Jordan River is a relatively short stream by American standards, about 355 kilometers (220 miles) long, that originates in Southern Lebanon and runs through the Sea of Galilee to the Dead Sea. It was also a border line between Israel and Jordan along a part of its course after 1948 and between the West Bank and Jordan after the 1967 Six Day War. The river basin area is shared by Israel (10 percent), Jordan (40 percent), Syria (37 percent), the Palestinian territory (9 percent), and Lebanon (4 percent). Israel built a series of canals, pipes, reservoirs, and pumping stations about 130 kilometers (80 miles) in length to transfer water from the Sea of Galilee to central and southern parts of the country. The National Water Carrier, initiated in 1953 and completed in 1964, provides up to 1.7 million cubic meters of water per day, most of it (80 percent) for irrigation. In response to this project, the Arab states proposed the Jordan Headwater Diversion Plan in the same year. It called for diverting 20 to 30 million cubic meters (5.3 to 7.9 billion gallons) of water from the Jordan River to Syria and Jordan as well as reducing the capacity of Israel's National Water Carrier by one-third and the country's water supply by over 10 percent. This led to a series of military confrontations between Israel and its neighbors and eventually to the Six Day War of 1967.

Israel destroyed these water diversion schemes after taking control of the Golan Heights from Syria. It also used water as a weapon in dealing with the Palestinians in the occupied West Bank. Their irrigation pumps were destroyed or confiscated, and they were prevented from using water from the Jordan River, had restrictions on using water from existing irrigation wells, and could not secure permits for new ones. These conditions existed until the mid-1990s when Israel recognized Palestinian water rights.

Most countries of the Arabian Peninsula have particularly limited freshwater supplies, and some, including Israel, obtain a large portion of their freshwater from desalination plants. The Ras al-Khair plant on the Eastern Saudi coast, just south of the city of Jubail, is the largest facility of this type in the world and produces 1 million cubic meters of water a day. About half of Saudi Arabia's water needs are met by over thirty desalination plants. The country is currently building the largest solar-powered desalination plant in the world near the city of Khafi on the Arab/Persian Gulf coast, which will provide 60,000 cubic meters (15.8 million gallons) of water a day. Israel is another Middle Eastern country that relies on water from such plants. About 80 percent of its domestic water needs are now met by five desalination plants.

ECONOMIC ACTIVITIES

Regional Contrasts in Development

The Middle Eastern countries can be divided into several groups with respect to the natural resource endowment and levels of development. First, there are six oil-rich countries in the Arab/Persian Gulf region: Bahrain, Kuwait, Oman, Qatar, Saudi Arabia, and the United Arab Emirates. These countries, with relatively small populations and large reserves of oil, have high per capita incomes, ranging from $34,000 to $100,000 (Fig. 5.37). Agriculture is not well developed and all these countries are food importers. Next, four poorer oil-exporting countries include Iran, Iraq, Algeria, and Libya. Although they have large deposits of oil (particularly Iran and Iraq), larger populations and histories of significant political instability and violence lower their income per capita to a third or a quarter of that of the previous group of countries. Third, the medium-developed countries of Morocco, Tunisia, Lebanon, Syria, Egypt, and Cyprus are characterized by a more balanced structure of their economies, although the service sector is the major contributor to the GDP. The income per capita ranges from $5,000 to $25,000 Cyprus and Lebanon are the most developed in this group. Recent political instability in Syria has put that country at the bottom of this group in terms of GDP per capita. The poor nations of the Middle East are Jordan, Yemen, Sudan, the Palestinian territories, and Western Sahara with a GDP per capita below 3,000 dollars. They have very little or no oil, and relatively fast growing populations offset any economic gains. The agricultural sector still plays an important role in the national economies and employs a relatively large portion of their labor force (almost 50 percent in Sudan). Finally, there are two countries with diverse economies, Turkey and Israel. Turkey is the largest economic power in the Middle East, but Israel is the most developed country in this region, and its level of development is similar to that of many Western countries. Both countries have a strong agricultural sector, a diverse industrial base, and close economic ties with Europe and other developed regions.

Agriculture and Irrigation

Considering the dominance of dry climates, it is not surprising that agricultural land occupies a small proportion (less than 8 percent) of the total land area in the Middle East (Fig. 5.38). Yet, agriculture is still the main source of living for one-fifth of the region's population. Three major types of farming are found in the Middle East: (1) the cultivation of rain-fed crops in humid and semi-humid regions of Turkey, Iran, the Atlas Mountains

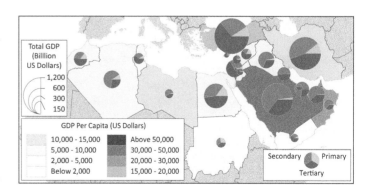

FIGURE 5.37 Gross domestic product by sector and per capita in the Middle Eastern countries, 2014. *Source:* CIA World Factbook 2014.

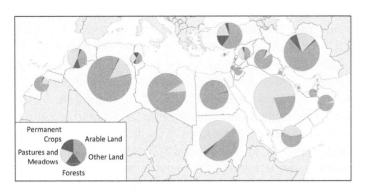

FIGURE 5.38 Land use patterns in the Middle East—The size of each pie chart is proportional to the country's land area. The large percentage of pastures and meadows in Saudi Arabia should be taken with some caution since most of the country is a desert. *Source:* CIA World Factbook 2014.

in Morocco, the Levant, and southwestern parts of the Arabian Peninsula; (2) irrigated farming in river valleys and parts of the Sahara and the Arabian Peninsula; and (3) livestock herding (pastoralism) in dry and semi-dry areas throughout the entire region. The first type is characterized by extensive small grain farming (mainly wheat, barley, millet, and sorghum) during the more humid (cool) season (Fig. 5.39). Wheat and barley are dominant crops in the northern parts of the region (Turkey, Iran, and the Atlas Mountains), while millet is prevalent in the hotter and drier southern regions, mainly Sudan and Yemen.

Mediterranean agriculture, another type of farming, is well known for the winter cultivation of small grains (mainly wheat) and horticulture, the cultivation of vegetables, fruits and nuts, often for export. Citrus fruits (mainly oranges), grapes, and olives are dominant crops, but figs and even bananas are grown on a smaller scale. A variety of nut tree orchards (hazelnuts, pistachios, and walnuts) can be found at higher and cooler places, mainly in Turkey and Iran. The olive tree is well adapted to the Mediterranean

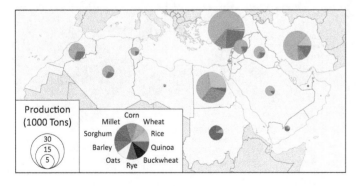

FIGURE 5.39 Production of major cereals in the Middle East, 2005–2013. *Source:* FAOSTAT.

region. It can grow in many types of soil, in rocky and hilly terrain (although it does not tolerate frost), and can produce, on average, ninety pounds of fruit every other year. It is also well known for its longevity—some trees may be 2,000 years old. Relatively small, humid parts of Turkey along the Black Sea and Northwestern Iran, areas with no dry season grow corn, tea, rice, and tobacco. The western slopes of the Asir Mountains in the southwestern part of the Arabian Peninsula, another small area with year-round precipitation, grows sorghum, coffee, and *khat* (*qat*). *Khat* is a flowering, slow-growing shrub whose leaves can be chewed for stimulating effects. It is very popular in Yemen, and its cultivation is the main source of income for many farmers. The area under *khat* cultivation has been rapidly increasing in recent years.

A typical farm in most Middle Eastern countries is very small by American standards, and its average size has been shrinking since at least the 1960s. The average farm size is just over 3 hectares (less than 8 acres). Very small farms (less than 1 hectare/2 acres) account for almost 60 percent of all landholdings but occupy less than 6 percent of the total farmland. Farm fragmentation is particularly acute in Egypt.

An interesting part of Israeli agriculture is the presence of two types of collective rural communities, *kibbutz* and *moshav*, which are, to some extent, similar to the collective farms established in the former Soviet Union. They began as utopian Jewish settlements based on socialist and Zionist ideas. A **kibbutz** (plural: *kibbutzim*) is a collective enterprise (predominantly agricultural) based on common ownership of resources and on the pooling of labor, income, and expenditure. In a traditional *kibbutz*, every member is expected to work to the best of his/her ability and is paid no wages but is supplied by the enterprise with all the necessary goods and services. It is based on voluntary action and mutual liability, equal rights, and full material responsibility for all its members. The first *kibbutz* was established by early Jewish immigrants to Palestine in 1921.[9] Their number and size had been increasing until the peak in 1989. There were 267 *kibbutzim* in Israel at the end of 2013, and they accounted for about 40 percent of the country's agricultural output. Some *kibbutzim* have been privatized in recent years. A moshav (plural: *moshavim*) is similar to the *kibbutz* collective settlement with one main difference—individual land ownership (but farms are equal in size). The first such settlement was established in 1921, and today Israel has over four hundred with stable numbers (unlike that of *kibbutzim*).

Irrigation is essential for growing crops in most parts of the Middle East; it was first invented there and has been practiced for thousands of years (Fig. 5.40 and

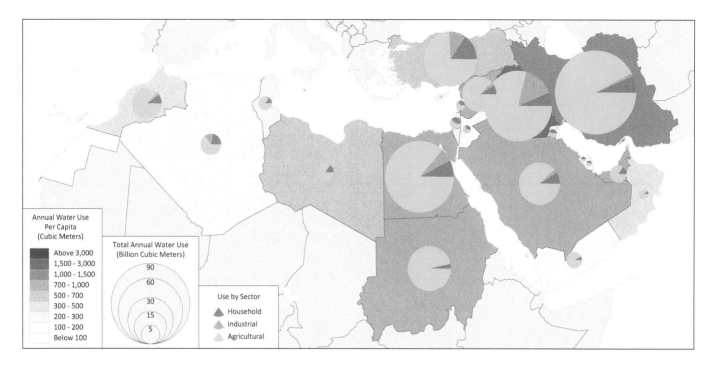

FIGURE 5.40 Fresh water usage in the Middle East, 2012—Notice the importance of irrigation in every country. At least 75 percent of freshwater, and in some cases much more, is used for agriculture in most countries. *Source:* FAOSTAT.

Fig. 5.41). Water for irrigation has been obtained from three sources: rivers, groundwater, and springs. The Nile and Tigris-Euphrates rivers, as well as many smaller streams, have sustained farming activities in Egypt, Mesopotamia, and other parts of the region since the beginning of written human history. The previously mentioned ancient description of Egypt as "the gift of the Nile" accurately reflects its dependence on water for survival. Groundwater found in aquifers and obtained through wells, some several hundred feet deep, is the second most important source of

FIGURE 5.41 An irrigation canal in Egypt—Irrigation is essential for farming activities in most parts of the Middle East where at least 75 percent of freshwater is used for that purpose. *Source:* Heike C. Alberts.

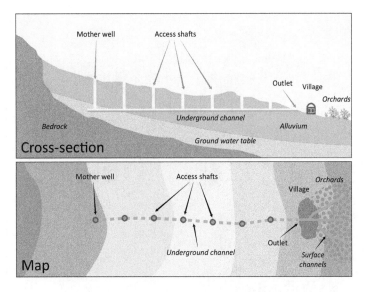

FIGURE 5.42 Profile of a qanat—Drawn after a similar image at Researchgate (www.researchgate.net/figure/242729587_fig1_Figure-1-Diagram-of-a-karez-qanat-in-cross-section-and-aerial-view).

water for farming in the Middle East. Agriculture in some parts of the Levant, the Maghreb, or the Arabian Peninsula would be impossible without access to this source of water. Springs, where water naturally comes to the surface, support human settlements and farming activities in many oases of the Sahara and the Arabian Peninsula. Several major irrigation methods and devices have been used by Middle Eastern farmers.

Basin irrigation had been practiced in the Nile River Valley and Delta for thousands of years, and Egyptian farmers were completely dependent on it for their survival.[10] Fields along the low banks of the river were divided into artificial basins by earth edges. Flood waters full of silt filled the basins during the flood stage in late summer and were kept there by the closure of ridge gates for six to eight weeks. The standing water gradually deposited a rich layer of sediment. After the standing water was drained away,

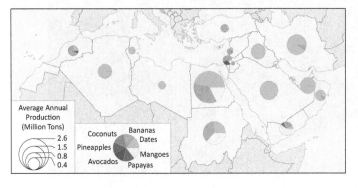

FIGURE 5.43 Production of selected fruits in the Middle East, 2000–2012—Notice the importance of dates in most countries. *Source:* FAOSTAT.

the field was ready for sowing and planting. This irrigation method had several disadvantages. The major one was that only one crop could be grown per year. Another problem was that fields located at slightly higher elevations could not be irrigated during less intensive floods. Basin irrigation was replaced by perennial irrigation after the completion of the Aswan High Dam and the creation of the Lake Nasser reservoir in 1970. Although fields can now be irrigated throughout the year, farmers have to depend on commercial fertilizers to maintain soil fertility since the flood water no longer carries any silt. The major advantages of perennial irrigation are the expansion of cultivable land and the possibility of harvesting two or even three crops from the same field. However, more intense soil erosion has been observed as water without silt runs faster.

In hilly and mountainous regions of the Middle East, water can be collected through a system of underground canals connected with the surface by a series of vertical wells. This system, known as **qanat**, probably originated in present-day Iran in the seventh century BCE and has spread throughout the region and beyond. It is usually found in areas with no major perennial rivers, pockets of fertile soil, dry climates with high evaporation rates, and deep aquifers (too deep for traditional water wells). Although *qanats* are associated with high construction and maintenance costs, very little water is lost due to evaporation. There were some 50,000 *qanats* in Iran at the beginning of the 20th century, but their number has decreased to about 20,000 today (Fig. 5.42).

A variety of plants can be grown on irrigated land, from grains to vegetables, fruits, and commercial crops. Climate, soil, terrain, cultural, and economic factors determine the type of cultivation. Wheat, corn, rice, and barley are the main grain crops. Date palms are common fruit trees in river valleys and other areas where water is accessible. They were domesticated in the Middle East and are well adapted to dry climate. Date palms require plenty of groundwater for growing and hot dry weather for producing fruit. A single plant can produce 150 to 300 pounds of fruit per harvest. It can also be a source of construction materials and fiber for making baskets and mats. Over 88 percent of world's date production comes from the Middle East. Egypt, Iran, and Saudi Arabia are the largest producers today (Fig. 5.43 and Fig. 5.44). Among specialty crops, cotton, tobacco, and sugar cane play the dominant role. Egyptian cotton is known for its high quality and demand around the world.

Livestock herding plays an important role in every part of the Middle East, and in most cases it is still the main subsistence activity. Although sheep and goats are the most common animals, cattle herding is developed on a larger scale in Turkey and Iran. The absence of hogs is

FIGURE 5.44 Date palm fruits—Date palms are well adapted to dry and hot climate but also require large amounts of water for growing and producing fruits. Dates used to be an important source of food for desert travelers. *Source:* Pixabay.

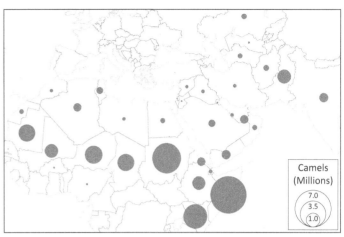

FIGURE 5.45 Camel population in the Middle East and surrounding areas, 2012. *Source:* FAOSTAT.

noticeable in most of the region except Cyprus and, to a lesser degree, in Israel, Lebanon, and Egypt. Dry climate and religious restrictions have prevented large-scale hog raising. Pigs do not do well in hot-dry climates, and Muslims and Jews do not eat pork. On the other hand, camels are well adapted to desert conditions and can be found in most parts of the Middle East. Contrary to popular belief, however, countries in the northern part of Sub-Saharan Africa and Pakistan have more camels than all Middle Eastern state except Sudan (Fig. 5.45). They need water and pasture every three or four days in the hot season but can go without water for a month in the cool season. Camels used to be important to the desert people in particular because they provided milk and meat, were reliable means of transportation (desert caravans), and could be used for military purposes (Fig. 5.46). Camel racing is a popular sport in much of the region, and the great wealth of some oil exporting economies has translated into astonishing prices for the most prized animals. In 2008, the crown prince of Dubai paid 2.7 million dollars for one during what was described as a "camel beauty pageant."

Livestock herding has also been closely associated with pastoral nomadism, a fairly common practice in the past but now a declining way of life in the Middle East and other dry regions. Pastoral nomads move their livestock herds from place to place in search of grazing lands and water. Three types of nomadism have been practiced in various parts of the region since ancient times: horizontal and vertical nomadism as well as semi-nomadism. The first type was characterized by an irregular but sometimes more organized movement of livestock across low-lying areas all year round. Vertical nomadism was practiced in mountainous regions, and it was a seasonal movement of animal herds between lower (cool season) and higher (hot season) elevation areas. Each environment was best utilized during its peak of productivity in this system. Finally, semi-nomadism could be found on the periphery of agricultural settlements, usually in river valleys or near other sources of water. It was a combination of sedentary farming and nomadism. A part of a village or clan was engaged in growing crops in the same area every year while the other part journeyed with its livestock through drier surrounding regions. Pastoral nomadism has been on decline throughout the entire region for some time, and it is practiced today

FIGURE 5.46 The camel, a desert animal—It is very well adapted to dry climate, and it has been an essential means of transportation across desert regions for millennia. *Source:* Pixabay.

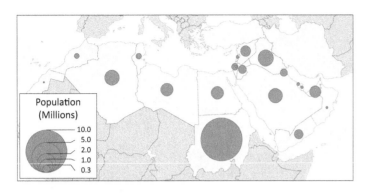

FIGURE 5.47 The distribution of the Bedouin population—The map shows the total estimated Bedouin population in each country. Not all of them are engaged in a nomadic way of life. *Source:* Joshua Project (joshuaproject.net).

Mineral Resources and the Importance of Petroleum

Although the Middle East has rather limited amounts of metallic and non-metallic ores, it is very rich in fossil fuels, particularly petroleum and natural gas. Turkey and Iran have the richest and most diverse deposits of metallic ores, including chromium, iron ore, copper, and lead. Morocco has been one of the leading producers of phosphates in the world. None of these deposits, however, compare to the reserves of petroleum found in this area.

The Arab/Persian Gulf region is the richest part of the world in regard to this resource (Fig. 5.48). Saudi Arabia has over 16 percent of global reserves, Iran and Iraq about 9 to 10 percent each, small Kuwait over 6 percent, and the United Arab Emirates slightly less than Kuwait. Together, these five countries control nearly half of the global oil. The Arab/Persian Gulf deposits are located in coastal areas and not very deep in the ground (Fig. 5.49). Consequently, production costs are substantially lower than those in the United States.[11] The first petroleum deposits were discovered and developed in Iran by British companies in 1901 and the first oil shipped through the port of Abadan in 1912.

by a very small segment of the population (quite often called Bedouins), perhaps no more than 5 percent of the total population (Fig. 5.47). Sometimes pastoral nomads could cross an international boundary during their journey, and the governments today want to prevent such activities and put pressure on nomads to switch to a sedentary life style.

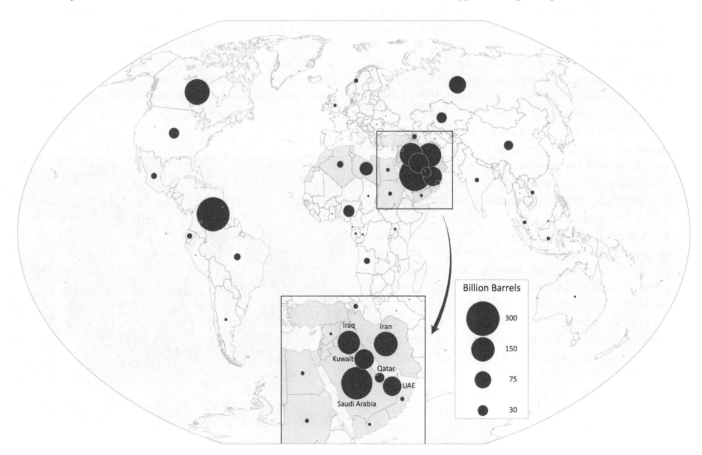

FIGURE 5.48 Proven petroleum reserves in the world, 2013. *Source:* U.S. Energy Information Administration.

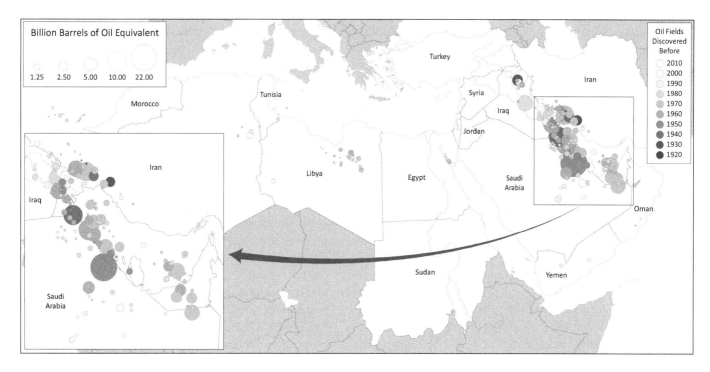

FIGURE 5.49 The distribution of major oil fields in the Middle East. *Source:* WorldMap (worldmap.harvard.edu/data).

Oil was subsequently discovered in Iraq (1928), Bahrain (1932), Saudi Arabia (1938), Qatar (1940), the UAE (1958), and Oman (1963). The other part of the Middle East rich in oil is Northern Africa, especially Libya and Algeria. However, the oil deposits found here are smaller, located in the interior, and were discovered later. Interestingly, the Middle East accounted for only 35 percent of global oil production in 2016, indicating that its reserves will last longer than those of some other major producers (e.g. Russia has 5 percent of proven oil reserves but accounted for 12 percent of production), although new production technologies (e.g. hydraulic fracturing) may change that picture.

Five Middle Eastern countries (Iran, Iraq, Kuwait, and Saudi Arabia) and Venezuela established the **Organization of Petroleum Exporting Countries** (OPEC) in 1960. Several other Arab countries joined OPEC: Qatar in 1961, Libya in 1962, the United Arab Emirates in 1967, and Algeria in 1969. The organization gained international importance in the 1970s after member-country governments took control of domestic production. When OPEC members act together they can strongly affect oil prices. That power was demonstrated to the world when in 1973 Arab states in OPEC imposed an embargo on the United States in retaliation for U.S. support of Israel in the Yom Kippur War. There were several more OPEC cuts in the 1970s so that oil prices were ten times higher in 1980 than they had been at the beginning of 1973. The price shock triggered a deep recession in the U.S. Yet in the 1980s,

oil prices tumbled as new sources (e.g. in the North Sea between Scotland and Norway) became available, as energy efficiency improvements diffused (e.g. small, fuel-efficient Japanese cars), and as economies slowed. There have been several more wide swings in oil prices since then. Oil prices posted their all-time high (as of 2018) at $147 per barrel in July 2008, but just a few months later in December 2008 they had collapsed to $34 per barrel as the global economy spun downward in the Great Recession. The story is broadly similar in the natural gas sector where the Middle East likewise plays an outsize role. In 2016, Iran had 17 percent of the world's proven gas reserves (second only to Russia who had 25 percent), and Qatar—a country smaller than Connecticut—had 13 percent. Overall, the Middle East contained just under half of proven reserves. Because natural gas is cleaner burning than oil and much cleaner than coal, it will likely play an increasing role in the 21st century, perpetuating the importance of the Middle East as a key energy source for much of the world.

Fossil fuel revenues comprise a large part of the gross domestic product in all Arab/Persian Gulf countries, so they are vulnerable to the gyrations in the market. The export of oil, natural gas, and refined petroleum products accounts for 87 to 99 percent of all exports in Iraq, Kuwait, Qatar, and Saudi Arabia; two-thirds in Oman; and half in the United Arab Emirates and Iran. The two major North African producers, Libya and Algeria, also derive most of their income from export of oil. To buffer their economies from price changes, most of these countries have built up large sovereign wealth funds in which they save oil profits. Qatar's fund had $335 billion in investments in 2017 or about $1.3 million per Qatari citizen. The fund owned large stakes in Volkswagen, a major Hollywood film studio, and much of the premium real estate in London—along with many other investments around the world.

At home, the income from oil has made several Middle Eastern countries, especially those with small populations, rich and able to offer a variety of welfare-type benefits to their citizens, including tax-free income, free health care and education, subsidized fuel, generous retirement plans, and interest-free home mortgages. They have invested vast sums of money into transportation infrastructure improvements, including the construction of new seaports, airports and highways, utilities (water and sewer systems and water desalination plants) and housing projects. The United Arab Emirates is an example of such a country. Its two major cities, Dubai and Abu Dhabi, have become large construction sites in recent years. The current tallest building in the world (830 meters/2,722 feet), completed in 2010, is the *Burj Khalifa* in Dubai.[12]

Considering the eventual depletion of fossil fuel resources and fluctuating prices, most countries have begun preparing by investing in projects that generate long-term income and employment. Dubai has ambitions to become a major global city and a financial center, as well as a magnet for tourists and wealthy foreigners. It wants to be known as a business-friendly city with limited regulations (no taxes and tariffs and few limits on banking transactions) on various types of economic activities. It will host the World Expo in 2020. *Dubailand*, the world's largest entertainment and shopping center (277 square kilometers/107 square miles), is under construction. The city of Abu Dhabi opened a large amusement park, Ferrari World, in 2010. All these, and other developments, far surpass the country's domestic needs but are good examples of what money (petrodollars) can do.

Manufacturing and Transportation

Although the region has a long industrial tradition going back to medieval times, today, complex and large-scale manufacturing activities—other than those in the petrochemical industry—are found in only a few countries, including Turkey, Iran, and Israel. Although Turkey is the largest industrial power in the region in terms of total manufacturing output, Israel has the most advanced and well-balanced manufacturing sector in the region. It is comparable to that of the most developed countries with respect to technological sophistication and productivity. The country is well known for its high-tech industry, mainly software, electronic, biomedical, pharmaceutical, communications, and military hardware sectors.[13] For example, Teva Pharmaceutical Industries is the world's largest generic drug maker, and Rafael Advanced Defense Systems is the inventor of the world's first operational air defense system (known as the *Iron Dome*) against short-range rockets and artillery shells. Israel is one of the two leading diamond processing centers in the world and has a well developed chemical industry.

Four Middle Eastern countries are producers of motor vehicles. The auto industry is fairly well developed in Turkey and Iran—each country makes over 1 million vehicles (passenger cars, light commercial vehicles, buses, and trucks) a year and is among the world's top twenty producers. Both countries are also major steel producers. Several oil-rich countries in the Arab/Persian Gulf region built a series of aluminum smelters (energy-hungry facilities) and today account for about 9 percent of the global production of aluminum. And of course the petrochemical industry has been well established in this region for several decades, with some eighty refineries spread from Morocco to Iran today.

Located at the junction of Europe, Asia, and Africa, the Middle East has been crisscrossed by important transportation corridors on land and sea for millennia. Camel caravans and sail boats used to be the major means of transportation in most parts of the Middle East until about a century ago. Much more recently air transportation has become vitally important. The most spectacular development occurred in the oil-rich Gulf States in the last twenty years. Some Middle Eastern airlines are considered the best in the world in terms of customer satisfaction. Qatar Airways, established in 1993, was the number one airline in terms of quality of service in 2015. Its modern fleet of over 150 planes connects this small country with all populated continents. Emirates Airlines, based in Dubai, has a fleet of over 250 planes and is the third largest international carrier by number of passengers. Some 120 planes of Etihad Airways, based in Abu Dhabi and established in 2003, connect this city with over ninety places on most continents. Turkish Airlines serve more countries (over 120) than any other airline in the world, and it is the world's second largest carrier of international passengers (after Emirates Airlines). These four airlines are so-called "superconnectors." The position of the Middle East relative to other population centers of the world and the great range of contemporary wide-body jets means that it is possible to travel from almost any large city on the planet to almost any other large city with one stop in the Middle East. To accommodate the resulting flow of people and cargo through the region, several large and modern airports were built in the Middle East as well. Dubai International was the third busiest airport in the world (after Atlanta and Beijing) in terms of passenger traffic (78 million) in 2015, and Atatürk International Airport in Istanbul served over 61 million passengers in the same year.

The Middle East attracts about 100 million tourists each year (Fig. 5.50). The number of visitors, however, can be strongly affected by political instability in various countries of this region. Tourism is an important source of income for several countries, including Egypt, Israel, and Tunisia, where it accounts for about 10 percent of gross domestic product and employment. Religious tourism is most important in Saudi Arabia and Israel. Several million Muslim pilgrims visit Mecca each year, and many Christian and Jewish visitors go to Israel to see sites associated with biblical events. Egypt attracts about 10 million visitors

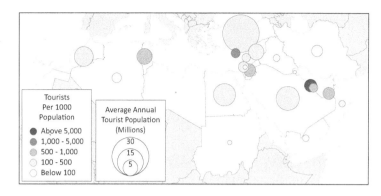

FIGURE 5.50 Tourism in the Middle East (tourist arrivals), 2005–2012. *Source:* World Bank.

interested in historical sites, such as the Pyramids and Great Sphinx in Giza (Fig. 5.51). Turkey is the major tourist destination in this region—it admits about 34 million visitors each year who come to visit various historic and religious sites, look for bargains in traditional marketplaces

FIGURE 5.51 Ancient Egyptian architecture and art—Numerous ancient structures, like the pyramids and the Sphinx shown in this image, attract millions of tourists to Egypt every year, and revenues from tourism account for over 10 percent of the country's gross domestic product. *Source:* Heike C. Alberts.

(bazaars), and enjoy sunny summer weather in many beach resorts along the Aegean and Mediterranean Seas. Tunisia and Morocco also attract many beach lovers. However, the number of tourists visiting some of these countries has declined in recent years in response to terrorist activities and threats.

FUTURE PROBLEMS AND PROSPECTS

The Middle East is confronted by daunting political, economic, and social issues. Political instability and frequent conflicts have caused tremendous human suffering and material damage in almost every country in the region.[14] The Jewish-Arab conflict has been the longest dispute in this region in recent history and, despite numerous attempts to solve it, will probably continue to cast a shadow on the daily lives of people directly affected by it. The persistence of extreme positions on both sides of the conflict and the intractability of certain specific issues (e.g. who gets to control Jerusalem, which both sides and Christians regard as sacred space) likely will preclude any durable solution for the foreseeable future. The spread of militant Islamism has contributed to widespread human tragedy in several parts of the region. ISIS activities in Iraq and Syria not only killed many innocent people and generated millions of refugees but also drew several major external powers in this conflict. Unfortunately, even if ISIS is defeated, it seems likely that other groups will emerge with similarly ruthless ideologies. One factor fueling such groups is pervasive authoritarian rule, which continues to be the norm rather than an exception in most Middle Eastern countries. Only Israel, a different country in many ways, is an effective democracy in this part of the world. Many hoped that the Arab Spring uprisings would bring democracy to most Arab states, but the results have been disappointing so far. The extremes of wealth clearly visible within and among several countries, have also generated a lot of popular resentment and hostility and have even led to military conflicts. The growing population pressure on limited natural resources is a major concern for many governments. The political turbulence in the Middle East is partly attributable to the "youth bulge" of the millions of young people at the bottom of this region's population pyramid. Providing education and employment to a high number of young people will be a real challenge, particularly in the less developed and conflict-prone regions. Finally, the shortage of water, due to dwindling aquifers and increased demand, may lead to tensions and even military conflict.

Still, while the experience of recent decades gives ample cause for pessimism about this region's future, a longer-term perspective provides at least some hope. This is the region where much of what is meant by the term *civilization* first began—farming, cities, science, and mathematics. It has given birth to religions that are a source of inspiration and guidance for half the world's people. The region's rich inheritance is one reason to hope that it will find civilized, effective responses to its 21st century challenges.

NOTES

1. Cohen, S. B. (2015). *Geopolitics: The geography of international relations* (3rd ed.) (pp. 382–390). Lanham, MD: Rowman & Littlefield.

2. Maddocks, A. (2013). Water stress by country. Retrieved from World Resources Institute website: http://www.wri.org/resources/charts-graphs/water-stress-country

3. Center for International and Regional Studies. (2008). *Migrant labor in the Gulf: Summary report.* Retrieved from Georgetown University School of Foreign Service in Qatar website: https://repository.library.georgetown.edu/bitstream/handle/10822/558543/CIRSSummaryReport2MigrantLaborintheGulf2011.pdf;sequence=5

4. Held, C. C., & Cummings, J. T. (2014). *Middle East patterns: Places, peoples, and politics* (6th ed.) (p. 127–131). Boulder, CO: Westview Press; Ziegler, D. J., Stewart, D. J., & Ali, A. K. (2012). Cities of the Greater Middle East. In S. D. Brunn, M. Hays-Mitchell, & D. J. Ziegler (Eds.), *Cities of the world: World regional urban development* (pp. 281–329). Lanham, MD: Rowman & Littlefield.

5. Council on Foreign Relations. (2018). Israeli-Palestinian conflict. *Global Conflict Tracker.* Retrieved from https://www.cfr.org/interactives/global-conflict-tracker#!/conflict/israeli-palestinian-conflict

6. Fearon, J. D. (2015). Instability in the Middle East. Defining Ideas. Retrieved from Hoover Institute website: https://www.hoover.org/research/instability-middle-east

7. The Arab Spring at five: a comprehensive look at how 2011 shaped the Middle East. (2016). *Foreign Affair Anthology Series.* Retrieved from https://www.foreignaffairs.com/anthologies/2016-02-29/arab-spring-five

8. Rababa's, G. I. (2012). Water conflict in the Middle East. *International Journal of Humanities and Social Science, 2*(21), 13–27.

9. Held, C. C., & Cummings, J. T. (2014). *Middle East patterns: Places, peoples, and politics* (6th ed.) (pp. 378–380). Boulder, CO: Westview Press.

10. Conniff, K., Molden, D., Peden, D., & Awulachev, S. B. (2012). Nile water and agriculture: Past, present and future. In S. B. Awulachew, V. Smakhtin, D. Molden, & D. Peden (Eds.), *The Nile River Basin: Water, agriculture, governance and livelihoods* (pp. 5-29). New York, NY: Routledge.

11. Russell, M. B. (2012). *The Middle East and South Asia* (47th ed.) (pp. 14–19). Lanham, MD: Stryker-Post Publications.

12. Khouri, R. (2008). The incredible development of the Gulf States. Retrieved from Belfer Center for Science and International Affairs website: https://www.belfercenter.org/publication/incredible-development-gulf-states

13. Held, C. C., & Cummings, J. T. (2014). *Middle East patterns: Places, peoples, and politics* (6th ed.). Boulder, CO: Westview Press, p. 385.

14. Fisher, W. B. (1989). The Middle East and North Africa: An introduction. In *The Middle East and North Africa 1990* (36th ed.) (pp. 3–21). London, UK: Europa Publications.

6

SUB-SAHARAN AFRICA

Among the ten major world culture realms discussed in this textbook, Sub-Saharan Africa is the largest in area and the third largest in population. It occupies one-sixth of the world's land area and is inhabited by one-eighth of its population. The equator divides the region, which extends for over 6,920 kilometers (4,300 miles) from east to west and 6,435 kilometers (4,000 miles) from north to south, into two almost equal parts. Although Sub-Saharan Africa shares a number of characteristics with other, particularly developing, parts of the world, it is also different from the rest of the world with regard to several environmental and human features (Fig. 6.1).

GEOGRAPHIC QUALITIES AND WORLD SIGNIFICANCE

Africa is considered a plateau continent with a simple outline. It has no major mountain ranges and wide coastal plains but is divided into a series of plateaus and basins. Although it is four times bigger than Europe in area, its coastline is much shorter since it has no prominent peninsulas, large islands (except Madagascar), or bays. The tropical hot climate is dominant in most parts of Sub-Saharan Africa; while average annual temperatures are high and do not vary much from place to place, precipitation is unevenly distributed—some parts are humid tropical rainforests while others are deserts. The region has a rich and diverse mineral resource base and is the major world producer of diamonds, gold, copper, uranium, and several strategic minerals. The export of these commodities has been the main source of income for many African countries.

A large and fast growing population is another geographic characteristic of this region. Sub-Saharan Africa has over 900 million people and is the third most populous region of the world (after South and East Asia). Its share of the global population has increased from 7 to 13 percent since 1950. With an annual rate of growth over 2.7 percent, Africa's population doubles almost every generation. Europe's population was over twice as large as that of Sub-Saharan Africa in 1950; today, it is the other way around. If these demographic trends continue, the region will have over two billion people by 2050 and will be the second most populous region of the world (after South Asia).

Sub-Saharan Africa is also well known for its great linguistic and ethnic diversity. Its residents communicate in over 2,000 languages, and this diversity has been one of several reasons for political instability in many African countries. The great linguistic diversity has also been responsible, to some degree, for choosing European languages as the official means of communication in many African countries since their independence.

The enslavement and forced removal of over 10 million Africans to other parts of the world prior to the mid-19th century (and the deaths of many more due to cruel treatment) had a devastating demographic and economic impact on the region. Most of Sub-Saharan Africa was under European colonial rule for several decades (until the 1960s and 1970s), and the imprint of this rule is still very strong in many parts of the realm. Some of these characteristics have also been partially responsible for the low levels of economic development and widespread poverty across the region. Although most Africans still engage in agricultural activities, periodic food shortages have led to high mortality and health problems as well as political instability in some parts of Sub-Saharan Africa.

The importance of this region can be expressed in several ways. First, it is the leading source of several major minerals. It has the largest reserves of gold, bauxite, chromite, cobalt, and diamonds in the world and accounts for over half of the global production of cobalt, diamonds, platinum, and chromium. It is also an important supplier of vanadium, copper, and gold. Second, Sub-Saharan Africa is an important supplier of several agricultural commodities, including cocoa (two-thirds of global production), some tropical fruits (e.g. bananas, mangos, and papayas),

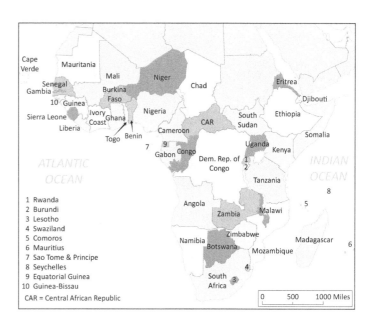

FIGURE 6.1 Countries of Sub-Saharan Africa—The region is divided into forty-eight independent countries and three dependent (British and French) territories.

nuts (groundnuts), and spices (cloves). The region also produces sizable amounts of tea and coffee for the world market. Third, due to its large and fast growing population, Sub-Saharan Africa may be an attractive source of cheap labor for Western companies and a large market for consumer goods. Fourth, poverty, political instability, periodic environmental disasters, and some of their outcomes (e.g. refugees, food shortages, and disease outbreaks) affect many countries in the region and beyond, particularly those in Europe. They also put pressure on the United Nations and many non-governmental organizations to find solutions to these problems. Fifth, Sub-Saharan Africa has been the center of the HIV/AIDS epidemic for the past three decades. Over two-thirds of people affected by it live in this part of the world, and only collective global action can bring any solution to this problem. Finally, the potential and innovation of Africa's large, fast-growing, and urbanizing population can benefit the region and the rest of the world in many ways.

PHYSICAL ENVIRONMENT

Landform Configuration

As indicated earlier, Africa is usually described as a plateau continent. It consists of a zone of narrow coastal plains (especially in its southern and eastern parts), a zone of relatively steep slopes parallel to the coastal plains, and the vast interior composed of a series of basins and uplands. Africa has fewer mountain ranges and lowland plains than

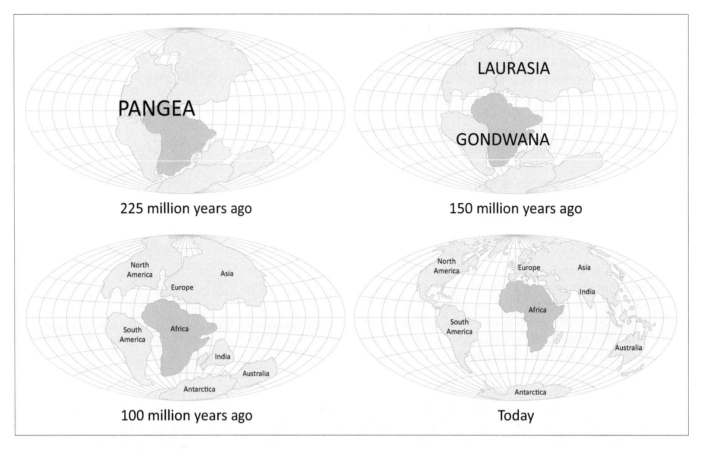

FIGURE 6.2 Continental drift theory—Africa is the only continent that has largely remained in its original place. The plateau-type landform configuration and the lack of major mountain ranges on its territory reflects the region's relative geologic stability. *Source:* drawn after a similar map in Encyclopedia Britannica.

any other continent. Considering its large territorial size, this is a remarkable physical feature. The explanation comes from **continental drift theory**, which was proposed by German geologist Alfred Wegener in 1912. According to this theory, all continents formed a large landmass called Pangea over 250 million years ago (Fig. 6.2). The break-up of this large continent began about 200 million years ago. It originally split into two parts, Laurasia and Gondwana. Laurasia later split into North America and Eurasia, while Gondwana split into Africa, South America, Australia, Antarctica, and the Indian subcontinent. As individual parts began moving away from their original place, mountain ranges formed on their peripheries. South America has moved west, and the Andes were formed along its western coast. The Indian subcontinent has drifted northeast and merged with Eurasia, and this led to the formation of the Himalayas. Australia has moved east, and a low mountain chain known as the Great Dividing Range was formed along its eastern periphery. Africa has not moved much from its original place over the past 250 million years, and therefore no prominent mountain ranges (except the Atlas Mountains) were formed along its periphery.

What proof do we have for this theory? First, the shapes of some continents (Africa and South America in particular) fit like pieces in a jigsaw puzzle. Second, the same freshwater animal fossils are found on continents on opposite sides of the oceans (i.e. Africa and South America). Third, some plant fossils are also found in Antarctica, Australia, South Asia, and South America. Fourth, similar rock layers are found on several separate continents. And fifth, glacial deposits are found in some tropical and desert regions on some of these continents.

With regard to landform configuration and average elevation, Sub-Saharan Africa is often divided into two regions, Low and High Africa. Both regions consist of a series of plateaus (uplands) and basins (Fig. 6.3). However, Low Africa, occupying the western and central parts of the continent, has much lower elevations, and basins (Congo, Chad, Djouf, and Sudan) are more prominent landform features there. High Africa, on the other hand, has much higher elevations, and more prominent plateaus (Ethiopian, East African, and Katanga) are the dominant landform features in this region occupying Southern and Eastern Africa. Most African plateaus are products of

FIGURE 6.3 Landform regions of Sub-Saharan Africa—The region is divided into Low and High Africa, and both parts are comprised of a series of basins and plateaus (highlands). *Source:* Natural Earth.

uplifting and of differential erosion of ancient rocks and volcanic activity (Fig. 6.4).

The **Great Rift Valley** is a distinctive landform and geologic feature of High Africa. This 9,650-kilometer (6,000-mile) long and 32 to 64 kilometers (20 to 40 miles) wide valley (much wider than the Red Sea) runs from the Sinai Peninsula in Egypt through Ethiopia to Malawi and Mozambique in southern Africa (Fig. 6.5). It splits into western and eastern parts in the East African Highlands. The lowest parts of the valley are filled with water and form a series of elongated lakes. The Great Rift Valley region is the most seismically active part of Sub-Saharan Africa. A series of dormant volcanoes is the most prominent seismic

FIGURE 6.4 A plateau region of Serra da Leba, Angola—It is part of High Africa, a region of plateaus and basins occupying the southern and eastern parts of the African continent. *Source:* Pixabay.

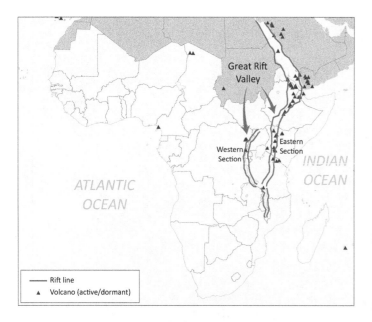

FIGURE 6.5 The Great Rift Valley—This landform feature is proof of continental drift theory. It may indicate a future separation of the eastern part of the continent from the rest of Africa.

Climatic Contrasts

Sub-Saharan Africa's location at low latitudes means that most of the region has a hot tropical climate. While there is relatively little variation in average annual temperatures from place to place, there are tremendous differences in the amount of precipitation various areas receive during the year (Fig. 6.6). In general, the climate becomes drier as one moves away from Central Africa or coastal areas of Western Africa. The tropical rainforest climate, characterized by high humidity and fairly constant high temperatures throughout the year, is dominant in the Congo Basin. Although there is no dry season in this region, precipitation is less evenly distributed over time, and one can identify two short, more-or-less rainy periods corresponding to the movement of the sun between the Tropics of Cancer and Capricorn. Tropical rainforest is the dominant type of vegetation associated with this climate. Areas north, east, and south of the Congo Basin have a tropical wet and dry type of climate. Two distinctive seasons, wet summer and dry winter, are associated with this climatic region. Average monthly temperatures are fairly high year around (slightly lower during the dry season) but the precipitation and humidity vary greatly between the two seasons. The rainy season is from June through August and from December through February in areas north and south of the Equator, respectively. The savanna type of landscape, tall grasses and scattered trees (some of them shedding leaves during the dry season), is characteristic of this climate (Fig. 6.7).

feature of this area. Mt. Kilimanjaro (5,895 meters/19,340 feet above sea level) in Tanzania, with its permanent snow cover, is a well known image of this region. Past volcanic activity is also responsible for large lava outpours and the formation of fertile soils in Ethiopia and parts of the East African Highlands.

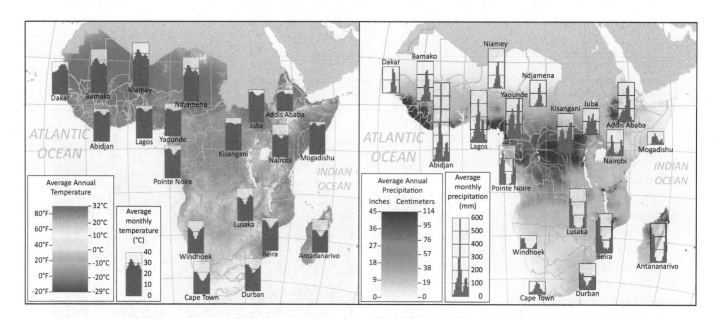

FIGURE 6.6 Sub-Saharan Africa: patterns of temperature and precipitation—There is less spatial variation in average temperature than precipitation patterns across the region. Monthly temperatures are quite consistent in equatorial areas but their variability increases at higher latitudes. A dry and wet season can be identified in most parts of the region, and the amount of precipitation generally decreases with increasing distance from the center of the continent and the Gulf of Guinea. *Source:* WorldClim-Global Climate Data.

FIGURE 6.7 Savanna landscape, Tanzania—These grasslands areas are found in semi-dry parts of Sub-Saharan Africa. Mount Kilimanjaro, seen in the background, is a dormant volcano and the highest peak on the African continent. *Source:* Jürgen Böhm.

Moving north, east, or south of the savanna region, the climate becomes much drier and the vegetation scarcer. Deserts occupy the northern, northeastern, and southwestern parts of Sub-Saharan Africa. The Sahara, as mentioned in the previous chapter, is the largest desert in the world. Most of Mauritania, Mali, Niger, and Chad are part of this very dry region. The Kalahari and Namib deserts stretch across parts of Botswana, Namibia, and South Africa. The Kalahari Desert occupies an interior basin that is greater in area than the state of Texas. It is not as dry as the Sahara and supported widely scattered groups of indigenous people almost completely dependent on hunting and gathering until recent decades. The Namib Desert, located west of the Kalahari Basin, is one of the driest places on Earth (Fig. 6.8). This 1,930-kilometers (1,200-miles) long and

FIGURE 6.8 Semi-desert landscape, Namibia—It is a transition zone between the savanna and desert (Kalahari) ecosystems. *Source:* Heike C. Alberts.

130 to 160-kilometers (80 to 100-miles) wide region along the Atlantic coast is almost uninhabited and devoid of any vegetation. Most of Somalia and Eastern Ethiopia, located in the Horn of Africa, also have a dry climate and are basically deserts. The southernmost part of the African continent (the coastal area of Southern Africa from Cape Town to Durban) lies in the zone of subtropical climate. Some areas have a Mediterranean climate with precipitation limited to the winter season (Cape Town), while others have a more even distribution (Durban). Most precipitation in Sub-Saharan Africa, regardless of climate type (the Mediterranean one might be the exception), comes in the form of torrential rains that are often associated with thunderstorm activity.

Altitude, ocean currents, and air pressure patterns are also important climatic factors in some parts of Sub-Saharan Africa. The Ethiopian Highlands, located fairly close to the Equator, have lower average annual temperatures than the surrounding regions. In Addis Ababa, the capital of Ethiopia located at an elevation of about 2,408 meters (7,900 feet) above sea level, daily maximum temperatures range from 20 to 25°C (68 to 77°F) and overnight lows from 5 to 10°C (41 to 50°F). The cold Benguela Current along the Atlantic coast of South Africa, Namibia, and parts of Angola is responsible for frequent fog and limited, erratic precipitation in the Namib Desert. A hot and dry northeasterly wind called the **harmattan** may occur during the winter season in parts of Western Africa. These strong winds can carry large amounts of dust over long distances and create problems for air transportation.

Water Resources

Sub-Saharan Africa has about 9 percent of global freshwater resources; they are unevenly distributed across the region. There is a fairly close correlation between the availability of surface freshwater and climate type. Humid tropical regions, such as the Congo Basin, have ample resources while some desert areas completely lack them. Sub-Saharan Africa has several major river systems and large lakes (Fig. 6.9). Most African rivers have poor navigability but great hydroelectric potential. The Congo River and its numerous tributaries form the second largest river system in the world in terms of water volume. It drains the humid and densely forested but sparsely populated Congo Basin region. Significant stretches of the river's course are not navigable due to the presence of several cataracts in the upper and lower sections of the stream, but these same cataracts give the river gigantic untapped hydroelectric potential. Several major cities are found along the Congo

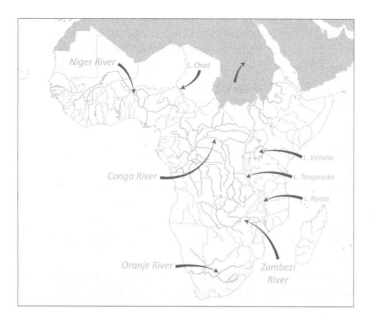

FIGURE 6.9 Major rivers and lakes of Sub-Saharan Africa—There is a strong relationship between the availability of surface water and climate type. The Congo River and its tributaries form one of the largest river systems in the world. Notice the absence of rivers in the dry parts of the region. Most large African lakes are located in the Great Rift Valley region.

FIGURE 6.10 Victoria Falls on the Zambezi River—One of the best known waterfalls in the world, it is on the Zambezi River between Zambia and Zimbabwe, and a major tourist attraction in Sub-Saharan Africa. *Source:* Pixabay.

River, including the capital cities of Kinshasa (Democratic Republic of Congo) and Brazzaville (Republic of Congo), which face each other on opposite banks.

The Niger River is a very important source of water and a navigation route for parts of Western Africa. It originates in the hills of Eastern Guinea and runs through the savanna lands of Mali and Niger and forms a large delta at its mouth in Southern Nigeria (a petroleum-rich region). The capital cities of Bamako (Mali) and Niamey (Niger) are some of the major urban centers along this river. Several advanced culture centers (briefly discussed later in this chapter) originated along the middle course of the Niger River in the past. The Zambezi River in South-central Africa is the fourth largest river system on the continent (the Nile, discussed in Chapter 5, ranks first). Its great hydroelectric potential has been harnessed by the Kariba and Cahora Bassa dams along the Zambia-Zimbabwe border and in Mozambique, respectively. The Victoria Falls between Zambia and Zimbabwe are one of Sub-Saharan Africa's major tourist attractions (Fig. 6.10).

Most African lakes (except Lake Chad) are located in the Great Rift Valley region. Lake Victoria is the third largest lake in the world (after the Caspian Sea and Lake Superior); it receives water from numerous streams but is drained only by the Nile River. It is different from other East African lakes in terms of size, shape, and depth. Lake Victoria is twice the size of the next largest lake, has a relatively compact

(round) shape, and is rather shallow (the average depth is 40 meters or 130 feet). Lake Tanganyika is the second largest and deepest body of surface freshwater in the world (after Lake Baikal in Russia). It contains one-sixth of global freshwater and its maximum depth is 1,469 meters (4,820 feet). Lake Nyasa (Malawi), like Lake Tanganyika, occupies the lowest parts of the Great Rift Valley, and is the ninth largest lake in the world. There are several smaller lakes in both sections of the Rift Valley, including Lake Rukwa, Albert, and Edward. Lake Chad, located in West-central Africa where four countries (Chad, Niger, Nigeria, and Cameroon) meet, used to be one of the largest lakes in Africa. Known for changing its size by season, it has shrunk in recent decades from about 17,600 to 1,550 square kilometers (6,800 to 600 square miles). Some scholars blame unsustainable water management while others hold climate change responsible for the lake's desiccation. Its waters and the surrounding areas are also known for great biological diversity, and the lake played an important role in the economic life of this semi-dry region in the past.

Vegetation and Soil

Vegetation and soil are closely related to climate and landforms in every part of the world. The amount and seasonal distribution of precipitation play an important role in determining vegetation types in Sub-Saharan Africa. Human activities have also modified the natural vegetation in many parts of the region. Tropical rainforest dominates the hot and humid region of Central Africa, some coastal parts of Western Africa, and the eastern coast of Madagascar.

Tropical rainforests are known for a great variety of plant species and are composed of three vegetation layers: the lower layer of shrubs and ferns; the middle layer of trees, palms, and lianas; and the upper layer (canopy) of broadleaf evergreen trees. Several tropical hardwoods (mahogany, rosewood, and ebony) and other commercially valuable plants (rubber tree and oil palm) are found throughout the forested areas but seldom form widespread homogeneous colonies. From a commercial point of view, these forests may be less productive than those in temperate regions characterized by the dominance of a single species over large areas.

Savannas comprise the most extensive landscapes in Sub-Saharan Africa and are the dominant types of vegetation in areas with wet and dry seasons. More humid regions will be associated with a mixture of scattered deciduous trees (e.g. widespread acacia and less common baobab) and tall grasses (woodland savanna), while drier areas will have fewer trees (also smaller in size) and shorter grasses. The savannas look quite different during the wet and dry season as many trees shed leaves and grasses die during the dry season. These areas are attractive to large numbers of herbivorous animals, such as antelopes, giraffes, elephants, buffalos, and zebras, as well as carnivores, including lions, hyenas, leopards, and cheetahs. As the climate becomes drier, the savanna landscape turns into grass steppe, a

semi-desert of small, thorny bushes and patches of short grasses and eventually into desert. A small southernmost part of Africa is a region of Mediterranean vegetation consisting of a great variety of plant species (about 8,700), many of them found nowhere else in the world.

Most African soils are not fertile. The soils of the tropical rainforests do not contain many nutrients—they are washed away from the top layer by frequent torrential rains. Such soils tend to be rich in iron oxides that give them a reddish or orange color. They can support dense, natural vegetation but are not suitable for the permanent cultivation of food crops. Conversely, desert soils lack moisture and organic matter. However, there are pockets of fertile soils across the region. Alluvial soils, formed by the deposition of silt and other material by running water, in some river valleys support intensive traditional and commercial farming. Areas along the Niger River between Bamako and Timbuktu in Mali, and along the White Nile and its tributaries in South Sudan, are just two examples of agriculturally productive regions associated with such soils. Soils formed on volcanic bedrock in tropical regions also tend to be fertile. The Great Rift Valley region, parts of South Africa, Zimbabwe, and Cameroon have such soils, and they support a variety of agricultural activities, including large-scale commercial farming (tea and coffee plantations).

HUMAN-ENVIRONMENT INTERACTION

Since most Africans are engaged in primary activities, they have a very close relationship with the natural environment and are directly dependent on it to a greater degree than residents of more developed countries. Yet, African environments can be very challenging and present numerous problems to rural and urban residents in many places. Desertification or the expansion of desert-like conditions has been the biggest challenge to semi-dry transition zones between deserts and savannas. It has contributed to soil erosion and the extinction of many plant and animal species. Some insects destroy crops, spread diseases, and cause other nuisances. Desertification, which greatly reduces the biological productivity of the land, has numerous causes, including climate change, deforestation, overgrazing, improper irrigation techniques, poverty, and political instability. Often it is a combination of these factors that leads to irreversible adverse environmental changes in many parts of Sub-Saharan Africa. As the vegetation cover gets thinner and larger areas of bare ground are exposed to weather elements, increased soil erosion leads to declining crop yields or even crop failure and a reduced amount of forage for domesticated animals. The thinned tree and

bush cover also contributes to the shortage of fuelwood and building materials, and residents have to devote more time and energy to collecting this important raw material needed for cooking and heating. Desertification is also responsible for the lowering of the groundwater level and limited water supplies for human and animal consumption and for irrigation.

The Sahel region, a transition zone between the Sahara to the north and the savanna land to the south, is particularly prone to desertification. This 965-km-wide and 5,310-km-long (600-mile-wide and 3,300-mile-long) zone extends from the Atlantic Ocean in Mauritania to the Red Sea in Sudan (Fig. 6.11). The region is known for strong climatic variations and irregular rainfall, and it remains dry for most of the year except for a short rainy season in the middle of summer (June–August). Short grasses, scattered thorny bushes, and acacias cover most of the area and are used for the grazing of livestock (cattle, camels, goats, and sheep). Its current population of about 60 million is one of the fastest growing in the world, and it may climb to over 100 million by 2025 and 200 million by 2050. Growing population pressure on limited vegetation cover has led to

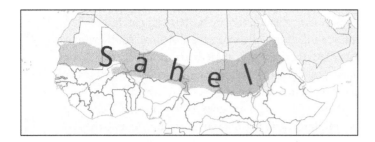

FIGURE 6.11 The Sahel region—The Sahel is an environmentally fragile region prone to droughts and pests, and it may be the poorest part of Sub-Saharan Africa. *Source:* Wikipedia.

soil erosion and desertification in many parts of the region. A severe drought in the late 1960s and early 1970s reduced the livestock herds (mainly cattle) by 50 to 70 percent and eliminated crop farming in many parts of the region. It resulted in over 100,000 deaths and forced many residents to move south. The Sahel is one of the least developed and poorest parts of Sub-Saharan Africa.[1]

Deforestation is also a serious and complex problem for some African countries. This region has one-third of the world's tropical rainforests but the deforestation rate has greatly exceeded the global annual average of 0.8 percent for the past few decades. While commercial logging and cattle ranching have been the leading causes of deforestation in other parts of the world, collection of fuelwood and subsistence farming have been responsible for most forest loss in Sub-Saharan Africa. Some 90 percent of the African

population relies on fuelwood for cooking and heating, and over half of all energy needs are met by burning wood and brush. Deforestation has particularly affected densely populated parts of Western Africa (Nigeria and Togo in particular) where almost 90 percent of the primary rainforest has been destroyed (Fig. 6.12). Growing population pressure and increased demand for additional farmland and fuelwood in Ethiopia have reduced the forest cover from 35 to 11 percent of the country's total area in less than a century. In addition to subsistence farming, illegal logging and mining have also been important causes of deforestation in the Democratic Republic of Congo which has the largest amount of forest in Sub-Saharan Africa. Despite various efforts to stop or reduce the pace of deforestation by African governments and international organizations, including stricter regulations on the logging industry (e.g. a ban on cutting certain types of trees), the development of forest protection schemes (e.g. creation of national parks and forest reserves), and addressing unsustainable human activities, little success has been achieved so far in most parts of the region. However, some countries have been able to reverse these unfavorable trends and expand the forested areas through reforestation projects since 1990. Most of them are small countries (Cape Verde, Rwanda, Swaziland, Lesotho, and Gambia). Ghana and Gabon are examples of larger states with some success in protecting their forests.

Numerous insects and other parasites are responsible for crop and infrastructure damage, spread of diseases, and even poverty across the region. Termites, for example, live in large colonies consisting of several million insects. Some species cause damage to wooden buildings and other structures (quite often undetected until it is too late to save them), crops (root and grain plants as well as fruit trees), and plantation forests (especially eucalyptus trees). Termite mounds in agricultural fields are obstacles to farm machinery. **Locusts**, a type of grasshopper found in semi-dry and dry regions, live in large swarms and can migrate long distances. The entire swarm can descend on a crop (usually when it is ready for harvest) and consume it in a matter of hours. One of the largest locust infestations occurred in Western and Northern Africa in 2004; it damaged half of the crop in some areas, especially Mauritania. A similar calamity occurred in Madagascar in 2013 when a large part of the rice crop was damaged. The **tse-tse fly** is an insect living in humid tropical Africa. It is responsible for spreading a disease known as sleeping sickness in humans and nagana in animals. Some consider this insect the major cause of rural poverty since it prevents livestock herding in many parts of Sub-Saharan Africa. The absence of cattle herding means no milk and meat for human consumption, no manure for fertilizing soils, and no draft animals for plowing the fields.

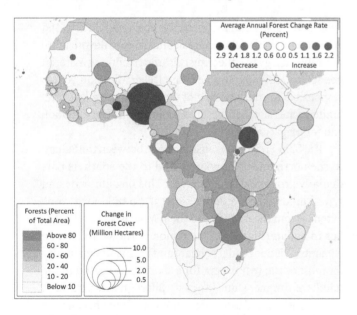

FIGURE 6.12 Deforestation in Sub-Saharan Africa, 1990–2015—Most countries have been losing forests for the past several decades, and some of the most densely populated countries (Nigeria, Uganda) have recorded the highest rates of deforestation since 1990. A few countries have been able to stop this trend (Gabon, Ivory Coast). *Source:* Mongabay.

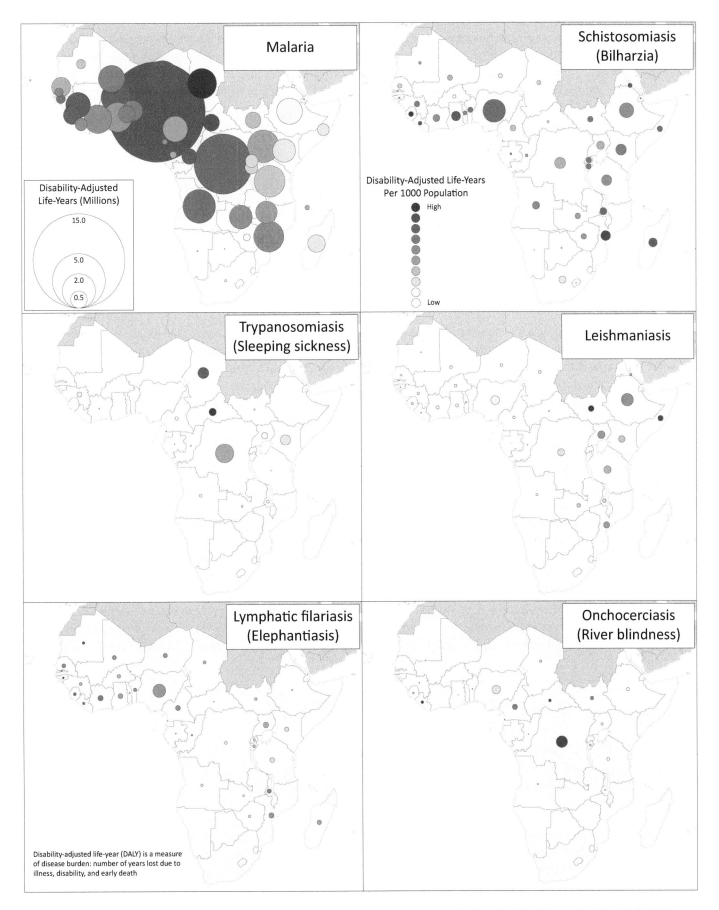

FIGURE 6.13 Selected tropical diseases in Sub-Saharan Africa—Malaria affects more people than the other diseases together. Notice that some diseases are spatially clustered and associated with specific natural environments. *Source:* World Health Organization.

Tropical environments provide favorable conditions for the spread of various infectious diseases caused by bacteria (e.g. cholera and leprosy), viruses (e.g. dengue, yellow fever and **Ebola**), and parasites (e.g. malaria, trypanosomiasis, leishmaniasis, schistosomiasis, and river blindness). They infect millions, kill thousands of people each year, and have a negative impact on worker productivity, agricultural output, and quality of life, among other things. Controlling the spread of these diseases and helping already infected people require significant financial and medical resources to which most African countries have limited access. **Malaria** is the most common tropical disease, and over 90 percent of global infections occur in Sub-Saharan Africa (Fig. 6.13). Each year 1 million people die from it, most of them children and the elderly. It is transmitted by mosquitos that thrive in hot and humid regions with pools of standing water. It can be controlled by spraying insecticides, draining swamps, pouring oil on standing water, and with the use of mosquito nets. According to some estimates, this disease alone is responsible for over 1 percent of annual reduction in economic growth for the countries most affected by it.[2]

Schistosomiasis or bilharzia, another fairly common tropical disease, is spread by contact with freshwater contaminated with a parasite found in water snails. Most infection occurs during regular farm activities, swimming, and fishing. The parasite can penetrate human skin and get to the liver and other internal organs via blood veins, and infected individuals may suffer from headaches, fever, chills, and joint and muscle pain. Some 85 percent of the world's infections occur in Sub-Saharan Africa, many of them among children under fourteen years of age. **Trypanosomiasis** or sleeping sickness, is carried by tsetse flies and found predominantly in rural tropical regions of Africa. Its initial symptoms include fever, headache, joint pain, and itching, but it can later lead to behavioral

changes, confusion, and insomnia (sleeping problems). Although sleeping sickness mortality rates have been declining in recent years (due to better surveillance and control methods as well as better access to medical technology), this disease still kills some 18,000 people a year. Leishmaniasis or black fever is spread through the bites of infected sand flies and results in skin sores on the legs, hands, and face that develop a few weeks after infection. Sub-Saharan Africa's annual death toll from this disease is around 14,000, which is about one-third of all global deaths. As Fig. 6.13 shows, Leishmaniasis is more common in the eastern than other parts of the region. Lymphatic filariasis or elephantiasis, spread by worms, is a painful and greatly disfiguring disease affecting people of all ages. Some of its symptoms (swelling of arms and legs) may be visible years after infection and cause temporary or permanent disability. Onchocerciasis or river blindness is the second most common cause of blindness in Africa. It is caused by bites of flies living near rapidly flowing rivers. The infected persons may suffer from severe itching and rashes, develop skin discoloration, and suffer eye disease that often leads to permanent blindness. Other tropical diseases, including cholera, yellow fever, dengue fever, and leprosy, are also found in parts of Sub-Saharan Africa. Although they are not as widespread as those discussed above and do not kill as many people as they did in the past, local periodic epidemics may occur and cause a lot of human suffering and other problems. The recent outbreak of the Ebola virus disease in Western Africa is an example of such an epidemic. This disease first appeared in two simultaneous outbreaks in what is now South Sudan and the Democratic Republic of Congo in 1976. The West African epidemic of 2014 was the largest and deadliest in history as it killed more people than all previous outbreaks of this disease together. Guinea, Sierra Leone, and Liberia were the most affected countries where over 28,000 cases and 11,000 deaths were reported.

POPULATION PATTERNS AND TRENDS

Sub-Saharan Africa's population has increased over five times during the past sixty-five years from 180 million in 1950 to 950 million in 2015, and the region has doubled its share of global population from 7 to 14 percent during the same period. As the fastest growing part of the world, Sub-Saharan Africa increases its population by 25 million each year; this is almost one-third of the total annual global increase. If this growth continues, the region will have almost four billion people and account for over one-third of the world's population by 2100.

Population Distribution and Growth

Nigeria and Ethiopia have the largest populations in Sub-Saharan Africa, 183 and 100 million, respectively, and they account for almost one-third of the region's population (Fig. 6.14). The next three largest African countries, the Democratic Republic of Congo (70 million), South Africa (53 million), and Tanzania (52 million) have a combined population of 175 million. Almost half of the region's

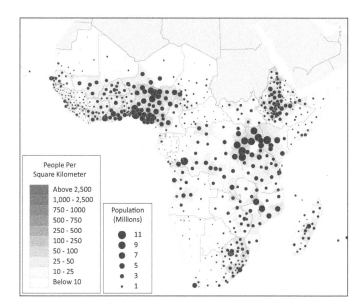

FIGURE 6.14 Population distribution in Sub-Saharan Africa—The eastern and coastal parts of West Africa (particularly Nigeria), the Ethiopian Highlands, and areas around Lake Victoria are the major population clusters. The eastern part of the Republic of South Africa and Malawi are also densely populated. Dry (the Sahara and Kalahari Deserts and the African Horn) and hot-humid (the Congo Basin) regions have the lowest population densities. *Source:* GeoHive (www.geohive.com) and statistical agencies of individual countries.

population lives in these five countries. The population distribution in Sub-Saharan Africa, like in any region, reflects environmental conditions, particularly precipitation, landforms, and soils, as well as historical and economic factors. The three major population clusters include Western Africa (particularly Nigeria), the Ethiopian Highlands, and the Great Lakes region of East-central Africa. Smaller pockets of high population densities are found in Malawi and eastern parts of South Africa. The West African cluster has about 250 million people. Coastal regions along the Gulf of Guinea from the Niger River Delta in Nigeria to the Ivory Coast and the highlands of Northern Nigeria have particularly high population densities exceeding 500 people per square kilometer (1,300 people per square mile) in some areas. Sufficient precipitation and fairly good soil support various types of agricultural activities from root crops (cassava and yams) and plantation crops (cocoa and oil palm) in the south to grains (sorghum and millet), groundnuts, and fiber crops (cotton) in the north.

The Ethiopian Highlands and the Great Lakes clusters have about 60 to 70 million people each. Population densities also reach 500 people per square kilometer (1,300 people per square mile) in some parts of both regions. Fertile soil formed on volcanic bedrock and a moderate climate (lower humidity and temperatures due to higher elevation) have supported dense populations in these two areas. The Ethiopian Highlands are also one of the early culture centers of Africa, so history played a role in attracting people to this region. Conversely, several large areas of low population densities are associated with either dry climate (Sahara, Kalahari, Namib, and the African Horn region) or dense tropical rainforests (the Congo Basin).

Sub-Saharan Africa has the fastest population growth rate in the world (2.7 percent), and its population has been doubling every generation since the 1950s. Most African countries entered the third stage of the demographic transition, characterized by declining fertility and mortality, just a generation ago or even later. Natural increase has been the major component of population growth in all but two or three countries over the past several decades. Sub-Saharan Africa has the highest fertility rates in the world—a typical woman has over 5 children as compared to the global average of 2.5 children (Fig. 6.15). The rate is over 6 children for several countries in Western and Central Africa and over 7 children in Niger. Several economic and cultural factors explain such high rates. Most Africans still live in the countryside and engage in primary activities, mainly agriculture. Farming families have a need for children to help parents with various domestic chores (e.g. fetching water, collecting firewood, and taking care of other children). A large number of children is also a symbol of prestige—it means higher social status and insurance for old age. The tradition of early marriage (the age of puberty is considered a proper age for marriage) and high infant and child mortality are other factors leading to high fertility. The knowledge of, access to, and use of contraception, which are generally very low in this part of the world, further explain high fertility among African women.

Mortality rates have been declining in all African countries for several decades, but they are still among the highest in the world in many states. Infectious diseases are responsible for approximately 60 percent, chronic diseases for 20 percent, and injuries for 10 percent of all deaths in Sub-Saharan Africa. As indicated earlier, tropical diseases, especially malaria, are major causes of death in many countries. Conflicts and food shortages may also occasionally contribute to higher mortality in some parts of the region. The 1991–92 famine in Somalia caused by drought and civil war that killed some 300,000 people, or the second Congo War of 1998–2004 that resulted in the death of over 3 million people due to starvation and disease, are examples of such mortality outbreaks.

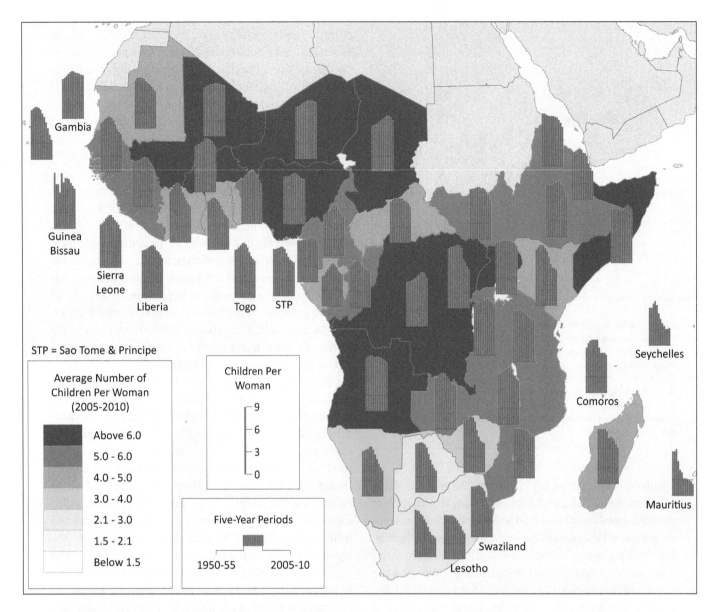

FIGURE 6.15 Total fertility rates in Sub-Saharan Africa, 1950–2010—Most countries have fertility rates well above the replacement level. These rates began to decline in many of them in recent years. Notice a number of countries with fertility rates of over six children per woman. *Source:* United Nations. Population Division. World Population Prospects 2012.

The HIV/AIDS Epidemic

Most scholars agree that the human immunodeficiency virus (HIV) was transmitted from primates (apes or monkeys) to humans probably during the hunting for or the handling of wild meat somewhere in Africa in recent times. The first HIV infections were found in humans in 1959 and 1960 in the present-day Democratic Republic of Congo, and about 2,000 people had probably been infected with this virus by the end of the 1960s. The first AIDS epidemic also occurred in the Democratic Republic of Congo in the 1970s when a sudden increase in several types of opportunistic infections was reported in Kinshasa. The

first large-scale epidemic then began in East Africa, especially around Lake Victoria, mainly among sex workers and their clients in the early 1980s. By 1990, there were about 6.9 million HIV-positive individuals in Sub-Saharan Africa, and they accounted for 75 percent of global infections. The infection rate rose rapidly for the next several years, and by 2000 the region had over 21 million people living with HIV (Fig. 6.16). Although the spread of infections has slowed down since that time, the number of HIV-positive persons in Africa has risen to over 23 million today (70 percent of the world's cases). Countries of Southern and Eastern Africa have been particularly affected by this epidemic. The Republic of South Africa has about 7 million infected people

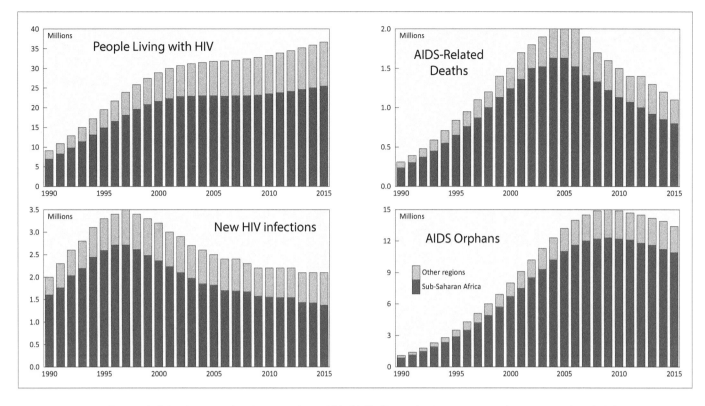

FIGURE 6.16 The HIV/AIDS epidemic in Sub-Saharan Africa, 1990–2015—The region has a disproportionate share of HIV/AIDS cases, deaths, infections, and orphaned children since the start of the epidemic. However, this epidemic may be slowly getting under control as the number of new infections and deaths has been declining. *Source:* UNAIDS.

(19 percent of its population), more than any other country in the world. The highest proportion (22 to 28 percent) of adult population living with HIV is found in other South African countries, mainly Botswana, Lesotho, and Swaziland (Fig. 6.17). Although West and Central Africa has been less impacted by this epidemic, Nigeria may have the second largest HIV-positive population in Sub-Saharan Africa.[3]

The HIV/AIDS epidemic in Sub-Saharan Africa is different from that in other parts of the world in at least two ways. First, it has mainly affected the heterosexual population (some 80 to 90 percent of all cases), while in other regions homosexuals and intravenous drug users have been its primary victims. Second, women comprise the majority of the HIV-positive population (about 60 percent) in Sub-Saharan Africa. The male-female gap is even higher among young adults (15 to 24 years of age); women account for over 66 percent of all cases in this age group.

Why does Sub-Saharan Africa have such a high infection rate? One reason is a culture of multiple sex partners, especially among truck drivers and miners. As they travel from place to place (truck drivers) or move away from home for a longer period (miners), they get infected and infect others through sexual contact with women along their travel routes or in mining towns and upon returning home.

Many refugees in politically unstable areas and temporary settlements, especially women and children, are vulnerable to sexual abuse by soldiers and even refugee camp workers. Reluctance to use or a lack of access to condoms, especially among men and the poor, respectively, is another factor in HIV transmission. Stigma associated with HIV/AIDS prevents many infected persons (mainly women) from revealing their health condition to their spouses or partners because of their fear of rejection and even expulsion from home. Low public awareness of the disease and the expensive medicine needed to treat it during the early stages of the epidemic also contributed to it spreading quickly.

The HIV/AIDS epidemic has impacted Sub-Saharan Africa in many ways. First, the health care sector has been severely impaired due to the shortage of hospital beds and health care workers (many of whom died after contracting the virus). Second, it affected the national economies of many countries because of lower productivity and high absenteeism among the infected employees. Third, it lowered household income of families with sick members (unable to work), limiting funds for purchasing basic necessities and causing higher healthcare expenses and funeral costs. Fourth, the epidemic has generated a large number of orphans. After their parents' death, many children had

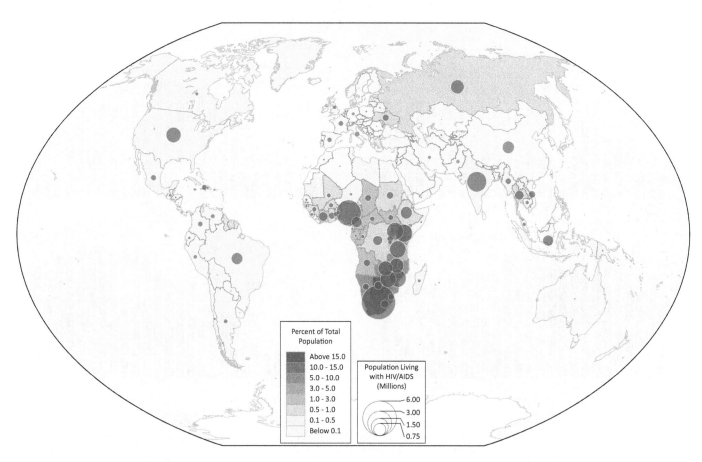

FIGURE 6.17 The HIV/AIDS epidemic around the world, 2012—Notice the large number of affected people in the countries of southern and eastern Africa and Nigeria. *Source:* UNAIDS.

to take care of their younger siblings and work instead of attending school. Many became homeless and vulnerable to various abuses as street children. Fifth, the educational sector has been handicapped by the decline in the number of students and the shortage of healthy teachers. Sixth, high mortality rates, especially among middle-aged individuals, resulted in a distorted age/sex population structure (characterized by relative shortages of economically active age groups) of several countries, especially those in Southern Africa. Although the worst seems to be over as far as the number of new infections and AIDS-related deaths are concerned, Sub-Saharan Africa has a long way to go before this epidemic is contained and eventually eliminated.

Migration Patterns

Although migration has been a minor component of population change in Sub-Saharan Africa recently, it has played an important role in the region's demographic history. Most importantly, as discussed later in this chapter, millions of people were forcibly moved from the region during the

centuries-long slave trade. Since the abolition of the slave trade during the early 19th century, large scale migration has been motivated by the political strategies of imperial powers, the pursuit of economic opportunities, and the flight from famine, persecution, and other push factors.

During the colonial era, imperial powers encouraged the immigration of Europeans to their African colonies. A seminal event in this period was the Great Trek (1835–40), a migration of about 6,000 Boers (descendants of Dutch immigrants who came to this region in the second part of the 17th century) from the coastal areas of the Cape region to the interior regions of Transvaal and Orange. This migration was spurred by tensions between the Boers and the British, whose power was expanding in South Africa. The Great Trek led to numerous conflicts between the Boers and indigenous Africans along the way.

Other areas of the region also attracted substantial European migration. For example, the Portuguese government supported white immigration to Angola and Mozambique in the early 20th century. By 1975, some 400,000 Portuguese lived in Angola and 350,000 in Mozambique. However, most left both countries and went either to Portugal or South Africa after the two Portuguese colonies gained independence in 1975. The Angolan economic boom has attracted some of them (and others) back in recent years, and currently there are about 20,000 whites in Angola. The British authorities had plans to make Southern Rhodesia (now Zimbabwe) a "white man's country" and encouraged immigration from the British Isles. By 1980, there were 240,000 Europeans in Zimbabwe. Most of them left the country because of increasing racial tensions and government policies of land redistribution after 2000, and the current white population in Zimbabwe is estimated at only 20,000.

The discovery of diamonds and gold and the development of mining have contributed to relatively large-scale migrations in some parts of Africa. The Transvaal gold rush of the second part of the 19th century attracted over 100,000 migrants from neighboring areas and Europe within a ten-year period. The number of African migrant workers in these mines ranged from over 170,000 in 1911 to 400,000 in 1979. About a half of them came from other parts of South Africa (mainly the former homeland of Transkei); a quarter from the neighboring states of Botswana, Lesotho, and Swaziland; and the remainder from countries to the north (Angola, Mozambique, Tanzania, Zambia, and Zimbabwe).[4] Although the number of foreign mine workers in South Africa has declined in recent decades (the production of gold has declined as well, as is briefly discussed later in this chapter), the country continues to attract migrants from other African, and even Asian, countries. Some 4 million immigrants have entered South Africa since 1985, 97 percent of them from other African countries. However, over 640,000 whites left the country during the same period. There are also about 500,000 to 1 million illegal immigrants in the country, most of them from neighboring Zimbabwe. Another major mining region of Sub-Saharan Africa, the Copperbelt of Zambia and the Democratic Republic of Congo, had also been a magnet for migrants, albeit on a much smaller scale than South Africa.

Not all economic migration has been driven by mineral resources. The Ivory Coast, a former French colony in West Africa, experienced an economic boom supported by cocoa and other tropical plantation crops (grown in the southern part of the country) during the 1960s and 1970s. Demand for labor in agriculture and other sectors was met by migrants from neighboring Francophone countries, particularly Burkina Faso and Mali; some Middle Eastern states (Lebanon and Syria); and even France. After a sharp decline of cocoa prices in the 1980s, the country's boom ended. The combination of economic decline, population growth, and migration led to widespread ethnic tensions

across the country in the 1990s[5]. These tensions reflect the local-versus-outsider (foreigner) rather than the south-(Christian)-versus-north (Muslim) divide responsible for numerous conflicts in the region.

Considering the political instability, poverty, and environmental stress in many parts of Sub-Saharan Africa, it is not surprising to see large numbers of Africans trying to leave their homeland in search of a better life in the developed world, particularly Europe. Some estimates put the number of African emigrants to over 8 million, most of them from West Africa.[6] A growing number of migrants attempt to reach Europe illegally through the Spanish enclaves of Ceuta and Melilla in Morocco, the Canary Islands (Spanish territory) west of Western Sahara, or Malta and the Italian islands of Sicily and Lampedusa in the Mediterranean Sea. To reach these points, they first must travel long distances via one of several routes through the Sahara or along the West African coast. Smugglers may charge each migrant several thousand dollars for a journey that is full of danger. Some of them perish along the way and never reach their destinations.

Sub-Saharan Africa has several million forced migrants, including 3.2 million refugees and 5.6 million internally displaced persons. Most of them are found in the Democratic Republic of Congo, Somalia, South Sudan, and neighboring countries. Their presence is associated with recent political instability (civil wars) in these three states.

Urbanization Trends and Patterns

Sub-Saharan Africa is the least urbanized region of the world; only 37 percent of its population is urban (Fig. 6.18). However, this population has been growing at a very fast rate, over 5 percent a year, and it has more than doubled in one generation. Despite low urbanization levels, urban traditions are fairly old in parts of the region. Western Africa was the major center of urbanization in the pre-colonial era. Several large cities in present-day Mali, including Kumbi, Timbuktu, Gao, Djenné, and Saleh, were centers of power and learning between 800 and 1500 CE. As centers of power, they were surrounded by walls and located at defensible sites. They also performed major economic functions as manufacturing and trading centers. A number of cities along the eastern coast of Africa (Kenya and Somalia), among them Mogadishu, Mombasa, and Kilwa, supported trade between Africa and the Middle East and South Asia. Some of them had impressive architecture (mosques and palaces) and flourished for many centuries. The city of Great Zimbabwe in Southern Africa might have had a population of 18,000 by the early 15th century.

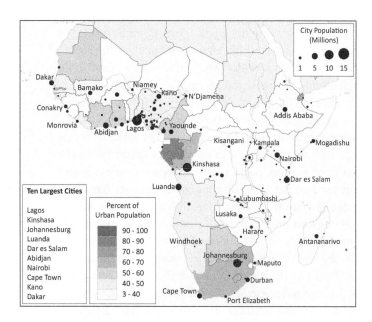

FIGURE 6.18 Urbanization levels in Sub-Saharan Africa—Most countries are predominantly rural. Relatively high urbanization levels in some of them reflect high levels of economic development (Republic of South Africa) or inhospitable natural environment (deserts and dense forests) unable to support high population densities across the entire area (Mauritania, Gabon, Republic of Congo). *Source:* United Nations. Population Division. World Urbanization Prospects 2014.

Europeans established a number of coastal cities for trading purposes (slaves and tropical agricultural products) during their early colonial expansion in the 16th and 17th centuries. St. Louis at the mouth of the Senegal River, Luanda and Benguela in Angola, and Lorenço Marques (now Maputo) in Mozambique were built by the Portuguese; Calabar in Nigeria by the British; Conakry in Guinea by the French; and Cape Town in South Africa by the Dutch.[7] After the colonization of the African interior in the second part of the 19th century, additional cities along the coast or railroad lines and in mining and plantation regions were built, especially in Southern Africa. Some of them became administrative centers of national or regional importance, others mining or plantation towns (Fig. 6.19). Most colonial cities consisted of neighborhoods segregated by race and ethnicity.

After independence, many cities upgraded their infrastructure by building new highways, airports, hospitals, and schools. Industrial parks on the periphery of larger cities were also established. Some African countries relocated their capital functions from coastal cities to newly built settlements in the interior for economic or political reasons. The city of Abuja in Nigeria became the new capital in 1991; Yamoussoukro has been the capital of Ivory Coast

FIGURE 6.19 The capital city of Harare, Zimbabwe—Founded by the British colonists in 1890 and known as Salisbury until 1982, it has a population of 1.6 million and is the economic and cultural center of Zimbabwe. *Source:* Pixabay.

since 1983; and Malawi moved its government to the city of Lilongwe in 1975. The city of Dodoma, established by the Germans in 1907, became the capital of Tanzania in 1996.

The largest cities in many African countries are primate cities. A primate city is several times larger in population size than the next largest city in the same country. The capital city of Djibouti has almost 60 percent of the country's total population. The cities of Brazzaville in Congo and Libreville in Gabon house 40 percent of those countries' total populations while the capital cities of Monrovia and Bissau have at least a quarter of Liberia's and Guinea-Bissau's populations, respectively. Luanda in Angola, Dakar in Senegal, and Abidjan in the Ivory Coast are other examples of African primate cities. The importance of primate cities in many countries has been increasing as the proportion of people living in them has also been increasing since independence. For example, Luanda had less than 8 percent of Angola's total population in 1970, but it is now a city of over 5 million people and houses a quarter of that country's population. Abidjan's population increased from half a million in 1970 to over 4 million in 2015 or from 10 to 22 percent of the Ivory Coast's total population. Migration from rural areas has been a very important component of urban population growth in most of Africa. However, many newcomers are unable to find employment and adequate housing and engage in the informal economy as petty traders and service providers. They have no choice but to live

FIGURE 6.21 The slums of Cape Town, Republic of South Africa—Over half of Sub-Saharan Africa's urban population lives in squatter settlements. In the economically most developed country of this region, the Republic of South Africa, a quarter of urban residents live in such conditions. *Source:* Heike C. Alberts.

in slums and **squatter settlements**, usually located in the least desirable areas such as poorly drained floodplains, abandoned industrial sites, or along railroad tracks. Residents of such neighborhoods comprise a large proportion of the urban population in many countries (Fig. 6.20 and Fig. 6.21). Cities in Sub-Saharan Africa face many other challenges, including air and water pollution, inadequate waste management, poor access to drinking water and electricity, and health-related issues. The majority of Africans still live in rural settlements, and most of these settlements face even more challenges, including poor access to health care and isolation (Fig. 6. 22).

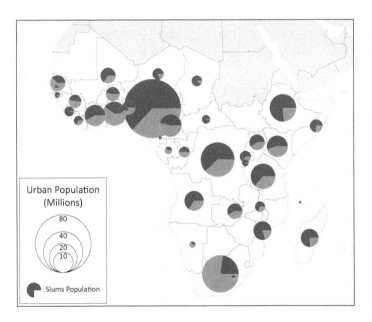

FIGURE 6.20 Urban squatter population in Sub-Saharan Africa, 2009—Notice that in many countries over half, and in some over three-quarters, of the urban population lives in squatter settlements. *Source:* UN Statistics Division. Millennium Development Goals Database.

FIGURE 6.22 Houses in an African village, Malawi—Most rural dwellings in Sub-Saharan Africa are made of local materials (adobe, clay, twigs, etc.), do not yet have access to electricity or running water, and are not divided into separate rooms. *Source:* Pixabay.

LANGUAGE AND RELIGION

Almost all countries in Sub-Saharan Africa are characterized by great ethnic diversity. European colonial powers considered ethnic identity as an objectively defined culture trait associated with a particular group of people and remained unchanged for a long time. Scholars today consider ethnic identity as a socially constructed concept that may change its meaning over time. As an example, the Hutu and Tutsi groups in Rwanda and Burundi speak the same language (known as Kinyarwanda in Rwanda and Kirundi in Burundi) and adhere to the same religion (Christianity) but have long been constructed as separate ethnic groups. Although there may be some differences in physical features, blood chemistry, lactose tolerance, and other genetic variables between the groups, differences in lifestyles and economic activities have also been important factors in the ethnic identity of both groups. Cattle ownership has been one of these factors—anyone with fewer than ten cows was considered a Hutu. The Tutsis have been engaged in cattle herding and were economically more prosperous than the Hutus who have practiced farming, which was considered a low class occupation by the Tutsis. The Hutus came to Rwanda and Burundi from present-day Chad; the Tutsis came from Ethiopia at a later time (14th and 15th centuries).[8] The German and Belgian colonial authorities emphasized differences between the two groups and favored the Tutsis as intermediaries between colonial administrators and the indigenous people. This example shows that ethnic identity and diversity is a very complex issue in many parts of this region.

Linguistic Patterns

Sub-Saharan Africa is one of the most (if not the most) linguistically diverse regions of the world. Its 950 million people speak over 2,000 languages that belong to four major and two smaller linguistic families (Fig. 6.23). The Niger-Congo family includes over 1,500 languages found in southern, central, and western parts of Sub-Saharan Africa, which are spoken by almost half of the region's population. The Bantu linguistic branch is dominant in Central and Southern Africa. One of the best known languages in this branch is Swahili, used by about 50 million speakers in parts of Eastern Africa. It originated as a trade language of the people inhabiting coastal areas of Kenya and Tanzania and later became the **lingua franca** for many residents of these and other neighboring states (Democratic Republic of Congo and Uganda). Its vocabulary contains many words

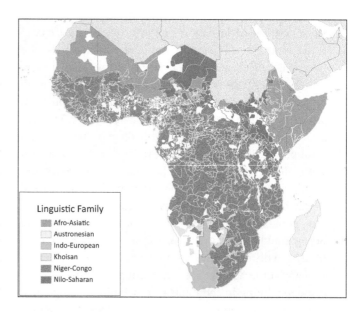

FIGURE 6.23 Distribution of major linguistic families in Sub-Saharan Africa—Each linguistic family is composed of numerous languages. Individual language boundaries are shown as thin white lines. *Source:* World Language Mapping System.

Linguistic Family
- Afro-Asiatic
- Austronesian
- Indo-European
- Khoisan
- Niger-Congo
- Nilo-Saharan

of Arabic origin. Other major languages belonging to this branch are Shona and Zulu, spoken in Zimbabwe and South Africa, respectively.

The Nilo-Saharan family includes about 200 languages spoken by 45 million people, mainly in Chad and South Sudan as well as parts of several countries in West and East-central Africa (Fig. 6.24). The Afro-Asiatic linguistic family is dominant in the northern part of Sub-Saharan Africa, including the Horn of Africa. The Semitic branch

FIGURE 6.24 The Maasai people of East Africa—One of the best known ethnic groups in Sub-Saharan Africa, the Maasai have a population of 1.6 million and inhabit parts of Kenya and Tanzania. *Source:* Pixabay.

includes the Arabic language spoken in several countries of the Sahara region, from Mauritania to South Sudan. Some 18 million residents of Madagascar speak Malagasy, a language that belongs to the Austronesian family of languages which are found mainly in Southeast Asia. The Khoisian languages spoken by some 400,000 inhabitants of the Kalahari Basin in Namibia and Botswana form a distinctive linguistic family. These languages are known for the common use of click consonants.

Afrikaans is a Germanic language of Dutch origin in the Indo-European linguistic family. It is the native tongue of over 7 million mainly white inhabitants of South Africa and Namibia. Although Afrikaans has borrowed words from Portuguese, English, and Bantu languages, it is still very similar to Dutch (in fact the two languages are mutually intelligible). It is one of eleven official languages in South Africa. English, another Germanic language, is the native language for over 3 million white residents of South Africa and smaller groups in a few other countries (e.g. Zimbabwe and Kenya).

A major feature of African linguistic geography is the fact that some major languages (e.g. Fulani, Hausa, and Swahili) are spoken in several countries; at the same time, most countries are inhabited by people speaking a number of languages (Fig. 6.25). The Fulani language, used by about 25 million people, is widely distributed across the Sahel region and is spoken in countries stretching from the Atlantic to the Nile. One of those countries is Benin, but the 10 million residents of Benin, one of the smaller African countries, use at least nine different languages on a daily basis. These two examples reflect complex linguistic patterns across Sub-Saharan Africa; these patterns became even more complex after the imposition of colonial boundaries on the region.

The great linguistic and ethnic diversity of African countries was an important factor in giving the languages of their former colonial powers official status or at least making them the languages of administration after independence (Fig. 6.26). English is the official language in 20 countries, French in 16 countries, and Portuguese in 5 countries. Several states gave the official status to two European languages: English and French in Cameroon, Rwanda, Madagascar, and the Seychelles; and Spanish and French in Equatorial Guinea (a former Spanish colony). Mauritania is the only country in Sub-Saharan Africa that did not give the language of its former colonial master (France) official status (Arabic is the official language in this country). Ethiopia is another country without a European language in official use, but it has never been a European colony except for a brief period of Italian rule just before World War II.

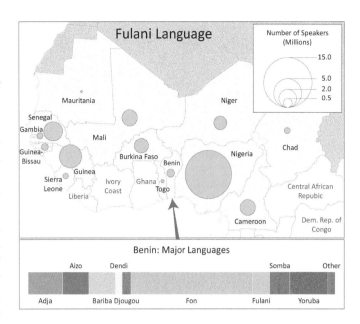

FIGURE 6.25 Distribution of the Fulani speakers and major linguistic groups in Benin—The Fulani language belongs to the Niger-Congo family and has over 25 million speakers in most countries of Western Africa. It is the dominant language in Guinea, and the second most important one in Burkina Faso, Gambia, Guinea-Bissau, and Senegal. Benin is an example of a linguistically diverse country. *Source:* Encyclopedia Britannica Book of the Year 2016.

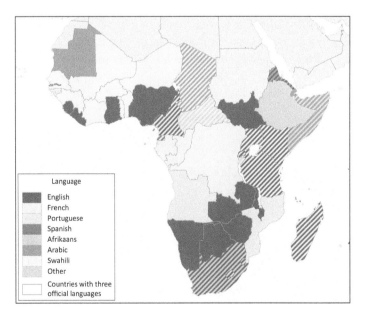

FIGURE 6.26 Official languages in Sub-Saharan Africa—Ethiopia is the only country in the region without any official status given to a European language (Amharic is its official language). A few countries have three or more official languages: the Republic of South Africa has eleven, while Comoros, Rwanda, and the Seychelles have three. Eritrea has no official but nine recognized national languages. *Source:* CIA World Factbook.

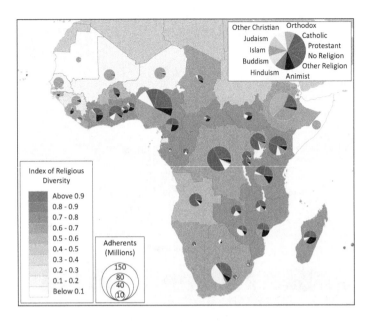

FIGURE 6.27 Religious affiliation of people in Sub-Saharan Africa—Nigeria, the Democratic Republic of Congo, and Ethiopia have the largest Christian populations in the region. Nigeria also has the largest Muslim population in this region. Most countries in Sub-Saharan Africa are religiously diverse with a few exceptions in the northern part of the region where Islam is the dominant religion. *Source:* Association of Religious Data Archives.

Religious Patterns

Sub-Saharan Africa is a region of two major religions, both of them imported from two nearby culture realms (Europe and the Middle East), which have, to a large degree, replaced the indigenous, mainly animistic, beliefs.

FIGURE 6.28 An Eritrean Eastern Orthodox procession, Eritrea—About half of the country's population adheres to Eastern Orthodox Christianity that was introduced to this region in the 4th century. *Source:* Pixabay.

About 60 percent of its population adheres to Christianity and 30 percent to Islam. Christianity is dominant in central and southern as well as coastal regions of Western Africa, while Islam is the majority religion in the northern parts of Sub-Saharan Africa, from Mauritania and Senegal to Chad and along the coast of Eastern Africa from Eritrea to Tanzania (Fig. 6.27). The remaining 10 percent of the African population follows various animistic traditions. **Religious syncretism** is relatively common in some parts of the region—Christians and Muslims may incorporate some elements of indigenous customs in their practices and beliefs. Christianity became a well-established religion in present-day Ethiopia by the beginning of the fourth century CE. The Ethiopian Orthodox Church is today the second largest Eastern Christian denomination after the Russian Orthodox Church; it has over 35 million believers, mostly in Ethiopia and Eritrea (Fig. 6.28). Western Christianity was introduced (on a limited scale) to Sub-Saharan Africa by European missionaries, both Catholic and Protestant, to coastal areas in the 16th through 17th centuries and to the interior of the continent in the 19th and 20th centuries. The diffusion of Christianity during the latter period was closely associated with the colonial advances of European powers. Catholic missionaries were more active in the French, Portuguese, and Belgian colonies, while Protestants spread their faith in the British and German possessions. Today, about 40 percent of the region's Christian population is Protestant, 35 percent is Catholic, and 8 percent Eastern Orthodox. The remaining 18 percent of the population belongs to other (mainly Evangelical and independent African) denominations. Nigeria and the Democratic Republic of Congo have the largest Christian populations on the continent, over 60 million in each country. Protestants comprise the majority of Christians in Nigeria and Catholics in the Democratic Republic of Congo.

Islam was first introduced to coastal areas along the Red Sea and was originally popular among the ruling class and other, more affluent social groups. Several medieval empires of Western Africa accepted Islam between the 10th and 15th centuries. The beginning of Muslim influence along the East African coast also began around that time. The Islamic religion also greatly expanded during the colonial era when it was often presented as a religion for black people, while Christianity was seen as a religion of white people, (i.e. European colonizers). Most Muslims in Sub-Saharan Africa (95 percent) follow the Sunni tradition. Nigeria has the largest Muslim population in the region (75 to 80 million), while over 99 percent of Somalia's population adheres to this faith.

Although animistic religions have been declining in importance throughout the region, they are still relatively strong in some West African countries (especially Guinea-Bissau and Togo), Madagascar, the Central African Republic, and South Sudan. Almost half of Guinea-Bissau's and one-third of Togo's populations practice traditional African religions.

Although Christians and Muslims have lived side by side in many parts of Sub-Saharan Africa for generations, religious tensions between the two groups have become more common in recent years. Some attribute this to the rapid growth of Muslim and Christian populations across the region, others to proximity to the Middle East and radicalization of certain segments of the Muslim people, and still others to authoritarian or weak governments and their inability to control parts of their territories. As discussed in the previous chapter, conflict in Sudan, which led to the separation of the predominantly Christian southern part of the country from the Muslim north in 2011, had a strong religious dimension. The tensions in Nigeria closely coincide with religious divisions in the country—a Muslim north and Christian south (Fig. 6.29). The most vivid example of such tensions is the Boko Haram terrorist insurgency group operating in the northeastern part of the country that has tried to impose strict Muslim law on Northern Nigeria.

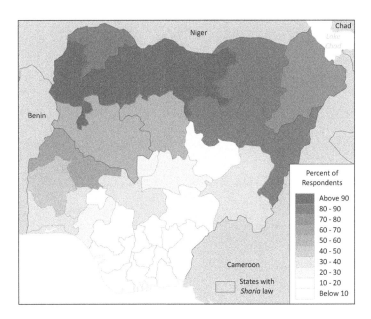

FIGURE 6.29 The Muslim population in Nigeria—The Muslim-Christian split has been responsible for serious tensions and conflict in recent years. Sharia law has been introduced in several northern states since 1999. *Source:* Wikipedia.

The former French colonies of Chad and the Central African Republic, as well as Kenya, have also been affected by sporadic Muslim-Christian tensions in recent years.

POLITICAL ORGANIZATION OF SPACE

Precolonial Sub-Saharan Africa

Several centers of plant domestication and complex political and social organization existed in various parts of Sub-Saharan Africa as early as 3000-2000 BCE and 1000 BCE, respectively. The shift from hunting and gathering to sedentary agriculture and pastoral nomadism first occurred in the parts of Western Africa where millet, sorghum, and certain varieties of rice were domesticated and grown around Lake Chad and along the Senegal and Niger rivers. Most people lived in villages and small cities and were governed by chiefs responsible to a hierarchy of regional leaders with a king at the top. They practiced various forms of animism and polytheism. The Trans-Saharan trade with Northwestern Africa was well developed—the West African region was an important source of gold and slaves for Mediterranean Africa and Europe. This trade also contributed to the development of urban centers (e.g. Timbuktu) in the desert-savanna transition zone; some of these early centers are fairly large cities today.

Prior to the establishment of the first European settlements along the African coast in the 16th century, several kingdoms and empires had emerged and fallen apart in some parts of the region (Fig. 6.30). The three largest and best known West African empires were the Kingdom of Ghana (900–1100), which controlled an area similar in size to Texas in parts of present-day Mauritania and Mali; the Kingdom of Mali (1200–1450) with the city of Timbuktu as its political, economic, and cultural center; and the Kingdom of Songhai (1464–1591), which at its peak was one of the largest states in African history with the city of Gao as its major center of power. All three empires had several things in common. First, their societies were highly stratified, composed of at least four major classes including the ruling class at the top, the merchants below it, then farm workers, cattle herders, and miners, and the slaves at the bottom of the social ladder. Second, the upper classes practiced Islam while the lower ones adhered to

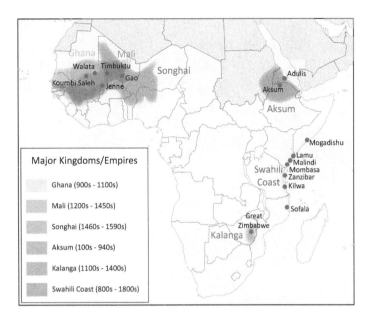

FIGURE 6.30 Selected pre-colonial African empires—This map shows only selected pre-colonial states. Considering their location, some scholars identified three regions where such states existed: the West African Imperial System, the Ethiopian Kingdoms, and the Bantu States of south-central Africa. *Source:* drawn after a similar map in Wikipedia.

traditional animistic beliefs. Third, they had a hierarchical administrative structure and system of taxation. Fourth, their economies were based on agriculture (cultivation of grain and root crops and livestock herding), mining (gold and salt), and trade (with the Mediterranean regions of North Africa).

To the east, the Kingdom of Aksum (ca. 100–940) in parts of today's Ethiopia, Eritrea, and Sudan, supported by advanced agriculture (cultivation of wheat and barley, crop rotation, and the use of the plow) and trade (with Europe and India), was the first Christian state in Africa. It was also the first African state to have its own currency. A series of city-states along the Indian Ocean, from Southern Somalia to Northern Mozambique, were supported by trade with the Mediterranean region, the Arabian Peninsula, and South Asia from early medieval times until the 19th century. Ivory, spices, incense, and slaves were exchanged for cotton, copper, and iron tools. Mogadishu in Somalia, Malindi and Mombasa in Kenya, Zanzibar and Kilwa in Tanzania, and Sofala in Mozambique were the largest trading centers. Finally, the Kingdom of Great Zimbabwe (1100–1450) was a powerful state in present-day Zimbabwe. Its Bantu-speaking inhabitants, who came to this region by the eighth century, practiced mixed farming, ironworking, and gold mining. The city of Great Zimbabwe with its dry-stone architecture was a political and religious center of the empire. The above examples indicate that

pre-colonial Sub-Saharan Africa had a rich history and three regions (West Africa, the Ethiopian Highlands, and South-central Africa) gave rise to a number of politically and economically complex states, some of which existed for centuries and maintained extensive links with the outside world.

The Slave Trade

Although slavery may be as old as written human history and was practiced in every part of the world at different times, the African continent was affected by this form of human cruelty to a larger extent than any other region. Slavery had a tremendous demographic, social, political, and economic impact not only on African societies but also on those in the Middle East and the Americas. The Trans-Saharan Slave Trade, practiced on a large scale between the 7th and 19th centuries, resulted in the forced shipment of over 9 million (usually young and healthy) people from Western Africa to the Mediterranean region of Northern Africa, Europe, and Southwest Asia. The journey across the Sahara was treacherous and responsible for the high mortality among the slave population. Women and children comprised about two-thirds of the slaves and were mainly used as concubines and domestic servants. Most male slaves were soldiers or courtiers. The East African Slave Trade between the 8th and 19th centuries forcibly displaced at least 5 million people from East Africa to the Arabian Peninsula, Persia, and South Asia. Like in the previous case, most slaves were women and children and were used for similar purposes. Most slaves sent to the Middle East were not allowed to reproduce, and their presence did not have a major long-term demographic impact on the region. The mortality among African slaves was also very high; by some estimates, only one in twelve slaves reached the destination area.[9]

The **Trans-Atlantic Slave Trade**, briefly discussed in Chapter 7, has been the best known and studied example of forced human migration in world history. Although shorter in its duration (the 16th century through middle of the 19th century) than the previous slave trades, it was the largest in magnitude and longest in terms of distance between the areas of origin and destination. The slave trade across the Atlantic began in 1510 when the Spanish king authorized the shipment of fifty African slaves to the Spanish colony of Santo Domingo in what is today the Dominican Republic. Some 4,000 slaves were sent to New Spain (Spanish colonies in the Caribbean and Central America) in 1518, and that year marked the beginning of the large-scale slave trade in which some 10 to 12 million slaves were shipped from Africa to the New World over the next 350 years. They were treated as a commodity that should be transported quickly and cheaply across the ocean. The harsh treatment of the slaves prior to boarding the ships and the miserable conditions (overcrowding, poor or no sanitation, and malnutrition) during the "middle passage" killed about two-thirds of them. The Trans-Atlantic Slave Trade removed 30 to 36 million inhabitants, most of them from Western and parts of Southern Africa (Angola and Mozambique), and impoverished the continent demographically and economically for many decades.

European Colonial Rule

Africa is located fairly close to Europe, yet it was colonized by European powers much later than the more distant Americas, Australia, and parts of Asia. Although the Portuguese, Spanish, and others began establishing coastal settlements along the Atlantic and Indian Oceans by the 15th century, the interior of the African continent was virtually unknown to them until the second part of the 19th century. However, there was a growing interest in this continent by the end of the 18th century for two reasons. First, several European travelers visited the interior of Africa and reported their findings in popular and scientific journals. Richard Burton (a British geographer and linguist) and John Speke (an officer in the British Indian Army) travelled to the source of the White Nile (Lake Victoria) in the 1850s. David Livingstone (a Scottish medical missionary) and Henry Stanley (a Welsh journalist) explored Central Africa around the same time. Second, there was also an increased interest in spreading Christianity through missionary posts across the continent and "civilizing" the African population. Europeans controlled only 10 percent of Africa around 1870 but over 90 percent by 1914.

The late European entry to Africa had several causes, including the desert barriers (Sahara and Kalahari/Namib), the nature of African rivers (difficult upstream navigation due to the plateau nature of the continent which results in numerous cataracts), the hot-humid tropical climate (resulting in high mortality among European settlers due to various tropical diseases—Africa was considered the "white man's grave"), opposition by slave traders (fears of disrupting their lucrative business), and the lack of readily available sources of wealth (minerals). However, when several European powers decided to partition and control Africa, they did it quickly at the **Berlin Conference** in 1884–85. Thirteen European countries and the United States attended the conference that became known as

the "Scramble for Africa." Most of Africa was partitioned into colonial zones among seven European powers—the United Kingdom, France, Belgium, Spain, Portugal, Germany, and Italy. Most of the imposed political boundaries showed little if any respect for ethnic and linguistic patterns; one-third of these boundaries were straight lines or arcs (Fig. 6.31). France controlled about 35 percent of Sub-Saharan Africa's area and 20 percent of its population by the turn of the 20th century. Most of the Western and parts of Central Africa, plus Madagascar, were French domains. The British were in charge of a quarter of the region's territory and about 45 percent of its population, including Nigeria, Ghana, and Sierra Leone in Western Africa and large segments of Southern and Northeastern Africa. Belgium, Germany, and Portugal together controlled about 30 percent of Sub-Saharan Africa's area and a quarter of its population. Germany lost its colonial possessions (present-day Tanzania, Namibia, Cameroon, and Togo) to France and Great Britain after World War I. Italy was in control of parts of Northeastern Africa (Eritrea and parts of Somalia), and Spain had a small possession in Central Africa (Rio Muni—present-day Equatorial Guinea). Only two Sub-Saharan African countries, Ethiopia and Liberia, avoided long-term European control. Italy was interested in

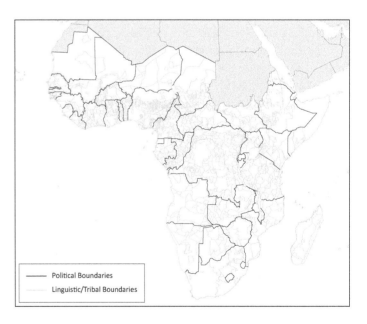

FIGURE 6.31 Linguistic/tribal and political boundaries in Sub-Saharan Africa—Most political boundaries imposed by colonial powers did not match linguistic and ethnic patterns. Over 170 major groups were split between two or more colonial empires, and about one-third of boundaries are arcs or straight lines. Almost every country is a collection of many ethnic groups speaking different languages and adhering to various cultural traditions. A weak correlation between political and ethnic boundaries has been one of several factors responsible for political instability in many parts of the region. *Source:* World Language Mapping System.

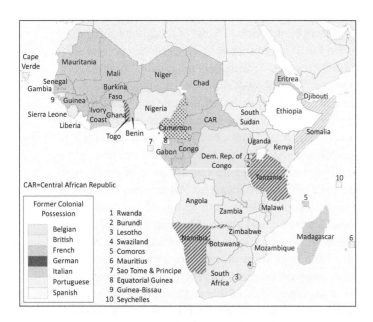

FIGURE 6.32 European colonization of Sub-Saharan Africa—Colonial boundaries were slightly different from present day boundary lines in a few cases (e.g. Cameroon, the Republic of Congo). Somalia was split into British and Italian parts. Germany lost its colonies after World War I. Only Ethiopia and Liberia avoided long-term direct European control.

controlling Ethiopia (known as Abyssinia at that time) but was unable to do so due to strong resistance of its population. Liberia was established in 1847 as a country for former African slaves living in the Americas who were interested in going back to their area of origin (Fig. 6.32).

European countries colonized Africa for two main reasons: to have access to raw materials for their expanding industries and to create markets for some industrial goods. To achieve these objectives, the colonial powers applied the "law and order" policy (strict criminal justice system and severe penalties for various challenges to the colonial rule) and developed economic and social infrastructure on a limited scale to serve their interests. The limited investment also reflected the policy of minimizing the costs of colonial administration. Four types of colonial rule could be identified in Sub-Saharan Africa: company, direct, indirect, and settler rule. Company rule was associated with the early stages of British colonialism and public colonial enterprises such as the Imperial British East Africa Company and the British South Africa Company that had numerous powers (e.g. taxation, custom duties, administration of justice) to act in the name of the colonial government. Direct rule was found mainly in French and Belgian colonies, and it was characterized by the presence of a highly centralized colonial authority at most territorial levels and the exclusion of indigenous people from the colonial government at all but the lowest levels. Under indirect rule, common in British colonies, traditional local government structures

were incorporated into the colonial system of government. Laws were created by colonial powers but enforced by local (indigenous) leaders who often had a few European "advisers." Settler rule was found in several parts of Southern Africa (British and Portuguese colonies) and was associated with a strong colonial government composed of only a European (white) population that denied political and many other rights to the indigenous residents who were also affected by harsh labor polices and ethnic dislocation.

Indigenous people periodically challenged European colonial rule by various means, including armed resistance. The Chimurenga Resistance (1896–97) was a revolt of the Ndebele and Shona groups against the British South Africa Company rule in present-day Zimbabwe. An armed uprising, known as the Maji Maji Rebellion, against German colonial rule in present-day Tanzania in response to forcing the African farmers to grow cotton took place in 1905–1907. The leaders of the rebels persuaded their followers that German bullets would turn to water and not harm them. That was not the case, and the death toll of this uprising exceeded 200,000. The Ashanti Resistance (1807–1874) in Ghana had been a series of conflicts between the British forces and Ashanti people and resulted in several thousand deaths. It took the British almost seventy years to defeat one of the strongest colonial resistance movements in Africa. Samori Toure (1830–1900), a Guinean Muslim cleric, became a powerful example of African resistance to the European (French) colonial rule. He had a well-disciplined army of 30,000 to 35,000 soldiers and was able to fight the colonial forces for several decades.

As indicated earlier, most African colonies supplied Europe with raw materials, mainly mineral resources and plantation crops. Colonial economic policy focused on the development of mines and plantations and limited transportation networks (mainly railroads) connecting the mining or plantation regions with coastal cities. The copper-rich parts of Zambia and the Katanga region of the Democratic Republic of Congo, sisal plantations of Tanzania, and tea plantations of Kenya are examples of such developments. Most plantations were established on the best lands forcibly taken from their African owners who had no choice but to cultivate less productive or marginal lands. West Africa had been a less attractive region to European settlers because of higher population densities and well-developed indigenous farming systems. However, African farmers were encouraged or forced to grow plantation crops (cotton and groundnuts) for European needs. The parts of Sub-Saharan Africa that were poor in mineral resources or fertile soil or were peripherally located (e.g. Mali, Niger, Chad, and Lesotho) became the sources of labor for various colonial projects.

Decolonization

The struggle for independence began quite early and was carried out on three fronts: intellectual, armed resistance, and passive resistance. The first, intellectual, was originally led by Africans educated in the United States or Europe who later became part of the Pan African movement calling for "Africa for the Africans," political unification of the entire continent, economic development based on socialist principles, and democratic forms of government. The second and third approaches of armed struggle, political agitation and civil disobedience, were carried out in several states and led to the independence of Portuguese and some French and British colonies. Although the Republic of South Africa gained independence from Great Britain in 1910 (then known as the Union of South Africa), the real decolonization process began in the 1950s when Sudan, Ghana, and Guinea became independent. Some thirty countries gained independence during the 1960s (Fig. 6.33 and Fig. 6.34). The Portuguese and Spanish colonies, as well as some small British and French colonies, obtained independence in the 1970s. Namibia became the last African country to obtain independence in 1990 after an over two-decades long guerilla war against the rule of South Africa. Eritrea and South Sudan are the youngest African countries; the former separated from Ethiopia in 1993 and the latter from Sudan in 2011.

Independence created numerous challenges for most African states. They faced important choices regarding their way to development: whether to give priority to agriculture or education, the urban or the rural sector; whether to have a one- or multi-party political system; and whether to promote national homogeneity or encourage ethnic and cultural diversity. Each choice offered opportunities and challenges. A one-party rule might give greater hope for uniting a country's population for common goals, while a multi-party rule might lead to greater ethnic and territorial fragmentation. One-party rule might also lead to a dictatorship and personality cult, while multi-party rule may result in ethnic tensions and political instability or even civil war. The road to democracy for most African countries has been fairly difficult. Some African political leaders considered Western democracy a concept foreign to their culture. For them, democracy was something more than periodic elections and competition for power among political parties. They emphasized economic democracy and the common good as more important goals than political democracy, individual rights, and freedom of speech. They also claimed that African countries were not yet ready for true Western-style democracy; instead, they needed strong leadership capable of maintaining economic, social, and political order in multi-ethnic societies. This system of government would somehow evolve into real democracy in the future; meanwhile, the one-man and one-party rule had to continue. Many African leaders have used this reasoning to justify their grip on power. Some of them were in charge of their countries for several decades and ready to crush

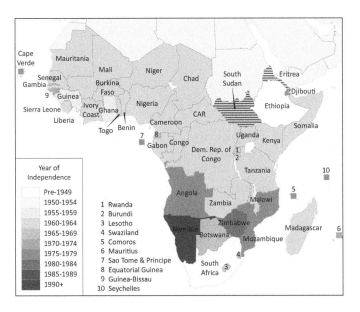

FIGURE 6.33 Decolonization of Sub-Saharan Africa—Eritrea and South Sudan were parts of Ethiopia and Sudan until 1991 and 2011 respectively. Namibia was a German colony until 1915, and was then administered by South Africa until 1990.

FIGURE 6.34 The Kwame Nkrumah Mausoleum and a Memorial Park in Accra, Ghana—It is dedicated to the first leader of independent Ghana and is located in the commercial district of the country's capital. *Source:* Pixabay.

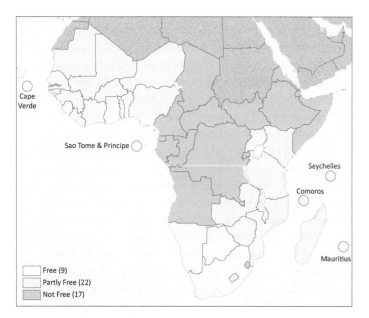

FIGURE 6.35 Political freedom in Sub-Saharan Africa, 2015—The classification of countries into three groups is based on the annual *Freedom in the World* report. It takes into account several variables reflecting political freedoms (electoral process, political pluralism and participation, and functioning of government) and civil liberties (freedom and expression of belief, associational and organizational rights, rule of law, and personal autonomy and individual rights). *Source:* Freedom in the World 2016.

any form of resistance with force. Nevertheless, political change has been coming to Sub-Saharan Africa, and there are more countries with democratic governments today

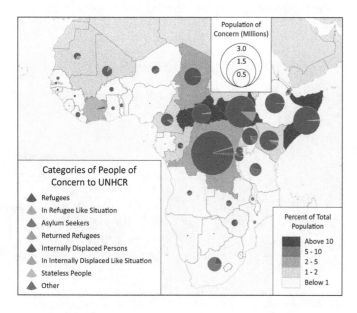

FIGURE 6.36 People of concern to the United Nations High Commissioner for Refugees, 2014—Most of these people are refugees and internally displaced persons. Notice their high numbers in countries (or their neighbors) affected by recent armed conflicts. *Source:* UNHCR Statistical Yearbook 2013.

than in the past. According to the 2015 Freedom House annual report, 12 percent of the population in the region lives in countries that were considered free (democratic), 49 percent in partially-free states, and 39 percent in not free ones (Fig. 6.35).

Political Instability

Sub-Saharan Africa has been plagued by political instability resulting from two major factors: great ethnic and religious diversity of the region and imposition of colonial boundaries which, in most cases, did not respect that diversity. The uneven distribution of important natural resources, ineffective leaders, and the adverse involvement of foreign powers, have also played key roles in determining political stability in parts of the region. Natural disasters have sometimes triggered human emergencies and instability. Some countries became politically unstable shortly after independence, and others experienced the instability after decades of relative peace and economic prosperity. In some states, the instability lasted for decades, while in others it was a short-lived problem. However, in many cases it resulted in staggering death tolls and forced migrations (Fig. 6.36 and Fig. 6.37). In this section we discuss five examples drawn from around the region, but unfortunately there have been many other conflicts not discussed here.

The Congo, which lies at the center of the Sub-Saharan Africa, has also been at the center of numerous conflicts in the region. Its unhappy history began shortly after independence for which this former Belgian colony was poorly prepared. Katanga, a mineral-rich province of the newly independent Congo, proclaimed independence, an idea supported by Belgium. The Congolese government asked the United Nations for peacekeeping forces to bring stability to the country, but there were differences of opinion between the president and prime minister on the use of force against the rebellious region. This conflict became a proxy war between the two Cold War superpowers, with the Soviet Union supporting the central government and the United States the Katanga region. The conflict ended after a military coup leader named Mobutu Sese Seko ousted both the president and prime minister and took control of the country. He renamed it Zaire, which he considered a more authentic name and also changed the names of some cities including the capital, which was changed from Léopoldville (named for a Belgian king) to Kinshasa. He stayed in power until 1997, and his rule could be described not only as a one-party dictatorship but also

FIGURE 6.37 A refugee settlement in Eritrea—Political instability and ethnic and religious conflicts in several parts of Sub-Saharan Africa have generated millions of refugees, many of them living in refugee camps with inadequate basic services and vulnerable to various forms of abuse. Source: Pixabay.

a kleptocracy (rule by thieves) as Mobutu enriched himself while his vast and mineral-rich country sank deeper into poverty. His successor changed the name of the country to Democratic Republic of Congo but conditions hardly improved for the Congolese. The initial success of the new government was challenged by a rebellion in the eastern part of the country, which led to a five-year civil war that drew neighboring countries into what became known as Africa's Great War. Forces from eight countries fought on Congo's soil, with the death toll soaring into millions, making it one of the deadliest wars on earth since World War II. The war ended in 2003 but Congo remains a deeply troubled, fragile, and impoverished country.

Nigeria, the most populous country in Africa, gained independence from Great Britain in 1960 (Fig. 6.38). The dominant ethnic groups include the Hausa and Fulani people in the Muslim north, the Yoruba in the southwest, and the Igbo in the oil-rich southeast parts of the country. Ethnic frictions between the Muslims and the more prosperous and better-educated Igbos turned into violence by the mid-1960s, followed by an unsuccessful coup by an Igbo general in 1966. A counter-coup supported by the Hausa, Fulani, and Yoruba groups took punitive action against the Igbos. In response, the Igbo-dominated southeastern province declared independence as Biafra, and this event marked the start of the Nigerian Civil War (1967–70). The federal government refused to recognize the new country and launched a full-scale

offensive against Biafra. The initial success of the Biafran troops turned into a defeat and the escape of its leader to the Ivory Coast. The conflict led to a large-scale famine as the Biafran people had no access to food and medicine. Although several African countries recognized Biafra's independence and France provided military support, the central government defeated the secessionist revolt by 1970 and the unity of Nigeria was preserved. Estimates of the death toll from this conflict range from half a million to 3 million. The Congo and Nigerian conflicts had at least one thing in common—both originated in resource-rich parts of each country; Katanga has large deposits of copper and Southeastern Nigeria is rich in oil; and both regions had not always been willing to share their mineral wealth with the rest of the country. Nigeria has been somewhat more successful in attaining a measure of peace; in the 2017 Fragile States Index from the nongovernmental organization Fund for Peace, Nigeria ranked thirteenth while Congo was seventh (South Sudan was ranked first).

Another fragile state, Somalia (second in the Fragile States Index) became an independent country after a British protectorate and adjacent Italian trust territory were merged into one political entity in 1960. Border clashes with Kenya and Ethiopia, and the Western support for these countries, prompted the Somali government to rely on Soviet military help. Chaotic elections in 1969 led to a military coup, and the new government established still closer ties with Communist countries, particularly the Soviet Union and China. In 1974, Somalia invaded Ethiopia's eastern province and controlled most of it by 1977. However, the Ethiopian government, which also had established close ties with the Soviet Union, received strong support from its new ally, and Somalia was forced to withdraw the following year. The Somali defeat brought about the collapse of the central government and the emergence of various clan rivalries, especially in the southern part of the country. Somalia became a collapsed or failed state—the central government was unable or unwilling to offer services and protection to its people throughout the entire country. Parts of the former British colony proclaimed independence as the Republic of Somaliland in 1991. The United States and several European countries tried to restore order in Somalia by sending 35,000 troops in 1992 but they were withdrawn two years later after a high number of casualties among the Western soldiers. Another part of the country, Puntland (parts of former British and Italian territories), became a self-governing unit in 1998. Numerous attempts to bring peace and stability to Somalia have been unsuccessful. Meanwhile, pirate attacks on ships in waters surrounding Somalia

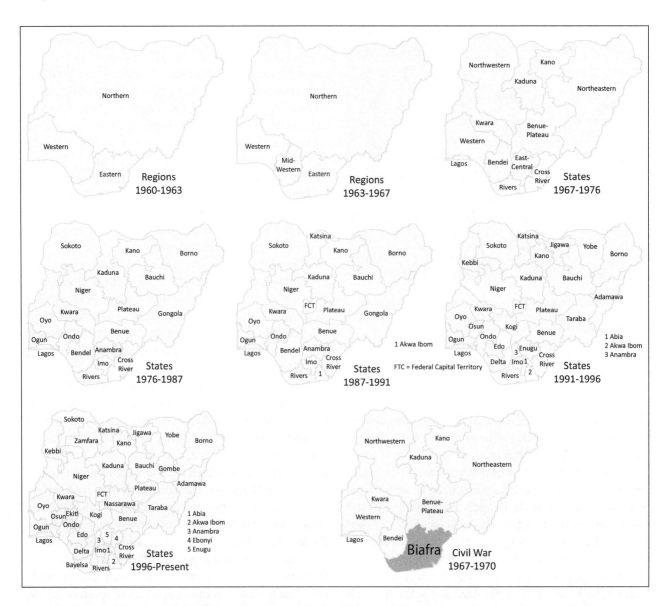

FIGURE 6.38 Administrative division in Nigeria since independence—There are at least eleven ethnic groups with a population of over 1 million each in Nigeria. The steady increase in the number of administrative divisions reflects Nigeria's complex ethnic patterns and the growing desire of many groups for official recognition in the form of an administrative unit. The number of such units has increased from 3 in 1960 to 37 now. *Source:* Wikipedia.

have also challenged international maritime transportation (Fig. 6.39).

On the opposite side of the continent, the people of Liberia have endured massive suffering from two civil wars in recent decades. The first war (1989–97) was an internal conflict that resulted in over 600,000 deaths, the second one (1999–2003) involved two rebel groups backed by Guinea and Sierra Leone (and indirectly by the United Kingdom and the United States) fighting the central government. Its death toll amounted to between 150,000 and 300,000. Both conflicts stemmed partly from the unusual history of Liberia and its connections to the United States. The American Colonization Society, established in 1816,

transported the first freed slaves back to Africa in 1822 after signing an agreement with local chiefs in what is now Liberia. The Society transported some 3,000 Africans by 1831 and another 2,000 by 1860. The colony was named Liberia and its capital Monrovia (after President Monroe), and it maintained strong economic ties with the United States as its new settlers preferred American foods and goods over the local ones. It became independent in 1847 and was quickly recognized by European powers and later (1862) by the United States. The Americo-African settlers had little knowledge of tropical agriculture, did not speak any local languages, and lived in urban settlements along the coast. The Firestone Tire and Rubber Company began

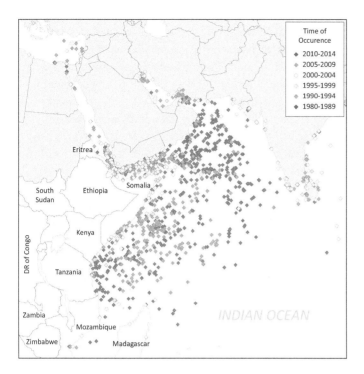

FIGURE 6.39 Piracy in waters northeast of Africa—Ships, including big oil tankers, travelling through the waters around the African Horn have been victims of pirate attacks in recent decades. This map shows that political instability in the region has extended to international waters around it. *Source:* National Geospatial Intelligence Agency.

establishing rubber plantations in 1926, and Liberia was the only source of natural rubber for the United States and its allies during World War II. Tensions between the Americo-Africans and the indigenous residents increased sharply after an officer of indigenous background staged a successful coup in 1980 and by the mid-1980s the country sank into a civil war that lasted for a decade. Its death toll amounted to over 5 percent of Liberia's population. About half a million people fled to neighboring states, and half of the remaining population was internally displaced. A 1997 election brought to power a leader whose rule was harsh and characterized by numerous human rights abuses. Another civil war began two years later and lasted until 2003. It killed a quarter million and displaced almost 1 million people. Various guerilla factions in both civil wars were supported by profits from diamonds and forced many children to participate in the fighting. The military use of children (child soldiers) has been strongly condemned by the international community. The 2005 presidential election brought the first woman to power. She has faced numerous challenges to put the country on the right path, including rebuilding the economic infrastructure (mining and rubber plantations), providing electricity and water to urban residents, and reintegrating former child soldiers.

The country ranked twenty-seventh in the 2017 Fragile States Index.

The Hutu-Tutsi conflict in Rwanda also has deep historical roots. The German (before World War I) and then Belgian colonial authorities favored the Tutsi minority over the Hutu majority. However, the numerically dominant Hutus began gaining more influence at the end of Rwanda's colonial rule, and this led to increased tensions and violence between the two groups. Waves of violence and retaliation between the two groups resulted in hundreds of thousands of mainly Tutsi refugees in neighboring countries.[10] The Rwandan Patriotic Front (RPF), under the leadership of Paul Kagame and composed mainly of the Tutsi refugees in Uganda, was formed in 1988. Its main objectives were to bring back the exiles and share power with the Hutu-dominated government. After it launched a major attack on Rwanda with about 7,000 fighters, the Rwandan government labeled all Tutsi residents RPF supporters and Hutu members of the opposition parties traitors. Despite the peacemaking efforts of the Organization of African Unity, some extremist members of the Hutu government tried to derail the peace process and began planning a campaign to exterminate their enemies, the Tutsis and moderate Hutus. The 1994 genocide was triggered by the deaths of the Rwandan (a moderate Hutu) and Burundian presidents in a plane crash caused by, according to government claims, an RPF rocket attack. During a three-month period (April 7–July 4, 1994), some 800,000 people, most of them Tutsis and moderate Hutus, were killed. It was an organized campaign supported by extreme elements of the Hutus and inflamed by propaganda from many media outlets (mainly radio). Some 200,000 Hutus participated (or were forced to take part) in the massacre. About 2 million people left Rwanda but were able to return a few years later. Many individuals responsible for this genocide were later tried in three types of courts, the International Criminal Tribunal for Rwanda based in Tanzania, the Rwandan national courts, and the local *gacaca* courts. Most were sentenced to death or prison terms but later pardoned and released. The reconciliation process will be painful and may take many years. Rwanda ranked thirty-fourth in the Fragile States Index.

Although the imposition of arbitrary political boundaries on Africa by the colonial powers has been a source of numerous problems, the Organization of African Unity (now the African Union) accepted them as the lesser evil. Trying to change them might create more problems than solutions. Nevertheless, tensions and conflicts in two countries led to the formation of two additional states since the beginning of the decolonization era over 60 years ago: Eritrea and South Sudan. Eritrea was an Italian colony until 1941 and was then controlled by Great Britain. It was merged with Ethiopia in 1950, forming a federation. However, Ethiopia imposed its rule on Eritrea and the latter's autonomy was abolished in 1962. In response, the Eritrean Liberation Front emerged as the leading force for independence, which was achieved in 1991. South Sudan was a part of Sudan from 1956 until 2011. When Great Britain gave independence to Sudan in 1956, it merged two different regions into one political entity. The northern part was predominantly Arabic and Muslim, while the south was African and Christian or Animist. The Muslim north had tried to impose its rule on the south, and this led to two civil wars (1955–72 and 1983–2005). South Sudan gained independence after a referendum approved by almost everyone in 2011. The new country has faced severe challenges since its independence, including internal security, a border dispute with Sudan, the presence of refugees on its territory, resource (oil) dependence, corruption, poverty, and poor health and education systems.

Political instability in some parts of Sub-Saharan Africa has also led to the emergence of terrorist groups trying to impose their ideology through violence. **Al-Shabaab** is a Somali-based Islamic militant group with links to Al-Qaeda. Its original goal was to maintain law and order in areas controlled by Islamic courts after the collapse of central government in 1991. It then devolved into a violent organization targeting the provisional United Nations-backed government and resorted to terrorism inside Somalia and neighboring Uganda and Kenya, killing hundreds of people at sites such as a shopping mall and a university in Kenya and a restaurant in Uganda. **Boko Haram**, another Islamic militant group, originated in northern Nigeria in 2002. Its name in the Hausa language means "Western education is forbidden." The group began relying on terrorist methods to achieve its main objective—the creation of an independent Islamic state—in 2009. It intensified the fighting and proclaimed *jihad* against Christians, the government, and anyone disagreeing with the group's policy. It kidnapped over two hundred school girls in northern Nigeria in 2014; some of them were released in 2017 but the fate of others remains unknown.

South Africa's Apartheid Policy

The Republic of South Africa used to be, and in some ways still is, a unique country in Sub-Saharan Africa. First, it became independent much earlier (in 1910) than the rest of the region. Second, its relatively high level of economic development has made it an African "superpower." Third, this development, to a large extent, has been based on one of the richest mineral resource bases on the African continent, particularly large deposits of gold and strategic minerals. Fourth, it has the largest population of European (white) origin, both in absolute and relative terms, of any African country. Fifth, it had an official policy of racial segregation, known as **apartheid**, for over forty years. This policy, in theory, supported separate development for different races but in reality was based on racial segregation and political and economic discrimination against the non-white, particularly African, population.[11]

Although the policy of apartheid was officially practiced from 1948 until 1992, it really began during the British colonial rule when laws regulating the movement of Africans to white areas were introduced at the end of the 19th century. Africans were not allowed to be in public places after dark in some parts of the colony. After independence from Great Britain in 1910, the Native Land Act (1913) established special areas (known as the African Reserves) for the Africans and denied them the right to purchase any land outside those areas (i.e. in white areas). The 1948 electoral victory of the National Party (representing the Afrikaans-speaking white population) marked the beginning of official apartheid. A series of laws were passed by the parliament to enforce this policy. For instance, the Prohibition of Mixed Marriages Act (1949) outlawed inter-racial marriages, particularly between whites and Africans. The Population Registration Act (1950) established a racial classification of the South African population into originally three (White, African, and **Coloured**) and later four (Asian was added) categories. The Bantu Education Act (1953) introduced segregated educational facilities and government control over the curriculum and resources to prevent educating Africans for jobs traditionally reserved for the whites. The Promotion of Black Self-Government Act (1958) created separate territorial units (homelands or *bantustans*) for the African population. These areas were supposed to become independent of the South African government. The Black Homeland Citizenship Act (1970) made all Africans citizens of their homelands and not of South Africa. In other words, Africans became foreigners in their own country.

Most scholars identified two types of apartheid. Petty apartheid was a set of laws and regulations governing the daily life of the South African population, particularly its black residents. The designation of separate amenities for whites and non-whites was the best example of this policy. Other examples of this discriminatory policy included the following: blacks could not employ white people; black police could not arrest a white person; a white taxi driver could not have a black passenger of the opposite sex in the front seat; and blacks were required to have a permit to be present in white areas for more than seventy-two hours. Grand apartheid meant residential segregation in urban

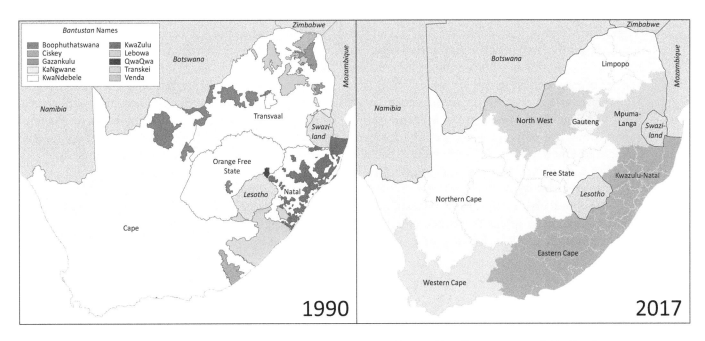

FIGURE 6.40 Apartheid-era and current administrative divisions in the Republic of South Africa—The country was divided into four provinces and ten Bantustans during the apartheid era (1948–92). Notice the irregular and fragmented shape of most Bantustans. Although they occupied only 13 percent of the country's area, they were supposed to house three-quarters of its population. The country has been divided into nine provinces since 1994. *Source:* Statistics South Africa.

areas and the creation of ten homelands for the African population (Fig. 6.40). These homelands occupied only 13 percent of the country's area, yet they were supposed to house over two-thirds of the South African population. In theory, they were supposed to become independent countries and be joined in economic union with white South Africa. In reality, no other country recognized their "independence," and they were too small, fragmented, and overcrowded to be economically viable entities. Some apartheid practices were arbitrary; for example, certain Asian groups—Japanese, South Koreans, and Taiwanese—were considered "honorary white" groups as their countries maintained diplomatic relations with South Africa; sometimes members of the same family were put into different racial categories, depending on the hair type (curly or straight) of each member.

Resistance to apartheid took various passive and armed forms, predominantly among blacks, but also among some whites. The South African Native National Congress was formed in 1912 to oppose certain discriminatory racial policies of the Union of South Africa. It was renamed the African National Congress (ANC) in 1923, and for the next fifty years it used peaceful protests and petitions to change the discriminatory laws and policies, although sporadic violent incidents occurred. In 1959, some ANC leaders formed the Pan-Africanist Congress (PAC), a more radical and militant organization counting on black supporters only. A turning point in the fight against apartheid was the

Sharpeville Massacre of 1960 when sixty-nine blacks were killed after white police opened fire on PAC demonstrators. The government banned the PAC and ANC and arrested

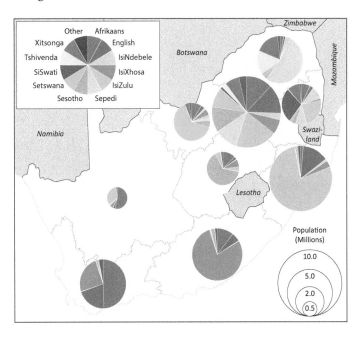

FIGURE 6.41 Linguistic diversity in the Republic of South Africa, 2011—Two African languages, Zulu and Xhosa, are spoken by 23 and 16 percent of the country's population respectively. Afrikaans and English are native tongues for 13 and 10 percent of its population respectively. Notice the concentration of speakers of some languages (Zulu, Xhosa, Afrikaans) in specific provinces. *Source:* Statistics South Africa.

many of their leaders. In response, the ANC began supporting the armed struggle against the government. One of its leaders, Nelson Mandela, was arrested and remained in jail for twenty-seven years.

There was also growing resistance against the apartheid policy around the world; it was considered a crime against humanity. Many countries imposed economic sanctions on South Africa in the early 1960s. The South African white government took the first steps to dismantle apartheid in 1990 when it lifted the ban on the ANC and other political organizations, released Mandela from prison, and eventually (after a referendum) repealed the policy of apartheid. It held its first multi-racial elections in 1994 in which the ANC received a great majority (63 percent) of votes and Mandela became the first black president of the country. The new South Africa was admitted to, or rejoined, many international organizations and established diplomatic relations with most African and other countries. It changed its administrative divisions from four to nine provinces, and it now has eleven official languages: English, Afrikaans, and nine different African languages (Fig. 6.41 and Fig. 6.42). However, political progress has not been accompanied by economic changes, and the black-white economic gap still remains. It may take a generation or more to erase these disparities.

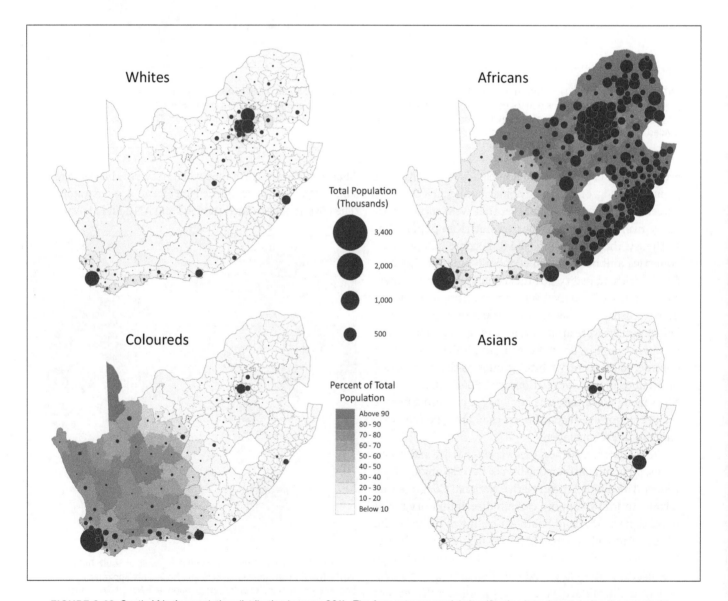

FIGURE 6.42 South Africa's population distribution by race, 2011—The four-category racial classification introduced during the apartheid era is still recorded in population censuses. These maps show the distribution of the four groups at the municipality level. Notice the distinctive spatial pattern for each group. Africans account for 79 percent of the total population while Whites and Coloureds account for 9 percent each. Asians and others account for the remaining 1 percent. *Source:* Statistics South Africa.

ECONOMIC ACTIVITIES

Sub-Saharan Africa remains one of the least developed world regions, with most of its labor force engaged in primary activities, mainly agriculture or mining, and a gross domestic product per capita below $2,000, well below the world average of about $10,000 (Fig. 6.43). One of the major features of the economy is the coexistence of economic growth and widespread poverty, with significant regional disparities in levels of development within and among countries. Most countries have been simultaneously pursuing natural resource development and economic diversification, and they have been stressing both autonomous development and international cooperation. Yet, there are still several obstacles to more sustained growth, including the high dependency of agriculture on weather conditions, high unemployment rates, low national savings and low domestic investment rates, heavy debt burdens, and high dependency on a single commodity.

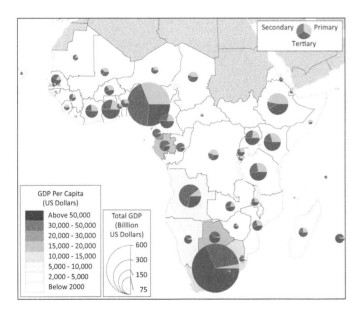

FIGURE 6.43 Gross domestic product by sector and per capita— The primary, secondary and tertiary sectors account for 20, 32, and 47 percent of the region's gross domestic product respectively. The island countries of Seychelles and Mauritius, oil rich Equatorial Guinea and Gabon, diamond-rich Botswana, and the Republic of South Africa have the highest GDP per capita (over $11,000). The Republic of South Africa and Nigeria are the largest economic powers in the region. Notice the significant differences in the importance of each sector in the national economies of the various countries. *Source:* CIA World Factbook.

Development Strategies

Many economic development strategies followed by African countries after independence could be divided into three categories. The free market or capitalistic approach, chosen by the Ivory Coast, Kenya, Gabon, Nigeria, and a few other countries, put emphasis on supporting the private sector, especially in agriculture and mining, and encouraging foreign investment albeit with relatively strong government interventionism. The belief was that the economic growth and efficiency would trickle down and eventually benefit all social groups and regions of the country. This approach initially produced favorable results but benefited mainly foreign companies and indigenous elites. The socialist road to development in several states, including Ghana, Tanzania, and Zambia, could be described as a combination of socialist ideas and African traditions (cooperative production, communal land ownership, and shared responsibility for welfare) for the benefit of all social groups in the country. It has been less successful than the free market strategy due to inadequate decision-making systems, too much emphasis on ideology, local (mainly rural) resistance to some policies, and unfavorable external economic conditions (low prices for many export commodities). The Marxist approach was modeled on the Soviet and Chinese examples and was supported by some Communist states through financial, technical, and military assistance. The major objectives were rapid economic growth and social progress (health care, education, and status of women). Failure to achieve them in Mozambique, Angola, Burkina Faso, Benin, and Ethiopia reflected, like in the case of the socialist approach, poor management, emphasis on ideology, resistance to collective farming, as well as the break-up of the Soviet Union and the end of assistance from former Communist states.

Regardless of their development strategies, most African countries became heavily indebted by the 1980s and 1990s, and low prices on many export commodities put a great burden on them. The economic policies imposed on Africa and other developing countries by the International Monetary Fund and the World Bank, known as structural adjustment, were supposed to stimulate economic growth and ease the burden of foreign debt. Most countries had no choice but to accept them and introduce major changes to their economies, including the privatization of many businesses; encouragement of foreign investment and greater role of market forces in the decision-making system; reduction of public sector employment; and various user fees for access to social amenities, health care, and education. Although some countries may have benefited from these policies, in most states, they led to serious economic problems as they were designed more to deal with the concerns of creditors than helping those in need.[12]

Agriculture

Most people in Sub-Saharan Africa engage in subsistence primary activities associated with food production, including several types of mixed crop and livestock farming, livestock herding (pastoralism), shifting cultivation, and tree crop farming. A typical African farm is characterized by small size, relatively low productivity, and a low level of mechanization. African agriculture is sensitive to weather conditions (droughts in particular) and various pests, and it is characterized by the practice of intercropping and a gender-based division of labor (Fig. 6.44).

As environmental conditions change from humid to dry moving from the center of the continent toward its periphery, so does the type of agricultural systems and the importance of crops and livestock as major sources of food and income (Fig. 6.45). Farming activities may also be influenced by terrain features (elevation), level of technology available, access to domestic and foreign markets, and a host of other factors. Shifting cultivation (slash and burn) is practiced in sparsely populated, humid, and densely forested regions of Central Africa (the Congo Basin). A piece of a forested land is cleared and burnt (ash enriches the soil) before planting of crops takes place. The most common root crops are cassava and yams, while maize and sorghum are popular grain crops; a variety of vegetables and pulses are also grown. After growing crops for two or three years, the field is abandoned and another one is prepared for cultivation. The abandoned field may again be used for cultivation after ten to twenty years; it is fully forested by that time, and the clearing/burning and planting/harvesting cycle will be repeated. Shifting cultivation is an example of best farming practices adapted to infertile tropical soils unable to support permanent cultivation. Other types of agricultural activities found in humid regions of Sub-Saharan Africa include tree crop farming, dominant in Western Africa in a belt about 320 kilometers (200 miles) wide, parallel to the Gulf of Guinea and extending from Liberia to Cameroon, and the rice-tree crop farming in parts of Madagascar. The former type is characterized by cultivation of industrial tree crops (cocoa, oil palm, rubber, and coffee) for sale and food crops (mainly yams and maize) for household consumption. The latter type is practiced on mostly small farms

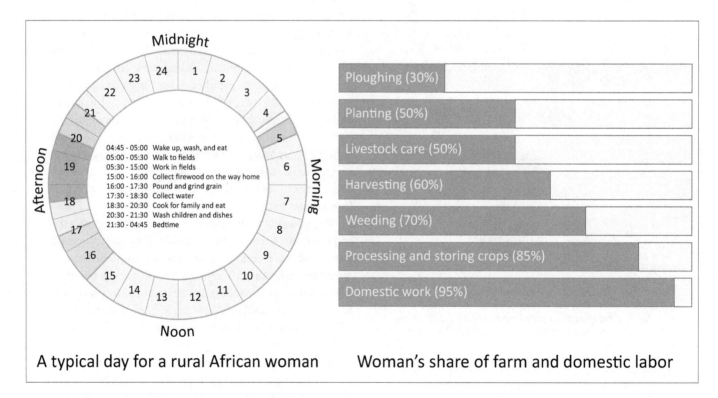

A typical day for a rural African woman

04:45 - 05:00 Wake up, wash, and eat
05:00 - 05:30 Walk to fields
05:30 - 15:00 Work in fields
15:00 - 16:00 Collect firewood on the way home
16:00 - 17:30 Pound and grind grain
17:30 - 18:30 Collect water
18:30 - 20:30 Cook for family and eat
20:30 - 21:30 Wash children and dishes
21:30 - 04:45 Bedtime

Woman's share of farm and domestic labor

Ploughing (30%)
Planting (50%)
Livestock care (50%)
Harvesting (60%)
Weeding (70%)
Processing and storing crops (85%)
Domestic work (95%)

FIGURE 6.44 Gender-based division of labor in Sub-Saharan Africa—Women produce most of the food in the region, and they devote fifteen to sixteen hours to farm work and various domestic chores each day. *Source:* drawn after similar images at the Rehydration Project website (rehydrate.org).

Region	Crop-livestock integration	Major crops and livestock	Major livestock outputs
Humid	Pure crop	Roots (cassava/yams) Cereals (maize/sorghum) Trypanotolerant livestock	Milk
Sub-humid	Crop-livestock	Cereals (maize/sorghum) Livestock (goats/sheep/cattle)	Meat, milk, power
Highland	Well integrated crop-livestock	Cereals (wheat/teff) Livestock (cattle/sheep/goats)	Power, meat, milk
Semi-dry	Livestock-crop	Cereals (sorghum/millet) Livestock (cattle/sheep/goats)	Milk, power
Dry	Pure livestock	Livestock (sheep/goats/camels)	Milk, meat

FIGURE 6.45 Major agricultural systems in Sub-Saharan Africa—The cultivation of tropical root crops and certain cereals is the dominant activity in humid regions. As the climate becomes drier, the importance of root crops decreases but that of livestock herding increases. Different grain crops are grown in more and less humid regions. *Source:* FAO.

growing rice, maize, cassava, and legumes as food crops and bananas and coffee as cash crops. Irrigation is fairly important in this type of farming, especially in areas devoted to rice farming (Fig. 6.46). Although livestock does not play an important role in any agricultural system in Africa's humid regions, farmers may raise trypanotolerant (nagana-resistant) species of cattle and goats, mainly for milk.

In the sub-humid (mainly savanna) regions of Western, Eastern, and Southern Africa several types of mixed cereal and root crop farming are found, and they support almost

FIGURE 6.46 Rice fields in Tanzania—Most African farmers engage in subsistence activities and grow a variety of cereals and root crops. Rice is an important crop in several countries, including Tanzania, the third largest producer of this commodity in Sub-Saharan Africa. *Source:* Pixabay.

one-third of the rural population in Sub-Saharan Arica. Maize, sorghum, and millet, as well as cassava and yams, are major crops. Groundnuts and beans may be common crops in certain parts of this region. Farmers may also grow some industrial plants, mainly tobacco, cotton, and coffee, and work part-time outside the farm. Root crops are dominant in the more humid parts of the savanna region, while a mixture of cereal and root crops is found in the drier parts. In the highlands of Eastern Africa (mainly in Kenya, Tanzania, Zambia, and Zimbabwe) maize is the main staple crop (Fig. 6.47 and Fig. 6.48). Livestock (cattle and goats) is also raised in this region, and it is a source of power (plowing), farm manure, milk, and meat, as well as bride wealth and insurance against crop failure.

Livestock herding or pastoralism is found in most dry and semi-dry regions of the savanna and desert that are too dry, rocky, or steep for farming. Cattle, goats, sheep, and camels are the dominant animals among African herders (Fig. 6.49 and Fig. 6.50). The size and quality of the livestock herd (particularly cattle) is quite often a measure of social status and wealth. People dependent on livestock herding consume dairy products (milk and yogurt) in larger quantities than meat. Animal blood can also be consumed on special occasions. Spatial mobility is an important part of a pastoralist life style, and the movement of herds in search of pastures and water can take several forms, including the movement between lower (river plains) and higher elevations during the dry and rainy season, between the areas free of tse-tse flies in the dry season and areas free of tse-tse flies in the rainy season, or between the more and less intensive farming regions during the dry and rainy season.

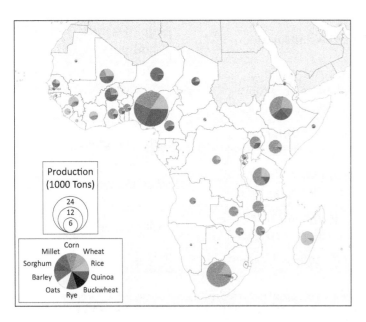

FIGURE 6.47 Production of cereals in Sub-Saharan Africa, 2005–2013—The dominant crops are maize (corn), sorghum, millet, rice, and wheat. The largest producers of maize are the South and East African countries and Nigeria. Sorghum is more important in West Africa and Ethiopia, and millet in the semi-dry parts of West Africa. Rice requires irrigation and is the dominant crop in humid coastal regions of West Africa and Madagascar. Wheat, a temperate climate crop, is grown in the drier and higher parts of East and South Africa. *Source:* FAOSTAT.

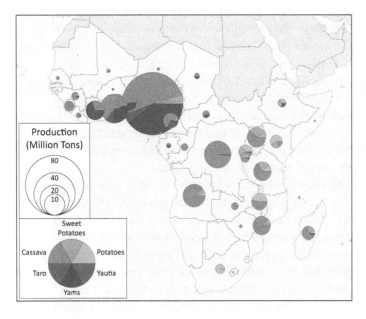

FIGURE 6.48 Production of root crops in Sub-Saharan Africa, 2005–2013—The major crops are cassava (manioc), yams, sweet potatoes, and taro (cocoyam). Cassava is by far the most popular crop and is grown across the entire tropical region. Yams and taro are mainly grown in Western Africa, and sweet potatoes in Eastern Africa. *Source:* FAOSTAT.

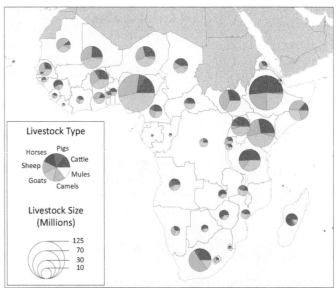

FIGURE 6.49 Livestock herding in Sub-Saharan Africa, 2014—Goats, cattle, and sheep are the most common domesticated animals in the region. Notice that the tse-tse fly prevents large-scale livestock herding in several Central African countries. *Source:* FAOSTAT.

FIGURE 6.50 Livestock herding in East Africa—This activity is dominant in semi-dry and dry parts of Sub-Saharan Africa, and the herd size is often a symbol of social standing and wealth. *Source:* Pixabay.

The major challenges facing African pastoralists, in addition to increasing restrictions on the movement of their herds, is the low productivity of livestock, unsustainably large herd sizes, and conflicts with sedentary farmers.

Highland perennial and temperate mixed farming, found in the fertile highlands of Ethiopia, Uganda, Burundi, Rwanda, and parts of Southern (Lesotho and Angola) and Western (Nigeria and Cameroon) Africa, occupies a relatively small area but supports high population densities.

It is characterized by intensive land use and very small farm size, cultivation of perennial crops (banana, plantain, and coffee), root plants (cassava and sweet potatoes), cereals (wheat and barley), and pulses (beans). Cattle are an important source of meat, milk, and power, while the sale of sheep, goats, wool, and pulses provides a source of cash.

Hunting and gathering have been declining in importance for some time but are still practiced in a few locations, mainly by the !Kung San people of the Kalahari Desert and the Mbuti (Pygmies) groups in the tropical rainforest of the Congo Basin. Men are mainly responsible for hunting and women and children for collecting fruits and nuts. There has been growing pressure on these groups to switch to a sedentary life style through such practices as fencing off cattle ranches and establishing game reserves, especially in the Kalahari Desert.[13]

Plantation agriculture in Sub-Saharan Africa may not be as well developed as in other tropical regions, but the region is an important producer of several industrial and food crops, including fiber plants (cotton and sisal) as well as coffee, tea, and cocoa. As indicated earlier, individual smaller farms grow some quantities of these crops as a source of cash, but a large portion of the production comes from plantations located in Kenya, Tanzania, Cameroon, and several other countries (Fig. 6.51).

Sub-Saharan Africa has been seriously challenged by periodic food shortages since independence, and it was the only major world region that recorded a decline in food production per capita during the second part of the 20th century. Although food production has been slowly increasing in recent years, it is still lower than it used to be in many countries several decades ago. Several factors, quite often working together, have been responsible for Sub-Saharan Africa's inability to feed itself. Some scholars blame the tropical climate for the low agricultural productivity; it is responsible for low soil fertility, fast weed growth, numerous pests and plant diseases, and quickly rusting machinery. Natural disasters, especially droughts, contribute to crop failures and high livestock mortality. Political instability (conflicts) forces many people to become refugees or internally displaced persons so they are unable to farm and become dependent on food from other sources. Limited access to cash prevents many farmers from purchasing fertilizers, pesticides, water pumps, and various farm implements and reduces their ability to buy food if they cannot grow it themselves. Rising global food prices create a big challenge to poor urban residents who may have to spend most of their meager income on basic nutritional necessities. Diseases such as the HIV/AIDS epidemic in Southern Africa and the recent Ebola outbreak in Western Africa affected farmers' abilities to produce or access adequate food supplies. The highest population growth rate in the world makes it even harder to keep increasing food production per capita. Finally, Africa benefited relatively little from the Green Revolution (see chapters 9 and 10). The region's poverty has made it difficult for African farmers

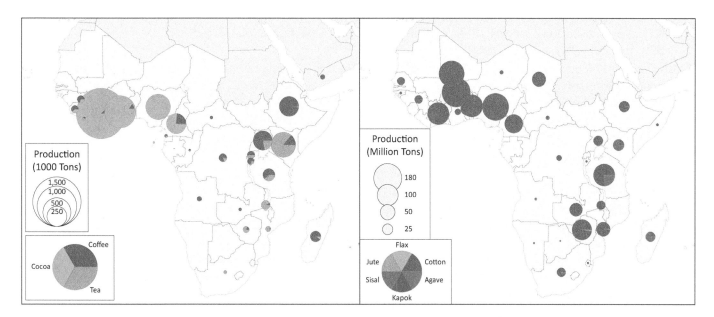

FIGURE 6.51 Production of cocoa, coffee, tea, and selected fiber crops in Sub-Saharan Africa, 2005–2013—Cocoa is grown in the hot and humid parts of West Africa, and the Ivory Coast is the world's largest producer. Coffee and tea are important crops in the less humid uplands of East Africa and Ethiopia. Cotton, the dominant fiber crop, is grown in both West and East Africa; like coffee and tea, it does well in a less humid climate. Tanzania, Kenya, and Madagascar are important producers of sisal, a less common fiber plant. *Source:* FAOSTAT.

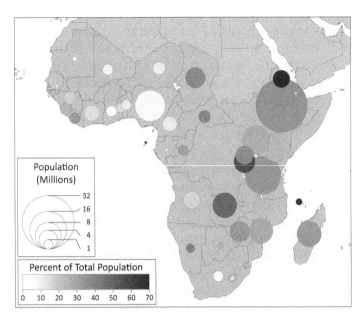

FIGURE 6.52 Undernourished population in Sub-Saharan Africa, 2010–2015—Eastern and northeastern Africa have the largest numbers (both in absolute and relative terms) of undernourished people. Almost 70 percent of Eritrea's population is in this category. No reliable data are available for the Democratic Republic of Congo, Somalia, and South Sudan. *Source:* Millennium Development Goals Indicators.

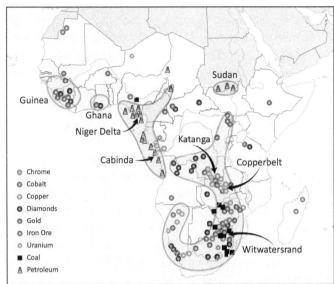

FIGURE 6.53 Major mining regions of Sub-Saharan Africa—Notice the variety of mineral resources in southern and south-central Africa and their almost complete absence in most of eastern Africa. *Source:* drawn after a similar map at the Le Monde Diplomatique website.

to afford the inputs (e.g. chemical fertilizers) necessary to take advantage of new high-yielding varieties. Also, the Green Revolution focused on rice, wheat, and corn; but as described above, these crops represent only a small part of the tremendous diversity of African agriculture.

Consequently, about one-sixth of the African population (160 million) is undernourished or malnourished, and large-scale food shortages and famines have occurred several times during the past fifty years (Fig. 6.52). The two best known examples of famine since the 1960s affected the two most populous African countries, Nigeria (late 1960s) and Ethiopia (mid-1980s). In both cases, it was a combination of natural (drought) and human (conflict) factors that led to about 1 million deaths in each case. Parts of the Sahel and the Horn of Africa, Sudan, and Uganda have also experienced serious food shortages in recent years. For example, the Somali food crisis of 2010–12, caused by drought and conflict, resulted in some 260,000 deaths, half of them children under age of six; 1 million refugees; and 1 million internally displaced persons. A similar catastrophe in the same area occurred in 1991–92 when 300,000 people died from starvation and 2 million people were displaced from their homes. Famines and other types of food shortages have killed over 4 million people in Sub-Saharan Africa since the beginning of the 20th century. Although more people died from famines in the rest of the world (mainly

Asia) during the same period, this region may be the only large part of the globe still seriously challenged by food shortages. Sub-Saharan Africa has 13 percent of the world's total population but has received over 40 percent of all food aid during the last fifteen years.

Mineral Resources

Mining is another important primary activity in several parts of Sub-Saharan Africa, and some countries are almost completely dependent on the export of mineral resources such as oil, gold, diamonds, or iron ore. Mining has attracted more foreign capital than any other sector, and several major conflicts began in areas rich in mineral resources. The Witwatersrand region of South Africa is considered one of the largest and richest mining areas on Earth (Fig. 6.53). It has the world's largest known deposits of gold; half of the gold ever mined comes from this region. Gold has been mined here since the early 1890s, and production peaked in the late 1960s and early 1970s when South Africa produced two-thirds of global output. However, there has been a steady decline in gold production since that time, and the region now accounts for only 6 percent of the global production and many mines have been losing money (Fig. 6.54). Higher operation (electricity and deeper mines) and labor (unionization and strikes) costs, instability of gold prices on the world market, and

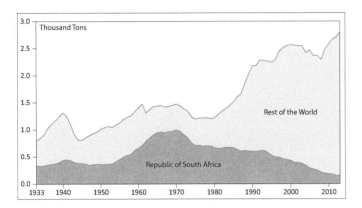

FIGURE 6.54 Gold production in the Republic of South Africa and the world, 1933–2013—Until the early 1970s, the Republic of South Africa was the largest producer of this commodity in the world. At the peak of gold mining, it supplied 60 percent of the global output. Notice the diverging trend since that time—declining production in the Republic of South Africa and increasing production in the rest of the world. *Source:* US Geological Survey. Minerals Yearbook.

increased production in other countries explain the absolute and relative decline of Witwatersrand's gold industry. Despite the declining importance of gold mining, the region remains the largest mining center in Africa as it is also rich in a variety of other metallic ores. It produces three-fourths of the platinum, over 40 percent of the chromium, and a quarter of the manganese in the world. The region's mining industry has attracted many migrants and investment over the years and has contributed to high urbanization levels and the establishment of many cities, including Johannesburg, one of the largest urban agglomerations in Sub-Saharan Africa.

Katanga province in the Democratic Republic of Congo and the Copperbelt province of Zambia form another major mining region of Africa. Although copper ore is the dominant resource here, cobalt and other metallic ores are also mined. The region produces almost 90 percent of copper and over 85 percent of cobalt in Africa (Fig. 6.55 and Fig. 6.56). The copper deposits were discovered here by the end of the 19th century, and the mining activities also attracted migrants and investments. The city of Lubumbashi in the Democratic Republic of Congo is the major urban agglomeration in this region.

The coastal areas along the Gulf of Guinea and the Atlantic Ocean, from the Niger Delta in Nigeria to the Cabinda exclave of Angola, is the largest petroleum producing region of Sub-Saharan Africa (Fig. 6.57). The search for oil in Nigeria began in the early 1900s, but sizeable deposits were not found until several decades later and large-scale production started in the late 1950s. The country today provides one-third of the region's total output, and the sale of petroleum accounts for 95 percent of all export value and 40 percent of government revenue in Nigeria. Port Harcourt is the center of the Nigerian oil industry. The Cabinda oil deposits were discovered in the late 1960s and early 1970s and made Angola an important producer by the mid-1970s.

Sub-Saharan Africa is a major producer of several other mineral resources. Guinea, for example, produces 90 percent of the African bauxite and is the fifth largest global producer of that commodity. Over half of the world's diamond production comes from Africa, and Botswana accounts for 40 percent of the region's output; South Africa and the Democratic Republic of Congo are other major producers. Almost all of Africa's iron ore comes from Mauritania, and Niger and Namibia provide over one-sixth of the global uranium output.[14] Sub-Saharan Africa is also a top producer of coltan (also known as tantalite), a strategic mineral used in modern technology, including cell phones and computers. The Democratic Republic of Congo and Rwanda account for over 80 percent of global production of this rare metal. Mining of this commodity has become a controversial issue as various reports revealed inhumane working conditions, violence, and environmental degradation associated with this activity.[15]

Manufacturing, Trade, and Tourism

Manufacturing accounts for only 10 percent of Sub-Saharan Africa's GDP—the lowest share of any major world region. African industries are mainly resource- and labor-oriented types of activities that focus on the processing of raw materials (agricultural commodities and minerals) and textiles. There are several obstacles to industrial development, including an unreliable power supply, inadequate network of domestic suppliers, high transportation (import/export and tariffs) costs, and poor physical infrastructure. Almost all African countries have a low manufacturing attractiveness index in comparison to other parts of the world. To attract foreign investment, some countries (South Africa, Kenya, the Ivory Coast, and Zambia) have established industrial parks and special economic zones.

Nigeria and South Africa have the largest industrial base in the region. Manufacturing contributes 9 percent to Nigeria's gross domestic product. Apart from the oil industry, food, beverage, and tobacco processing are the major branches of manufacturing, accounting for over half of the country's industrial production. The automotive sector is growing in importance; the country began producing its first vehicles in 2015.

South Africa used to be the largest industrial power in Africa, but it now ranks second. However, it has the

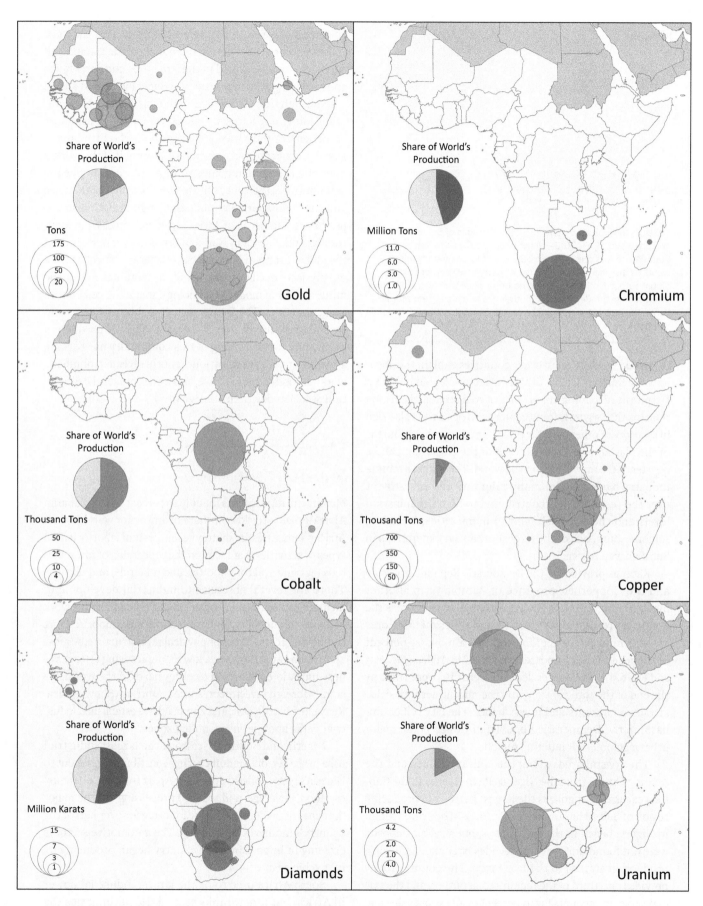

FIGURE 6.55 Production of selected mineral resources in Sub-Saharan Africa—Notice the region's global importance in the production of selected strategic minerals (chromium and cobalt) and diamonds. *Source:* US Geological Survey. Minerals Yearbook.

FIGURE 6.56 A former diamond mine, Republic of South Africa—Sub-Saharan Africa is the major supplier of several mineral resources to the developed world. The Republic of South Africa is particularly well endowed with a variety of minerals, including gold and diamonds, and mining has been the basis of the country's economic prosperity for decades. *Source:* Pixabay.

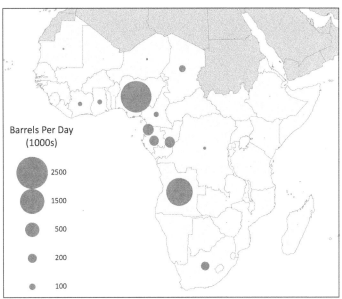

FIGURE 6.57 Production of petroleum in Sub-Saharan Africa, 2009–2013—Nigeria and Angola have been the leading African producers of oil. However, the production of oil has slowed down in both countries during the past several years. *Source:* U.S. Energy Information Administration.

most diverse and technologically advanced industries on the continent. Food and beverages; petroleum, chemicals, rubber and plastic products; and metal and metal products are the major industrial sectors, and its steel and automotive industries are the largest in Africa. Several European, Japanese, and American automotive companies built assembly plants that depend on parts supplied by domestic manufacturers.

Sub-Saharan Africa plays a minor role in global trade. It accounts for less than 2 percent of the world's total imports and exports, and its share has been declining since the 1960s when it amounted to about 5 percent. Most countries export raw materials (agricultural items or minerals), and many depend on one or two commodities for most of their revenues; many of these commodities are price-inelastic (i.e. a price decline is not followed by increased demand) (Fig. 6.58). African countries import various industrial goods, and often face unfavorable terms of trade. Their economies were designed to depend on the colonial master for almost all imports and exports before independence, but their trade links have expanded since that time. Countries that are rich in mineral resources usually have a positive balance of trade (unless a significant drop in the price of their export commodity occurs). South Africa, Nigeria, and Angola are the largest trading countries in the region (Fig. 6.59). Trade with China, which is now the largest trading partner of Sub-Saharan Africa, has been quickly growing in recent decades. China imports mainly raw materials and exports machinery, transportation, and communication equipment, various consumer goods, and

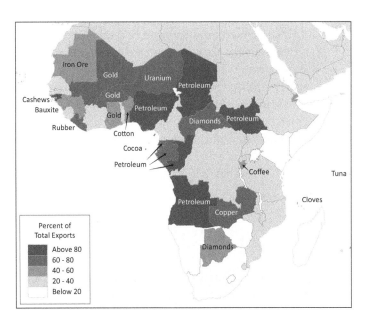

FIGURE 6.58 One commodity economies in Sub-Saharan Africa—Some twenty countries depend on the export of a single commodity for at least half of their revenues. In most cases, it is a mineral resource. Angola and South Sudan derive 95 percent of their earnings from petroleum. The small country of Sao Tome and Principe is almost totally dependent on export of cocoa, and Guinea-Bissau gets 90 percent of its earnings from export of cashew nuts. A high dependence on an agricultural commodity makes a country vulnerable. *Source:* Encyclopedia Britannica Yearbook 2014.

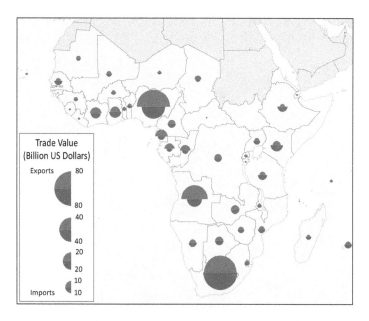

FIGURE 6.59 Foreign trade of countries in Sub-Saharan Africa, 2005–2013—Notice the positive balance of trade (greater value of exports than imports) for most oil-exporting countries and a negative one for countries dependent on export of agricultural commodities. *Source:* 2013 International Trade Statistics Yearbook.

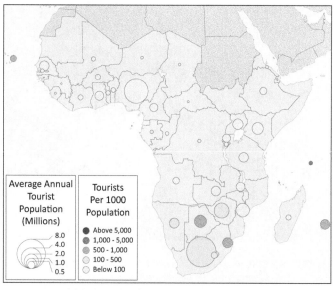

FIGURE 6.60 Tourism in Sub-Saharan Africa (tourist arrivals), 2005–2012—Countries with the best tourist infrastructure and environmental attractions (beaches and wildlife reserves) are visited by many tourists. Notice the high per capita tourist population in small island countries as well as Botswana and Swaziland (eSwatini). *Source:* World Bank.

textiles. It has also been providing loans to develop mineral resources and has developed special trade (economic) zones in several countries.

Africa attracts only 3 percent of the world's tourists, but their number has almost tripled during the past two decades, from 11 to over 30 million. South Africa is the major tourist destination visited by over 9 million travelers each year (Fig. 6.60). It has a fairly good tourist infrastructure and many natural attractions such as national parks. Safari tours are popular in the savanna regions of Eastern and Southern Africa (Kenya, Tanzania, and Botswana). Beaches of small island nations (e.g.

Seychelles, Mauritius, and Comoros) also bring many sun lovers from Europe, Asia, and Australia. Although cultural tourism has been less popular in Sub-Saharan Africa, it has been growing in importance, especially among African Americans who visit places associated with the slave trade (e.g. Elmina and Cape Coast in Ghana and the island of Gorée in Senegal). A country's tourist attractiveness may also reflect its visa and other travel-related policies. Most countries of Central Africa have rather restrictive visa policies while others (e.g. Botswana, Mauritius, and Seychelles) require no visas or require them for tourists from just a few countries.

FUTURE PROBLEMS AND PROSPECTS

Many books and articles have been written on African development that try to explain why this region is less economically developed in comparison to Europe and other developed parts of the world. These explanations could be grouped into three major categories. First, traditional explanations blamed the tropical environment, slavery, and colonialism. Second, failed development policies after independence, mainly corruption and incompetence among government officials, are responsible for widespread poverty. Third, weak links to the world economy, including the high dependence on a single export commodity

(crop or mineral) and unfavorable terms of trade with the rich world, partly explain Sub-Saharan Africa's inability to catch up with the rest of the world. However, things may be changing as the region has experienced one of the fastest rates of economic growth in the world during the past ten years. It has also been rapidly urbanizing in recent years, and some experts predict that Sub-Saharan Africa will have higher urbanization rates than Asia by 2030.

Despite favorable economic prospects for most of the region, high unemployment is the top concern in many countries.[16] A recent survey revealed that over 80 percent of respondents in nine African countries listed the lack of employment opportunities as their major problem. The highest unemployment rates (over 40 percent of the total labor force) in the world are found in Zimbabwe, Djibouti, Senegal, Kenya, and Swaziland. Providing jobs to large, and sometimes still growing, numbers of young people will be a real challenge to many African governments. At the same time, demographic ageing in the developed world puts Sub-Saharan Africa in a favorable position as a supplier of a young and cheap labor force for the global economy.

Better access to health care and the fight against the HIV/AIDS epidemic is also a high priority for this region. Lowering infant mortality and eradicating or reducing the prevalence of many infectious diseases will require enormous efforts on the part of African governments and the global community. Although the spread of HIV infections and AIDS-related deaths has been declining for the past 10 to 20 years, there are still over 23 million people living with HIV and over 1 million AIDS-related deaths a year. The number of physicians per capita is ten times lower than the world average and the number of hospital beds three times lower. Reducing this gap even partially will require tremendous effort on many fronts.

The poor quality of many schools and limited access to education, reflected in the highest illiteracy rates in the world, as well as a lack of competitive higher education systems and an exodus of many educated individuals (**brain drain**) may become major barriers to technological innovation and the development of the world's third most populous region. If Sub-Saharan Africa is to become "the next frontier" or "the tech industry's next China" in the foreseeable future, as some experts predict, its educational system has to receive major attention through more funding and structural change.

Government corruption, administrative incompetency, and questionable election results have been responsible for frequent violent and peaceful protests across the region, from economic protests in the Ivory Coast or Ghana to political ones in Zimbabwe or South Africa. Although democracy has been well established in some countries, authoritarian leaders are still in power in others and care more about their personal fortunes than the lives of their subjects. Much more remains to be done before the region becomes democratic and prosperous.

NOTES

1. Potts, M., Henderson, C., & Campbell, M. (2013). The Sahel: A Malthusian challenge? *Environmental & Resource Economics, 55*(4), 501–512.

2. Mestrovic, T. (2015). What are tropical diseases? *News Medical Life Sciences*. Retrieved from https://www.news-medical.net/health/What-are-Tropical-Diseases.aspx

3. Kagaayi, J., & Serwadda, D. (2016). The history of the HIV/AIDS epidemic in Africa. *Current HIV/AIDS Reports, 13*(4), 187–193. doi:10.1007/s11904-016-0318-8

4. Harington, J. S., McGlashan, N. D., & Chelkowska, E. Z. (2004). A century of migrant labour in the gold mines of Souith Africa. *The Journal of the South African Institute of Mining and Metallurgy, 50*(2), 65–71

5. Lewis, M. W. (2011). The demographic dimensions of the conflict in Ivory Coast. *GeoCurrents*. Retrieved from http://www.geocurrents.info/geopolitics/the-demographic-dimensions-of-the-conflict-in-ivory-coast

6. Flahaux, M.-L., & De Haas, H. (2016). African migration: Trends, patterns, drivers. *Comparative Migration Studies, 4*(1), 1. doi:10.1186/s40878-015-0015-6

7. Myers, G., Owusu, F., & Subulwa, A. G. (2012). Cities of Sub-Saharan Africa. In S. D. Brunn, M. Hays-Mitchell, & D. J. Ziegler (Eds.), *Cities of the world: World regional urban development* (pp. 331–378). Lanham, MD: Rowman & Littlefield.

8. Stock, R. (2013). *Africa south of the Sahara: A geographical interpretation* (pp. 89–90). New York, NY: Guilford Press.

9. Stock, R. (2013). *Africa south of the Sahara: A geographical interpretation* (pp. 177–181). New York, NY: Guilford Press.

10. United Nations. (2005). Rwanda: A brief history of the country. Retrieved from http://www.un.org/en/preventgenocide/rwanda/education/rwandagenocide.shtml

11. History.com. (2010). Apartheid. Retrieved from https://www.history.com/topics/apartheid

12. Stock, R. (2013). *Africa south of the Sahara: A geographical interpretation* (pp. 298–307). New York, NY: Guilford Press.

13. Mohammed-Saleem, M. A. 1995. Mixed farming systems in sub-Saharan Africa. In R. T. Wilson, S. Ehui, & S. Mack (Eds.), Livestock development strategies for low income countries. Rome: Food and Agriculture Organization. Retrieved from http://www.fao.org/Wairdocs/ILRI/x5462E/x5462e0e.htm.

14. Stock, R. (2013). *Africa south of the Sahara: A geographical interpretation* (pp. 451–464). New York, NY: Guilford Press.

15. Grant, R. (2015). *Africa: Geographies of change* (pp. 70–72). New York, NY: Oxford University Press.

16. Pew Research Center. 2015. Health care, education are top priorities in Sub-Saharan Africa: Most are optimistic about economic future. Retrieved from http://www.pewglobal.org/2015/09/16/health-care-education-are-top-priorities-in-sub-saharan-africa/

7

LATIN AMERICA

L atin America is a very large region located south of the United States. It occupies the continent of South America and the southern part of the North American continent, including the Caribbean Islands, and is one of only two major world realms located on two continents (the other one is the Middle East). It is divided into two major parts, South America and Middle America (Fig. 7.1). The second region is further subdivided into Mexico, Central America, and the Caribbean Islands. Finally, the Caribbean Islands consist of the Greater Antilles, the Lesser Antilles, and the Bahamas. To make things even more complex, the Lesser Antilles are often divided into the Windward and Leeward Islands. There are over thirty independent countries and ten dependent territories in this region, and they vary significantly in area and population. Some countries are among the largest in the world (Brazil and Mexico), while others are tiny islands of a few square miles in area inhabited by a few thousand people.

GEOGRAPHIC QUALITIES AND WORLD SIGNIFICANCE

One of the most apparent physical qualities of Latin America is its great latitudinal extent, larger than that of any other region. It stretches from 30°N in Northern Mexico to 55°S in the southernmost parts of Argentina and Chile, an extent of almost 90 degrees, the equivalent of the distance from the Equator to the North or South Pole. It should be no surprise that the great diversity of natural environments, especially of climates and landforms, is another quality of Latin America. The longest and second highest mountain range in the world (the Andes) and one of the largest plains on Earth (the Amazon Basin) are found here. Some parts of the region are very hot and humid (the Amazon Basin), while others, located not far away from them, are considered the driest places in the

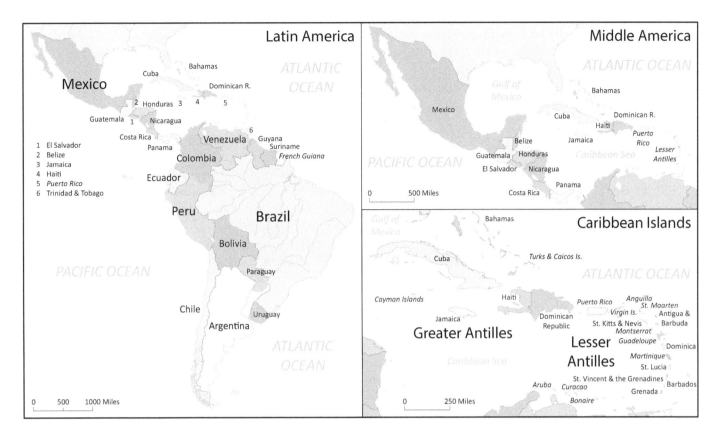

FIGURE 7.1 Countries of Latin America—The region is divided into 32 independent countries and 14 dependent territories (shown in italics). Most of the dependent territories are located in the Caribbean Islands.

world (the Atacama Desert). Areas along the Pacific coast and parts of the Caribbean Islands are seismically active, known for strong earthquakes and active volcanoes. On the other hand, the eastern and central parts of South America are geologically stable areas. Tropical storms (hurricanes) may cause a lot of damage in parts of Middle America but do not occur in the rest of the region.

Latin America is also well known for its rich natural resource base. It has large amounts of various metallic ores (copper, silver, bauxite, and iron) and fossil fuels (petroleum). The Amazon Basin is the largest tropical rainforest region in the world, an important source of timber (tropical hardwoods), medicinal plants, and oxygen for the Earth's atmosphere. The rich soils of the Pampas and grazing lands in other parts of the region are important agricultural resources for many Latin American countries. Unlike its natural resources, human resources have been wasted through limited educational opportunities, social barriers, and corruption. Consequently, Latin America is a region of great social and economic inequalities, such as inequalities in land ownership, levels of development, and social and racial contrasts, particularly visible in urban areas. These inequalities have periodically led

to political instability and conflict in some countries of the region.

Latin America is characterized by significant cultural uniformity, especially with regard to language and religion. The main reason for calling this region Latin America is the dominance of the Spanish and Portuguese languages (both derived from Latin) and the Roman Catholic religion (Latin is the traditional language of the church). Although some parts of the region have been influenced by British, French, and Dutch culture, these areas comprise a relatively small part of Latin America, both in area and population.

In contrast to its cultural uniformity, the great ethnic diversity of Latin America is the result of large-scale human migrations, both voluntary and forced, that have taken place during the past five centuries. Several waves of European migrants, the forced relocation of Africans during the slave trade era, the importation of indentured Asian laborers after the abolishment of slavery, and the mixing of every group with each other and the native Amerindian people have resulted in a region that is at least as diverse ethnically and racially as North America.

Another geographic quality of Latin America is its high level of urbanization. It is the most urbanized developing part of the world with over 75 percent of the population living in cities. Four of these metro areas (São Paulo, Mexico City, Buenos Aires, and Rio de Janeiro) have over 10 million inhabitants and are among the largest urban agglomerations in the world. Social and economic contrasts are especially visible in most large Latin American cities where affluent districts can be located next to squatter settlements.

Because of its geographic location, Latin America has been an especially important region to the United States. First, it has been the major source of immigrants to this country for several decades. Since about 2000, the majority of U.S. immigrants (legal and illegal combined) have been from Middle America, particularly Mexico. The Hispanic population has become the largest minority group in the United States, and its share of the total U.S. population will continue to increase. Second, Latin America is a major tourist destination for Americans and Canadians. The Caribbean Islands attract millions of visitors from both countries every year, particularly during the winter season, and tourism is the major source of revenue for many small Caribbean islands. Third, the United States has been politically and militarily involved in the affairs of many Latin American countries for over a century. Political and sometimes military intervention has changed the course of events in some countries. Fourth, Latin America provides many raw materials for the U.S. economy, including fossil fuels (oil), metallic ores (e.g. copper, bauxite, and iron), and agricultural commodities (meat, fruits, and coffee). It produces about 40 percent of the copper and silver and 60 percent of the coffee in the world. Fifth, the Panama Canal is a strategic waterway that shortens intercontinental voyages and cuts transportation costs for ships travelling between Atlantic and Pacific ports in the United States and other countries.

PHYSICAL ENVIRONMENT

Landform Configuration

Latin America can be divided into three major landform regions: the Eastern Highlands, the Central Lowlands, and the Western Mountains. The Eastern Highlands region, the oldest part of the South American continent from a geological point of view, is composed of three parts, the Brazilian Highlands, the Guiana Highlands, and the Patagonian Plateau. The Brazilian Highlands occupy over one-third of Brazil, including its eastern and most of its central and southern parts (Fig. 7.2). They are rich in mineral deposits, particularly iron, bauxite, and some strategic minerals (titanium, manganese, chromium, molybdenum, and tungsten). These deposits have made Brazil one of the world's major exporters of mineral resources and have provided a foundation for domestic industrial development. Some parts of the highlands have fertile soil, formed on volcanic bedrock, that has attracted various types of agricultural activities, including cultivation of coffee, soybeans, and sugarcane. Several major rivers draining the region have formed numerous waterfalls, including Iguaçu Falls (Fig. 7.3), the world's largest system of falls; their great hydroelectric potential has been utilized by Brazil, Paraguay, and Argentina. The Guiana Highlands, located in the northern part of South America, are also an old geologic formation known for distinctive flat-topped mountains and high waterfalls, including Angel Falls in Venezuela, the highest waterfall in the world. These highlands are rich in iron ore and bauxite, but they do not have fertile soil, except in the coastal parts of Guyana, Suriname, and French Guiana. The Patagonian Plateau is a cool, dry, and windy region in Southern Argentina. It is sparsely populated and offers limited agricultural opportunities (mainly sheep herding). It also has reserves of petroleum and natural gas, including the Vaca Muerta deposit in northern Patagonia, an important resource made more viable through hydraulic fracturing.

The Central Lowlands occupy the largest portion of South America and are composed of four parts. The Orinoco River Plain, located in the northern part of the continent between the Andes and the Guiana Highlands, is a flat and sparsely populated area, covered with tall grasses and scattered trees. The grasslands are known as *llanos*. The eastern part of the plain has large deposits of petroleum. The Amazon Basin, one of the largest plains in the world, occupies most of Northwestern Brazil and parts of the neighboring countries (Bolivia, Colombia, Peru, and Venezuela). It is also a sparsely populated but densely forested and well-watered region. One-third of the world's tropical rainforest is found here. The Amazon River and its tributaries contain about 20 percent of all surface freshwater in the world. It is navigable up to the city of Iquitos in Peru. The city of Manaus, once the world's leading exporter of natural rubber, located in the center of the Amazon Basin (1,285 kilometers/800 miles from the Atlantic Ocean), is

FIGURE 7.2 Landform regions of Latin America—*Source:* Natural Earth.

FIGURE 7.3 Iguaçu Falls—The Iguaçu Falls between Argentina and Brazil are the largest waterfall system in the world and a major tourist attraction. *Source:* Wikimedia Commons.

accessible by large ocean-going vessels and is considered a sea port. Although many tributaries of the Amazon River are not navigable for most of their course, they have great hydroelectric potential. The Paraguay-Pilcomayo Rivers Plain, also known as the Gran Chaco region, is located between the Central Andes and southwestern parts of the Brazilian Highlands and is similar to the Orinoco River Plain in vegetation, climate, soil types, population densities, and economic (agricultural) activities. The La Plata Basin or the Pampas is a region in East-central Argentina, Uruguay, and the southernmost part of Brazil. Because of its fertile loess soil, it has been called the breadbasket of Latin America and is known for wheat farming and cattle ranching. It is similar in many ways to the Great Plains in the United States.

The Western Mountains region extends from the southern fringes of Chile and Argentina to Northern Mexico and is composed of two parts: the Andes in South America and the mountain ranges and uplands of Middle America.

As mentioned earlier, this is a seismically active area with numerous volcanoes and frequent and sometimes devastating earthquakes. The Andes, which parallel the Pacific coast, are the longest and one of the highest mountain ranges in the world (Fig. 7.4). The southern parts of the chain in Chile are similar to the Alaskan/Canadian and Norwegian coastal areas and contain numerous fjords and islands. The Central Valley of Chile is a densely populated and agriculturally productive (irrigated horticulture) region of the Andes. Some of the tallest peaks in the entire Andean range, including Aconcagua, are found along the central part of the Chilean-Argentine border. The Altiplano is a high plateau region located in parts of Peru and Bolivia; it is surrounded by mountain ranges on the eastern and western sides. Lake Titicaca, located in this region, is the largest freshwater lake in the Andes and one of the highest in the world (Fig. 7.5). The Andes split into three ranges in Colombia—ranges separated by the densely populated and economically productive Cauca and Magdalena River

FIGURE 7.4 The Andes in Chile—The Andes stretch the entire length of the South American continent. *Source:* Pixabay.

FIGURE 7.5 Lake Titicaca—Lake Titicaca is a large high-altitude (3,812 meters or 12,507 feet above sea level) lake in Peru and Bolivia. *Source:* Heike C. Alberts.

Valleys. The eastern range further splits into two parts, separated by the Maracaibo Basin in Western Venezuela. The part located east of the Maracaibo Basin extends along the Venezuelan coast and through some islands in the Lesser Antilles archipelago.[1]

The landforms of Middle America are extensions of the western mountain ranges of South America. Central America and Mexico are composed of two coastal plains along the Pacific Ocean and the Caribbean Sea and the Gulf of Mexico; these plains are separated by interior mountain and upland ranges. The Pacific coastal plains are narrower and drier than those on the Caribbean and Gulf of Mexico side. The interior highlands of Central America are fertile and densely populated areas and have many active volcanoes. Parts of the Mexican interior highlands, especially the central plateau, are also very fertile and densely populated. Mexico City, the largest urban agglomeration in the Western hemisphere, is located there. The Yucatan Peninsula is a flat region known for karst topography; it has numerous sinkholes and underground streams. Most of the Caribbean Islands are extensions of the western mountain ranges of South America.

Climatic Contrasts

Latitude and landform configuration are major factors that explain the great climatic diversity of Latin America; the former is of greater importance in the eastern and central regions of South America and the latter in the Western Mountains zone. Ocean currents and wind patterns also influence the climate in some parts of this region. Some of the wettest and driest areas in the world, sometimes not far away from each other, are found in Latin America. Most of the Amazon Basin is located in the tropical rainforest climate (Fig. 7.6), which is characterized by a high average annual temperature and high precipitation and humidity. While there is little difference in monthly temperature patterns, precipitation is more unevenly distributed, and most comes in the form of torrential convectional rain (caused by rising warm air which then cools down and condenses), quite often accompanied by thunderstorms (Fig. 7.7). The climate becomes slightly drier, and the seasonal distribution of precipitation is more pronounced as one moves north or south of the Amazon Basin. Tropical savanna climate is dominant in South-central and North-eastern Brazil

FIGURE 7.6 The Amazon rainforest—The Amazon rainforest is the largest rainforest in Latin America, but rainforests also exist on some Caribbean islands such as Puerto Rico. *Source:* Wikimedia Commons.

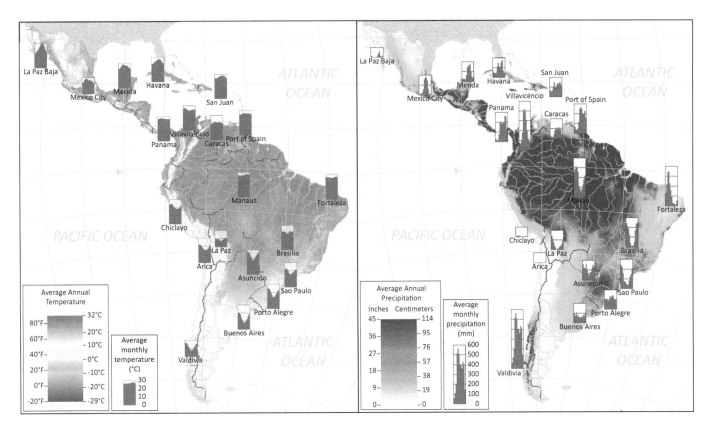

FIGURE 7.7 Latin America: patterns of temperature and precipitation—Notice the small monthly temperature variations in equatorial regions and increasing summer-winter differences with increasing distance from the equator, especially in South America. The seasonality of precipitation is well visible in most parts of the region. Also notice the proximity of very dry and humid areas in Peru and southern Chile and Argentina. *Source:* WorldClim-Global Climate Data.

and in parts of Venezuela and Colombia. Again, there is little difference in average monthly temperatures (although they are lower than those in the tropical rainforest region), but there are two distinctive seasons with regard to the amount of precipitation: dry winters and wet summers. Some trees lose leaves during the dry season and certain farming activities are correlated with temporal rainfall patterns. Moving south, average temperatures decline and winter-summer temperature ranges increase. Northeastern Argentina, Uruguay, and Southern Brazil are located in the warm temperate climate zone, similar to the Southeastern United States. The climate becomes cooler and drier south of this region, especially in Patagonia. This area is located in the rain shadow of the Andes; eastward moving moist air masses encounter a barrier of high mountains and deposit most of their moisture on the western slopes of the Andes. Southern Chile is one of the wettest places on Earth while Patagonia, located on the opposite side of the same range, is quite dry.

Moving north along the Pacific coast in Chile, the climate becomes drier as well. It also becomes warmer. The Central Valley of Chile has a Mediterranean climate similar to that in parts of coastal California. The Atacama Desert of Northern Chile and Southern Peru is one of the driest places on Earth. The extremely low and erratic precipitation is the outcome of four factors. First, around the world, the latitude band of about 20 to 25°S is associated with high pressure and dry air having to do with global circulation patterns. This band is home not only to the Atacama but also Africa's Namib and Kalahari Deserts and Australia's Great Sandy and Great Victoria Deserts. Second, at the latitude of the desert, prevailing winds come from the east and therefore the Atacama lies in the rain shadow of the Andes. Third, the cold ocean current offshore (the Peru or Humboldt Current), running from south to north and parallel to the coast, cools coastal air masses, making them less able to hold moisture and deliver it to the desert as precipitation. Indeed, the air over the Atacama is so dry that it sucks moisture out of the landscape. Finally, much of the desert is at a high altitude, where humidity is naturally lower.

Most of Middle America is part of the tropical climate region. Average monthly temperatures are fairly high and consistent throughout the year, while most of the unevenly distributed precipitation comes during the summer months. Warm trade winds coming from the northeast create sharp contrasts in climate and vegetation between the windward and leeward parts of many Caribbean Islands. For instance, San Juan in the northeast corner of Puerto Rico has an average annual precipitation of nearly 177 centimeters (66 inches), while Ponce near the southwestern corner of the island gets just 94 centimeters (37 inches). Hurricane season from June through November is another climatic feature in this part of Latin America. Several hurricanes occur every year, and a few can be quite strong. For example, Hurricane Mitch hit parts of Central America (mainly Honduras and Nicaragua) and killed over 11,000 people in 1998. Hurricane Patricia (2015), which formed southwest of Mexico, was the strongest hurricane ever recorded, with sustained winds of 346 km/hour (215 miles/hour). Fortunately, it did not cause as much damage as originally feared after making landfall along the less densely populated Pacific coastal parts of Mexico. Hurricane Maria (2017), one of the strongest tropical storms in recent history, caused a lot of damage to Puerto Rico, including over a thousand deaths.

Altitude is the most important climatic factor in mountainous regions, particularly the tropical parts of the Andes and Central America. Since elevation moderates climate, temperatures and humidity will decline as one moves up from coastal regions to high parts of the mountains. Five vertical zones have been identified in these regions. The altitude and vertical extension of each zone is a function of several factors, mainly latitude. In equatorial regions, each zone will be vertically wider than the same zone in temperate parts of the mountains. There is no sharp distinction between these zones in most areas either. Rather, a zone of transition will separate adjacent vertical belts.

Each zone is associated with a specific climate regime, natural vegetation, and economic activities (Fig. 7.8). The lowest zone, known as *tierra caliente* (hot land), is a hot and humid, densely forested, and rather sparsely populated area where both commercial and traditional tropical agriculture are practiced. This is the zone of sugarcane and banana plantations, as well as some root crops (cassava, sweet potatoes, and yams) and grains (maize and rice) grown on small peasant landholdings. The *tierra templada* (temperate land) zone, characterized by lower temperatures and humidity, has become an important producer of coffee, cotton, and maize. It is a relatively densely populated region that attracted many people of European origin. Most of the large interior Latin American cities are also located in this zone. The third permanently inhabited mountainous zone is *tierra fria* (cool land). Natural

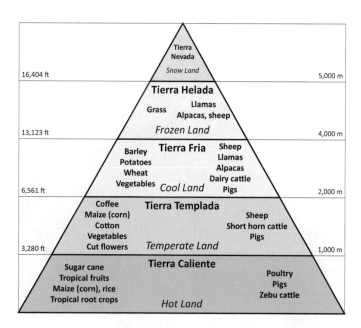

FIGURE 7.8 Vertical zonation in the mountainous regions of Latin America—The five distinctive natural zones, particularly in terms of climate and vegetation, are well pronounced in the equatorial parts of the Andes and mountains of Central America. The three lowest zones are permanently inhabited, and each zone is associated with different types of agricultural activities.

conditions of this region favor the cultivation of several temperate crops, including wheat, barley, and potatoes. Some Andean parts of *tierra fria* (e.g. the Altiplano) are also densely populated, mainly by people of Amerindian origin (Fig. 7.9), and some large cities (Mexico City, Bogota, and Quito) are found in this zone. The *tierra helada* (frozen land) zone is an uninhabited region located above *tierra*

FIGURE 7.9 Amerindians in Bolivia—Indigenous peoples in the Andes often wear traditional dress such as these three Quechua women in Bolivia. *Source:* Heike C. Alberts.

fria. It may be utilized as grazing land during warmer parts of the year. It is called *paramo* or *puna* in various parts of the Andes. Finally, the *tierra nevada* (the land of permanent snow) zone occupies the tallest parts of the mountains and is devoid of any vegetation and economic activities.[2]

HUMAN-ENVIRONMENT INTERACTION

Latin America has the largest area of tropical rainforest in the world. This forest, also known as *selva*, is the habitat for over half of the world's plants and animals and regulates the Earth's climate by producing oxygen and absorbing carbon dioxide. The forest is a source of many medicinal plants, but only a tiny fraction of its vast biodiversity has been assayed for beneficial health effects. Some tropical hardwoods, including mahogany (native to this region), resistant to rotting and cracking, are used in the production of expensive furniture and cabinets. The balsa tree, a source of soft and light lumber, is another valuable commodity from this region. Finally, the tropical rainforest is home to many indigenous Amerindian groups who are dependent on it for their survival.

Unfortunately, the area of tropical rainforest in Latin America has been shrinking for decades (Fig. 7.10).

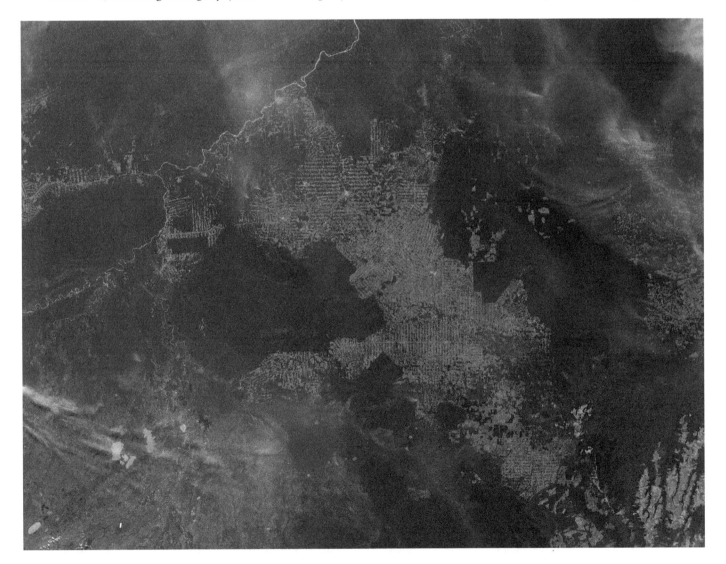

FIGURE 7.10 Deforestation in the Amazon region—Large areas of the Amazon rainforest have been deforested, but deforestation rates are fluctuating. *Source:* Wikimedia Commons.

The good news, however, is that the region's rate of deforestation has slowed considerably. Between 2010 and 2015, the forested area was cut by about 0.2 percent per year; a decade earlier the rate was more than double, with deforestation advancing at 0.5 percent per year between 2000 and 2005. In fact, the region no longer ranks first in the world in pace of deforestation. Between 2010 and 2015, Sub-Saharan Africa had more rapid deforestation both in terms of the absolute number of hectares lost per year, and in the percentage rate of reduction. The deceleration in Brazil has been especially important. While the Amazon giant still ranks first in the world among individual countries in forest loss per year, it has slowed dramatically: between 2010 and 2015, an area roughly the same size as Puerto Rico was cleared each year, but a decade earlier the rate was more than three times as fast. Unfortunately, deforestation rates have been once again on the rise since 2016.[3] The demand for additional grazing land by cattle ranchers and arable land by small-scale subsistence farmers have been responsible for over 90 percent of the forest loss. In addition to agricultural expansion, wood extraction and infrastructure expansion (road construction) are other direct causes of tropical deforestation; indeed deforestation is strongly concentrated along roads through the Amazon. Another factor is Brazil's weak system of land titles. Many people in the Amazon do not have a clear title to the land they occupy, and therefore they have little incentive to protect it for the future. However, spurred in part by concern about global climate change and the country's aim to be a "green superpower," Brazil has begun to address the land ownership problem, to invest more heavily in the enforcement of forest protection laws, and to set aside more land in parks and reserves.

The western fringes of Latin America are part of the seismically active Pacific Ring of Fire, a zone associated with frequent earthquakes and periodic volcanic activity. The coastal areas from central Chile through central Peru and in Northern Ecuador are particularly prone to devastating earthquakes (Fig. 7.11). Out of the thirty strongest earthquakes on record, thirteen occurred in the Latin American part of the Pacific Ring of Fire. The strongest earthquake on record occurred in Chile in 1960 (the Valdivia earthquake of magnitude 9.5); it killed at least 2,200 people. The offshore Arica earthquake of 1868 in Northern Chile had an estimated magnitude of 9.0 and killed over 25,000 people, and the 1906 Ecuador-Colombia earthquake with a magnitude of 8.8 left about 1,000 people dead. The 2010 offshore earthquake in Central Chile was the fifth strongest quake on record; fortunately, it claimed

only 525 lives. Some of these earthquakes also generated tsunamis that affected coastal areas on both sides of the Pacific Ocean. Relatively strong earthquakes may also occur in the coastal areas of Southern Mexico and parts of the Greater Antilles. Tragically, an earthquake with a magnitude of 7.0 that struck Southwestern Haiti in 2010 killed an estimated 100,000 to 300,000 people. The death toll was so high because the area most impacted by the earthquake was densely populated and very poor and had little recent experience with seismic activity. Conversely, the Chilean earthquake that same year struck a more lightly populated and richer area with better built infrastructure, and Chile has considerable experience with managing seismic risks.

Three clusters of active volcanoes are found in the southern Andes along the southern half of the Chile-Argentina border, the central Andes along the Chile-Bolivia border and in Southern Peru, and in the northern Andes in parts of Ecuador and Colombia. Other lines of active volcanoes are in Central America and Mexico and in the Lesser Antilles. The Galapagos Islands are also known for volcanic activity. The 1902 Mt. Pelée eruption in Martinique in the Lesser Antilles destroyed the entire island and killed approximately 30,000 residents. More recent volcanic eruptions occurred in 1982 in Mexico (Mt. El Chichón) and in 1985 in Colombia (Nevada del Ruiz) and killed approximately 3,500 and 25,000 people, respectively.

Most of the Middle American region is also threatened by strong hurricanes. Those formed in the Atlantic Ocean pass through the Caribbean Islands and sometimes reach coastal regions of Central America and Mexico. The Pacific coast of Southern and Central Mexico lies in another hurricane zone. Poverty and deforestation exacerbate the hazard posed by hurricanes. For instance, Hurricane Jeanne, Latin America's deadliest since 2000, traveled through the Caribbean before crashing into Florida. While Jeanne would ultimately strengthen to a Category 3 hurricane just as it hit the Florida coast, it was only a tropical storm as it passed over Haiti. Yet, the storm killed more than 3,000 Haitians and only five Americans. The severely deforested landscape of Northern Haiti could not absorb the more than 33 centimeters (13 inches) of rain that Jeanne dropped in some areas, and many people died in the resulting mudslides. Further, Haiti's status as the poorest country in the Western Hemisphere meant that many victims lived in poorly constructed homes and had little access to health care in the storm's aftermath.

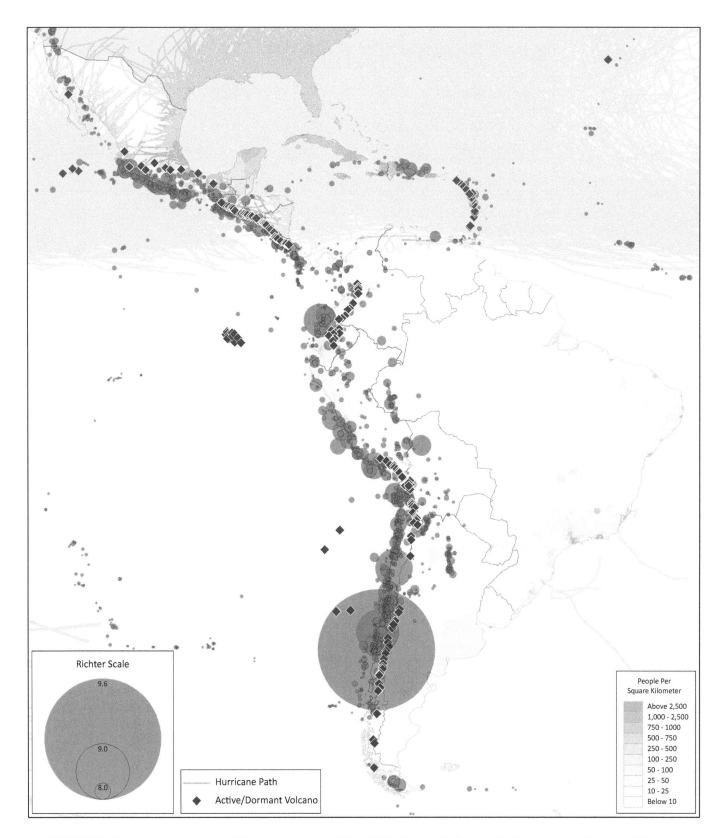

Richter Scale

9.6

9.0

8.0

——— Hurricane Path

◆ Active/Dormant Volcano

People Per
Square Kilometer

Above 2,500
1,000 - 2,500
750 - 1000
500 - 750
250 - 500
100 - 250
50 - 100
25 - 50
10 - 25
Below 10

FIGURE 7.11 Selected natural hazards (20th century) and population distribution in Latin America—Notice a strong positive correlation between population densities and probability of seismic hazards in the Andes, Central America, and parts of the Caribbean Islands. *Source:* NOAA National Climatic Data Center; Earthquake Hazards Program; GeoTech Center Data Library.

POPULATION PATTERNS AND TRENDS

Considering its size and natural resource base, Latin America is a relatively sparsely populated part of the world. Its population density of 30 persons per square kilometer (75 persons per square mile) is lower than that of all major world regions except Oceania, the Russian Realm, and the United States and Canada. By comparison, South Asia, the most densely populated region, has ten times more people per unit of land than Latin America does. Brazil and Mexico have the largest populations in the region (205 and 125 million, respectively) which account for over half of Latin America's inhabitants.

Population Distribution and Growth

The Latin American population of 630 million is very unevenly distributed. Its distribution can best be described as peripheral and clustered. This pattern of distribution is especially visible in South America (Fig. 7.12). The northern half of the Andes, from Peru through Ecuador and Colombia to Venezuela, forms one such population cluster. The coastal areas of Brazil, particularly those in the southeast, form another cluster. Two smaller population clusters can also be found in Central Chile and Northeast Argentina. About 80 to 90 percent of South America's total population is located in these four coastal clusters.

Middle America has slightly different population distribution patterns. In Mexico, the majority of the population lives in the interior cluster around the capital of Mexico City, while in Central America the highest population densities are found along the Pacific coast. The Caribbean Islands are the most densely populated parts of Latin America. Population densities on Barbados, Grenada, and Hispaniola are over ten times greater than the region's average. The population distribution reflects the natural environment and historical patterns of European settlement. The highest population densities in the northern Andes are found in the *tierra templada* and *tierra fria* zones. Since elevation moderates climate in tropical areas, these relatively warm and less humid areas have attracted both native and European settlers. Fertile volcanic and alluvial soil in many parts of these zones support subsistence and commercial (plantation) agriculture. Mineral resources (silver in particular) have also attracted many settlers for the past five centuries. Most of South America's interior is sparsely populated. The hot-humid and densely forested Amazon River Basin is inhabited by only about 10 million

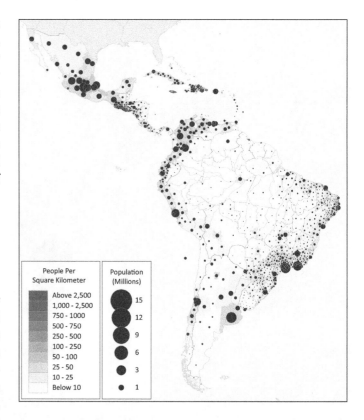

FIGURE 7.12 Population distribution in Latin America—The peripheral and clustered population distribution in South America is well visible on this map. The interior population clusters in Mexico and Central America are also visible on the map while high population densities in the Caribbean Islands, especially the Lesser Antilles, are less visible due to the small size of those islands. *Source:* GeoHive (www.geohive.com) and statistical agencies of selected countries.

people. For instance, 90 percent of Brazil's population still lives within a 321-kilometer (200-mile) belt along the coast despite government efforts (e.g. building a new capital city of Brasilia) to attract more people to the interior. The dry regions of Latin America, particularly the Atacama Desert and Patagonia, and to a lesser degree Northwestern Mexico, also have very small populations.

Latin America's population has more than tripled for the past two generations, from about 170 million in 1950 to over 630 million today. Latin America had the highest fertility rate in the world in the 1950s and the early 1960s (Fig. 7.13). In most countries, a typical woman had at least six children. Only Argentina, Chile, and Uruguay as well as a few Caribbean Islands had lower fertility rates at that time. Population control programs were not popular in Latin America in those days for several reasons, including

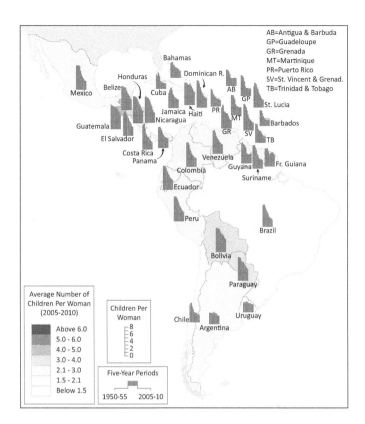

FIGURE 7.13 Total fertility rates in Latin America, 1950–2010—Fertility rates have significantly declined in most Latin American countries during the past six decades. Notice the low rates in Argentina and Uruguay during the entire post-World War II period. *Source:* United Nations. Population Division. World Population Prospects 2012.

the tradition of *machismo* (male dominance) and the influence of the Catholic Church. Fertility rates, however, have been steadily declining in most countries for the past four decades due to growing popularity of family planning programs, increasing educational levels and secularization, among other things, and are close to the replacement level today. They are even below that level in Cuba, Puerto Rico, and a few other Caribbean islands. As fertility has dropped, population growth rates have slowed, though they are still over 1 percent per year. This means an annual addition of over 6 million people.[4]

International and Internal Migration

Latin America was one of the major destinations for European migrants between the 17th and the early 20th centuries. The Spanish and Portuguese colonization of the region brought thousands of usually young and adventurous individuals, most of them from Southern Spain and Northern Portugal, ready to establish a new life in the initially little-known land. After the independence of most Latin American countries in the early 19th century, migrants from other parts of Europe, mainly Italy and Germany, also began moving to this region, especially its temperate southern parts (Argentina and Brazil). While most people who migrated to Latin America from Europe did so voluntarily, those who came from Africa and Asia did so mainly through enslavement or indentured servitude, respectively. The rapid large-scale decline of the Amerindian population in the 16th century, resulting mainly from high mortality due to infectious diseases brought by the Europeans, led to the forced migration of 10 to 12 million Africans. The Trans-Atlantic slave trade, also discussed later in this chapter, had a tremendous demographic and economic impact on both Latin America and Africa. Over 40 percent of African slaves were shipped to present-day Brazil, another 40 percent to the Caribbean Islands (British, French, and Dutch colonies), and the rest to Spanish parts of Latin America (12 percent) and British North America (4 percent). After the abolition of slavery, indentured Asian laborers were brought to some parts of the region. Most South and Southeast Asian migrants landed in the British-and Dutch-controlled Caribbean Islands and the Guianas, while East Asians went to Brazil, Peru, and a few other parts of former Spanish America.

From being a significant destination for migration flows (forced or voluntary), Latin America shifted to becoming a region of emigration after World War II. The volume of emigrants had been steadily increasing for most of the post-1950 period, from approximately 200,000 a year half a century ago to over 400,000 today (Fig. 7.14). Poor economic conditions, political instability, and high crime rates in some parts of the region encouraged or forced many residents to look for a better future somewhere else. Mexico has been the largest supplier of migrants to the United States for decades. Most countries of Central America and the Greater Antilles region have also become important origins of economic, political, and environmental migrants to this country. Emigration from Peru reached relatively high levels between the mid-1990s and mid-2000s as well. Political instability and the drug wars in Colombia also pushed thousands of residents to other countries, especially in the 1970s and 1980s. There are over 28 million Latin Americans living outside their home countries today.[5] Despite the negative net-migration balance for the entire region for the past half century, some Latin American countries attracted migrants from neighboring countries or even from other continents at various times after World War II. Venezuela's oil industry attracted some migrants from neighboring Colombia and the Caribbean Islands in the 1950s. Argentina received over 450,000 migrants, some from other Latin American

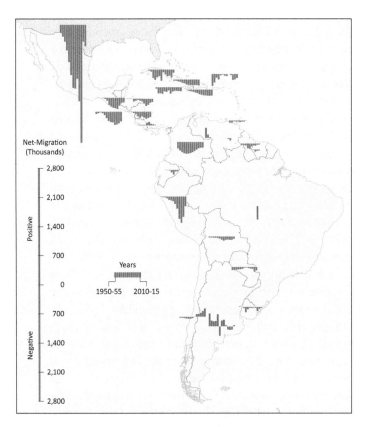

FIGURE 7.14 Net migration in Latin America since 1950—Over 34 million people have left the region since that time. Mexico generated one-third of the migrants, and most of them went to the United States. Only a few countries have had a positive migration balance. Data for Brazil and Venezuela are incomplete. *Source:* United Nations. Population Division. World Population Prospects 2012.

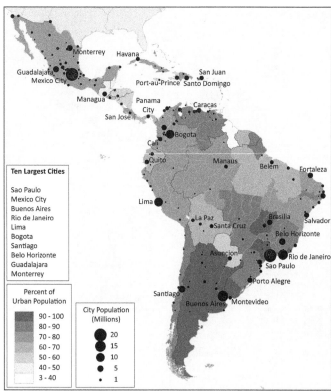

FIGURE 7.15 Urbanization levels in Latin America—The region has more megacities than other parts of the world of similar population size. *Source:* United Nations. Population Division. World Urbanization Prospects 2014.

countries and some from Europe, during the 1950s and 1960s, and Costa Rica has attracted over 280,000 migrants since the early 1980s. Chile has also become more attractive to migrants in recent years.

High Levels of Urbanization

Latin America is the most urbanized part of the developing world, with over 75 percent of its population living in cities today (Fig. 7.15). The urbanization levels are similar to those in Europe and other developed regions. In some Latin American countries (Argentina and Uruguay) over 90 percent of the population is urban. The proportion of the urban population in the region has doubled since 1950. Although some Caribbean countries and Belize are still predominantly rural, the urbanization process seems to be unstoppable. The preference for urban residence goes back to early colonial times when towns and cities were crucial tools for the administration of colonial territories and for

sites where the indigenous population could be more easily converted to Christianity. Cities also had high social status. This tradition has continued after independence, and today Latin America struggles to cope with rapid urban growth. In most Latin American societies, urbanization is considered a positive process despite many drawbacks such as crime, poverty, and environmental degradation. It is expected that 90 percent of the region's total population will be living in cities by 2050.

A distinctive feature of Latin American urbanization is the presence of several megacities, urban agglomerations of over 10 million people. Mexico City in Mexico and São Paulo in Brazil have a metropolitan population of about 21 million each. Buenos Aires, the capital of Argentina, is a metropolis of 15 million residents, and Rio de Janeiro, the former capital of Brazil, is inhabited by 13 million people. Lima in Peru and Bogota in Colombia are approaching the 10 million mark. There are over sixty cities with a population of 1 million or more, and they have one-third of the region's total population.

Another characteristic of the Latin American urban network is the dominance of primate cities in most countries. A primate city is a settlement that is several times

bigger in population than the next largest
city in a specific country or region. It is
usually the economic, political, and cultural
center of the country. The presence of a
primate city sometimes indicates regional
inequalities in development, resulting in
an overdeveloped core and an underdevel-
oped periphery. In Latin America, Buenos
Aires in Argentina, Santiago in Chile, and
Lima in Peru are good examples of large-
size primate cities. Each of them has about
one-third of the respective country's total
population. Several smaller-sized primate
cities have an even greater proportion of the
national population; Montevideo is home to
almost half of Uruguay's population.

Latin American cities are also known
for economic polarization and spatial
segregation. Great inequalities in wealth
and a high percentage of residents living
in squatter settlements are especially visible in large cities. Squatter settlements,
known as *barrios, ranchos, barriadas,* or

FIGURE 7.16 Favela in Brazil—Favelas are squatter settlements (shantytowns) in
Brazil. Many are located on very steep slopes. *Source:* Wikimedia Commons.

villas miserias in the Spanish-speaking regions and *favelas* in Brazil (Fig. 7.16), are parts of the urban landscape in
almost every Latin American country. About 170 million
people, or one-third of the urban population, lives in such
settlements in this region (Fig. 7.17). Haiti and Jamaica have
the highest proportion of urban residents living in such
settlements: 70 and 60 percent, respectively. The squatter
settlements first appeared as communities of poor former
slaves at the end of the 19th century, and they became
visible parts of the urban landscape between the 1940s
and 1970s during the large-scale migration from rural to
urban areas. Confronted with very expensive urban real
estate, these migrants began erecting makeshift structures from collected and sometimes stolen materials of
various types, including cinder blocks, bricks, and sheet
metal, usually on marginal, environmentally hazardous,
and otherwise undesirable sites (steep hillsides, polluted
wetlands and/or floodplains), frequently located on the
urban periphery. Today, these areas tend to have inadequate
infrastructure, and land tenure is insecure. Limited (if
any) access to running water, sewage, electricity, garbage
collection, and public transportation services as well as
high crime rates, illegal drug trade, and vulnerability to
natural hazards (mudslides) make life for their residents
very challenging. Although rural-to-urban migration, poverty, and the lack of low-cost housing have been responsible
for the emergence of squatter settlements, other factors,
such as the inability of local governments to manage urban

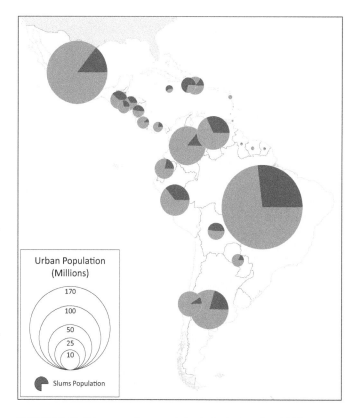

FIGURE 7.17 Urban squatter population in Latin America, 2009—
About a quarter of urban residents in the region lives in shantytowns. However, over half of Haiti's and Jamaica's urban population
lives in such neighborhoods. *Source:* United Nations Statistics
Division. Millennium Development Goals.

growth, natural disasters, and politics, may also be partially responsible for this problem. Most countries have been attempting to solve it through infrastructure development, demolition of poorly built structures, and relocation of residents to public housing projects or back to rural areas. These attempts are time-consuming, expensive, and sometimes controversial projects. For instance, residents of one *favela* slated for clearance before the 2016 Rio Olympics resisted the government's plans to destroy their homes, even though they were promised better quality homes in a new neighborhood. However, in many instances the squatters themselves have improved their communities, so that some scholars are now optimistic about their long-term development.[6]

LANGUAGE AND RELIGION

Dominance of Spanish and Portuguese Languages

Considering its territorial and population size, Latin America is characterized by remarkable linguistic uniformity. Spanish and Portuguese are the dominant languages spoken by about 90 percent of the population. Spanish is the official language in all former Spanish colonies, and Portuguese has the same status in Brazil. Both languages, in addition to the Catholic religion and other elements of Iberian culture, were imposed on the indigenous people. European settlers had little appreciation for indigenous languages and began implanting a sense of shame of their languages and cultures among some groups. In some cases, indigenous people were forbidden to use their native language. Furthermore, the decimation of indigenous populations also undermined the viability of many of their cultural traditions. Together, these circumstances resulted in the partial or total assimilation into Spanish or Portuguese culture. Most people of mixed race, especially of European and Amerindian or African origin, used Spanish or Portuguese at home and with others. Although some indigenous languages are still used in several parts of Latin America, knowledge of the Spanish or Portuguese language is considered an asset, especially when seeking employment in urban areas. Today, the largest number of Spanish speakers in the world is in Mexico, and the largest number of Portuguese speakers is in Brazil. Indeed, Latin America is almost solely responsible for the fact that Spanish and Portuguese are among the ten most commonly spoken languages in the world.

English, Dutch, and French are spoken in parts of Latin America that were or still are controlled by the United Kingdom, the Netherlands, or France, respectively. English is widely used in one South American and several Caribbean countries, including Antigua and Barbuda, the Bahamas, Barbados, Belize, Dominica, Guyana, St. Kitts and Nevis, St. Lucia, St. Vincent and the Grenadines, and Trinidad and Tobago, as well as the British dependencies of Anguilla, British Virgin Islands, Cayman Islands, Montserrat, and the Turks and Caicos Islands. The Dutch language is used in Suriname and the Netherlands Antilles, which include the islands Aruba, Bonaire, Curaçao, Sint Maarten (the Dutch part of the island), Saba, and Sint Eustatius. The French territories of French Guiana, Guadeloupe, Martinique, and Saint Martin are the French-speaking parts of Latin America. Most people in Haiti, a former French colony and the first independent country in Latin America, speak French Creole, a language derived from 18th-century French with influences from Spanish, Portuguese, and some West African languages. English Creole has about 5 million speakers in Jamaica. Papiamento, another Creole language, is spoken in parts of the Netherlands Antilles. It is a mixture of Portuguese and West African languages with influences from several Amerindian and other European languages. The last three languages belong to a larger group of Creole languages that are also spoken in parts of Africa, Asia, and Oceania. They are simplified mixtures of two or more non-native languages adapted by the next generation of speakers as its first language.

Native Amerindian Languages in the Andes and Central America

At least 15 million people in Latin America use several indigenous languages on a regular basis. Most of them live in rural areas where the Inca, Aztec, and Mayan cultures flourished during pre-colonial times (Fig. 7.18). Quechua is spoken by 10 million people in Peru, Bolivia, Ecuador, and Argentina, and Aymara has over 2.5 million speakers in Bolivia and Peru. Both languages are official, in addition to Spanish, in the last two countries. Guarani is an official language in Paraguay (in addition to Spanish), and has about 2.5 million speakers. Various Mayan languages are still used by about 6 million people in the Yucatan Peninsula

FIGURE 7.18 Distribution of major linguistic families in Latin America—*Source:* World Language Mapping System.

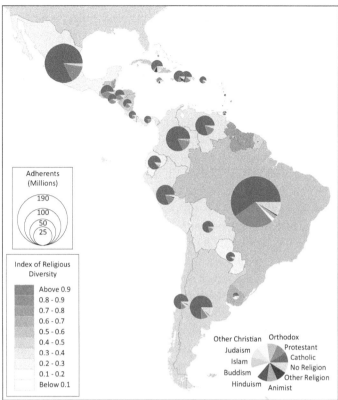

FIGURE 7.19 Religious affiliation of people in Latin America—Paraguay and Ecuador are the least diverse countries where Roman Catholics comprise 87–88 percent of the total population. Trinidad and Tobago, Guyana, and Suriname have a mixture of Christians (Catholics and Protestants), Hindus, and Muslims. *Source:* Association of Religious Data Archives.

of Mexico, Guatemala, and Belize. Oto-Manguean languages are spoken by approximately 2 million people living in Southern and Central Mexico and Uto-Aztecan languages by a similar number of speakers in Northern and Central Mexico. Arawak languages are spoken by about 600,000 speakers in Eastern Venezuela and the Guianas, and 250,000 people speak Chibcha languages in Colombia, Panama, and Costa Rica.

Roman Catholicism and Other Religions

Approximately 90 percent of Latin America's population is Christian, including 70 percent Roman Catholics and over 18 percent Protestants (Fig. 7.19). Catholics comprise the majority of the population in twenty-five countries; in Paraguay, Ecuador, Mexico, Colombia, Peru, and Bolivia over 80 percent of the population is Catholic. Protestant churches are dominant in several former British possessions in the Caribbean region. The most secularized country is Cuba where a quarter of the population is nonreligious.

Indigenous people at the time of European conquest adhered to various types of polytheistic religions, and some groups, especially the Aztecs, practiced ritual human

sacrifice. Roman Catholicism became the dominant religion shortly after the imposition of Spanish and Portuguese rule on most of the region. Indigenous people converted to the religion of the colonial power in large numbers, quite frequently without understanding the principles of their new faith. Religious syncretism (i.e., the mixing of native and Catholic beliefs and practices) became fairly common among indigenous groups. Churches and other religious structures were often built on native religious sites. The Catholic Church began facing several challenges at that time, including the perception of the new religion as a culture trait rather than a specific system of beliefs; the shortage of clergy, especially the lack of clergy of native or mixed-race origin; a fairly relaxed moral discipline among the clergy; and the perception of the institutional church as an extension of the colonial government.

The Catholic Church became a powerful institution through land ownership in rural and urban areas and through close ties with the government elites in colonial times and has retained this status until recent decades. Latin American Catholicism has several distinctive features, including a relatively low attendance at religious services (10 to 15 percent of the total population) and widespread veneration of saints and the Virgin Mary. Some scholars have identified three types of Catholics in Latin America.[7] Formal Catholics comprise about 10 to 20 percent of the total faithful and are found mainly among the urban rich. They regularly attend religious services, participate in other church-sponsored activities, and make significant financial contributions to support the church. About 60 to 70 percent of the Latin American population could be described as nominal Catholics. The majority of the urban middle and lower class, as well as peasants, belongs to this group which is characterized by sporadic church attendance and limited financial contributions. Folk Catholics, today found mainly among isolated indigenous and African groups, incorporate a mix of animistic and Catholic practices and have been declining in numbers over time, especially among Amerindian groups.

By 2010, when Buenos Aires cardinal Jorge Bergoglio was elected pope, Latin America was the single largest concentration of Catholics in the world. Bergoglio, who took the name Francis as pope, was the first non-European chosen to lead the church in more than 1,200 years. His selection reflected the shift of Catholicism to the global South.

Nevertheless, the rapid spread of various Protestant denominations in predominantly Catholic regions of Latin America is one of the greatest challenges to the Catholic Church as an institution. Most Protestant missionaries came to this area from the United States and quickly found many followers, especially among the urban and rural poor. There is a lot of emphasis on fundamentalist charismatic beliefs and practices as well as voluntary and widespread engagement in church activities. Protestant denominations are also characterized by a high degree of local autonomy, fragmentation, and internal competition. The traditionally Catholic countries of Guatemala, Honduras, Brazil, and Nicaragua have provided the most fertile ground for Protestant conversions. About 40 percent of the Guatemalan and one-third of the Honduran population is now Protestant. These countries are home to new Evangelical megachurches which vie with ancient Catholic cathedrals for the devotion of the faithful.

POLITICAL ORGANIZATION OF SPACE

Pre-Columbian America: Three Complex Cultures

Estimates of the number of native people inhabiting Latin America at the time of European discovery (1492) vary from 12 million to almost 100 million. The largest population clusters were found in present-day Mexico and the central Andes (Peru and Bolivia). These two areas may have had three-fourths of the entire region's population. The native population was linguistically diverse and divided into over 5,000 ethnic groups. There were also important differences with regard to the social and political organization as well as the spatial interaction among these groups. Some groups lived in isolation and depended on hunting and gathering for their survival while others developed into complex societies with advanced technology. The three most sophisticated civilizations that emerged in this region prior to the European conquest were those of the Mayas in present-day Southeastern Mexico, Guatemala, Honduras, and Belize; the Aztecs in what is now Central Mexico; and the Incas in the Andean region of Peru and Bolivia.[8]

The Maya civilization may have been the only major culture in the world that originated in the tropical rainforest region and developed ingenious adaptations to the difficult environment.[9] It is known for its impressive urban architecture; the numerous pyramid-like stone structures required a large and well-organized labor force for their construction (Fig. 7.20). Mayan culture is also associated with great achievements in mathematics and astronomy; it developed two calendar systems, one for religious (260 days) and one for secular (365 days) purposes. The 260-day calendar was probably based on the number of days between the sun transiting directly overhead at a Mexican site called Izapa. Located near the Guatemalan border and along the Pacific coast, Izapa is at the core of the Mayan world and seems to be where the sacred calendar was adopted. Because Izapa lies between the Equator and the Tropic of Cancer, the sun passes directly overhead twice each year: on April 30th and then 260 days later on August 13th.

The Aztec civilization flourished in Central Mexico. It was also known for significant achievements in urban planning and development. Tenochtitlan was a large city of over 200,000 inhabitants (but only 13 to 21 square kilometers or 5 to 8 square miles in area) located where Mexico City is found today. The Aztecs had a fatalistic concept of the universe. They could placate their gods

FIGURE 7.20 Maya Pyramid at Chichén Itzá—The pyramid known as El Castillo dominates the Maya city of Chichén Itzá on Mexico's Yucatán Peninsula. *Source:* Heike C. Alberts.

by practicing human sacrifice on a large scale (20,000 to 50,000 a year); most, if not all, of the victims came from subjugated neighboring ethnic groups. The Aztecs also developed a unique system of cultivation known as *chinampa*, the cultivation of maize and other crops in rectangular fertile fields built on shallow lake beds. It was an example of an intensive type of farming as these fields could be cultivated on a continuous basis. They also possessed knowledge of leather and woodworking, textile manufacturing, metallurgy, and pottery.

The Inca empire occupied large parts of the Andes with its center in present-day Peru and Bolivia. It had a strong central government that fully controlled the life of its subjects. Each individual was permanently tied to a certain occupation. There was no private property, and people were required to provide labor to the state which, in turn, was responsible for feeding and protecting them. The empire had a well-developed network of paved roads and suspension bridges and a communication system that used human messengers. Although the Incas did not develop a

writing system, they practiced recordkeeping on knotted strings attached to cords or ropes called *quipus*. They also developed a mortar-less stone construction technology. The ruins of Machu Picchu and the Inca capital Cuzco provide good examples of this technology (Fig. 7.21). The Incas also domesticated llamas and alpacas, two animals well adapted to mountainous terrain.

The Mayan, Aztec, and Inca cultures have several things in common. One of them was communal land ownership and collective labor arrangements. Although each culture had its own version, emphasis on the common good rather than individual rights characterized all of them. Another common feature was an emphasis on crop cultivation (grains and tubers) rather than on livestock herding. The Amerindians possessed solid knowledge of advanced land management techniques, including irrigation, terracing, and shifting cultivation. Rigid social stratification, practice of slavery, and warlike relations with their neighbors also characterized the three Amerindian cultures. Finally, none of them discovered a practical use of the wheel.

FIGURE 7.21 Machu Picchu, Peru—Machu Picchu is the most famous Inca site in the Peruvian Andes. It is a UNESCO World Heritage Site. *Source:* Heike C. Alberts.

European Conquest and Colonial Rule

Spain and Portugal established full control over most of Latin America within several decades after Columbus's discovery of the New World. They accomplished this through exploration, conquest, and colonization. The initial center of Spanish control was Santo Domingo on the island of Hispaniola. From there, European colonizers explored the Caribbean coast of Central America from Honduras to the Orinoco River Delta in Eastern Venezuela. Santa Maria in present-day Colombia was the first Spanish settlement on the American continent.

Hernando Cortés conquered the Aztec Empire with a small number of soldiers and with the help of neighboring Amerindian tribes by 1521. Cortés had first reached Tenochtitlan in 1519. The Spaniards were amazed at the magnificence of the city; and although they had slaughtered many Amerindians in crossing Mexico, the conquistadors

were initially greeted peacefully by the Aztec ruler Moctezuma, who showered Cortés with lavish gifts. In return, the Spanish unknowingly infected the Aztecs with European diseases to which the Aztecs had little resistance. Smallpox, a human disease closely related to an affliction in cattle, which had been domesticated thousands of years earlier in Eurasia, tore through the vulnerable Aztec population killing large numbers of people. The fact that Europeans were largely unaffected exacerbated the psychological effect of the epidemic. When Cortés returned in 1521, the conquistadors and their Amerindian allies defeated the Aztecs with relative ease.

The conquest of the Inca Empire by Francisco Pizarro in 1533 was even more astonishing and again disease played a decisive role. Evidence indicates that European diseases traveled overland faster than the Spanish themselves, so when Pizarro finally reached the Inca realm, which the Inca called Tawantinsuyu, smallpox was already wreaking havoc there. With the unwitting support of disease and European technological advantages (writing, steel weapons and armor, horse-mounted soldiers, and ocean-going ships), Pizarro and a small force thousands of miles from home defeated South America's greatest empire. With such an arsenal of factors in their favor, the Spanish swept north and south. By the 1540s, about fifty years after Columbus first reached Hispaniola, the Spanish reigned across a large area of the Americas.

The other main European power in the region was Portugal. These had been the first two European states to undertake large-scale exploration and colonization in the 15th century. To avoid any conflicts between them, Pope Alexander VI persuaded both countries to sign the **Treaty of Tordesillas** in 1494. This treaty divided the entire non-Christian world into Spanish and Portuguese spheres of influence along the 46°W meridian. Any newly discovered land west of this line would automatically belong to Spain, and any land east of the line would be a Portuguese possession. The division gave Portugal dominion in Africa and much of Asia, but almost all of Latin America lay on the Spanish side of the line. The only exception was the eastern third of what is now Brazil (the meridian passes just to the east of São Paulo). Portugal was gradually able to expand its control beyond the dividing meridian and incorporated vast interior areas of present-day Brazil into its colonial empire.

Early Spanish and Portuguese colonizers came to the New World in pursuit of the "three Gs": gold, God, and glory (i.e., to get rich and famous by acquiring a lot of precious metals (gold and silver) and to spread Christianity in the new lands). In Spanish-controlled areas, these objectives were served by the *encomienda* system, an economic and social institution in the form of a royal grant designed to control and exploit native people through their labor and tribute (taxation) in exchange for instructing them in the Spanish language and Catholic religion. This system of forced labor was widely abused by the *encomenderos* (individuals in charge of *encomiendas*) and strongly criticized by religious and some civil authorities in the colonies. It was gradually replaced, first in the more densely populated and economically developed areas, by the *repartimiento* system. This too was a forced-labor system but with government in control instead of individuals. Each native settlement was required to provide a certain number of workers for specific tasks every year. A similar institution called *mita* (based on the pre-existing Incan labor tax) was developed in parts of the Andean region and was used to extract native labor in silver mines. Both systems were later abolished in response to, among other things, a limited supply of labor resulting from the large-scale indigenous population decline.

FIGURE 7.22 Spanish and Portuguese colonial rule in Latin America—The administrative boundaries were subject to frequent change, and some boundary lines shown on this map are approximate. Drawn after several similar images in Jackiewicz, E. L. and F. J. Bosco. (2016). *Placing Latin America: Contemporary themes in geography.* Lanham: Rowman & Littlefield; and at the Wikimedia Commons Atlas of colonialism at https://commons.wikimedia.org/wiki/Atlas_of_colonialism" \I "Maps_of_colonialism" https://commons.wikimedia.org/wiki/Atlas_of_colonialism#Maps_of_colonialism

The Spanish colonies in Latin America were originally divided into two viceroyalties (administrative units). New Spain was centered on Mexico City (built on the same site as Tenochtitlan) and Peru had its capital in Lima (Fig. 7.22). The first administrative region, established in 1535, included most of Middle America and the northern parts of South America, and the second one, established in 1542, consisted of the remaining Spanish possessions in South America. Two additional viceroyalties were established later. The viceroyalty of New Granada with its capital in Bogota became the third center of power in 1717; it was formed from the southern parts of New Spain. Finally, the viceroyalty of Rio de la Plata, first governed from Buenos Aires and later Montevideo, became the fourth major center of power in 1776.

The centuries of European colonial rule in Latin America that followed 1492 had profound consequences for the region and the rest of the world, among them the large-scale decline of the indigenous population, the forced transfer of millions of Africans, and the introduction

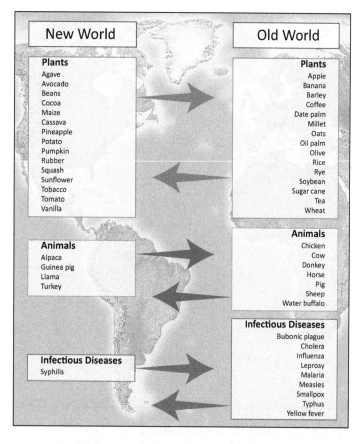

New World

Plants
Agave
Avocado
Beans
Cocoa
Maize
Cassava
Pineapple
Potato
Pumpkin
Rubber
Squash
Sunflower
Tobacco
Tomato
Vanilla

Animals
Alpaca
Guinea pig
Llama
Turkey

Infectious Diseases
Syphilis

Old World

Plants
Apple
Banana
Barley
Coffee
Date palm
Millet
Oats
Oil palm
Olive
Rice
Rye
Soybean
Sugar cane
Tea
Wheat

Animals
Chicken
Cow
Donkey
Horse
Pig
Sheep
Water buffalo

Infectious Diseases
Bubonic plague
Cholera
Influenza
Leprosy
Malaria
Measles
Smallpox
Typhus
Yellow fever

FIGURE 7.23 The Columbian Exchange—While a similar number of plant species were exchanged between the Old and New Worlds, more animal species and infectious diseases were brought to the Americas, and they had a much greater impact on the population and the economy of the New World than the other way around. *Source:* Wikipedia.

of the Roman Catholic religion and Spanish and Portuguese languages to the New World. Other consequences included the Columbian Exchange of plants and animals between the New and Old World, the introduction of new types of farming and expansion of mining, and the strong social and racial stratification of Latin American societies (Fig. 7.23).

Estimates of Latin America's indigenous population at the time of European discovery vary tremendously, from 10 to about 100 million, although most scholars today concur that the region had about 37 to 50 million inhabitants, including 6 million in the Aztec Empire, 11 million each in the Mayan region and in the Inca Empire, a similar number in present-day Brazil, and 0.3 million in the Caribbean Islands.[10] The population in most of these areas declined by 80 to 90 percent during the following century; in other words, the population was literally decimated or reduced by a factor of ten. Various infectious diseases (e.g. influenza, measles, and smallpox) brought by the

Europeans were mainly responsible for the high mortality among the indigenous people who had no immunity to them. Forced labor, particularly in mines, and massacres also killed many native residents. Starvation and famines, caused by the displacement of the native farmers from the most fertile to marginal and remote areas, added to the total death toll.

The indigenous population decline created severe labor shortages, and the European response to this problem was the importation of African slaves. The Trans-Atlantic Slave Trade, practiced for almost three centuries, resulted in the forced migration of 10 to 12 million, usually young and healthy, Africans to the New World (Fig. 7.24). Twice as many may have died along the way because of harsh treatment, poor diet, and unsanitary conditions. Most worked on sugar plantations, where the brutal way of life extracted a high death toll, fueling the demand for still more slaves. The slave trade was finally banned in the 19th century when Brazil became the last country to make the importation of slaves illegal. In 1888, Brazil also became the last country in the Americas to make slavery itself illegal. Now, more than a century later, the high proportion of people of African origin in Brazil and the Caribbean, areas still known for sugar, is the result of the past slave trade.

Even after the abolition of slavery, much of rural Latin America remained dominated by very large landholdings including plantations and *haciendas*, especially in coastal and other fertile areas (Fig. 7.25). Plantations were commercial farms producing one commodity, such as sugar cane, bananas, and coffee, almost exclusively for export (Fig. 7.26). All three of these crops are examples of the Columbian Exchange in that they were first domesticated on the other side of the Atlantic and were unknown in the Americas until after 1492. Haciendas were large landed estates, usually located in the interior, characterized by extensive cultivation and livestock herding. For hacienda owners, prestige from land ownership was more important than its productivity. Severe inequality in land ownership reinforced other forms of inequality.

A typical Latin American society was divided into several major and dozens of minor racial and/or social groups called *castas*. Among those with less mixed ancestry, the population was divided into Peninsulares (Spaniards) and Criollos (Spanish Americans), Indios (Amerindians), and Negros (Africans). People of mixed races were classified into numerous groups, among them Mestizos (Amerindian and Spanish), Mulattos (African and Spanish), and Zambos (African and Amerindian). The offspring of Spanish and Mestizo heritage were called Castizo while those of Mestizo and Amerindian origin were known as Cholo. Some

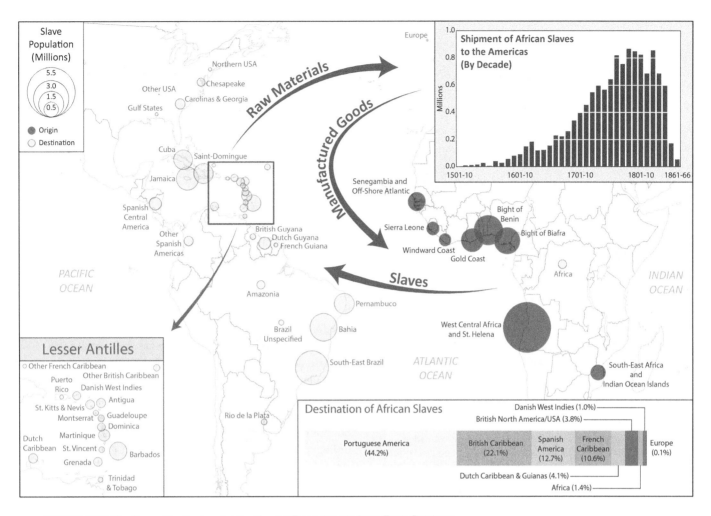

FIGURE 7.24 The Trans-Atlantic slave trade—*Source:* Trans-Atlantic Slave Trade Database.

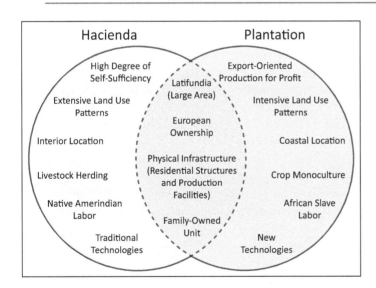

FIGURE 7.25 Characteristics of haciendas and plantations—Some scholars claim that the hacienda is a South European (Spanish and Portuguese) while the plantation is a West European (British, French and Dutch) invention. Although plantations played a greater role in the economies of West European colonies, they also comprised an important part of Spanish and Portuguese colonial agriculture.

FIGURE 7.26 Banana plants and sugar cane in Martinique—Cash crops such as bananas and sugar cane play an important role in the Latin American economy. *Source:* Wikimedia Commons.

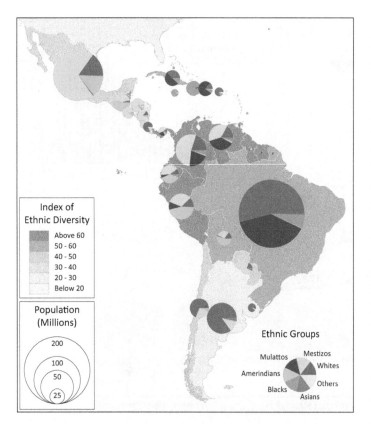

FIGURE 7.27 Distribution of ethnic groups in Latin America—Although the complex system of ethnic classification developed under the Spanish colonial rule is no longer practiced in Latin America, some ethnically mixed groups such as Mestizos and Mulattos are widely recognized and even recorded in census publications of many countries. However, there are significant differences among scholars and other authoritative sources regarding the size of some ethnic groups in several countries. *Source:* CIA World Factbook 2014; Encyclopedia Britannica Yearbook 2014; Wikipedia.

of these groups had different names in various parts of Spanish America. Some of these racial groups (e.g. Mestizos or Mulattos) are still officially recorded in censuses and other government publications (Fig. 7.27).

Early Independence and Political Instability

Several factors contributed to the early independence of Latin American countries compared to many other parts of the global periphery under European control. First, the population of Spanish origin was divided into two groups, Peninsulares and Criollos; between them a growing hostility emerged that would undermine Spanish control. The first group included Spaniards born in the Iberian Peninsula, and the second those born in the New World. The Peninsulares comprised a numerically small but politically influential group—all high civil and ecclesiastical

positions were reserved for them, and Criollos saw them as representatives of distant Spanish rather than local interests. The ideas of the American and French Revolutions inspired Criollos to further resist Spanish control. Second, Spain and Portugal were deeply involved in affairs on the European continent and had less time and energy to control their colonial possessions in Latin America. The Spanish monarch was exiled between 1808 and 1814 by Napoleon; the increasingly absolute rule by the king after 1814 strengthened Criollos' desire for self-rule and independence. By the 19th century, Spain and Portugal were weak and marginal European powers, ill-equipped to hold on to vast colonial empires. Third, the increasingly powerful United States considered Latin America a part of its sphere of influence and would not tolerate any European incursions. The Monroe Doctrine (1823) may have helped newly independent countries preserve their freedom from Spain.

Independence came quickly to most Spanish and Portuguese colonies. Between 1810 and 1825 all continental colonial possessions of both countries became independent states (Fig. 7.28). While Spanish colonies divided into several independent countries, mostly along administrative boundaries of former vice-royalties and smaller colonial units, Portugal's colony stayed together and formed one gigantic country: Brazil. The country had been less politically polarized than most former Spanish colonies. Brazil was originally a monarchy and nearly seventy years of the royal "moderating power" of Dom Pedro II (1831–1899) may have contributed to Brazilian unity.

Elsewhere in the region, the early years of independence were associated with political instability and changing alliances, and the political map of this region was in a state of flux for the next several decades. For example, most of Central America, after declaring independence from Spain in 1821, formed one country called the United Provinces of Central America or the Federal Republic of Central America. The new country was absorbed by the Mexican Empire in 1822 but separated from it the following year. This union was dissolved in 1839 after individual parts began declaring independence. Seven new countries emerged from this union, but some of them were later absorbed by or merged with their neighbors.

Another new country established in 1819, Gran Colombia, included present-day Colombia, Venezuela, Ecuador, Panama, and parts of Peru, Brazil, and Guyana. A dispute led to the break-up of the federation and the formation of Ecuador and Venezuela in 1830. The United Provinces of the Rio de la Plata (1810–31) were a relatively short political union of parts of Argentina, Uruguay, Bolivia, Brazil, and Paraguay. Frequent disputes among its members

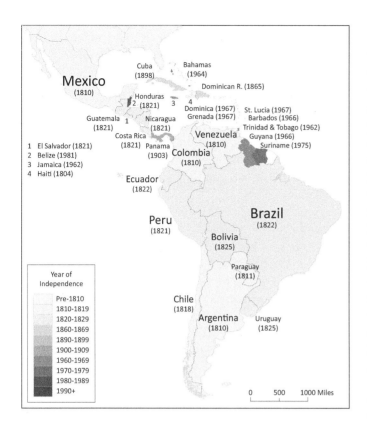

FIGURE 7.28 Independence dates of Latin American countries—Haiti, a former French colony, was the first country in the region to gain independence after a successful slave revolt. Belize gained independence from the United Kingdom in 1981.

from the beginning led to the dissolution of this union two decades later.

The War of the Triple Alliance (1865–70) or Paraguayan War was a conflict between Paraguay on one side and Argentina, Brazil, and Uruguay on the other. Its outcome was about 400,000 deaths, making it Latin America's deadliest war. The dead included most of the Paraguayan male population; so near the war's end, Paraguay fielded armies of children. Paraguay lost and ceded territory to Brazil and Argentina, leaving the landlocked country weaker and poorer. The 19th century also weakened Latin America's other landlocked country, Bolivia. It was also part of a brief Peru-Bolivia Confederation (1836–39) but was invaded by Peru after the dissolution of the confederation. Both countries later participated in the War of the Pacific (1879–83), a conflict between Bolivia and Peru on one side and Chile on the other. Its result was Bolivia's loss of the Antofagasta Corridor, a mineral-rich part of the Atacama Desert, to Chile. Peru also lost two southern provinces, Tarapaca and Arica, to Chile in that war. The loss also left Bolivia landlocked, a disadvantage that continues to thwart development.

International conflict among the young countries continued into the 20th century. One example was the Gran Chaco War (1932–35) between Bolivia and Paraguay. The war ended in Bolivia's loss of two-thirds of the disputed area of Gran Chaco that was believed to have deposits of petroleum. This conflict resulted in 50,000 to 80,000 deaths on the Bolivian side and 35,000 to 50,000 deaths on the Paraguayan side. The Soccer War (1969) between Honduras and El Salvador, triggered by a soccer match, was a brief conflict over economic issues, especially the status of approximately 300,000 Salvadoran immigrants in Honduras, who made up a fifth of the country's population. The Falkland War (1982) between Argentina and the United Kingdom was another, more recent example of political and economic instability in this region. Argentina invaded the islands which have been under British rule since 1833. This war was the Argentine military government's attempt to divert attention from worsening economic conditions at home. It led to Argentina's defeat and the re-establishment of the civilian rule the next year.

The U.S. has also been involved in numerous conflicts in the region, the most significant being the Spanish American War of 1898. In the early 19th century, only two Spanish colonies in Latin America did not proclaim independence: Cuba and Puerto Rico. Spain recognized the strategic and economic importance of these islands after it had lost the rest of Latin America and was determined to control them at any cost. However, conflicting Spanish and American interests led to the 1898 war. Spain was defeated in this conflict and lost control of both islands. Puerto Rico became a United States possession; today it is termed a "commonwealth" or a free associated state of the United States. United States citizenship was granted to residents of Puerto Rico in 1917, so there are no legal restrictions on their migration to other parts of the U.S. Puerto Ricans do not pay federal income tax, do not have a voting representative in U.S. Congress, and do not have a vote in the Electoral College that chooses the U.S. president; however, most federal laws (e.g. the U.S. minimum wage) do apply in Puerto Rico. As mentioned in Chapter 2, there have been periodic calls for changing Puerto Rico's political status and making it the fifty-first state of the United States. Puerto Ricans seem to be evenly split on this issue; half of the population would like statehood; the other half wants to maintain the island's current status. A small segment of the population is interested in complete independence. Puerto Rico is much poorer than any U.S. state, and the majority of its population is fluent in Spanish only.

Cuba was under direct American military control for the first few years after the Spanish-American war and later had limited self-government (1902–34). During the

Batista rule (1952–59), political repression and widening socioeconomic inequalities inspired Fidel Castro and his supporters to challenge the Cuban government. Castro came to power in a military coup in 1959. Shortly after, Cuba became a Communist state and established close ties with the Soviet Union. The Cuban Missile Crisis of 1962, caused by the secret installation of nuclear-armed Soviet missiles on the island, led to a brief political and military standoff between the two Cold War superpowers. In response to the Soviet move, the United States imposed a naval blockade on Cuba and was ready to use military force to protect its strategic interests in this part of the world. The crisis ended after the Soviets agreed to remove the missiles from Cuba in exchange for the American promise not to invade Cuba and to remove U.S. missiles from Turkey. Castro's ties to the Soviet Union and his government's poor human rights record led to a decades-long embargo on U.S. trade and travel with the island country. Those restrictions were loosened somewhat in 2014.

Political struggles between states in Latin America generally have been dwarfed by the often violent political struggles within them. An almost perpetual tug of war between the conservatives (federalists) and liberals (centrists) has developed in most states. The first group favored the church-aristocracy alliance, a weak national government with more power given to the provinces, while the second favored a secular state with a strong central government and free trade. The Mexican Revolution (1910–1917) is one of the best examples of internal political instability in Latin America. At the time, the country was a land of inequalities (1 percent of the population controlled 70 percent of the land), Roman Catholicism was the official religion, and the church and state worked together. The indigenous Indian population had very limited rights and lived in almost slave-like conditions. Most of the natural resources were controlled by foreign interests.[11] The revolution began as a protest against fraudulent elections but soon became a widespread movement demanding "Land

and Liberty." Seven years later, the revolution had brought about a number of changes including (1) a major land reform that divided large estates and redistributed the land among landless peasants and established *ejidos* (communal land ownership by villagers); (2) the confiscation of church property and the restriction of church influence on education and government; (3) the right to own land and vote for the Mestizo and Indian population; (4) the nationalization of natural resources; and (5) limits on military and presidential powers.

Frequent military takeovers of the government have also been a common feature of the political landscape in Latin America. For example, Haiti, the first independent country in the region, has had twenty-five government takeovers since its independence. The emergence of insurgency movements in several countries at various times has been another component of the Latin American political landscape. For instance, the Revolutionary Armed Forces of Colombia, known by its Spanish acronym FARC, waged a fifty-two-year insurgency against the Colombian government before finally agreeing to lay down its weapons in 2016. As with similar insurgency groups in El Salvador and Guatemala, FARC is expected to transition toward becoming a more conventional political party that advances its aim through ballots rather than bullets, but with so many grievances built up over a half century of violence, maintaining the peace will be difficult.

The good news is that Latin America today, with some important exceptions, is a relatively peaceful, democratic region. According to Freedom House, a U.S.-based nongovernmental organization that rates every country in the world in terms of civil liberties and political freedoms, most Latin American countries, including some like Peru and El Salvador with very violent recent histories, were rated "free" (the same category as the U.S. and Canada) in 2017. A handful of Latin American countries, including Mexico and Colombia, were rated "partly free." Only Cuba and Venezuela were judged to be "not free."

ECONOMIC ACTIVITIES

The turn towards greater peace and democracy described at the end of the last section ought to help accelerate economic development in Latin America. The region's political turbulence is one reason why Latin America fell behind the U.S. centuries ago. When Europeans first arrived in the Americas, Central Mexico and Highland Peru almost certainly had higher levels of development than North America, and as late as 1700 Mexico in particular was probably still richer

in terms of per capita GDP than the British colonies that became the U.S., but since then, the U.S. economy has far outpaced those of the main Latin American countries. By 2016, Mexico's GDP per capita was just 19 percent of the U.S. level, and no sizeable country in the region was much higher (Fig. 7.29). The five-to-one gap is not just due to political troubles in Latin America. Other obstacles have been severe: inequality rooted deep in the region's history,

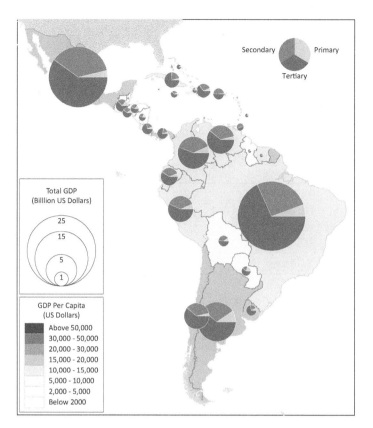

FIGURE 7.29 Gross domestic product in Latin American countries—Most countries, except a few small Caribbean dependent territories, are in the group of middle-income nations with their GDP per capita below $20,000. Haiti, with a GDP per capita of $1,600, ranks last in the region. Agriculture is the least important sector in all Latin American economies. It may employ a relatively large proportion of the labor force, but its contribution to the GDP is rather small, usually below 15 percent. *Source:* CIA World Factbook 2014.

poor quality infrastructure, weak educational systems, ineffective government intervention in the economy, and **brain drain**—especially the loss of many highly qualified people via migration to the U.S. Recent decades have brought progress on these fronts, but daunting development challenges remain.

Primary Activities: Mining, Agriculture, and Fishing

Mining has been an important economic activity in some parts of Latin America since early colonial times. The Spanish quest for precious metals led to the exploitation of mines originally developed by indigenous people prior to European conquest, as well to as the opening of new ones. Most labor was provided by Amerindian people. Mexico and the central Andes region became the two major silver mining centers in the New World, and Latin America has

been producing more silver than the rest of the world for centuries. Brazil became another important mining center by the end of the 17th century where first gold and later diamond mines were opened.

Later mineral commodities valuable to industry took center stage. For instance, the guano boom of the 1850s and 1860s brought great wealth to Peru. Guano, the hardened remnant of bird droppings, was mined from islands off the Peruvian coast where the upwelling of nutrients provided a rich environment for fish and the birds who fed on them. Guano became a lucrative, internationally traded fertilizer at a time when agriculture was being turned into an industry. In his 1850 State of the Union Address, U.S. President Millard Fillmore declared, "Peruvian guano has become so desirable an article to the agricultural interest of the United States that it is the duty of the Government to employ all the means properly in its power for the purpose of causing that article to be imported into the country at a reasonable price."[12] Later, guano was supplanted by chemical fertilizers (though guano is still used in organic farming), but other mineral resources continued to be central to Peru's economy, including nitrates. The mining of nitrates and copper made Chile another major Latin American mining center. Interestingly, the territory lost by Bolivia and Peru in the War of the Pacific contains much of Chile's mineral wealth. But by the early 20th century, Bolivia had become one of the world's principal sources of a different resource: tin.

In northern South America, Venezuela became the setting for a great oil boom in the 1920s, and within ten years the country became the second largest oil producer in the world. Mexico also emerged as a significant oil producer. In both countries, the government nationalized the oil industry, meaning the government took over the exploration, drilling, production, and refining of oil. Mexico kicked out foreign oil companies in 1938 and Venezuela in 1976. In both countries, nationalization meant that a higher proportion of oil revenues stayed in the domestic economy, but the oil industry has suffered from a lack of investment and technical know-how that the world's major oil companies could bring. The two countries now seem to be headed in opposite directions as oil producers: Mexico's production has declined steadily since 2004 due to the exhaustion of some of its major fields, but Venezuela is now ranked first in the world in proven oil reserves, ahead even of Saudi Arabia. To try to revitalize its oil sector, Mexico loosened some restrictions on foreign investment in 2014. Meanwhile, Ecuador and Brazil also have significant oil resources.

Today, mining plays an important role in the economy of several other Latin American countries. Chile is the world's largest producer of copper, providing one-third of the global production, and the export of this commodity accounts for over 50 percent of the country's total exports. Brazil is the third largest producer of bauxite in the world, but export of this mineral (used in the production of aluminum) is also very important for the economies of Jamaica and Suriname. Mexico is the world's largest producer of silver, and Latin America accounts for almost half of the world's total production. Other important mineral resources of Latin America are iron ore (Brazil is the third largest world producer) and lithium, which is used in many electronic batteries. Over half the world's reserves are found in the so-called Lithium Triangle of Argentina, Bolivia, and Chile.

Land Reforms

From early colonial times through the first decades of the 20th century, agricultural production units in Latin America were divided into large landed estates (plantations or haciendas) called *latifundia* and small peasant holdings known as *minifundia*. Most of the rural land belonged to a relatively small number of *latifundia*-type estates while a much greater number of *minifundias* comprised a small fraction of the land in almost every country. Haciendas and plantations utilized indentured and slave labor or employed nearby *minifundia* cultivators in exchange for usually meager wages and/or access to some of the estate resources. The *latifundia* owners had a lot of political and economic power and shaped the agricultural institutions in their own interest.[13] This system of production and land ownership brought about tremendous inequalities in wealth and strong social stratification magnified by racial divisions.

Western European and North American ideas of democracy and equality began finding fertile ground in some countries, and fears of social dissatisfaction and unrest, as well as external pressure, prompted some governments to introduce at least limited land reforms. These reforms aimed at land redistribution and change in power relations in favor of landless peasants and small farmers at the expense of large estate owners and their associates. The transfer of landed property occurred through confiscation (no compensation), expropriation (compensation), progressive taxation, and the development of public lands.

Mexico was the first Latin American country to introduce a large-scale land reform (Fig. 7.30), which was an outcome of the Mexican Revolution of 1910–17. The new constitution of 1917 and the land reform law of 1922 supported the principle of ownership of the land by those who work it. The real reform began in the 1930s and led to the redistribution of 45 million acres of land to about 800,000 rural families and the establishment of the *ejido* system, based on collective or communal land ownership.

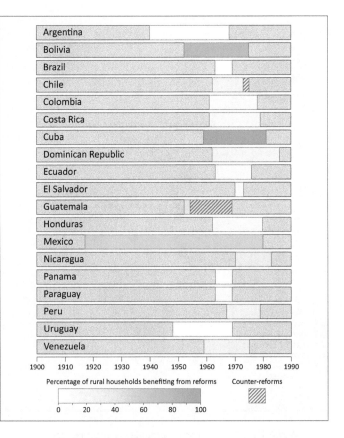

FIGURE 7.30 Land reforms in Latin America—The Mexican, Bolivian, and Cuban reforms benefited the largest proportion of peasants in the region. *Source:* Wikipedia.

An *ejido* was an agrarian community (village) where the land was divided into two parts: one part was land that was accessible to all members of the village, and the other part consisted of parcels assigned to individual families. Although these families did not own the land (it was state property), they had the right to use it and transfer this right to other family members. At the end of the reform, just over half of the Mexican-cultivated land was under the *ejido* system. This popular reform gave the Institutional Revolutionary Party, known by its Spanish abbreviation PRI, almost uncontested power for the next seven decades. However, the *ejidos* suffered from low productivity and restrictions on their privatization were lifted in the 1990s.

Because land reform meant taking a source of wealth from the most powerful interests in society, it often encountered severe resistance, as the case of Guatemala illustrates. Although Guatemala was one of the richest Central American countries, it was characterized by enormous inequalities in land ownership as 2 percent of the population controlled over 70 percent of the arable land; only about 12 percent of that land was cultivated. The agrarian reform began in 1952, and over 2 million acres of land were redistributed among approximately 100,000 families (about 40 percent of the rural population) during the eighteen-month period. Some of the redistributed land was owned by American corporations, including the United Fruit Company, well known for its Chiquita brand bananas. The land reform was aborted in 1954 after the U.S. supported a coup that ousted the democratically elected president. The new government annulled the land expropriation and returned most of what had been taken to the previous owners and its military supporters.

In contrast, the Cuban government introduced the most widespread land reform in Latin America after the Communist victory in 1959, which completely upset the established order on the island. Land reform consisted of the confiscation of all foreign-owned (mainly American) land, restrictions on the size of private farms (originally 990 and later 165 acres), the conversion of public lands to state farms, expropriation of *latifundias* and distribution of that land (now state-owned) to peasants, conversion of sugar cane plantations to cooperative farms, and nationalization of cattle ranches.

Despite land reforms in most Latin American countries, there are still inequalities in land ownership in some countries. Unequal land ownership feeds broader inequalities. For the most recently available data ranking the world's countries in terms of how equitably income is divided among the population, six of the fifteen most unequal societies were in Latin America including Haiti, Colombia, Guatemala, Paraguay, Panama, and Chile. Conversely, the most equitable Latin American country, El Salvador, still had greater income inequality than seventy countries from other world regions.

Commercial and Subsistence Agriculture

Although agriculture accounts for a relatively small proportion of the total gross domestic product in almost every Latin American country today, the region is a major producer and exporter of several plantation crops (bananas, coffee, and sugarcane), cereals (wheat and corn), fruits, and animal products (beef and wool). Plantation agriculture, well established in the tropical coastal parts of the region, has played an important role in the Latin American economy since early colonial times. Family-owned plantations were dominant through the late 19th century; corporate farms became more important through the mid-20th century, and today there is a mixture of transnational and native ownership of these production units. Native farmers focus on the production of crops while transnational corporations specialize in exporting and marketing

them. Sugarcane was the first major plantation crop, grown mainly in the Caribbean region, Northeastern Brazil, and the Guianas. Fertile volcanic or alluvial soil and a warm to hot climate with wet and dry seasons (growing and harvesting) made cultivation of this plant very profitable. Almost all work in the fields (planting and harvesting) and sugar mills (sugar extraction) was done by African slaves. The cultivation of sugarcane significantly increased after the 1520s, in response to a high demand for sugar in Europe. Although slavery has long since been outlawed, Latin America remains a key source of sugar, producing about one-sixth of the global sugarcane output since the 1960s. Brazil is by far the largest producer in the region (and the world) today—it harvests over ten times more than Mexico, the second largest sugarcane producer in the region. Over half of Brazil's sugarcane is now used for ethanol production.

Banana plantations were first established in the western parts of the Caribbean region, including Jamaica and coastal areas of Central America, in the 1870s. After the plants were decimated by the Panama disease in the 1930s, production was relocated to the Pacific coast of Central America. When disease-resistant varieties of the banana plant were found and introduced to the region in the 1960s, production again shifted to the Caribbean coast. The production and marketing of this fruit has been controlled by three American companies: Chiquita (formerly United Fruit), Dole (United Standard), and Del Monte, for decades. Most Central and South American bananas are exported to North America while those produced in the Caribbean Islands are sold to Europe. Today Ecuador and Brazil are the largest Latin American producers of bananas (Fig. 7.31). The economy of most Central American countries has been dependent on banana exports for years, and this dependency was associated with the derogatory term "banana republics" in the past.[14]

There are two major coffee growing regions in Latin America, one in Southern Mexico, Central America, and Colombia where shade-grown varieties are grown on small- and large-holder farms, and the other in Southern Brazil, particularly in the Sao Paulo area, where sun-grown varieties on large farms are dominant. The shade-grown varieties, harvested by traditional methods (hand-picked ripe berries), are considered to be of higher quality than those mechanically harvested at various stages of ripeness. Coffee became Colombia's dominant export commodity by the 1860s. The Brazilian coffee industry began in the 1720s, and the country has been the world's leading producer since 1845. Mexico, Honduras, and Guatemala are other important coffee producers in the region. The last two countries have significantly increased their production in the past

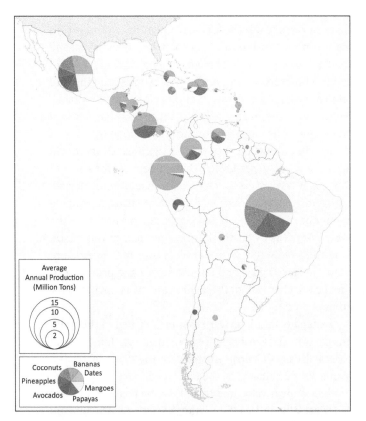

FIGURE 7.31 Production of selected tropical fruits in Latin America, 2005–2013—The banana is the most important tropical fruit plant grown in the region. Brazil, Mexico and a few other countries produce a greater variety of fruits while most Central American countries, Ecuador, and the Lesser Antilles depend on monoculture of bananas. Since only tropical fruits are shown on this map, it understates the importance of other countries, especially Chile, as fruit producers and exporters. *Source:* FAOSTAT.

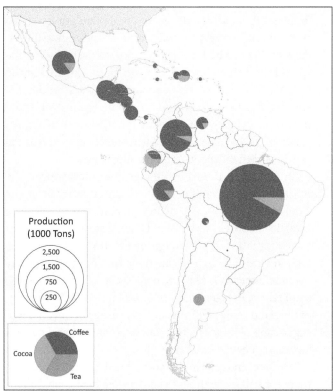

FIGURE 7.32 Production of cocoa, coffee, and tea in Latin America, 2005–2013—Although cocoa was domesticated in the New World, it is a relatively unimportant crop in this region except in Ecuador and the Dominican Republic. Coffee has been the dominant beverage crop for decades, particularly in Brazil, Colombia, and Central America. Argentina is the only important producer of tea in Latin America; it is made from *yerba mate*, a plant native to the Americas. *Source:* FAOSTAT.

few decades. However, the share of Latin America's global production has declined from 75 percent in the early 1960s to just over 50 percent today (Fig. 7.32) as other producers such as Vietnam have come on board.

Chile, Mexico, and a few other Latin American countries are important producers of fruits and vegetables, most of them for export to the United States. Most of the Chilean production is concentrated in the Central Valley region known for its Mediterranean climate that is well suited for this type of agriculture. A rapid expansion of Chilean horticulture occurred in the 1980s in response to a shift in consumer preferences to healthier diets, supportive government policies, and the correlation between the harvest seasons in the southern hemisphere and the increased demand for these commodities in the northern hemisphere. Indeed, Chile has been one of the biggest beneficiaries of the advent of permanent global summertime (availability of fresh fruits and vegetables to consumers all year round) in affluent northern hemisphere markets.

The export of table grapes, apples, plums, and peaches/nectarines permit American consumers to enjoy these fresh fruits year-round, even in the depths of winter. Mexico is another major supplier of fresh fruits and vegetables for the American market. Production is more dispersed than in Chile, and avocados and tomatoes are the dominant export items.

Commercial grain farming has been well established in the Pampas region of Argentina, Uruguay, and southern Brazil for some time. The fertile soils and warm to mild climate have made this region the breadbasket of Latin America. Argentina is now the world's sixth largest exporter of wheat. The cultivation of soybeans has also significantly increased in Brazil and Argentina in recent decades. Both countries, in addition to the United States, are leading global exporters of this crop.

The fishing industry has been an important component of Peru's and Chile's economies for some time (Fig. 7.33). The Peruvian and Chilean coastal waters are productive fishing areas due to the Humboldt Ocean Current that runs

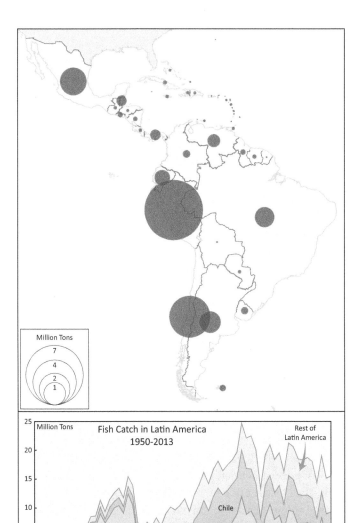

Million Tons

7

4

2

1

Million Tons

Fish Catch in Latin America
1950-2013

Rest of
Latin America

Chile

Peru

FIGURE 7.33 Fish catch by country—Peru's fishing industry began developing very rapidly in the late 1950s, and the country's annual fish catch amounted to almost 90 percent of the region's total catch during the next decade. Although it has recovered after a spectacular decline in the early 1970s, other countries, especially Chile, have increased their fish catch since that time. Peru still has the largest fishing industry in Latin America but its fish catch now amounts to only about 40 percent of the region's catch. *Source:* FAOSTAT.

parallel to their coast. This cold current contains large amounts of plankton, which attracts various species of fish, including anchovy. Peru ranks second in total fish caught in the world (after China), and it is the largest exporter of fishmeal in the world. Fishing is the second highest source of foreign currency after mining. However, the fish catch declines during El Niño years as warm waters brought to this part of the Pacific Ocean have fewer nutrients. El Niño is a periodic climatic phenomenon associated with

abnormally warm waters brought to the equatorial parts of the eastern Pacific from the western Pacific and characterized by wet weather in parts of the Americas.

Industrial Development Policies

Although the colonial powers discouraged the development of manufacturing activities in Latin America to protect these industries at home, the processing of plantation crops (sugarcane), non-ferrous metallic ores, dye plants (indigo), and insects (cochineal, from which a dark red pigment was extracted) flourished in the region. After independence, the policy of laissez-faire (minimal governmental interference in economic affairs) attracted American and European (British, French, and German) capital mainly to the agricultural and mining sectors, including the production of bananas and coffee in Central America, Colombia, and Brazil; beef and wheat in Argentina; sugar in Cuba and Puerto Rico; silver in Peru; nitrates in Chile; and copper in Mexico. Foreign investment gave these countries some access to advanced technology, helped to establish transportation networks and improve infrastructure, created better employment opportunities, and led to the growth of the urban middle class. On the other hand, this policy also led to greater income inequality, resentment toward foreign interests, and more frequent labor-management disputes.

During the 1920s and 1930s, Latin American countries began to support **import-substitution industrialization**, which emphasized domestic industrial development to lessen the dependence on imported goods and raise the standard of living for their citizens. During the first stage of this program, the development of labor-intensive textiles, pharmaceuticals, and food processing industries was emphasized. Later, governments supported the development of durable consumer goods industries making such items as household appliances, TV-sets and radios, and automobiles. They allowed the import of parts for these goods, but the export of finished products was discouraged. Next, the development of intermediate industries producing parts and other items for the industries, established during the first two stages, was encouraged. The final stage of this policy was characterized by the establishment of heavy manufacturing such as the iron and steel industry and the production of mining and transportation equipment. This policy also imposed quotas and high tariffs on imported goods to protect domestic industries in their initial stage of development.

Although the import-substitution policy allowed large countries (Brazil, Mexico, and Argentina) to expand their industrial base, it also led to economic inefficiencies resulting in low-quality finished products, government bureaucracy, decreased foreign investment, impoverishment of the rural population because of low prices for food items and high costs for farming equipment and fertilizers, and large foreign debts in the 1980s and 1990s through dependence on imported raw materials for these industries. For instance, in the mid-1970s Mexico began investing heavily in a brand new steel mill on the Pacific coast 320 kilometers (200 miles) north of Acapulco. The mill had been a dream of a former Mexican president, and the new city that grew up around the mill was named for him, Lazaro Cardenas. The idea was to use an iron ore deposit near the plant to make steel, to use the site's naturally deep harbor to create the largest port on Mexico's Pacific coast, and to jump-start development in the poor region. The multibillion dollar steel mill, funded by Mexico's oil revenues, was built on the site of a coconut plantation; and because it was built in a rural area far from the industrial regions in the middle of the country, the plant got off to a difficult start. It lacked good transportation access by rail to the rest of Mexico, and so the raw materials had to be imported and the finished steel exported. The project generated far less steel and far fewer jobs than had been hoped.

Thirty years later, however, the Mexican economy had been transformed to much more strongly emphasize exports, including automobiles and appliances. These represented a significant market for steel and made the Lazaro Cardenas plant, by then Mexico's largest producer, an attractive enterprise. The state-owned company was privatized, and the plant was ultimately acquired by Luxembourg-based ArcelorMittal, the world's largest steel company. The transition from a state-owned company meant to create jobs, accelerate regional development, and feed the domestic economy to a foreign-owned plant providing steel for export-oriented manufacturers was emblematic of a larger shift in the Latin American economy. The policy of **export-promotion manufacturing** was introduced by some countries in the region as early as the 1950s and 1960s and supported the export of locally produced goods by domestic or foreign companies. Foreign businesses were attracted to these countries by tax incentives, limited regulations on the import of raw materials and the export of finished products, looser policies on the movement of capital and people, and low labor costs and weaker unionization.

Operation Bootstrap, for example, transformed Puerto Rico from an agricultural island of sugarcane plantations to an industrial and service-based economy in the early 1950s. It encouraged American companies to establish textile, food, leather, and other labor-intensive industries and created thousands of new jobs. Good relations between the government and labor unions contributed to the early success of this program. However, increased competition from Asian countries weakened Puerto Rico's comparative advantage and led to higher unemployment and strained government-labor relations. In response, the economy shifted to capital-intensive industries such as pharmaceuticals, petrochemicals, and electronics. Today Puerto Rico has a developed economy in which agriculture contributes less than 1 percent to its gross domestic product, while manufacturing accounts for almost half of it.

The Border Industrialization Program in Mexico encouraged the construction of mainly foreign-owned assembly plants (*maquiladoras*) along the U.S.-Mexican border that would produce goods from imported raw materials and export them to other countries (Fig. 7.34). The program had its roots in another U.S.-Mexico agreement known as the Bracero Program. Beginning in 1942, Mexican migrants were allowed to work on American farms, initially to make up for labor shortages during World War II. But that program was abruptly terminated in 1964 by the U.S., and thousands of Mexicans returned home.[15] A year later, the government of Mexico introduced the *maquiladora* program to create jobs for these people. Foreign companies were encouraged to establish assembly plants along the U.S.-Mexican border through various types of government subsidies and generous tax incentives. The construction of such plants was rather slow at the beginning of the program but accelerated in the 1970s and 1980s after the liberalization of government regulations regarding plant ownership and location. The reforms allowed *maquiladoras* to be completely foreign-owned and located anywhere in Mexico.

Two major clusters of maquiladoras eventually emerged, one along the northern border and the other in the central part of the country. The first and original cluster emphasized the production of electronic goods and heavy machinery, while the interior one specialized in textiles and food processing industries. Originally, American ownership was dominant but Mexican- and Asian-owned factories became more common with the passage of time. Currently, there are about 5,000 *maquiladora* establishments, and they employ over 2 million workers. Mexico and foreign companies claim that this program has been a successful venture for both sides. For Mexico, it has provided employment opportunities for many individuals and contributed to the growth of the middle class; for American and other foreign corporations, the lower labor costs, less restrictive labor laws, and lower degree of labor unionization reduced production costs and supplied the markets with cheaper consumer goods. Critics of the program point to weak Mexican environmental regulations and subsequent serious

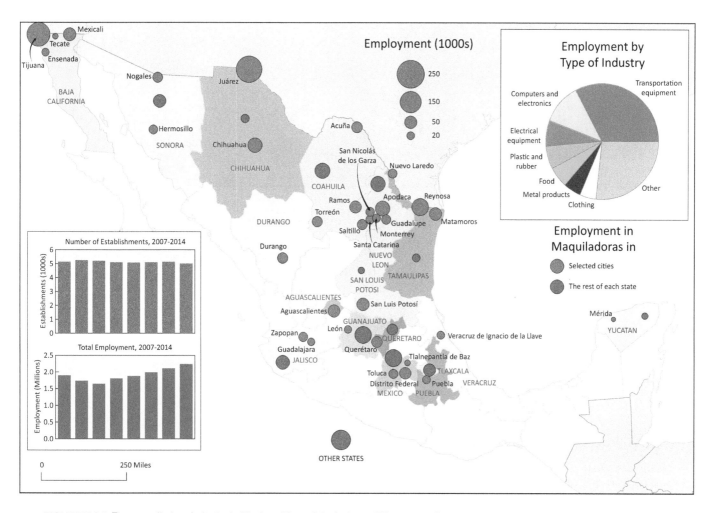

FIGURE 7.34 The maquiladora industry in Mexico—Most of the industry (56 percent of the total employment) is located in the northern states. The city of Juarez in the state of Chihuahua has over 300 and Tijuana in the state of Baja California over 550 maquiladora plants. Both states employ over a quarter of the maquiladora labor force. *Source:* Mexico. Instituto Nacional de Estadistica y Geografia.

environmental pollution in the *maquiladora* regions, the exploitation of a largely female workforce, and the exportation of American jobs.[16]

More broadly, Latin American manufacturing is concentrated in several countries. Brazil, Mexico, and Argentina have about 70 percent of all industries in the region; an additional 15 percent is found in Colombia, Venezuela, Chile, and Peru. Most industries are also found in large urban agglomerations and provincial capitals. Several Latin American countries produce automobiles; Brazil and Mexico are the seventh and eighth largest car manufacturers in the world, and both countries make over 3 million vehicles a year. The Brazilian aerospace and defense company Embraer produces about 200 passenger jets a year. JBS, based in Sao Paulo, is the largest meat processing company in the world, and Cemex, based in Mexico, is the second largest building materials maker in the world.

Illegal Drug Production

Latin America is one of three major centers of illegal drug production and distribution in the world (Fig. 7.35 and Fig. 7.36). While the **Andean Ridge** of Bolivia, Colombia, and Peru has been the largest global cocaine producer for years, Middle America, and particularly Mexico, has become the major transit zone for distributing drugs to the United States and Europe in recent years. As drug use became more popular in the United States in the 1960s, poor rural communities in Latin America saw economic opportunities in exporting this commodity to the American market. Illegal small shipments of cocaine began in the early 1970s. High profits from exporting it encouraged small groups of smugglers to consolidate and expand their operations and form powerful drug cartels. The Medellin and Cali Cartels in Colombia controlled most of the cocaine production and distribution by the mid-1980s. Early drug shipment

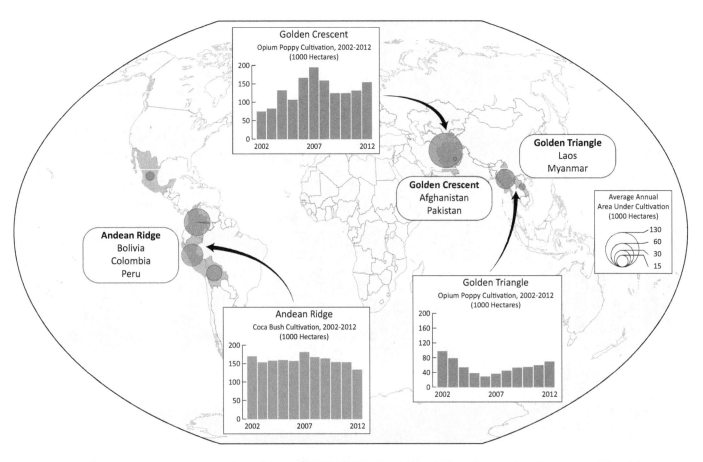

FIGURE 7.35 Illegal drug production around the world, 2002–2012—The Andean Ridge is the most important center of illegal drug production in the world. Despite numerous government efforts to eradicate the cultivation of coca, the area devoted to this crop has not decreased much (if at all) in recent years. *Source:* World Drug Report 2014.

routes went through the Caribbean Islands into Miami. The Colombian government, with strong support from the United States, challenged the drug cartels' criminal activities by targeting their leaders and infrastructure and eradicating the coca crop in the 1990s. The partially successful U.S.-backed war on drugs led to the gradual relocation of the drug trafficking centers from Colombia to Mexico. The Guadalajara Cartel, formed in the 1980s, established a dense network of connections, routes, and smugglers, and controlled most of the drug trafficking to the United States a decade later. This and other Mexican drug cartels, like their Colombian predecessors, became very powerful organizations. Their power and political influence have been achieved through bribery of corrupt officials and police, threats and/or use of violence, and (in Colombia) alliances with various guerilla movements. As competition among various drug cartels became more intense, violence, including killings, kidnapping, and human trafficking, became more common and brutal as well. Over 164,000 people were killed in Mexico's drug war between 2007 and 2014, more than in the U.S.-led wars

in Afghanistan and Iraq (Fig. 7.37). The three countries with the world's highest murder rates in 2015—El Salvador, Honduras, and Venezuela— and the most dangerous cities are all in Latin America, and the drug trade is an important reason.[17]

Offshore Financial Services, Tourism, Trade, and Transportation

One corollary to the drug trade has been the rise of offshore financial services. Not all of the money flowing through these centers is illicit, but a portion is. The Cayman Islands, Bermuda, and Panama have become major centers of offshore financial services in recent decades. These services, offered to individuals and companies regardless of their legal status at home or abroad, include banking services, insurance services (medical malpractice and product liability), and registration of ships and companies. There are

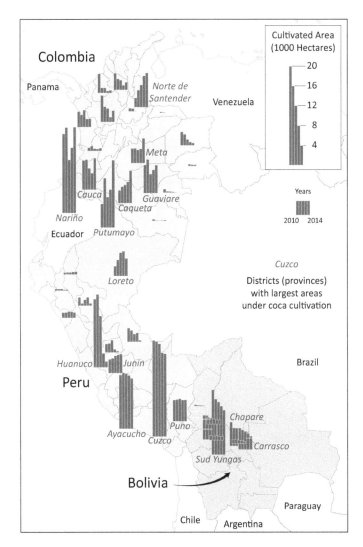

FIGURE 7.36 Coca cultivation in the Andean Ridge—The cultivation of the coca plant is more clustered in Bolivia and Peru than in Colombia. While the Bolivian states have recorded a decline in the area under coca cultivation, its cultivation has expanded in several Colombian states in recent years. *Source:* World Drug Report 2014.

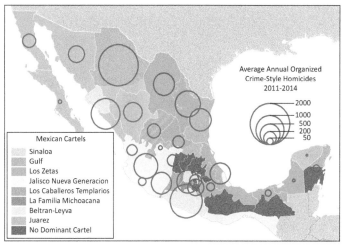

FIGURE 7.37 Drug cartels and drug-related violence in Mexico—Although the number of drug-related deaths has been declining in most parts of the country for the past few years, almost 8,000 people lost their lives in drug-related violence in 2014. A quarter of such deaths occurred in only two states, Chihuahua and Guerrero. *Source:* Drug Violence in Mexico. Data and Analysis Through 2014.

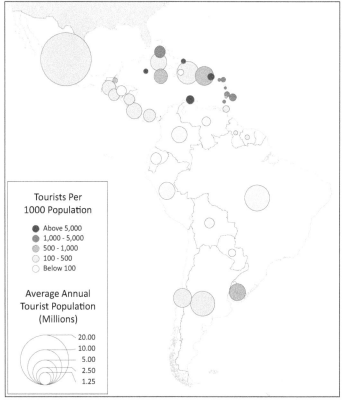

FIGURE 7.38 Tourism in Latin America (tourist arrivals), 2005–2012—Although the region's relative world importance as a tourist destination has slightly decreased since 2005, the number of tourist arrivals has increased from 47 to 80 million during the same period. *Source:* World Bank.

some 70,000 registered companies, including over 400 banks and 700 insurance firms, in the Cayman Islands, and the offshore financial services generate almost half of this British territory's total gross domestic product. A single building in the Caymans is the legal address for nearly 19,000 companies, almost all of which set up their headquarters in the islands to lower their tax burden at home. The Bahamas and Panama generate approximately one-third and one-fifth of their income from such services, respectively.

Some of the same economies that host offshore financial services are significant tourist destinations. Overall, however, Latin America, in comparison to Europe or Asia, is not especially prominent in international tourism flows as it captures only about 7 percent of the global tourist

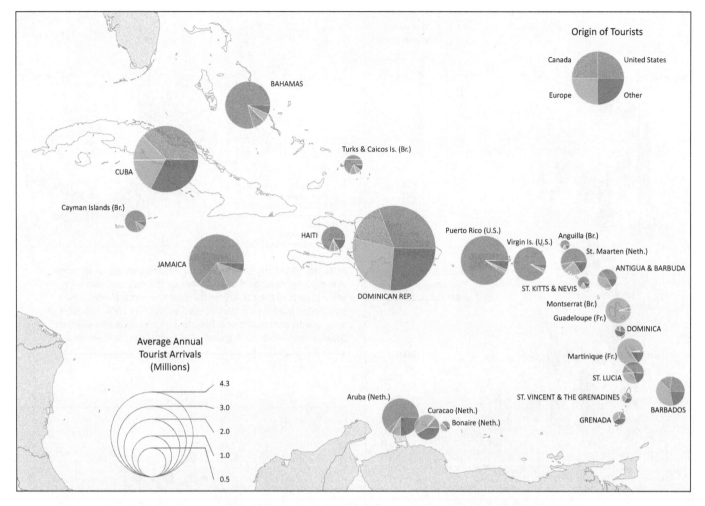

FIGURE 7.39 Tourism in the Caribbean Islands, 2009–2013—The region is the second most important (after Mexico) tourist destination in Latin America. *Source:* Caribbean Tourist Organization.

market. Yet, some 60 to 80 million visitors come to this region every year. Although Mexico attracts more visitors than any other Latin American country, the Caribbean Islands, particularly the small ones, are most dependent on tourism (Fig. 7.38). The year-round warm climate, nice beaches, and proximity to the United States and Canada have made this region a major tourist destination in the Western Hemisphere. Tourism can be both a blessing and a curse for the countries dependent on it. On the one hand, it provides employment (albeit quite often seasonal) to many local residents and supports home-grown businesses, but it is also sensitive to local weather conditions and natural disasters (hurricanes) and vulnerable to change in destination popularity. Tourism also exposes wealth inequalities (rich tourists versus poor locals), contributes to environmental degradation, socioeconomic discrimination (public beaches and other facilities may not be accessible to local residents), and the displacement of some people by tourist infrastructure expansion. Cuba used to be the major tourist

destination for Americans before the Cuban Revolution in 1959. Today, the Dominican Republic attracts the largest number of visitors (Fig. 7.39). Most Americans go to the Bahamas, Puerto Rico, Jamaica, the Virgin Islands, and Aruba, while Canadians prefer Cuba (until recently, it was illegal for U.S. citizens to visit Cuba as tourists). Some parts of the Lesser Antilles (e.g. Martinique, Guadeloupe, and Barbados) are popular destinations for European tourists. Several Latin American countries, especially Costa Rica, have been promoting ecotourism in recent years.

Tourism flows are among the forces that increasingly bind the Americas more closely together. To further that integration, the United States, Canada, and Latin American countries have formed several supranational organizations designed to develop economic and political ties among member states. The United States, Canada, and Mexico formed the **North American Free Trade Agreement** (NAFTA) in 1994. It is a union of countries with significantly different levels of development, and it has many supporters and opponents, especially in the United States. Large corporations were the strongest supporters of this agreement, claiming that it would transform Mexico into a more developed country, create markets for U.S. exports, and generate more jobs in the U.S. The opponents, including labor, consumer, religious, and environmental groups, claimed that NAFTA would lower wages and destroy many U.S. jobs and lower health, environmental, and food safety standards. The facts are that NAFTA created jobs, attracted foreign investment, contributed to a higher GDP per capita in Mexico, and led to economic development in Mexican states along the border with the United States. But it also created pockets of economic decline in Southern Mexico, hurt small farmers in Mexico through the influx of subsidized U.S. food products, contributed to environmental degradation in some parts of Mexico, and led to traffic congestion and delays at border crossings between Mexico and the United States. Concerns about job losses to Mexico remain a potent political issue in the U.S., as the 2016 presidential election illustrated. **Mercosur** (Southern Common Market) is a regional trading bloc and a customs union of five countries (Argentina, Brazil, Paraguay, Uruguay, and Venezuela) established in 1991 to promote the free movement of goods, services, and people between member states; to establish common trade policies and external tariffs; and to coordinate economic policies to assure free competition within the bloc. Most Caribbean countries are now members of the **Caribbean Community** (CARICOM), another regional organization to promote economic integration and cooperation, established in 1973. After redefining its original objectives in 2001, CARICOM members would like to strengthen economic and political ties and become an organization similar to the European Union.

The enlarged flows of people and goods through Latin America require better transportation infrastructure. The biggest transportation project in the region's recent history has been the widening of the Panama Canal, completed in 2016 (Fig. 7.40). In 2014, the canal celebrated the centennial of its opening. The appeal of a canal across the narrow Isthmus of Panama to link the Atlantic and Pacific Oceans was clear by the mid-19th century. A French company began working on the project in 1876, but unexpected technical difficulties, limited engineering expertise, and tropical diseases led to the suspension of the project after eight years of work. Another French attempt to complete it was also unsuccessful. Later the United States became interested in finishing the project, but the isthmus was part of Colombia at the time, and the Colombian government did not approve the U.S. plan. In response, the United States supported an insurgency movement, which led to the independence of Panama in 1903. The new country quickly granted the

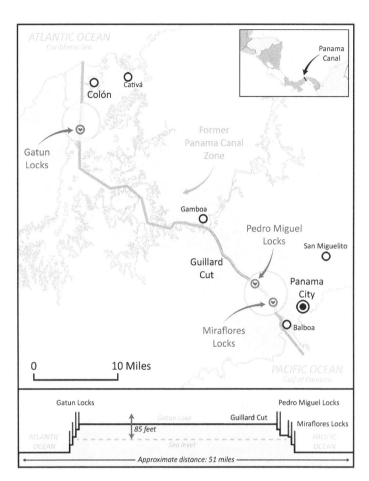

FIGURE 7.40 The Panama Canal—*Source:* drawn after a similar image in Wikipedia.

United States permission to build the canal; the work began in 1904 and was completed in 1914. The United States was in full control of the Panama Canal Zone until 1999. Today the canal is a major source of revenue for Panama. Some 12,000 ships (most of them American, Chinese, and Chilean) carrying various commodities, including grain, petroleum, and containers, pass through it every year.

This waterway was recently modernized and expanded by the completion of two additional sets of locks at both ends of the canal, and by deepening and widening the Atlantic and Pacific coast entrance channels to allow even larger ships to pass through the Panama Canal.[18] The project was Panama's biggest construction project since the original work on the canal, but it was important to Panama and the global economy. Already by the 1980s, what were then the largest containerships in the world, holding as many as 5,000 twenty-foot equivalent units (TEUs, a measure of standard shipping containers), could barely squeeze through the locks (Fig. 7.41). But containerships continued to get bigger as global trade boomed and shipping lines searched for economies of scale. The widened canal can

FIGURE 7.41 The Gatun Locks, Panama Canal—The original locks, shown in this photo, have become too small for modern ships. So as part of the recent expansion of the canal, another much wider set of locks were opened north of the site shown here. *Source:* Pixabay.

accommodate ships carrying as many as 12,500 TEUs. That is still not enough for every ship in the world; in 2017, a handful of containerships carried more than 20,000 TEUs each, but the new Panama Canal is wide enough for all but a small fraction of ships. The widened canal is expected to bring more traffic and more revenue for the government of Panama. The largest ships passing through the canal pay a toll of about $1 million each. Overall, tolls amounted to about $2 billion in 2016, helping to make Panama one of Latin America's most prosperous societies.

FUTURE PROBLEMS AND PROSPECTS

As mentioned at the beginning of this chapter, significant socio-economic inequalities characterize most Latin American societies. About a quarter of the population still lives in poverty, including 10 percent in extreme poverty. Only some countries in Central and Southern Africa have similar or greater levels of income inequality than most Latin American states. The United Nations and World Bank reports consistently list Haiti, Colombia, Honduras, Brazil, Panama, and Guatemala as among the countries with the most unequal income distribution. Although various poverty alleviation programs have been introduced in many Latin American states, there is still plenty of room for improvement, especially in terms of employment opportunities and gender equality.

Drugs, organized crime, and corruption have plagued several Latin American countries for decades. Colombia and Mexico are the leading centers of illegal production and distribution of cocaine in the world. The Sinaloa drug cartel based in Mexico (with annual revenues of about $3 billion) is considered the world's fifth largest organized crime network. Some drug eradication programs, supported by the United States, had a rather limited effect on restricting this illegal activity. Widespread corruption and high crime rates in several Latin American countries, particularly in Venezuela, Haiti, Honduras, and El Salvador, are another major challenge to their governments.

More attention to education and technological innovation is required to improve Latin American countries' competitiveness in the global economy. Although the years of schooling for the adult population have increased in recent decades, they are still below the world average. Latin American countries are characterized by a deficit of schooling of 1.4 years in comparison to their GDP per capita, and this deficit has not decreased much since 1960. Although some Latin American countries spend more on education than other developing countries, the distribution of these funds is skewed in favor of urban schools. Brazil, Mexico, Chile, and El Salvador introduced reforms attempting to correct this problem. Relatively low computer penetration rates, research spending per worker, and number of filed patents point to challenges in the area of skills development that many Latin American governments will have to deal with in the foreseeable future.

Creating a better business climate for improving competitiveness and attracting international companies is another challenge for many Latin American governments. Better transportation infrastructure, more investment in research and development, and better logistics are particularly important to reach these objectives. More needs to be done to clarify "poorly-defined property rights, complex and inconsistently applied regulations, [and] unpredictable judicial systems."[19] Several Latin American countries (Panama, Brazil, and Mexico) have introduced development plans for modernizing their infrastructure.

Despite these and other challenges facing Latin American countries, the region has great potential to improve its attractiveness and competitiveness in the global economy. The rich natural resource base, steady progress toward democracy, greater emphasis on education, and introduction of various socio-economic reforms and some innovative business models should pave the road to a better future for many people in the region.

NOTES

1. Clawson, D., & Tillman, B. (2018). *Latin America and the Caribbean*. Oxford, UK: Oxford University Press; Kent, R. (2006). *Latin America. Regions and people*. New York, NY: Guilford Press.

2. Clawson, D., & Tillman, B. (2018). *Latin America and the Caribbean*. Oxford, UK: Oxford University Press.

3. Fearnside, P. (2017). Business as usual: A resurgence of deforestation in the Brazilian Amazon. Retrieved from https://e360.yale.edu/features/business-as-usual-a-resurgence-of-deforestation-in-the-brazilian-amazon

4. Juarez, F. & Gayet, C. (2016). Fertility transition: Latin America and the Caribbean. In *International encyclopedia of the social & behavioral sciences* (2nd ed.). Atlanta, GA: Elsevier.

5. Economic Commission for Latin America and the Caribbean. (2014). Around 28.5 million Latin American and Caribbean people live outside their native countries. Retrieved from http://www.cepal.org/en/pressreleases/

6. Neuwirth, R. (2005). Rio de Janeiro: City without titles. In *Shadow cities. A billion squatters, a new urban world* (pp. 25–65). New York, NY: Routledge.

7. Clawson, D., & Tillman, B. (2018). *Latin America and the Caribbean.* Oxford, UK: Oxford University Press.

8. Encyclopedia Britannica. (2018). Pre-Columbian civilizations. Retrieved from https://www.britannica.com/topic-browse/History/Ancient-World/Pre-Columbian-Civilizations

9. Demarest, A. (2005). *Ancient Maya: The rise and fall of a rainforest civilization.* Cambridge, UK: Cambridge University Press.

10. McEvedy, C., & Jones, R. (1978). *Atlas of world population history.* New York, NY: Penguin.

11. Smith, J., & Smith, L. (1980). *Essentials of world history.* Hauppauge, NY: Barron's Educational Series.

12. Quoted in Rimas, A. & Fraser, E. (2010). *Empire of food: Feast, famine, and the rise and fall of civilizations* (p. 134). New York, NY: Free Press.

13. Barraclough, S. (2007). The legacy of Latin American land reform. Retrieved from https://nacla.org/article/legacy-latin-american-land-reform

14. Kent, R. (2006). *Latin America. Regions and people.* New York, NY: Guilford Press.

15. The Bracero Program was criticized for adversely affecting the wages, working conditions, and employment opportunities of American farm workers.

16. Clawson, D., & Tillman, B. (2018). *Latin America and the Caribbean.* Oxford, UK: Oxford University Press.

17. The Economist. (2017). The world's most dangerous cities. Retrieved from https://www.economist.com/blogs/graphicdetail/2017/03/daily-chart-23

18. Canal de Panama. (2018). The expanded Panama Canal. Retrieved from http://micanaldepanama.com/expansion/

19. Ody, A., & Ferranti, D. (2006). Key economic and social challenges for Latin America: Perspectives from recent studies. Retrieved from https://www.brookings.edu/research/key-economic-and-social-challenges-for-latin-america-perspectives-from-recent-studies

8

EAST ASIA

Some geographers divide the Asian continent into three climatic regions: cold, dry, and monsoon. Most of Siberia and the Russian Far East, covered in the chapter on the Russian Realm in this textbook, comprise Cold Asia. Certain parts of this region, particularly Eastern Siberia, are the coldest spots on the Earth outside Antarctica and Greenland. Southwestern Asia is a dry region and considered part of the Middle East. Most of this land is a sparsely and unevenly populated desert. Most of the remaining (and largest) parts of Asia are affected by a **monsoon** climate. This climate, characterized by two distinctive seasons and specific wind patterns and discussed in greater detail in the next chapter, influences the agricultural cycle and many aspects of life for almost half of the world's population. Due to its large territorial extent, Monsoon Asia is usually divided into three smaller parts: East, South, and Southeast Asia. Each of these regions is discussed in separate chapters. This chapter focuses on East Asia.

East Asia occupies over half of Monsoon Asia's territory and has more than 40 percent of its population. There are only five countries in this region, but one of them (China) has the largest population, the second largest economy, and the third largest area in the world (Fig. 8.1). Another country, Japan, although much smaller in area, is the world's third largest industrial power. South Korea has been rapidly catching up with the developed world as well, while North Korea remains the most isolated and one of the poorest nations in the world. Mongolia, a large landlocked country, has established stronger ties with the rest of the world after several decades of relative isolation under Communist rule. This densely populated region of great physical contrasts has become one of three centers of global economic power despite its limited natural resource base. Indeed the economic ascendance of the region over the past century has been described as "Asia coming full circle" as East Asia returns to the economic and technological leadership it enjoyed before being overtaken by Europe and then North America in the last half millennium.[1]

Although East Asia is incredibly dynamic today, its historic legacies still matter. Ancient Chinese philosophies and forms of government still impact the culture and environment of most of East Asia, and several culture traits, such as the emphasis on the

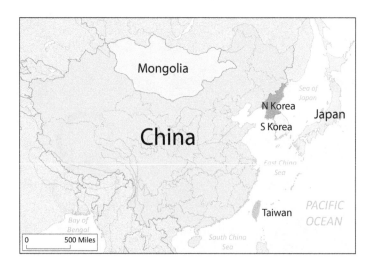

FIGURE 8.1 Countries of East Asia—The region is divided into five countries and the territory of Taiwan, whose unusual status in the world political geography is discussed more fully later in the chapter.

common good, close family life and kinship links, similar writing systems, and a mixture of indigenous and Buddhist beliefs, give the region a distinctive character. Unlike the rest of Monsoon Asia, this area's large population is characterized by remarkable linguistic and ethnic uniformity. Nevertheless, despite many cultural similarities, the five countries in this region can be placed on opposite sides of the political and economic spectrums.

PHYSICAL ENVIRONMENT

East Asia is a region of great physical contrasts with respect to landform configuration, climate, vegetation, and water resources. The differences are particularly pronounced between the western and eastern parts of the region. The west is known for high elevations (mountains and plateaus), dry, and in many areas, cold climates (at least in winter), extensive deserts, poor soil, and limited forests. The east, on the other hand, comprises a series of large plains associated with several major river systems, hill regions, and lower mountain chains. The relatively humid climate and large areas of fertile soil make this part of the region favorable to human settlement.

Landforms and Climate

Some geography textbooks identify three distinctive landform regions in Monsoon Asia: an inner arc of geologically young and high mountains, high plateaus, and intermountain basins; a middle arc of river plains and hills formed by the deposition of eroded material from the inner arc; and an outer arc of islands (Fig. 8.2).[2] In East Asia, western China and Mongolia occupy most of the inner arc. A few large plateaus and basins are separated from each other and the neighboring regions by chains of mountains of various lengths and heights (Fig. 8.3). One of them, the Plateau of Tibet, comprises one-fourth of China's territory (Fig. 8.4). This geologically young and uplifted region was formed by the collision of the Indian and Eurasian tectonic plates about 65 million years ago. It borders the Himalayas, the world's highest mountain range, along its southern periphery, and the Kunlun Shan, an over 1,930 kilometers (1,200 miles) long but slightly lower mountain range, to the north and northeast.

The rest of China and the Korean Peninsula comprise the middle arc in East Asia. The most important landform here is the North China Plain, a flat and fertile area similar in size to California. The plain was prone to frequent river flooding in the past. It is the birthplace of Chinese civilization and has been densely populated and economically productive for millennia. The plain is comprised of fine windblown soil, called **loess**, which is easily worked (helping to explain why this is one of the world's earliest areas of agriculture) but also easily eroded. The Northeast (Manchurian) Plain, slightly smaller in area but higher in average elevation than the North China Plain, is also known for fertile soil. It was formed by the deposition of eroded material by several rivers originating in the surrounding hills and mountains.

Farther south and toward the center of China, the Sichuan Basin is another area whose fertile soil supports diverse agricultural systems and a very large population. The basin is composed of hills and alluvial plains located between 180 and 610 meters (600 and 2,000 feet) above sea level. Still farther south, the Wuyi Shan region in Southeast China is known for its beautiful landscapes of dome-shaped and columnar cliffs, rugged terrain, and winding river valleys. Its topography was one of several factors in designating this region a UNESCO World Heritage Site.

Meanwhile, about 70 percent of the Korean Peninsula, particularly its northern and eastern parts, is hilly or mountainous. However, the highest elevations do not exceed 2,750 meters (9,000 feet). The eastern coast has a simple outline and offers few suitable sites for seaports; the western coastline is much more complex and its wider coastal plains are more densely populated.

Japan, the Ryukyu Islands, and Taiwan are parts of the outer arc of islands, encircling East Asia along its eastern

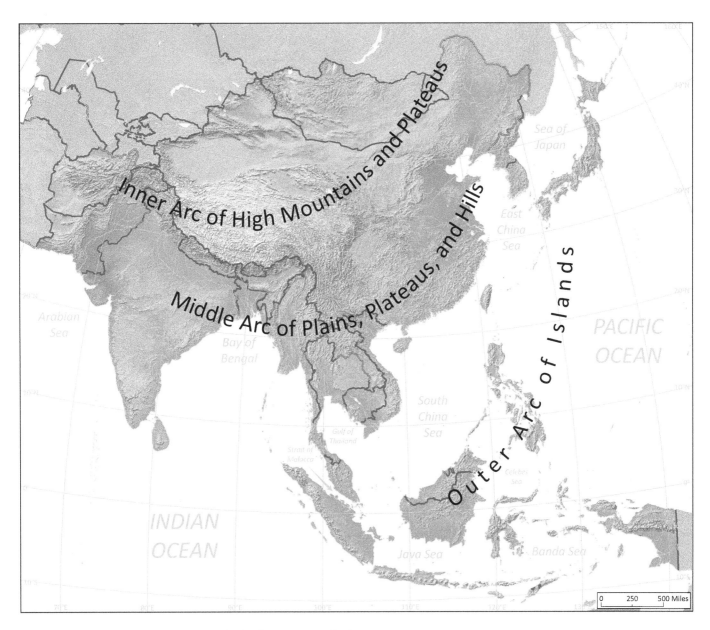

FIGURE 8.2 The three landform arcs of Asia—*Source:* Natural Earth.

periphery. This seismically active region, known for frequent and sometimes strong earthquakes and dozens of dormant and active volcanoes, is composed of six large islands (from north to south, Hokkaido, Honshu, Shikoku, Kyushu, Taiwan, and Hainan) and hundreds of small islands. These mainly mountainous islands with numerous small and narrow coastal plains were formed by recent tectonic activities. Mt. Fuji (3,776 meters/12,388 feet in elevation) in Japan is the best known example of volcanic activity in this region. The mountain is an icon of Japan; its familiar shape has been invoked to symbolize ideas as varied as Japanese nationalism in World War II and environmental conservation today (Fig. 8.5).

The influence of the monsoon climate in East Asia declines with distance from the Pacific Ocean, both in terms of the amount of precipitation and its seasonal distribution. The outer arc of islands and Southeastern China receive the greatest amounts of precipitation, mainly in the form of rain in the summer months, although heavy snow is common in Northern Japan during the winter season (Fig. 8.6). Moving northwest, the climate becomes drier. As mentioned earlier, large parts of Western China and Mongolia are deserts where low and erratic precipitation is a barrier to large-scale human settlement and rain-fed agriculture. Latitude and elevation are the main determinants of temperature patterns in the eastern and western parts

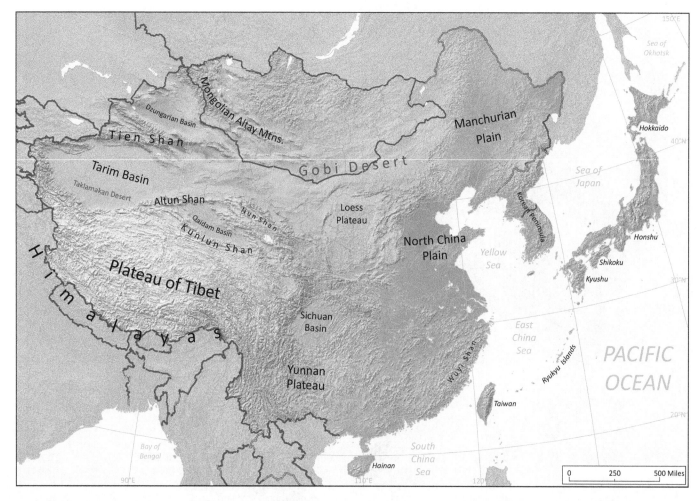

FIGURE 8.3 Landform regions in East Asia—The western half of China and Mongolia are part of the inner arc of high mountains and plateaus while the rest of the region is part of the middle arc of river plains and hills and the outer arc of islands. *Source:* Natural Earth.

FIGURE 8.4 A train on the Tibetan Plateau—Rail service to Lhasa in Tibet (Xizang) began in 2006. *Source:* Wikimedia Commons.

FIGURE 8.5 A Buddhist pagoda near Mt. Fuji—At 3,776 meters (12,389 feet), Mt. Fuji is the tallest mountain in Japan. One of more than one hundred active volcanoes in the country, it last erupted in 1707. *Source:* Pixabay.

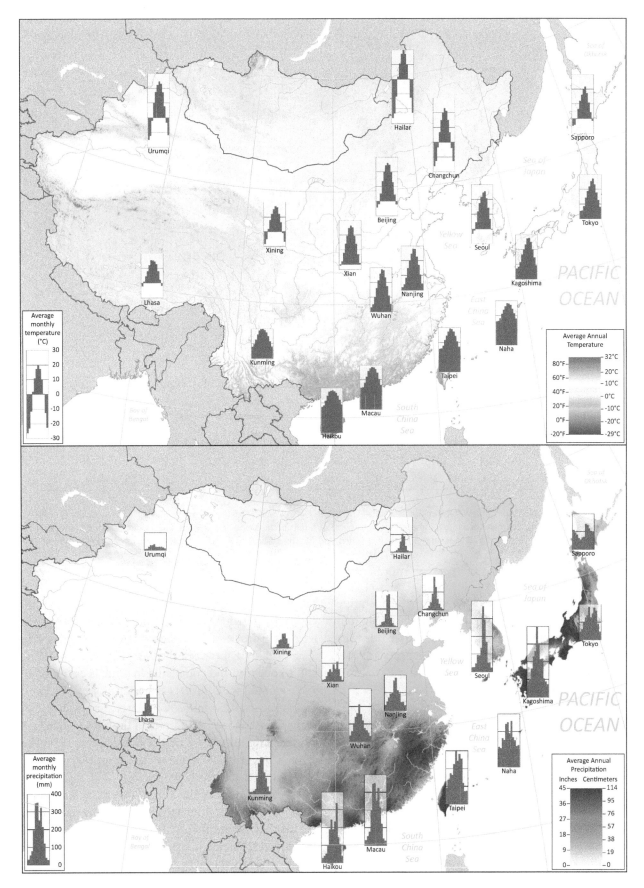

FIGURE 8.6 East Asia: patterns of temperature and precipitation—Notice the strong influence on temperature patterns of landform configuration in the western parts and of latitude in the eastern parts of the region. Precipitation patterns are more correlated with distance from the ocean than landforms. *Source:* WorldClim-Global Climate Data.

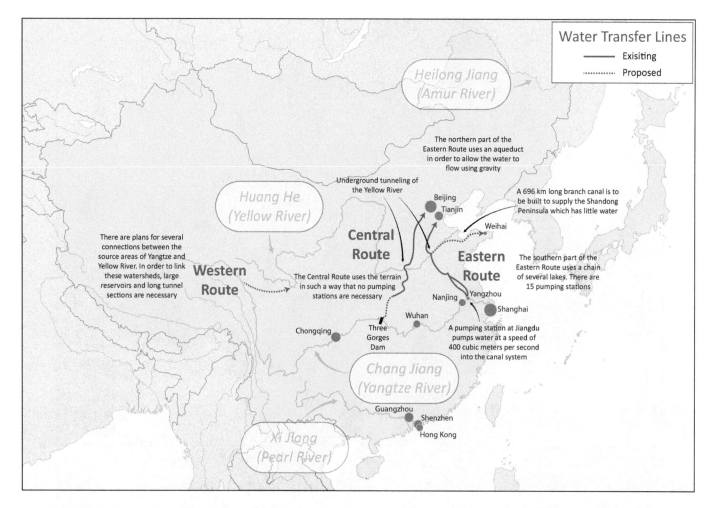

FIGURE 8.7 China: major rivers and water transfer projects—The South-North Water Transfer Project will divert large amounts of water from the Yangtze River to the major urban agglomerations in the northern part of the North China Plain. This controversial project will lead to the resettlement of several hundred thousand people. It is scheduled for completion by 2050. *Source:* drawn after a similar map in Wikipedia.

of East Asia, respectively. The winter-summer temperature ranges also increase with distance from the ocean and latitude. The greatest differences are found in Mongolia and the northeastern part of China where January and July average temperatures range from –30°C (–22°F) to 20°C (68°F), respectively.

Major Rivers

East Asia has ample but unevenly distributed freshwater resources, and this distribution is closely associated with the climatic differences between the western and eastern parts of the region. While there are no large lakes in any East Asian country, several major river systems have played a profound role in Chinese history and the economy. The Chang Jiang or the Yangtze River (6,300 kilometers/3,915 miles) is the longest river in Asia and the third longest in

the world. Its watershed area is inhabited by one-third of China's population (Fig. 8.7). The river is also known for its great hydroelectric potential—the Three Gorges Dam, located half way between the two major cities of Wuhan and Chongqing and completed in 2012, is currently the world's largest water power generation project. The river is also a major transportation route; by passing through locks at the dam, large vessels can reach the city of Chongqing, located 2,250 kilometers (1,400 miles) upriver. Shanghai, China's largest city and one of the largest seaports in the world, is located at the river's mouth.

The Huang He or the Yellow River, the second longest river in China, drains the north-central uplands and the northern part of the North China Plain. The easily eroded loess that dominates the region through which the river flows gives the river its yellow color and means that it carries a very heavy **sediment load** (Fig. 8.8). As the river slows nearer its mouth at the Yellow Sea (yellow for

FIGURE 8.8 The Yellow River near the border of Shanxi and Henan Provinces—The erosion of fine silt from the surrounding landscape gives the Yellow River (Huang He) its distinctive color. *Source:* Wikimedia Commons.

the same reason), some of the sediment is deposited on the riverbed, raising the bed over time and making the communities near its banks highly flood prone. Known as "China's Sorrow," the Huang He has been responsible for frequent flooding and its lower course has changed on several occasions in the past. The 1931 flood affected an area similar in size to South Carolina; it killed perhaps as many as 4 million people and made another 80 million homeless. Similar large-scale floods occurred in 1887 (2 million deaths) and 1938 (900,000 deaths). Although the riverbed towers above the surrounding landscape in some places by as much as 11 meters (35 feet), today catastrophic floods are less likely. Complementing thousands of miles of levees built over the centuries, a series of flood-control projects completed by the mid-1950s has protected the surrounding densely populated areas from flood disasters.

The Xi Jiang or the Pearl River in Southern China is much shorter than the Huang He and Chang Jiang but of great economic importance to the densely populated, highly urbanized, and productive areas around Hong Kong. The Pearl River Delta, inhabited by over 40 million people, is the fastest growing urban and industrial region in the country. The Heilong Jiang or the Amur River forms the border between Russia and China along a part of its course. The economic importance of this river diminished during the Soviet-Chinese tensions from the 1960s through the 1990s but has increased recently as both countries established closer ties and began working together on projects related to navigation, hydropower, and marshland reclamation.[3]

HUMAN-ENVIRONMENT INTERACTION

For millennia, East Asia has witnessed extensive purposeful efforts to transform the environment. Those efforts accelerated in the last half century as the region's population and economic clout grew. Asia's rapid economic development has also brought vast unintended environmental problems. Today, however, there is a greater emphasis on trying to manage and mitigate the ecological impacts of Asia's more broadly shared prosperity.

East Asia was among the earliest centers of plant and animal domestication. Most significantly, people living in the east-central parts of China (the North China Plain and the lower Yangtze River Plain) domesticated certain types of rice and millet about 8,000 years ago, and the knowledge of rice farming spread to the southern parts of the region by 3000 BCE and to the Korean Peninsula and Japan about 2,000 years later. Rice can produce more calories per unit of land than other staple grains, fostering population growth. And, in turn, high population densities and the significant water requirement for rice cultivation led to a very intensive use of limited land resources, including the conversion of hill slopes to terraces and the establishment of elaborate irrigation systems. For instance, in 256 BCE a dike was built in the Min River, a tributary of the Chang Jiang, to reduce spring flooding and to divert a portion of the flow through an artificial channel cut in nearby mountains so that the water could irrigate a swath of arid land on the Chengdu Plain. This project, called Dujiangyan, and other water management projects that came later, could only be completed and maintained by collective efforts (Fig. 8.9). Dujiangyan employed tens of thousands of people for years.

More commonplace was the everyday cooperation of entire villages to terrace hillsides, plant seeds, transplant seedlings, harvest the rice crop, and do the other work to extract a livelihood from the land. Some scholars see a connection between this history of environmental management by (sometimes very large) groups of people and the emphasis on cooperation, deference to authority, and the common good rather than individual rights in the region's cultural traditions, especially Confucianism.

High population densities and the shortage of flat land in many coastal areas have compelled some governments to reclaim land from the sea. Japan has the longest tradition of land reclamation in East Asia. The first major project, a small island in the city of Kobe, was completed in the 12th century. Other important reclamation schemes were implemented in the 16th through 19th centuries, including an inlet and a series of island forts near Tokyo and an island near Nagasaki. However, most of the country's land reclamation projects were undertaken after World War II. There are over 245 square kilometers (95 square miles) of reclaimed land in the Tokyo Bay area alone, and most of it has attracted various industries and transportation

FIGURE 8.9 Dujiangyan, an ancient irrigation system in China—This ancient structure on the Min River, a tributary of the Yangtze River, was built two millennia ago to divert water on an arid plain. The main channel of the Min is in the background and the diversion channel is in the foreground. *Source:* Wikimedia Commons.

FIGURE 8.10 Kansai International Airport—Kansai International Airport, the main gateway to the city of Osaka, is built on an artificial island and is among the most expensive airports ever built. Source: Wikimedia Commons.

facilities. The three artificial islands in Osaka Bay, built between 1966 and 2005, have also attracted similar activities, including an international airport (Fig. 8.10). Two of these islands also have residential districts. Meanwhile, China has the largest area of such land in the world, mainly along the Yellow Sea and in the metropolitan areas of Shanghai, Macau, Hong Kong, and a few others. For example, the Hong Kong International Airport (Chek Lap Kok), opened in 1998, is located partly on reclaimed land. And South Korea ranks third in the world (after China and the Netherlands) regarding the area of reclaimed land. Seoul's main airport is located on an artificial island as well.

As East Asian societies have transformed their environments through dikes, dams, artificial islands, and other artificial structures, they have also imposed a heavy burden on the region's air, land, and water resources through overuse, misuse, and unintended consequences. For instance, high demand for wood products (e.g. China produces as many as 80 billion pairs of wooden chopsticks per year) led to large-scale deforestation in recent history. Forest loss endangered the habitats of many species, including giant pandas, and contributed to intense river flooding, especially of the Chang Jiang, and to desertification, soil erosion, and

dust storms, mainly in the northern regions. In response, the Chinese government has taken a series of measures. Several afforestation schemes (programs to establish tree cover in new areas) have been under development since the 1970s. The best known is the **Green Belt**, a 4,500-kilometer (2,800-mile) long belt of planted trees roughly paralleling the Great Wall to stop the expansion of the Gobi Desert and China's other northern deserts. Although China's forest cover has increased from 16 to 22 percent since 1990, some critics say there is too much emphasis on planting trees and not enough on restoring natural forest habitats. Meanwhile, both Japan and China have been criticized for protecting their own forests at the expense of increased deforestation in other regions, especially Southeast Asia.

Air quality is another concern in East Asia. Particularly during the winter months when monsoon wind currents blow from the middle of Eurasia towards the sea, air quality in many cities deteriorates.[4] This is the time of the so-called "yellow dragon" (yellow again because of the fine particulate matter it carries) that beleaguers Beijing and other population centers. Massive coal burning (in recent years, China has accounted for half of global coal use) and heavy industrialization compound these problems. Furthermore, especially during winter, China's air quality problems become the problems of its neighbors too as the winds carry pollution east toward the Korean Peninsula, Japan, and even North America.

Water pollution, both of the region's lakes and rivers and of coastal areas, is also a pervasive concern. Particularly in Northern China, overuse of limited water resources has depleted aquifers and has caused the Huang He to dry up before it reaches the Yellow Sea. In 2007 the river failed to reach the sea for 277 consecutive days. Today, Beijing and other northern cities are severely water stressed. To counter this challenge, China has embarked on the largest water management project in its long history—a massive scheme to divert water from the Chang Jiang basin to the Huang He basin.[5] The first of three routes for the South-North Water Transfer Project near China's east coast began moving water north in 2013, and the middle route did so in 2014. The western route is still in the planning stage. So far, China has spent $62 billion dollars on the project, making it one of most expensive engineering undertakings in history. The first two routes are designed to move nearly 28 billion cubic meters (989 billion cubic feet) per year (enough to refill the Aral Sea to its 1960 volume—see Chapter 4—in forty years). The project has required the relocation of more than 300,000 people and raised serious concerns about the adequacy of water supplies in the south.

POPULATION PATTERNS AND TRENDS

East Asia is one of the world's two largest population clusters. It occupies less than 9 percent of the total land area but has almost 22 percent of the population (1.6 billion). China is still the largest country in the world, but its population of almost 1.4 billion has been growing at a relatively slow rate. Japan's population (126 million) has already begun to decline. South Korea, the third largest country in the region, has over 50 million inhabitants, while its neighbor North Korea has only 25 million. Taiwan has a slightly smaller population of 23 million, and Mongolia, the region's second largest country in area, is inhabited by only 3 million people (Fig. 8.11).

FIGURE 8.11 Gers in the Mongolian countryside—Although Mongolia's economy has grown rapidly in recent years, many of its people still live in traditional gers, a tentlike structure. *Source:* Stefan Fischer/Henrik Watzke.

Population Distribution and Growth

The region has one of the most uneven population distribution patterns in the world and can be clearly divided into the sparsely populated west and the densely populated east (Fig. 8.12). The east-west dichotomy reflects natural conditions, mainly landforms and climate. The western half of the region, inhabited by only 5 percent of its total population, is high and dry, while the eastern half, with 95 percent of the population, is more humid and lower in elevation. Further evidence of the uneven population distribution is the fact that half of the region's population lives on 12 percent of the land and half of that population (or a quarter of the total population) occupies only 4 percent of the land area. Parts of the North China Plain, Sichuan Basin, and coastal areas of China and Japan have densities of over 1,000 persons per square kilometer or 2,590 persons per square mile (denser than the densest U.S. state, New Jersey). Fertile alluvial or volcanic soil, availability of water for rice farming, and historical patterns of settlement have contributed to high densities in these regions. Some urban areas are much more crowded with densities of over 5,000 persons per square kilometer (12,950 persons per square mile). On the other hand, Xizang (Tibet), China's second largest province, and Mongolia are inhabited by only 3 million residents each, and their population densities are below 3 persons per square kilometer or 8 persons per square mile (similar to Montana).

Although East Asia's population has increased from 658 million in 1950 to over 1.6 billion today, the region's global share has dropped from 26 to 22 percent. Population growth rates have been declining in all East Asian countries in recent decades and now amount to less than 0.5 percent per year on average. Fertility rates have been below the replacement level in most countries for some time (Fig. 8.13). Japan began losing population around 2011 and, if nothing unexpected happens, it may have only 107 million by the middle of this century (Fig. 8.14). Natural increase has been the major component of population change in most countries; migration played a more important role (in relative terms) only in Mongolia during the 1990s, shortly after the collapse of communism, when many younger, usually better-educated people left for other Asian and European countries in search of employment opportunities.

International and Internal Migration

The significance of international migration will likely be on the rise as East Asian societies are reaching demographic

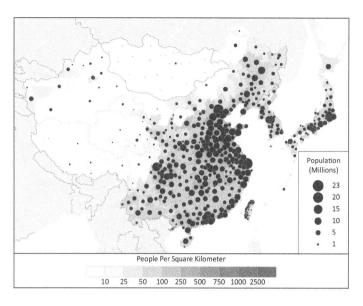

FIGURE 8.12 Population distribution in East Asia—The dry and high western part of East Asia occupies over half of the region's area but contains only 5 percent of its total population. The North China Plain, the Sichuan Basin, and the coastal areas of China and parts of Japan are very densely populated. *Source:* GeoHive (www.geohive.com).

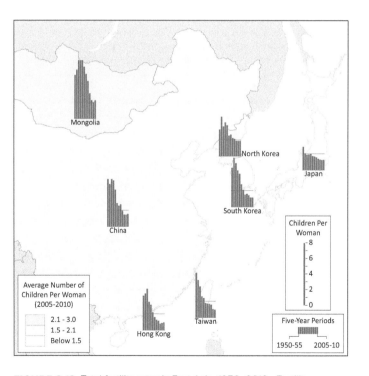

FIGURE 8.13 Total fertility rates in East Asia, 1950–2010—Fertility rates have been declining in every country during the past several decades, and they are now below or at the replacement level in every country of this region. Notice the particularly low rates in Japan. *Source:* United Nations. Population Division. World Population Prospects 2012.

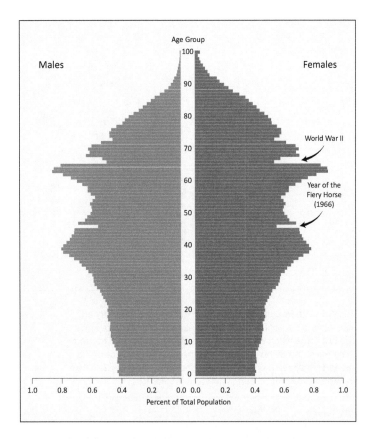

FIGURE 8.14 Japan: population pyramid, 2012—This is a typical pyramid for a demographically mature society. Notice the population loss during World War II and in 1966—the Year of the Fiery Horse. Many Japanese couples avoided having children during that year (occurring every 60 years) due to the belief that those children will have bad luck. *Source:* Japanese Statistics Bureau.

maturity, and the labor pool in the region's most economically developed countries has already begun to shrink. Unlike Western European countries, Japan did not rely on imported labor to rebuild its devastated economy after World War II. However, the number of foreigners has slowly increased in recent years, and there are currently some 2.23 million migrants in Japan, 60 percent of them from three countries: China, South Korea, and the Philippines. Japanese society is becoming more immigrant-friendly; a recent survey indicates that over half of its population supports increasing immigration to deal with labor shortages. Similar trends can also be observed in South Korea which also has over 2 million foreigners, about half of them from China. Even China has begun attracting migrants from other parts of Asia. Its aggressive economic development during the past three decades has attracted migrants from Vietnam and other Southeast Asian countries, most of them of Chinese ancestry, who can easily blend with the local population and be employed for half the cost of Chinese workers.

A numerically small but risky migration from North Korea across the Yalu River into China is another recent phenomenon. These mostly illegal migrants are considered economic refugees and face deportation if found by the Chinese authorities. Some lucky ones able to find refuge in embassies of other countries are usually allowed to leave the country for South Korea.[6]

Internal migration was strictly controlled in China until the late 1970s. When the Communist government was established in 1949, almost 90 percent of the population lived in rural areas. The early program of economic development emphasized heavy manufacturing, and millions of peasants moved to cities to find employment in the industrial sector. The rapid urbanization and lower priority given to agriculture led to food shortages and food rationing in all major cities by the early 1960s. To deal with this problem, some 24 million urban residents were forcibly transferred to the countryside in the early 1960s. Later, millions more Communist Party members, intellectuals, and young people were sent for political re-education and work on state farms known as **people's communes**. As a result of these actions, the urban share of the population remained low and unchanging.

Only in the late 1970s did large-scale migration to urban areas resume, a pattern that continues to the present time. Some 260 million rural residents have moved to cities in search of better employment opportunities during the past three decades, making for what has been described as the largest migration in human history. Yet, many of the migrants, even though they have been instrumental in China's economic success, have been considered illegal, deprived of any benefits available to urban residents, and often blamed for high crime rates and unemployment.

An internal passport system known as *hukou*, introduced in 1958 to control rural-urban migration and population distribution, was responsible for the second-class status of many internal migrants. It classified all individuals as rural or urban residents who were required to live and work in their designated areas. Access to most social services (health care, education, employment rights, etc.) was tied to the individual's residence status. Permission was required to permanently move from a rural to an urban area; a move without permission deprived migrants of these benefits. The *hukou* system favored urban residents as they had access to better services. The preferential treatment of urban dwellers was believed to reduce the risk of anti-government activities, which would be harder to control in large cities than among more dispersed peasants. Although the *hukou* system has been gradually reformed since 1984, access to social benefits still remains tied to a person's residence. And while changes in the policy have encouraged the movement of rural people to towns and small cities, restrictions remain on migration to large cities.

Population Policies in China

When Communists came to power in China in 1949, the country had a population of about 540 million. Their leader Mao Zedong was originally against any type of population control as he considered Chinese people producers rather than consumers. An aphorism credited to Mao expresses his views: "Every stomach comes with two hands attached"[7], meaning that each additional person had to be fed but more importantly could also do work. By the time Mao died in 1976, the country's population had swelled to 931 million and was growing by one person every two and a half seconds (Fig. 8.15).

Even before Mao's death, other Communist leaders were emerging who took population control more seriously. In 1971, the government began advocating later marriage (recommended marriage age of 25 to 28 for men and women in urban areas and 23 to 25 in rural areas), longer intervals between births (at least 4 years for urban and 3 years for rural couples), and fewer children per couple (2 for urban and 3 for rural couples, later reduced to 2 children for all couples). To enforce this program, local authorities kept detailed information on the reproductive behavior of women of child-bearing age and exercised strong pressure on couples breaking the rules by recommending or coercing

abortion, sterilization, or IUD (intra-uterine device) insertion. Despite a significant decline in fertility rates, from 5.6 children per woman in 1969 to 2.7 ten years later, in 1980 the Communist leadership introduced much stronger measures of population control: the One-Child Policy. The new policy called for one child per couple, achieving zero population growth rate by the year 2000, and keeping China's population below 1.2 billion in 2000. At the time the policy was introduced, the forecast was for China to have 1.6 billion at the turn of the millennium.

The new rules required the authorization of every pregnancy through the issue of birth coupons (required to obtain the birth certificate for a newly born infant), allocation of annual birth quotas for each administrative unit, mandatory IUD insertion for women who already had one child and monitoring of women's menstrual cycles. Couples with one child could apply for a one-child certificate, also known as the glory certificate, which entitled them and their child for some benefits in exchange for the promise not to have more children. Higher wages/salaries and pensions and larger housing units for parents, longer maternity leaves and better health care for mothers, and priority in admission to nurseries, kindergartens, and schools and in job assignments for children were examples of such

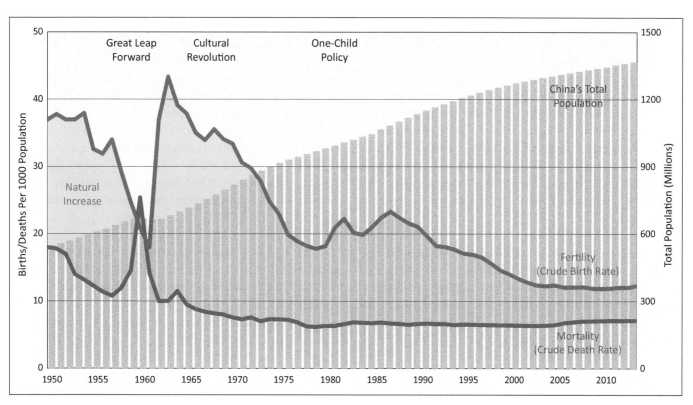

FIGURE 8.15 Fertility and mortality trends in the People's Republic of China, 1950–2013—Notice a sharp drop of fertility and a sharp increase of mortality rates during the Great Leap Forward program during which millions of people died due to food shortages. Also, notice a moderate increase of fertility rates on two occasions shortly after the One-Child Policy was introduced. *Source:* China's National Bureau of Statistics.

benefits. In case the promise was broken, the couple lost the benefits and had to pay a fine amounting to their income for two or three years.

These policies were more strictly enforced in urban than in rural areas, but families tended to be smaller in cities anyway. In fact, fertility already fell below replacement level in urban areas in 1976 but did not do so in rural areas until 1991. Since the late 1990s, China's overall fertility rate has remained steady at between 1.5 and 1.6 births per woman. Note that if the One-Child Policy were followed perfectly, the fertility rate would be close to 1.0.

Although the policy was not fully successful, it probably did play some role in further slowing the country's growth. China's population reached 1.266 billion in 2000—far below the predicted total of 1.6 million but still over the government's target by a number greater than the whole population of France. Despite some successes, China ended the policy in 2015 following a series of reforms that loosened its strictures as mounting evidence underlined the negative outcomes of this massive government intervention in the reproductive behavior of hundreds of millions of people. Most importantly for government authorities, some areas of China began to experience serious labor shortages, undermining the country's economic development model.

But there were other more damaging social effects, too. First, the policy has created an elite based on birth right—children from families with a one-child certificate have come to expect preferential treatment in education and, when grown up, employment. Second, it produced a generation of spoiled children known colloquially as "little emperors," who, without any siblings and pampered by both parents and four grandparents, could become adults unable to cope with setbacks and lacking a sense of fairness. Third, it led to high female infanticide and sex-selective abortion rates in favor of boys. The strong preference for sons among many couples, a preference deeply rooted in Chinese culture, resulted in failing to register newly born girls or abandoning them or, in extreme cases, killing them through exposure to cold, drowning, or other drastic measures. Many women resorted to abortion to ensure they had a son. Fourth, the One-Child policy was responsible for an imbalance between the sexes. The sex ratio at birth (number of boys per one hundred girls born in one year) is about 105 in most societies, but it is 116 in China and 140 in some parts of the country (Fig. 8.16). Again, the preference for sons explains this precarious demographic phenomenon. There are concerns that a growing army of single men (known as "bare branches") will be unable to find wives or life partners, and this, in turn, may lead to higher rates of prostitution, sex trafficking, crime, or other hard-to-predict outcomes.[8]

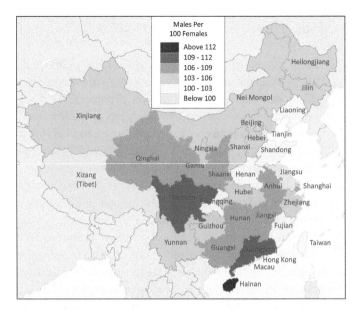

FIGURE 8.16 Sex ratios in China's provinces, 2012—Hainan Island, Sichuan, and Guangdong provinces have the highest surplus of males, while Tibet, Jiangsu, and the city of Tianjin have a surplus of women. The sex ratios are close to 140 in some parts of the country. *Source:* China's National Bureau of Statistics.

To deal with these worsening outcomes, the Chinese government gradually introduced several changes to its one-child policy since the mid-1980s. For example, it permitted rural families with "difficulties" (e.g. sick or disabled parents) and those with a girl, and later all couples with a girl, to have another child. Ethnic minorities could also have two (and sometimes three) children. Couples where at least one of the parents was the only child were also exempted from these restrictions. Finally in 2015, the government declared that all couples would be allowed to have two children. However, because reproductive behavior changes slowly and because China has become an increasingly urban country where space is expensive, the end of the One-Child Policy is not expected to dramatically change the country's demographic outlook. China's working age population peaked in 2011, and its overall population is projected to peak in 2030 at 1.45 billion. As the country approaches and goes beyond that peak, it will age rapidly.

Japan's experience may give a foretaste of China's future in this regard. Japan's working age population peaked in the mid-1990s, and not coincidentally, the country's economy has struggled since then. Japan has one of the highest shares of elderly people of any country: 26 percent in 2015 versus 10 percent in China. South Korea and Taiwan are also ageing rapidly. High life expectancies in the region (e.g. 84 years in Japan) are a great achievement but pose significant social and economic challenges.

Urbanization Trends and Patterns

While East Asia has been a predominantly rural, agrarian region for most of its history, it has also been a region with very large cities. A thousand years ago, the largest city on Earth was Kaifeng, the imperial capital at the time; Kaifeng is located inland near the Huang He. Three hundred years ago, Edo—now called Tokyo—was the world's largest city. As other regions overtook East Asia in development, other cities took the top rankings (e.g. London and New York), but now Asian metropolises are back on top. About 60 percent of East Asia's population is urban today, up from 18 percent in 1950. Japan and South Korea are among the most urbanized nations in the world, and many of China's cities have quickly increased their size in recent years.

Urbanization trends in East Asian countries have several things in common. First, industrialization was the main catalyst of urban growth. It led to rapid urbanization in Japan after World War II, in South Korea after the Korean War, and in China after the major economic reforms at the end of the 1970s. Second, regional disparities in urban growth have occurred in each country. Most of that growth has taken place in the Pacific Belt, stretching from the Tokyo region in the northeast to the Osaka-Kobe area in the southwest in Japan, around the Busan and Seoul agglomerations in the southeastern and northwestern parts of South Korea, respectively, and in coastal regions of Eastern and Southeastern China (Fig. 8.17). Third, national policies of urban growth and management have been introduced in each country albeit with a varying degree of success. Japan and South Korea, for instance, emphasized the relocation of some activities to other regions, construction of new cities, and the establishment of a green belt around major cities.

China has witnessed particularly sharp shifts in policies toward cities. As China was incorporated into the world economy from the 18th century, a dual urban hierarchy emerged consisting of administrative centers in the

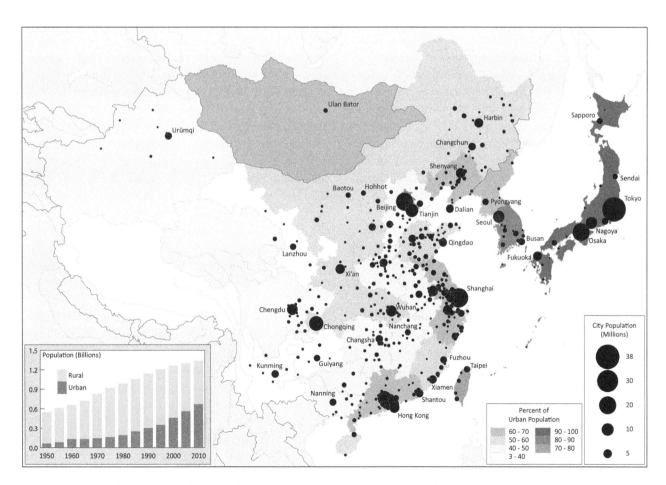

FIGURE 8.17 Urbanization levels in East Asia—The proportion of the urban population has increased from 18 to 60 percent since 1950. The increase was particularly significant in China (12 to 56 percent). Notice the significant contrasts between some interior and coastal Chinese provinces. *Source:* China. National Bureau of Statistics (www.stats.gov.cn); United Nations. Population Division. World Urbanization Prospects 2014.

interior and thriving coastal port cities, especially after the increased European influence in the second part of the 19th century.[9] The Communist government put emphasis on more balanced urban growth after 1949. The growth of large, mainly coastal, cities was restricted through the *hukou* system described earlier, and most funds for urban development were allocated to urban centers in the interior. Communist symbolism became evident in city centers in the form of large public squares used for mass government-sponsored gatherings and military parades. The squares were often surrounded by large structures of political and cultural importance.

China's urban development after 1978 was guided by a mixture of centrally planned and free market principles. This period has witnessed the intertwined trends of massive Chinese economic growth and the vast increase of its urban population, especially in coastal cities (Fig. 8.18). These forces have transformed Chinese cityscapes. Massive infrastructure and housing projects and numerous businesses and service centers have changed the urban morphology of many large cities and made them, in some ways, similar to their Western counterparts. Clusters of high-rise office structures, networks of highways and subways, shopping centers, and specialty districts have completely reshaped many cities during the past twenty to thirty years. At the same time, the influx of migrants from rural areas and smaller cities has created an army of second-class citizens and led to the emergence of dilapidated residential neighborhoods. Some urban problems of Western cities such as traffic congestion, air pollution, residential segregation, and higher crime rates have also been affecting Chinese cities.

China's urban network is at least somewhat balanced however in that there are several leading centers including Beijing, Shanghai, the Pearl River Delta, and Chongqing. The urban networks in Japan, South Korea, and Mongolia, conversely, are characterized by **urban primacy**. Thirty percent of Japan's and 20 percent of South Korea's population resides in the Tokyo and Seoul metropolitan areas, respectively. The metro area of Mongolia's capital Ulan Bator has almost 50 percent of the country's total population and is over ten times larger than its second largest city.

There are at least seven mega-cities in East Asia. Although Tokyo had been considered the world's largest city for some time, a recent United Nation report lists the Pearl River Delta's cluster of several cities (Dongguan, Foshan, Guangzhou, and Shenzhen) in Southeastern China as the world's largest urban agglomeration in area (2,700 square km or 1042 square miles) and population (41 million).[10] It displaced Tokyo from the first place

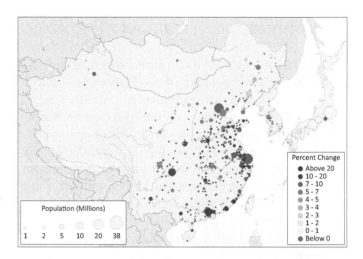

FIGURE 8.18 East Asia: population growth in cities over 300,000 inhabitants, 1980–2015—Most Japanese and Korean cities as well as Hong Kong have been growing very slowly, while many Chinese coastal and interior cities recorded rapid population growth. *Source:* United Nations. Population Division. World Urbanization Prospects 2014 Revision.

sometime between 2000 and 2010. One of its major cities, Shenzhen, located just across the border from Hong Kong, grew from a settlement of 333,000 people in 1980 to a metropolis of over 10 million in 2010, a thirty-one-fold increase (Fig. 8.19). It has attracted a variety of industries, and its total economic output is greater than that of Vietnam or Ireland. Its subway system, opened in 2004, now consists of six lines and over 140 stations. Guangzhou, the largest city in this agglomeration (13 million people), is a major port and transportation hub as well as a commercial and manufacturing center in China. It used to be the only Chinese city open to foreigners for trading purposes in the 19th century. Today it is the largest city in what has been described as the workshop of the world—an area linked to the whole world through its manufacturing output.

Outside the Pearl River Delta, Shanghai is the largest (24 million people) and most rapidly growing city in China. It is the commercial and financial center of the country and the world's busiest container port. The city's economic importance in the 18th century reflected its favorable location at the mouth of the Chang Jiang. Despite restrictions on its growth during the Mao Zedong era (1949–76), the city quickly regained its economic importance through reforms adopted in recent decades. The skyline of the city's new downtown in the Pudong district is particularly impressive. Its two landmarks, the Shanghai Tower (632 meters/2,073 feet high) and the Shanghai World Financial Center (492 meters/1,614 feet high) are among the ten tallest buildings in the world (Fig. 8.20).

FIGURE 8.19 The urban edge in Shenzhen, China—Shenzhen has experienced the most explosive growth of any large city in world history. Here, in a photo taken from one of its many skyscrapers, is a view of the edge of the rapidly expanding urban area. *Source:* Pixabay.

FIGURE 8.20 Shanghai's financial district—Shanghai has rapidly emerged as one of the world's top financial centers, with much of that activity concentrated in the new skyscrapers in the Pudong district. The building soaring above its neighbors at the right, the Shanghai Tower, was the second tallest building in the world in 2018. *Source:* Pixabay.

Still farther north and about 150 kilometers (90 miles) inland from the shore of the Yellow Sea, the capital city of Beijing has over 20 million people in its metro area. This historic city, established some 3,000 years ago, has been the political, cultural, and educational center of China for centuries. It has a mixture of traditional and modern architecture, including seven UNESCO World Heritage Sites. It is also a forward-looking innovation center, with six major high-tech development zones on the city's periphery. Its airport is currently second only to Atlanta in passengers per year.

The rise of China and its major cities has created new rivals for Tokyo as one of the leading economic centers of East Asia. The Tokyo metropolitan area has 38 million residents. It became Japan's capital in 1868, but it had already played an important political role prior to that date. Like many other East Asian cities, it has a mixture of traditional and modern architecture and economic activities. Tokyo is an economic and financial center of global importance (which is somewhat ironic given the city's location in a seismically active region and its vulnerability to strong earthquakes), and headquarters of many well known Japanese corporations are located here. It has a well-developed public transportation network with its subway system that has thirteen lines and over 280 stations. Tokyo is one of the world's most expensive cities to live in; the average monthly rent for a housing unit of 84 square meters (900 square feet) varied from $1,500 to $2,800 in 2017.

Strategically positioned between Japan and China, Seoul, the capital of South Korea, is also an old city, established over 2,000 years ago, and has a mixture of old and modern structures, among them five UNESCO World Heritage Sites. The city proper has about 10 million inhabitants, but the Seoul Capital Area, which includes neighboring Incheon, Suwon, and a few other cities, has 24 million people, almost half of the country's total

FIGURE 8.21 Monumental architecture in Pyongyang—Modeled on the L'Arc de Triomphe in Paris, a similar structure in Pyongyang commemorates the struggle of the Korean people against Japanese colonialism and is an example of the monumental architecture of the North Korean capital. *Source:* Pixabay.

population. It is the largest economic center where most Korean global corporations (e.g. Samsung) are headquartered and is considered the world's most wired city by some technology experts. By contrast, Pyongyang, the capital of North Korea, is larger in area but much smaller in population. Established in the 12th century, it is now the major industrial center of the country. It is very different from other capital cities of East Asia as it is full of Communist-style monuments, including a towering statue of the country's founder Kim Il-Sung at the foot of which many North Korean newlyweds pay their respects (Fig. 8.21). The city's tree-lined boulevards have very little traffic as most North Koreans do not own cars. Again in sharp contrast to other cities in the region, Pyongyang is a quiet city with a limited network of service (retail) facilities.

LANGUAGE AND RELIGION

Relative Linguistic Uniformity

Considering its population size and territorial extent, East Asia is characterized by remarkable linguistic uniformity. In Japan and both Koreas, 99 percent of the population speaks Japanese and Korean, respectively, Mongolian is a native language for about 95 percent of Mongolia's population, and more than 1 billion people, including the majority of China's population, speak Mandarin. Mandarin (*Putonghua* or *Guoyu* in Chinese) is the official language of China, has the largest number of speakers, and is the mother tongue in the northern, central, and southwestern parts of the country (Fig. 8.22). Southeastern China is home to a number of other languages including Cantonese (Yue), the dominant language in Hong Kong and the rest of the Pearl River Delta, though Mandarin serves as a lingua franca (a language

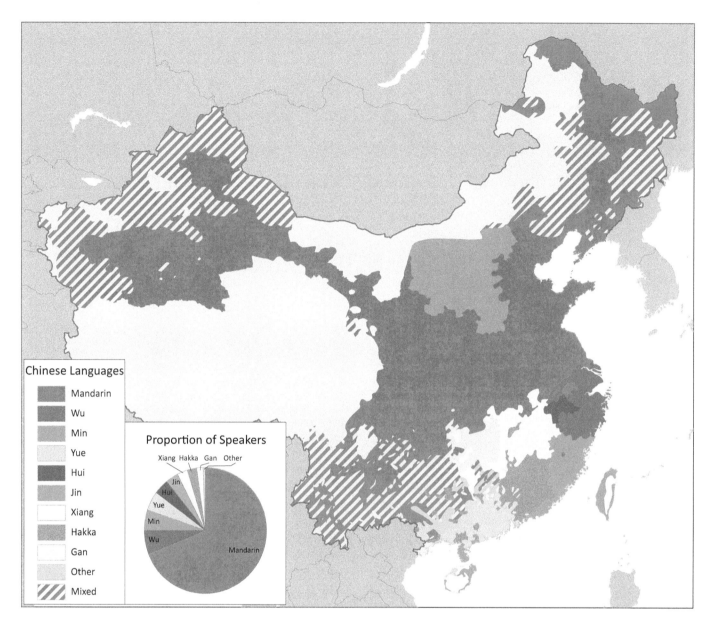

FIGURE 8.22 China: Chinese language patterns—Although spoken Chinese consists of over a dozen dialects, most of them mutually unintelligible, all Chinese speakers use the same system of ideograms and can easily communicate with each other in writing. The Chinese script was a major force of national unity in ancient times. Chinese Mandarin, spoken by about 65 percent of the Chinese population, is the official language of China. *Source:* Digital Language Atlas of China at ACASIAN GIS Data Archive.

used to communicate between people whose own native languages are mutually unintelligible) among the many migrants to this dynamic area.

Most of the languages spoken in China are members of the Sino-Tibetan family, the second largest linguistic family in the world (Fig. 8.23). Although there are numerous Chinese languages, they all use the same system of writing, which is based on over 10,000 (some claim as many as 50,000) **ideographs**, symbols representing ideas and not individual letters like in English and most other languages. A highly literate person might know several thousand ideographs; however, knowledge of about 2,500

of the most commonly used characters is sufficient to write and read a Chinese text today. There are traditional and simplified forms of Chinese characters; the former are used in Taiwan and the latter in China. Simplified characters were introduced in the 1950s to promote literacy and have spread to Chinese communities elsewhere in the world (e.g. Singapore).

Japanese belongs to the Japanese-Ryukyuan family of languages spoken in Japan and the Ryukyu Islands. It is the world's ninth largest language in terms of number of speakers (127 million). There are three systems of writing known as *kanji*, *hiragana*, and *katakana*. The *kanji* system uses

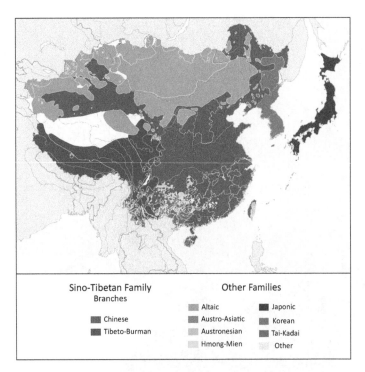

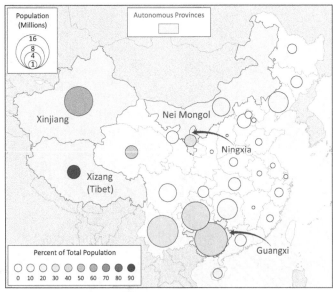

FIGURE 8.23 East Asia: linguistic patterns—Considering its population size, East Asia is characterized by a remarkable linguistic uniformity. China is the most linguistically "diverse" country where only 8 percent of the population do not speak Chinese as a native tongue. Source: World Language Mapping System.

FIGURE 8.24 Ethnic minority population in the People's Republic of China, 2012—China recognizes fifty-six ethnic groups that account for about 8 percent of the country's population (110 million). Half live in five autonomous provinces located in peripheral parts of the country. These areas are of great strategic importance to the Chinese government as they are rich in minerals and function as buffer zones between China and neighboring countries. *Source:* China's National Bureau of Statistics.

Chinese characters for nouns and adjectives and reflects the ancient legacy of Chinese cultural influences in Japan; the *hiragana* system is composed of forty-six characters for verb endings and particles placed after nouns to indicate their case; and the *katakana* system has forty-eight characters used for foreign words and names. Partly because of this multiplicity of writing systems, many scholars consider Japanese one of the most difficult languages for foreigners to learn.

Most people in North and South Korea speak Korean. The Korean alphabet (*hangul*) has twenty-four letters, which, in clusters of two, three, and four, form syllables and words. Almost half of the Korean vocabulary consists of imported Chinese words. Koreans use a hybrid system of writing where words of Chinese origin are written in Chinese ideographs and the Korean ones in *hangul*. Interestingly, the decades of separation between North and South Korea have fostered a growing number of differences that distinguish the Korean language north and south of the border. The North Korean dialect now sounds old fashioned or quaint to people in the south.

Despite such differences, a high degree of linguistic uniformity in most countries of East Asia also means that there are relatively few minority groups in this part of the world. Only China, where over 8 percent of the

population belongs to one of the fifty-six officially recognized ethnic minority groups, is diverse. Although 8 percent does not seem to be a high number, this represents 110 million people in absolute terms. About 40 percent of that population lives in five autonomous regions (provinces) located on the periphery of the country: Xinjiang and Xizang (Tibet) in Western China, Nei Mongol (Inner Mongolia) and Ningxia in the north, and Guangxi in Southern China (Fig. 8.24). Most of the remaining minority population is found in adjacent provinces, particularly those around Guangxi.

The Hui people (over 10 million) are Chinese Muslims, almost all of them Sunni; and they are widely dispersed throughout the country, although one-third of them live in the northwestern and north-central parts of the country. Their culture is different from the mainstream Chinese way of life with respect to diet (no pork, which is very popular among other Chinese people) and dress (men wear white caps and women scarves). The Zhuang people comprise the largest minority group, and 85 percent of them (out of 17 million) are found in the Guangxi Autonomous Province. Their language, a member of the Tai-Kadai family, consists of several mutually unintelligible dialects, and members of various groups communicate in Chinese among themselves today. Most Zhuang people used to follow traditional animistic religions.

FIGURE 8.25 Uighur women, Kashgar, Xinjiang Province in China—In this photo from 2009, a group of Muslim women are wearing head-scarves in the ancient city of Kashgar, Xinjiang in far western China. In 2017, the Chinese government put some restrictions on expressions of Islamic faith in Xinjiang. *Source:* Wikimedia Commons.

Almost all Uighurs (10 million) live in the southwestern part of Xinjiang (Fig. 8.25), and cotton farming is their main livelihood. Their language belongs to the Altaic family and uses the Arabic script. Uighurs converted to Islam in the 11th century. They have had a tense relationship with the Chinese Han majority and have challenged the central government on several occasions since 1912. After its incorporation to China, the region became an autonomous prefecture. However, the Chinese government has kept a tight lid on the Uighur people and their culture by forbidding daily calls to prayer and Ramadan fasting, as well as banning children from entering mosques, in recent years as part of its fight against Islamic terrorism—at least that is the official explanation for these restrictions on Uighur identity.

Over 70 percent of China's total Mongol population (6 million) lives in the Nei Mongol region bordering Mongolia to the north. Many of them engage in livestock herding, particularly horse raising, and they were known for their nomadic way of life until recent decades. There are twice as many Mongols in China as in Mongolia.

Over 6 million Tibetans, the best known of China's minority groups, live in Xizang (43 percent of its total number), Qinghai (25 percent), and Gansu (22 percent) provinces. Tibetans had their own state on several occasions after the sixth century CE, as well as their own system of weights and measures, an alphabet, calendar, and laws. At other times, they came under direct or indirect Mongol and Chinese control. Although Tibetans received political recognition in the form of the Xizang autonomous region in 1952 and some cultural autonomy in recent years, their relations with the Communist government are strained and sometimes violent. The Dalai Lama, the spiritual leader of Tibetan Buddhists, who has lived in exile in India for decades, has called for greater autonomy. A significant issue both for Tibetan Buddhists and for the Uighurs is the migration of ethnic Han Chinese (the country's majority population) into these peripheral regions. For instance, Han Chinese dominate economic life in Lhasa, the religious and administrative capital of Tibet (Fig. 8.26), and they comprise as much as 40 percent of Xinjiang's population.

Native and Imported Religions

Several indigenous folk religions and ethical systems, as well as one major outside religion (Buddhism), have influenced East Asian culture for over 2,000 years. China is the

FIGURE 8.26 Potala Palace, Lhasa, Tibet, China—Situated at an altitude of 12,140 feet (3,700 meters), this palace in Lhasa, Tibet was the winter residence of the Dalai Lama until 1959 when the current Dalai Lama fled Chinese oppression. *Source:* Pixabay.

birthplace of Confucianism and Taoism, while Shintoism is a native religion to Japan. Although their importance for daily life and the system of government has varied through time and across the region, the origin of many contemporary East Asian culture traits can be traced back to these old systems of belief and codes of behavior.

Several Chinese ethical systems originated or gained fairly wide support during a politically unstable era in China's history between the fifth and third centuries BCE. Each system sought the best road to a peaceful and prosperous society. **Confucianism** was based on the teachings of Confucius (551–479 BCE), the best known Chinese philosopher. According to Confucius and his followers, peace and prosperity could be accomplished through a hierarchical system of responsibilities (proper superior-inferior relationships) in private and public life; filial piety based on devotion and respect for parents; and kindness or humaneness based on the virtues of courtesy, righteousness, proper conduct, wisdom, and trustworthiness. When a proper hierarchical relationship within the family is maintained (i.e., when each member performs his or her duties and responsibilities correctly and shows respect to those above and below him or her), the family will be harmonious and happy. By the

same logic, the family model of proper relationships could be extended to the public (political) arena and produce a wise and virtuous leader acting as a father to his subjects. In this model, the government is accountable for people's conditions who, in turn, show respect and loyalty to their rulers. Human virtues, not birth rights, should determine an individual's place in society, and these virtues could be perfected through education, which for Confucius meant the acquisition of knowledge and the building of character. Confucian ideas have formed the basis for the design and operation of the Chinese state for about 2,000 years. Although Confucianism was suppressed under early Communist rule and blamed for China's backwardness, it has been tolerated and even praised for its emphasis on loyalty and obedience to government in recent years.

Lao Tzu (604–531 BCE), the founder of **Daoism (Taoism)**, another ethical system of the same era, believed that a simple life in harmony with nature and a disengagement from worldly affairs would bring peace and harmony to Chinese society. The principle of *Tao* (the way of nature) is the foundation of this ancient philosophy. It can be compared to water, which flows everywhere and is considered weak (yields to pressure) but in reality is one of the strongest natural forces. Taoism advocated humility and self-improvement, indirectly changing the world for the better by changing oneself.

While most scholars do not consider the Chinese ancient ethical systems to be religions, they agree that Shintoism, a native Japanese ethical system, which has no known founder and sacred texts, is a polytheistic religion as it recognizes the presence and worship of numerous gods, known as *kami*, living in natural objects (trees, streams, mountains, etc.). Numerous Shinto shrines have been built for worshipping one or more specific gods, and the *torii* gates of orange-red and black color at the shrine entrance symbolize separation of the physical and spiritual worlds (Fig. 8.27).

Buddhism, discussed in greater detail in Chapter 10, is the major "imported" religion in East Asia. It originated in northern India in the sixth century BCE. One of its early major branches, Theravada, which puts emphasis on monastic life and meditation as a way to enlightenment, spread to most of Southeast Asia and Sri Lanka. The Mahayana branch emerged in the first century BCE and spread from Northern India to China, Korea, and Japan. It believes that enlightenment can be achieved through normal daily activities and community engagement rather than strict monastic life. In Japan, Mahayana Buddhist deities that intercede between the human and divine worlds, may also be worshiped as Shinto *kami*. The statement that many Japanese people "live like Shintoists and die like Buddhists" may indicate the incorporation of some beliefs and practices from both religions by many individuals. Some scholars even say that these two religions form a single system of belief. Tibetan Buddhism incorporates some teachings and meditation techniques from the Mahayana and some philosophical and cosmological ideas from the Theravada branches. Lamas (spiritual teachers), who train future religious leaders by empowering them with spiritual energy and wisdom, play an important role. Tibetan Buddhism was not well known in other parts of the world until the Communist takeover of the region in 1950. Ironically, though, suppression by Chinese authorities since then has helped to make the religion widely known. Many Tibetan religious leaders went into exile to Northern India, including the Dalai Lama. He left in 1959 and has been living in Dharamsala (Northern India) for over half a century, but his work on behalf of the Tibetan cause and toward peace has made him one of the world's most recognizable people.

FIGURE 8.27 Miyajima Torii, Itsukushima, Japan—Miyajima Torii, or the "Floating Torii," is a spectacular example of a torii, a gate that represents the passage to sacred space at a Shinto shrine. *Source:* Pixabay.

Unlike the three Western exclusivist religions (Judaism, Christianity, and Islam), most Asian religions or ethical systems are more tolerant of theological differences and diversity of worship practices, and there has been a relatively high degree of religious syncretism in East Asian societies. Chinese folk religions represent a mixture of Confucian, Taoist, and Buddhist ideas, along with practices like ancestor worship, magic, shamanism, astrology, and worship of animal totems. Although the Communist government considered Chinese folk religions to be feudal superstitions and strongly discouraged or even banned their practice, there has been some religious revival in recent decades, and the number of their followers has increased since the mid-1990s. By some accounts, about 80 percent of Chinese people believe in some type of traditional folk religion.

In addition to these older religious and philosophical affiliations, Christianity is on the rise. Christian missionaries arrived in the region from Europe in the 16th century, but until recently there were few Christians here. Today, however, about 30 percent of South Koreans are Christian and so are about 5 percent of people in China, or nearly 70 million people, meaning that China—in addition to its many other superlatives—is home to the largest Christian minority population in the world. Some have argued that continued dissatisfaction with life in China, after decades of unprecedented economic growth, has led people to look elsewhere for answers, including religion.

Church-state Relations in China

Although the Chinese constitution guarantees freedom of religious belief and the government allows state-registered religious organizations to possess property, publish literature, train and approve clergy, and collect donations, church-state relations have been problematic for decades.[11] Human rights organizations claim that activities of many religious groups have been severely curtailed or even banned and some of their members jailed or put under house arrest. The Communist government recognizes only five religions: Buddhism, Taoism, Catholicism,

Protestantism, and Islam. Any organizations associated with these faiths must register with the appropriate state-approved patriotic religion association. Although the practice of other religions is officially prohibited, there is limited tolerance of activities by various groups associated with Chinese folk religions. In fact, there has even been some tacit support for these beliefs as they can help slow down or reverse the country's "moral decline" and create a more harmonious society. On the other hand, some 90 million members of the Communist party are discouraged from holding any religious beliefs and their families are precluded from participating in religious activities, and in some provinces applicants for party membership are screened for signs of religiosity.

The government has also taken a less tolerant approach to certain Muslim and Christian groups. As indicated earlier in this chapter, the relations with the Uighur minority have been tense for decades. In response to several terrorist attacks in Xinjiang and other parts of China in recent years, blamed on Uighur Islamist militants, the government restricted certain Muslim religious practices among members of this minority group. It believes that Islam should only be considered a culture trait rather than a symbol of ethnic or religious identity and Islamic religious practices should be corrected if they contradict state policies or impede progress toward national unity. Periodic hostilities toward Christian groups have also arisen, including a 2014 campaign to remove hundreds of rooftop crosses from church buildings and the imprisonment of prominent Christian leaders for "disturbing public order."

China's rule in Tibet gives it considerable control of Tibetan Buddhism, even though the Dalai Lama has lived in exile in India since 1959.[12] Tibetan Buddhists believe that the spirit of the Dalai Lama will be reincarnated into a child after the Dalai Lama's death. But to discern who that child is, the spiritual elders look for signs in the Tibetan landscape including a lake near Lhasa, the capital. China controls that landscape and therefore may be able to govern the process leading to the selection of the next Dalai Lama. Controlling the selection process would make it easier for China to impose limits on the cultural, and especially the political aspirations, of the Tibetan people.

POLITICAL ORGANIZATION OF SPACE

Comprising just five states (and Taiwan, which has an indeterminate status in global politics), East Asia is the least politically fragmented region in the world. The dominance of large states is a long-standing feature of its political

geography. By the beginning of the first millennium CE, imperial China controlled a vast swath of Asia encompassing 2,590,000 square kilometers or 1 million square miles and 50 million people. In its spatial extent and population, the Han dynasty's dominion at the time was comparable to the Roman Empire, its contemporary on the other side of Eurasia. But whereas Europe would fragment into hundreds of pieces by the Middle Ages, China has remained largely unified for most of its long history. Japan, likewise, has an ancient history as one sovereign power.

Between China and Japan lies the Korean Peninsula. With its powerful neighbors (also including Russia), the peninsula has been repeatedly subject to external control. In response, Korea isolated itself for much of its history, becoming the so-called Hermit Kingdom. Japan and China, too, have gone through long periods of self-enforced isolation, reflecting a sense of cultural superiority and a fear of foreign influence.

Today, in a region that has harnessed international trade to propel stunning economic development, only North Korea remains isolated. The country is one of the most secluded places in the world, and the border that separates it from South Korea is among the most heavily militarized on the planet. But it is not the only trouble spot in the region. In particular, long running tensions between the People's Republic of China and Taiwan comprise another important challenge in East Asia's political geography. Meanwhile, within the states in the region, there is great political diversity. China and North Korea are two of the few remaining Communist countries in the world and provide little freedom for their citizens; North Korea in particular is the least free country in the world. Yet South Korea, Japan, Taiwan, and even Mongolia are democracies.

The Political Geography of Ancient East Asia

China claims to have the oldest continuous civilization in the world, dating back about 4,000 years. Most of Chinese history can be summarized as a series of governments called dynasties that originally ruled over a part of the North China Plain and gradually expanded their control over adjacent territories to form one of the largest states in human history (Fig. 8.28). Thirteen dynasties ruled the Chinese people between 2100 BCE and 1911 CE. Some stayed in power for several centuries; others for just a few decades. Likewise, some made great contributions to culture and development, while others suffered political or social instability and territorial loss. The Han dynasty (202 BCE–220 CE) is considered one of the four great Chinese dynasties. During its rule, the country experienced a period of peace and prosperity. Sericulture (production of silk) spread from the Huang He region to Southern China

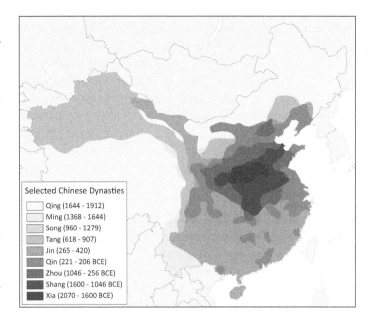

FIGURE 8.28 Territorial expansion of the Chinese state during the past four millennia—The map shows the approximate territorial control of present day China by selected dynasties. The Chinese state sometimes controlled additional areas, including Mongolia and parts of Russia and Central Asia.

and beyond, and silk export including over the **Silk Road** to Central Asia and Europe was an important source of income. Paper, invented around 100 CE, became the major medium of written communication.

During the Tang dynasty rule (618–907 CE), China was probably the most advanced civilization in the world. This period, sometimes called the Golden Age of Ancient China, witnessed an impressive development of arts, poetry, and technology. Gunpowder was invented around 850 CE and was initially used in fireworks displays and later by the military. Woodblock printing was another useful invention of this era, and it was the dominant printing technology on textiles and paper in this region until the 19th century.

The Song dynasty rule (960–1279) was associated with economic prosperity and technological development. Irrigation was expanded and new varieties of rice resulted in greater food surpluses and subsequent population increases. Granaries for emergency relief were established across China. The invention of the compass, first used in divination and later in navigation, was another important achievement of this era. This dynasty is also credited with expanding the educational system and creating a bureaucratic class to help emperors in ruling the country.

Under the Ming dynasty (1368–1644), the introduction of new crops from the Americas (sweet potatoes, corn, and peanuts) led to agricultural expansion into regions not suitable for growing rice. In this way, China was one of the greatest beneficiaries of the Columbian Exchange, and some Chinese cuisines, such as fiery Sichuan dishes, would be unimaginable without American ingredients. Yet China undertook its own great voyages at this time too. Under Admiral Zheng He, Chinese expeditions at the beginning of the 15th century visited ports in Southeast Asia, South Asia, the Arabian Peninsula, and Eastern Africa. With hundreds of ships and as many as 28,000 men under his command, Zheng He led the largest fleet the Pacific would see until World War II, and the largest of his ships dwarfed those that would carry Columbus to the New World at the end of the 15th century. The size of Zheng's fleet and the reach of his seven voyages illustrate what a unified China could achieve.

So do the Great Wall and Grand Canal. Construction of the Great Wall, whose many segments stretch from near the present-day North Korean border to the far southwestern frontier of the Gobi Desert, began in the second century BCE and was designed to protect China from attacks from its northern nomadic neighbors. A large army of soldiers, convicts, and peasants was used to build it, and some 400,000 workers died during its construction. The wall, 4.5–15 meters (15 to 50 feet) wide and 4.5-9 meters (15 to 30 feet) high, is considered one of the most ambitious construction projects in human history. It was designated a UNESCO World Heritage Site in 1987 and is a major tourist attraction today, particularly the section northwest of Beijing. The **Grand Canal**, the world's longest artificial waterway, connects the cities of Beijing in the north and Hangzhou in the south. The 1,800-kilometer (1,100-mile) long canal was constructed during the sixth century CE to transport grain from Southern China to the capital city and northern regions to feed the soldiers guarding China's northern frontiers. It took six years and millions of workers, many of them forced laborers, to build. Now it is a key component of the eastern route of the South-North Water Transfer Project previously discussed.

Many scholars attribute the political and cultural unity of ancient China for much of its long history to three factors: (1) the country's administrative structure, composed of a powerful and effective central political apparatus as well as a large, well-educated, and efficient bureaucratic class; (2) the common system of writing as a symbol of national unity; and (3) Confucian philosophy which, as indicated earlier, emphasized moral standards, a well-ordered society, and loyalty to the state. Alternatively, Jared Diamond in the influential book *Guns, Germs, and Steel* argues that China's smooth coastline, lack of large offshore islands, and lack of mountains in the densely populated east part of the country favored political integration.

Japan, conversely, is inherently fragmented, and for much of the last millennium, the Japanese emperor was fairly weak as more power was concentrated in the hands of regional landowners across the mountainous archipelago and their private armies of samurai (professional soldiers). When the Portuguese reached Japan by 1542, they introduced various items including tobacco, sweet potatoes, and guns. They also tried to convert the Japanese people to Catholicism, and Nagasaki in the far southwest of Japan became the center of their missionary activities. The introduction of new military technology (guns) allowed some regional leaders to increase their power and political influence over large parts of the country. Fear of Western influence, however, provoked the shoguns (military rulers who governed in the name of the emperor) to almost completely isolate the country from 1639 until 1853. For most of this two-century long period, the only contact with Europe was two Dutch ships per year, allowed to dock at an artificial island in Nagasaki's harbor.

Far to the west, the Mongolian people could not so readily isolate themselves and experienced remarkable swings from dominating large areas of Eurasia to being dominated by outsiders themselves. Chinggis Khan (also spelled Genghis Khan), who became the ruler in 1206 CE, controlled a vast empire from the Pacific Ocean to Eastern Europe and parts of the Middle East, which was later fragmented into four parts (khanates) (Fig. 8.29). His grandson, Kublai Khan, became the ruler of one of the khanates and established the Yuan dynasty in China in 1271 (Fig. 8.30), the first Chinese dynasty of foreign origin. But by the time of the Ming dynasty, the tables were turned and China controlled Mongolia.

China and Japan in the Modern World

At the beginning of the 17th century, the English scientist Francis Bacon opined that the three greatest inventions in history to that time were gunpowder, printing, and the compass. Bacon did not know it, but all three were invented in China. Yet crucially, Europe would go on to use these inventions more effectively than China. European countries fought more wars with one another and with the rest of the world, using gunpowder to conquer much of the Earth. Europeans printed more books and developed more literate, knowledgeable societies. And Europeans ultimately sailed farther and more often, using the Chinese-invented compass to extend European empires to the far side of the planet. The disparity between the origins of these inventions and where they were used most effectively illustrates a larger pattern: beginning about five hundred years ago East Asia declined

FIGURE 8.29 Chinggis Khaan International Airport in Ulan Bator, Mongolia—Named for Chinggis Khaan (also spelled Ghengis Khan), who ruled a vast empire stretching across Eurasia, this airport is an important gateway between Mongolia and the rest of the world. *Source:* Wikimedia Commons.

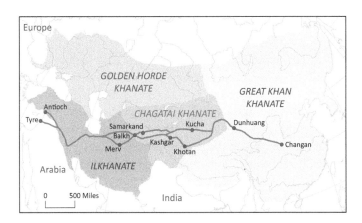

FIGURE 8.30 The Silk Road—The Silk Road was a trade route connecting medieval China with the Middle East and Europe. The vast Mongol Empire under the leadership of Chinggis Khaan and his successors controlled most of East Asia for a few centuries.

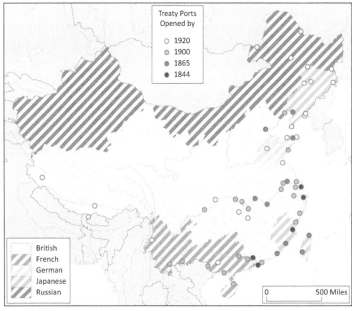

FIGURE 8.31 China: foreign influence, 19th century—Large parts of China were under the direct or indirect control of several European powers and Japan during the 19th and early 20th centuries. Many coastal and border cities and cities along the Yangtze River were centers of foreign control or at least open to foreigners for trade. *Source:* drawn after a similar map at www.portsmouth-peacetreaty.com/process/causes/causes2.html.

in technological, economic, and political power in the world as it was overtaken by the West. The reasons for this shift in power are complex but one key factor was the earlier development of capitalism in Europe, which was a catalyst for more dynamic, prosperous societies.

Nevertheless, Europe continued to want Chinese goods, including silks, tea, and porcelain. Because China had little interest in European products, however, the result was a widening trade deficit. To close the gap, Britain began exporting opium from British-controlled India to China. This trade became very profitable to the British but the widespread addiction to opium had a disastrous effect on Chinese society. To contain the effects of rampant drug abuse, the Chinese government banned the import and smoking of opium in 1800 and 1813, respectively, which prompted military retaliation by the British. These disputes are known as the Opium Wars of 1839–42 and 1856–60. Reflecting the degree to which it had been eclipsed technologically, China lost both wars and was forced to sign a series of unequal treaties, ceding direct or indirect foreign control over parts of its territory (Fig. 8.31). Most importantly, these wars led to British control of Hong Kong.

China's decline left it vulnerable not only to Western powers but also to a newly powerful Japan. The 1894–95 Sino-Japanese War resulted in the loss of Taiwan and increased Japanese economic expansion in China. Chinese resentment of the growing foreign influence and widespread discontent within China led to an uprising that quickly gathered strength, especially in the southern part of the country. The last dynasty collapsed in 1912, and China descended into semi-anarchy.

Two political parties emerged from this chaos as dominant forces in the country by the late 1920s: the **Chinese Nationalist Party** (Kuomintang), first under Sun Yat-Sen's and later under Chang Kai-shek's leadership, and the **Chinese Communist Party** under Mao Zedong's leadership. While both parties originally cooperated and even briefly joined forces to fight the Japanese, ideological differences between them led to numerous skirmishes in the early 1930s. The Long March (1934–35) of the Communist forces from Southern China to the north-central parts of the country, an outcome of such skirmishes, strengthened the position of Mao Zedong and the support for Communist ideas, especially in the rural regions. A civil war erupted between the two sides after 1945. While the nationalist forces originally had the upper hand in this conflict, the Communists recovered from the early setbacks and took control of mainland China by 1949, establishing the People's Republic of China. The Kuomintang forces fled to Taiwan and proclaimed the Republic of China a few months later.

The changes in Japan during this period were even more jarring. The growing 19th-century Western (mainly American) pressure on Japan to open its markets for imported goods and the superiority of Western military technology persuaded Japan to sign a series of treaties with several European countries (France, Great Britain, the Netherlands, and Russia) granting them trading rights,

coaling ports, and protection for shipwrecked sailors. These unequal and humiliating treaties greatly weakened the power of the shoguns. Pro-emperor forces gained control of the country, and the Emperor Meiji decided to aggressively modernize the country by adopting Western technology and opening it to outside influence.

The Meiji Restoration (1868–1912) was a policy of economic (technological) modernization and of establishing closer trading and political ties with the outside world, especially with Western powers. The Japanese government supported industrialization through generous loans and grants to the private sector. The military forces were reformed along German army and British navy lines in 1878, and compulsory education was introduced in 1872 and the Western calendar a year later. The royal family accepted the Western dress code, and the country developed a constitution (modeled on the German one) and created an elected parliament (Diet) by 1889. Japan emulated the Western powers in another way too: building up a colonial empire. By the end of the 19th century, Japan controlled Taiwan and a key port in China and was making inroads in Korea. Japan's victory over Russia in the 1905 Russo-Japanese War was a shocking outcome for the West, given the prevailing racist views about the inferiority of Asians. The war freed Japan to further extend its power in Korea and Manchuria in Northeastern China. In the 1930s, Japan swept through more of Eastern China and then on toward Southeast Asia (Fig. 8.32).

To stem Japan's advance in Asia, the United States banned the export of oil to Japan at a time when American exports met 80 percent of Japan's needs. The Japanese response was the attack on Pearl Harbor and proclamation of war against the United States (December 7, 1941). Japan continued to expand its territorial control of Asia by capturing Singapore, the Philippines, and most of Indonesia by 1942. The turning point for the Japanese military was the battle of Midway Island in 1942 where it lost four aircraft carriers. It began gradually losing other occupied territories as well. The dropping of two American atomic bombs on the cities of Hiroshima and Nagasaki in 1945 forced the Japanese to capitulate and surrender (Fig. 8.33). But within a generation, Japan would be hailed as a miracle economy. In the course of a century then, Japan went from ending centuries of self-imposed isolation to frenetic industrialization and militaristic expansion until its empire encompassed much of East Asia and the Western Pacific. It then endured a shattering defeat only to rise from the ashes as one of the world's great economies and a peaceful society, as the pacifist constitution imposed during the U.S. occupation (1945–1952) took hold.

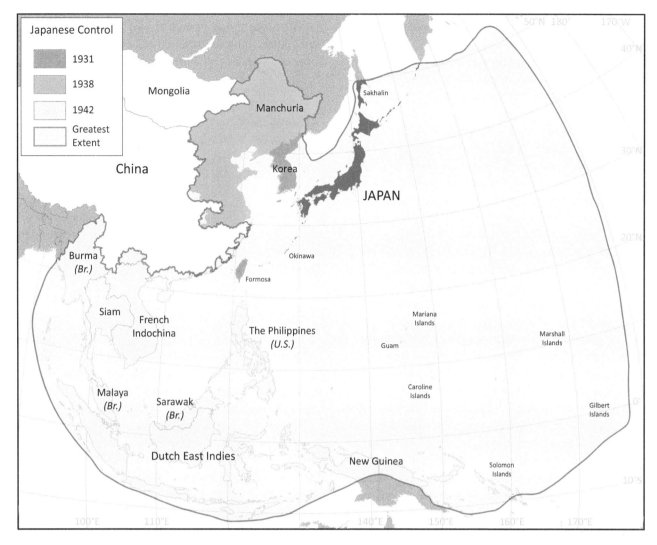

FIGURE 8.32 Japan's territorial expansion, 1875–1942—The Japanese Empire stretched over several thousand miles across East and Southeast Asia and the western Pacific Ocean. At the peak of its expansion, it was many times larger than the four major Japanese Islands. Drawn after a similar image at Grand Alliance Wiki at http://the-grand-alliance.wikia.com/wiki/File:P_D-614_map_Japanese-expansion_1931-42.jpg.

FIGURE 8.33 Nagasaki Hypocenter Park—A simple black monolith marks the hypocenter (the point directly beneath the detonation) of the atomic bomb dropped on Nagasaki. In the foreground are many colorful strands of one thousand paper cranes each, offered as a symbol of peace. *Source:* Wikimedia Commons.

Communism in China

The introduction of the Communist system in mainland China after World War II had a pervasive impact on the Chinese people. Communist rule resulted in several major positive social changes, including higher literacy rates, better health standards, and equal rights for women. On the other hand, the Communist government denied many people basic political rights, such as freedom of expression and religion. The Chinese Communist Party era can be divided into two major parts: the Mao Zedong (1949–76) and the post-Mao Zedong (1976–present) phases. The former phase was associated with harsh political rule and catastrophic failures in the attempt to recast China in the mold of a Communist society. The latter phase has brought economic modernization and globally unprecedented rates of growth but also controversial population policies (discussed earlier in this chapter) and the continued suppression of political dissent.

As in the Soviet Union (see Chapter 4), remaking Chinese society to fit Communist ideals brought tremendous upheaval and loss of life. The most cataclysmic period was the Great Leap Forward (1958–60), a program whose goal was to make China self-sufficient in agricultural and industrial goods. The collectivization of agriculture, implemented by establishing large farms known as people's communes, was supposed to achieve the first objective. Some 53,000 communes (occupying 98 percent of the total farmland) were established. A typical commune had about 25,000 members and was divided into ten to thirty production brigades, each production brigade into ten to twenty production teams, and each production team was composed of one hundred to two hundred people. A strong emphasis on collective life in the people's communes led to the establishment of large communal dining halls, child care centers, and other facilities that were supposed to diminish or eradicate the role of the individual family as the basic unit of society. Farmers remained loyal to their families however, and in the run-up to collectivization they used up their stored grain and slaughtered their livestock rather than turn over their possessions to the state. Then, once the collectives were in place, there was pervasive over-reporting of how much food was actually being produced in the new system, which led the country's leaders to make ruinous miscalculations in determining how much land to plant in which crops. The resulting calamity was compounded by the diversion of labor to serve the second objective of this program: industrial self-sufficiency. This was to be achieved through the increased production of iron and steel, mainly through a network of backyard furnaces across the country. Huge numbers of people were devoted to such enterprises, but the result was great economic inefficiency and poor quality output—one-third of pig iron produced in the backyard furnaces was simply useless. By piling mistake upon mistake, the Great Leap Forward precipitated one of the greatest famines in human history, killing as many as 10 to 30 million people.

To silence his critics, Mao Zedong launched another disastrous campaign known as the Cultural Revolution in 1966. The campaign of wiping out the "four olds" (ideas, customs, culture, and habits) led to anarchy, terror, mass executions, torture, imprisonment, public humiliation of many individuals, and the widespread destruction of property and many cultural relics and historical sites. Bands of young people (many of them university students) known as the Red Guards roamed across the country in search of "state enemies," including landlords, rich peasants, counterrevolutionaries, bad elements, and rightists.[13]

This ill-conceived campaign of political indoctrination, xenophobia, and international isolation also led to economic collapse, famine, and the death of 1.5 million people.

One of the many targeted during the cultural revolution was Deng Xiaoping, who had become a key economic leader in China after the failure of Mao's Great Leap Forward. Mao felt threatened by Deng, so he stripped him of his position in Beijing and sent him to work as a regular worker in a faraway tractor factory. Deng staged a remarkable comeback, however, and within two years of Mao's death in 1976, Deng had become China's paramount leader. A much more pragmatic man than Mao, Deng emphasized economic issues and established the foundations for China's spectacular economic growth during the past three decades. His policies are discussed later in this chapter.

Unresolved Cold War Conflicts

Although the **Bamboo Curtain** (analogous to the Iron Curtain in Europe) that once separated China and its allies from capitalist democracies has fallen with greater economic integration, several Cold War conflicts remain unresolved. First, the status of Taiwan remains unsettled. The Chinese Nationalist government under Chiang Kai-Shek, his defeated army, and 2 million of his supporters fled to the island in 1949 and proclaimed the Republic of China. Chiang stayed in power until his death in 1975, and his harsh dictatorial rule became known as "white terror." Like the Japanese who had colonized Taiwan for a half century, however, he strongly supported economic growth and made Taiwan one of the **"Four Tigers"** of Asia- economies that were small but began to grow very rapidly in the 1960s: Hong Kong, Singapore, South Korea, and Taiwan. Chang Kai-shek's successors gradually relaxed political restrictions, allowed the formation of opposition political parties, and introduced democracy by 1986. Now, democratization has become one of a growing number of factors distinguishing Taiwan from the rest of China, making future reunification more problematic.

When two separate states were established in 1949 (the People's Republic of China on the mainland and the Republic of China in Taiwan), both claimed to represent the entire Chinese population in the international arena. The Nationalist government in Taipei was a member of the United Nations until 1971 and had the strong support of the United States and other Western countries. But the growing international importance of Communist China eventually persuaded the United States to switch its diplomatic support and recognize the Communist government in Beijing as the sole representative of the Chinese people.

The Shanghai Communiqué of 1972, issued by the United States and the People's Republic of China, stated that there is "one China and Taiwan is a part of China."[14] Most other countries followed suit and established diplomatic relations with Communist China. Despite the lack of diplomatic recognition of Taiwan, the United States is committed to the military protection of the island in case of Chinese attempts to take it by force. Meanwhile, a significant proportion of Taiwanese people now support independence for the island. At the same time, however, political and economic ties between China and Taiwan have been increasing in recent years, and it looks like neither side is rushing to solve the "one China" issue in the immediate future.

A thousand miles to the north lies another unresolved Cold War conflict. The Korean Peninsula was divided into Soviet and American spheres of influence along the 38th parallel of latitude after the defeat of Japan in 1945; as in Germany, the defeated territory of an Axis power (in this case Japan's colony of Korea) was occupied by rival Allied powers (in this case the US and the USSR). In 1948, the Soviet Union helped Kim Il-Sung, a Korean nationalist and Communist, come to power in the new Democratic People's Republic of Korea in the north, and the U.S. helped install a pro-American figure as leader of the new Republic of Korea in the south. The Communist victory in China a year later, and its support for the North Korean invasion of the south (with the Soviet Union also in support), led to the three-year long Korean War. North Korea launched a surprise attack on the south in 1950 and quickly took control of most of the country. The United States formed a coalition of seventeen countries and slowly began regaining lost territory. After American forces crossed the 38th parallel and pushed the Communist invaders further north (close to the Chinese border), China entered the conflict by sending some 300,000 troops. They pushed the American and South Korean forces back to the original borderline along the 38th parallel. The war, which resulted in 4 million deaths, ended in 1953 more or less along the same line that had divided the two sides at the outset. Although both countries reached a ceasefire agreement, they have never signed a peace treaty and, technically, have been in a state of war since that time (Fig. 8.34).

Today the two countries are separated by a 250-kilometer (160-mile) long and 4-kilometer (2.5-mile) wide zone known as the **Demilitarized Zone** (DMZ), whose purpose was to create a buffer between the hostile powers (Fig. 8.35). Immediately north and south of the DMZ are some of the most heavily mined, barbed-wire fenced, and militarized areas in the world. There are only two settlements inside the DMZ, one on the South Korean side (Daeseong-dong or Freedom Village) and the other on the North Korean side (Kijong-dong or Peace Village). Both settlements have

FIGURE 8.34 The Korean Peninsula—North and South Korea are separated by the Demilitarized Zone (DMZ) along the 38th parallel of latitude. Communist North Korea is divided into eleven administrative units, including the capital city (Pyongyang), a special city (Rason), and nine provinces, while South Korea consists of seventeen units, including a special city (Seoul), six metropolitan cities, one metropolitan autonomous city (Sejong), eight provinces, and one special self-governing province Cheju (Jeju). *Source:* Natural Earth.

FIGURE 8.35 The Demilitarized Zone—The Demilitarized Zone on the border of North Korea and South Korea is ironically one of the world's most heavily militarized borders, but it is also a significant tourist destination. *Source:* Wikimedia Commons.

tall flagpoles and loudspeakers used for broadcasting propaganda messages. The North Korean village is an empty settlement built for propaganda purposes to show the "good life" in this isolated Communist state.

Despite the claims in its official name to be a democracy and a republic, many scholars consider North Korea a Communist monarchy where power has been transferred from father to son and grandson and where the leader's whim has frequently been the law of the land. Its founding father, Kim Il Sung, stayed in power until his death in 1994. His son, Kim Jong-Il, ruled the country until his death in 2011. Kim Jong-Un succeeded his father as the third leader of North Korea and has gradually consolidated power. While South Korea is the most "wired" (i.e., the highest level of Internet and mobile connectivity) nation on Earth and another of Asia's Four Tigers, North Korea is a kind of new Hermit Kingdom. Its official ideology is called *juche*, which can be summarized as political independence, economic self-sustenance, and military self-reliance. This country of 25 million people has the fourth largest army in the world—over 1 million soldiers and 5 million reserves. Military service is compulsory at the age of seventeen and lasts

for ten years. Approximately one-fifth of all North Korean men are on active duty at any time. The country has been developing and testing nuclear weapons and long-range missiles in recent years, developments many consider a serious threat to peace and stability in East Asia and beyond.

As in the case of Taiwan and China, the longer the two Koreas remain apart the more they diverge in ways that will make eventual reunification more challenging. In the case of the Korean Peninsula, the nearly impermeable border hastens the two countries down their separate trajectories.

Administrative Structure of China

Although China is approximately the same size as the United States, its internal political geography is quite different. The world's third largest country in area has several hierarchies of administrative units (Fig. 8.36). The top provincial-level consists of thirty-four units, including twenty-two provinces, five autonomous regions (Guangxi, Nei Mongol or Inner Mongolia, Xizang or Tibet, Xinjiang, and Ningxia), four municipalities (Beijing, Tianjin,

FIGURE 8.36 Administrative divisions of the People's Republic of China, 2012—China is divided into 22 provinces (23 if Taiwan is included), 5 autonomous regions, 4 municipalities, and 2 Special Administrative Regions (Hong Kong and Macau). *Source:* China's National Bureau of Statistics.

FIGURE 8.37 Hong Kong and Macau—Hong Kong is divided into three parts, Hong Kong Island (1.2 million people), Kowloon Peninsula (2.2 million), and the New Territories (3.8 million). Its area is about six times larger than the District of Columbia. Macau includes the Macau Peninsula (divided into five parishes) and the three islands of Taipa, Coloane, and Cotai, and its land area is only one-third of the District of Columbia.

Shanghai, and Chongqing), two special administrative regions (Hong Kong and Macau), and one claimed province (Taiwan). Most of the autonomous regions were established during the Communist era and were modeled after the Soviet republics created for various ethnic groups.

Two special administrative units, Macau and Hong Kong, deserve some attention. Macau was under Portuguese control for over five centuries. This coastal urban settlement in the Pearl River Delta was the last overseas Portuguese colony when it was given back to China in 1999 (Fig. 8.37). By then it had become Asia's major gambling center, and that industry has grown much larger since the return of Chinese control. There are over thirty casinos and 14,000 slot machines, and annual gambling revenues amount to over $40 billion, several times more than those of Las Vegas. The gambling industry employs some 19,000 people, almost a quarter of the total labor force. Macau is also a tourist magnet—it attracts 30 million visitors a year, two-thirds of them from mainland China. The gambling industry has also attracted organized crime and prostitution; however, the Chinese government launched an anti-corruption campaign in 2013 aimed mainly at Chinese officials visiting Macau, some of whom participated in these illegal activities.

Hong Kong became a British possession in 1843. It originally included only the island of Hong Kong given to Britain after the First Opium War. The nearby Kowloon Peninsula was added in 1860 after the Second Opium War. Both of these were given to the British in perpetuity (i.e., forever). Then in 1898, Britain was given a lease on the adjacent New Territories for ninety-nine years. Hong Kong thrived as a major trans-shipment port for trade with China until the Communist Revolution on the mainland forced Hong Kong to find a new economic engine. It turned to manufacturing, originally in the textile and garment industries, and later furniture, toys, and sporting goods manufacturers, as well as electronics and optical goods makers. Hong Kong's success in this endeavor made it still another of the Four Tigers.

Ties with China were gradually reinstated after 1978, and later many Hong Kong manufacturers relocated their production facilities to the nearby Pearl River Delta to take advantage of lower labor costs. Those ties strongly affected Sino-British negotiations over the future of Hong Kong in the 1980s. China's initial negotiating position was that British control of the colony was an affront to Chinese sovereignty and that the whole territory had to be returned to Chinese control in 1997 when the New Territories lease expired. Britain's initial negotiating position was that all of the territory should remain under British control, with the lease being extended. In the end, China received most of what it wanted, partly because by then Hong Kong's economy, its water and food supply, and its future vitality were tied inextricably to the rest of China. On June 30, 1997, the British flag was lowered and the Chinese flag raised over the former colony. However, the Hong Kong Basic Law called for a separate political status for the territory under the formula "one country, two systems" (meaning Hong Kong is part of one country, China, but there are two political and economic systems in that country—one for Hong

FIGURE 8.38 Housing in Hong Kong—Hong Kong is among the most densely populated places on earth. *Source:* Pixabay.

Kong and one for the rest) for fifty years. The Hong Kong Special Administrative Region (SAR) has its own currency (Hong Kong dollar), police, administration, legal system, and free market economy. The Beijing government is only responsible for Hong Kong's foreign policy and defense. However, tensions between the central government and local residents have developed over the election process and political power of the SAR's chief executive in recent years. The Chinese Communist government is unwilling to tolerate much political independence in Hong Kong fearing that these ideas might spill to the mainland and challenge the leading role of the Communist party (Fig. 8.38).

ECONOMIC ACTIVITIES

East Asia, as indicated earlier in this chapter, has become one of three global centers of economic power in recent decades. Its spectacular rise to this prominence, known as the Asian economic miracle, was first associated with Japan's recovery after World War II and its economic acceleration by the early 1970s, followed by Four Tigers' aggressive development and growing share of the world's economy since the mid-1980s, and finally China's fast rate of growth during the past two decades and its emergence as the second global economic power after 2010. East Asia's share of the global gross domestic product has been steadily increasing during the past five decades, from about 8 percent in 1960 to over 22 percent today.

Japan's Post-WW II Recovery

Japan's economy was seriously handicapped at the end of World War II. First, the country lost several territories acquired after 1894, including the Kurile Islands to the Soviet Union, the Ryukyu Islands (including Okinawa) to the United States, and Taiwan to China. Second, its infrastructure, mainly transportation and industries, was severely damaged, particularly in urban areas (among major cities, only the ancient capital of Kyoto was spared from large-scale destruction). Third, about 13 million people were unemployed, including people released into the workforce by the disbanding of the armed forces and the loss of military-related jobs. Over 1 million people living in the former occupied territories (e.g. Korea) were forced to return and join the ranks of the unemployed. Fourth, shortages of food and energy resulted from a sharp decline in the production of rice and coal. Fifth, labor strikes were rampant, further crippling the economy.

Yet despite WW II's death toll of 1.8 million in Japan and its economic destruction amounting to a quarter of the national wealth, Japan recovered from its war-related calamities within a short time like the proverbial phoenix rising from the ashes. Several factors played a major role in this process. American help in the form of financial aid ($4.8 billion by the early 1960s), U.S. purchases of Japanese goods, transfer of American technology, and military protection were of great importance. One might wonder why the United States was so generous to its former enemy. Perhaps the sense of guilt after dropping two atomic bombs on Hiroshima and Nagasaki and fear of Japan becoming a Communist state if left alone explain this generosity.

Strong government support for big (private) business, investment of public funds in industrial growth, and the export-oriented strategy of Japanese companies were other factors responsible for the rapid development. Favorable external conditions for economic growth, such as the Korean War, played a role as well. United States' forces in Korea became a huge market for struggling Japanese manufacturers. The management and employment practices of many big corporations, characterized by lifetime employment security in exchange for loyalty to employers, also contributed to this success. Many scholars point to the relatively cheap (at the beginning of its economic recovery) and skilled labor force, stable family structure, and emphasis on education as factors contributing to growth. Indeed, while Japan's infrastructure had been shattered by the war, its human resources—including managers, engineers, scientists, and technicians—largely survived to aid in the rebuilding.

The post-war Japanese economic boom was associated with the development of the cotton textile and clothing industries in the 1950s; iron and steel, chemicals, and shipbuilding in the 1960s; electronics and automobiles during the next decade; and computers and robotics in the 1980s. Japan became the world's second largest economic power by the early 1970s, and it maintained that position until overtaken by China in 2010. However, the high rate of economic growth of over 10 percent a year during the 1960s slowed down to about 5 percent by the early 1980s and zero a decade later, making the 1990s Japan's "lost decade."

Much like the earlier "miracle" economy, the more recent slowdown in Japan's economy has numerous causes. The rapid rise in land prices and labor costs during the boom encouraged many firms, such as the main automakers, to shift production abroad. Japanese auto assembly plants in places like Kentucky, Ontario, England, and Thailand are examples of what has been called the hollowing out of Japan's economy. The close relationship among big businesses, big banks, and government during the years of rapid growth has become a problem in the past two decades as Japanese banks have been hobbled by many bad loans and government has been undermined by numerous instances of corruption. Similarly, the high savings rate of Japanese families, which was advantageous when Japan's economy needed money to invest in new infrastructure and factories, has become disadvantageous now that what is needed to drive the economy is consumer spending. Most fundamentally, the decline in Japan's working age population, and rapid ageing of the population since the mid-1990s, have slowed the economy. More recently, other factors have played a role, including the Tohoku "triple disaster" of 2011 which began with a massive 9.1 magnitude earthquake, followed by a catastrophic tsunami, and then radioactive contamination from the destroyed Fukushima nuclear power plant.

China's Four Modernizations Program

At the time of Mao Zedong's death in 1976, China was the eighth largest economy in the world in terms of gross domestic product, which amounted to only one-tenth of the United States' GDP. The unprecedented average annual growth rate of over 10 percent since the early 1990s has made China the world's second largest economic power today (Fig. 8.39). Most scholars attribute this phenomenal development to the policy of Four Modernizations, a mixture of centrally planned and free market economic reforms introduced by Deng Xiaoping in 1978. He and his supporters believed that China could advance economically only by opening itself to the rest of the world and modernizing its industrial base by adopting Western technology and management styles. His famous phrase that "it does not matter if a cat is black or white as long as it catches mice"[15] expressed the pragmatic foundation of this program, which targeted four sectors for accelerated growth, namely agriculture, industry, the military, and science and technology.

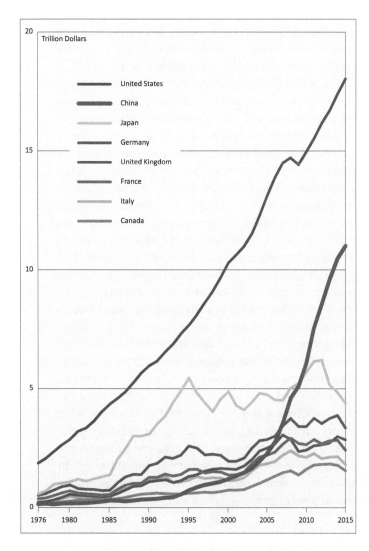

FIGURE 8.39 Economic growth of China and the world's other largest economies, 1978–2015.—Notice China's very rapid growth since 2000 and its rise to the rank of the world's second largest economy in about a decade. *Source:* World Bank.

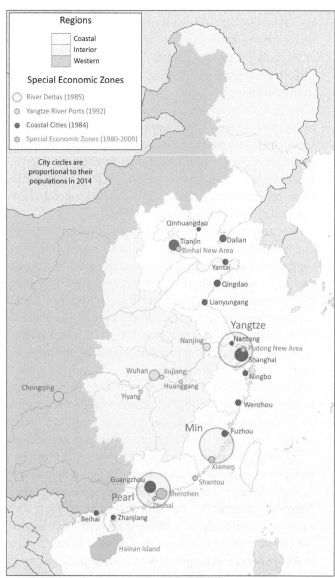

FIGURE 8.40 China's special economic zones—Notice that all these zones are located along the coast or the Yangtze river. *Source:* China's National Bureau of Statistics.

The household responsibility system became the cornerstone of agricultural modernization and virtually replaced the highly inefficient people's commune system by the end of 1983. Cultivated land could be subcontracted to families who would be responsible for meeting certain production targets at agreed prices and could keep the surplus for themselves, either for home consumption or to sell on local markets. Similar schemes were developed for animal husbandry, mainly raising pigs and poultry.

The modernization of the industrial sector called for, among other things, the decentralization of the decision-making system, establishment of joint ventures with Western companies, privatization or joint ownership (state-individual or state-foreign) of some small state-owned enterprises, and creation of **special economic zones** (SEZs)[16]. These zones represented a crucial break

with what has been called Mao's Closed-Door policy in which China aimed for economic self-sufficiency and had very little trade with the rest of the world. The shift to an Open-Door policy under Deng was somewhat tentative, however, in that only four small SEZs were opened initially and they were deliberately situated far from the core of power in Beijing. The first four SEZs were established in coastal areas of Southeastern China: Zhuhai (next to Macau), Shenzhen (next to Hong Kong), and Shantou and Xiamen (in proximity to Taiwan) in 1980 (Fig. 8.40). Hainan Island became another SEZ in 1988 and the Pudong New Area (in Shanghai) in 1990. These specially designated areas for foreign investment were supposed to attract and utilize foreign capital, encourage the establishment of joint ventures and foreign-owned enterprises, emphasize production for export, and have their economic activities be driven by market forces. The government would provide special tax incentives for foreign investments and give these zones more independence in international trading activities. The initial success of these reforms led to the establishment of additional zones for foreign investment. Together these various special economic zones now account for almost a quarter of China's GDP, 45 percent of foreign direct investment, and 60 percent of exports.

The modernization of science and technology focused on creating incentives for developing and sharing domestic technology and securing access to foreign world-class technology for economic development. It also called for state sponsorship of technological innovation, increased funds for research and development, created competitive procedures for funding public research projects, relaxed travel restrictions for Chinese scientists, and sent thousands of Chinese students for studies abroad. One measure of the success of these efforts is that China now leads the world in the number of patents issued each year.

Finally, the modernization of defense was prompted by the poor military performance of the armed forces during a Soviet-Chinese border conflict in the mid-1970s and a border war with Vietnam in 1979. It led to the dismissal of many top-ranking officers by the end of the 1970s, the restructuring of army leadership, an increase of military salaries, the appointment of more officers to government positions, and an investment in the modern weapons industry. As an illustration of its progress, China deployed its first aircraft carrier, the Liaoning (named for a province in the northeastern part of the country), in 2016.

Although the program of Four Modernizations made China the world's second largest economic power and improved the lives of many families and individuals, it has also contributed to greater regional inequalities in development and wealth distribution, particularly between the coastal provinces and major urban areas on the one hand and the interior rural areas on the other (Fig. 8.41).

Agriculture in East Asia

A small proportion of farmland (below 20 percent of the total land area) and severe land fragmentation characterize agriculture in most East Asian countries. Over 90 percent of Chinese, two-thirds of Japanese, and 60 percent of South Korean farms are very small (below two acres). The main challenge to most governments in this region is to feed large populations from shrinking areas of cultivated land

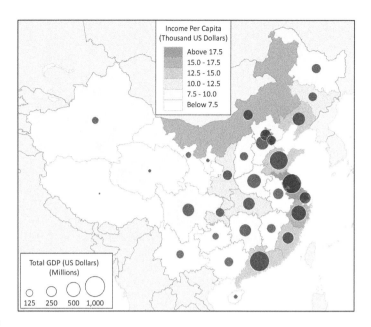

FIGURE 8.41 Gross domestic product in China's provinces, 2012— The cities of Beijing, Shanghai, and Tianjin have the highest GDP per capita in the country (over twice the national level), while Tibet, Yunnan, Gansu, and Guizhou have the lowest (below 60 percent of the national average). *Source:* China's National Bureau of Statistics.

with declining freshwater availability and a declining and ageing farming population.

The region can be divided into two parts from an agricultural point of view. The west, characterized by a dry climate and high elevations, is mainly associated with extensive livestock herding (cattle, horses, yaks, sheep, and goats), while the east, comprised of river and coastal plains interspersed by hills and low mountains, is used for more intensive agriculture based on the irrigated and rain-fed

FIGURE 8.42 Rice paddies in Yunnan Province in southern China—Growing rice in standing water allows the seedlings to outcompete weeds, keeps animal pests in check, and keeps the plants at a moderate temperature. *Source:* Pixabay.

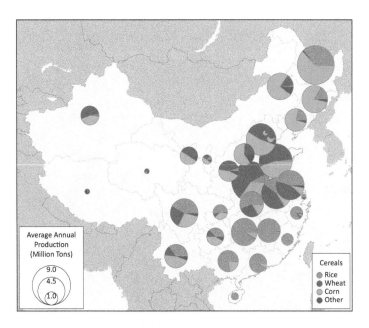

FIGURE 8.43 Production of cereals in China, 2013—Rice is the dominant crop in southeastern China and wheat in the North China Plain. Corn is the most widespread grain crop. *Source:* China's National Bureau of Statistics.

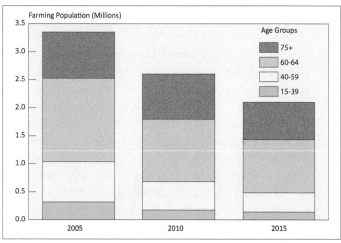

FIGURE 8.44 Farmers by age in Japan, 2005–2015—Japan has a rapidly declining population interested in farming, and its average age has been rapidly increasing. *Source:* Statistics Japan.

cultivation of cereals, root and oil plants, some cash crops, as well as livestock herding (pigs, cattle, and poultry). Both parts closely correspond to the major landform regions; the western agricultural region coincides with the inner arc of high mountains and plateaus and the eastern one with the middle arc of river plains, valleys, and hills and the outer arc of the islands (Fig. 8.42).

Southeastern China is associated with wet-rice cultivation, while the northeast is the land of wheat and corn farming (Fig. 8.43). Wet-rice cultivation is also the dominant type of farming in Japan, Taiwan, and South Korea. A variety of secondary crops is grown across the eastern half of East Asia, including corn, millet, sorghum, soybeans, sweet potatoes, sugar cane, cotton, and tea. The importance of each crop is determined by the climatic conditions, soil quality, landform configuration and altitude, dietary preferences, and a host of other factors. China leads the world in the production of several agricultural commodities including rice, wheat, sweet potatoes, cotton, tea, and pork. It is self-sufficient in wheat, rice, and cotton but dependent on imports of soybeans, mostly from the United States.

Despite China's great agricultural successes in recent decades, there are other major obstacles to achieving and maintaining its food self-sufficiency, among them the lack of land security. The land still belongs to the state (a legacy of communism) and can only be leased for a period of thirty to fifty years. Although recent changes allow farmers to

trade, rent, sub-contract, and transfer land rights, the lack of private land ownership has been responsible for weak investment incentives among farmers and forms an obstacle to the consolidation of fragmented plots into larger and more efficient farms. The dominance of small farms has also been responsible for a growing number of part-time farmers who engage in non-agricultural activities in nearby cities to supplement their meager incomes. Large-scale irrigation has led to water shortages, particularly in Northeastern China.

The ageing of agricultural labor force is an issue in China, South Korea, and Japan. The average age of a Japanese farmer is 66 years, and one-third of the farming population is over 75 years of age (Fig. 8.44). Additionally, heavy government regulations and subsidies to protect farmers from foreign competition have led to high food prices (especially of rice) in Japan.

North Korea continues to depend on large collective or state farms (like those in the former Soviet Union and in China under Mao) for its food needs. It is one of the few countries in the world where basic food items are rationed. The mechanization level is low and the heavy reliance on manual labor means that agricultural productivity is also very low. Some urban residents (mainly students) are sent to state farms to help with harvesting crops each fall. Despite its policy of self-sufficiency in food, North Korea had to cope with a major food crisis and famine during the 1990s. The collapse of communism and the end of Soviet subsidies, as well as the reduced support from China after 1994, meant that there was too little fuel to produce electricity, which crippled irrigation systems. A series of natural disasters (floods and drought), combined with economic mismanagement and high defense spending, halved the North Korean gross domestic product between 1992 and 1998 and resulted in widespread starvation and the death of up to 3 million people. International food aid from South Korea, Japan, the United States, and few other countries lessened the impact of this calamity, but North Korea's food security remains precarious.

Manufacturing in East Asia

While the Industrial Revolution came to East Asia relatively late, first to Japan in the second part of the 19th century and to China and the Korean Peninsula in the early 20th century, it made this region a major center of manufacturing in a much shorter time than it had Europe or the United States. Japan became the second largest industrial power in the 1970s, China surpassed Germany, Japan, and the United States in industrial production (as measured by the value added in manufacturing index) around 2000, 2006, and 2010, respectively, and South Korea is now the

tenth largest industrial power in the world. East Asia is the leading producer of many industrial goods, including ships (92 percent of global production), steel (60 percent), aluminum (46 percent), and motor vehicles (43 percent).

Most of Japan's modern manufacturing plants are found in the coastal areas of the country's industrial core region, stretching from the Kanto Plain around Tokyo to the Kitakyushu region in the northern part of Kyushu Island. Four major industrial clusters can be identified in this region, each one associated with a large urban agglomeration. The Tokyo-Kawasaki-Yokohama region, also known as the Keihin Industrial Zone, is the largest cluster. A variety of heavy and light industries (steel mills, shipbuilding, textiles, food processing, consumer electronics, household appliances, oil refineries, and robotics) are located here. Several land reclamation projects in the Kawasaki-Yokohama harbor created room for industrial expansion. The Osaka-Kobe-Kyoto region (or Keihanshin Industrial Zone) is the oldest and now Japan's second largest cluster of manufacturing. Cotton textiles and porcelain used to be the leading industries there, but the region's industrial

FIGURE 8.45 The Boeing Dreamlifter, Nagoya, Japan— A specially modified Boeing 747 is used to ferry wings of the Boeing 787, which are manufactured in Nagoya, Japan, to assembly plants in Washington State and South Carolina. *Source:* Wikimedia Commons.

base is much more diverse now. The major challenge to industrial expansion is the shortage of suitable land. The Nagoya region (Chukyo Industrial Zone) has attracted a host of industries, from textiles (silk, cotton, and wool) to motor vehicle and aircraft plants. Interestingly, the wings for the Boeing 787 are manufactured in Nagoya and then flown on a specially modified 747 to Washington State or South Carolina for assembly with the rest of the aircraft (Fig. 8.45). The Northern Kyushu region around the city of Fukuoka is a cluster of various heavy (iron, steel, and chemicals) and light (porcelain and pottery) industries. Nagasaki is in this region. The historically significant gateway to Japan became a major shipbuilding center in the 20th century (which is why it was targeted by one of the atomic bombs dropped in 1945), and it resumed that role after World War II, but Japan's shipbuilding industry has been overtaken in recent decades, first by South Korea and now China.

South Korea's progress in industrialization after World War II was like that of Japan but began about a decade later. Most of its industries are concentrated in the Seoul and Busan regions. Both areas have a large and diverse manufacturing base, including shipbuilding, chemicals, steel, oil refining, and motor vehicle companies. Hyundai's plant at Ulsan, not far from Busan, is the largest auto assembly plant in the world, producing a car every ten seconds.

China's manufacturing geography is more complex. The Communist government expanded the industrial base to several interior regions for strategic and ideological reasons. Then, the more recent phenomenal growth in export-oriented industrialization drew manufacturing to the coast; but now, in search of lower cost labor, manufacturing is moving back toward the interior.

There are many significant industrial regions in China (Fig. 8.46). The Manchurian industrial region, rich in iron ore and coal, is the largest resource-based cluster of heavy manufacturing in the country. Producing iron and steel, chemicals, railway equipment, and military hardware, it has been called China's Rust Belt but remains important. The Tianjin-Beijing cluster of industries is known for heavy manufacturing (metallurgical and engineering industries) and recently developed high-tech industrial parks around the capital city of Beijing and around the Binhai New Area, China's newest special economic zone. The country's oldest industrial region, open to foreign influence in the second part of the 19th century, is the Lower Yangtze region. Its cotton textile and silk, food processing, and leather industries were developed first; they were followed by steel, petrochemical, shipbuilding, electric appliances, and high-tech industries. There were restrictions on industrial growth in this area during the Mao Zedong era for the sake of more regionally balanced development across the country. The Pearl River Delta region, a labor- and transportation-based industrial cluster, is the most rapidly developing part of China. Its proximity to Hong Kong and abundant cheap labor force has attracted numerous Chinese and foreign companies to build textile (cotton, silk, and jute) mills, food processing and household appliances plants, shipyards, and a variety of other industries. The region is the largest center of electronics manufacturing in the world.

Yet much of China's manufacturing capacity takes place beyond these zones. For instance, the largest single iPhone assembly plant in the world is operated by a Taiwanese company called Foxconn near the airport in Zhengzhou, China. The city is located about 620 kilometers (385 miles) southwest of Beijing and offers lower costs than the Pearl River Delta where Foxconn previously concentrated such work. A growing number of Chinese workers do not want to migrate far from their families to work on the booming coast. In response, some manufacturing is coming to them.

Transportation: Accelerating East Asia

Railways and roads are the major modes of transportation in East Asia. Japan and South Korea have a dense and modern network of transportation routes, and China has rapidly expanded and modernized its transportation system during the past few decades. High-speed trains are a

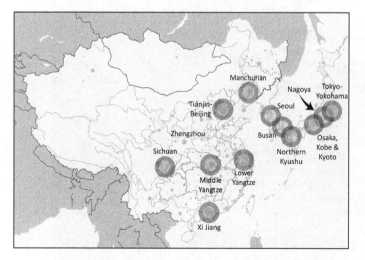

FIGURE 8.46 East Asia: major industrial regions—Although various industries are widely distributed across the eastern part of the region, most of them are located in six Chinese, four Japanese, and two South Korean clusters.

prominent feature of this region. The Japanese high-speed train network (Shinkansen) was opened in 1964. It now has seven major lines extending from Kyushu to Hokkaido, and carries over 300 million passengers a year. In South Korea, the Korea Train eXpress, opened in 2004, consists of two high-speed train lines from Seoul to Busan and from Osong to Gwangju-Songjeong in the southwestern part of the country. Even Taiwan has a high-speed line between its two main cities. Most spectacularly, starting from zero in 2007, China now has a more extensive high-speed rail network than the rest of the world combined (Fig. 8.47).

Not all of China's impressive rail lines are high-speed. In 2006, the country completed a normal-speed line from Golmud in the center of the country to Lhasa in Xizang (Tibet). The line is the highest altitude passenger train in the world, requiring oxygen to be pumped into the pressurized cars. The train better links the remote province to the rest of the country and facilitates tourism, but it may undermine Tibet's autonomy and cultural distinctiveness. Another impressive achievement is the so-called New Silk Road, a freight rail service linking China and Europe via a 12,000-kilometer (7,500-mile) route through Central Asia.

The importance of rail transportation in China is long-standing but now other modes are growing rapidly. Although many Chinese roads are still of low quality (unpaved), the rapid expansion of the country's expressway network, which is now longer than that of the United States, is impressive. And China is now the top vehicle producer in the world, manufacturing more cars each year than the U.S. and Japan together. Rapid industrial development and growing levels of motorization though have led to serious air pollution, especially in urban areas (Fig. 8.48). Meanwhile, although rail passenger-kilometers (a measure of traffic produced by summing the distance traveled by all passengers) more than doubled in China between 1990 and 2016, the number of air passenger-kilometers grew nearly thirtyfold over the same time period.

Several East Asian airlines and airports are major players in the global air transportation system. Three Chinese state-owned airlines, China Southern Airlines based in Guangzhou, China Eastern Airlines headquartered in Shanghai, and Air China with its major hub at Beijing Capital International Airport, are among the ten largest air carriers in the world in terms of passenger traffic. Other large airlines based in this region include two from Japan, two from South Korea, and one from Hong Kong. Each of these carriers serves at least 30 million passengers a year. Out of the world's ten largest airports, three are in China and one in Japan. Beijing Capital International, Hong Kong International (Chep Lap Kok), Shanghai Pudong International, and Tokyo Haneda serve some

FIGURE 8.47 High speed trains at Shanghai—China has a more extensive network of high-speed rail services than the rest of the world combined. *Source:* Wikimedia Commons.

65 to 95 million passengers a year. Several of these airports have been opened in the last two decades, and others have significant new terminals. In aviation, as in other forms of transportation, one advantage for East Asia is that so

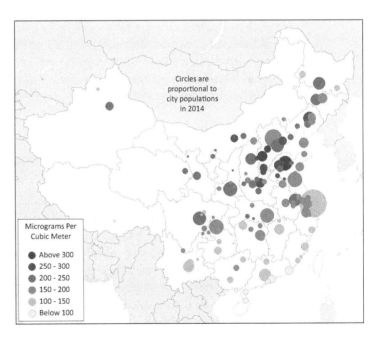

FIGURE 8.48 China: average annual concentration of air pollutants in major cities, 2014—The highest concentration of major pollutants (sulfur and nitrogen dioxides) is found in cities with heavy manufacturing, most of them in the North China Plain. Notice the relatively low pollution in cities that became special economic zones that have attracted more high-tech and other less polluting industries. *Source:* China's National Bureau of Statistics.

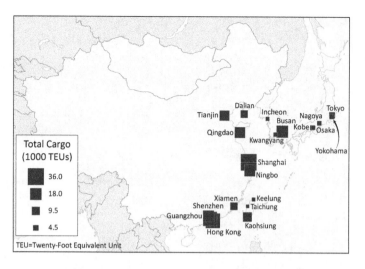

FIGURE 8.49 East Asia: largest container ports, 2011—*Source:* Wikipedia.

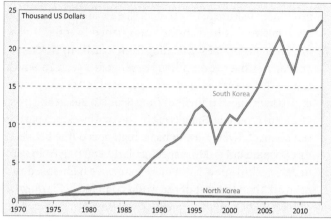

FIGURE 8.50 North and South Korea: GDP per capita, 1970–2013—North Korea had a higher income per capita until the mid-1970s. However, its stagnant economy lags behind that of South Korea, and today the gap is larger than ever before. *Source:* Hyundai Research Institute.

much of its infrastructure is new and incorporates the latest technology.

About half of global maritime cargo traffic goes through East Asian seaports. Seven Chinese and one South Korean port are among the world's top ten busiest container seaports (Fig. 8.49). The Shanghai deep-water port facilities at Yangshan were opened in 2005 and are connected with the city via the Donghai Bridge (the world's longest sea bridge). This seaport handles more cargo traffic than any other port in the world, and the shipment volume has doubled since 2005. Three seaports in the Pearl River Delta (Shenzhen, Hong Kong, and Guangzhou) together handle twice as many container shipments as the Shanghai port.

The Korean Peninsula: Contrasts in Development

When the United States and the Soviet Union partitioned the Korean Peninsula in 1945 and established two separate states, Communist North Korea had several advantages over its southern neighbor. Most of the mineral wealth (coal, iron ore, and some other metallic ores), hydroelectric power, forests, and industries were found in the north while the south was an overcrowded and predominantly agricultural region. Yet, different economic and political systems introduced in both countries have led to diametrically opposed outcomes. South Korea is one of the world's most developed countries while North Korea remains the most isolated and one of the poorest states in the world (Fig. 8.50).

The centrally planned economy of North Korea, modelled after its two Communist neighbors (the Soviet Union

and China), has emphasized the development of heavy industries and paid little attention to consumer needs. The policies of *juche* and *songun* (military first), the rigidity of the North Korean central planning system, and more recent emphasis on nuclear weapons over economic development have left the North Korean economy stagnant for decades, particularly since the collapse of the Soviet Union in 1991. While the North Korean government introduced limited reforms to boost its ailing economy in recent years, among them some tolerance for semi-private markets and the establishment of several special economic zones to attract foreign investment, they have had a limited impact on economic growth so far.

Although South Korea's economy was not in much better shape for a decade or so after the Korean War, and its rates of economic growth and income per capita were below those of North Korea prior to the early 1970s, the country has experienced a long period of impressive economic growth since that time. This growth, known as the "Miracle on the Han River," has made South Korea one of the technologically most advanced countries and the tenth largest economic power in the world (Fig. 8.51). Strong government support for big privately-owned conglomerates known as *chaebols*, including Hyundai and Samsung, has contributed to that success. The rate of economic growth has slowed down in recent years, in response to lower levels of domestic consumption and investment, and the South Korean economy, like that of Japan, is facing several challenges, among them the ageing labor force and great dependence on exports.

Despite some shortcomings of the South Korean economy, there are stark differences between the two Koreas in

FIGURE 8.51 Seoul, South Korea—Seoul is located on the Han River. The North Korean border lies just 30 miles (48 kilometers) to the right (north). The Olympic Stadium for the 1988 Summer Games is in the foreground. *Source:* Pixabay.

	South Korea	North Korea
Population (Thousands)	51,015	24,779
Gross national income (Billion won)	1,565,816	34,512
Income per capita (10,000 won)	3,094	139
Foreign trade (100 million $)	9,633	63
Energy production: capacity (1,000 kW)	97,649	7,427
Energy production: actual (100 million kWh)	5,281	190
Rice production (1,000 tons)	4,327	2,016
Fish catch (1,000 tons)	3,342	931
Coal production (1,000 tons)	1,764	27,490
Iron ore production (1,000 tons)	445	4,906
Non-ferrous metal production (1,000 tons)	1,597	398
Motor vehicles (1,000s)	4,556	4
Steel production (1,000 tons)	69,670	1,079
Cement production (1,000 tons)	52,044	6,697
Chemical fertilizer (1,000 tons)	1,982	528
Chemical fibers production (1,000 tons)	1,340	23
Railroads (km)	3,874	5,304
Roads (km)	107,527	26,183
Cargo handling capacity in ports (1,000 tons)	1,140,917	41,560

0   200   400   600   800   1000   1200
Magnification factor

FIGURE 8.52 North Korea and South Korea compared, 2015—North Korea is ahead of its southern neighbor only in coal and iron ore production and the length of railroads. *Source:* Statistics Korea.

many areas (Fig. 8.52). One example of such disparities is the GDP per capita. It is about twenty to thirty-six times higher in South Korea, depending on the source of information and method of calculation. There is little reliable information published by the North Korean government; hence, it can be risky to make comparisons between the two countries, especially using data expressed in monetary units. Food shortages in North Korea led to widespread malnutrition, particularly among children, and stunted growth. On the average, North Koreans are two to eight centimeters (one to three inches) shorter than their South Korean counterparts. Life expectancy is about ten years lower and the infant mortality rate is seven times higher in the north. Over 80 percent of South Koreans have access to the Internet, while less than 1 percent of North Koreans do. These kinds of differences make the North Korea-South Korea border the starkest in the world in terms of development differences.

FUTURE PROBLEMS AND PROSPECTS

Although East Asia has to a considerable degree "come full circle" returning to near its former position of economic and technological leadership in the world, the region faces great challenges in the 21st century. First, while East Asia has over 1.6 billion people today, its population is expected to decline to 1.2 billion by 2100. The shrinking of the labor force and the growing number of the elderly are the two major demographic challenges for this region. The working age population is projected to decline by half and the elderly group to triple in size by the end of this century. There will be one dependent person (children and the elderly) for each economically active individual. Japan and South Korea will reach this unfavorable condition sooner than China, but the working-age cohort has already begun to shrink in all three countries. The introduction of population policies encouraging higher fertility is one solution to this problem (China has already ended its strict one-child policy). Raising the retirement age and encouraging immigration are other proposed solutions. Partly due to labor shortages, Japan is a world leader in robotics, and China is moving in the same direction. A Ford factory in the Lower Yangtze Industrial region, for instance, has 650 robots and 2,800 workers in one of the most advanced auto assembly plants in the world.

Second, the nuclear ambitions of North Korea threaten to destabilize regional and global security. The country has been developing and testing nuclear weapons since 2006. Despite promises to halt the development of these weapons on several occasions (in exchange for food and other aid from several neighboring countries and the United States), the program has accelerated under Kim Jong-Un. North Korea has also tested ballistic missiles and developed long-range types that can reach the United States. It probably has chemical and biological weapons. The government claims that its nuclear program is for self-defense purposes and blames the United States for destabilizing the Korean Peninsula. Although China has some leverage to pressure the North Korean government to abandon its weapons of mass destruction program, it has been reluctant to do so out of fear that if the government in Pyongyang is toppled, millions of North Korean refugees could cross the border into China.

Third, China's growing influence (economic, political, and military) is a concern to the United States and its Asian allies, mainly Japan and South Korea. China is displacing the United States as the main trading partner for many Asian countries, and the Chinese model of development is becoming popular in the developing world, especially Africa. Territorial claims to the Spratly Islands in the South China Sea (see Chapter 10), and the program of building-up artificial islands and runways there, are some examples of growing Chinese influence beyond East Asia.

Fourth, the dependence on imported energy sources, most of them from the Middle East, is one of the major economic weaknesses of this region. About three-fourths of its energy needs are met by burning fossil fuels, and only China has significant, albeit insufficient, amounts of oil and natural gas. Reducing this dependence through the development of alternative sources of energy is a major challenge, especially to Japan and South Korea. Before the 2011 Tohoku triple catastrophe, nuclear energy accounted for about 30 percent of all electricity in Japan and in South Korea. However, many Japanese plants have been shut down since then and the probability of natural hazards (earthquakes, tsunamis, and typhoons) is an obstacle to the further expansion of the nuclear energy program in Japan. Hydroelectricity is currently the most important renewable energy source, particularly in China and North Korea.

Fifth, serious environmental pollution in East Asia is closely connected with the rapid economic development and high dependence on fossil fuels for energy production. China is the world's largest producer of greenhouse gases. Its reliance on coal-fired plants and recent increase in motorization of Chinese society have led to high air pollution levels, well above safety norms in many cities. Chinese-origin acid rain and smog periodically affect the environment and people in neighboring countries (South Korea and Japan). Water depletion and contamination is another environmental challenge to the region, especially China. About two-thirds of Chinese cities suffer from water shortages, and some politicians claim this problem challenges the survival of the Chinese nation.

Moving towards the middle of the 21st century, East Asia faces significant challenges. It is also a region with great questions hanging over some of the most basic features of its future. Will the two Koreas reunify? Will Taiwan be reunified with the rest of China? If these changes happen, will they be peaceful or violent? The answers to these questions will matter not just to East Asia, but to whole world.

NOTES

1. Jones, E., Frost, L. & White, C. (1993). *Coming full circle: An economic history of the Pacifc Rim.* Boulder, CO: Westview Press.

2. Robinson, H. (1967). *Monsoon Asia: A geographical survey.* New York, NY: Praeger.

3. Muranov, A.P., Owen, L. & Greer, C.E. (2017). Amur River. *Encyclopedia Britannica.* Retrieved from htps://www.britannica.com/place/Amur-River

4. Delang, C.O. (2016). *China's air pollution problems.* New York, NY: Routledge.

5. Carle, D & Carle, J. (2013). *Traveling the 38th Parallel: A water line around the world.* Berkeley, CA: University of California Press.

6. Skeldon, R. (2011). China: An emerging destination for economic migration. Migration Policy Institute. Retrieved from https://www.migrationpolicy.org/article/china-emerging-destination-economic-migration

7. Quoted in Hutchings, G. (2000). *Modern China: A guide to a century of change* (p. 164). Cambridge, MA: Harvard University Press.

8. Hudson, V.M. & den Boer, A.M. (2004). *Bare branches: Te security implications of Asia's surplus male population.* Cambridge, MA: MIT Press.

9. Veeck, G., Pannell, C.W., Smith, C.J., & Huang, Y. (2011). *China's geography: Globalization and the dynamics of political, economic, and social change.* Lanham, MA: Rowman & Litlefeld.

10. World Bank. (2015). *East Asia's changing urban landscape: Measuring a decade of spatial growth*. Washington, DC: World Bank Group.

11. Albert, E. (2015). Religion in China. Council on Foreign Relations. Retrieved from htp://www.cfr.org/china/religionchina/p16272

12. Wong, E. (2009, June 6). China creates specter of dueling Dalai Lamas. *New York Times*, A6.

13. Veeck, G., Pannell, C.W., Smith, C.J., & Huang, Y. (2011). *China's geography: Globalization and the dynamics of political, economic, and social change*. Lanham, MA: Rowman & Litlefeld.

14. Kan, S. (2001). China/Taiwan: Evolution of the "One China" policy – Key statements from Washington, Beijing, and Taipei. Congressional Research Service Report for Congress. 7-5700. RL-30341.

15. Quoted in Chen, F. (1995). *Economic Transition and Political Legitimacy in Post-Mao China* (p. 60). Albany, NY: State University of New York Press.

16. Zeng, D.Z. (2010). *Building engines for growth and competitiveness in China: Experience with special economic zones and industrial clusters*. Washington, DC: World Bank.

9

SOUTH ASIA

GEOGRAPHIC QUALITIES AND WORLD SIGNIFICANCE

South Asia consists of eight countries: India, the realm's dominant country; two other countries that flank India and also rank among the world's ten most populous—Pakistan and Bangladesh; three landlocked and mountainous countries—Afghanistan, Nepal, and Bhutan; and two island countries—Sri Lanka and the Maldives (Fig. 9.1). South Asia is possibly the world's most culturally diverse world region. Even though the region is separated from other regions by impressive mountain chains, foreign influences have contributed to the diverse cultural setting. As a region, South Asia is united by its past as a part of the British Empire, which directly or indirectly controlled the entire realm and left a strong legacy.

During colonial times, the British exploited the riches of India, but toward the end of the colonial time and after India's independence in 1947, South Asia was politically and economically weak and its population poor and hungry. However, South Asia is emerging from its peripheral position in the world. The region has a large share of the world's population, with India alone being home to 1.3 billion people, and Pakistan and Bangladesh together add nearly another 400 million. India, the region's most important power, has had a difficult relationship with neighboring Pakistan since the two countries were formed through the partition of British India in 1947. Since both countries today possess nuclear weapons, the conflict between them would have global significance. Terrorism is a major problem in India, which suffers more terrorist attacks than any other country in the world, and Pakistan and Afghanistan are known to harbor terrorist groups that pose a global threat. On the positive side, India has become a major economic power. While the outsourcing of work by U.S. and other Western companies to India is controversial, it is a testament to India's well-trained work force. Advances in science, engineering, and computer technology even more clearly show the potential of this region.

PHYSICAL ENVIRONMENT

Landform Configuration

The landforms of South Asia can be divided into three main regions: the inner arc of high mountains, the middle arc of river plains and hills, and the outer arc of islands (Fig. 9.2). The Himalayas, the most prominent feature of inner arc, separate the Indian subcontinent from the rest of Asia[1]. The tectonic collision that has formed the world's highest mountain chain has been millions of years in the making and is still underway. When Pangaea broke apart about 200 million years ago, the Eurasian continent was part of the northern supercontinent Laurasia, while South Asia was part of the southern supercontinent Gondwanaland. About 120 million years ago, India and its neighbors split from Gondwanaland and travelled northward. Some 50 million years ago, the Indian subcontinent collided with the Eurasian continent, forming the Himalayas. As this upheaval is still ongoing, the Himalayas grow about 5 millimeters (0.2 inches) per year. Their rapid uplift is evident in steep and jagged peaks and deep valleys and river gorges cut by erosion (Fig. 9.3).

The Himalayas cover a vast area of Northern India, Nepal, and Bhutan. The range forms a crescent shape and can be subdivided into three different mountain belts (Fig. 9.4). The northern belt is called the Great or High Himalayas as it has the highest average elevation (over 6,000 meters; 20,000 feet) and contains the highest mountains in the world, several of which are over 8,000 meters (26,246 feet) high, led by Mount Everest at 8,848 meters (29,029 feet). The second belt, the Lesser Himalayas, is somewhat lower in elevation, and the third belt, the sub-Himalayas, forms the foothills composed of sediments carried down from the erosion of the higher Himalayas belts.

The second major mountain range in South Asia is the Karakoram, which covers parts of Pakistan and India and extends into Afghanistan and China. The Karakoram is home to K2 (8,611 meters; 28,251 feet), the second highest peak in the world after Mount Everest, and four peaks over 8,000 meters are located in close proximity. The Karakoram is the most heavily glaciated mountain range in the world outside the polar region. The Siachen Glacier stretches over 76 kilometers (47 miles) and Biafo Glacier over 63

FIGURE 9.1 Countries of South Asia—South Asia consists of eight countries. India is the dominant country in this realm; colonial India encompassed most of the region.

kilometers (39 miles), making them the second and third longest glaciers in the world (Fedchenko Glacier in Tajikistan is the longest at 77 kilometers or 48 miles).

The Hindu Kush is the third major mountain range in South Asia. It stretches over 800 kilometers (500 miles) along the Afghanistan-Pakistan border. The highest peak in the Hindu Kush is Tirich Mir (7,708 meters; 25,289 feet) in Pakistan, and the average altitude is about 4,500 meters (14,764 feet). The Hindu Kush is a formidable obstacle to transportation; most mountain passes are at elevations of about 4,000 meters (13,123 feet) and can only be traversed in late spring and in summer. The most famous mountain pass is the Khyber Pass, which connects Pakistan and Afghanistan; its relatively low elevation (1,070 meters; 3,510 feet) helps to explain its historic importance.

The middle arc of river plains, hills, and plateaus is located south of the major mountain chains. The river plains are a thick accumulation of sediments that have been eroded from the mountains. Together the plains of the Ganges, Indus, and Brahmaputra rivers form the Indo-Gangetic Plain. The Ganges and Brahmaputra plains are characterized by fertile alluvial soil, while the Indus Plain has dried out and become a desert. Peninsular India and Sri Lanka largely consist of plateaus, including the vast Deccan Plateau, which covers most of Central and

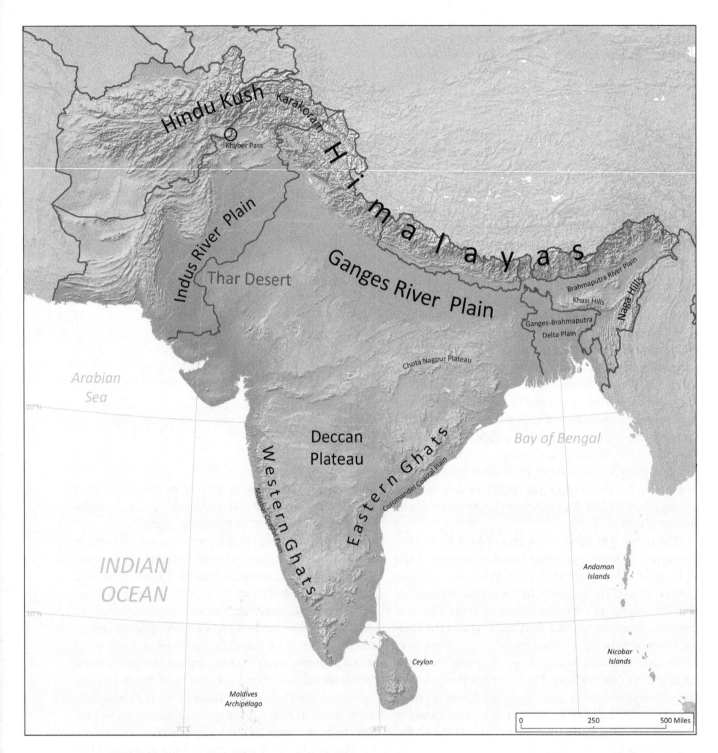

FIGURE 9.2 Landform regions in South Asia—The most defining landforms in South Asia are the high mountain systems at its northern edge as well as the plains of the major rivers. *Source:* Natural Earth.

Southern India. The plateau is higher on the western side; and in the southern half of the subcontinent it is lined by *ghats* (steps) toward the narrow coastal plains.

The island arc consists of several archipelagos of smaller islands. The Maldives comprises almost 1,200 islands spread over an area of 90,000 square kilometers (35,000 square miles). The islands consist of coral reefs and sand bars that sit atop a submarine ridge that rises from the Indian Ocean. At an average elevation of less than two meters (over six feet) above sea level, the Maldives is the

FIGURE 9.3 The Himalayas in Northwestern India—A flock of goats on the move at nearly 18,000 feet (5,400 meters) in the Himalayan landscape of Indian Kashmir. *Source:* Pixabay.

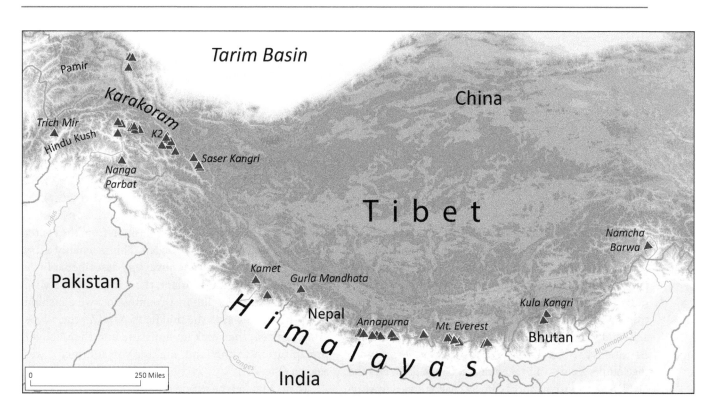

FIGURE 9.4 The Himalaya and Karakoram Mountains—The Himalayas and the Karakoram contain the world's highest mountains such as Mt. Everest, K2, and Nanga Parbat. *Source:* Natural Earth; OpenDEM.

FIGURE 9.5 The low-lying Maldives—Malé, the capital and largest city of the Maldives, illustrates the country's vulnerability to climate change-induced sea level rise. *Source:* Wikimedia Commons.

lowest-lying country in the world (Fig. 9.5). The highest "peak" of the Maldives is 2.4 meters (7.9 feet) above sea level. Despite protective measures, the country is at high risk of being submerged as the sea level rises due to global warming[2]. If the sea level rises at current rates the Maldives may be uninhabitable by the end of the century. To draw attention to the threat of the rising sea levels, the Maldives government held an underwater meeting in 2009, with political leaders sitting around a table on the seafloor in diving gear and signing papers with waterproof ink.

Climate

Due to its vast size, South Asia has several distinctive climate types influenced by the impact of monsoons, proximity to the coast, and altitude (Fig. 9.6). In the inner arc of high mountains climatic conditions change dramatically with altitude. Outside of the high mountains, Northern India and parts of Nepal and Bhutan have a humid subtropical climate characterized by hot and humid summers and mild winters. Farther south, the subtropical climate transitions to tropical climates. The western coast of India, the southern parts of Sri Lanka and Bangladesh, and the Maldives have an equatorial climate characterized by year-round heavy precipitation (no dry season). Most of India, Bangladesh, and Sri Lanka have pronounced wet and dry seasons and can best be described as tropical savanna environments. The wide range of climate types and associated biomes means that South Asia is one of the ecologically most diverse regions in the world, with biomes ranging from high mountains to extensive **mangrove** swamps, and from deserts to rainforests. This ecological kaleidoscope is home to some of the world's most iconic animals such as the snow leopard (found in the Hindu Kush and Himalayas), water buffalo (India), one-horned rhinoceros (Northern India and Nepal), Asian lion (India), Bengal tiger, Irrawaddy dolphin, and Asian elephant.

While diversity in climates, biomes, and wildlife is a major characteristic of South Asia, a commonality for most of the region is the influence of the monsoon[3]. The word monsoon comes from the Arabic word *mawsim* meaning season. In South Asia there are two great seasons with different precipitation patterns. In winter, strong winds blow in a clockwise fashion from the center of Asia towards the Indian Ocean. This is usually a dry time in South Asia but not always as described a little further below. In the summer, the winds reverse with strong currents blowing in a counterclockwise fashion from the sea towards the middle of Asia. As the winds cross the sea, they pick up moisture and then deliver precipitation to the land, making the summer a wet season (Fig. 9.7).

To understand the nature of the monsoon climate, one should be familiar with the basic physical properties of land and water. Land absorbs and releases heat quickly, while water warms up slowly and retains heat for a longer time. The interior of Asia is very cold in winter; cold air

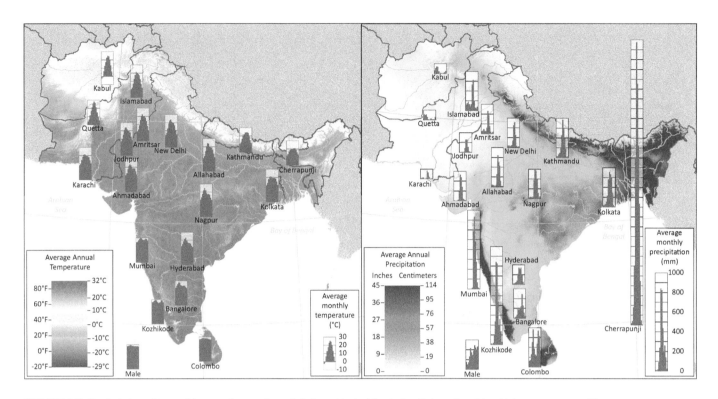

FIGURE 9.6 South Asia: patterns of temperature and precipitation—Most of the Indian Subcontinent has high average annual temperatures with the exception of the high mountains in the north. Precipitation is much more variable, with most of Afghanistan, Pakistan, and northwestern India receiving low to moderate amounts of precipitation while the Ganges River Plain and Bangladesh receive high amounts. *Source:* WorldClim-Global Climate Data.

is heavy, sinks, and forms a high-pressure cell over the center of the continent (Fig. 9.8). Out over the sea, it is still warm, and air is therefore rising over the water leading to lower pressures. The winds move from the land to the sea to equalize the pressure. As they do, they are deflected away from a straight path by the **Coriolis Effect** (an apparent deflection from a straight line) induced by the Earth's rotation, giving rise to the clockwise pattern described earlier. These conditions are reversed in summer. The surface of the land warms up faster, heating the air above it, which rises and forms a low-pressure area over the northwestern part of the region. The ocean's surface conversely is still cool as the sun's rays penetrate deeper into the water and heat is dissipated by waves. The air near the surface is cooler too, and therefore sinks and creates higher pressures. The seasonal wind blows from the sea to the land to balance this pressure differential. As the air masses are drawn towards the land, they move over the Indian Ocean and pick up moisture through evaporation. When the air masses then rise over the warmer land, the moisture is released as rain.

The seasonal alteration in monsoon wind currents creates distinct precipitation patterns. Mumbai, for instance, averages 84 centimeters (33 inches) of rainfall in July and virtually zero from November to May. An even starker

FIGURE 9.7 An Indian couple braves the monsoon in Bangalore—Bangalore gets about 831 millimeters (33 inches) of precipitation per year, about the same as Detroit, but while the Michigan city gets a fairly even distribution of precipitation through the year, in Bangalore 85 percent of rain falls between May and October. *Source:* Wikimedia Commons.

example is Cherrapunji, India, sometimes considered the wettest place on Earth. The town is located in northeastern India in the Himalayan foothills just across from the Bangladeshi border. Moisture-laden airmasses get trapped by the towering mountains and deliver incredible amounts

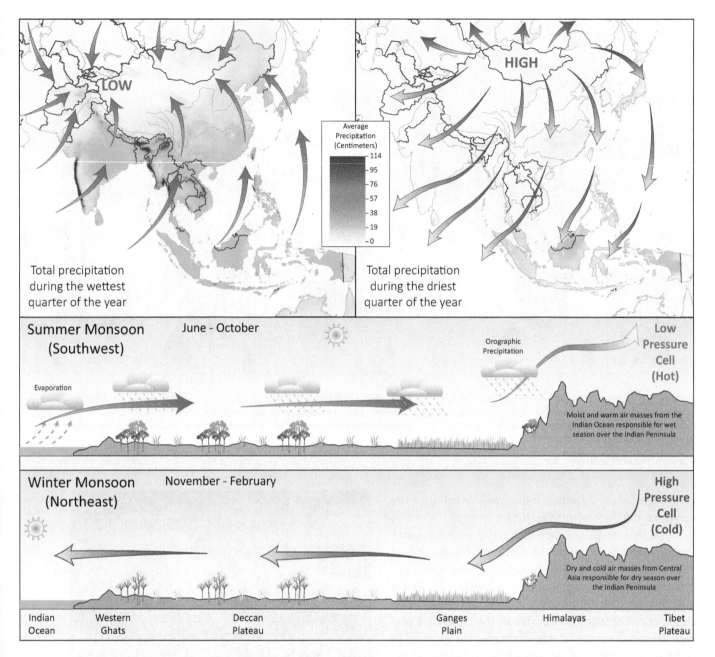

FIGURE 9.8 Monsoon climate: temperature, precipitation and wind patterns—Notice the great contrasts in precipitation between the wet and dry season, particularly in South Asia, Indochina, and Eastern China. *Source:* WorldClim-Global Climate Data; profile drawn after a similar image in *Diercke International Atlas.*

of rain to the community and others nearby. More than 270 cm (106 in) fall in July alone on average, but almost nothing during the winter months. For the year, Cherrapunji averages 996 cm (33 feet!). More generally, for most of South Asia, the wettest months are in summer. On the east side of the peninsula, however, the pattern is more complicated; Chennai receives 33 cm (13 in) in November as winter monsoon currents sweep clockwise over the Bay of Bengal, picking up moisture, and then move back over the coast near Chennai. The city also gets quite a bit of precipitation from the summer monsoon, but less; for instance, the average for July is just 11 cm (4 in).

South Asia depends heavily on the torrential rainfalls associated with the monsoon. Most of the region does not have elaborate irrigation systems or productive aquifers, so the region relies on the summer rains to replenish its water resources. Rice and tea, as well as many other crops, could not be grown without the monsoon rains. Industries and cities also rely on the monsoon rains, as hydroelectric plants depend on the water stored during the wet season. While a weak monsoon can result in large agricultural and economic losses, heavy monsoon rains can also be devastating when entire neighborhoods and villages flood and mudslides cover farmland and villages.

FIGURE 9.9 The ghats in Varanasi, India along the Ganges River—Munshi ghat is one of dozens of similar sites along the Ganges in Varanasi where people bathe, carry out religious rituals, and occasionally cremate the dead. *Source:* Wikimedia Commons.

Rivers

The Ganges River (*Ganga* in Hindi) is a wide and sluggish stream that flows through some of the most fertile and densely populated areas in the world: the Northern Indian plain. Compared to other major rivers, it is relatively short at 2,510 kilometers (1,560 miles), but it is of tremendous importance to the millions of people who live close to it. It originates in the Himalayas in the borderlands between India and Tibet. Its volume increases substantially as it enters the area of heavier rainfall and is joined by several tributaries. Once the Ganges crosses into Bangladesh, a number of distributaries branch off from it and flow to the south towards the Bay of Bengal (a **distributary** is a branch of a river that does not return to the main stem). About 100 kilometers (160 miles) from its mouth, the Ganges is joined by the Brahmaputra, and the combined stream forms a vast delta. The Ganges-Brahmaputra system is the third largest river system in the world measured by average discharge. During the monsoon season, much of the delta region floods to a depth of over a meter, so people must settle on elevated land and can travel only by boat. In addition to seasonal flooding, the delta is also frequently hit by storm surges associated with strong **cyclones** (the term used in the Indian Ocean basin for what are termed

hurricanes in the Atlantic and eastern Pacific and typhoons in the western Pacific). The severe flooding from these events often results in severe loss of life, homes, livestock, and agricultural crops.

The Ganges was the heartland of a series of successive civilizations[4]. For example, the Ganges Plain was the focus of historic Hindustan, the Mughal Empire was centered on Delhi and Agra in the western part of the Ganges basin, and Dhaka in the delta became a center of the Muslim era which began in the 12th century. Today many important cities are lined up along the Ganges, its tributaries, and distributaries such as Agra (the site of the famous Taj Mahal), Kolkata (formerly called Calcutta), and Dhaka. Another city of importance along the banks of the Ganges river is Varanasi (or Benares), a sacred Hindu city. In fact, most of the important places for Hindu pilgrimages are located along the Ganges, making the Ganges the most important river for any religion in the world. During religious festivals, thousands of pilgrims take ceremonial baths in the river. Hindus also place the ashes of the dead into the river with the belief that this allows them to travel directly to heaven. Therefore, large numbers of cremation ghats (the word means "step" in this context, too, as with the ghats that flank the Deccan Plateau previously discussed) can be seen along the river (Fig. 9.9).

The seaward part of the delta, called the Sundarbans, contains large areas of mangrove forest that have been designated a UNESCO World Heritage Site. The forest is inhabited by tigers and numerous other kinds of wildlife and provides livelihoods ranging from fishing to farming to tourism. But the Sundarbans are gravely threatened by rising sea levels, the incursion of saltwater farther upstream due to reduced freshwater flow in some distributaries, overfishing, and other environmental issues.

Other environmental concerns in the greater Ganges watershed include the construction of hydroelectric dams, whose costs include habitat destruction and the disruption of water supplies. Of even greater concern, however, is water quality. Dozens of cities and towns pump untreated sewage into the river. Additional pollution comes from agricultural and industrial runoff, but also from partially cremated or unburned bodies. As a result, the Ganges is heavily polluted by disease-causing bacteria, as well as by toxic substances—an ironic and dangerous situation given the hundreds of millions of Hindus who believe that bathing in the river is spiritually purifying[5].

The Brahmaputra flows through China, India, and Bangladesh, and is therefore known by many different names. It originates in Tibet, slices through the Himalayas in impressive gorges, and eventually flows south through Bangladesh where it joins with the Ganges. The river is prone to flooding during the snow melt in spring; its volume can increase to five times the normal flow. The periodic flooding of the river is important to deposit alluvium and replenish the fertile soils, but deforestation in the Brahmaputra watershed is contributing to catastrophic flooding. For example, in a 1998 flood, about two-thirds of Bangladesh was flooded and almost 1,000 lives were lost. A 2004 flood affected 36 million people and made over 1 million people homeless.

Thousands of schools were destroyed, millions of latrines washed away, and water wells were contaminated. As a result, water-borne diseases such as cholera broke out. Despite some efforts to manage the floods, the threat has not yet been brought under control.

The Indus River gave India its name, but it is located in modern-day Pakistan. It originates on the Tibetan Plateau, is fed by the snows and glaciers of the Karakoram, Hindu Kush, and Himalayas, flows for 3,200 kilometers (2,000 miles) through Kashmir, and then traverses the entire length of Pakistan where it enters the Arabian Sea close to Karachi. Due to global warming, the glaciers are melting at alarming rates. The rapid melting of the glaciers contributes to river flooding; in the long run, however, meltwater flows will decrease as glaciers disappear, reducing the flow volume of rivers they feed. Today, the Indus is Pakistan's lifeline, as it supplies the water for the breadbasket in Punjab and Sindh provinces, which account for most of the agricultural production in Pakistan. Much of its water is used for irrigation as rainfall is scarce in the lower Indus valley. The first irrigation canals had already been built by the Harappans around 3300 BCE, making this one of the earliest irrigated areas in the world. Later civilizations expanded and improved this system, allowing food production and population to grow but also increasing the region's dependence on this vital resource. After the partition of India, the use of the Indus waters became a point of contention between India and Pakistan. In particular, Pakistan was concerned that India might build dams on some of the river's tributaries that would reduce the water flow. The issue was largely settled in the Indus Waters Treaty of 1960. Other modern concerns center on the extensive deforestation and industrial and agricultural pollution that affect the Indus.

HUMAN-ENVIRONMENT INTERACTION

South Asia is extremely vulnerable to natural disasters as the region is marked by high population densities, high rates of poverty, and a lack of coping capacities. Bangladesh is ranked among the ten most disaster-prone countries in the world.

By number of deaths, the most devastating natural disasters in South Asia in the last twenty-five years were the 2004 Indian Ocean tsunami (over 200,000 deaths), Cyclone Nargis (over 130,000 deaths in Sri Lanka and Myanmar), and the 2005 Kashmir earthquake (over 70,000 deaths). The 2015 earthquake in Nepal killed nearly 9,000 people and resulted in enormous damage (Fig. 9.10). While

more people die from seismic disasters (earthquakes and tsunamis) or from cyclones, floods and droughts often affect much larger numbers of people. For example, a 2002 flood in India affected 42 million people and a 2003 flood in Bangladesh 36 million. Even more significant, the 2002 drought in India is estimated to have impacted the lives of 300 million people. Droughts do not claim many lives or result in catastrophic destruction, but they destroy the livelihood of those who depend on agriculture, so they have huge social and economic impacts.

The 2004 Indian Ocean tsunami resulted in major loss of life in South Asia[6]. It was triggered by a 9.1 magnitude

FIGURE 9.10 Durbar Square, Kathmandu, Nepal—This plaza near the old royal palace in Nepal is popular with tourists and pigeons. The 350-year old pedestal in the foreground once carried a statue of a great Nepali king but it fell over during the country's devastating 2015 earthquake. *Source:* Michael Pease.

earthquake off the west coast of Sumatra, Indonesia and killed between 230,000 and 280,000 people in fourteen countries. Indonesia was the most severely impacted country, but Sri Lanka and India were also hit hard. Interestingly, there were only a few casualties in Bangladesh even though it was located close to the epicenter. This has been explained by the north-south orientation of the fault that triggered the earthquake, which sent the strongest tsunami toward the east and west; the wave height in Bangladesh to the northwest of the epicenter was slight. Even though the tsunami only reached India and Sri Lanka 90 to 120 minutes after the earthquake, people were taken by surprise as no tsunami warning system existed at the time. In Sri Lanka, thousands of people died as the tsunami travelled up to two kilometers inland in some places. It inundated hundreds of settlements and struck a train traveling along the coast, killing almost all of the 1,700 passengers on board. The country's agricultural sector suffered from the salinization of rice paddies, deposition of debris, and the destruction of farm equipment and drainage systems. In India, the Andaman and Nicobar Islands were particularly affected due to their closeness to the epicenter. It has been estimated that the tsunami reached a height of 15 meters (49 feet) in the Nicobar Islands. Approximately one-fifth of the population was reported dead or missing.

The 2005 Kashmir earthquake (magnitude 7.7) resulted in widespread devastation in Northern Pakistan and Kashmir (with an estimated death toll of over 70,000 in Pakistan, with another 1,400 dead in Indian-administered Kashmir), but also caused damage in Afghanistan and Northern India. The earthquake hit during the holy month of Ramadan on a school day, so many people were either killed by collapsing school building or were resting in their homes. It is estimated that in some areas over 60 percent of buildings collapsed, explaining the vast majority of deaths and injuries. One of the major problems was that the landslides triggered by the earthquake blocked access routes to the destroyed villages, and rescuers lacked heavy equipment to clear the roads making it difficult to bring relief to remote settlements. Aftershocks also hampered the rescue efforts. Furthermore, the earthquake occurred just prior to the winter snows in the Himalayan region and left millions of people without adequate shelter. Exposure to winter weather, coupled with the danger of diseases spreading, made providing help to the survivors particularly urgent. One positive outcome of the earthquake was that India and Pakistan overcame their hostility regarding the political status of Kashmir (discussed later in this chapter) to provide help to the people affected. They opened five border crossings along the Line of Control in Kashmir to allow relief goods to reach the victims and make it possible for families to check on relatives. The United States also participated in the relief effort, which helped to improve tense relations with Pakistan that stemmed from the War on Terror.

The 2015 Nepal earthquake killed nearly 9,000 people. The loss of life could have been even worse had the earthquake not occurred at a time when farmers were working outdoors. Some 3.5 million people were made homeless when entire villages were destroyed. The earthquake also triggered several avalanches that killed both villagers in the Langtang Valley and mountaineers on Mount Everest. Beyond destroying many buildings, including UNESCO World Heritage sites in the Kathmandu Valley, the earthquake also resulted in major social costs. For example, human trafficking increased as traffickers took advantage of the chaos in the aftermath of the earthquake and preyed on poor women who had lost their homes. Similarly, it has been reported that rapes and domestic violence have increased. Furthermore, disease, mental health problems, and malnutrition have also become worse. Nepal is one of Asia's poorest countries, so financing the reconstruction poses a major challenge.

Bangladesh is among the most vulnerable countries in the world, as it is exposed to earthquakes, tsunamis, and typhoons as well as sea level rise related to global warming. About one-fifth of Bangladesh is flooded in an average year, while during severe floods three-quarters of the country can be under water[7]. Most of Bangladesh's land area is barely above sea level, and nearly all is classified as floodplain because Bangladesh is essentially the delta of some of the world's largest rivers. During the snow melt in the Himalayas, these rivers have dramatically increased flow rates, but the heavy sediment load makes them more prone to flooding; the sediment is deposited as the rivers slow upon reaching Bangladesh's flat terrain and so river channels become shallower and broader and the deltas more expansive. Further, Bangladesh is located in a monsoon climate, so seasonal rainfall (as well as orographic rainfall created by the Himalayas) adds even more water. In addition to these diverse physical circumstances, human factors also play a role. Deforestation in the Himalayas increases runoff, and the sea level rise from global warming results in coastal flooding. Most floodplain communities are only protected by embankments made from soil and turf built by farmers.

In addition to seasonal flooding, longer-term changes in Bangladesh's watery landscape threaten many. The constant movement of Bangladesh's coastline and the changing course of rivers compel thousands of people to give up their land every year. At the same time, however, some lands are created through sedimentation, and people settle in these newly emerged lands called *chars* (Fig. 9.11). The Char Development and Settlement Project supports people in building their lives on the chars, which are often only accessible by foot or boat. Gaining a foothold in such a capricious landscape is difficult. The land is flooded regularly, and there are no public services such as safe drinking water, sewage removal, or electricity. There are also no markets, schools, or medical facilities. Despite all these problems, the chars are often the only option available to people who have lost their land.

It is widely believed that the disastrous flooding in the Ganges and Brahmaputra plain in Bangladesh is in part due to the deforestation in the Himalayas. The argument is that the cutting of trees by mountain peoples leads to hydrological changes such as increased river flow speed, and more deposition of sediments eroded in the Himalayas causes or strengthens floods in the lowlands. However, some people argue that there is no direct link between human activities and floods in Bangladesh, as precipitation and runoff from the Himalayas may contribute less to the flooding than previously thought. While a more sustainable use of the mountain forests will not solve the flooding issue in Bangladesh, it is important for other reasons.

One of the main concerns is that the deforestation in the Himalayas may lead to the extinction of dozens of animal species and hundreds of plant species. Since the 1970s, an estimated 15 percent of forest cover has been lost in the Himalayas, and if current deforestation rates continue, two-thirds of the forests may be gone by the end of this century. The Himalayas are considered one of the world's biodiversity hotspots, with some experts saying that the watersheds in the Himalayas are biologically richer than the Amazon region[8].

In addition to flooding, Bangladesh also frequently suffers from tropical cyclones, which in addition to strong winds and storm surges cause tidal bores in the funnel-shaped northern portion of the Bay of Bengal[9]. A tidal bore occurs when the leading edge of a tide forms a wave

FIGURE 9.11 The Sundarbans, Bangladesh—The Sundarbans are a low-lying area of small islands, many of which are temporary chars, and mangroves near the mouth of the Ganges River. *Source:* Pixabay.

that travels against the river's direction of flow. Cyclones in Bangladesh are often associated with high numbers of casualties. It has been estimated that the 1970 Bhola cyclone claimed over 300,000 lives. More recently, the 1991 Bangladesh cyclone reached wind speeds of around 250 kilometers (155 miles) per hour and a storm surge of 6 meters (which was further amplified by the high tide). It killed over 138,000 people and 10 million became homeless as entire villages were inundated. Some of the offshore islands lost their entire populations.

Afghanistan is also highly vulnerable to natural disasters. Floods are common when the snow melts and heavy rains fall. Since Afghanistan is located in a seismically active region, earthquakes and associated landslides are common. In winter, avalanches are frequent. In 2008 Afghanistan experienced a ferocious blizzard. Temperatures dropped to –30°C (–22°F), and 3 meters (10 feet) of snow fell. Over 900 people died, and many more had to be treated for pneumonia and other respiratory infections.

Many people also suffered severe frostbite, as they were walking barefoot in the snow and lived in structures that offered little protection from the extreme cold. Over 100,000 sheep and goats, as well as over 300,000 cattle, also died.

The above discussion has focused on the multiple threats that the environment poses to South Asians, but the relationship is often the other way around: human activities comprise a significant and expanding threat to the environment. For instance, 29 of the 50 cities that the World Health Organization has ranked as having the world's worst air pollution (2010–2014 data) are in South Asia. Some of the region's most important rivers are severely polluted. The stunning diversity of wildlife is similarly endangered. A key challenge for South Asia then is to use the financial resources generated by its expanding economies to protect its natural resources. In the meantime, the continued growth of the region's population, as discussed in the next section, will make its environmental challenges even more difficult.

POPULATION PATTERNS AND TRENDS

Population Distribution and Growth

South Asia is home to three of the ten most populous countries in the world. With a population of over 1.3 billion India is the second largest country in the world (after China), and Pakistan (203 million) and Bangladesh (163 million) rank sixth and eighth. Afghanistan (33 million), Nepal (28 million), and Sri Lanka (21 million) also have fairly large populations. By contrast, Bhutan (800,000) and the Maldives (400,000) are among the least populous countries in the world.

Population density is lowest in Bhutan and Afghanistan and highest in the Maldives and Bangladesh (Fig. 9.12). In fact, Bangladesh is the tenth most densely settled country in the world. Remarkably, all the countries with higher densities (such as Monaco, Singapore, or Malta) are much smaller in population and area, so Bangladesh is the most densely settled country with a large population. The Maldives, conversely, have a small population which is squeezed onto a very small land area. The largest island in the archipelago is just 8 kilometers (5 miles) long and 3 kilometers (2 miles) wide.

Many parts in South Asia have very high physiological densities. For example, large portions of Pakistan have mountains and deserts, Nepal is very mountainous, and the Maldives have hardly any arable land as they consist of coral reefs. It is important to remember that the physiological density (like arithmetic density) describes the *average* population density for a country, so the population densities in the fertile river valleys and lowlands are even higher.

As previously mentioned, India is currently the second most populous country in the world. Its population has nearly quadrupled in size since the 1930s and currently represents about 15 percent of the world's population. Due to the rapid growth of its population, India was the first country to implement an official family planning program to slow population growth in the 1950s. Hospitals and health care facilities provided information about birth control, but there was no real push to convince people to limit the number of their children.

By the 1970s the Indian government understood that birth rates would only drop if the standard of living increased, so India integrated programs for development with those for family planning. One part of this was to educate the population about the problems associated with rapid population growth. Another part was providing sterilization, usually for women (sterilization of men is often interpreted as a threat to their masculinity, so there is a strong preference for the sterilization of women despite the associated health risks). Health workers were given incentives for carrying out sterilizations. This target-driven approach meant that women were often pressured into sterilizations or not properly informed about the risks. In the 1980s, the central government delegated family planning programs to state governments who provided family planning services through local health care facilities, designated hospital facilities for sterilizations, and promoted the use of intra-uterine devices. In the 1990s, India moved away from target-driven approaches.

Despite India's attempts to curb population growth, the population grew rapidly until the 1990s. In India, women marry young and therefore start having children early in their lives, often in their late teens or early twenties. In the 1990s, many women who agreed to sterilizations did so only after having four children of which at least two were sons. The strong desire to have sons is rooted in culture, but also seen as an economic necessity. Sons are expected to provide for ageing parents, so parents want at least two. Furthermore, in rural areas children, especially sons, are needed as workers. While girls contribute to the family when they are young (household chores or agricultural labor), their labor is lost to the family when they get married as they are then

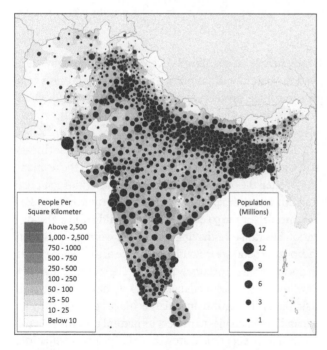

FIGURE 9.12 Population distribution in South Asia—The population distribution in South Asia is uneven. Notice the population clusters in the river plains and the much lower population densities in the desert and mountain areas. *Source:* GeoHive (www.geohive.com).

obliged to contribute to the husband's family. Traditionally, girls also require a **dowry**, a payment from the bride's family to the groom's family to cement the relationship between the two families. Technically, demanding dowries is no longer allowed but in practice it is still common; so many families see boys as economic assets and girls as an economic drain. The strong preference for sons has led to an imbalanced sex ratio, with significantly more men living in India than women (in most countries, by contrast, there are slightly more women than men). Part of the imbalance in India can be attributed to poor nutrition, poor health care, and high maternal mortality rates. However, sex-selective abortions (where female fetuses are aborted while male fetuses are carried to term) and female infanticide (killing female babies through neglect or direct action) are common. Human rights organizations estimate that female infanticides still number in the thousands every year.

Since the 1990s India's fertility rate has been decreasing. In the mid-1990s, India's total fertility rate was already lower than that of other South Asian countries. Today, India's fertility rate is reported as 2.3 children per woman, which is just above replacement level. Nevertheless, India is projected to experience continued population growth through the middle of the 21st century, and current projections call for India to pass China as the world's most populous country in 2021. Meanwhile Nepal and Bangladesh are also at 2.3, and Bhutan and Sri Lanka's rates are 2.1, so their population is stabilized. The Maldives are at 2.5 and Pakistan's population is growing rapidly due to a total fertility rate of 3.7. Afghanistan has a very high fertility rate of 5.3 (Fig. 9.13).

Gender, Health, and Poverty

As previously explained, there is a strong preference for sons in India. The same is true for the other Asian countries for similar reasons as described in previous sections. More generally, gender inequality is widespread in South Asia[10]. To cite just one example, women in South Asia face huge barriers to education. One major obstacle is that girls marry young, effectively ending their education (if they had a chance to attend school before). As a result, about half of the world's illiterate women live in South Asia. In India, where 72 percent of the population is literate, only 63 percent of women can read (compared to 81 percent of men) (Fig. 9.14 and Fig. 9.15). In Pakistan, the overall literacy rate is 56 percent (70 percent for males, 43 percent for females), and in Afghanistan the rate is 38 percent (53 percent for males, 24 percent for females). These are among the largest gender differentials in literacy in the world, especially in Afghanistan, where the Taliban forbids the education of girls. Men in Muslim countries are often educated in **madrassas**, schools that focus on teaching the

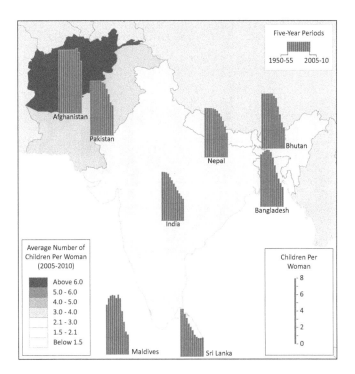

FIGURE 9.13 Total fertility rates in South Asia, 1950–2010—While fertility rates have dropped in most South Asian countries, they remain high in Afghanistan. *Source:* United Nations. Population Division. World Population Prospects 2012.

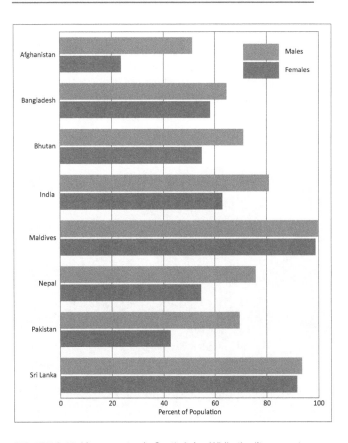

FIGURE 9.14 Literacy rates in South Asia—While the literacy rates for males and females are similar in the Maldives and Sri Lanka, many more women than men are illiterate in most South Asian countries. *Source:* World Bank.

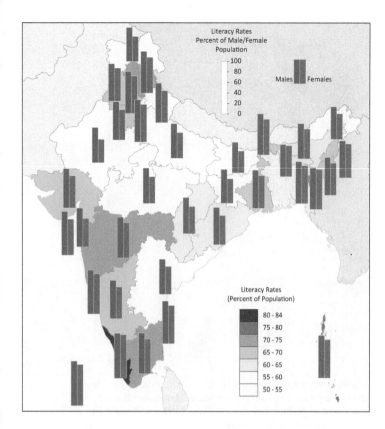

FIGURE 9.15 Literacy rates in India—Notice that the literacy gap between men and women is highest in the parts of India that have overall lower literacy rates. *Source:* Census of India.

Koran, so that their education is mostly a religious education. Differential access to education is not the only form of gender discrimination in South Asia. Women are also severely underrepresented in politics, even though several South Asian countries had or have female political leaders

FIGURE 9.16 Afghan women in burqas—A group of Afghan women, most of whom are wearing burqas, take part in a U.S.-run livelihood program that has taught them beekeeping. Each stands before beekeeping equipment given to graduates of the program. *Source:* Pixabay.

such as Indira Gandhi (1966–1977; 1980–84) in India or Benazir Bhutto (1988–1990; 1997–1999) in Pakistan (both were daughters of former prime ministers).

Women in South Asia also face other limitations, including limited freedom of movement. For example, in India only a third of the women are allowed to go to the market without permission of their husband, and only a quarter can visit friends and family when they want. In Pakistan, misinterpretations of the Koran are used to justify the subordination of women to men. As a result, there are high rates of domestic abuse, rape, and other violence against women. Forced marriages and child marriages (technically illegal for girls under the age of sixteen but often done much earlier) are common as well. In rural areas, young girls are sometimes forcibly married off to resolve feuds between different clans. Disputes over dowries can lead to dowry killings (estimated to number about 2,000 per year), and women who bring shame to their families through illicit relations with men (even when the "relationship" is being raped by the man) may fall victim to **honor killings**. Technically honor killings have been outlawed in Pakistan since 2004, but there are legal loopholes so that men carrying out the killings are not punished. Women face similar issues in Afghanistan. During the rule of the Taliban (1996–2001) women were treated worse than during any other time in Afghan history[11]. Women were forbidden from getting an education, working, leaving the house without a male guardian, or seeking medical help. They were also forced to wear the **burqa**, a tent-like dress that completely covered their bodies, including a mesh over their eyes (Fig. 9.16). If a woman committed adultery or was raped, she would be stoned to death. Since the fall of the Taliban, the situation has improved somewhat, but both Afghanistan and Pakistan are among the most dangerous and oppressive countries for women in the world.

Arranged marriage is a different dimension of gender relations in which South Asia is distinctive. Worldwide more than half of all marriages are arranged, but in India, the rate is close to 90 percent. In most cases, parents and other relatives decide on a suitable partner. Factors taken into consideration include religion, caste, culture (e.g. how conservative or liberal a family is), education and profession (especially to make sure that the future husband can provide for his wife), skin color and other physical attributes (e.g. fair-skinned women are preferred), and the horoscope. It has often been argued that the arranged marriage system works well, as less than 2 percent of marriages in India end in divorce (partly because getting a divorce is a long, complicated, difficult process). Even though the vast majority of Indians still marry partners chosen by their families, match-making now increasingly occurs via websites that take on the role of family members. Arranged marriages are also common in the other South Asian countries, but love matches are slowly becoming more accepted.

South Asia still faces some significant health challenges at least partly related to the gender inequality. For example, infant mortality rates in Bangladesh (38 per 1,000 births), India (40 per 1,000), and Bhutan (44 per 1,000) are fairly high, and they are very high in Pakistan (67) and Afghanistan (68); the comparable rates are 6 in the U.S. and 9 in China. About a third of maternal deaths worldwide occur in South Asia, and about half of all low birthweight babies are born in the region (a quarter of these weigh less than 2,500 grams or 5.5 pounds at birth). Unequal access to education, nutrition, and health care for women helps to perpetuate these problems.

More generally, South Asia's pervasive poverty is evident in problems that affect men, women, and children, including a relatively low life expectancy, high rates of malnutrition and anemia, and high incidence rates of diseases such as tuberculosis and HIV/AIDS. South Asia struggles with poor access to healthcare services, lack of sanitation, and great poverty, making it the second most vulnerable world region after sub-Saharan Africa. In regards to sanitation, South Asia has made considerable progress over the last two decades, but substantial challenges to providing clean drinking water and adequate sanitation remain. For example, a much smaller proportion of people in South Asia has access to toilets than elsewhere in the world. While the proportion of people practicing open defecation has fallen rapidly, it is estimated that more than half a billion people do not have a toilet. About a third of the schools in South Asia lack basic sanitation. The dearth of basic sanitation in South Asia imposes a great health and economic cost on the region as diseases related to poor sanitation are widespread.

The good news is that the proportion of people living in extreme poverty is falling in South Asia; it is estimated that about 15 percent of people lived below the poverty line of $1.90 a day in 2013, down from 56 percent in 1981. However, while the progress in reducing extreme poverty is impressive, South Asia is still home to a large share of the world's poorest people. Over the last few years, a substantial middle class has developed in India, but there are large disparities within the country and the region as a whole. Even though South Asia is more developed than Sub-Saharan Africa, it is believed that it has more people living in extreme poverty.

Migration Patterns

Over time, several major international migration flows out of South Asia can be identified: indentured labor to the Caribbean and Africa, pre-and post-colonial migrations to the U.K., labor migrations to the Middle East, and migrations to the United States, Canada, Australia, and New Zealand.

Between 1834 and 1918, Britain transported about 2 million **indentured laborers** from India to its other colonies.

Indentured labor developed because, after the abolition of slavery, the newly freed African slaves refused to work on the sugar plantations in the British West Indies. Indentured laborers (also called by the derogatory term *coolies*) were recruited to work for a fixed time (five years or more) on the sugar, cotton, and tea plantations in British colonies in the West Indies (e.g. Trinidad, Jamaica, and Guyana), Africa (e.g. Uganda, Kenya, and South Africa), and Southeast Asia (e.g. Malaya). Indentured laborers were supposed to receive free passage and wages, but they were often exploited. The indentured labor system left a legacy of a large Indian **diaspora** (a dispersed population), spread over parts of the tropics and subtropics[12].

Another colonial factor in the creation of that same diaspora was the British East India Company's recruitment in India of crewmen for their ships. Since their passage back to India was not paid, many did not have a choice but to settle in Britain. Some Indians, especially domestic servants and nannies, also accompanied their wealthy British employers back to Britain, and some returning British soldiers brought Indian-born women with them. After India's independence, Indian migration to the United Kingdom increased. Some Indian workers were recruited to fill the labor shortages that resulted from World War II. Others arrived in the 1950s and 1960s to work in industrial jobs in the British Midlands, and in later decades many have found jobs with the U.K.'s National Health Service and in other service industries (Fig. 9.17).

In recent decades, the Middle East has been a nearer destination than the U.K. and its former colonies for millions of South Asian migrants. While some South Asian migrant workers in the Gulf States (e.g. United Arab Emirates, Saudi Arabia, and Qatar) are highly skilled professionals and enjoy a high standard of living in their host countries, the vast majority are low-skilled workers employed in construction and domestic work who live and work in difficult conditions. Large-scale labor migrations to the Gulf States began in the early 1970s. Increasing oil prices led to a rapid rise in the standard of living in the Gulf States, resulting in a demand for improved infrastructure and domestic help. By the early 21st century the workforce in the Gulf States consisted mostly of foreigners. For example, almost 90 percent of the workforce in the United Arab Emirates consists of migrant workers, and most of these are South Asians. As a result, almost half of the entire population of the UAE is South Asian. Both construction workers and domestic workers are frequently exploited and abused. Much of the exploitation is attributed to a sponsorship system that gives employers a lot of leverage over their workers. For example, under this system, workers cannot change employers or leave employment. The employers, by contrast, can cancel work contracts at any time and often keep their employees' passports to prevent them from leaving.

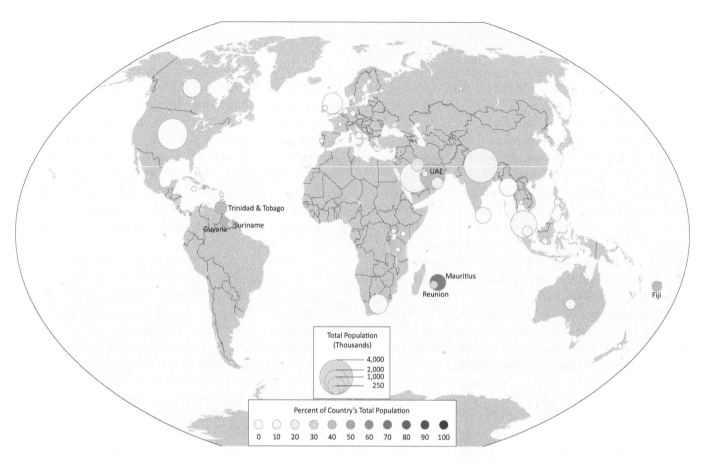

FIGURE 9.17 The Indian diaspora—People of Indian origin are found in every major part of the world except the Russian Realm and East Asia. They comprise 68 percent of Mauritius' population and about 40 percent in Guyana, Trinidad & Tobago, Fiji, and the United Arab Emirates. *Source:* Nonresident Indians Online.

In the last few decades, large numbers of South Asians have migrated to the United States and other English-speaking countries such as Canada, Australia, and New Zealand. In the United States, the passage of the 1965 Immigration and Nationality Act opened the door to migrants from Asia. Numerically, Indians are the second most important group of immigrants in the United States after Mexicans. Like other Asian migrants in the United States, South Asians tend to be more highly educated, are more likely employed in professional jobs, and have higher incomes than the general population. South Asians are the fastest growing population group in the United States.

The large number of Indians leaving India for education and work in rich (mostly English-speaking) countries, resulted in a large-scale brain drain. Tens of thousands of Indians who went abroad for their studies preferred to stay in their host countries because of the better job opportunities and higher standard of living. However, while large numbers of Indians are still going abroad, more and more are returning home after some years as more attractive employment opportunities have become available in India. Other reasons for their return are the desire to be with their families, obligations to take care of ageing family members, or feeling more comfortable in their native country. This relatively new phenomenon is called the reverse brain drain (emphasizing that highly educated people are returning to India and boosting its economy rather than contributing long-term to the country they had migrated to before) or **brain exchange** (emphasizing the connections that migrants create between their two countries).

While the previous examples described largely voluntary migration flows, other people were forced to leave their homes. As described in more detail later in this chapter, the partition of India in 1947 into a predominantly Hindu state (today's India) and a Muslim state (today's Pakistan and Bangladesh) resulted in one of the largest migration flows in human history as millions of Muslims migrated from India into what is now Pakistan and Bangladesh, and Hindus and Sikhs moved in the opposite direction. Even though Hindus, Muslims, and Sikhs had lived together in the same land for hundreds of years, the partition resulted in an outbreak of violence, especially in the border regions that included massacres, abductions, arson, and sexual violence. Ultimately over 17 million people migrated and at least 1 million people died. For Indians, Pakistanis, and Bangladeshis the partition is the pivotal historical event in 20th century South Asia, an event that brings painful memories and clouds the relationship between these countries to this day.

Although the population transfer between Pakistan and India is unparalleled in the region in terms of the number of people affected and the brutality that accompanied it, there are also more current examples of South Asians having to leave their native countries. Afghans have the longest history of fleeing their home country and seeking refuge in other countries. The first major refugee wave developed after the 1979 Soviet invasion of Afghanistan, with most refugees fleeing to neighboring Iran and Pakistan. When the Soviets withdrew from Afghanistan, some refugees returned to Afghanistan, but a new refugee wave developed when the Taliban took over Afghanistan in 1996. A third wave developed during the War on Terror after 2001. At the peak of the Afghan refugee crisis, about 6 million Afghans lived in Pakistan and Iran. For over three decades Afghanistan produced more refugees than any other country, and even today Afghans are the second largest refugee group after Syrians (Fig. 9.18).

Today it is believed that about 3 million Afghan refugees reside in Iran. Even though many of them have been born in Iran, they are still considered citizens of Afghanistan. Iran originally practiced an open-door policy towards Afghan refugees and provided them with support, but more recently, Iran has limited access to services such as education and tried to encourage the repatriation of Afghan refugees. Similarly, Pakistan has repatriated Afghans since 2001, but over 2 million are believed to be in Pakistan to this day, continuing to impose a heavy economic and financial burden on the country. Since the Taliban attacked a school in the Pakistani city of Peshawar in 2015, Pakistan increasingly sees the presence of Afghan refugees as a security threat. While Pakistan would like to have the Afghans return to Afghanistan, Afghanistan is struggling to meet the needs of the returning refugees. A solution to this refugee crisis must therefore balance the needs of both countries.

A less well known refugee flow and one that has a surprising origin is the flight of people from Southern Bhutan. The small Himalayan country has become famous in recent years for its promotion of "gross national happiness" (discussed below), but in the 1990s, over 100,000 southern Bhutanese of Nepali ancestry fled to refugee camps in Nepal after Bhutan passed a new citizenship law. This new law denied the refugees citizenship based on their ancestry and took away people's right to work or own land, so they had to leave Bhutan. After attempts to repatriate the refugees to

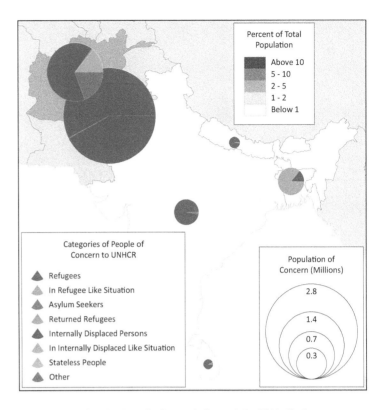

FIGURE 9.18 Distribution of refugees in South Asia, 2014—Notice the high number of refugees and other people of concern in Afghanistan and Pakistan. *Source:* United Nations High Commissioner for Refugees.

Bhutan failed, most have now been resettled to the United States, Australia, Canada, and New Zealand. Despite the large number of people affected, the Bhutanese refugee situation has faded from public consciousness.

With the world's spotlight currently on the plight of Syrian refugees, another recent refugee crisis in South Asia is often overlooked as well. As described later in this chapter, the civil war in Sri Lanka between the Sri Lankan government and the Tamil Tigers resulted in about 145,000 refugees and 300,000 internally displaced people. Most of the refugees fled to India, especially to the southern state of Tamil Nadu, where about 60,000 Sri Lankans live in refugee camps. However, more recently, Sri Lankan Tamils who are unwelcome in India and face persecution in Sri Lanka, have tried to reach Australia in boats.

Urbanization and Cities

Urbanization rates in South Asia are low compared to most other world regions. Pakistan and Bhutan are both at about 39 percent, India and Bangladesh at 33 percent, Afghanistan at 27 percent, and Nepal and Sri Lanka below 20 percent

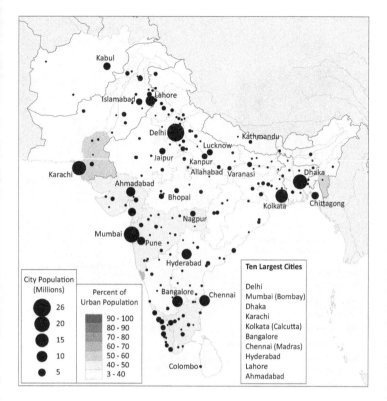

FIGURE 9.19 Urbanization levels in South Asia—Notice that the largest cities are located in Pakistan, India, and Bangladesh. Despite a large urban population, South Asia has a relatively low urbanization rate. *Source:* United Nations. Population Division. World Urbanization Prospects 2014; Census of India.

(Fig. 9.19). These low percentages of urban populations obscure two factors. First, urbanization has progressed significantly in South Asia. For example, Bhutan had a rate of only 4 percent in 1960, Bangladesh 5 percent, and Afghanistan 8 percent. Second, in absolute numbers, South Asian cities are growing very fast. Between 2001 and 2011 South Asia's urban population grew by 130 million and is expected to rise by about 250 million by 2030. Third, even though urbanization rates are low, South Asia is home to several large cities. These cities struggle with providing their inhabitants with adequate housing, public services, and urban infrastructure. South Asia's urbanization has been described as messy because cities are unplanned and chaotic, and the growth of South Asia's cities has resulted in vast slum areas. According to estimates, over 130 million South Asians live in substandard settlements.

South Asia currently has six cities with metropolitan populations of 10 million or more: Delhi, India (26 million); Mumbai, India (21 million); Dhaka, Bangladesh (18 million); Karachi, Pakistan (17 million); and Kolkata, India (15 million) are the biggest. Lahore, Pakistan and several other Indian cities (Bangalore, Chennai) are also considered megacities. Many of these cities also have very high percentages of people living in slums. According to estimates, 40 percent of the inhabitants in Dhaka live in slums, about 50 percent in the Indian capital Delhi, and up to 60 percent in Mumbai.

In many Indian cities **pavement dwellers** are a common sight[13]. The term refers to people who live on the sidewalks of cities by building simple shelters that use the walls or fences of existing buildings as part of the structure they make from cardboard, wood, plastic sheets, or cloth (the settlements are also called hutments). Many pavement dwellers work as day laborers and cannot even afford the cheapest housing and therefore end up sleeping, cooking, and washing on the street. Many families have to share a public water pump and a public toilet. Most pavement dwellers have been on the street for two or three decades with little hope of moving to better housing. Most Indian cities do not have well developed policies to address the problems of slums and pavement dwellers. While Indian cities offer more and more amenities for the middle and upper classes, the poor are left behind. The relocation of the poor to better areas and the redevelopment of slums cannot keep pace with the high numbers of people living in substandard dwellings. The United Nations estimates that over a quarter of all slum dwellers in the world live in South Asia, and the vast majority of those in India.

Many South Asian cities could be described in detail, but the four examples that follow demonstrate the wide range of urban experiences in large South Asian cities—the great contrasts of wealth and poverty in Mumbai, the capital functions of the Pakistani cities of Karachi and Islamabad, and the urban cultural heritage in Kathmandu.

Mumbai (previously known as Bombay) is the capital city of the Indian state of Maharashtra, located on India's western coast. Originally it was located on seven islands, but land reclamation projects have connected the islands over time. Mumbai is not only the second most populous city in India, but also its financial, commercial, and entertainment capital, as well as the richest city in India. Due to the economic opportunities and high standard of living, Mumbai attracts migrants from all over India and has become a melting pot of different cultures. Architecturally the city is also diverse. British colonialism left a legacy of Gothic Revival buildings reflecting various European influences such as German gables and Swiss timbering, but it also reflects traditional Indian features. The main train station built during the British period is a UNESCO World Heritage Site. However, Mumbai has another side as well: It suffers from widespread poverty, poor public health and education levels, and substandard housing. As an example of the sharp disparities in the city, Antilia, a $2 billion dollar private skyscraper owned and occupied by a single extremely wealthy family (Fig. 9.20) lies just 12 kilometers (7 miles) from Dharavi, a slum area home to an estimated 700,000 poor people crowded at densities of up to 18,000 people per acre (Fig. 9.21).

FIGURE 9.20 Antilia Tower in Mumbai—Antilia, the 27-story residence of an Indian billionaire, is one of the world's most expensive homes but it lies just a short distance away from extensive slums in Mumbai. *Source:* Wikimedia Commons.

FIGURE 9.21 Dharavi settlement in Mumbai—Dharavi is a vast squatter settlement in Mumbai. Notice, however, that many homes have satellite dishes. *Source:* Wikimedia Commons.

After Pakistan's independence, the coastal city of Karachi became the first capital of the country. Today, the city is one of the largest cities in the world (and the second largest city in the Muslim world after Dhaka). Karachi is Pakistan's economic center and most cosmopolitan and religiously and socially liberal city. In the 1960s, Islamabad was purposely built as the country's new capital city. Islamabad is an example of a **forward capital**. It is located close to the contested territory of Kashmir in order to increase Pakistan's control over the region. Furthermore, its name

Islamabad is also a political statement as it is located close to Hindu India. The design of Islamabad is based on a detailed plan that divided the city into eight functional regions (e.g. administrative, industrial, and residential) and includes several universities, large parks, as well the Faisal Mosque—the largest mosque in South Asia, which is named for King Faisal of Saudi Arabia who paid for its construction. Islamabad is mostly inhabited by well-off people and is considered one of the safest cities in South Asia.

Kathmandu, the capital city of Nepal, is the largest city in the Himalayan region. It is located at an elevation of about 1,400 meters (4,600 feet) in the bowl-shaped Kathmandu Valley. Kathmandu has a multiethnic population and is the cultural and economic center of the country. As the gateway to the Nepalese Himalayas, the city has become an important tourist destination, but it also attracts visitors with its cultural riches. Kathmandu was once located along an ancient trade route between India and Tibet, so its architecture is a blend of local and imported cultural traditions. The city's architectural treasures are now a UNESCO World Heritage Site, but the stunning sites are surrounded by serious environmental problems. Kathmandu frequently experiences temperature inversions that trap air pollution. Factories pour waste products into rivers, and most homes are not connected to the sewage system. Many people also deposit household trash in rivers.

LANGUAGE AND RELIGION

Linguistic Patterns

India is known for its great linguistic diversity (Fig. 9.22). Over 400 languages are spoken in India; 24 of these have more than 1 million speakers, and another 114 more than 10,000. India's languages belong to two major linguistic families: Indo-European and Dravidian, spoken by about 75 and 20 percent of the population, respectively.

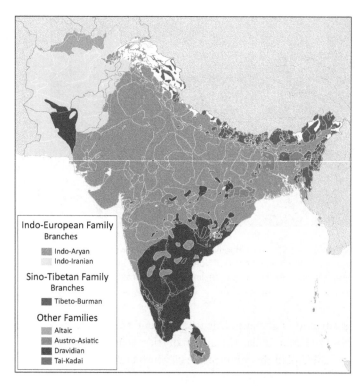

FIGURE 9.22 Distribution of major linguistic families in South Asia—Most languages in the northern part of the region belong to the Indo-European family, while the Dravidian languages are dominant in the south. *Source:* World Language Mapping System.

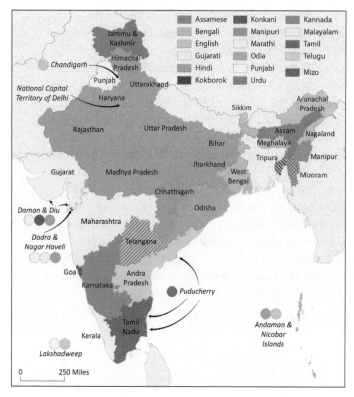

FIGURE 9.23 Official languages in India—Hindi is the official language in several Indian states, but many states have their own official languages.

The Northern Indian languages evolved from Old Indo-Aryan languages such as Sanskrit. The development of distinctive languages was due to contact with speakers of other languages through trade or conflict. For example, Hindi is strongly influenced by Persian and Arabic. By about 1000 CE, Hindi, Marathi, Punjabi, and Bengali had emerged as separate languages. The origin of Dravidian languages, as well their development over time, is less clear. The most important Dravidian languages are Telugu, Tamil, Kannada, and Malayalam. The languages spoken in India and other South Asian countries have distinctive scripts. Urdu (the language of Pakistan identical to Hindi in India) and sometimes Kashmiri, Sindhi, and Punjabi are written in modified Arabic script. All other Indian scripts are native to India. Brahmic scripts are used to write several Indian and Nepali languages such as Hindi, Marathi, Bengali, Assamese, and Nepali.

Hindi is the official language of the Indian government, and English continues to be used for official purposes, but an individual state can adopt a regional language as the official language of that state (Fig. 9.23). As a result, the Indian Constitution recognizes 23 official languages. For example, Hindi is the official language in nine states including Uttar Pradesh, Bihar, and Rajasthan as well as the National Capital Territory of Delhi. Tamil is the official language in Tamil Nadu, Puducherry, and the Nicobar Islands (Fig. 9.24).

Since both Pakistan and Bangladesh were once part of British India, English is important in both countries. The Pakistani Constitution was originally written in English and later translated into local languages. English is also

FIGURE 9.24 A multilingual road sign near Chennai—A road sign on Chennai-Bangalore highway in Tamil Nadu state shows the different forms of writing for two of the main languages in the country, including Tamil at the top and Hindi in the middle. *Source:* Wikimedia Commons.

widely used in the education system and spoken by the elite. The second official language of Pakistan is Urdu. Despite its status as a national language of Pakistan, less than 10 percent of Pakistanis speak Urdu as their mother tongue; the vast majority speaks it as their second language. The Pakistani government is promoting the use of Urdu to foster national solidarity. The most important regional languages of Pakistan are Punjabi, Sindhi, and Baluchi (each associated with particular provinces in Pakistan: Punjab, Sindh, and Baluchistan) and Pashto, the official language in neighboring Afghanistan. Since Pakistan is a Muslim country, Arabic also plays an important role as religious texts are taught in that language. In Bangladesh, Bengali is the official language, with virtually all people, regardless of their native language, speaking the language fluently; the smaller size and much flatter terrain of Bangladesh favor greater cultural homogeneity than in mountainous Pakistan. English has no official status in Bangladesh, but is widely used in government, law, the media, and education.

Religious Patterns

India is characterized by great religious diversity (Fig. 9.25). In addition to several Indian religions (Hinduism, Jainism, and Sikhism), India is also home to substantial numbers of Christians and Muslims. The most important religion in India (as well as in neighboring Nepal) is Hinduism. Hinduism is considered to be the oldest religion in the world, as its practices date back several thousand years. It is closely related to the other Indian religions but also has some unique features that sometimes clash with the views of these other religions. Most notable among these is the division of Hindu society into hereditary social classes called castes (explained in more detail later in this chapter), while the other religions emphasize that all humans are equal. Hinduism defies an easy definition because there is such a great diversity in beliefs, practices, and rituals within the religion. This is largely because Hinduism, as opposed to many other religions, does not have a single founder, a single scripture, or a single teaching. Therefore, Hinduism is often described as a way of life rather than a single religion.

Hinduism originated in the Indus River Valley in modern-day Pakistan, though it has little influence in the valley today. Most Hindus believe in a supreme god as well as a multitude of deities that represent the supreme god's various qualities and forms (Fig. 9.26). Brahman is the supreme godly force present within all things, and accordingly early Hinduism was called Brahmanism. Hinduism recognizes three main gods: Brahma (not to be confused

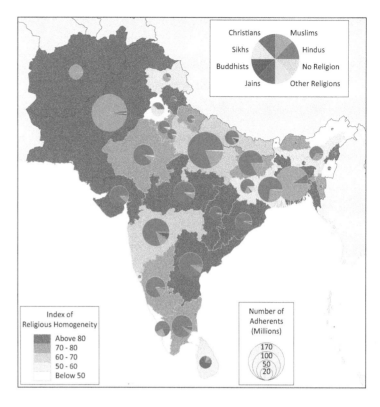

FIGURE 9.25 Religious affiliation of people in South Asia—While Afghanistan, Pakistan, and Bangladesh are predominantly Muslim countries, Hindu India has large numbers of Muslims as well. *Source:* Association of Religious Data Archives; Census of India.

with Brahman) is the creator god, Vishnu is the preserver of the universe, and Shiva destroys and recreates the world. Each god has particular characteristics. For example, Shiva is believed to have strong passions, leading him to extreme behaviors. Similarly, each god is presented with particular

FIGURE 9.26 A Hindu temple in Southern India—Hindu temples, like this one devoted to Vishnu, tend to be colorful, exuberant places. *Source:* Wikimedia Commons.

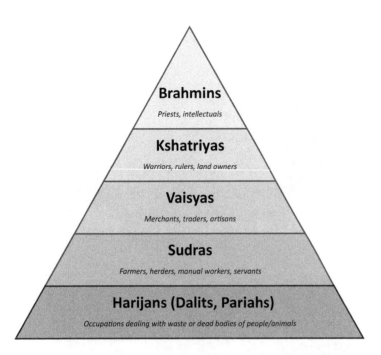

FIGURE 9.27 The Hindu caste system—The different castes are tied to specific occupations.

features. Shiva is represented as a man with a blue face. He has a third eye (representing wisdom), a cobra necklace (representing power), and carries a trident to represent the three functions of the Hindu triumvirate (three deities). As in other Indian religions, one of Hinduism's core beliefs is the existence of a cycle of birth, death, and rebirth, with the rebirth determined by one's karma (one's actions in a previous life). Most Hindus follow a common set of values known as dharma. Dharma, translated as "code of conduct" or "duties," is discussed in the *vedas*, the sacred Hindu texts written in Sanskrit. Dharma means that all people have to behave virtuously, but what is considered virtuous behavior is not identical for all people, as people have different duties depending on their age, gender, and social position.

Hindus celebrate many festivals, of which Diwali, the Festival of Lights, is the most well known. Diwali extends over five days. Because the festival (which is also celebrated by Jains and Sikhs) involves lights, fireworks, and sweets, it is beloved by children. It symbolizes the victory of good over evil and light over darkness. Hanuman Jayanti is a popular festival celebrating the monkey god, Hanuman. A sacred text is recited and offerings are made to the monkey god. In many Indian cities, colorful processions take place where people carry idols of the Hanuman or wear masks and tails to imitate the god.

Communal worship is not practiced in Hinduism; instead Hindus worship individually at a shrine at home (which can be a dedicated room or simply a statue of a deity) or in a temple and make offerings of water, fruit,

flowers, and incense to the deity. Some Hindus also worship a sacred thread made from cotton for the priests and different materials for people of other castes. Hindus carry out three different kinds of rituals: small daily rituals involving offerings at the home shrine, rituals at festivals, and pilgrimages. For example, every twelve years, millions of people gather in Allahabad (at the confluence of the Ganges and Jumna rivers) for ritual bathing, which is believed to wash their sins away.

As previously explained, dharma (duties) is an important concept in Hinduism, and it is also at the core of the Hindu **caste** system that divides Hindus into hereditary hierarchical social groups[14]. It is believed that the system has been in existence for over 3,000 years. The system recognizes four main categories: the Brahmins (priests), Kshatriyas (warriors and rules), Vaisyas (merchants), and Sudras (workers). These main castes are further divided into *jatis* according to occupations, which are split into thousands of sub-castes according to family lineage and place of birth. For centuries caste has dictated all aspects of a Hindu's life. There was a strict segregation of the castes, especially in rural areas, with people of different castes living in different communities and only marrying within their own caste (Fig. 9.27).

Some people are considered to be so low in the social hierarchy that they are not part of the caste system. In the past, they have frequently been called "untouchables", a term that reflects their outcast status. The untouchables had to do all the dirty work such as dealing with sewage, working with animal skins, or anything else that is associated with pollution or disease. Brahmins were considered to be absolutely pure, so they had to avoid contact with untouchables to preserve this purity. For example, some Brahmins felt obligated to take a bath if they were touched by the shadow of an untouchable. Even today, there are reports of untouchables having to sit on the floor of their classroom or being forbidden from using communal wells for fear that they may pollute the water. Mahatma Gandhi, who opposed the caste system, called the untouchables *Harijans* (children of god). Nowadays, they call themselves **Dalits** ("those who have not been broken," or "the oppressed").

The system has often been criticized for allowing higher caste people to oppress lower class people. Mahatma Gandhi wanted to abolish the caste system, and India's constitution bans discrimination based on caste. In an attempt to improve the situation of the disadvantaged, the Indian government implemented quotas for employment and places in schools. The quotas reserve spaces not just for Dalits but also for other disadvantaged castes and tribal groups (poor, often isolated indigenous populations, such as the sixteen different tribes found in a small, mountainous state called Nagaland on the border with Myanmar). More than 70 percent of India's population may be in one of these categories. The quota system has paradoxical effects. On the one hand, India's status as the world's largest democracy gives the hundreds of millions people in these categories significant political power. On the other hand, the Indian government's plan to right historical wrongs through job quotas for the disadvantaged keeps social stratification alive.

In recent decades the importance of caste has declined somewhat, especially in cities where the social and spatial separation that defines the caste system is less pronounced. It is more common for urban Indians of different castes to interact with one another, live in the same neighborhoods, and intermarry. However, there are still reports of caste-related violence including homes being burned and even murder. Many Dalits have converted to Buddhism in hopes of escaping the oppression they experience.

Sikhism was founded in the Punjab region in the 16th century. To this day, most of the world's 20 million Sikhs live in the Punjab, which is split between India and Pakistan. Sikhism is a monotheistic religion in which God is believed to have no shape or gender. Similar to other Indian religions such as Hinduism and Jainism, Sikhs believe that there is a cycle of birth, life, death, and rebirth, and that the quality of life depends on karma, or how a person behaved in the previous life. Therefore, Sikhism emphasizes that it is not enough to carry out rituals; it is more important to actually do good things, such as treat everyone equally, live an honest life, work hard, be generous toward others, help others, and keep God in heart and mind at all times. Sikhs avoid the five vices: lust, greed, anger, pride, and attachment to things. Sikhs can be identified by the five Ks: *kesh* (uncut hair), *kara* (steel bracelet), *kanga* (wooden comb), *kachera* (cotton underwear), and *kirpan* (sword). Sikhs worship at *gurdwaras*, which do not have a particular architectural style, but always contain the Granth Sahib, the Sikh scripture (which Sikhs consider a living guru and therefore respect the same way they would a human being) on a throne, under a canopy, with a Sikh flag on top of the building (Fig. 9.28). People from all faiths are welcome in *gurdwaras* and are invited to eat vegetarian meals there. Many *gurdwaras* also have a library, a nursery, and meeting rooms. Sikhism is sometimes falsely described as a combination of Islam and Hinduism. It shares some commonalities with both religions but also differs in some crucial ways. For example, as opposed to Hindus, Sikhs do not worship multiple gods or practice the caste system. On the contrary, Sikhism considers all human beings equal regardless of caste, race, or gender.

FIGURE 9.28 The Golden Temple in Amritsar, India—This temple is the holiest site in the world for Sikhs. *Source:* Pixabay.

Several decades ago, a Sikh nationalist movement wanted to create an independent Sikh state called Khalistan, resulting in violent clashes between supporters of the movement and the Indian army. The Indian army damaged the Golden Temple at Amritsar (the holiest *gurdwara* of Sikhism) and desecrated it. Indian Prime Minister Indira Gandhi was assassinated by her Sikh body guards, and thousands of Sikhs were killed in the following riots. By now, the militant Khalistan movement has weakened considerably, and even though some demands for an independent Sikh homeland remain, the situation in Punjab is now largely peaceful.

Over 4 million people in India are adherents of **Jainism** (and 6 to 7 million worldwide, with most followers outside India in Europe and North America). The core belief of this ancient Indian religion is that all living beings, people, animals, and plants, have souls. Therefore, they should be treated with respect and compassion. Because of the concern for all living beings and the universe itself, Jains are strict vegetarians, committed to non-violence, and try to minimize their use of resources as much as possible. Mahatma Gandhi was a great admirer of Jainism and adopted the Jain principles of compassion for all living beings: self-discipline, vegetarianism, and tolerance for people of different faiths.

Zoroastrianism or Parsiism was founded in ancient Iran by the Prophet Zarathustra (or Zoroaster) about 3,500 years ago. It is believed that Zoroastrianism is the world's oldest monotheistic religion. Zoroastrianism was once one of the major religions in the world but is now one of the smallest with about 200,000 followers. Today, the Zoroastrians are split into two groups: the Iranian Zoroastrians and the Indian Parsis, who are descendants of Zoroastrians

FIGURE 9.29 A Buddhist statue in Sri Lanka—Many of the tallest statues in the world depict the Buddha, including this 49 meter (160 foot) tall statue in central Sri Lanka, a predominantly Buddhist country. *Source:* Stefan Fischer/Henrik Watzke.

Mumbai. Fire is of great importance to Zoroastrians, and no ceremony or ritual takes place without a sacred fire. Zoroastrians pray multiple times per day facing the sun, a fire, or another source of light. Sacred fires are maintained in fire temples and never extinguished. In the West, Zoroastrians are probably most known for their tradition of laying out the dead in special towers so that they are exposed to the sun and eaten by vultures.

In addition to the Indian religions described above, India is also home to a significant number of followers of Islam, Christianity, and Buddhism. Even after the 1947 partition of British India and the large-scale population transfer, large numbers of Muslims remain in modern-day India. In fact, today Islam is the second largest religion in India, with over 170 million people (over 14 percent of the population) following this religion. Islam first reached India through Arab traders in the seventh century in coastal areas. With about 10 percent of the world's Muslims, India now has the third largest Muslim population after Indonesia and Pakistan. With close to 28 million followers, Christianity is the third largest religion in India. Roman Catholicism was introduced to India by Jesuits, who founded numerous Christian schools and hospitals. Later missionaries brought Protestantism to India and translated the Bible into Indian languages. Today Christians form a significant minority in India.

Even though Buddhism arose in what is now India, the religion's importance declined in India for centuries, with the exception of the Himalayan region. However, more recently, Buddhism is reemerging due to the conversion of lower caste Indians to Buddhism and due to the significant numbers of Buddhist Tibetan exiles (including the Dalai Lama himself) living in India (Fig. 9.29).

Across the entire South Asian region, close to two-thirds of people are Hindus (mostly in India and Nepal as well as 25 percent of the population in Bhutan), close to one-third are Muslim (Afghanistan, Pakistan, and Bangladesh are Muslim countries, but as previously explained India also has a large Muslim population), with other religions such as Buddhism (mostly Sri Lanka and Bhutan), Christianity, and Sikhism accounting for roughly 2 percent each.

who fled from Iran in search of religious freedom. It is estimated that the population of Parsis in India may dwindle to fewer than 30,000 people in the near future due to the very low birth rate and the high age of the community. Parsis are known for their high education levels (their literacy rate is 98 percent) and almost all live in urban areas, especially in

POLITICAL ORGANIZATION OF SPACE

Precolonial India

The Indus Valley civilization arose in India in about 2500 BCE (the third major civilization in the world after Mesopotamia and Egypt). People in the Indus Valley practiced agriculture, raised cattle, used bronze tools, spun cotton, and traded with other civilizations. Increasingly people lived in cities, of which Harappa (which gave the Indus

Valley civilization its other name: Harappan civilization) and Mohenjo-Daro were the most important ones. The cities consisted of brick buildings lining streets, laid out in a grid pattern. They had a citadel as well as granaries, and provided running water, a sewage system, and garbage collection. Around 1700 BCE the Indus Valley civilization declined, possibly due to climate change or the Indus River changing course. People moved back into rural areas, and the Indus Valley civilization eventually vanished. It was not rediscovered until the 20th century.

After 1500 BCE Aryans from central Asia migrated into the area. Originally the Aryans were nomadic, but they eventually settled and a hierarchical society evolved, with the Aryans forming the elite (priests, rulers, warriors, and merchants) and the conquered people being laborers and slaves. Hinduism evolved at that time, as did the caste system that was based on these social hierarchies. Over time, India once again became a highly civilized society with people living in cities.

Over the next few millennia, several empires rose and fell in India. One was the Mauryan Empire (fourth century to second century BCE) in Northern India, which stretched from the Hindu Kush in the west to the Bay of Bengal in the east. The Mauryans were successful traders and accumulated great wealth. The greatest Mauryan leader, Asoka, pacified the empire, converted to Buddhism, and made it the religion of the empire. He also built public infrastructure such as wells and hospitals. Asoka's seal (showing four lions) later became India's national emblem. After a period of chaos, the Guptas united India again and made it prosperous. The Gupta era (early fourth century to late sixth century CE) produced great advances in the sciences, literature, and medicine and is known as India's Golden Age. The Muslim Mughal Empire controlled vast areas in South Asia by the late 17th century and brought Persian influences to the region. During this time, one of India's most recognizable buildings was erected: the Taj Mahal. After a series of invasions from Persia and Afghanistan, the Mughal Empire declined. European powers took advantage of the situation. The Portuguese had already begun to import spices from India in the 15th century, but in the 17th century the British Empire took control of India.

European Colonial Rule

Until 1858 British possessions in India were administered by the British East India Company. In 1600 Queen Elizabeth of England granted a royal charter to the company to organize the trade in cotton, tea, and indigo with India. Within a few decades, it had established trading posts in Bombay

(now Mumbai), Calcutta (now Kolkata), and Madras (now Chennai). The Company's role expanded from an economic one to a political one when King Charles II granted it the rights to acquire and control more territory.

After an insurrection of Indians against the British East India Company (Indians resented the exploitation by the Company as well as the influx of cheap clothes manufactured in Britain from raw materials that had been grown in India), which came to be known as the First War of Indian Independence, the British government gained direct control over Indian territories. British colonial rule over India (the British Raj) lasted from 1858 to 1947 and included present-day India, Pakistan, and Bangladesh. Nepal, Bhutan, and the Maldives were under British influence as well, but were not formally part of the Raj. The Raj included areas directly administered by Britain, as well as princely states governed by rulers on behalf of the British crown. Britain followed the divide and rule policy, pitting one Indian ruler against another, in order to exercise control over India.

Over time, however, Indians gained more control over India. Mahatma Gandhi led the peaceful resistance movement against British rule. The 1930 Salt March in protest of the British controlling the salt trade became the most famous example of Gandhi's civil disobedience against the British. Growing popular resistance undermined the legitimacy of the Raj. External factors also played a role, especially the exhaustion of British human and financial resources during World War II. Britain granted India independence in 1947.

British colonial rule over India brought both negatives and positives. For Britain, India was the "jewel in the crown" as it was a source of great wealth for Britain. India benefited from the construction of transportation infrastructure (roads and railways) and communication systems (telephone and mail) that were built under the British, as well as from the transfer of modern industrial machinery (for manufacturing cars, steam engines, guns, vaccines, etc.). Hygiene, sanitation, and medical services improved under the British. The implementation of the British education system, transfer of ideas about science, medicine, and technology, and the widespread use of English helped the country develop. In modern times India has an advantage over other countries because of the widespread use of the English language, which has helped India attract many call centers and other support functions for global companies in India. It also facilitated the development of high-tech jobs. On the other hand, Britain ruined India's native economy by forcing India to import goods from Britain and export raw materials for little money, making the country dependent on Britain. The colonizers also encouraged the farmers to grow cash crops, resulting in widespread starvation among the poor who could not afford the higher prices.

Partitions

The British Raj was dissolved by the Indian Independence Act in 1947. Since Muslim leaders felt that they were not adequately represented in India, they called for the creation of a separate Muslim state upon India's independence. Hindu leaders, such as Mahatma Gandhi and Jawaharlal Nehru, had wanted to keep India as a unified country. In the end, the Act stated that two independent countries, India and Pakistan (then consisting of West Pakistan, which is modern-day Pakistan, and East Pakistan, which is modern-day Bangladesh) would be created (Fig. 9.30). The partition displaced over 17 million people (7.3 million Muslims moved from India to West Pakistan and 1.3 million to East Pakistan; 5.3 million Hindus moved from West Pakistan to India and 3.6 from East Pakistan to India). The large-scale population transfers were accompanied by massive violence and resulted in a refugee crisis. The violent nature of the partition resulted in hostilities between India and Pakistan that continue to this day.

In 1947 Pakistan became the first modern state that has ever been created to separate a religious group (Muslims) from others. India, by contrast, had a Hindu majority but was multi-religious and secular-minded. Furthermore, India consisted of a single territory, while Pakistan was split into West Pakistan and East Pakistan separated by 1,600 kilometers (1,000 miles) of Indian territory, with the capital Karachi (and later Islamabad) located in West Pakistan. West Pakistan was politically and economically dominant, but East Pakistan had a larger population and had to transfer resources to West Pakistan. There were also cultural differences: West Pakistan was religiously more conservative and overwhelmingly Muslim, while East Pakistan (Bengal) was religiously more liberal and more mixed (15 percent were Hindu). Urdu was the main language in West Pakistan, but most people spoke Bengali in East Pakistan. The tense situation boiled over when a cyclone (the Bhola cyclone mentioned earlier in this chapter) cost 300,000 lives and West Pakistan failed to provide sufficient disaster relief. Violence soon broke out as East Pakistan rose up against West Pakistan. In 1971 East Pakistan gained independence after a brutal war, in which India fought on East Pakistan's side (aiming to weaken its adversary Pakistan), and became Bangladesh.

Political Instability

Even today, ethnic and religious conflicts continue to plague South Asia. Some have lasted for decades, and even though several have officially ended, tensions still remain.

For a long time, Afghanistan has been entangled in the conflicts of other powers[15]. In the 19th century, Afghanistan was a buffer state between Russian and British imperialist interests, during the Cold War it was a battleground for the Soviet Union and the United States, and more recently it became a focus of the United States-led War on Terror. Afghanistan's struggles began in the 1830s, when it was invaded by British forces. In 1919 Afghanistan regained independence and was governed as a monarchy. In the 1950s Afghanistan turned to the Soviet Union for military and economic assistance and carried out some social reforms. Notable among these was the abolition of **purdah**, the practice of secluding women. Over time, political reforms were carried out as well, and Afghanistan first became a constitutional monarchy in 1964 and then a republic in 1973.

In 1978 a pro-Soviet coup was carried out, giving the Soviet Union an excuse to invade Afghanistan to support the Communist government. The **mujahedeen** (the term means "fighters for Islam") put up a fierce resistance against the Soviet invaders who in turn used indiscriminate bombings of villages as a way to suppress the insurgency and terrorize civilians. Despite their much larger numbers and better training, the Soviets were never able to defeat the

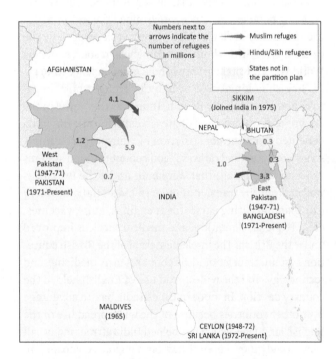

FIGURE 9.30 The Partition of South Asia—The 1947 partition of what had been a large British colony and other areas under British influence created the modern states of India and Pakistan. Until a civil war in the early 1970s broke the country apart, Pakistan comprised two very different regions separated by the vast expanse of India. *Source:* Drawn after a similar image at Course-Works@Columbia (http://www.columbia.edu/itc/mealac/pritchett/00maplinks/modern/maps1947/maps1947.html).

mujahedeen, partly because the rebels were armed by the United States, Pakistan, and several other (mostly Muslim) countries. The United States supplied the mujahedeen with Stinger missiles, which allowed them to shoot down the Soviet helicopters that carried out the bombing campaigns. In 1988, the Soviet forces began to withdraw. They left behind a country devastated by war, with large proportions of the population killed, displaced within Afghanistan or to neighboring countries as refugees, or mutilated by mines.

With the withdrawal of the Soviets (completed in 1989) the mujahedeen lost their common enemy. As a result, divisions among Afghan peoples came to the forefront again. Furthermore, Islamic fundamentalism emerged in the refugee camps in neighboring Iran and Pakistan, and part of the mujahedeen developed into a new group, the Taliban ("religious students"), who were educated in madrassas (religious schools) in Pakistan. When the Taliban seized control of the Afghan capital Kabul in 1996 they brought with them a hardline version of Islam that banned girls from education and women from work; forced women to wear the burqa; forbade all kinds of entertainment (such as music, dancing, and even kite-flying—an iconic Afghan pastime); and introduced *sharia* punishments such as amputating the hands of thieves or stoning adulterers. By 1997 the Taliban controlled about two-thirds of the country.

Among the mujahedeen who had come to fight the Soviet Union was Osama bin Laden, an affluent and well-connected Saudi who formed the militant Islamist group al-Qaeda in 1988. After spending some time in Sudan, bin Laden established his new base in Afghanistan. In 1996, the same year that the Taliban took control of Kabul, he initiated a series of bombing attacks and declared war against the United States. For example, it is claimed that bin Laden funded the Luxor, Egypt massacre in 1997 and organized the bombing attacks on United States embassies in Dar es Salaam, Tanzania, and Nairobi, Kenya in 1998. By 2000, the Taliban controlled about 90 percent of Afghanistan. Relationships with the Western world continued to worsen, not just because attacks were being carried out in third countries, but also because of the policies the Taliban implemented in Afghanistan. The Taliban earned global scorn when it ordered the destruction of the famous giant Buddha statues in the Bamiyan Valley that the international community had asked the Taliban to spare.

Less than a month after the terrorist attacks against the United States on September 11, 2001, the United States launched Operation Enduring Freedom against Afghanistan. By the end of the year, over 12,000 bombs (including cluster bombs) had already been dropped on Afghanistan. Over the next few years, the United States sent more and more troops to Afghanistan, reaching 100,000 in 2009, but by the early 2010s foreign troops began to withdraw from Afghanistan, country by country (e.g. France in 2012, the United States and Britain in 2014). In 2014, NATO formally ended its thirteen-year combat mission in Afghanistan and handed the country over to Afghan forces, but some foreign troops remained. The bloodshed continued, and 2014 is believed to have been the bloodiest year in Afghanistan since 2001. In 2014 the Islamic State (IS) emerged in Eastern Afghanistan and captured large areas previously controlled by the Taliban. So the Afghan government, the United States, and their allies still face the Taliban, the Islamic State, and even a remnant of al-Qaeda (whose operations have mainly moved to other world regions) in Afghanistan.

For decades, Afghanistan has been among the poorest and least developed countries in the world. Afghanistan has some of the highest infant, child, and maternal mortality rates in the world. It also lacks access to clean water, adequate sanitation, and reliable food supplies. These difficult conditions, coupled with substandard health services, mean that less than three-quarters of the children born in Afghanistan reach age five, and infectious diseases kill many more afterward. The education system is also in shambles. Before the Soviet invasion, hardly any schools existed, and most were religious schools where education consisted of memorizing the Koran. During the Soviet invasions, many schools were destroyed, and most of the teachers fled to neighboring countries. By the end of the 1980s, less than a quarter of Afghan children received an education. After the U.S. invasion of Afghanistan in 2001, schools reopened, but most did not have any teaching materials and the teachers had little education themselves. Over the decades of conflict, Afghans became one of the largest refugee groups in the world. Since 2001, about 5 million Afghans have been repatriated from Pakistan and Iran. Nevertheless, as noted earlier, Afghans today are still the second largest refugee group after Syrians.

The Sri Lanka conflict between the Sri Lankan government and the Liberation Tigers of Tamil Eelam (Tamil Tigers) lasted for almost three decades and is therefore one of the longest civil wars in Asia. It stemmed from both religious and linguistic differences. During British colonial rule, Hindu Tamils had migrated from India to Ceylon (as Sri Lanka was then called) to work on tea plantations. Eventually the Tamils made up close to 10 percent of the Sri Lankan population and were favored by the British colonial authorities. When Ceylon became independent in 1948, the original population, Buddhist Sinhalese, disenfranchised the Tamils and made Sinhala the country's official language. Tensions between the two groups increased, and the Tamil Tigers began campaigning for a Tamil homeland in Northern Sri Lanka called Tamil Eelam

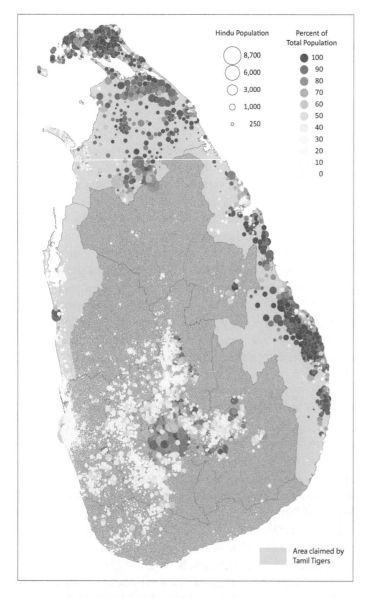

Hindu Population	Percent of Total Population
◯ 8,700	● 100
◯ 6,000	● 90
◯ 3,000	● 80
○ 1,000	● 70
∘ 250	● 60
	● 50
	40
	30
	20
	10
	0

Area claimed by Tamil Tigers

FIGURE 9.31 The Tamil population of Sri Lanka—While Hindus are clustered in the areas that the Tamil Tigers claimed as the Tamil homeland, some other regions also have high percentages of Hindus. *Source:* Sri Lanka. Department of Census and Statistics.

(Fig. 9.31). In 1983 riots broke out after the Tamil Tigers ambushed an army convoy. Despite the deployment of an Indian peacekeeping force violence escalated.

The Tamil Tigers turned into a feared terrorist group, which became known for high-profile assassinations (including India's Prime Minister Rajiv Gandhi), the use of suicide bombers, and the recruitment of child soldiers. In the late 2000s the Sri Lankan government launched another brutal campaign against the Tamil Tigers and declared in 2009 that it had defeated them. Human rights organizations have accused both the Tamil Tigers and the Sri Lankan army of serious human rights violations. For example, they alleged that the army indiscriminately shelled a supposed no-fire zone where 50,000 Tamils were

trapped. Sri Lanka now faces the challenge of dealing with both these human rights violations and the continuing tensions between the majority Sinhalese and minority Tamils.

The conflict in Kashmir dates back to the partition of India and Pakistan in 1947 and adds fuel to the strained relationship between the two countries. After the partition, several hundred small states run by princes had the option to decide which country they wanted to join or whether they wanted to remain neutral. Because of its location bordering both India and Pakistan, the ruler of Kashmir decided that Kashmir would remain independent. In October 1947, however, Pakistan took over Kashmir, and the Kashmiri ruler (a Hindu, even though the vast majority of Kashmiris were Muslim) asked India for military help and signed over Kashmir to India. The United Nations asked Pakistan to withdraw its troops and wanted to hold a referendum to let the Kashmiris decide, but the referendum never took place. In 1949 there was an agreed-upon ceasefire, with Kashmir divided between India (65 percent of Kashmiri territory) and Pakistan (35 percent). In the 1950s China occupied some areas in Eastern Kashmir (Aksai Chin). In the 1960s China and India fought over control of Aksai Chin (Sino-Indian War), and a year later Pakistan ceded some Kashmiri territory to China as well. In the 1960s and 1970s India and Pakistan fought two brief wars over Kashmir and finally signed the Simla Agreement in 1972. The agreement meant that the temporary ceasefire line became the permanent Line of Control, the de facto border between the two countries, and established that the two countries would solve conflicts in a peaceful manner.

The Simla Agreement did not lead to permanent peace in the region. Indian and Pakistani troops regularly exchanged shots at the Line of Control, but the conflict became a potential global threat after both India and Pakistan tested nuclear weapons in 1998. In the 2000s the peace process renewed. Some progress was made, especially after the devastating earthquake in Kashmir in 2005, but there were also setbacks, especially after the 2008 attacks on the Indian city of Mumbai that had been orchestrated by Pakistan. The Kashmir conflict has lasted over six decades and led to an estimated 70,000 deaths. Despite a renewed interest in finding a peaceful solution, there are still claims that the ceasefire is not being respected. Furthermore, Kashmir still remains divided between three major powers, as India administers 43 percent of the region, Pakistan controls 37 percent, and China 20 percent (Fig. 9.32). Kashmiris are also split; some of those living under Indian control would like to join Pakistan due to the shared Muslim heritage, others want to remain part of India, and still others would prefer complete independence. Pakistan, to strengthen its claims for the Kashmir region, relocated its government from Karachi to Rawalpindi and finally to the newly built city of Islamabad, which is very close to the disputed area (Fig. 9.33).

Pakistan's Federally Administered Tribal Areas (FATA) are semi-autonomous regions in the Pakistani-Afghan borderlands with a total population of roughly 3.3 million people. The FATAs are often described as lawless areas. For example, many people in Waziristan, one of the tribal areas, supplement their meager incomes from agriculture with smuggling and processing illicit drugs. Due to its location along the Afghan border, Waziristan became one of the destinations for refugees during the Soviet occupation of Afghanistan. Later Waziristan became an area of refuge for the militant Islamist Taliban and al Qaeda, making the region a battleground in the War on Terror, as Pakistan and the United States searched for al Qaeda fighters. Pakistan and the United States have a difficult relationship with one another. On the one hand, Pakistan supported the U.S.-led invasion of Afghanistan after 9/11 and tolerated U.S. missile attacks against the Taliban and al-Qaeda in Pakistan's FATAs. On the other hand, Pakistan sheltered Taliban and al Qaeda leaders.

Militant Islamists remain a powerful force in Pakistan and have been responsible for numerous acts of terror within the troubled country. In a 2017 rating of the world's most fragile states, Pakistan ranked eighteenth, by far the worst score for any country with a nuclear weapons arsenal. India, by contrast, ranked seventy-second (out of 178 countries ranked). The country's democratic system—India is the world's most populous democracy—helps to diffuse some tensions.

In Sri Lanka, India, Pakistan, and the rest of the region, addressing ongoing conflicts and resolving difficult political legacies of the past will be eased with higher levels of economic development and strong trade ties within the region. Intra-regional trade currently accounts for just 5 percent of trade for South Asian countries, versus 25 percent for countries in Southeast Asia. Low levels of intraregional trade are both a reflection of persistent political tensions and an obstacle to easing those tensions. Trading patterns are a feature of the region's economic geography, to which we turn next.

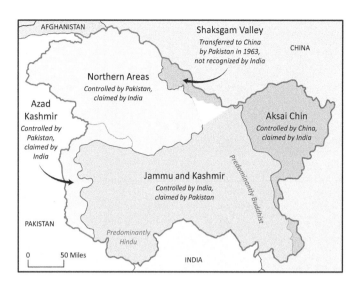

FIGURE 9.32 Kashmir: a disputed territory between India and Pakistan—Kashmir is divided into a Pakistan- and an India-administered part. However, China also claims some parts of Kashmir. *Source:* drawn after a similar map in Hobbs, J. 2013. *World Regional Geography.* Brooks/Cole.

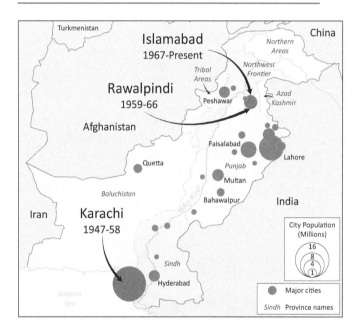

FIGURE 9.33 Pakistan's provinces and capital cities—Pakistan's capital moved multiple times. Islamabad, the current capital, has a smaller population than Lahore and the former capital Karachi. *Source:* United Nations. Population Division. World Urbanization Prospects 2014.

ECONOMIC ACTIVITIES

Agriculture

Agriculture has always played an important role in South Asian countries. Even today, the majority of the population depends on agriculture as their livelihood, and agricultural commodities account for about a third of South Asia's exports. India is the most important producer of agricultural products in the region, especially of wheat, rice, and

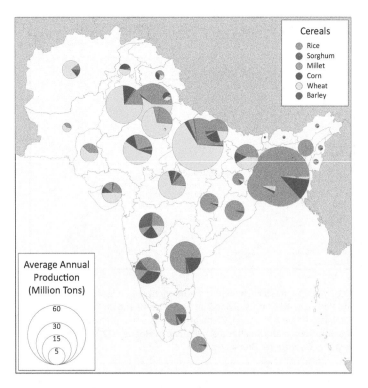

FIGURE 9.34 Production of cereals in South Asia, 2010–2012—Rice is the dominant crop in the regions most strongly affected by the monsoon; the drier regions have much lower agricultural productivity overall. *Source:* Statistical Yearbook of India; FAOSTAT.

millet (Fig. 9.34). India is also the world's largest producer of tea and jute (a coarse fiber used to make sacks, packaging, rugs, and other products) and is a major source of spices, tobacco, cotton, and oil seeds.

Tea has been consumed in India for thousands of years, but commercial production of tea did not begin until the British East India Company converted large land areas to tea production. More than two-thirds of the tea produced in India is also consumed in India, but nevertheless India is

FIGURE 9.35 A woman tends the crop at a tea plantation in Sri Lanka—Sri Lanka ranks fourth in the world in tea production, after China, India, and Kenya. *Source:* Pixabay.

a major exporter of tea and has developed a technologically advanced system of tea production, certification, and export. India is most famous for Assam and Darjeeling teas that grow exclusively in India. Neighboring Sri Lanka is known for Ceylon tea (Ceylon is Sri Lanka's former name). Ceylon tea is recognized for its rich aroma and strong taste. Tea is one of the main sources of income for Sri Lanka and tea production employs about 1 million people there (Fig. 9.35).

India is the world's most important producer, consumer, and exporter of spices, accounting for half of the world's spice trade. The varying climatic conditions in India make it possible to cultivate about one hundred different spices. The spice industry is technologically advanced and strives to provide high quality products, and organic spice farming is becoming increasingly common. India exports whole spices, spice mixes, extracts, and essential oils. Almost a quarter of the chili powder used in the world originates in India, and India also controls a significant market share of mint, cumin, pepper, and turmeric.

The cultivation of cotton, the world's most important textile fiber, has a long history in India. Based on the length and structure of the fiber, different types of cotton are distinguished. About half of India's cotton production is of long staple cotton, the highest quality fiber. India is the only country in the world that grows all types of cotton, and it has devoted the largest area of land to cotton cultivation (however, China and the United States produce more cotton). Pakistan is also a major producer of cotton. Jute is the second most important natural fiber after cotton. Almost 85 percent of the world's jute is grown in the Ganges Delta of India (West Bengal) and Bangladesh, but some is also grown in Pakistan, Nepal, and Bhutan. Similar to tea, India has developed advanced production techniques for jute and dominates the global jute market. By law, jute has to be used as packaging material in India, making India both the largest producer and consumer of jute. Bangladesh is known for producing the highest quality jute, and therefore is the largest exporter of jute fiber (Fig. 9.36).

Despite its agricultural productivity, South Asia has a long history of food insecurity. In the early 1960s India was facing famine. In order to increase food production, high-yield wheat seeds developed by the International Maize and Wheat Improvement Center in Mexico were introduced. Later, both India and Pakistan also began planting high-yield varieties of rice. The rice variety IR8, developed at a research institute in the Philippines (see Chapter 10), yielded up to 10 tons of rice per hectare under optimal conditions, about ten times more than traditional rice. Accordingly, IR8 became known as "miracle rice". In the first few years the production of wheat and rice increased at rates of over 20 percent per year. By the 1980s three fourths of the wheat and about half of the rice grown in

India were high-yield varieties. The research, development, and planting of high yield varieties became known as the **Green Revolution**. The Green Revolution comprised the use of high-yield varieties in concert with the application of chemical fertilizers and other agricultural chemicals (such as pesticides), irrigation, and mechanization. Norman Borlaug, the father of the Green Revolution, received the Nobel Peace Prize for his work, as he was credited for saving millions of people from starvation[16]. While South Asia was one of the main beneficiaries of the Green Revolution, millions of people in the region remain poorly fed. Specifically, in 2015, the proportion of people who were undernourished was 15 percent in India, 16 percent in Bangladesh, 22 percent in Pakistan, and 27 percent in Afghanistan. Among the sixteen countries in East and Southeast Asia, only North Korea, Laos, and Timor-Leste had rates as high as India.

About one-third of the cattle in the world lives in India (Fig. 9.37), three times as many as in the United States. However, large numbers of India's cattle are zebus, which do not produce much milk, and cattle breeds that would produce more milk are not well suited to tropical or subtropical environments. Cows are also important in rural areas as bulls plow the fields and transport goods. Cow dung is used as a fuel (to generate heat and electricity), fertilizer (it is rich in minerals), and as insulation material in homes. Because of the religious as well as practical importance of cows, slaughtering a cow and eating its meat is forbidden in many parts of India. Protected by their sacred status, cows are allowed to roam around freely, even if they block traffic in the busy streets of Indian cities. Sustaining a large population of cows diverts grain from the human food supply, and belching Indian cattle are a factor in global production of methane, a potent greenhouse gas (GHG); though to put things in perspective, in 2010, it was estimated that Indian cattle accounted for less than half a percent of global GHG emissions from all sources.

Mineral and Energy Resources

India has the region's most significant mineral resources. It is an important producer of iron ore, coal, mica, and manganese (all produced in the northeastern part of the Deccan Plateau), and it also has significant reserves of limestone and bauxite (mostly in Rajasthan and Gujarat). India has larger mineral resources than most European countries and Japan, but it lacks petroleum. So India has had to import most of its energy but is actively pursuing the development of offshore fields along the western coast and is exploring offshore opportunities near the Ganges Delta. Pakistan has some gas and petroleum, as well as iron ore and coal. In Afghanistan, vast reserves of iron, copper, gold, lithium, and other minerals have been found. The

FIGURE 9.36 Moving the jute harvest in rural Bangladesh.—About 95 percent of the world's jute, which is used to make a wide range of products from sacks to cosmetics, comes from Bangladesh and India. *Source:* Wikimedia Commons.

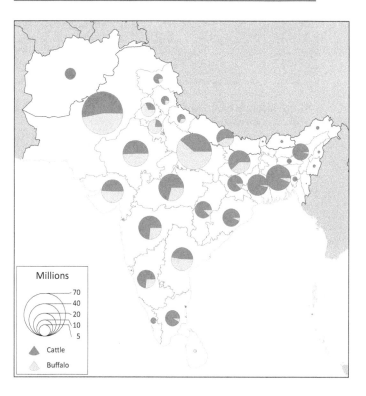

FIGURE 9.37 Cattle and buffaloes in South Asia, 2012—South Asia has large numbers of cattle. In the east cattle is dominant, but towards the west, buffaloes account for a significant percentage of livestock. *Source:* Statistical Yearbook of India; FAOSTAT.

reserves are so large and resources like lithium so critical to modern industrial economies that Afghanistan may become an important mining center in the future. So far, almost constant war has prevented the development of resources, but they could help Afghanistan to significantly strengthen its economy and lessen its dependence on drugs and foreign aid.

Apart from coal, energy resources are poorly developed in South Asia. India generates some hydroelectric power,

FIGURE 9.38 An Isuzu plant near Chennai, India—This plant, which opened in 2016, produces pickups and other light trucks for the Indian market. *Source:* Wikimedia Commons.

and there is the potential to develop more hydroelectric power in the Himalayan region of India and Nepal as well the mountains of Sri Lanka. However, development is difficult, not just because of political resistance but also due to geographical factors, such as lack of access to suitable locations and climatic fluctuations. Adding to the region's electricity generating capacity and improving transmission infrastructure are vital challenges. Currently, the demand for electricity often exceeds the available energy supply, resulting in frequent power blackouts. Many millions of people still live without any access to electricity. Both India and Pakistan are looking into adding to the existing nuclear generation capacity. In 2010, Pakistan opened a new plant built with Chinese assistance as part of a broader increase in economic and strategic cooperation between the two countries.

Manufacturing and High-Tech Industries

Since independence, industrialization has progressed more rapidly in India than in other South Asian countries. Now India is among the top ten countries in terms of industrial output. However, only a modest percentage of its labor force is employed in factories. The vast majority of Indians and other South Asians in the manufacturing sector work in small workshops in both rural and urban areas that produce textiles (cotton, silk, and rugs), wood and metal wares, and other goods for the local market. Those who work in small factories now produce items such as electrical appliances, bicycles, and tools. In recent times, the more widespread use of electricity has helped expand these factories.

Governmental support in India has led to the expansion of heavy industries. Machinery (including transportation, military, and energy production equipment), as well iron, steel, and chemicals, are all under government control. One of the main motivations to put these industries under the state was import substitution industrialization, a strategy aimed at reducing imports from other countries and making domestically produced goods available. The government also helps to protect industrial outputs, such as cars, aircraft, and electrical appliances, from foreign competition by imposing high tariffs on imported goods. These policies have succeeded in transforming India from a country that was almost completely dependent on imports to an exporter that is competitive on the global market (Fig. 9.38).

While India's economy is now diversified, and India boasts three major industrial regions (Fig. 9.39), the other South Asian countries depend heavily on just a few products and have only small industrial bases. Pakistan produces cement and fertilizer, and Bangladesh's economy is based on jute and other textile products (textile products account for about 80 percent of the country's exports), as well as rice milling and some production of steel. Bangladesh also has a large fishing industry focused on fish and shrimp, and over 10 million people, mostly women, depend on the fish industry. Sri Lanka continues to produce plantation crops such as tea and rubber and has developed some industries based on processing these raw materials.

South Asia is home to several centers in the ship-breaking industry[17], in which the purpose is the opposite of most manufacturing: rather than making products, the industry tears them apart (Fig. 9.40). Vast numbers of workers use brute force and simple equipment to tear apart old ships that are deliberately beached. Specifically, three main sites in the industry are Gadani, Pakistan; Alang, India; and Chittagong, Bangladesh. In 2015, these three countries accounted for just over 60 percent of all dismantled ships. On the positive side of the ledger, the industry recycles metals and other valuable materials inside often gigantic ships and creates jobs. On the negative side, working conditions are often extremely dangerous, and workers are poorly protected (they may even be barefoot!). The surrounding environment is threatened with pollution from the toxic materials, such as asbestos and heavy metals, released during the breakdown.

Exploitative work conditions are still widespread in South Asia. Of particular concern is debt bondage, a form of modern slavery. **Debt bondage** is a situation where a person is forced to work off a debt, and virtually all the money they earn goes towards paying off these debts. Often entire families end up being enslaved because of a loan taken out by a family member, and the debt gets passed from parents to children, keeping families enslaved for generations. Examples of bonded labor (including child labor) include the silk industries in India, rug- and brick-making in Pakistan; fish processing in Bangladesh; and agriculture in India, Pakistan, and Nepal. While many poor people are vulnerable to bonded labor, the caste system makes it easy for the ruling classes to exploit the poor, especially the Dalits. Bonded labor is technically illegal, but existing laws are rarely enforced, leaving millions of people trapped.

At the same time that these miserable conditions persist, however, India has also become a location for high tech industries. The Indian technology industry began when Western countries began to outsource basic IT work as well as call centers to India in the 1990s. A decade later, India provided higher-level information technology tasks, developed consulting services in the high-tech field, and became a location for advanced research and development. More recently, India is developing innovative high-tech products, such as medical diagnosis equipment and other

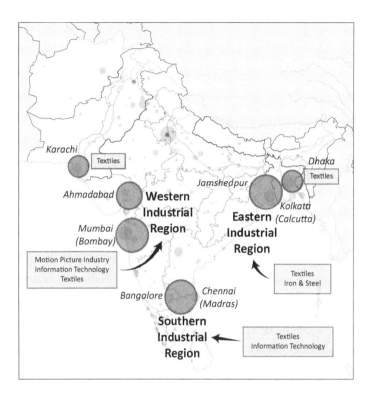

FIGURE 9.39 Industrial regions of India—Two of India's three main industrial regions are focused on information technology, while the third is dominated by the iron and steel industries. *Source:* drawn after a similar map in Nijman, J., P. Muller, and H. de Blij. 2016. *The World Today: Concepts and Regions in Geography.* Wiley.

high-value products. Most of this development is centered on the city of Bangalore (also spelled Bengaluru), which has become known as the science and technology capital (sometimes the term Indian Silicon Valley is also used).

FIGURE 9.40 Shipbreaking in Bangladesh—The beach in Chittagong, Bangladesh is one of the world's top sites for ship-breaking. The industry got its start there when a Greek ship washed ashore during a cyclone in the 1960s. *Source:* Wikimedia Commons.

The city is home to several prestigious institutions such as the Indian Institute of Science and the Indian Space Research Organization, as well as a range of companies in the biotechnology, avionics, information technology, and engineering fields. India is highly competitive in software development and IT because it has a wealth of well-educated, technically talented people. Since computer work does not require transportation infrastructure, the lack of such infrastructure does not pose an obstacle as it does for the development of many other industries.

Media and Tourism

Mumbai is the focus of the Indian film industry, producing nearly 1,000 films per year, most in Hindi. The industry produces movies in other Indian languages (e.g. Tamil and Telugu) and has other production sites, but the term "Bollywood" (derived from Bombay and Hollywood) is often used to refer to Indian cinema more generally (Fig. 9.41). Bollywood is one of the largest film production centers in the world, producing about twice as many as in Hollywood. Bollywood films are mostly musicals, with music and dance woven into the storyline. Many Bollywood plots are melodramatic and focus on love triangles, big sacrifices, and dramatic reversals of fortune.

Tourism has become an important source of income for several South Asian countries. In India, tourism generates close to 10 percent of the country's GDP. The big cities Delhi, Mumbai, Chennai, Agra, and Jaipur attract most foreign visitors, but the single most known tourist site is the Taj Mahal, a mausoleum built in 1631. It is considered one of the Seven Modern Wonders of the World (an honor it shares with Machu Picchu in Peru, the Colosseum in Rome, and the Great Wall of China) and a UNESCO World Heritage Site. India is also home to several other UNESCO World Heritage Sites, such as the Fort at Agra, the Mountain Railroads, the Elephanta Caves in Mumbai's harbor,

FIGURE 9.41 Bollywood film posters—Several posters advertise the drama Jodhaa Akbar, a 2008 Bollywood romantic blockbuster set in 16th century India. *Source:* Pixabay.

and Sundarbans National Park, which protects mangrove forests and is a tiger reserve. India has also become a popular destination for specialized forms of tourism, such as **spiritual tourism** (where people seek spiritual experiences, often in the homeland of a particular spiritual practice) and **medical tourism** (where people travel to seek cheaper or high-quality medical treatments abroad).

Sri Lanka is highly ranked as a tourist destination due to its scenic beauty and rich cultural heritage. Despite its small size, Sri Lanka is a biodiversity hotspot with numerous endemic species of flora and fauna and protects more than a tenth of its land area as national parks or other wildlife reserves. Furthermore, Sri Lanka has almost 1,600 kilometers (1,000 miles) of tropical beaches and a rich (mostly Buddhist) cultural heritage. Sri Lanka has recently been labeled one of the world's best tourist destinations, and its tourism industry is growing rapidly. Tourism is also important in Nepal, where it is the largest source of revenue. Nepal attracts adventure tourists (mountain climbing, rock climbing, and trekking) as well as cultural tourists (who visit places such as Lumbini, Buddha's place of birth). In Nepal, tourism is a double-edged sword: It provides much-needed revenue and jobs but also imposes a great environmental cost on fragile high-mountain environments and leads to the exploitation of locals, especially the Sherpas, who work as guides and load carriers on trekking and mountain climbing expeditions. Concerns about the costs of tourism in Nepal are among the reasons Bhutan, which was already a difficult to reach country, has imposed very high fees on visitors to deter so-called "hippies" and backpackers (Fig. 9.42).

Illicit Drugs

Asia has two major areas of illicit drug production: the Golden Triangle in Southeast Asia and the **Golden Crescent** in South Asia. The Golden Crescent refers to the borderland

FIGURE 9.42 Paro Airport, Bhutan—Paro is home to the only international airport in Bhutan. The proximity of high mountains near the runway make it one of world's most challenging places for commercial aircraft. *Source:* Wikimedia Commons.

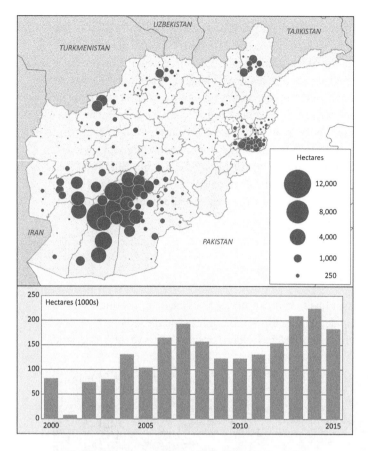

FIGURE 9.43 Cultivation of opium in Afghanistan, 2000–2015—Opium is produced in most of Afghanistan. There are several clusters in the north and east, but the center of opium production is the south-west. *Source:* World Drug Report 2016.

to support their families. As soon as the Taliban regime collapsed after the United States-led invasion in 2001, farmers once again began to grow poppies. Today, more land is devoted to cultivating opium poppies in Afghanistan than for coca cultivation in Latin America, about 3.3 million Afghans are involved in producing opium, and it is estimated that roughly half of Afghanistan's GDP is generated by the drug trade (Fig. 9.43). Programs aimed at eradicating the cultivation of opium poppies have largely failed. One reason is corruption in the government, but even more important is that the opium cultivation is so profitable that it is difficult to convince farmers to grow other crops.

Gross National Happiness

In 1979 the King of Bhutan said that the Bhutanese "do not believe in Gross National Product, Gross National Happiness is more important."[18] With this statement, the king made it clear that economic development was not the most important goal, but the happiness of the people. This concept was included in Bhutan's 2008 Constitution. **Gross National Happiness** is a holistic concept, as it refers to four different kinds of wellbeing: sustainable development, good governance, cultural preservation, and environmental conservation. The Gross National Happiness Index is measured on thirty-three indicators that fall under these four categories. The surveys conducted to measure happiness provide a rich dataset that reveals differences among demographic groups. For example, it shows that on average men are happier than women, people in urban areas are happier than rural dwellers, and that people with some education are happier than those with little or no education. By now, there are also efforts to measure happiness globally. In 2017 the fifth World Happiness Report was released. According to this report, the Scandinavian countries are the happiest in the world. Bhutan ranked ninety-seventh, which was better than other South Asian countries except—surprisingly—Pakistan.

of Afghanistan, Pakistan, and Iran. Afghanistan now produces over 90 percent of the world's heroin (opium) and is also the world's largest producer of cannabis (hashish). Opium poppy cultivation accelerated in Afghanistan in the 1990s, at the same time as its cultivation declined in the Golden Triangle and in Pakistan (where the United States helped to eradicate opium). In 2001 the Taliban banned poppy cultivation. As violators were severely punished, this ban was effective but deprived many farmers of a way

FUTURE PROBLEMS AND PROSPECTS

South Asia still faces a number of challenges, such as the impact of climate change, population growth, international migration, development, terrorism and political instability, and human rights. South Asia is threatened by some serious environmental issues connected to global climate change. The increased melting of the Himalayan glaciers causes flooding in the short-term but will result in much-reduced

water flow in the long run. Furthermore, low-lying parts, such as Bangladesh (which already experiences serious flooding) and the Maldives, are at great risk. It is likely that the region will eventually become a producer of **climate refugees** even as rising development levels and dependence on coal-fired electricity in India in particular make the region a more significant producer of greenhouse gases.

South Asia also continues to face population challenges. While fertility rates have declined in most of the region, they remain high in Pakistan and Afghanistan. Even with reduced fertility rates, most South Asian countries struggle with providing education, health care, and public services (especially clean water and adequate sanitation) for their populations, and they still have large numbers of people living in poverty and sub-standard housing. India, Pakistan, and Bangladesh are still scarred by the brutal population transfer associated with independence, but they also face modern migration challenges such as the out-migration of their elites (brain drain) and the treatment of their citizens who are guest workers in the Gulf region. While there are several refugee issues in the region, the plight of Afghans overshadows all the others, as Afghans are still among the largest refugee groups in the world.

Serious human rights issues persist. For example, gender-based violence (e.g. domestic violence, honor killings, and rapes) are still a problem in several South Asian countries. Terrorism and unrest also continue to trouble Afghanistan and Pakistan in particular, but are also possible in India, Sri Lanka, and Nepal. Drug production in Afghanistan remains high, as alternative ways to make a living are lacking for large parts of the population.

Despite all these problems, there are some positive developments. Most South Asian countries have reduced their population growth rates and have been successful in bringing millions of people out of poverty. In India, a large middle class has developed. While many people still leave the region in search of opportunities abroad, an increasing number of people return home and contribute to the economic and technological development of their countries. India in particular has developed into a major economic power and is among the world's leaders in the development of some technologies. And, even though there is still a significant amount of political instability in the region, some long-running conflicts have ended or abated.

NOTES

1. Zurick, D. & Karan, P.P. (1999). *Himalaya: Life on the edge of the world.* Baltimore, MD: Johns Hopkins University Press.

2. Stojanov, R., Duží, B., Kelman, I., Němec, D., & Procházka, D. (2017). Local perceptions of climate change impacts and migration patterns in Malé, Maldives. *The Geographical Journal,*183(4), 370–85.

3. Pant, G.B. & Kumar, K.R. (1997). *Climates of South Asia.* Chichester, NY: Wiley.

4. Chapman, G. (2009). *The geopolitics of South Asia from early empires to the Nuclear Age.* Burlington, VT: Ashgate.

5. Colopy, C.G. (2012). *Dirty, sacred rivers: Confronting South Asia's water crisis.* New York, NY: Oxford University Press.

6. Athukorala, P.-C. & Resosudarmo, B.P. (2005). The Indian Ocean tsunami: Economic impact, disaster management, and lessons. *Asian Economic Papers,* 4(1), 1–39.

7. Bradnock, R.W. & Saunders, P.L. (2002). Rising waters, sinking land? Environmental change and development in Bangladesh. In R.W. Bradnock and G. Williams (Eds.), *South Asia in a globalising world: A reconstructed regional geography* (pp. 51–77). London, UK: Routledge.

8. Owen, J. (2006, May 30). Himalaya forests vanishing, species may follow, study says. National Geographic News. Retrieved from https://news.nationalgeographic.com/news/2006/05/060530-himalaya.html

9. Paul, B.K. & Rashid, H. (2017). *Climatic hazards in coastal Bangladesh: Structural and non-structural solutions.* Amsterdam, Netherlands: Butterworth-Heinemann.

10. Raju, S. (Ed.). (2011). *Gendered geographies: Space and place in South Asia.* New Delhi, India: Oxford University Press.

11. Kaur, H. & Ayubi, N. (2008). Status of women in Afghanistan. In Rennie, R. (Ed.), *State-building, security, and social change in Afghanistan: Reflections on a survey of the Afghan people* (pp. 89–111). Washington, DC: The Asia Foundation.

12. Oonk, G. (2007). *Global Indian diasporas: Exploring trajectories of migration and theory.* Amsterdam, Netherlands: Amsterdam University Press.

13. Davis, M. (2006). *Planet of slums.* New York, NY: Verso.

14. Blackwell, F. (2011). *India: A global studies handbook.* Santa Barbara, CA: ABC-CLIO.

15. Williams, B.G. (2012). *Afghanistan declassified: A guide to America's longest war.* Philadelphia, PA: University of Pennsylvania Press.

16. Hesser, L.F. (2006). *The man who fed the world.* Dallas, TX: Durban House.

17. Buerck, R. (2006). *Breaking ships: How supertankers and cargo ships are dismantled on the beaches of Bangladesh.* New York, NY: Chamberlain Brothers.

18. Quoted in Munro, L.T. (2016). Where did Bhutan's gross national happiness come from? The origins of an invented tradition. *Journal of Asian Affairs,* 47(1), 71–92.

10 SOUTHEAST ASIA

On Monday, November 10, 2014, passengers arriving on an AirAsia flight from Malaysia's capital Kuala Lumpur to Myanmar's capital Naypyitaw were surprised when, shortly after landing, their jet was greeted by a water cannon salute from an airport fire truck. Only then did they learn that theirs was the first international flight at Naypyitaw's airport and thus the traditional aviation honor for historic flights. The flight was noteworthy in other ways, too—ways that serve as a useful introduction to the remarkable dynamism of Southeast Asia.

First, it linked two starkly different cities. Kuala Lumpur was established in the 19th century as a British colonial trading center for what would become the booming tin mining industry in the area. From the start, the city was connected to the international economy. By the early 21st century, Kuala Lumpur was home to a pair of the tallest buildings in the world (the Petronas Towers were the world's tallest buildings from 1998 until 2004) and was a globally significant financial center. Naypyitaw, conversely, is a new capital city that replaced Yangon as the center of government in 2005. Its development largely kept secret until its unveiling, Naypyitaw was built in the center of the country in contrast to coastal Yangon, and the motivation for the new city was believed to have been to isolate and insulate the military junta then in charge of the country. For years after it opened, Naypyitaw remained largely off-limits to the country's own people and foreigners alike, evoking images of a ghost town. But beginning in late 2010, Myanmar began to open-up, culminating in—among other things—the new AirAsia flight. A similar type of opening-up has—to varying degrees—transformed Vietnam, Laos, and Cambodia and their relations with the broader world, narrowing the gap between states that were once shut and those already plugged into the global economy.

Second, the new flight was launched in conjunction with a November 2014 summit of the **Association of Southeast Asian Nations (ASEAN)** in Naypyidaw. The summit, which drew together leaders of the ten-country grouping, as well as U.S. president Barack Obama, signaled a new phase in the integration of Southeast Asia. ASEAN had begun as an anticommunist political organization, but by late 2014 was on its way towards becoming an

FIGURE 10.1 An AirAsia jet departs—AirAsia is the largest of several low-cost carriers in Southeast Asia whose many flights have helped to tie the region more strongly together. *Source:* AirTeamImages.

FIGURE 10.2 A family on motorbike in Ho Chi Minh City—Ho Chi Minh City has been described as a city of 9 million people and 30 million motorbikes. Here a family of four shares one motorbike. Their mobility is emblematic of a region on the move. *Source:* John T. Bowen.

integrated market. The new flight was made possible by the loosening of restrictions on flights within the region. This "open skies" policy has fostered dozens of new international flights (like Kuala Lumpur-Naypyitaw) drawing a once-fractious Southeast Asia more closely together. Southeast Asia is now a more integrated region than at any other time in its history.

Third and finally, the AirAsia flight was one small example of a region in motion, especially in the air. AirAsia's logo "Now everyone can fly" is emblazoned on all of its nearly 150 jets (Fig. 10.1). Though that claim is hyperbole, there is little doubt that AirAsia and other **low-cost carriers** in the region—such as VietJet, Thai Smile, and Indonesia's Lion Air—have done much to make air travel more affordable since the region's budget airline craze took off

around 2000. New highways and railways and port complexes are likewise speeding the movement of people and goods in Southeast Asia.

And so, a single flight serves as an apt metaphor for a dynamic region. From its political divisions to its economic landscapes to the ways of life for its people, Southeast Asia is on the move (Fig. 10.2).

GEOGRAPHIC QUALITIES AND WORLD SIGNIFICANCE

Southeast Asia has been profoundly influenced by its geographic situation, south of China and east of India (Fig. 10.3). The region's religions, languages, and technologies have been shaped by its giant neighbors over the past two millennia. Hinduism came to Bali; Islam to the Malay Peninsula and many of the islands of Southeast Asia; and Buddhism to Myanmar, Cambodia, Thailand, and Laos—all through India. The Pallava influence on the written forms of Thai, Khmer (the language of Cambodia), Lao, and Burmese (the main language of Myanmar) also originated in India. Meanwhile, many people in Southeast Asia are of Chinese ancestry, and the many shipwrecks in the Philippines and elsewhere in the region containing Chinese bronze guns and porcelain

are a legacy of the ancient flow of technology from China to Southeast Asia.

More recently, Southeast Asia's position has given it global strategic significance. The Straits of Malacca linking the South China Sea and the Andaman Sea comprise one of the world's most heavily trafficked chokepoints. Specifically, as much as 40 percent of world trade flows through the Straits of Malacca. Meanwhile, the combination of massive trade flows, substantial fossil fuel resources, and competing historic claims has made the South China Sea a pivotal area. Southeast Asia today and for many centuries has been a trade crossroads. The flows through the region have made Singapore's port the world's second busiest (after Shanghai) and have contributed to Singapore's

FIGURE 10.3 The situation of Southeast Asia—Southeast Asia's geographic situation between India and China has profoundly influenced its development.

countries where Buddhists comprise at least 50 percent of the population), and the most populous predominantly Catholic country (the Philippines) outside of Latin America. Hundreds of languages are spoken with particularly great linguistic diversity on the many islands of the Indonesian and Philippine archipelagoes.

These two island groups, comprising more than 20,000 islands, are part of maritime Southeast Asia. In addition to Indonesia and the Philippines, maritime Southeast Asia also includes Brunei, Timor-Leste, Singapore, and the parts of Malaysia on the island of Borneo. The rest of region is termed mainland Southeast Asia. It is the southeastern-most extent of the vast Eurasian landmass and includes Peninsular Malaysia, Thailand, Cambodia, Vietnam, Laos, and Myanmar.

Together, this culturally, economically, and physically diverse region is more integrated than ever before. A key force in this regard has been ASEAN. When the organization was formed in 1967, it had five members (Indonesia, Malaysia, the Philippines, Singapore, and Thailand) and was intended mainly as a bulwark against the expansion of communism. At the time, Vietnam was in the midst of a great civil war between the Communist north and the U.S.-allied south; Cambodia and Laos were also roiling with Communist insurgencies; and Myanmar (then known as Burma) was decades into long self-enforced isolation. In the decades since, Southeast Asia has changed profoundly politically. The wars of the 1960s and 1970s are over, and their bitter legacies (including unexploded bombs and land-mines) are receding into the past; these countries are more open economically and are making progress on democrati-zation, albeit very unevenly. All of these countries are now members of ASEAN as is tiny Brunei. In fact, the only state in Southeast Asia that has not joined the organization is Timor-Leste, a tiny country that successfully broke away from Indonesia in 2002—making it the newest country in Asia.

wealth; it ranks among the richest countries in the world. So does Brunei Darussalam, a small, oil-exporting country in the region. But the eleven countries in Southeast Asia also include Cambodia and Timor-Leste (formerly East Timor), which are among the poorest places outside of Sub-Saharan Africa. In fact, measured by the range of values for gross domestic product per capita, Southeast Asia is the second most diverse region in the world after the Middle East; and, like the Middle East, Southeast Asia has an overall medium level of economic development.

Southeast Asia is also culturally diverse. It has the world's most populous predominantly Muslim country (Indonesia), the second most populous predominantly Buddhist country (Thailand, second after Japan among

PHYSICAL ENVIRONMENT

Landform Configuration

Mainland Southeast Asia is part of the great middle arc of river plains, hills, and plateaus that stretches from South Asia, through Southeast Asia, and then East Asia (Fig. 10.4). Countercockwise through the region, the major rivers are the Irrawaddy River, the Salween River, the Chao Phraya, the Mekong River, and the Red River. All of these except the Chao Phraya have their headwaters in China, illustrating

Southeast Asia's environmental dependence on its giant neighbor to the north. For instance, hydroelectric power developments along the Chinese section of the Mekong River (called the Lancang in China) imperil the delivery of nutrient-rich sediment to downriver countries. The dams also threaten fish populations in the world's richest inland fishery.

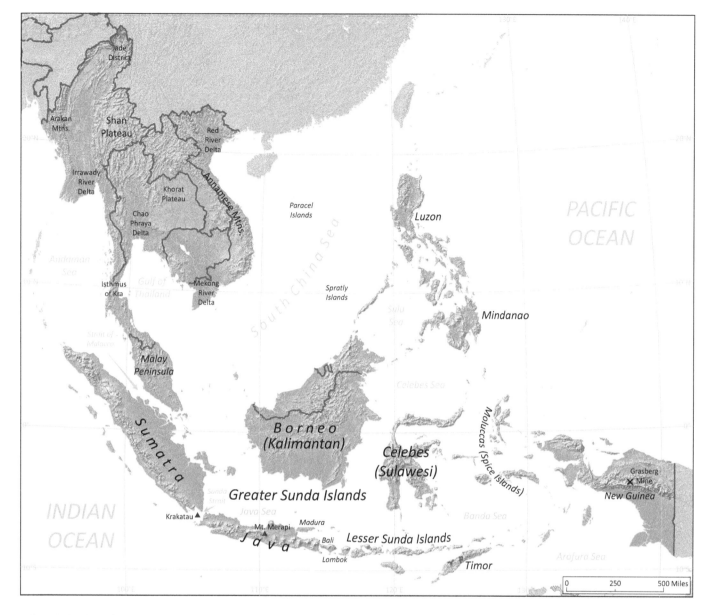

FIGURE 10.4 Landform regions of Southeast Asia—Unlike other world regions, Southeast Asia is located almost entirely in the tropics. *Source:* Natural Earth.

In 2016, all six operating dams on the Mekong were in China, as were six of the seven dams then under construction (the exception was the hugely controversial Xayaburi Dam in Laos); but ten of the eighteen additional planned dams were farther south—in Laos, on the Lao-Thai border, or in Cambodia. The Mekong descends 4,900 meters (16,100 feet) in its course from Tibet to its many distributaries in Southern Vietnam, offering tremendous potential energy. So, in their pursuit of greater material wealth, the countries of the Mekong Basin have rushed headlong into exploiting and undermining one of the region's richest sources of natural wealth. The same is true to a lesser degree on the other primary rivers of mainland Southeast Asia.

Between the river basins are the highlands of Southeast Asia. From east to west, the region's great mountain chains include the Annamese Cordillera along the border of Vietnam and Laos; the low mountains that separate the remote, arid Khorat Plateau in Northeastern Thailand from the central part of that country; the Shan Hills and other highlands along the frontier of Thailand and Myanmar; and finally the Arakan Mountains in Western Myanmar. The Annamese Cordillera (also called the Annamite Mountains) has played the greatest role in the region's history, including as a cultural barrier to influences from the west. During the Vietnam War, it was the forbidding terrain traversed by the Ho Chi Minh Trail that linked North Vietnam and

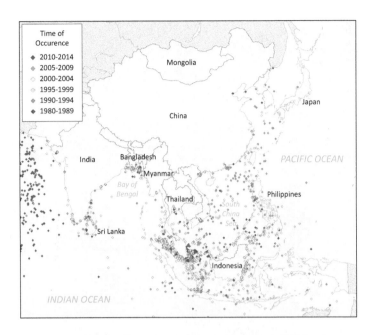

FIGURE 10.5 Piracy in Asian waters—In the early 2000s, piracy was a significant problem in the Straits of Malacca and South China Sea. Concerted efforts by governments in the region helped to suppress the problem, and piracy has been concentrated between India and the Arabian Peninsula in recent years. *Source:* National Geospatial Intelligence Agency.

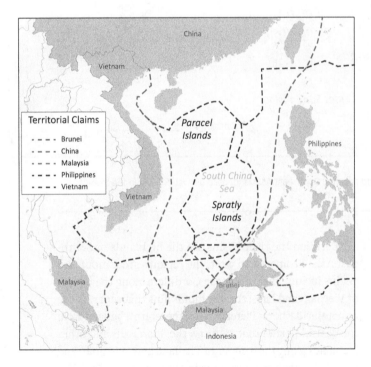

FIGURE 10.6 Territorial claims to the South China Sea—Several countries have overlapping claims in the South China Sea, a body of water important in international trade and potentially in fossil fuel resources. To strengthen its claims, China has expanded islands in the Spratly archipelago through land reclamation and then built airstrips, radar domes, lighthouses, and other infrastructure on the enlarged islands. *Source:* Drawn after a similar map in Wikipedia.

Communist rebels in the south during the Vietnam War, and then as the setting for camps to which class enemies of Vietnam's government were sent for re-education after the Communists' victory.

The southernmost extent of Mainland Southeast Asia is the Malay Peninsula (itself a part of the much larger Indo-China Peninsula). A striking feature of the Malay Peninsula is its narrowing at the Isthmus of Kra, which at just 44 kilometers (27 miles) across separates the Gulf of Thailand and the Andaman Sea. For centuries, there have been proposals to construct a canal across the isthmus to permit ships to avoid the densely trafficked Straits of Malacca. Middle East oil shipments to China and Japan would save 1,200 kilometers (745 miles), for instance[1]. Furthermore, a canal would circumvent the often pirate-infested strait (Fig. 10.5), but so far the multibillion dollar idea remains on the drawing board.

Maritime Southeast Asia, a central part of Asia's outer arc of islands, comprises more than 20,000 islands arrayed in a great half circle from Luzon in the north down through New Guinea (the eastern half belonging to Papua New Guinea and the west to Indonesia) and off to the west to Sumatra. Within the circle lies the South China Sea, one of the most hotly contested bodies of water in the world. At least five countries along the sea have overlapping claims to its resources; China alone lays claim to a vast tongue-shaped swath of the sea descending from Hainan Island (Fig. 10.6). The sea is a corridor through which much of Asia's trade (especially much of the oil supply for China, Japan, and South Korea) flows, and deep beneath its surface lie vast, untapped oil and natural gas resources.

The islands in the region include several of the largest in the world including New Guinea (second largest after Greenland); Borneo (third) shared by Indonesia, Malaysia, and Brunei; Sumatra (sixth); Sulawesi (eleventh); Java (thirteenth); and Luzon (fifteenth). Amid these are thousands of much smaller islands, which contribute to Southeast Asia's cultural diversity but also to some of the development challenges and political instability the region continues to face.

Climatic Contrasts

The Equator slices through Southeast Asia, and all but Northern Myanmar lies between the Tropic of Cancer (23.5°N) in the north and the Tropic of Capricorn (23.5°S) in the south. The position of Southeast Asia within the tropics strongly influences its climates; much of the region is warm throughout the year and receives ample precipitation (Fig. 10.7).

Throughout the region, the monsoon is a defining feature of climate. Even along the Equator, there are noticeable

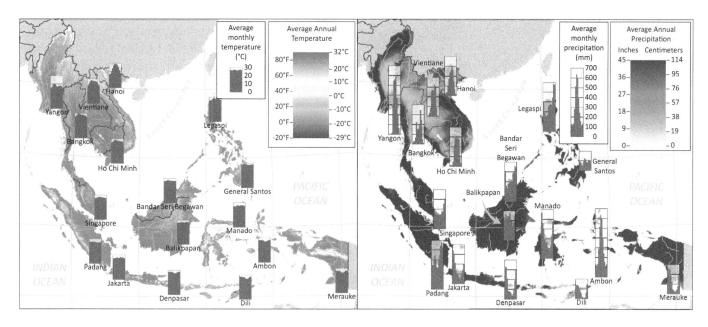

FIGURE 10.7 Southeast Asia: patterns of temperature and precipitation—With few exceptions, Southeast Asia is a warm and wet region. Away from the Equator, precipitation is strongly seasonal, though the month of maximum precipitation varies across the region. *Source:* WorldClim-Global Climate Data.

differences in precipitation patterns. For instance, in Singapore, November, December, and January are the wettest months of the year with more than 250 millimeters (10 inches) of precipitation in each month while May, June, and July receive fewer than 170 millimeters (7 inches) in each month. The wetter weather at year's end brings a modest but welcome relief from the typically punishing heat of the city-state's equatorial climate. Away from the Equator, the seasonality of the monsoon is more sharply expressed. In Manila, for instance, August averages 441 millimeters (17 inches) of precipitation versus just 8 millimeters (0.3 inches) in February.

The difference between Singapore and Manila is not just in the degree of seasonality but also in the timing of the wet versus dry season. Manila is characteristic of much of Southeast Asia in having the wettest season of the year in the northern hemisphere's summer months, but Singapore and cities south and east of the South China Sea, such as Bandar Seri Begawan (the capital of Brunei) have their heaviest precipitation in the northern hemisphere's winter months. The winter monsoon currents also influence Indonesia, though as the winds cross the Equator they are deflected towards the east. Nevertheless, most Indonesian cities have their heaviest precipitation during the winter monsoon. For Jakarta (6°S latitude), January is easily the wettest month of the year; this is also true for Dili, the capital of Timor-Leste.

Much of Southeast Asia is vulnerable to tropical storms, the most powerful of which are termed cyclones in the Indian Ocean and typhoons in the Pacific. For instance, Cyclone Nargis devastated Southern Myanmar in early May 2008. The storm passed near Yangon and other densely populated areas in the Irrawaddy delta, killing nearly 140,000 people. The military junta in control of the country at the time may have compounded the disaster by initially resisting offered foreign aid. At the other end of the region, the Philippines has been named the most typhoon-exposed country in the world. In November 2013, Typhoon Haiyan (called Yolanda in the Philippines) swept through the Visayas, an area of many small islands in the middle of the country, killing at least 6,300 people (Fig. 10.8). When it made landfall on the island of Samar, Haiyan had the strongest sustained one-minute wind speeds (315 kilometers per hour; 195 miles per hour) ever recorded at that time (though as described in Chapter 7, Hurricane Patricia off Mexico in 2015 had even stronger winds).

HUMAN-ENVIRONMENT INTERACTION

Tropical storms are just one of the natural hazards facing the people of Southeast Asia. Much of the region is also threatened by volcanoes and earthquakes, especially the swath of maritime Southeast Asia lying along the Pacific Ring of Fire (Fig. 10.9). Most of Southeast Asia sits on the Sunda Plate. The plate boundaries to the east, south,

FIGURE 10.8 Typhoon Haiyan approaches the Philippines—Typhoon Haiyan, known as Yolanda in the Philippines, made landfall on the island of Samar (upper left corner of this satellite image) on November 8, 2013 as one of the most powerful tropical storms ever recorded. *Source:* NASA Earth Observatory.

and west are complex and active. The configuration of plate boundaries means that earthquakes and active volcanoes are common along a semicircle through maritime Southeast Asia. Between 2001 and 2016, there were about 200 earthquakes in the region measuring at least 6.5 on the Richter scale, and they had epicenters in Myanmar, Indonesia (including very near Timor-Leste), and the Philippines. None occurred in the region's other countries, but the rest of Southeast Asia is hardly immune to these disasters, as illustrated by the catastrophic earthquake and Indian Ocean tsunami on December 26, 2004. At just before eight o'clock in the morning local time, an earthquake with a magnitude of 9.1, the strongest anywhere on Earth in more than forty years, ruptured an area of the Earth's crust 1,200 kilometers long (745 miles) and 100 kilometers (62 miles) wide off the northwest coast of Sumatra. The shaking lasted several minutes and released

an amount of energy equivalent to 23,000 Nagasaki atomic bombs, shifting a vast block of the Earth's crust ten meters (33 feet) to the west-southwest and uplifting it several meters. Simultaneously, a colossal volume of water in the Indian Ocean was displaced too, and the result was one of the world's most devastating tsunamis. The giant wave swept outward across the Indian Ocean. Within half an hour it had struck nearby Banda Aceh, Indonesia with waves up to ten meters (33 feet) in height, killing more than 130,000 people. After an hour and a half, the tsunami struck Southern Thailand, killing more than 5,000. After two hours, it struck Sri Lanka and India, killing 40,000 more people. More than seven hours after the initial earthquake, the tsunami reached East Africa, killing 150 people in Somalia on the opposite side of the Indian Ocean from the earthquake's distant epicenter. In all, an estimated 230,000 people lost their lives across fourteen countries (including Thailand and Malaysia, which typically face a very low earthquake hazard). The death toll was magnified by the lack of a tsunami warning system in the Indian Ocean basin (in contrast to the Pacific) so that coastal populations thousands of kilometers and hours away from the epicenter were tragically taken by surprise.

Within a few years, the devastated landscape left by the tsunami had been largely rebuilt. Before December 26, 2004, the region nearest the epicenter, a province called Aceh, had been home to a long-running conflict with the Indonesian government, but the tsunami disaster brought the rebellion to a swift end. The locally based rebels were much more adversely affected by the tsunami (many drowned) than the Indonesian army, and the government was forced to open up the region to much needed foreign assistance. And so in August of 2005, prodded by some of the outside forces, the two sides agreed to a peace deal in which the rebels would lay down their weapons (many had been destroyed anyway) and the government would withdraw some of its forces and give the region greater autonomy. The case of Aceh illustrates one of the myriad ways in which the physical environment—in this case via a catastrophe—influences human geography.

At the opposite end of Sumatra in the Sunda Strait lies a volcanic island called Krakatau. On August 28, 1883 at 10:02 in the morning, Krakatau erupted with unimaginable force[2]. Indeed, the eruption is considered the loudest sound in recorded human history; it was clearly heard hours later (given the speed of sound) in distant Australia and on the island of Rodrigues on the opposite side of the Indian Ocean (nearly 5,000 kilometers or 3,000 miles away). The eruption vaporized a chunk of the Earth's crust and caused a

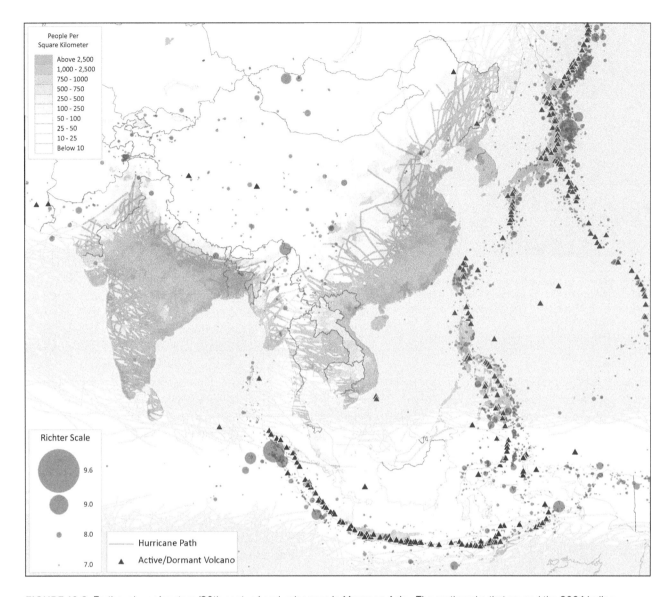

FIGURE 10.9 Earthquake epicenters (20th century) and volcanoes in Monsoon Asia—The earthquake that caused the 2004 Indian Ocean tsunami had an epicenter under the Indian Ocean off the northwest coast of Sumatra. *Source:* NOAA National Climatic Data Center; Earthquake Hazards Program; GeoTech Center Data Library.

devastating tsunami that swept over the nearby shorelines of Sumatra and Java.

Krakatau remains one of many active volcanoes through island Southeast Asia (Fig. 10.10). Their most significant legacy may be the fertile soil of the region and its rugged topography. Volcanic soils are usually rich in nutrients and contribute to the agricultural productivity of islands like Java and Luzon. At the same time, however, the geologically young region has many high volcanic peaks and rough terrain. In a region where wet-rice cultivation has long been the principal source of the staple food, people have dealt with the lack of flat land on which to situate rice paddies by constructing terraces. For instance, the Banaue rice terraces in the middle of Luzon are recognized

FIGURE 10.10 Krakatau—Although Krakatau was obliterated in a volcanic eruption in 1883, a new smaller volcano has grown up over the same "hot spot" in the earth's crust. *Source:* Wikimedia Commons.

FIGURE 10.11 The Banaue rice terraces—A village is perched amid the rice terraces in central Luzon. The terraces extend over a large area and have been designated a World Heritage Site. *Source:* John T. Bowen.

as a UNESCO World Heritage Site (Fig. 10.11). They were constructed more than 2,000 years ago without the help of heavy machinery. Over many generations, the terraces have been maintained against the forces of erosion through massive human effort, though now the migration of young people from the area to Manila and other cities is seen as a significant threat to their future integrity. The terraces,

FIGURE 10.12 Workers on an oil-palm plantation, Sabah, Malaysia—Oil-palm plantations have been expanded rapidly in Southeast Asia. The fruit of the oil-palm is processed into a widely used oil. *Source:* Wikimedia Commons.

which are only the most spectacular example of a land use pattern found throughout much of the region including Java and Bali, express—in the words of the World Heritage List—"the harmony between humankind and the environment."[3]

Today, it is harder to see that harmony. Indeed, Southeast Asia is home to several significant environmental issues. These include the dams on the Mekong previously mentioned, severe pollution of mangroves (trees and shrubs that grow in brackish water along coastlines) in Thailand that have been converted to shrimp farms, and overfishing—especially by Chinese boats—in the South China Sea[4]. Perhaps the most pressing is deforestation. The warm wet conditions found across most of Southeast Asia mean that the dominant natural land cover is tropical rainforest, and, as in tropical Africa and Latin America, deforestation has been rapid in recent decades. The broad forces behind deforestation are similar across these areas: population growth, expanded rural road networks, weak governance, and uncertain land ownership.

In Southeast Asia, a more specific factor has been the global surge in demand for palm oil. Oil-palm plantations have been planted across thousands of hectares of cleared forests, especially in Indonesia and Malaysia (Fig. 10.12). Palm oil is used in myriad products from soap to pizza and is regarded by some as healthier than other vegetable oils. Banks, both in Asia and the West, have invested heavily in supporting the expansion of oil-palm plantations, but the success of those investments has come at a heavy price. It has been estimated that daily emissions from burning in the Indonesian rainforest—much of it to clear land for plantations—at times exceeded emissions from all economic activity in the U.S. in 2015. The fires create choking haze across parts of Indonesia and its neighbors, especially during the monsoon dry season in the area (June, July, and August). For instance, on June 21, 2013, Singapore's Pollution Standards Index hit an all-time high of 401, far above the "hazardous" threshold of 300. The smoke closed schools in the region, caused flight delays at major airports, and compelled many to don facemasks to leave their homes. The clearing of the forests has also been devastating for the orangutan (a Malay word meaning "forest person") population in the region. Much of their habitat has been destroyed, pushing the International Union for the Conservation of Nature in 2016 to designate the animal as critically endangered.

By 2012, Indonesia had achieved the dubious distinction of having the fastest rate of tropical deforestation in the world, surpassing Brazil in this regard[5]. Geographers using remotely sensed satellite data have been instrumental in assessing these changes. By 2010, only 50 percent of Indonesia's primary forest (that is, original forest) remained, but that was still the highest in the region (by contrast, less than 1 percent of Vietnam's primary forest remained); primary forest is especially important in preserving Southeast Asia's remarkable biodiversity.

Many of the region's environmental problems, including deforestation, are likely to be eased by higher levels of economic development (as people value environmental protection more highly) and by slower population growth. Population change is the next theme.

POPULATION PATTERNS AND TRENDS

In 2016, the eleven countries of Southeast Asia had a combined population of 633 million people, or almost exactly the same as Latin America (Fig. 10.13). But while Southeast Asia extends over an immense area (for instance, Indonesia's east-west extent is about the same as the contiguous U.S.), much of that space is open water. Its land area is relatively small, and the result is that Southeast Asia's population density is three times that of Latin America. Compared to recent decades, the region's population is growing relatively slowly but remains highly dynamic given the mobility of Southeast Asians; many people live in countries other than those in which they were born.

With 259 million people, Indonesia is by far the most populous country in the region and the fourth most populous in the world, and the Philippines has just over 100 million people. At the other end of the spectrum, Brunei Darussalam has fewer than 500,000 people, and Timor-Leste just 1 million.

Population Distribution and Growth

Southeast Asia has highly uneven population density (Fig. 10.14). For instance, the island of Borneo—which is bigger than California and Nevada combined—had a population of about 22 million in 2015. By contrast, the much smaller island of Java—about the size of North Carolina—had a population of 141 million. Indeed, Java is among the most densely populated places on Earth.

These patterns in population distribution are readily explained by differences in soil fertility, accessibility, and development. As described above, Java's volcanic landscape is highly fertile and the island has long been home to well-organized, advanced societies. For instance, the Buddhist Borobudur temple complex, which, like the Banaue rice terraces is a UNESCO World Heritage Site, was begun

FIGURE 10.13 Southeast Asia reference map—Southeast Asia comprises eleven countries.

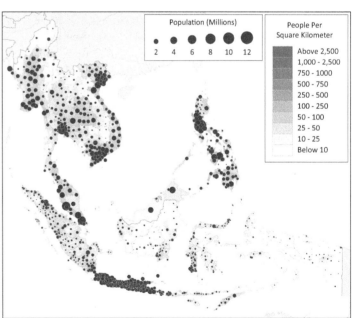

FIGURE 10.14 Population distribution in Southeast Asia—Java, Luzon, and the major river deltas on the mainland are the most densely populated parts of Southeast Asia. *Source:* GeoHive (www.geohive.com) and statistical agencies of selected countries.

FIGURE 10.15 Borobudur—Borobudur, an ancient Buddhist temple on the island of Java, is Indonesia's most popular tourist destination. *Source:* Wikimedia Commons.

in 750 CE in the shadow of Mount Merapi, Indonesia's most active volcano (Fig. 10.15). Conversely, Borneo's soils are mainly nutrient-poor soils found in wet, broadleaf forests and peat (a thick layer of partially decomposed organic matter). For much of its history, the island—especially its enormous interior—was very lightly populated by Dayaks, a loosely related group of indigenous peoples who traditionally lived in longhouse communities and practiced shifting cultivation. More generally, densely populated areas of Southeast Asia include those with volcanic soil, river valleys and deltas, highly accessible islands such as Singapore, and areas of historic labor-intensive plantation and mining activities (e.g. parts of Malaysia).

Across the region, population growth rates are generally modest. In 2016, the natural increase rate was 1.2 percent for the region as a whole. By contrast, thirty years earlier, the region was growing nearly twice as fast at 2.3 percent per year. Similarly, over the same period, the total fertility rate in the region fell from an average of just over four children per woman to 2.4. The reduction in family size is hardly unique to Southeast Asia, but the process is happening faster, partly because the region's economic development has been faster as well (Fig. 10.16).

Within the region, there is considerable variation in population growth due to natural increase. In Timor-Leste, the population is expanding at a rapid 3 percent per year, a rate at which the doubling time is just twenty-three years. No other country in the region has a rate as high as 2 percent, and several are much lower. In particular, Singapore's rate of 0.4 percent is characteristic of the rich countries elsewhere in the world that are like it.

The Philippines and Thailand offer an instructive demographic contrast. In 1950, the two countries had nearly identical populations of about 20 million each; but since then the Philippines has grown more rapidly, so much that by 2016 the Philippines had 103 million people and Thailand had 65 million. Demographic projections for mid-century call for the Philippines to have 149 million people, while Thailand's population will have already peaked and be on its way down at about 63 million. The different trajectories of the two countries reflect Thailand's more successful economic development and perhaps cultural differences. In particular, the powerful Catholic Church in the Philippines has used its clout to discourage contraception. In 2016, 38 percent of Filipino women of reproductive age used modern forms of contraception versus 77 percent of Thai women.

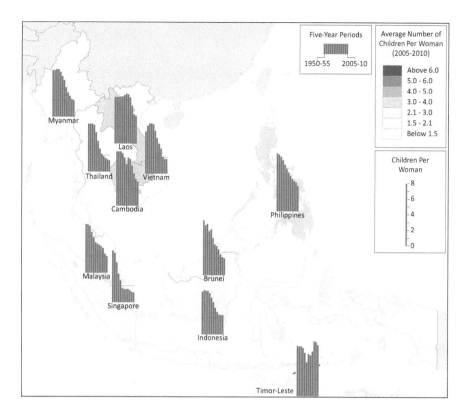

FIGURE 10.16 Total fertility rates in Southeast Asia, 1950–2010—Fertility rates have been declining across the region. In Singapore, Thailand, and Vietnam, fertility has now fallen below replacement level. *Source:* United Nations. Population Division. World Population Prospects 2012.

The faster population growth in the Philippines is likely one factor in its slower development, since it is harder for an economy to keep pace with a surging population, but in the 21st century, it is poised to be one of the world's economic stars because of its favorable demography. Much of Asia, including Thailand, is rapidly ageing; but the Philippines will remain a young country and will have a highly advantageous dependency ratio through the middle of the 21st century. The **dependency ratio** contrasts the number of people in dependent age groups, specifically young people aged 14 and under and the elderly aged 65 and over, with the number of people in the prime working-years, aged 15 to 64. In 2050, there will be 50 dependents for every 100 working-age people in the Philippines; in Thailand, there will be 75 dependents for every 100 working-age people.

The less favorable dependency ratio for Thailand in the decades ahead will mainly be driven by the country's rapid ageing. Singapore faces a similarly formidable problem on that front. In 2050, it is projected that Thailand will have 53 people aged 65 years and over for every one hundred working-age people, Singapore will have 49, Indonesia 24, and the Philippines just 14. Singapore has the advantage of great wealth with which to battle the challenges of an older population, but Thailand is among the growing number of middle-income countries confronted by the accelerated graying of their people.

International and Internal Migration

Southeast Asia has long been a significant destination for migrants. As Jared Diamond explains in *Guns, Germs, and Steel*, millennia ago people from China migrated into mainland Southeast Asia.[6] The earlier development of agriculture, writing, technology, and government in China gave the Chinese an advantage in outcompeting and ultimately displacing much of the indigenous population of the region. Therefore, Southeast Asians ended up looking much like the Chinese farther north. A few remnants of the original population remain; Malaysia's Orang Asli (meaning "original people" in Malay), for instance, numbered just over 100,000 people in 2003[7]. They tend to have darker skin and curlier hair than most Southeast Asians and have been subject to discrimination because of their supposed backwardness and the loss of their traditional lands.

In more recent centuries, migration from China has continued. Beginning in the 17th century and continuing through to the victory of the Communists in the Chinese

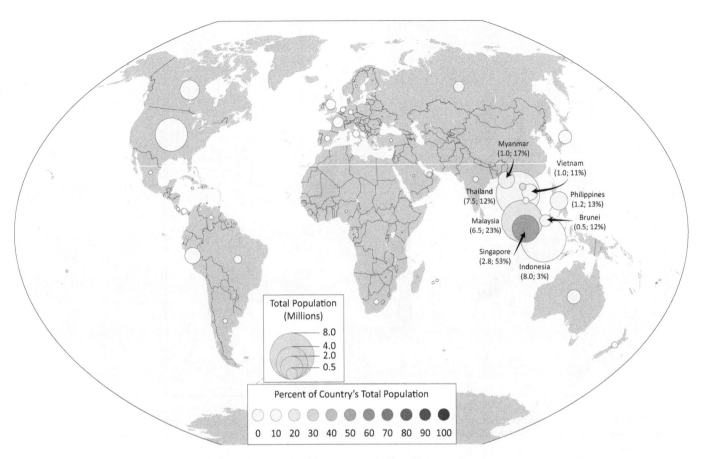

FIGURE 10.17 Distribution of the Overseas Chinese in Southeast Asia—Ethnic Chinese people are a significant minority across Southeast Asia except Singapore, where they comprise the majority of the population. *Source:* Poston, D. L. and Wong, J. H. 2016. "The Chinese diaspora: The current distribution of the overseas Chinese population" at http://journals.sagepub.com/doi/full/10.1177/2057150X16655077.

civil war in the 20th century, millions of so-called **Overseas Chinese** migrated in a great diaspora from Southern China to Southeast Asia. In 2011, there were 40.3 million Overseas Chinese (defined as people of mainly Chinese ancestry living outside China) worldwide, and 69 percent lived in Southeast Asia[8]. The largest communities were in Indonesia (8.0 million), Thailand (7.5 million), and Malaysia (6.5 million). Singapore is distinctive as the only majority Overseas Chinese country in the region (Fig. 10.17).

The Overseas Chinese are generally more affluent than other groups in Southeast Asia, partly because they have settled in cities that tend, in any case, to be richer than the surrounding countryside (Fig. 10.18). Additionally, the multiscalar business networks of the Chinese (e.g. links among Chinese-speaking people within Bangkok, within Thailand, across Southeast Asia, and globally) have contributed to their relative prosperity.

The Overseas Chinese have been subject to significant discrimination and exclusion, partly justified by their supposed loyalty to China rather than the societies in which they have settled. For instance, in the mid-1960s, thousands of ethnic Chinese Indonesians were killed and others forcibly expelled during a time of anticommunist purges in the country. The Overseas Chinese were also singled out for particular persecution after Communists gained control of Southern Vietnam in the 1970s. Many were sent to re-education camps and many others took their chances as "boat people"—refugees who, if they survived the dangerous escape by sea—ended up in places like the U.S. and Australia. Even in more recent years, the wealth of the ethnic Chinese has made them a scapegoat in economically difficult times. For instance, there were violent riots against Chinese-owned shops in Indonesia during that country's financial crisis in the late 1990s.

China was not the only significant source of migration flow to Southeast Asia in the past. Many Indians also migrated to what was then called Malaya and Singapore in 19th century. In Malaya, they worked in tin mines and rubber plantations as the British colony became incorporated into the world system. Today, both Malaysia and Singapore have sizeable Indian minorities, and, like

FIGURE 10.18 Gateway to Worarot district, Chiang Mai, Thailand—Many cities across Southeast Asia have a traditional Chinatown. Here is a gateway to the Chinese commercial district in Chiang Mai, Thailand. *Source:* John T. Bowen.

the Chinese, they tend to be better off than the region's indigenous population.

Southeast Asia is no longer a major destination for migration from other world regions, but smaller numbers of people continue to arrive. In particular, net migration to Singapore has been about 50,000 people per year. The migrants come from all over the world and are very diverse in contrast to the generally impoverished migrants of the past. There are poor people who work as maids and construction workers, but many of the foreign nationals are bankers, financial analysts, engineers, and other professionals. With Singapore's fertility rate stuck at a level far below replacement level (it was 1.2 in 2016, one of the lowest in the world), the migrants are vital to Singapore's continued prosperity, but they are controversial. Indeed, one of the few large public protests in Singapore in recent years was prompted by a government plan to increase the island's population from 5.3 million in 2014 to 6.9 million in 2030, by which time migrants would account for half the population. Bearing signs with messages like "Singapore for Singaporeans," thousands gathered to protest what they saw as unfair bias in favor of foreigners and the rapidly rising cost of living in an already crowded city-state.

Internal migration within Southeast Asian countries, meanwhile, is fairly modest except for rural-to-urban migration (discussed more fully below). In the past, several of the region's governments have sought to redistribute population toward less densely settled areas. In particular, Indonesia's government continued a program, called **transmigration**, begun under Dutch colonialism, to move people from the country's crowded Inner Islands (Java, Madura, Lombok, and Bali) to the Outer Islands (Fig. 10.19). The government helped transmigrant families clear plots of land in places like Sumatra and Papua and gave them resources to tide them over until they could be self-supporting farmers. In practice, many of the transmigrants ended not much better off than they had been in their provinces of origin. Often the areas into which they were moved were lightly populated because the soil was poor. Furthermore, shifting large numbers of people from one part of the country into another often exacerbated ethnic

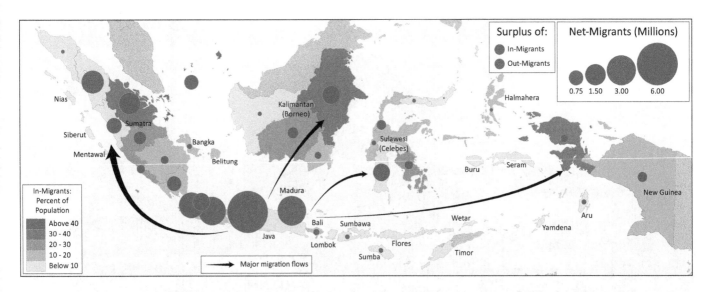

FIGURE 10.19 Migration flows within Indonesia, 1980–2010—The flow of migrants within Indonesia shows both the influence of the government's transmigration policy and the rural-to-urban migration that is common throughout the developing world. Notice the in-migration to places in Sumatra, Kalimantan, and Sulawesi but also to areas of west Java near Jakarta. *Source:* Statistics Indonesia.

tensions because the migrants typically differed in religion, language, or cultural traditions from the communities by which they were now surrounded. Some people in the Outer Islands perceived transmigration as a government attempt to control them by moving Javanese migrants into their communities.

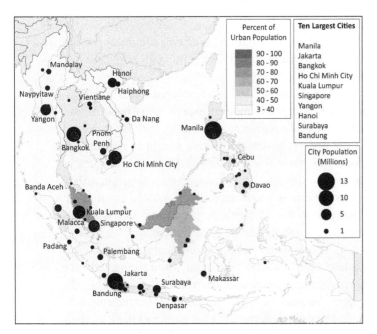

FIGURE 10.20 Urbanization levels in Southeast Asia, 2010—Urbanization rates are highest in the more developed parts of the region. *Source:* United Nations. Population Division. World Urbanization Prospects 2014; statistical agencies of individual countries.

In the late 1990s, as Indonesia tumbled into the Asian Financial Crisis, the transmigration program was abandoned. By then the program had cost billions of dollars and only resettled 4.5 million people in thirty years—a number equivalent to about two years' worth of net population growth in Java alone—and the resettlement of the families had cost the Indonesian government up to $27,000 each. Transmigration had proven an expensive, controversial, and ultimately ineffectual remedy for the population pressure in the country's Inner Islands. More recently, however, a more decentralized form of transmigration has emerged. In order to make up for labor deficits, districts in lightly populated areas of the country where oil palm plantations have been established have helped to sponsor the resettlement of families from some of the same sending regions that were prominent in the old transmigration program.

Primate Cities, Megacities, and World Cities

Southeast Asia is still a predominantly rural region but it is urbanizing quickly (Fig. 10.20). In 2016, 48 percent of the region's population lived in cities and towns, up from 39 percent a decade earlier. Such a difference means that thousands of people per day have been moving away from the bucolic rice paddies and lush forests of the countryside and into the bustling, noisy, and often chaotic cities from Yangon in the west to Manila in the east, from Hanoi in the north to Jakarta in the south, and to many other places in between. Naypyitaw, the city with which this chapter began, grew from essentially nothing to more than 1 million people in fewer than fifteen years.

A common theme of Southeast Asian urbanization is high rates of urban primacy. One way of measuring primacy is to contrast a country's largest city with its second largest. For instance, Metro Manila is eight times larger than the Davao metropolitan area, a city on the island of Mindanao. By comparison, Ho Chi Minh City is only twice as large as Hanoi (and New York City's metro population is only about 50 percent larger than that of Los Angeles). Manila is clearly a primate city; Ho Chi Minh City is not.

High rates of primacy are often considered problematic. The primate city absorbs too many resources, including a country's human resources as brain drain draws the best educated away from the rest of a country. Primate cities—which are usually political capitals too—also absorb disproportionate shares of government investment in schools, transportation, and other infrastructure. Such imbalances contribute to starkly uneven levels of development.

The problems of primacy are compounded when the primate city is also a mega-city. In 2015, there were two mega-cities in Southeast Asia: Manila (metro population 11.9 million) and Jakarta (10.3 million); and a third city—Bangkok (9.3 million)—was just below the threshold. Mega-cities, by their very concentration of activity, are rich with opportunities but typically suffer crushing traffic congestion, high land costs, severe air and water pollution, and are often surrounded by squatter settlements. The TomTom Traffic Index for 2017, which uses in-car global positioning system (GPS) data to measure congestion, rated Bangkok second worst in the world and Jakarta third after Mexico City (Manila was not included in the study).

Singapore is an example of how urban growth can be managed without succumbing to such problems, but as a city-state Singapore has a great advantage in that it can more easily control its growth. For instance, people who want to move to Singapore need a visa. Further, Singapore's government is highly competent but not democratic. This combination of circumstances has permitted the country to address some problems in ways that would be much more difficult in other cities. For instance, Singapore has managed traffic congestion (it ranked fifty-fifth in the TomTom study) by heavily taxing cars, investing massively in public transportation, and planning land use so that more people live close to their places of work. In mid-2017, a Toyota Corolla—which might retail for about $19,000 dollars in the U.S.—cost $70,000 dollars in

Buying a Toyota Corolla in Singapore, Mid-2017	
Item	**Cost (US Dollars)**
Open Market Value	14,381
Certificate of Entitlement	32,519
Registration Fee	245
Additional Registration Fee	14,381
Customs Duty	2,876
General Sales Tax	1,007
Road Tax	612
Dealer Profit	9,510
Total	**75,531**

FIGURE 10.21 Buying a car in Singapore, 2017—Singaporeans who wish to purchase a car must first bid for the right to own one. This right, called a Certificate of Entitlement, cost about $33,000 for a small car in mid-2017. A car buyer must also pay a variety of taxes, which raise the cost of the vehicle far above its open market value (what the car itself costs to produce). *Source:* John T. Bowen.

Singapore, with the difference almost entirely due to government-imposed taxes (Fig. 10.21). The heavy taxes have helped to pay for one of the densest, most efficient public transportation systems in the world, making the fact that many middle class Singaporeans cannot afford a car (or a second car like many American households) more politically palatable.

Limiting congestion is important to Singapore because it is engaged in a ferocious international competition for status, talent, and foreign investment, like several other cities in the region. Singapore is a world city, a command-and-control center of the global economy. In fact, Singapore is one of the most important cities of this kind. Scholars who study the global financial system classify world cities into several layers, with the two most powerful classified as Alpha++ cities: London and New York; but, Singapore ranks third as first among the Alpha+ cities[9]. Jakarta and Kuala Lumpur are not too far behind, and then farther back lie Bangkok and Manila. These cities mediate the flows of money, information, and ideas that comprise the lifeblood of the global economy, and they are constantly jostling with one another for position. High-quality infrastructure, good quality of life, and the "buzz" of a vibrant economy are important to holding onto and improving one's position.

The success of these cities ensures that they will remain magnets for future rural-to-urban migration, further shifting the balance of population in these countries and the region. Within a few years, Southeast Asia will for the first time be a predominantly urban region, rich with opportunities but burdened by the persistent problems of unbalanced growth, too.

LANGUAGE AND RELIGION

Southeast Asia's crossroads situation has contributed to its extraordinary cultural diversity. Millennia of diffusion from China in the north and India in the west have shaped its religious and linguistic geography. The connection to the Muslim Middle East on the other side of the Indian Ocean is also ancient. More recently, European colonization, U.S. postwar dominance of the Pacific Basin, and myriad foreign influences from around the world have added to the cultural mix.

Linguistic Diversity

Southeast Asia is home to four main language families (Fig. 10.22). In the western part of the mainland, several Sino-Tibetan languages are spoken, including Burmese, Thai, and Lao. Farther east on the mainland are many languages of the Austro-Asiatic language family including Mon (a language spoken on the border of Myanmar and Thailand), Khmer (the main language of Cambodia), and Vietnamese. Mon, Khmer, and related languages are among the oldest languages spoken in Southeast Asia and were once more widely dominant, but they were displaced by languages that diffused from China a little more than 2,000 years ago. For instance, Thai evolved from a language that

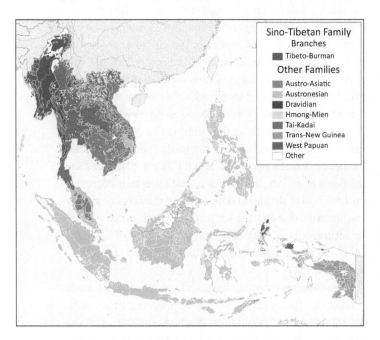

FIGURE 10.22 Distribution of major linguistic families in Southeast Asia—The distribution of the main languages in Southeast Asia shows the distinction between mainland and maritime parts of the region. Source: World Language Mapping System.

originated in Southern China. Thai is the main language in the Tai-Kadai language family, which dominates the center of mainland Southeast Asia.

In maritime Southeast Asia, a different language family, Austronesian, is dominant. The family includes Tagalog and the many other languages of the Philippines; Balinese, Javanese, and hundreds of other languages in Indonesia; and Malay, which is spoken on both sides of the Straits of Malacca. This family too traces its origins to China, specifically Taiwan. From there, beginning about 6,000 years ago, the language family diffused in clockwise fashion across Southeast Asia, nearby areas of the Pacific (including Hawaii), and across the Indian Ocean to Madagascar—fragmenting into hundreds of distinct languages along the way[10].

The tremendous linguistic diversity of the region—especially the two great archipelagic countries—has posed a significant challenge for nation-building. The Philippines has two official languages, partly in response to this challenge: Tagalog and English. Tagalog is the most widely spoken Philippine language and is dominant in the most densely populated parts of the country on the island of Luzon. English is a kind of lingua franca, widely used by Filipinos to speak with one another when their own mother tongues are mutually unintelligible. English was introduced into the country by the U.S., which colonized the Philippines in the first half of the 20th century; and since then the U.S. has remained a major factor in the Philippine economy and culture. A 2008 survey found that about 75 percent of Filipinos could read and speak English, compared to about 85 percent who could speak Tagalog (though only about 38 percent speak Tagalog as a mother tongue).

In Indonesia, conversely, the language of the former colonial power, Dutch, is not common at all. In fact, Dutch colonial authorities discouraged those they ruled from learning the language because they feared losing power in the East Indies. Somewhat ironically, the independence struggle against the Dutch was the catalyst for the emergence of what would become Indonesia's sole national language and its lingua franca: Bahasa Indonesia, which means the "Indonesian Language." Bahasa Indonesia has its roots in Malay, which was traditionally spoken in parts of Sumatra and on the Malay Peninsula. For thousands of years, Malay had been used as traders' lingua franca by the merchants plying routes among the thousands of islands in the region. As nationalism grew in the colony in the early 20th century, Malay was adopted as the basis for the new Bahasa Indonesia because it was easy to learn—in contrast to the more popular Javanese, for instance—and could more readily unify the disparate forces struggling against foreign rule. Once independence was secured in 1949, Bahasa Indonesia was taught in all schools across the country, its spelling was standardized, and its vocabulary greatly enlarged to accommodate a wider variety of uses. Still Bahasa Indonesia is not dominant as a mother tongue; in the country's 2010 census, only 43 million people (about 17 percent of the total) spoke it as a native language, but another 155 million spoke it as a second or third language in the country.

Singapore has embraced a different approach for dealing with linguistic diversity. Despite its small size, the city-state has adopted four official languages: English, the language of the former colonial power (Britain); Mandarin Chinese, a language of the ethnic Chinese majority; Malay, the chief indigenous language in the Straits of Malacca region; and Tamil, a language brought to the city-state by migrants from Southern India in the 19th century. Interestingly, Mandarin was not widely spoken among Singaporean Chinese until recent decades. The Overseas Chinese (see above) who came to the island in the 19th and 20th centuries spoke diverse languages of Southern China, including Cantonese (dominant in and around Hong Kong). But the government of Singapore, through its "Speak Mandarin Campaign," has promoted Mandarin for decades as a means of unifying its ethnic Chinese population, facilitating second language education, and leveraging Singapore's prominent place within the Overseas Chinese business networks.

In mainland Southeast Asia, there is less linguistic diversity, though the highlands that ring the great river basins of Myanmar and Thailand are certainly home to numerous linguistic minorities. Another noteworthy feature of language there is the different writing systems in use in this part of Southeast Asia. Burmese, Thai, Lao, and Khmer are all written with variations of Pavalla script, a form of writing that diffused from India in about the sixth century CE. Vietnamese, conversely, is written with a kind of modified Roman script called Quoc-ngu, which was first developed by Portuguese Christian missionaries in the mid-17th century and later refined by a French missionary.

Religious Diversity

As with language, Southeast Asia's religious patterns reflect the external forces that have washed over the region from myriad directions (Fig. 10.23). The earliest of these forces (but one now almost completely absent) was Hinduism. Two thousand years ago, Hinduism began to influence elites

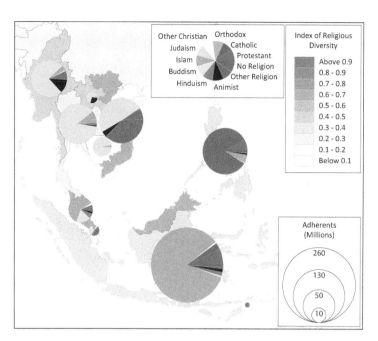

FIGURE 10.23 Distribution of major religions in Southeast Asia—Mainland Southeast Asia is predominantly Buddhist while Maritime Southeast Asia is mainly Muslim except for the predominantly Catholic Philippines and Timor-Leste. *Source:* Association of Religious Data Archives.

in both mainland and maritime Southeast Asia. Spectacular legacies of that influence are evident at sites like Angkor Wat in Cambodia and Prambanan in Indonesia, both of which are UNESCO World Heritage Sites today. Angkor—at the center of which is Angkor Wat—was the capital of a great Khmer kingdom, which at its height reigned over a broad stretch of Southeast Asia from modern-day Myanmar to Vietnam. Built over the 9th to 15th centuries CE and home to up to 750,000 people, it may have been the largest city in the world in its heyday. The kingdom was Hindu in orientation, and Angkor Wat—the most famous part of the city—was built as a temple of the Hindu god Vishnu. More than 2,000 kilometers (1,200 miles) to the southeast lies Prambanan, built in central Java in the eight to ninth centuries. It is a spectacular testament to the long-ago devotion of people in this area to the Hindu pantheon. Both temples are towering structures richly adorned with bas-relief carvings relaying the Hindu epics and local histories.

Today, however, few Southeast Asians are Hindu. The island of Bali, just east of Java, is the most enduring remnant of the religion's former sway in the region. About 84 percent of Balinese are Hindu. Elsewhere in the region, there are significant Hindu minorities wherever large numbers of Indians settled during the colonial period, including Singapore (5 percent) and Malaysia (6 percent).

Divisions in Buddhism

Theravada	Mahayana
Southern	*Northern*
Way of the Elders	Greater Vehicle

Ultimate purpose of life and the way to attain it

Seek *enlightenment* first to become a perfect saint (arhat), then help others to achieve enlightenment and *nirvana*	Help others first by becoming a saint (boddhisatva) who unselfishly delays *nirvana* to help others, then achieves *nirvana*
Intense, dedicated, and time-consuming effort required to attain enlightenment	Enlightenment achieved through a normal life with varying degrees of spiritual involvment
Enlightenment cannot be achieved in one life cycle	Enlightenment can be achieved in one life cycle
Emphasis on monastic life and silent meditation	Emphasis on daily activities and mantras and chanting
Politically conservative	Politically liberal
Sri Lanka, Thailand, Myanmar, Cambodia, Laos	Japan, China, Tibet, Mongolia, Korea, Vietnam

FIGURE 10.24 Divisions of Buddhism—About 85 percent of the world's Buddhists practice either the Mahayana or Theravada form of the religion. *Source:* World History Religions Projects: Buddhism at https://buddhism-korea.weebly.com/index.html

As with Hinduism, the extent of Buddhism was once far greater than its current geography. Not far from Prambanan lies Borobudur in the middle of Java. It is the world's largest Buddhist temple, but it lies in an overwhelmingly Muslim region today. In fact, after Java's rulers adopted Islam, Borobudur fell into disuse and was largely swallowed by ash and

FIGURE 10.25 Buddhist monks check their cell phones in Myanmar—A pair of monks wear traditional saffron robes but also show the arrival of mobile phone technology in what was until recently one of the world's most isolated states. *Source:* Larissa Krüger.

the encroaching rainforest. The site was reclaimed during European colonial rule and has been restored. Today, it is Indonesia's most popular tourist destination.

Buddhism never relinquished its grip on the cultures of mainland Southeast Asia. The main form of Buddhism here is Theravada (see Chapter 8 for more on the branches of Buddhism), similar to Sri Lanka on the other side of the Indian Ocean. The other main branch is Mahayana, which is more common in Northeast Asia but diffused from there into Vietnam (Fig. 10.24). A hallmark of Theravada is the monastic way of life. Many boys and men live as Buddhist monks for a time (Fig. 10.25); and a smaller proportion of girls and women likewise choose to be nuns. For instance, in Thailand there were approximately 300,000 monks and novices in 2012. This number may seem small in relation to Thailand's population of 65 million, but most adult men spend only a few months as a monk; so, at any given time, there are relatively few monks, but over time many people share in this experience. In Thailand's poorer neighbors, the appeal of the monastic life is even greater, especially for young people because the monasteries offer an avenue toward education and the opportunities to which education leads. Wearing their striking saffron-colored robes, monks can be seen early in the morning walking barefoot on their alms round. Buddhist lay people place rice in the monks' cups and sometimes give small bags of curries or flowers or little packets of money. Doing so allows ordinary Buddhists to "make merit" for a more favorable station in the next life after reincarnation. The monks bless those who make offerings and then return to their monasteries. Monks are not permitted to handle money directly and are allowed only two meals per day, the last of which must be consumed before noon. Much of each day is devoted to prayer, chanting, and meditation. Meanwhile, lay people help to clean temples as another way of making merit (Fig. 10.26).

Although the monastic way of life is simple, the reverence with which monks are treated by the local population gives them considerable political power. In 2007, massive protests against the military junta in Myanmar were led by thousands of Buddhist monks. The Saffron Revolution, named after the color of the monks' robes, was sparked by economic problems in the country and the violence the regime had used in crushing earlier protests. The Saffron Revolution was aggressively suppressed too, but just four years later the country embarked on its promising turn towards democracy.

A focal point for the 2007 protests was the gold-leaf-covered Shwedagon Pagoda in Yangon (Fig. 10.27), which was the tallest structure in the country until 2017. The other predominantly Buddhist countries have their own famous religious structures. For instance, That Luang—also

FIGURE 10.26 Making merit in Myanmar—Buddhists, such as these women at the Shwedagon Pagoda in Yangon, Myanmar, can gain spiritual favor for a better life now or in the future by doing good deeds, including keeping this sacred site clean. *Source:* Larissa Krüger.

FIGURE 10.27 Shwedagon Pagoda, Yangon, Myanmar—The 99-meter (326-foot) tall pagoda, which is covered in gold leaf and studded with diamonds, dominates the skyline of Yangoon. Deep within the pagoda lies a vessel containing eight hairs from the head of the Buddha. *Source:* Larissa Krüger.

FIGURE 10.28 Muslim girls in Indonesia—Muslim women and girls usually wear a headscarf, called a jilbab, in Indonesia. *Source:* Wikimedia Commons.

covered in gold—in Vientiane is a revered symbol of Laos. Farther north in Luang Prabang, the ancient capital of a Buddhist kingdom, are numerous Buddhist temples or wats that now attract millions of visitors annually. In Thailand, Bangkok's Wat Traimit contains the world's largest solid gold statue—a statue of the Buddha, of course.

While Buddhism dominates much of the mainland, Islam reigns across most of maritime Southeast Asia. There are several competing ideas for when and how Islam arrived in the region. The most widely held view is that it was carried across the Indian Ocean by Muslim traders from the Arabian Peninsula and India reaching Sumatra in the seventh or eighth centuries CE. Others contend that it may have come to the region via China or may have come earlier. In any case, Southeast Asia's first Islamic kingdom had been established in Sumatra by the 13th century. Islam spread slowly, however, as Buddhism and Hinduism were already entrenched across the region, including in Java.

Today, Islam is dominant across almost all of Indonesia, the Malay Peninsula, Brunei, the southern Philippines,

Southern Thailand, and Western Myanmar. The principal form of Islam in the region is Sunni (see Chapter 5), as is true across most of the Muslim world. Indonesia is the world's most populous predominantly Muslim country (87 percent of Indonesians are Muslim), but it has not made Islam its official state religion. Instead, the country's early nationalist leadership adopted as its official ideology Pancasila, which means "five principles." Among these is "belief in one God," a statement vague enough to be compatible with faiths beyond Islam.

By contrast, Islam is the official state religion in Malaysia and Brunei. The case of Malaysia, which is among the most diverse countries in the region, is especially interesting. Only about 61 percent of the population is Muslim, yet Islam has been privileged—just as Malay has been named the country's official language. These designations reflect the preference given to the ethnic Malays in the country. For complex historical reasons, the Malays were disadvantaged when the area was under British colonial rule. Since Malaysia gained its independence in 1963, the interests of Malays have been put first in numerous ways.

In much of Southeast Asia, the practice of Islam is moderate[11]. For instance, it is common for an Indonesian woman to wear a headscarf (called a *jilbab* in local parlance) but also to wear a colorful, form-fitting blouse-dress combination called a *kebaya* or even to wear blue jeans (Fig. 10.28). And in contrast to some other parts of the Muslim world, in Indonesia and Malaysia educational attainment for boys and girls is nearly identical. Sharia law is practiced in some regions (like Aceh in Northern Indonesia) but is not the norm.

However, Islamic fundamentalism has been on the rise in recent years and militant Islamists (the use of violence or the threat of violence to advance a radical Muslim ideology) have been active. Stronger connections, via mass media and frequent air travel, to the Arabian Peninsula have helped to propagate a more puritanical version of Islam to Southeast Asia[12]. Islamist terror groups have carried out bombings and other attacks. The deadliest of these was the nearly simultaneous bombing of a discotheque and bar in Bali in 2002. The attack, for which a group linked to Al Qaeda claimed responsibility, killed more than 200 people, among whom were many foreign (mainly Australian) tourists. Still, Islamists are weaker here than in some other regions, partly because Southeast Asia is far from the core of the Muslim world[13].

The last religion of great significance in the region is Christianity, especially Roman Catholicism. European colonial powers, and later American missionaries, brought the religion to Southeast Asia beginning in the 16th century. The impact was greatest in the Philippines (Fig. 10.29), where the lack of a deeply entrenched prior religious tradition meant relatively little resistance to the diffusion of Christianity. But by the time Catholic missionaries arrived in the Philippines, the diffusion of Islam had already reached the southern islands. Today, there is an important cultural cleavage through the southern Philippines between the dominant Christian north and center and the majority Muslim south, and violence between the national government and Muslim rebels on Mindanao and other nearby islands along this cleavage is a recurring theme in recent Philippine history.

The Spanish reorganized the Filipino population in order to facilitate conversion, regrouping the dispersed rural population into compact settlements. At the center of each village was the church. The forced urbanization of the colonial population was a catalyst for broader Hispanization of the Philippines as well. Many Filipinos, for instance, have Hispanic surnames; recent presidents of the independent Philippines had the following surnames: Aquino, Arroyo, Ramos, and Marcos.

The church remains strongly influential in everyday life. For instance, in 2015 the Pew Research Center found that among forty countries surveyed, the Philippines had the strongest opposition to divorce and especially

FIGURE 10.29 The history of the Manila cathedral—The plaque on the front of the Manila Cathedral attests to the country's long history of Catholicism and the many natural and human hazards the region has faced. *Source:* John T. Bowen.

abortion—views that are in line with church teaching. Furthermore, the largest papal mass in history took place when Pope Francis visited Manila in January 2015, with more than 6 million in attendance.

Beyond the Philippines, other significant Christian areas include Timor-Leste, which is also overwhelmingly Catholic, and remote areas elsewhere in the region. Christian missionaries have been active in highlands in mainland Southeast Asia, for example. And Singapore, too, has a growing Christian community. The city-state is now home to several Christian megachurches. City Harvest Church, for instance, offers services in multiple languages at a centrally located convention center seating more than 6,000 people. The increased popularity of evangelical Christianity as Singapore's wealth has grown suggests that other parts of the region might become more Christian, too, as their own economies continue to expand.

POLITICAL ORGANIZATION OF SPACE

Southeast Asia's political geography has followed a trajectory somewhat like Europe: from great fragmentation among many different state centuries ago, and a long history of violent conflict to increased unity today. The Association of Southeast Asian Nations (ASEAN), introduced at the beginning of this chapter, is not as powerful as the European Union, but it does draw together a once fractious region in the pursuit of shared goals—especially economic development. Like Europe, a region once beset by innumerable wars, Southeast Asia has become a largely peaceful region today.

Kingdoms at Sea and on Land: Southeast Asia before European Imperialism

A thousand years ago, much of Southeast Asia was lightly populated and its people lived largely beyond the reach of any effective state. Both on land and at sea, states rose and fell, but their dominion was limited. At the beginning of the 11th century CE, the two most powerful states included one whose power was mainly exercised at sea and one firmly anchored on land. Srivijaya, from its base in the city of Palembang on Sumatra, was a sea-based empire. It controlled the vital Straits of Malacca and coastal areas in present-day Java, Borneo, and the Malay Peninsula. Srivijaya was predominantly Buddhist, and it was one of the kingdom's rulers who ordered the construction of Borobudur.

In mainland Southeast Asia, the most powerful kingdom at the beginning of the 11th century CE, was the Khmer Empire. The kingdom emerged near the Tonle Sap, a lake in the middle of what is now Cambodia. During the summer monsoon, the Tonle Sap River, which normally drains the lake and serves as a tributary of the Mekong, reverses direction. The swollen Mekong then pours into the Tonle Sap River, making the river a distributary. The river flows into the Tonle Sap, greatly enlarging the lake. Indeed, the Tonle Sap increases in size from a low of about 1,000 square kilometers (390 square miles) during the dry season to about 4,000 square kilometers (1,540 square miles) during the June–November wet season. The annual cycle of flooding makes the surrounding landscape difficult to manage, but it is also highly fertile. The lake, too, is remarkably rich in resources (Fig. 10.30). From this advantageous base, Angkor

FIGURE 10.30 A fishing village on the Tonle Sap, Cambodia—Kompong Phluk is located on the northern shore of Tonle Sap, not far from the ruins of Angkor. *Source:* Pixabay.

extended its reign across much of mainland Southeast Asia at its height.

Yet much as Tonle Sap expands and contracts, these early states expanded and ultimately contracted too. Srivijaya was eventually displaced by a Java-based kingdom, and the Khmer lost power to an expansive Thai state. States rose and fell, their capitals shifted positions, and frontiers (there were almost no well-defined borders) were pushed back and forth. And much of the region—especially highland areas—remained outside state control. This dynamic political geography would be profoundly reshaped by the arrival of European powers beginning in the early 16th century.

European Imperialism in Southeast Asia

In Eastern Indonesia between Sulawesi and New Guinea lies a group of a thousand or so islands called the Maluku Islands (also known as the Moluccas). One of the smallest of these is an inconspicuous place called Pulau Run (or Run Island). About three kilometers (1.9 miles) long and a little more than a kilometer (0.6 miles) across, the little island is remote: to get there from New York City in 2017 would require flying for a day and a half via Tokyo and Jakarta to the eastern Indonesian city of Ambon; and then taking a five- to six-hour boat ride from Ambon to Pulau Run's neighbor, Bandaneira; and then finally taking another two-hour boat ride from Bandaneira to Pulau Run. With time waiting between flights and boats, it might reasonably take three days to get from the island of Manhattan to the island of Run. Yet, Pulau Run was once among the most important places in the world and has a striking connection to Manhattan[14].

In the 17th century, the Moluccas were the world's principal source of highly sought-after spices, especially nutmeg, which was found only on Pulau Run and other nearby islands. Nutmeg, then, was prized for its medicinal properties, including claims that it warded off the plague. At its height, demand for the spice was such that the price in Europe was 60,000 times higher than price in the Moluccas. The vast profits to be made stirred a great competition among European powers to find and control the "Spice Islands." The Portuguese got there first in 1511 but did little more than trade with the local people. Almost a century later, the Dutch arrived and compelled the local rulers to agree to a monopoly, but then the English showed up on the scene and traded at even better prices. The Dutch East India Company responded ruthlessly, eventually laying siege to Pulau Run and burning its nutmeg trees. The English

FIGURE 10.31 European imperialism in Southeast Asia—By the end of the 19th century, Europeans controlled much of Southeast Asia. Laos, Cambodia, and Vietnam comprised French Indochina. Britain dominated Burma, Malaya, and Singapore. The East Indies were a Dutch possession except for the Portuguese colony of Timor. The Philippines were under Spanish rule but the U.S. would gain control of the archipelago in the early 20th century.

relented but did not give up their claims to Pulau Run until the 1667 Treaty of Breda in which England ceded control of the faraway spice island in exchange for Holland ceding control of New Amsterdam—that is, Manhattan.

By the early 19th century, the spice trade was fading in importance. The Moluccas' monopoly on nutmeg, for instance, was broken when nutmeg trees were smuggled out by the French to Madagascar and later to other places. The value of nutmeg fell as did that of other spices. More generally, the first period of colonialism in Southeast Asia—**merchant colonialism**, in which colonies were economically valuable principally for the precious and exotic goods such as spices they supplied to European powers—was ending. In its place, a new model—**industrial colonialism**—emerged based on Southeast Asian colonies producing raw materials and in turn becoming markets for European manufactured goods. For instance, Malaya became a vital source first of tin and then rubber, and, in turn, it absorbed British manufactures like machinery.

At the same time, the extent of European control over the region continued to grow (Fig. 10.31). Near the end of the 19th century, Britain controlled Burma and Malaya, France controlled **Indochina** (out of which would be carved Vietnam, Laos, and Cambodia), and the Netherlands dominated the East Indies (much of present-day Indonesia).

Spain was ending nearly four centuries of control in the Philippines, and Portugal still held Timor. Only Thailand, partly through the skillful machinations of the Thai king keeping European powers at bay, managed to avoid direct Western colonization.

In the 20th century, two new Pacific powers entered the fray. American victories in the Spanish-American War and then the Philippine-American War (the latter being one of the least known conflicts in U.S. history) led to U.S. control of the Philippines. Because the U.S. was a country whose national identity was based on ideals of freedom and independence, possessing a colony on the far side of the Pacific was a deeply ambivalent experience. Mark Twain wrote at the time, "We cannot maintain an empire in the Orient and maintain a republic in America."[15] The U.S. sought to be a different sort of colonial power than the Europeans elsewhere in the region; more Filipinos were incorporated into the colonial bureaucracy, and the U.S. more strongly emphasized public education (but the school curriculum sang the praises of the U.S.). The U.S. granted the Philippines its independence as promised on July 4, 1946. Today, the date passes largely unnoticed there. Instead, Filipinos commemorate June 12—the anniversary of the 1898 declaration of independence from Spain.

A different rising power, imperial Japan, would usher in an end to Western imperialism in Southeast Asia. On July 27, 1940, Japan declared the formation of the Greater East Asia Co-Prosperity Sphere, a Japanese-dominated economic region whose boundaries encompassed most of Asia, including all of Southeast Asia. The stated purpose of the sphere was integrated economic development. In reality, Japan sought to supplant rule by Western countries with its own power. In fact, that is just what Japan did. In September 1940, Japan invaded French-controlled Vietnam just months after Japan's ally Germany invaded France. And then in December 1941, almost simultaneous with the attack on Pearl Harbor, Japanese aircraft bombed the Philippines, Malaya, Singapore, and Thailand (because of the International Date Line, the attacks in Asia occurred on December 8th rather than December 7th, the "day of infamy" in the U.S.). By early 1942, Japan controlled much of the region.

Ultimately, the Japanese would prove unable to hold onto their territorial gains in Southeast Asia, but their astonishing victories early in the war shattered the myths of white supremacy upon which Western imperialism had been partly based. After the Japanese were repulsed from the region in 1945, the old colonial powers attempted in various ways to return to their positions of power, but every place in Southeast Asia—except East Timor—would be politically independent within a generation. Unfortunately,

the transition to sovereignty would become a violent cataclysm in much of the region, with a death toll that climbed into the millions.

From Falling Dominoes to Falling Borders: Southeast Asia's Political Geography Since 1945

On September 2, 1945, on the same day the Japanese formally surrendered on the deck of the USS Missouri ending World War II, the Vietnamese nationalist Ho Chi Minh stood before a crowd of thousands in Hanoi and declared independence for the Republic of Vietnam from France. In his second sentence, he quoted Thomas Jefferson in the American Declaration of Independence: "All men are created equal; they are endowed by their Creator with certain inalienable Rights; among these are Life, Liberty, and the pursuit of Happiness." Ho hoped to win the support of the U.S., which emerged from the war as the world's foremost superpower; but as soon as one war ended, another—the Cold War—began. The U.S. needed the support of France in the new conflict and so refused to acknowledge Vietnam's independence. Ironically, the American response helped to push Vietnam deeper into the arms of the Communists.

By the end of 1946, the First Indochina War had broken out between the Communist Viet Minh and the French government. Fighting was concentrated in the northern third of Vietnam but also spilled over into other parts of Vietnam and neighboring Laos and Cambodia. In the end, the French suffered a crushing defeat at Dien Bien Phu, a base in the hills of Northwestern Vietnam. In response, the two sides agreed in the 1954 Geneva Accords that all French forces would be withdrawn from Indochina and that Vietnam would be split in two along the 17th parallel with the Viet Minh under Ho governing the north and a U.S.-backed government controlling the south.

Just two years later, the Second Indochina War began, with the U.S. and its allies fighting the Viet Minh and other Communist forces. Inexorably, the U.S. found itself dragged even deeper into the region and its conflicts as American policy was shaped by the Domino Theory, the idea that the fall of Russia to the Communists in 1917 and China in 1949 would be followed by other "dominoes" falling unless the U.S. intervened to prop up its allies. And so, an initial influx of U.S. advisors supporting South Vietnam in the early 1960s evolved into a massive American force by the late 1960s. Ultimately, nearly 60,000 Americans were killed in the war and more than 1 million Vietnamese. The result was another victory for Communist forces, who rolled into the southern capital Saigon (later renamed Ho Chi Minh City) on April 30, 1975, reuniting the fractured country under a single government for the first time since the 1940s.

During the Second Indochina War (known as the American War in Vietnam and the Vietnam War in the U.S.), fighting was concentrated in Vietnam (especially the south) but spilled over into Laos and Cambodia when the U.S. undertook massive bombing of the Ho Chi Minh Trail, a supply route to Communist insurgents in Southern Vietnam that passed through Laos and Cambodia. Between 1964 and 1973, the U.S. dropped 2,093,100 tons of bombs on Laos—one-third more than had been dropped on Nazi Germany and three times higher than the tonnage unleashed during the Korean War. In both Laos and Cambodia, the devastation of the war helped garner popular support for Communist insurgencies with the Pathet Lao seizing control of Laos and the Khmer Rouge (the "Red Khmer") prevailing in Cambodia.

The **Khmer Rouge** was an especially virulent force. Its leader Pol Pot declared Year Zero, evacuated cities, and began mercilessly persecuting so-called "class enemies"—doctors, teachers, engineers, and factory owners, as well as ethnic minorities (e.g. the country's Overseas Chinese community). As a measure of the devastation inflicted on the country, of 485 doctors in 1975 only forty-three lived to see the end of the Khmer Rouge era. More than 1 million people were murdered in killing fields, sites around the country where mass executions were carried out. Another 1–2 million died due to starvation and disease as the Khmer Rouge's disastrous policies crippled the country. The Khmer Rouge genocide only ended when Vietnam invaded Cambodia in 1978 in retaliation for a series of increasingly hostile border conflicts.

The Cold War-infused conflicts between Communists and their political adversaries were not limited to Indochina. In all of the larger countries in Southeast Asia, there were significant ideological conflicts in the decades after World War II. In Indonesia, perhaps as many as 1 million Communists—many of them ethnic Chinese—were killed by the army and vigilantes in 1965–66. Smaller-scale violence broke out in Thailand, Malaysia, and the Philippines.

By the 1980s, however, the region was moving towards peace. The end of the Cold War accelerated these changes and led to a period of new openness and economic vibrancy in the region. Vietnam adopted *doi moi* or renovation in 1986, which began to liberalize the economy. Similarly, Laos began to break with a decade of self-enforced isolation and a rigidly state-controlled economy with the implementation of what its government called "New Thinking", also in 1986.

Signaling how far the political divisions of the Cold War had retreated into the past, Southeast Asia took a big

FIGURE 10.32 The ASEAN Economic Community—The ASEAN Economic Community has lowered trade barriers among its members since 2015. *Source:* John T. Bowen.

step forward toward integration when Vietnam (1995), Laos (1997), Myanmar (1997), and Cambodia (1999) joined ASEAN. A primary purpose of ASEAN's formation in the 1960s had been to contain the threat of communism; now, three decades later, the group was admitting four countries, three of which were in various stages along the transition from Communist to free-market economies.

Along with ASEAN's enlargement has come a significant change in the organization's economic integration. In 2015, the group implemented the ASEAN Economic Community (AEC), which relaxes barriers to the movement of goods, labor, and investment capital within the region—in other words, it lowers the borders separating the member states (Fig. 10.32). Even before the AEC was implemented, about 70 percent of trade within ASEAN was tariff-free (a **tariff** is a tax on trade). As one example of the AEC's significance, in 2016 the group implemented a Single Aviation Market, making it easier for any airline from any member country to serve any city or route in the region.

The integration of Southeast Asia does not go as far as that of Europe but is still remarkable for a region that just a few decades ago was aflame with numerous wars. The economic ties and spirit of cooperation that characterize much of Southeast Asia have given rise to what one writer calls a "Pax ASEANA"—an ASEAN peace[16].

Uneven Democratization and Persistent Conflicts

Southeast Asia's political geography still has two troublesome features. First, the region's progress toward democratization is far from complete. Laos, in particular, is a totalitarian dictatorship. Vietnam and Cambodia are not much better. Interestingly, even the region's richest state is not particularly democratic; Singapore has been essentially a one-party state since gaining its independence in 1965, and there are significant limits on freedom of speech, assembly, and press. In other parts of the world, except the Middle East, wealth is usually correlated with political freedom. Moreover, as some countries in the region move forward, others retreat. A decade ago Thailand was a much freer country than Myanmar. In the interim, Myanmar began to open up. The military junta freed Aung San Suu Kyi, a woman who has long been a powerful voice for democracy and who had spent most of the previous quarter-century under house arrest. By 2017, Suu Kyi was the most powerful politician in the country, and her party controlled most of the seats in the legislature, though the military remained important. Conversely, a military coup in Thailand toppled a democratically elected government in 2014.

A second political challenge for the region is the many conflicts that remain unresolved, especially in peripheral areas of the larger countries. Among the most significant of these conflicts are the following:

- A long-standing rebellion by militant Islamist groups in the Southern Philippines: While the conflict has raged intermittently for decades, since 2015 the Islamic State (IS) has become involved, encouraging Muslims who cannot make it to the Middle East to go to the Philippines to fight on behalf of IS there.
- The brutal treatment of the Rohingya in Western Myanmar: The government claims the Rohingya, a Muslim minority group, is comprised of illegal migrants from neighboring Bangladesh.
- Conflicts between the government of Myanmar and sixteen different ethnic groups located in border regions mainly in Northern and Eastern Myanmar: Some of the ethnic militias are involved in illegal activities, including drug smuggling.

- A rebellion against the Thai government in predominantly Muslim areas near the Malaysian border.
- Conflicts between Papua, the Indonesian section of the island of New Guinea, and the central government in Jakarta: Papua is ethnically distinct from the rest of Indonesia and the lightly populated province is very rich in mineral resources, but much of the resulting wealth flows to the national capital.

One remedy for these varied disputes would be political decentralization. In Indonesia, for instance, decentralization since 1999 has turned the country's political system from a unitary state, in which political power was strongly concentrated in the national capital, to a federal state in which subnational units—in the Indonesian case, provinces—have considerable autonomy. The shift in organization has helped to defuse some conflicts in the vast archipelago. Once it was feared that Indonesia might fracture into many different pieces, especially after East Timor successfully broke away to become the independent country of Timor-Leste in 2002. But decentralization has helped to avoid that feared breakup.

In fact, East Timor was fundamentally different from all the other restive provinces of Indonesia. The territory had been a Portuguese colony for more than 400 years and was overwhelmingly Catholic as a result. East Timor only became part of Indonesia in 1975 when Portugal departed the distant colony and Indonesia invaded. Despite the differences with other provinces, however, East Timor's independence set a dangerous precedent for Indonesia. Accordingly, in 1999 (the same year that Timorese voted overwhelmingly in favor of independence), Indonesia embarked on a radical decentralization that pushed government decision-making and public tax revenues out to the provinces. The Philippines has also adopted devolution with some success, and the idea has been proposed as a means of alleviating similar strains in Thailand and Myanmar.

ECONOMIC ACTIVITIES

One feature of Southeast Asia that makes political cohesion difficult both within countries and across the region is the remarkably uneven pattern of economic development. Measured by GNI PPP per capita, Singapore was nearly twenty-five times as rich as Cambodia in 2016. Within

Indonesia, meanwhile, the disparity between the richest province (the capital district around Jakarta) and the poorest (a region just to the west of Timor-Leste) was ten to one. By comparison, the gap between the richest and poorest states in the U.S. is about two to one. Yet across Southeast

Asia's diverse economic landscapes, the past few decades have brought rapid development.

Explaining Development Patterns

What explains the pattern of spatial inequality in Southeast Asia? This important question can be addressed by focusing on the region's most developed country: Singapore. Why is Singapore rich? Six factors are particularly important, and the absence or weakness of those factors in other parts of the region helps to explain their comparative lack of development.

First, Singapore has an advantageous geographic situation. Its position at the narrow end of the Straits of Malacca helped it become Southeast Asia's most important entrepôt in the 19th century (an entrepôt is a transshipment port where goods are brought from different directions to be traded and then sent onward to their final destinations) and the second busiest port in the world. All that commerce passing through its waters has propelled Singapore's economy to ever greater heights. Conversely, the poorest parts of Southeast Asia (e.g. distant islands in Indonesia, including the Moluccas) tend to be remote from the world's trade corridors.

Second, Singapore benefited more than other parts of the region from foreign imperialism. Singapore was essentially the administrative center for the British Empire in Southeast Asia, and as a consequence the British invested more in its infrastructure (e.g. seaport, airport, water, and electricity systems) and public education than other areas in the region. Those investments gave the city-state a development head start when it became independent in 1965. Other parts of the region had a less favorable colonial legacy.

Third, in sharp contrast to many other areas in Southeast Asia, Singapore has been almost completely spared the destructive violence of ethnic conflict and ideological warfare. It is no coincidence that the region's poorest country, Cambodia, was devastated by the Indochinese wars. Singapore is an ethnically mixed country but the government leverages the fact that most people live in government-built apartment buildings (though in contrast to public housing elsewhere, most Singaporeans own the apartments in which they live) to ensure that every neighborhood is mixed, rather than having separate ethnic enclaves (Fig. 10.33). If a particular neighborhood is close to breaking out of government set thresholds and ceilings on what proportion of people must be Chinese, Malay, and Indian (the three main groups in the population), then an apartment-for-sale advertisement in that neighborhood

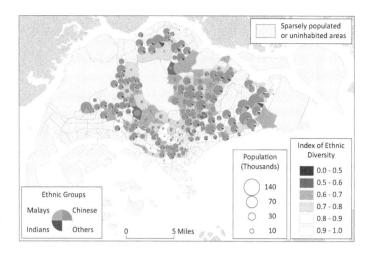

FIGURE 10.33 Ethnicity in Singapore—Nearly 80 percent of Singaporeans live in government-built high-rise apartment buildings in which the government ensures that the population is ethnically mixed. As the map indicates, there are no strongly homogeneous ethnic enclaves in Singapore today. The map also shows the areas in which few people live including areas set aside in the northwest and center for catching fresh water, the huge airport on reclaimed land in the northeast, and the central business district and port along the southern coast. *Source:* Department of Statistics Singapore.

will not only list the apartment's square footage and other features but also what ethnic groups are allowed to buy it.

Fourth, Singapore has been a great beneficiary of in-migration. It has a large Overseas Chinese population and many people of Indian ancestry too. These communities tend to be entrepreneurial and have favorable business connections to other parts of the world—especially China and India. And, Singapore remains an important migration destination. Although migration is controversial in the city-state as previously discussed, the influx of human capital—or **brain gain**—unquestionably helped to enrich the country. Conversely, poorer parts of the region have been undermined by brain drain.

Fifth, Singapore has been well-governed. Although the country is not very democratic, the government has staked its legitimacy on achieving steady development gains. Singapore's government ranks very well for its transparency and for the ease of doing business. Corruption in the city-state is rare.

Sixth and finally, Singapore has a remarkably open economy that has attracted billions of dollars in investments and encouraged vast volumes of trade. Under the umbrella of ASEAN, more of the region is opening up too, but some countries—especially Laos, Cambodia, Vietnam, and Myanmar—are still relatively closed.

Together these factors not only explain the wealth of Singapore; they also explain the success of Malaysia. More broadly, while other parts of Southeast Asia cannot

FIGURE 10.34 Rice processing in central Thailand—In Thailand, which ranks second in the world after India by volume of rice exports, rice production is concentrated in the Chao Phraya basin in the middle of the country where two crops per year can be harvested. *Source:* Stefan Fischer/Henrik Watzke.

change their geographic situations or their histories, they can change their policies, and to a varying degree the policy decisions that have fueled Singapore's growth have been adopted in other Southeast Asian states, too.

Primary Activities: Agriculture, Fishing, and Mining

As a resource-rich region at an overall medium level of development, it is unsurprising that the primary sector—especially agriculture—represents a large share of employment in much of Southeast Asia. In 2010, the proportion of employed adults who worked in agriculture was 71 percent in Laos, 54 percent in Cambodia, and 51 percent in Timor-Leste. Even in the region's more moderately affluent countries including Indonesia, the Philippines, and Thailand, the proportion was between 30 and 40 percent. These shares have fallen in recent decades with mechanization and the growth of the manufacturing and service sectors, but farming remains the primary livelihood for millions of people in Southeast Asia.

Rice is the dominant agricultural land use in Southeast Asia, accounting for about 40 percent of the total area harvested in any crop. Bright green rice paddies are a frequent scene across the region's rural landscapes. Rice production is concentrated in the great river basins including the Mekong, Irrawaddy, and Chao Phraya; but as noted earlier in the chapter, terracing has long been used to extend the rice crop high into the hills and mountains that dominate much of the region. Importantly, the productivity of paddy land has increased in recent decades so that Southeast Asia's food supply has outpaced rapid population growth. Between 1964 and 2014, the average rice yield in the region soared from 1.7 metric tons per hectare (0.7 metric tons per acre) to 4.3 metric tons per hectare (1.7 metric tons per acre). Over the same period, the average number of kilocalories of food consumed per person per day in Southeast Asia climbed from about 1,900 to about 2,700; the average person needs at least 2,000 to 2,500 kilocalories per day for good health.

In fact, Southeast Asia was one of the greatest beneficiaries of the Green Revolution. Perhaps not coincidentally, the International Rice Research Institute (IRRI), where much of the ground-breaking work on new high-yielding varieties of rice has been done, is located in Southeast Asia—specifically in Los Baños, just south of Manila (Fig. 10.34). It was at IRRI that so-called "miracle rice" was created in 1966, by crossbreeding an Indonesian variety that grew vigorously with a Taiwanese dwarf variety that was short and strong. The result was called IR8, a new variety that could effectively use ample applications of fertilizer to produce a big, heavy head of grain without falling over and dying before harvest. Since then, IRRI has developed many other high-yielding varieties that have permitted the food supply in Southeast Asia and other rice-dependent regions to grow faster than population without committing much additional land to the crop (Fig. 10.35).

Meanwhile, the second most significant agricultural land use in Southeast Asia is oil palm, which accounted for about 11 percent of all harvested land, but a much higher share in Malaysia (more than 67 percent) and Indonesia (18 percent). In contrast to rice, the area of land devoted to this crop has risen rapidly in the past decade with significant environmental implications as previously described.

Other significant agricultural land uses in the region include corn (almost all of which is fed to animals), rubber, coconuts, beans, cassava, and sugar cane. In some of the smaller countries, other crops are noteworthy. For instance, the main agricultural land use in Timor-Leste is coffee. In the northern part of mainland Southeast Asia where Myanmar, Laos, and Vietnam meet, lies the **Golden Triangle**,

FIGURE 10.35 High-yielding rice—IR8, developed in 1966, was a revolutionary high-yielding variety that boosted rice productivity. This photo was taken at the International Rice Research Institute in Los Baños, the Philippines.

Source: IRRI, "High-Yielding Rice," http://irri.org/our-impact/reducing-poverty/rice-breeding-creates-billion-dollar-impact. Copyright © by International Rice Research Institute (IRRI). Reprinted with permission.

FIGURE 10.36 The Golden Triangle—The Golden Triangle lies where Myanmar, Thailand, and Laos meet. This photo taken in northern Thailand shows Laos on the other side of the Mekong River. This region has long been one of the world's principal sources of opium. *Source:* John T. Bowen.

FIGURE 10.37 Fishing in Myanmar—A fisherman on Myanmar's Inle Lake uses a traditional conical net to catch carp, a staple of the local diet. *Source:* Larissa Krüger.

notorious for a different kind of agriculture (Fig. 10.36). The area is the second most important opium-producing region in the world after Afghanistan. It is also a significant source of illegal amphetamines. These drugs are smuggled into China, Thailand, and other markets. Like other illegal drug-producing areas, the Golden Triangle is remote, mountainous, weakly governed, and poor.

The other components of the primary sector—fishing and mining—are far less significant than agriculture for the region as a whole, but locally they can be very important. Only China had a larger marine catch (wild seafood caught at sea) than Indonesia in 2014, and only China outranked Myanmar in the size of its catch in inland waters (Fig. 10.37). In terms of aquaculture, the top five countries globally include three from Southeast Asia: Indonesia (second after China), Vietnam, and the Philippines.

Despite the productivity of the region's waters, seafood accounts for a small share of food consumption. For Southeast Asia as a whole, average seafood consumption amounted to 63 kilocalories per person, per day in 2014 or about 2 percent of the total. Of course, for coastal communities the share is higher. And much of the region's output

is exported into the world market. Vietnam in particular has emerged as the second-largest seafood exporter in the world after China.

There are unfortunately numerous problems in the seafood industry, including illegal fishing by boats outside their territorial waters, widespread coastal pollution, unsustainable harvest rates, and labor abuses. The latter issue often involves illegal migrants from poorer countries (e.g. Myanmar) working without pay and in miserable conditions on boats registered in Thailand and other countries.

Finally, Southeast Asia contains a wide variety of mineral resources, and mining is significant in several of the region's economies. Brunei ranks among the world's richest countries because of its oil wealth. It is not a major oil producer (its output in recent years has been similar to that of Kansas), but the small population (less than half a million people) means the per capita production is high. The Sultan of Brunei and the rest of the royal family have captured much of the resulting wealth. Timor-Leste is also quite dependent on oil resources found in the Timor Gap that separates the country from Australia, but for the region's newest country, oil revenues have not been sufficient enough to alleviate its poverty. Moreover, Timor-Leste's small oil reserve will not last deep into the 21st century.

Indonesia and Malaysia are far more significant oil producers, but they have much larger populations. Indonesia, in fact, became a net oil importer in 2009 and consequently withdrew from the Organization of Petroleum Exporting Countries (OPEC) (it rejoined for a while later but is out again). Indonesia and Malaysia are also the region's most significant natural gas producers, and Indonesia is the world's fifth largest coal producer, with much of that resource found in Kalimantan (Indonesia's part of Borneo).

Beyond fossil fuels, the region contains numerous other riches. Papua, the contentious eastern region of Indonesia mentioned earlier, contains Grasberg, the world's richest gold mine and third-largest copper mine. The mine is leased by an American company, and controversies over how the wealth from the large site (it features a mile-wide open pit mine) is distributed have been prominent in the reasons for rebellion against Jakarta. At the opposite end of the region in far Northern Myanmar lies the Jade District. It is estimated that jade mining in the area, which involves both heavy machinery and large numbers of poor people mining by hand, produces more than 30 billion dollars in revenue per year. Almost none of that money ends up in the pockets of ordinary people. Instead, it is syphoned off by the army, drug lords, smugglers, and other "crony tycoons". The situation is not helped by the fact that the Jade District is located in one of the war-torn, ethnic minority regions near Myanmar's border.

In these two far-flung mining areas as in others across the region, the challenges include ensuring that the natural wealth of Southeast Asia benefits the broader public and that mining is done in a way that is respectful of the environment.

Secondary Activities: Manufacturing Dynamism

Southeast Asia is not yet one of the world's principal manufacturing regions, but it may become one. In 2014, the eleven-country region accounted for about 4 percent of value-added manufacturing worldwide. To put that proportion in perspective, Southeast Asia's share is less than the share of Latin America and five times smaller than the share of China alone. However, the rapid growth of manufacturing in the region and the region's relatively young population make it likely that Southeast Asia's share will continue to grow.

Manufacturing is very unevenly developed in Southeast Asia. Because this sector requires good infrastructure (roads, electricity, etc.), workers, and access to markets, it is strongly concentrated in the main cities and their surrounding metropolitan areas. For instance, in Vietnam, the southeast region around Ho Chi Minh City and the Red River Delta (which includes Hanoi) accounted for 75 percent of manufacturing activity in 2010. As examples of the kinds of manufacturing found in these areas, seven of the ten largest (ranked by employment) factories producing goods for Nike in 2016 were located in and near Ho Chi Minh City; the other three in the top ten were located near Jakarta. Collectively, the seven factories near Ho Chi Minh City employed 140,000 people making shoes. By comparison, the entire U.S. footwear industry employed just 14,000 people in 2016.

The labor-intensive work of sewing, gluing, inspecting, packaging, and shipping running shoes in these Nike plants is characteristic of much of Southeast Asia's manufacturing sector. But not all of the region's manufacturing is labor-intensive. Thailand, for instance, is a major center for the auto industry. In 2013, the country ranked ninth in the world in passenger car production and fifth in commercial vehicle production. Thailand, which has been described as the "Detroit of the East," has no auto producers of its own, but most major manufacturers (led by Isuzu, Mitsubishi, and Toyota) have plants in the country, mainly in the industrial zone east of Bangkok along the Gulf of Thailand.

The most sophisticated manufacturing operations in Southeast Asia are found in Malaysia, and especially Singapore. For instance, these two countries are the only places in Southeast Asia with wafer fabrication plants, which produce the silicon wafers from which computer chips are cut. Wafer fabrication plants typically require several billion dollars each in investment and employ highly paid engineers and technicians. Singapore's first wafer fabrication plant opened in 1984 and Malaysia's in 2000. Both countries formerly specialized in labor-intensive activities within electronics global production networks, but they have moved on to more specialized, higher value-added activities since then by improving their infrastructure, raising education levels, and adopting favorable government policies. Meanwhile, the labor-intensive operations have moved on to lower-cost locations. For instance, Intel's largest assembly and test plant, where more routine steps in making computer chips are done, is now located in an export processing zone near Ho Chi Minh City (not far from the Nike plants).

Singapore is not only an advanced manufacturing base for the electronics industry. It is also a center in aerospace manufacturing, petroleum refining, and pharmaceutical production. These are capital-intensive (using lots of expensive and highly automated equipment) rather than labor-intensive activities. The city-state not only carries out manufacturing operations; it is also a center for research and development in these industries. Singapore's fifty-year trajectory toward progressively more sophisticated manufacturing is a model that the other, less-developed countries in the region aim to emulate.

Tertiary Activities: Jobs of the Future

In Southeast Asia's most developed economies, tertiary activities (i.e., services) dominate. In Singapore, 69 percent of working people were employed in the services sector in 2010 versus just 20 percent in Laos. Tertiary activities are concentrated in cities and in wealthier countries, helping to explain this disparity. As the region becomes more urbanized and more developed, the tertiary sector is likely to continue to grow in importance.

Tourism is a significant services sector industry in most countries in the region. Beach resort areas such as Boracay in the Philippines and Koh Rong in Cambodia, the numerous UNESCO World Heritage Sites previously identified, and the region's main cities are among the most popular tourist destinations. Ranked by the number of overnight visitors, Bangkok was the top destination among all the world's cities in 2016. Although people come from all over the world to visit the region, other ASEAN countries and nearby China typically rank high as sources of visitor arrivals.

Retail sales comprise another kind of services activity. In Southeast Asia, this includes everything from vendors selling vegetables and other fresh produce in vibrant, open-air markets to the glittering shopping malls in the major cities. In fact, several of the largest malls in the world are found in the Philippines. They are owned by SM Prime Holdings, which was founded by an Overseas Chinese entrepreneur, named Henry Sy. Born to a poor family in Southern China, Sy migrated with his family to the Philippines while still a toddler. After World War II, he began peddling shoes in Manila and then later set up a shoe store (called Shoemart, from which the SM abbreviation comes) and then a chain of shoe stores, and then a network of large malls in the Philippines and China. Now a billionaire, Sy has long ranked as the Philippines richest person.

Transportation and logistics comprise another vital component of the services sector. Singapore in particular is a key hub both for aviation and for maritime traffic. Interestingly, both Changi Airport and the main container-port terminals in Singapore are built almost entirely on reclaimed land. Bangkok and Kuala Lumpur are also key transportation and logistics centers. As in the Middle East, the region's most successful airlines, especially Singapore Airlines, Malaysian Airlines, and Thai International, operate networks that encompass the globe and help to drive economic development.

Yet in the last decade, the region has also witnessed the spectacular growth of new **low-cost carriers** (LCCs) that mainly carry traffic within the region, such as AirAsia mentioned at the beginning of this chapter. LCCs have brought massive increases in air traffic. For instance, in 2013, there was more airline capacity between Jakarta and Surabaya in Indonesia than between Los Angeles and San Francisco, despite the fact that Los Angeles is bigger than Jakarta, San Francisco is bigger than Surabaya, the two California cities are closer together than the two Javanese cities, and the U.S. is much richer than Indonesia. Ho Chi Minh City—Hanoi, Manila—Cebu, and Bangkok—Chiang Mai are other very densely trafficked air corridors where the LCCs have taken off. Weak ground transportation has propelled the growth of the budget airlines. Their positive effects include greater mobility for more middle class Southeast Asians, but they also bring increased pollution and even their very low fares are beyond the reach of the region's many poor people.

Finally, two of the largest parts of the services sector, health care and education, are also likely to expand with the region's continued development. As Southeast Asia ages, health care will become a larger and larger industry. And, as the people in this dynamic region seek better jobs, they will spend longer periods in school. According to *US News & World Report* rankings[17], only two of Asia's twenty-five best universities were in Southeast Asia in 2016 (both are in Singapore). That is bound to change.

FUTURE PROBLEMS AND PROSPECTS

Southeast Asia is more integrated, more peaceful, and more affluent than at any time in its modern history. Can the positive trends of recent decades continue? And what problems lie on the horizon?

First, the integration of ASEAN is likely to continue. One advantage to ASEAN's approach is that it has never moved particularly fast. The group emphasizes consensus and noninterference in its member states' affairs. In contrast to the European Union, ASEAN is cautious and has narrower aims (e.g. there is no prospect of a single ASEAN currency). In the not too distant future, Timor-Leste is likely to join ASEAN as its eleventh member; in 2011 Indonesia dropped its opposition to the country's membership.

A key challenge for ASEAN, however, is the rise of China and especially China's claims to a vast swath of the South China Sea. The resulting territorial disputes are very troubling, especially to Vietnam and the Philippines. Indonesia, too, has tangled with China over Chinese fishing in Indonesian territorial waters. Conversely, other countries in Southeast Asia, especially Laos, care much less about these disputes and look to China as a crucial investor and market. Divisions over how to deal with China have already strained ASEAN.

Second, while the ghastly Indochinese wars of the 1940s–1970s have retreated into history, the region is not completely peaceful and important flashpoints remain. In addition to the South China Sea disputes, numerous conflict zones are found along the borders of the mainland countries. ASEAN's nature means that it is unlikely to be assertive or effective in trying to calm these differences. Furthermore, the involvement of outside Islamist forces in the Southern Philippines and Indonesia risk entangling the region more deeply in the larger global struggle against Islamist terror.

Third, the region has come very far in terms of economic development, and recent growth rates indicate that further gains are in store. Moreover, as China increasingly becomes a higher-cost location, some of its businesses (e.g. in electronics) are likely to shift south into Vietnam and other countries in the region. And ASEAN's further integration should open new opportunities. Southeast Asia does face some economic challenges, however. Several countries in the region, especially Singapore and Thailand, are ageing rapidly, which may translate into worker shortages. Environmental concerns may impede some forms of development (e.g. rapid conversion of forest to palm plantations) that would have been tolerated in the past. Rising inequality may tear at the fabric of Southeast Asian societies.

Nevertheless, the outlook for Southeast Asia is largely positive. Discussions of Asia and its future often focus on its two giants—India and China. But between them lies a remarkably diverse region that has been drawn together under the umbrella of ASEAN. The region has a young and highly mobile, rapidly urbanizing population. And while openness has been a hallmark of the region's most successful societies for decades, today, openness is a more general characteristic of Southeast Asia. Diversity, youth, and openness are ingredients for a successful regional future.

NOTES

1. Sulong, S.R. (2013). The Kra Canal and Southeast Asian relations. *Journal of Southeast Asian Current Affairs* 4, 112–25.

2. Winchester, S. (2005). *Krakatoa: The day the world exploded.* New York, NY: HarperCollins.

3. World Heritage Center. (2017). Rice terraces of the Philippine Cordilleras. Retrieved from http://whc.unesco.org/en/list/722

4. Bale, R. (2016). One of the world's biggest fisheries is on the verge of collapse. *National Geographic.* Retrieved from https://news.nationalgeographic.com/2016/08/wildlife-south-china-sea-overfishing-threatens-collapse/

5. Margono, B.A., Potapov, P.V., Turubanova, S., Stolle, F., & Hansen, M.C. (2014). Primary forest cover loss in Indonesia over 2000–2012. *Nature Climate Change,* 4, 730–5.

6. Diamond, J. (1999). *Guns, germs, and steel: The fates of human societies.* New York, NY: W.W. Norton.

7. Aiken, S.R. & Leigh, C.H. (2011). In the way of Development: Indigenous land–rights issues in Malaysia. *The Geographical Review* 101(4), 471–96.

8. Poston, D. L. and Wong, J. H. (2016). The Chinese diaspora: The current distribution of the overseas Chinese population. Retrieved from http://journals.sagepub.com/doi/full/10.1177/2057150X16655077.

9. GaWC. (2017). The world according to GaWC 2016. Retrieved from http://www.lboro.ac.uk/gawc/world2016t.html

10. Diamond, J. (1999). *Guns, germs, and steel: The fates of human societies.* New York, NY: W.W. Norton.

11. Kaplan, R. (2011). *Monsoon: The Indian Ocean and the Future of American Power.* New York, NY: Random House.

12. Kaplan, R. (2011). *Monsoon: The Indian Ocean and the Future of American Power.* New York, NY: Random House.

13. Kaplan, R. (2011). *Monsoon: The Indian Ocean and the Future of American Power.* New York, NY: Random House.

14. Milton, G. (1999). *Nathaniel's nutmeg: Or the true and incredible adventures of the spice trader who changed the course of history.* New York, NY: Penguin.

15. Quoted in Merry, R.W. (2005). *Sands of empire: Missionary zeal, American foreign policy, and the hazards of ambition* (p. 77). New York, NY: Simon & Schuster.

16. Khanna, P. (2016). *Connectography: Mapping the future of global civilization.* New York, NY: Random House.

17. US News & World Report. (2017). Best global universities in Asia. Retrieved from https://www.usnews.com/education/best-global-universities/asia

11

AUSTRALIA AND OCEANIA

Australia and Oceania comprise a region different from most other world culture realms in several ways. First, it has by far the smallest population (39 million) of any region. If Oceania were one country, it would be the world's thirty-sixth most populous, placed behind Algeria and before Iraq. Second, it is located on both sides of the Equator and the International Date Line. In other words, it is in the northern and southern as well as the eastern and western hemisphere. Third, most of its countries are very small in area and population and have no land boundaries (with one exception). Fourth, it has more dependent territories (eighteen) than independent states (fourteen). Finally, many parts of the region (islands) were populated quite late in human history, some as recently as eight centuries ago.

GEOGRAPHIC QUALITIES AND WORLD SIGNIFICANCE

The most conspicuous geographic quality of Oceania is its great territorial extent. Although it occupies just over 6 percent of the world's land area (not counting Antarctica), it stretches over 160 degrees of longitude (as much as the Russian Realm), from the western coast of Australia to Easter Island in the Pacific Ocean (Fig. 11.1). Its latitudinal extent of over 75 degrees, from Midway Island in the north to the South Island of New Zealand in the south, is comparable to that of Latin America. The region can be conveniently divided into two major parts: Australia (a continent) and the Pacific Islands. The islands are divided into three archipelagos: Melanesia, Micronesia, and Polynesia. Its peripheral location, an example of relative geographic location, is another geographic quality of this region. While Europe is in the center of the **land hemisphere**, Oceania, located on the opposite side of the globe, is in the center of the **water hemisphere**[1]. Imagine rotating a

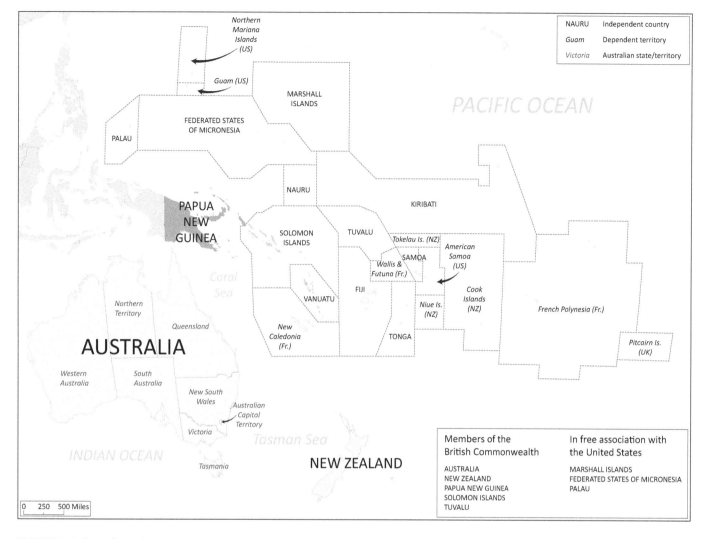

FIGURE 11.1 Countries and dependent territories of Australia and Oceania—The region consists of fourteen independent countries and ten dependent territories.

globe such that one side has as much land as possible and the other side has as much water as possible; the center of the water hemisphere would be just east of New Zealand's South Island. As mentioned in the first chapter, the relative location of a place may change over time. Considering the growing importance of Asia in world affairs and Oceania's proximity to that region, the notion of its peripheral location may lose its validity in the future.

Oceania is a land of great physical and human contrasts. The physical contrasts are most visible between Australia on the one hand, and the rest of the region on the other. While the former is large in area, relatively flat, low in elevation, and mainly dry, the latter is small, more diverse in topography, and more humid. In regard to human geography, Australia and one part of Oceania, New Zealand, share much in common and are part of the Western world, while the rest of Oceania is part of the economically developing world. While the population is of European origin and the English language and the commercial economy are dominant

in Australia and New Zealand, the Pacific Islander ethnicity and subsistence economy characterize much of the rest of the region. Despite differences in levels of economic development, natural resource-based economies are prevalent across the region. For example, Nauru, New Caledonia, and Papua New Guinea derive most of their revenues from exporting mineral resources; Tonga and Kiribati from agricultural commodities; Micronesia and American Samoa from fish products; and the Solomon Islands from timber. Even Australia and New Zealand built their prosperity mainly on the export of agricultural and mineral commodities.

Despite high population densities on some islands, small populations characterize all political entities in this region. Australia, similar in size to the continental United States, has only 23 million people. Tuvalu, Nauru, and Palau are among the least populous countries in the world. Pitcairn Islands, a British-dependent territory in Eastern Polynesia, has fewer than sixty inhabitants. However, high fertility rates are recorded in many parts of Oceania, particularly in Melanesia. In some countries (Samoa and the Solomon Islands) women have, on average, over four children. Only women in Sub-Saharan Africa and the Middle East have more children. The high fertility may reflect low levels of urbanization in these countries, past population decline due to infectious diseases brought by the Europeans over one hundred years ago, and high emigration to other parts of the region and North America.

Although Australia and Oceania form a peripheral region, its global importance is expected to increase as the world's attention has been shifting to Asia (mainly China) in recent years. Australia and Oceania together have large reserves and comprise a major supplier of many minerals to booming Asian economies, including uranium, diamonds, iron ore, bauxite, lead, and zinc, just to mention a few. The region is also a significant producer and exporter of food items (wheat, meat, and dairy products). Australia and New Zealand are also destinations for many Asian migrants. The region has been of military importance (military bases and weapons testing sites) to the United States, the United Kingdom, and France for decades, and considering the growing tensions in parts of Asia, this importance may even increase in the foreseeable future. Rising sea levels threaten many Pacific countries, and their pleas for help and global action should be taken seriously by the rest of the world. Oceania's great cultural diversity, especially that of Melanesia, enriches the rest of the world and should be preserved in the era of globalization.

PHYSICAL ENVIRONMENT

The region's great east-west and north-south extent, equivalent to about 12,550 and 8,530 kilometers (7,800 and 5,300 miles), respectively, is not necessarily reflected in great diversity of its physical environments. Most of

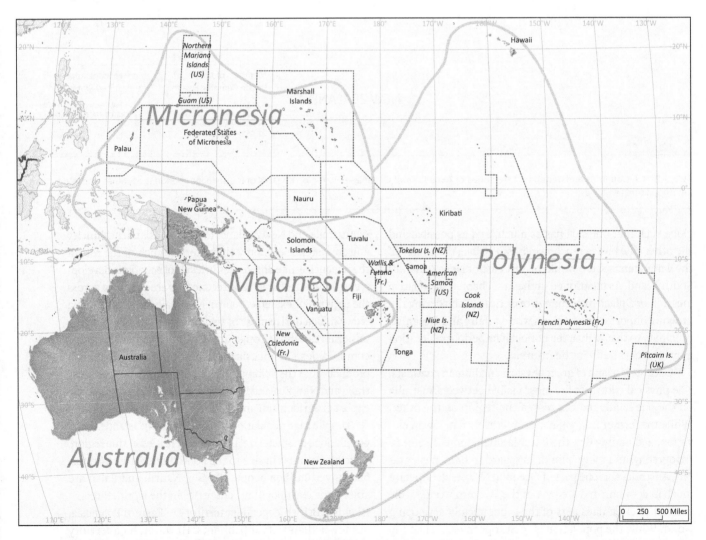

FIGURE 11.2 Physical regions of Australia and Oceania—Australia is a continent similar in size to the continental United States. Oceania is divided into Melanesia, Micronesia, and Polynesia, and its land area is similar in size to Texas and Louisiana. *Source:* Natural Earth.

Australia is low and flat, and the mountain ranges along its eastern coast are unimpressive by global standards. Although some Pacific islands (New Guinea and New Zealand) have more diverse topography, this diversity is of local importance. Climatic conditions are even less diverse across the entire region as most of Australia is dry and most of the Pacific world lies in the tropical rainy climate zone. Oceania's original flora and fauna, though perhaps less diverse than that of other regions, is highly endemic (i.e., unique to this region) and reflects a long (by geological standards) separation of this region from the rest of the world. A convenient way of exploring the physical geography of Oceania is to divide it into two parts: the continent of Australia and the Pacific islands (Fig. 11.2).

Landform Configuration

Australia, the smallest continent, separated from Gondwanaland some 60 million years ago, drifted northeastwards until it began colliding with the southwestward moving Pacific Plate about 25 million years ago. This collision resulted in the formation of the mountain chains of New Guinea and other Melanesian islands, as well as those of New Zealand and the Tonga archipelago in Polynesia. For most of its geological history, Australia has been a relatively stable landmass infrequently affected by tectonic and volcanic activity. Consequently, its landform configuration is relatively simple, and most of its topographic variations are products of weathering and erosion rather than plate tectonics (Fig. 11.3). Nevertheless, the continent can be divided into four parts of various size, shape, and elevation[2]. The Western Plateau occupies over half of Australia, and this old geologic shield is relatively flat and low in elevation. A few uplifted areas in the interior diversify the monotonous topography of this region. Some isolated mountains (weathered granite or sandstone monoliths), including the well known Uluru (Ayers Rock) and Kata Tjuta (Mt. Olga), located in the central part of the Western Plateau, are sacred places for indigenous people and

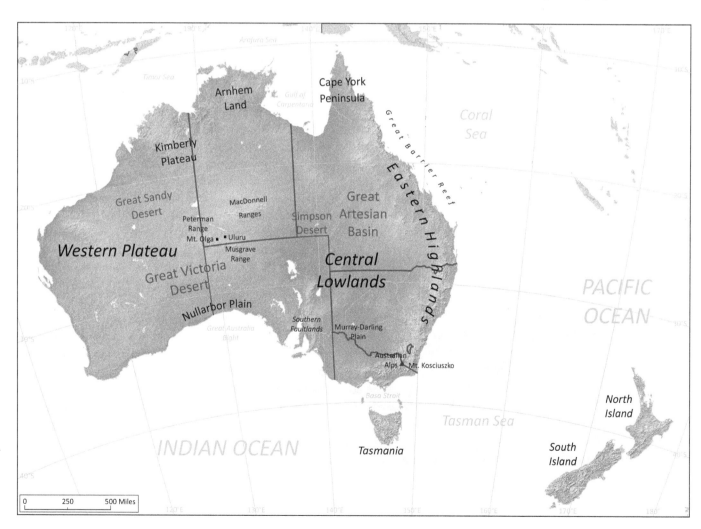

FIGURE 11.3 Physical regions of Australia and New Zealand—Australia is relatively flat while New Zealand is mountainous, especially the South Island. *Source:* Natural Earth.

FIGURE 11.4 Uluru or Ayers Rock, Australia—This remote feature, an 863-meter (2,830-foot) sandstone monolith rising out of the Australia desert, is sacred to the local Aboriginal population. *Source:* Pixabay.

major tourist attractions (Fig. 11.4). The Central Lowlands comprise about a quarter of the continent and stretch in a north-south direction from the Gulf of Carpentaria in the north, to the Indian Ocean shores between the cities of Melbourne and Adelaide in the south. The Great Artesian Basin, an area of horizontal layers of sedimentary rocks with the water- or wind-deposited materials on the surface, is the largest part of this region. Large amounts of underground (artesian) water support large-scale livestock herding in this area. The Murray-Darling Plain, located to the south of the Great Artesian Basin, is another agriculturally productive part of the Central Lowlands. The Southern Faultlands are a small part of South Australia located to the north of the state capital Adelaide and comprise a series of hilly ranges separated by rift valleys. Some

FIGURE 11.5 Tavurvur, an active volcano near Rabaul, Papua New Guinea—Located on the northern tip of New Britain, an island near New Guinea, this volcano is the most active and dangerous in Papua New Guinea. *Source:* Wikimedia Commons.

hills reach 914 meters (3,000 feet) in elevation. The Eastern Highlands stretch along the Pacific Ocean coast from the York Peninsula in the north to the southernmost part of Australia, around the city of Melbourne and the island of Tasmania. This region of relatively complex geology, also known as the Great Dividing Range, is characterized by steep escarpments along the coast, especially in its southeastern part, and by gentle slopes toward the interior, which are interspersed with high plateaus in the central part. Mt. Kosciuszko (2,228 meters/7,310 feet), located in the southeastern part of the region known as the Australian Alps, is the highest peak in Australia.

Oceania is a region of about 10,000 islands that comprise an area of 822,000 square kilometers or 317,700 square miles (similar in size to the country of Namibia). These islands are grouped into three regions: Melanesia (the name means black islands), Micronesia (small islands), and Polynesia (numerous islands). New Guinea, the second largest island in the world (after Greenland), Solomon Islands, and Fiji are the most important parts of Melanesia. Micronesia includes several archipelagos north of Melanesia, among them the Caroline Islands (which are divided among the Federated States of Micronesia and the Mariana Islands which include the U.S. territory of Guam). Polynesia, the largest of the three regions and triangular in shape, extends from the Hawaiian Islands in the north to New Zealand in the southwest and Easter Island (part of Chile) in the east.

There are three major types of islands in Oceania. **Continental islands** such as New Guinea used to be part of the Australian continent before changes in sea levels and continental drift and are parts of the Pacific Ring of Fire. Examples include the two islands of New Zealand (North and South Islands). They have mountainous terrain and are affected by seismic activity (Fig. 11.5). **High islands** are characterized by relatively large size, diverse topography, and steep slopes and most are of volcanic origin and are seismically active (Fig. 11.6 and Fig. 11.7). Some are made of single dormant or active volcanic peaks (e.g. Moorea in French Polynesia), others of two or more peaks (e.g. Bougainville in Papua New Guinea), and still others of mountain ranges (e.g. New Caledonia). Most Melanesian and some Micronesian (Guam) and Polynesian (Tahiti and Samoa) islands belong to this group. **Low islands**, most of them coral **atolls**, are made of a build-up of coral on top of submerged dormant volcanic craters. They are of low elevation, form irregular rings, and have inside lagoons. Nauru, Makatea in the Tuamotu Archipelago (French Polynesia), Tongatapu in the Tonga Islands, and Banaba or Ocean Island in Kiribati are examples of such islands.

Oceania has the largest collection of **coral reefs** in the world. The Great Barrier Reef along the northeastern coast of

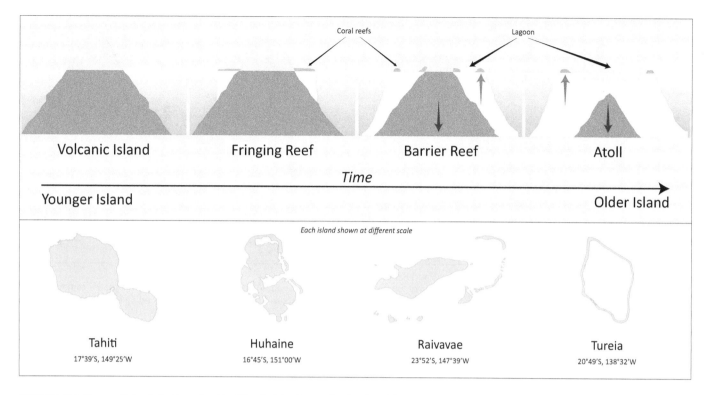

Coral reefs · Lagoon

Volcanic Island · Fringing Reef · Barrier Reef · Atoll

Time

Younger Island · Older Island

Each island shown at different scale

Tahiti
17°39'S, 149°25'W

Huhaine
16°45'S, 151°00'W

Raivavae
23°52'S, 147°39'W

Tureia
20°49'S, 138°32'W

FIGURE 11.6 Types of islands in Oceania—Most Pacific islands are of volcanic origin; their typology is closely related to the age of volcanic mountains. Drawn after a similar image at Tahiti: Le Blog (https://tahitileblog.fr/histoire-geographie/formation-iles-atolls-polynesie).

Australia (Queensland) is about 2,250 kilometers (1,400 miles) long and occupies an area of 345,000 square kilometers (133,000 square miles). It became a UNESCO World Heritage Site in 1981. The Great Barrier Reef is the world's largest collection of living organisms, and most of it is protected as a marine park (Fig. 11.8). This natural wonder faces various challenges from tourism, climate change, and pollution.

Climatic Contrasts

Although most of Australia and Oceania is in the tropical and subtropical climate zones, the former part is characterized by significant variations in its climate and is predominantly dry, while the latter region has a more uniform and humid climate. Australia's climate can be briefly

Tupai

Maupiti

Bora-Bora

Tahaa

Huahine

Raiatea

0   10   20 Miles

FIGURE 11.7 Types of islands in French Polynesia—The six islands shown on this map are part of the Society Islands in French Polynesia and exemplify the types of islands represented in the previous illustration.

FIGURE 11.8 Great Barrier Reef, Australia—Though it is threatened by numerous forces from climate change to agricultural run-off, the Great Barrier Reef remains an area of rich diversity and great beauty. *Source:* Wikimedia Commons.

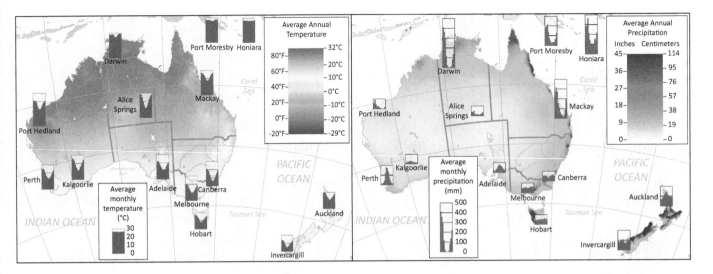

FIGURE 11.9 Australia and New Zealand: patterns of temperature and precipitation—Australia has a much warmer and drier climate than New Zealand. Notice the more seasonal distribution of precipitation in northern Australia which is influenced by the same monsoon patterns as nearby Indonesia. *Source:* WorldClim-Global Climate Data.

described as tropical in the north, dry in the interior, and temperate in the south. Latitude is the main climatic control in this region, but landform configuration, air pressure, wind patterns, and ocean currents also play a role in climate formation. About 80 percent of Australia receives less than 60 centimeters (24 inches) of precipitation a year (about the same as Abilene, Texas), and half of the continent gets less than 30 centimeters (12 inches) (about the same as Tucson, Arizona) (Fig. 11.9). The country's aridity is partly attributable to its location on the surface of the Earth: global air circulation patterns create a belt of dry, high pressure systems at about 30°S latitude. So Australia's interior deserts, including the Great Sandy Desert and Great Victoria Desert, are at about the same latitude as the Kalahari in Africa and the Atacama in South America. However, tropical air masses penetrate the dry interior of Australia so its deserts are not as dry as the Atacama.

The monsoonal north has well-defined wet (summer) and dry (winter) seasons. Summers are hot and humid, have frequent thunderstorms and periodic tropical storms (cyclones), while winters are dry and warm (pleasant) with plenty of sunshine. The low humidity and lack of precipitation cause frequent bush fires during the winter season. The humid east coast along the Great Dividing Range has a tropical climate in the north and a temperate one in the south. Summer is the rainy season in the former part and winter in the latter one. Annual temperature variations increase moving from north to south, and occasional droughts occur in this region. A Mediterranean climate is found in two parts of the continent, one in the southwest (around the city of Perth) and the other in the south (around the city

of Adelaide). These two regions have dry and hot summers and wet and mild winters. The most densely populated part of Australia, the southeast coast, has a mild, moist oceanic climate, somewhat similar to the Pacific Northwest in the U.S. or to Northwestern Europe. This type of climate occurs on the eastern coast of Australia rather than the west because of prevailing easterly winds at that latitude.

Most islands of Oceania have a tropical rainy climate characterized by high temperatures and humidity year round. Precipitation is more unevenly distributed across space and time. Northern Melanesia (Papua New Guinea and Solomon Islands) and Micronesia are the wettest parts of Oceania while the islands in Eastern and Central Polynesia are the driest. There are significant differences in precipitation amounts between high and low islands. The high islands receive much more rain than low coral atolls, as higher elevation and mountainous terrain are more conducive to moisture condensation. Consequently, many low islands experience freshwater shortages. In extreme cases, inhabitants of low islands depend on imported bottled water for their survival. New Zealand lies in the subtropical and temperate zones and has a much cooler climate than the rest of Oceania. Its location in the westerly wind flow zone and its diverse topography create a rain shadow effect responsible for great local differences in precipitation amounts. While the western slopes of the South Island receive over 600 centimeters (236 inches) of precipitation a year, the eastern coastal areas get less than 80 centimeters (31 inches) (Fig. 11.10). The east-west differences in New Zealand's climatic conditions are greater than the north-south ones.

FIGURE 11.10 Franz Josef Glacier in New Zealand—New Zealand has more than 3,000 glaciers, mainly on the western, wetter side of the South Island. The one shown here is unusual because its tongue advances down amid temperate rainforest. Notice the tourists on the bottom right side of the image. *Source:* Stefan Fischer/Henrik Watzke.

Flora and Fauna

Australia's and Oceania's long separation from the rest of the world has produced a unique flora and fauna in both places, with a high proportion of endemic species (not natively found in other regions). Among some 25,000 plant species found in Australia, 80 percent are endemic. Another characteristic of the Australian flora is the scarcity of dense forests and the presence of large areas of grasslands, shrublands, and open woodlands with two species, eucalyptus and acacia trees, widely dispersed. The absence of native cacti is another unique feature of the Australian flora. A high proportion of New Zealand's and many other Pacific islands' plants are also endemic. Fern trees of New Zealand are one example of such species. The uniqueness of Australia's native fauna is expressed, among other things, in the absence of many mammal species, including primates (e.g. no native monkeys), ungulates (e.g. no native cattle, deer, or pigs), mustelids (e.g. no native badgers, ferrets, or mink), and canids (e.g. no native dogs, wolves, or foxes).

Australia's famous dingoes are related to dogs but are relatively new to the continent, having only arrived in the last few thousand years.

On the other hand, **marsupials** and **monotremes** are common in this region. Marsupials first carry their young in the womb and then in a pouch. Kangaroos, koalas, and wallabies are the best known examples of this group of mammals. Monotremes are mammals that lay eggs instead of giving birth to their young. The duck-bill platypus and long-beak anteater are popular examples in this group. An interesting fact about Australia's and New Zealand's fauna is the presence of numerous reptiles, including many venomous snakes, in Australia and their almost complete absence in New Zealand. Another example of New Zealand's unique fauna is the presence of flightless bird species such as the kiwi (the country's official symbol). In general, the diversity of Oceania's flora and fauna decreases as one moves from New Guinea to the north and east. There is also a marked difference in the diversity of species between high islands (more diversity) and low islands (less diversity).

FIGURE 11.11 Invasive species control in New Zealand—The stoat, an animal related to the weasel, was introduced into New Zealand in the 19th century to control the population of rabbits (another introduced species). Stoats have now emerged as the number one threat to birds in the country, and in response efforts are underway in places such as the Abel Tasman National Park on the South Island to control their population. *Source:* Stefan Fischer/Henrik Watzke.

Some exotic (i.e., non-native) animals (and perhaps plants) were introduced by the first migrants to Australia about 50,000 years ago and much later by others to the Pacific islands. The European discovery and colonization of the region was also accompanied by the introduction of many new plants and animals, both domesticated and wild, which in some cases displaced or eliminated native species (Fig. 11.11). For example, the Dingo Fence (or Dog Fence), an over 5,600-kilometer (3,500-mile) long barrier to protect sheep from dingo dog attacks (both are exotic species brought to Australia by the Europeans and the Aborigines, respectively), has resulted in an increased number of rabbits, kangaroos, emus (ostriches), and other species in the "dingo dog-free zone" (Fig. 11.12). The island of Guam provides another example of the devastating impact of an exotic species on the native bird population. The brown tree snake, a creature native to parts of Australia and Melanesia, was accidently brought on a ship to Guam in the 1950s and quickly multiplied in the absence of natural predators. There may be as many as fifteen to twenty snakes per acre in some parts of the island. This nocturnal and slightly venomous snake can reach a length of 1.8 to 2.1 meters (6 to 7 feet). It has been blamed for the extinction of many native bird species and frequent power outages as it likes to climb electric poles.

HUMAN-ENVIRONMENT INTERACTION

The introduction of new species and the extinction of native species are just two examples of human-environment interaction in Australia and Oceania. The small size and isolation of many of the islands that comprise this region make them especially vulnerable to overuse of resources. Mining activities on the island of Nauru are a good example. Nauru is a small island (21 square kilometers/8 square miles) and an independent country. It was once very rich in phosphate (guano, the residue of bird droppings left over many centuries), which is used in the production of fertilizers and explosives. The mining of this resource began in the early 20th century

FIGURE 11.12 The Dog Fence, Australia—The fence runs east-west across Australia from the coast of South Australia to the coast of Queensland and was built to keep dingoes out of the rich agricultural land in the southeastern part of the country. *Source:* Wikimedia Commons.

and continued at increased rates after independence in 1968 until almost nothing was left. Today, 80 percent of the island is a wasteland as phosphate found between walls and columns of coral deposits was removed through strip mining. Revenues from exporting this resource made Nauru one of the richest countries (measured by GDP per capita) in the world in the 1970s and the early 1980s. However, corrupt and incompetent governments spent the money on various extravagant and often foolish programs. For instance, the tiny country's national airline grew to have a fleet of seven aircraft large enough to hold 10 percent of Nauru's population at one time. Air Nauru lost vast sums of money and its failure was among the reasons the country became bankrupt by 2000.

Prior to the phosphate boom, agriculture and fishing supported the island's population. Since little can be grown on the island today, Nauru's 10,000 inhabitants depend on imported and highly processed canned and frozen food. Consequently, over 90 percent of the residents are overweight and over 70 percent of them

obese[3]. The island is almost completely dependent on support from Australia, New Zealand, and Taiwan. The government of Nauru began looking for various sources of income in recent years. Selling passports to foreigners for a high fee ($10,000 to $50,000), which started in 1998, is one of them. Recognizing two Russian-backed breakaway republics of Georgia—Abkhazia and South Ossetia—for about $50 million dollars in aid from Russia is another. Housing a refugee-processing center for Australia in exchange for millions of dollars in aid is one more example. This short story of Nauru's phosphate mining is probably the best example of recent unsustainable development in Oceania.

The ecological tragedy of Easter Island (Rapa Nui) is an example of unsustainable development in the past[4]. This small island (165 square kilometers/64 square miles) is the most isolated inhabited place on Earth, located 4,000 kilometers (2,300 miles) from Chile and 2,100 kilometers (1,300 miles) from Pitcairn. Its subtropical climate and fertile volcanic soils supported a population

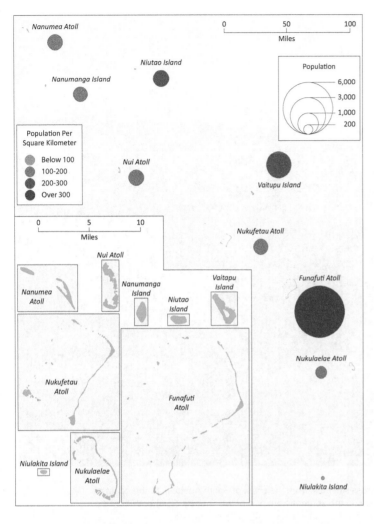

FIGURE 11.13 Tuvalu islands and their population—Tuvalu is a collection of nine low islands, also known as Ellice Islands, whose total area is 10 square miles. Over half of its residents live on the Funafuti atoll where population densities are over 2,310 persons per square kilometer (6,000 per square mile). *Source:* Encyclopedia Britannica 2017 Book of the Year.

a few centuries earlier. The island became a part of Chile in 1888, and tourism is the main source of income for its 3,000 inhabitants today.

The shortage of freshwater on many islands is another serious environmental issue in Oceania. Rising sea levels are responsible for increased salt content in groundwater supplies on most low islands, which also generally receive less precipitation than high islands. Rising demand for water due to population increase (some islands are very densely populated) and modern uses further magnify the water problem. Most Tuvalu residents, for instance, collect rain water in roof storage tanks and use it for household needs and limited farming activities, mainly growing taro and other plants in pits (known as *pulakas*) filled with organic matter and water as there is no natural soil on most islands (Fig. 11.13). Tokelau and other low islands have also experienced serious water shortages in recent years.

Several types of natural hazards affect people and economic activities in many parts of the region. Droughts are most common in Australia, and they have been occurring in severe form every eighteen years on average since the mid-19th century. The first decade of the 21st century was associated with the worst drought in the country's recorded history. It most affected the southeastern parts of Australia and had a very adverse impact on agricultural activities, especially dairy and cotton farming. Many scholars connect the increase in drought severity with global warming and El Niño/La Niña events. Droughts can also happen in Oceania and can lead to severe water shortages.

Bushfires are frequent events in Australia. They occur almost on a regular basis during the dry monsoon season in Northern Queensland and the Northern Territory and periodically in other parts of the country and can do a lot to damage to human life and property. Ironically, bushfires are beneficial to some types of vegetation as a means of reproduction. The Black Saturday Bushfire (2009) in Victoria affected an area of over 1 million acres and caused 173 deaths and over 400 injuries and damaged over 3,500 structures.

Tropical storms, called cyclones or typhoons in this part of the world, are most likely to affect Northern Australia, Southern Melanesia, and Northern Micronesia (Fig. 11.14). The strongest cyclone ever recorded in the southern hemisphere hit Fiji in 2016. Most of Melanesia and Western Polynesia are parts of the Pacific Ring of Fire and can be affected by strong earthquakes or volcanic eruptions. While fatal seismic events in Oceania are relatively rare due to the small populations of many islands, some of these geologic events can be very strong.

of at least 7,000 (some claim up to 20,000) during its peak of development around 1200–1500 CE. It had thick subtropical vegetation, numerous land and sea birds, and fish and dolphins in the surrounding waters. However, a few centuries after the arrival of the original settlers, the forests began to shrink as trees were used for canoe and house construction, the transport of huge stone statues, and as firewood. An alternative explanation for the abrupt deforestation is that the Polynesians who first settled in the island inadvertently brought rats with them. Facing no natural predators, the rats rapidly multiplied and fed on the palms that had covered the island. Whatever the cause, a once flourishing society was reduced to abject poverty and hunger. When Dutch explorers reached the island on Easter Day in 1722, it had only about a quarter (about 3,000 to 3,300) of its highest population number

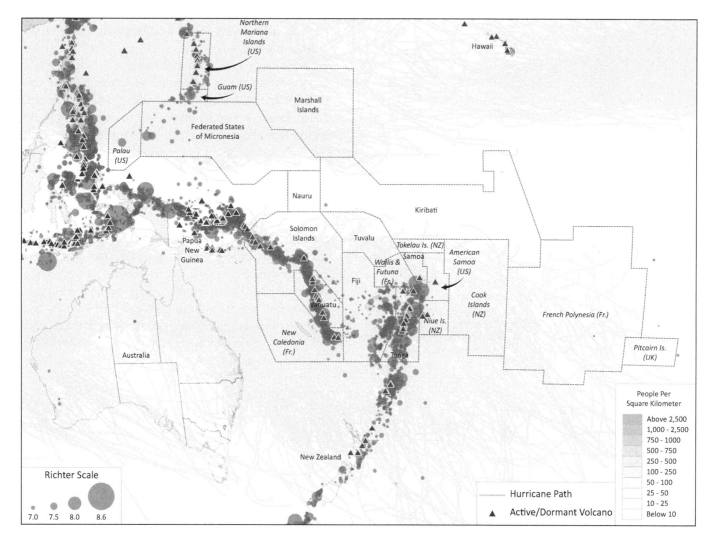

FIGURE 11.14 Selected natural hazards (20th century) and population distribution in Australia and Oceania—Most Micronesian and Melanesian islands (except New Guinea and the Bismarck Archipelago) can be affected by hurricanes (typhoons). The border between the Indo-Australian and Pacific tectonic plates is a seismically active area. Vanuatu, Solomon Islands, Tonga, and parts of Papua New Guinea and New Zealand are particularly prone to earthquakes. Guam and the Northern Mariana Islands, which lie along the borderline between the Philippine and Pacific tectonic plates, are also prone to seismic activity. *Source:* NOAA National Climatic Data Center; Earthquake Hazards Program; GeoTech Center Data Library.

POPULATION PATTERNS AND TRENDS

Australia and Oceania together have the smallest population size (39 million) and form the least densely populated (5 persons per square kilometer; 13 per square mile) world culture realm. It occupies over 6 percent of the total land area but has less than 1 percent of the world's total population. The region's population has tripled since 1950, and most of that growth resulted from high fertility, although migration has also played an important role in Australia. Oceania's population is about five years younger than that of Australia and New Zealand as measured by the median age (33 and 38 years, respectively). A twenty-year gap in life expectancy exists between Australia (82 years) and Papua New Guinea (62 years). About two-thirds of the region's population is of European origin, almost one-third of the Pacific Islander origin, and most of the remainder of Asian origin.

Population Distribution and Growth

Australia has 60 percent (23.7 million) of the region's total population, and 80 percent of the remaining population lives in Papua New Guinea (7.5 million) and New

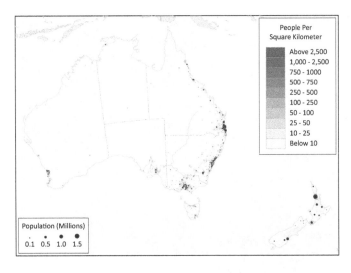

FIGURE 11.15 Population distribution in Australia and New Zealand—Peripheral and clustered distribution can be easily observed in Australia. However, New Zealand's peripheral distribution cannot be detected due to its smaller size and larger size of territorial units for which data were collected. *Source:* GeoHive (www.geohive.com); Australian Bureau of Statistics.

Zealand (4.5 million). The rest of Oceania has just over 3.1 million inhabitants.

Australia's population distribution can be best described as peripheral and clustered, and it clearly reflects the natural conditions of the continent (Fig. 11.15). More humid coastal areas, especially those in the eastern highland region, have attracted over three-fourths of the country's total population. Five major clusters, each associated with a large coastal city (Brisbane, Sydney, Melbourne, Adelaide, and Perth), can be identified. The dry interior, on the other hand, is very sparsely populated, and its population distribution can also be described as clustered. The interior's much smaller population clusters are mainly associated with mining activities. Although Australia's population density is one of the lowest in the world (lower than the Dakotas in the U.S.), its predominantly dry environment is the major obstacle to increasing that density. The carrying capacity (the maximum population size an area can support without adverse impact on its natural environment) of this continent has been a controversial issue for decades. Some

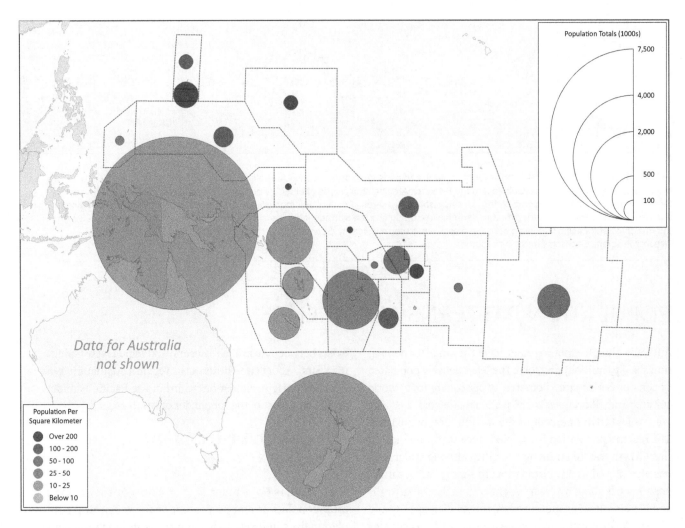

FIGURE 11.16 Population size and density in Oceania—Notice the largest populations are in Melanesian countries but the highest population densities are in Micronesia and Polynesia. *Source:* United Nations. Population Division. World Population Prospects 2014.

favor large-scale immigration and claim that Australia can support 36 million people by 2050. Others claim that the current rates of population growth (much higher than in other developed countries) will lead to an even bigger Australia (45 million people) and, therefore, something has to be done to limit the high growth rate. The opponents of "big Australia" associate higher population densities with permanent water shortages, loss of limited farmland to urban expansion, higher pollution levels and urban congestion, and many other problems[5].

The population distribution patterns across Oceania show significant variations from region to region and island to island (Fig. 11.16). Micronesia is the most densely populated archipelago (166 persons per square kilometer; 64 per square mile) while Melanesia's density is about nine times lower (18 persons per square kilometer; 7 per square mile). Papua New Guinea's population distribution pattern is opposite to that of Australia. The highest densities are found in the mountainous interior, while coastal regions are less attractive to people. Elevation (which moderates climate), soil quality, and certain economic activities (mining) are major determinants of the population distribution in this tropical country. Although New Zealand's population distribution is also peripheral and clustered, like that of Australia, the mountainous terrain, especially in the South Island, is the main reason for low densities in the country's interior regions. Several small Pacific islands are very densely populated, including Nauru (511 persons per square kilometer or 1,323 persons per square mile, denser than New Jersey which is the densest U.S. state), Tuvalu (330/855, denser than Massachusetts which is second to New Jersey in U.S. state population density), and Guam (314/813). Some of these islands are coral atolls and high population densities exacerbate water shortages discussed earlier in this chapter.

Australia and Oceania are above the world-average rates of population growth, and there are significant disparities in these rates among the countries and dependent territories of the region, regardless of their levels of economic development (Fig. 11.17). Even though Australia and New Zealand are developed countries, their populations have been increasing at higher rates than those of some poorer nations (e.g. Tuvalu, Tonga, and the Federated States of Micronesia). Migration is the most important component of population growth in Australia, and natural increase in the rest of the region. Several countries, particularly the Federated States of Micronesia, Tonga, and Samoa, have recorded major emigration in recent years.

Indigenous People

Australia was populated about 50,000 years ago by migrants from Southeast Asia who came here via the land bridge

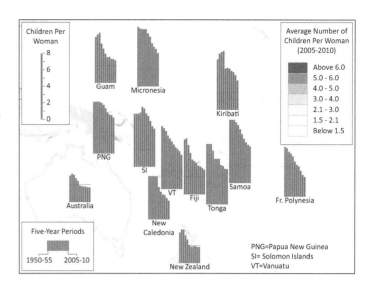

FIGURE 11.17 Total fertility rates in Oceania, 1950–2010—Fertility rates have been declining in all parts of Oceania but they are still above the replacement level and among the highest in the world. *Source:* United Nations. Population Division. World Population Prospects 2012.

connecting both regions when the sea level was much lower than it is today. Most of Oceania was settled much later, some islands as late as 1,000 years ago (Fig. 11.18). When Europeans "discovered" Australia and New Zealand in the 18th century, they encountered two major groups of indigenous people: the Aborigines in Australia and the Maoris in New Zealand. The **Aborigines** lived in small groups as hunters and gatherers and had no concept of private property. The land seizures by the European settlers led to violence and clashes in the frontier regions by the 1840s, particularly in Queensland and South Australia. One example of the harsh treatment of Aborigines was a New South Wales law that allowed for taking children from their parents; this practice was legal until 1969. There are over half a million Aborigines in Australia today, and they comprise 2.5 percent of the country's total population (Fig. 11.19). Most of them live in major cities and regional urban centers, the rest in remote areas, mainly in the Northern Territory. The Aborigine people have higher fertility rates than the rest of Australia's population. Most have been assimilated to some degree as only 10 percent still communicate in their native language at home and 60 percent do not speak any native language at all.

The **Maori** people came to New Zealand from other parts of Polynesia about 1,000 years ago, perhaps earlier, and their original livelihood was based on the hunting of birds and fishing (Fig. 11.20). At the time of the European encounter, some 100,000 to 200,000 Maoris lived on the two major islands, and most of them practiced shifting cultivation. The major event in the Maori-European relationship was the Treaty of Waitangi (1840) signed by the British and over forty Maori chiefs from the North

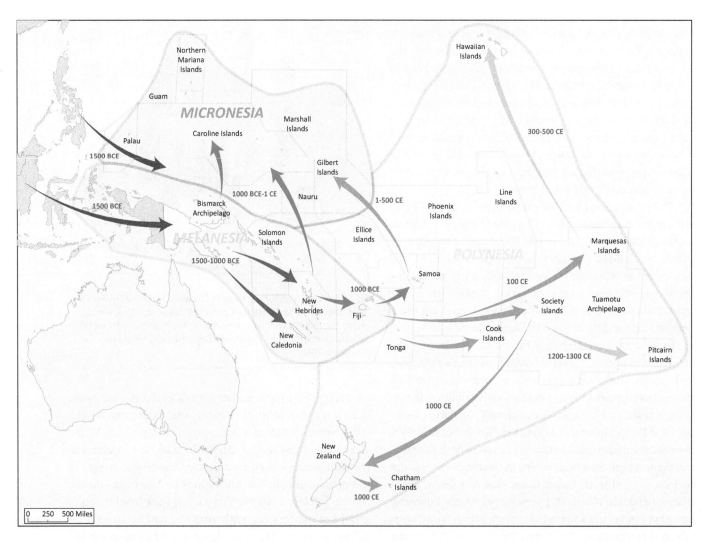

FIGURE 11.18 History of settlement in Oceania—Notice the late population of New Zealand and the Hawaiian Islands and other parts of Polynesia. Source: Drawn after a similar map at https://teachingpolynesia.weebly.com.

Island. It established British rule over New Zealand. The Maoris were guaranteed land ownership and the rights of British subjects in exchange for recognizing the British monarch as their ruler. Two versions of the treaty, one in English and one in Maori, were interpreted differently by each group. The Maoris understood it as giving the British permission to use their land, while the British believed they received complete sovereignty over the Maori people and their land. Disputes over the interpretation of the treaty led to the New Zealand Land Wars in the 1840s and 1850s, resulting in casualties on both sides. The New Zealand government did not respect many treaty rights given to the Maoris for decades. Finally, the Waitangi Tribunal, designed to reconsider many of the treaty provisions, was established in 1975, but it has not yet resolved all the disagreements[6]. The Maoris comprise about 15 percent of the country's total

population and most live on the North Island (Fig. 11.21). They are better integrated with the rest of New Zealand society than the Aborigines of Australia.

European Settlement and Australia's Immigration Policy

Early British visitors, like their Dutch predecessors, did not have a positive opinion of Australia. However, James Cook, who spent some time in the newly discovered land, provided a favorable report about parts of Australia to the British monarch in 1770. British colonization began after these reports, and the first settlers (736 prisoners and 294 free individuals) came to the Bay of Botany (near the city of Sydney) on eleven ships in 1788. Other British settlements, also consisting of many prisoners, were established

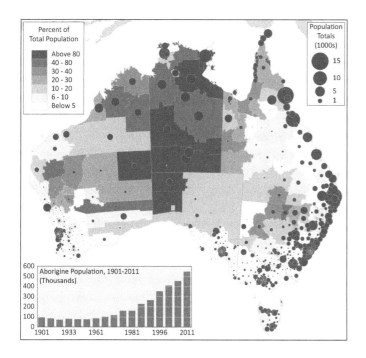

FIGURE 11.19 The Aborigine population in Australia, 2011—Although most of the Aborigines live along the eastern coast, the Northern Territory has the highest proportion. Notice a significant increase in their numbers after the 1960s. *Source:* Australian Bureau of Statistics.

FIGURE 11.20 The Maori warrior dance or *haka*—Warriors played an important role in traditional Maori culture, and the warrior dance or haka remains a part of Maori customs today. *Source:* Pixabay.

in other coastal locations. Although most of the early British immigrants were convicts (165,000 during the 1788–1868 period), free settlers began outnumbering them by the 1830s. The Victoria gold rush of the 1850s brought migrants from other parts of Australia and other countries, including 20,000 Chinese, and the population of that state increased from 70,000 to 500,000 in less than a decade. Another major gold rush occurred in Western Australia in the early 1890s and brought thousands of migrants, including 35,000 in just one year (1896). The first European settlement in New Zealand was a whaling station established in 1792, but large-scale colonization began in the 1840s, and there were six settlements by 1850. As the British immigrants began coming to Australia in large numbers after the gold rushes, some colonies introduced anti-Asian legislation, first against the Chinese, and later against the Japanese, South Asians, and Pacific Islanders. These legislative acts became known as the **White Australia Policy**[7]. However, the policy became less popular after World War II, and several changes relaxing the restrictions were gradually introduced. The official end to this policy occurred in 1973 when legislation prevented the use of race in any immigration decision.

Most immigrants coming to Australia today are from Asia, mainly from India, China, the Philippines, Sri Lanka,

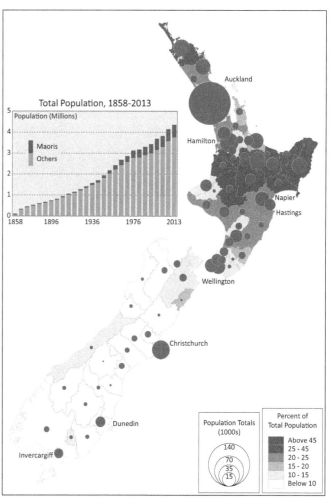

FIGURE 11.21 The Maori population in New Zealand, 2013—The North Island has over 85 percent and the Auckland urban agglomeration about a quarter of the total population. *Source:* Statistics of New Zealand.

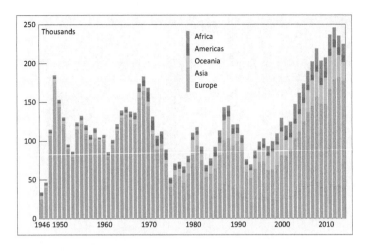

FIGURE 11.22 Immigration to Australia by area of origin, 1946–2014—Migration from Europe, particularly the British Isles, was dominant during the White Australia Policy. Notice the growing importance of Asian migration since the abolition of that policy in the early 1970s. *Source:* Australian Bureau of Statistics.

Malaysia, South Korea, and Vietnam (Fig. 11.22). The percentage of British immigrants has fallen to 15 percent. There has also been an influx of refugees from Asia in recent decades. Most of them originate in Afghanistan, Myanmar, and Iraq. The Australian government has opened several offshore immigration-processing centers in response to increased refugee inflow. The Regional Processing Center on the island of Nauru, in existence since 2001, has been the most controversial of these centers as claims of harsh conditions and mistreatment, including sexual abuse, have been publicized.

Past settlement patterns of indigenous people and much later influx of the Europeans and Asians have created a mosaic of ethnicities and cultures across the region. Australia and New Zealand are predominantly European, with European ancestry people comprising 90 and 70 percent of their populations, respectively. The rest of Oceania, on the other hand, has only a tiny proportion

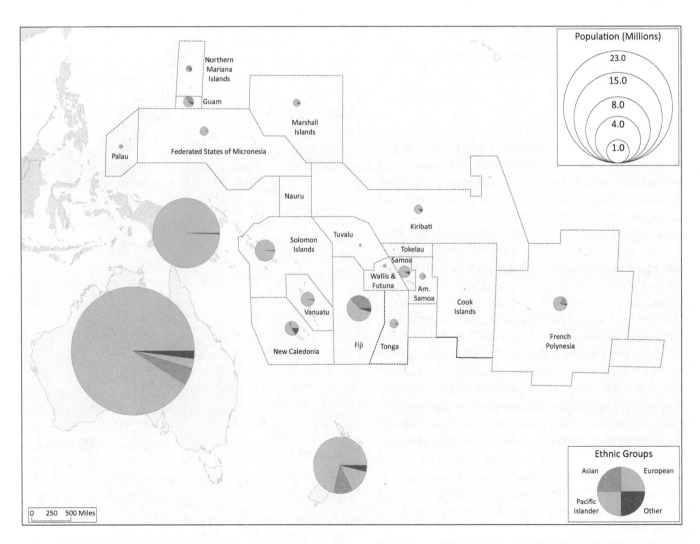

FIGURE 11.23 Distribution of ethnic groups in Australia and Oceania—Europeans comprise 65 percent of the total population, Pacific Islanders about 28 percent, and Asians just over 5 percent. *Source:* CIA World Factbook.

(1 percent) of white population, although one-third of the French territory New Caledonia's population is also of European origin. For Oceania as a whole, over 90 percent of the population are people of the Pacific Islander ethnicity (Fig. 11.23). Asians comprise about 5 percent of the region's total population, but they account for half of Northern Mariana Islands' population, over 35 percent of Fiji's, and a quarter of Guam's.

High Levels of Urbanization

Australia and Oceania comprise one of the most urbanized world culture realms with 80 percent of its population living in cities. However, there is a clear distinction between Australia and New Zealand on the one hand and the rest of the region on the other regarding urbanization patterns and processes. Australia and New Zealand have a high percentage of urban population, and their cities are similar in many ways to those in other parts of the developed world. Oceania is much less urbanized (with a few exceptions), and its cities are much smaller in size, less diverse from an economic and social point of view, and less connected with the rest of the world.

The most distinctive feature of Australia and New Zealand's urbanization is the dominance of several large cities, located along the coast and comprising the majority of their populations[8]. These cities are relatively young, established by the Europeans in the first part of the 19th century, and have become important regional centers of economic and political power with increasing global connections. They are similar to cities in the United States and Canada in terms of their layout and functions, including the concentration of high-rise structures in the central business district (CBD) and residential areas of different socioeconomic status dominated by single-family dwellings spreading for miles from the urban core. Sydney and Melbourne occupy the top of Australia's urban hierarchy, followed by Brisbane, Perth, and Adelaide (Fig. 11.24 and Fig. 11.25). These five cities have almost 60 percent of the country's total population. Sydney, established by the first European settlers in a deep and protected bay in 1788, is the country's leading commercial center and one of two major industrial centers (Fig. 11.26). It is known around the world for several of its iconic landmarks, including the Harbor Bridge and the Opera House (a UNESCO World Heritage Site). The city, which hosted the Summer Olympic Games in 2000, is increasingly multiethnic and renowned for its high quality of life in terms of natural environment (open spaces, parks, etc.) and cultural

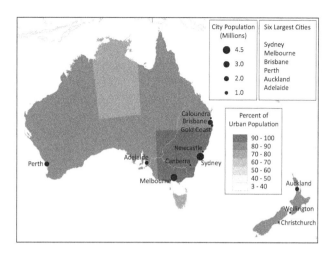

FIGURE 11.24 Urbanization levels in Australia and New Zealand—Australia has only five cities with a population of over 1 million but they comprise over half of the country's total population. Auckland is by far the largest urban center in New Zealand. *Source:* United Nations. Population Division. World Urbanization Prospects 2014; Australian Bureau of Statistics.

CITY	POPULATION	PERCENT OF STATE'S POPULATION
Sydney	5,005,358	65
Melbourne	4,641,636	76
Brisbane	2,349,699	49
Perth	2,066,564	79
Adelaide	1,326,354	78
Canberra	396,294	99
Hobart	222,802	43
Darwin	143,629	59
AUSTRALIA	16,152,336	67

FIGURE 11.25 Population of major cities in Australia, 2016. *Source:* Australian Bureau of Statistics.

FIGURE 11.26 Sydney harbor—Famed for the Opera House at the left, Sydney has benefited from its site on one of largest natural harbors in the world. *Source:* Pixabay.

amenities. Melbourne was established in 1835 and like Sydney is a major global financial center. Highly ranked for its educational, health care, research and development, tourism, and sports activities (it hosted the 1956 Summer Olympic Games), it is also considered one of the most livable cities in the world. It was also the temporary capital of Australia between 1901 and 1927. Sydney and other cities wanted to be the capital of the new country, too. To balance these competing forces and to place the government in a cooler, highland location, Canberra was developed as a compromise capital, a category that also includes Washington, DC (sited to balance north and south in the early U.S.). Canberra is the only major city located in the interior of Australia.

Increasing costs of living in major urban areas have encouraged many Australians to relocate to smaller coastal cities. This movement, known as the "sea change," was originally popular among the older and retired generations but is now also attracting young professionals able to work from home. Some coastal cities have been growing very fast in recent decades. For example, Gold Coast and Sunshine Coast, two cities located about 95 kilometers (60 miles) south and north of Brisbane, have populations of over 580,000 and 340,000 people, respectively. A similar but smaller-scale phenomenon known as the "tree change," characterized by the movement of urban dwellers to regional and rural towns, has been taking place in some parts of Australia. Cheaper real estate and open space have attracted predominantly younger migrants to these places.

Auckland is by far the largest urban agglomeration in New Zealand as it houses one-third of the country's total population. Established in 1840, it occupies an isthmus with good natural harbors on both sides. Its population of over 1.3 million is of diverse backgrounds and makes it the most cosmopolitan city in New Zealand. It has the largest number of Pacific Islander people in the world.

The lower levels of urbanization in most of the Pacific island countries and territories reflect their small populations and lower levels of economic development. Melanesia is the least urbanized with only one-fifth of the population living in cities. Port Moresby, the capital of Papua New Guinea, is the largest city in this region. However, most of its 345,000 residents live in inadequate housing with poor access to basic amenities and other services, and a large proportion is unemployed. There are three additional cities in Micronesia and Polynesia with populations of over 100,000: Noumea (181,000 inhabitants), the major urban center of New Caledonia, Suva (176,000) of Fiji, and Papeete (133,000) of French Polynesia. The largest cities on other islands are very small by most standards. The capital cities of Tuvalu (Funafuti) and the Federated States of Micronesia (Palikir) have less than 10,000 inhabitants each.

LANGUAGE AND RELIGION

Although the linguistic patterns in large parts of this region may not be as complex as those of South Asia or Sub-Saharan Africa, there are extreme differences among countries and territories regarding the number of languages in use. Melanesia is probably the most linguistically diverse part of the region, while Polynesia, considering its territorial extent, shows remarkable linguistic uniformity. Following the European colonization of the region, English or French have become official languages in almost every part of Oceania. Likewise, Christianity, introduced by European missionaries, became the dominant religion in most countries, and today about 70 percent of the region's population adhere to this faith. The three other major world religions, Buddhism, Islam, and Hinduism, have a much smaller number of followers here—only 5 percent of the total population claims membership in all of them together. A quarter of the region's population, mainly in Australia and New Zealand, has no religious affiliation.

Linguistic Diversity

Over 1,000 or almost one-sixth of all languages used in the world today are found in the three Melanesian countries: Papua New Guinea (840 languages), Vanuatu (117), and the Solomon Islands (73). They are among the four linguistically most diverse countries in the world (together with Cameroon)[9]. Mountainous terrain, dense forests, and a subsistence economy have contributed to the isolation of small groups of people who speak a bewildering variety of languages. Consequently, many languages have fewer than 1,000 speakers, and residents of neighboring villages may not understand each other. Most of these languages belong to a variety of the Trans-New Guinea

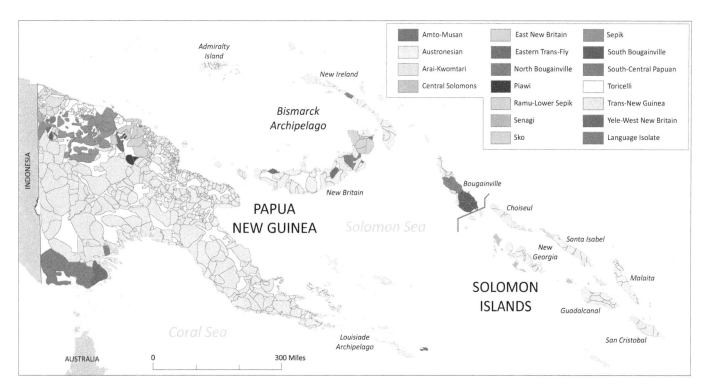

FIGURE 11.27 Linguistic diversity in Papua New Guinea and the Solomon Islands—These two countries are the most linguistically diverse in the world. Their residents speak over 900 languages belonging to about 20 linguistic families. *Source:* World Language Mapping System.

linguistic families, but some are members of the Austronesian linguistic family, which also includes languages spoken in the rest of Oceania, in Southeast Asia, and in Madagascar (Fig. 11.27). New Guinea today is perhaps the part of the world affected most severely by language extinction, as better education and connections to the broader world lead young people to learn one of a handful of global languages (especially English) instead of their parents' mother tongues.

The European colonization of Australia and Oceania and subsequent importation of Pacific Islander laborers speaking various languages to sugar cane plantations in Queensland (Australia), Fiji, Samoa, and New Caledonia led to their mixing and the subsequent emergence of several pidgin languages as the means of communication (i.e., lingua franca) among the laborers and the Europeans. Most of the pidgin vocabulary was derived from the English language; some words from German, Portuguese, French, and Malay, and various languages of the laborers were also added. When the pidgin languages become the main means of communication among the descendants of the original speakers, they are called Creole languages. Three Creole languages, in addition to English, have gained official status in these countries: Tok Pisin in Papua New Guinea, Bislama in Vanuatu, and Pijin in the Solomon

Islands. Several million people, mainly urban residents and government employees, use them, although not all speakers know them well. All three languages are closely related, and some scholars consider them dialects of the same language.

In order to protect them from extinction, numerous indigenous languages have been given official status across the region, including Samoan in Samoa and American Samoa, Carolinian in the Northern Mariana Islands, and Maori in New Zealand. The Maori language received official status in 1987, and most New Zealand government documents are now published in English and Maori. Aotearoa, which can be translated as "the long white cloud," is the Maori name for New Zealand. About a quarter of the Maori population can hold a conversation in this language, but a much smaller proportion can claim fluency in it. Some 250 Aboriginal languages were used by the indigenous residents of Australia at the time of European arrival. The colonial authorities and later the Australian government encouraged and quite often forced their speakers to learn English. Today less than fifty languages have more than one hundred speakers each, and many languages may become extinct after their very few old-age speakers are gone.

One of two European languages, English or French, is the official language in every country or territory in

FIGURE 11.28 Men's house near the Sepik River, Papua New Guinea—Such houses are used for rituals such as coming of age ceremonies in the community. *Source:* Wikimedia Commons.

the region. While English is the native tongue for most residents of Australia and New Zealand, and French for a large proportion of people in New Caledonia and French Polynesia, both languages are native only for very small numbers of residents on the remaining islands.

Religious Patterns

Prior to contact with European missionaries, most residents of Australia and Oceania adhered to various animistic beliefs. According to the Aborigines' beliefs, the mythical Dreaming Era was associated with powerful spirit-beings who came out of the earth or the sea and created humans, animals, and plants. They moved across the vast Australian land and created various topographic features, some of which are considered sacred sites (e.g. Uluru). People can connect with the beings through rituals, ceremonies, art, and music and maintain a close relationship with nature since they share their ancestry with plants and animals. Maori polytheistic religions recognized a series of gods in charge of various natural and human features and events. Both humans and natural objects could have mysterious qualities known as *tapu*, which made them sacred or unclean, and psychic power or *mana*[10]. Both qualities could be enhanced or diminished during one's lifetime, and any violations of rules concerning their nature would automatically lead to problems such as sickness or death. Various ceremonies to appease the Maoris' gods were performed in public and private places. Similarly, traditional religious beliefs of residents of other islands were associated with numerous deities and spirits of different characters and roles with powers of creation, life, prosperity, etc. that had to be placated through various rituals and sacrifices to assure prosperity and good fortune. Although the number of adherents to such animistic beliefs has decreased significantly during the past two centuries, some 310,000 people, over half of them in Papua New Guinea, still identify with these religious beliefs (Fig. 11.28). Between 4 and

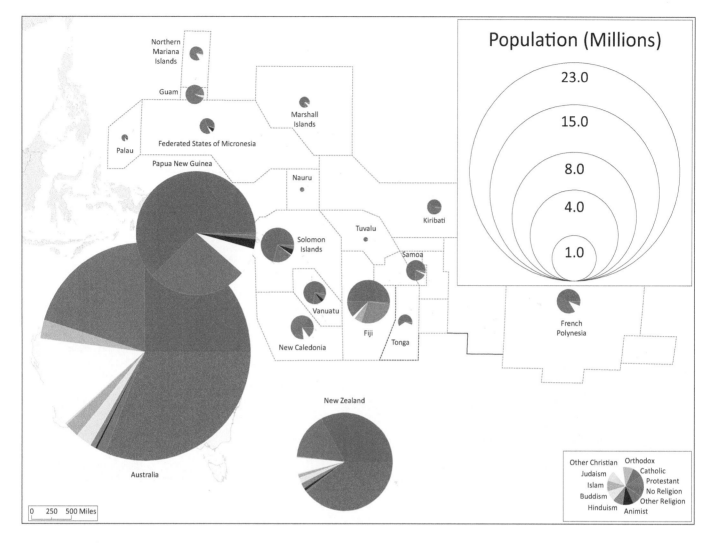

FIGURE 11.29 Religions in Australia and Oceania—Notice the high proportion of non-religious population in Australia (30 percent) and New Zealand (40 percent). *Source:* Association of Religious Data Archives.

8 percent of the total population in the Solomon Islands, Vanuatu, the Federated States of Micronesia, and Palau are followers of animistic traditions.

The arrival of Europeans and Christian missionaries to the region one or two centuries ago, as well as the early migration of indentured workers and more recent influx of other migrants from Asia to this region, has permanently changed its religious geography. Christianity is now the dominant religion in every country and territory of Australia and Oceania as 70 percent of its total population adheres to various Protestant denominations and Roman Catholicism (Fig. 11.29). Most of the former or current British possessions are predominantly Protestant while the former Spanish (later American) and current French territories have Catholic majorities. For example, over 95 percent of Tuvalu's population and 70 to 75 percent of residents of the Marshall Islands, Samoa, the Solomon Islands, and Vanuatu are Protestants.

On the other hand, most people in New Caledonia, Palau, and Kiribati are Roman Catholic (Fig. 11.30).

Buddhism, Islam, and Hinduism have similar numbers of followers, about half a million each. Sizable Buddhist populations are found in Australia and New Zealand, and most Buddhists are recent immigrants from Southeast Asia or their descendants. Islam is a significant minority religion in Australia, New Zealand, and Fiji. While most Muslims in the first two countries are also recent immigrants, most of those in Fiji are descendants of plantation workers brought from South Asia in the 19th century. Fiji also has the largest number of Hindus in the entire region, which account for 28 percent of its total population. Most are also descendants of 19th century South Asian labor migrants. Finally, a quarter of the region's inhabitants can be classified as non-religious; 44 percent of New Zealand's and 30 percent of Australia's population are in this category.

FIGURE 11.30 A view towards the harbor in Noumea, New Caledonia—The Roman Catholic cathedral overlooks the city's harbor and illustrates the importance of Christianity in the French colony. *Source:* Wikimedia Commons.

POLITICAL ORGANIZATION OF SPACE

Prior to European control of Australia and Oceania, various parts of the region had different types and levels of political organization. Both the Aboriginal population of Australia and the Maoris of New Zealand were divided into politically autonomous tribes. Each tribe occupied a certain area and generally respected loosely defined territorial boundaries of neighboring groups. Councils of men (community elders) made major decisions, and there was a system of checks and balances to control their powers. There was no concept of private land ownership. The other islands of Oceania had varying levels of autonomy. In some cases, neighboring islands easily accessible from each other and inhabited by culturally related people were organized into one strong political entity, even kingdoms. The Hawaiian and Tongan islands are examples of such relatively complex traditional political systems.

Australia

The British colonization of Australia began after the establishment of the first settlement near present-day Sydney in 1788. By the end of the 1850s, the continent was divided into several colonies, including Van Diemen's Land, later renamed Tasmania (1825), Western Australia (1827), South Australia (1836), Victoria (1851), and Queensland (1859). During the colonial period (1788–1901), each colony maintained closer ties with Great Britain than with each other. One expression of the limited internal contacts were separate railroad systems; some colonies had a narrow-gauge network (Queensland), others a standard-gauge one (New South Wales and South Australia), and still others a wide-gauge network (Victoria).

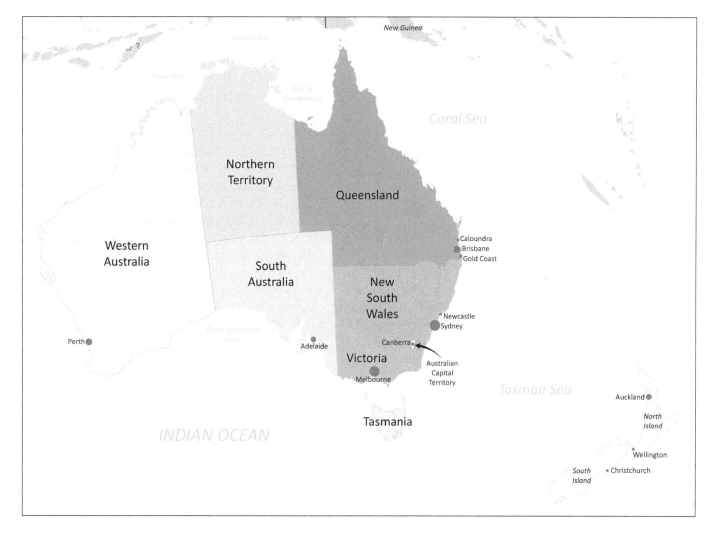

FIGURE 11.31 Administrative divisions of Australia—Australia is a federal country and is divided into six states and two federal territories. New Zealand is a unitary state.

The political maturity of these colonies and the desire to form some type of federation among them led to their independence in 1901 as the Commonwealth of Australia, a federation of six self-governing colonies (New South Wales, Queensland, South Australia, Tasmania, Victoria, and Western Australia), which became states in the new federation (Fig. 11.31).

The British monarch is the official head of state, and Queen Elizabeth II's image appears on all Australian coins and the five-dollar note. In recent years, a popular movement has emerged to change the country's status from a commonwealth to a republic with an elected Australian citizen as head of state. In 1999, a referendum to make the change failed, with 45 percent of voters in favor and 55 percent against. Some opponents, known as royalists, supported maintaining the historic connections to Britain, and others disliked the proposed means of electing the president[11]. Support for the republic has grown a little since then. In polls conducted in 2016, about half of Australians favored making the move, and some observers expect the idea to gain majority support after the reign of Queen Elizabeth II.

Oceania

New Zealand became a British colony in 1841 after it was separated from the Australian colony of New South Wales. It gained independence in 1907 as the Dominion of New Zealand. Like in Australia, the British monarch is the head of state and appoints a governor general on the advice of the country's prime minister. Unlike Australia, however, New Zealand is a unitary state; while there are units of government below the level of the national government in Wellington, the regions and territorial authorities have no power to make laws.

Beyond Australia and New Zealand, several European powers and the United States imposed their control on most of Oceania by the early 19th century, and in some cases even earlier. By the end of the 19th century, Spain, Germany, the United Kingdom, and France all controlled various islands across the vast expanse of the Pacific. Spain lost its possessions to the U.S. after being defeated in the Spanish-American War. Similarly, Germany lost its territories after World War I. Later in the 20th century, most of the island societies became independent countries, and today, only France, the United Kingdom, the United States, Australia, New Zealand, and Chile have territories in the region. The French territories include New Caledonia, Wallis and Futuna, and French Polynesia, the most famous part of which is Tahiti. The British still control Pitcairn Island, the place to which a handful of the seamen who mutinied against Captain Bligh on the *Bounty* fled in 1789, along with a small group of Tahitians. The U.S. possessions include, but are not limited to, American Samoa, Guam, the Northern Mariana Islands, and several uninhabited islands. Australia and New Zealand each control a number of small islands in Polynesia. Finally, in the Eastern Pacific lies the Chilean territory of Easter Island.

The dependent territories are small entities in area and population, have very limited (if any) natural resources, and would have great difficulty functioning as independent states. New Caledonia, French Polynesia, and Wallis and Futuna are "overseas collectivities" or DOM-TOMs (*Départements et Territoires d'Outre-Mer*) of France, have representatives in the French parliament, and their residents are French citizens. American Samoa, Guam, and the Northern Mariana Islands are self-governing, unincorporated territories of the United States. While their residents have similar rights and responsibilities as the rest of Americans, certain constitutional provisions may not be applicable to them (e.g. no one in these islands can vote for the U.S. president, and they do not have a voting representative in the U.S. Congress).

Except Australia and New Zealand, the remaining states across the region became independent relatively late in comparison to other parts of the world. Specifically, the Solomon Islands, Tuvalu, Kiribati, Palau, Vanuatu, Marshall Islands, and the Federated States of Micronesia became independent between 1978 and 1986. Three of them, the Marshall Islands, the Federated States of Micronesia, and Palau have special relations with the United States. They receive substantial American economic aid, and their citizens have access to some U.S. domestic programs and can live and work in the United States. The United States also guarantees military protection for these countries in exchange for the right to use their territories for specific military purposes.

Political Instability and Nuclear Tests

Several Pacific islands and desert sites in Australia were testing sites for nuclear weapons during the Cold War[12]. The United States, Great Britain, and France conducted over 330 tests between 1946 and 1996, with serious consequences for the environment and residents of some islands (Fig. 11.32). The United States conducted over one hundred nuclear and hydrogen bomb tests on Bikini and Eniwetok atolls in the Marshall Islands during the 1946–58 period and on Christmas (Kirimati) Island (present-day Kiribati) and Johnston Atoll in 1952. Great Britain started atmospheric nuclear tests on the Montebello Islands (Western Australia) and at Maralinga and Emu Fields (South Australia) in 1952; it conducted twelve tests before 1957. The French testing sites on Mururoa and Fangataufa atolls in French Polynesia were used for over 190 nuclear tests between 1966 and 1996. There was a series of widespread protests, organized by church groups, trade unions, women's organizations, high-profile individuals, and environmental groups against nuclear tests in the region. A Greenpeace vessel (*Rainbow Warrior*), taking part in some protests, was sunk by French agents in Auckland Harbor (New Zealand) in 1985. Some inhabitants of the Marshall Islands and in French Polynesia have been adversely affected by such tests and have developed numerous health problems (mainly cancer). Several states in the region signed the Rarotonga Treaty (1985) to establish the South Pacific Nuclear Free Zone in which the possession, testing, and use of nuclear weapons by member states and territories is banned.

Although Australia and Oceania form a more politically stable region than most other parts of the world, some countries had to deal with internal tensions that sometimes led to violence and government overthrow. Fiji is a country divided along ethnic and religious lines. This former British colony brought large numbers of South Asian (mainly Indian) workers, most of whom were employed on sugar cane plantations during the second part of the 19th and the early 20th centuries. The proportion of the Indian population and its control of the national economy had been steadily increasing over time, and Fiji Indians outnumbered the indigenous Fijians by 1956. At the time of independence in 1970, political power was allocated on the basis of ethnic background and a certain number of parliamentary seats were reserved for each group. However, two military coups in 1987 led to civil

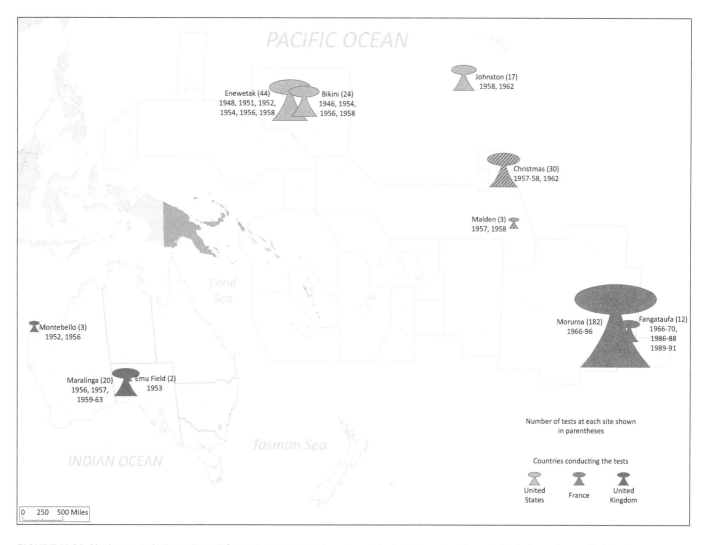

FIGURE 11.32 Nuclear tests in Australia and Oceania—Nuclear tests were conducted at ten sites, three in Australia and seven in Oceania. Notice the high number of such tests in French Polynesia. *Source:* Wikipedia.

unrest and the emigration of many Indian Fijians. Consequently, the indigenous Fijians became the largest group, and the new constitution of 1990 assured their dominance in the country's political system. Tensions between both groups, despite some reconciliation attempts, continued and led to another coup and military mutinies in 2000. In response to these developments, Fiji was briefly suspended from the Commonwealth of Nations, and some countries also suspended diplomatic relations with Fiji. Finally, after four decades of political turmoil, democratic elections were held in 2014, and political stability has been established.

Papua New Guinea, whose people speak numerous languages and practice various customs, was a politically unstable country for a decade or so in the late 1980s and most of the 1990s. The conflict began when a large open-pit copper mine in Panguna on Bougainville was opened in 1972 and attracted migrants from other parts of Papua New Guinea. It accounted for 45 percent of the country's export revenues at one time. The influx of migrants, outflow of profits, and environmental concerns prompted indigenous residents to challenge the central government. The Bougainville Revolutionary Army proclaimed independence and controlled the island for a short time in 2000. The conflict resulted in 15,000 to 20,000 deaths and ended with the island gaining some autonomy in 2001. The peace accord provided a five-year window for a referendum on the question of Bougainville's independence, which has recently been scheduled for 2019.

During the early stages of the Cold War, Australia and New Zealand formed military alliances with the United States to keep the spread of communism across the region in check. One example of such cooperation was the ANZUS Treaty on collective security, signed by the three countries in 1951. It called for military cooperation among its members in the Pacific region and assisting each other in meeting common threats. Soldiers of both countries fought alongside the U.S. forces during the Korean and Vietnam Wars. Later on, however, Australia had some reservations

about the U.S. intercontinental ballistic missile program and was opposed to proposed tests in the Tasman Sea. New Zealand, on the other hand, in response to French nuclear tests in Polynesia, declared its territory a nuclear-free zone, and prevented U.S. warships from entering its seaports. The United States suspended its treaty obligations toward New Zealand and labelled it a friend but not an ally.

ECONOMIC ACTIVITIES

Australia and Oceania generate only a small fraction of the global economic output (about 1.3 percent), and over 95 percent of it comes from two countries in this region, Australia and New Zealand. Their economic prosperity has been mainly based on the development of primary activities—agriculture and mining in Australia and agriculture in New Zealand. Although most of the remaining countries in Oceania have also relied on the primary sector, tourism and other tertiary activities have become important components of development in some island states and territories in recent decades. There are significant disparities in levels of economic development among these

countries, at least in terms of GDP per capita, ranging from $1,800 to over $30,000 (Fig. 11.33).

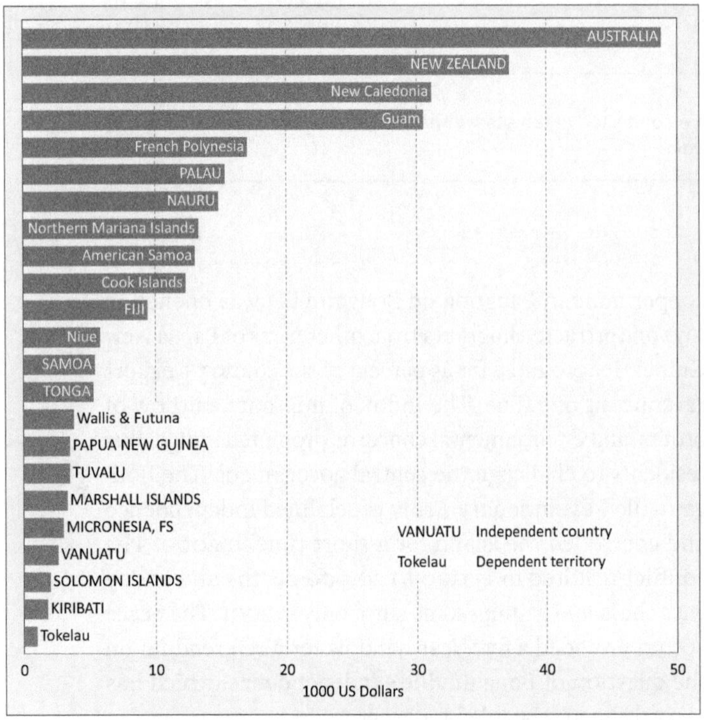

Primary Activities

Mining activities began shortly after the establishment of the first British settlements in Australia[13]. Coal was discovered in New South Wales by the end of the 18th century and was used as a source of energy, and lead was mined in South Australia by the early 1840s. The Victorian gold rush of the 1850s attracted many immigrants and made Melbourne a boom town. As much as 2 tons of gold per week flowed through Melbourne at the peak of the gold rush, and Victoria's output was second only to California, which experienced its own gold rush around the same time. Mining activities continued expanding rapidly after 1870 when additional gold fields and other metallic ores were discovered in several parts of the country. A relative decline of the mining sector in the early 20th century was followed by its resurgence in the 1960s after the mining of iron ore in Western Australia (the Pilbara region) began (Fig. 11.34). Australia is one of the richest places in the world in terms of mineral wealth per capita, which is one reason why it has been nicknamed "The Lucky Country."[14] It has the largest reserves of diamonds, gold, iron ore, lead, nickel, uranium, zinc, and zircon, and the second largest amounts of bauxite, cobalt, copper, manganese, silver, and tungsten in the world. Its mineral wealth is concentrated in several regions, including Broken Hill in New South Wales (mainly lead and zinc), Mount Isa in Queensland (lead and zinc), the Eastern Goldfields (Kalgoorlie) in Western Australia (gold and nickel), the Olympic Dam in South Australia (gold, copper, and uranium), the Pilbara region in Western Australia (iron ore), and Hunter Valley in New South Wales (coal) (Fig. 11.35). Most of the country's mineral wealth used to be shipped to Europe; East Asia is the major destination for these items today. Mining accounts for over 8 percent

FIGURE 11.33 GDP per capita in Australia and Oceania—Disparities in GDP per capita among various countries are greater in this region than most other parts of the world. *Source:* CIA World Factbook.

FIGURE 11.34 An iron ore train in northwestern Australia—Australia is the top source of iron ore in the world and more than 90 percent of its output comes from the Pilbara region located in the country's northwest. *Source:* Wikimedia Commons.

of Australia's gross domestic product, although it employs just over 2 percent of its labor force.

Mining accounts for an even greater share (22 percent) of Papua New Guinea's GDP, despite employing less than half a percent of its labor force. Copper, found on the island of Bougainville, is among the country's main mineral resource and is the leading source of income for the government. As discussed earlier, copper mining has been a politically charged activity. Papua New Guinea is also an important producer of gold and petroleum—these commodities generate tree-quarters of its exports. Three Pacific islands, Nauru, Banaba in Kiribati, and Makatea in French Polynesia, used to be rich in phosphates. Banaba and Makatea have suffered the same sort of environmental devastation as Nauru, which was discussed earlier in the chapter.

Fishing plays an important role in the economies of several Pacific states and territories, including the Federated States of Micronesia where export of tuna accounts for almost 90 percent of its total exports, the Marshall Islands with about 45 percent of revenues derived from exporting frozen fish, and American Samoa where canned tuna accounts for 99 percent of all exports. Although these and other small countries do not catch large amounts of fish even by regional standards, fishing is important as

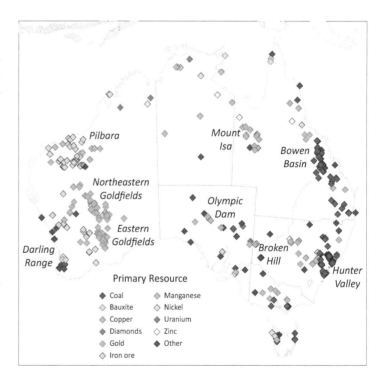

FIGURE 11.35 Mineral resources of Australia—Each symbol shows an active mine. Some mines produce several minerals but only the dominant one is shown for each mine. *Source:* Australian Bureau of Statistics.

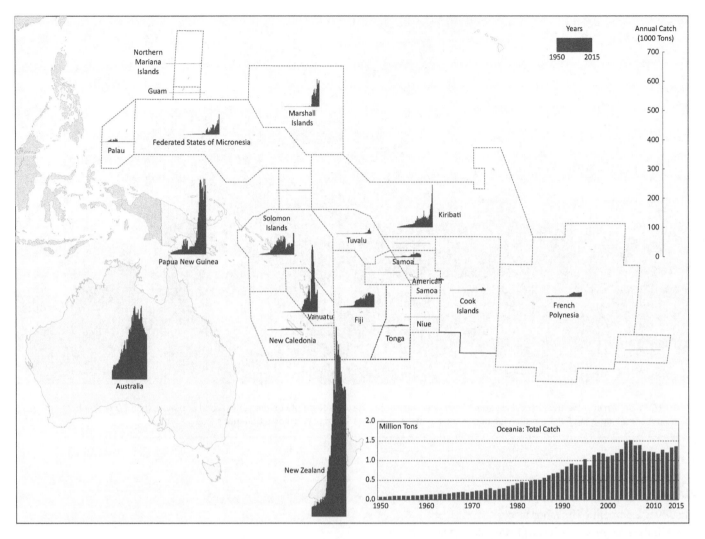

FIGURE 11.36 Fish catch in Australia and Oceania, 1950–2015—Notice the dominant role of New Zealand and a recent sharp increase in fish catch in Papua New Guinea and Kiribati. *Source:* FAOSTAT.

a source of income and food for large segments of their residents (Fig. 11.36).

Australia and New Zealand have been important producers and leading exporters of several agricultural commodities, among them wheat, wool, meat, and dairy products, for over 150 years. Agriculture, like mining in Australia, began playing an important role in their economies from the start of the British colonization of both areas. Sheep herding was developed in the semi-dry southeastern interior and, on a smaller scale, in southwestern parts of Australia and across New Zealand. Both countries became important exporters of wool by the mid-1850s and have maintained their dominant position ever since, despite periodic drops in production. There are about 72 million sheep in Australia and 30 million in New Zealand now, but their numbers have been declining since the 1970 peak in Australia (180 million) and the 1982–83 peak (70 million) in New Zealand. A declining demand for wool and lower prices on the world market have been responsible for shrinking sheep herds in both countries. Europe used to be the main destination for wool from this region, but most of it is now exported to China and other Asian countries and used for carpet making.

Cattle ranching was well-developed in Western and Northern Queensland by the 1860s (Fig. 11.37). This warmer and more humid region, with distinctive wet and dry seasons, was better suited for beef cattle than sheep raising. Australia is the second largest beef exporter in the world today, and most of it goes to the United States, Japan, and South Korea. Raising beef cattle is also an important rural activity in New Zealand, most of it is concentrated on the North Island. About 70 percent of exported red meat is shipped to the United States for use in hamburgers. Dairy farming was established in the more humid and milder parts of Southeastern Australia and across New Zealand

FIGURE 11.37 Distribution of selected farm animals in Australia—Sheep and cattle dominate the livestock economy in Australia. Notice different spatial patterns of both types of animal herding. *Source:* Australian Bureau of Statistics.

to meet the demand for milk and dairy products among the growing urban population. Most of the production was originally for the domestic market, but the invention of refrigeration in the 1880s opened markets for Australian and New Zealand dairy products and meat in Europe. The export of refrigerated goods to Europe, especially the United Kingdom, had been an important source of revenue for both countries for decades. After the United Kingdom

was admitted to the European Union in 1973, Australia and New Zealand had to find other markets for their agricultural exports because other EU states gained preferential access to the British market. Today, 80 percent of Australia's dairy exports go to Asia, while the U.S. is the top market for New Zealand's dairy exports.

Wheat farming was developed on a large scale only in Australia, mainly within a semi-circular belt from Central

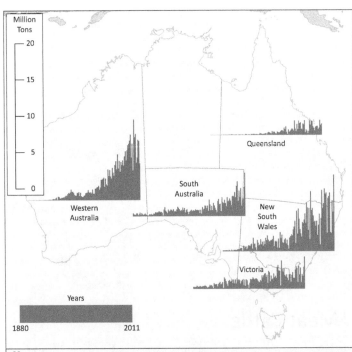

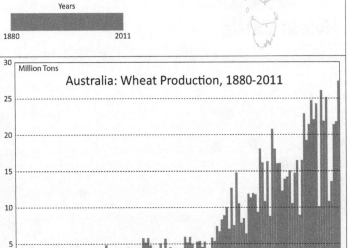

FIGURE 11.38 Wheat production in Australia, 1880–2014—Notice great annual fluctuations in production and the growing importance of Western Australia as a wheat producer. *Source:* Australian Bureau of Statistics.

FIGURE 11.39 An Australian vineyard—Australia ranks fifth in the world for wine exports after France, Italy, Spain, and Chile. *Source:* Pixabay.

FIGURE 11.40 In search of coconut sap—A man collects toddy, coconut sap, in Kiribati. Toddy is drunk fresh from the tree or fermented into coconut wine. *Source:* Wikimedia Commons.

Queensland through New South Wales and Victoria to South Australia and later in Western Australia, which is now its largest producer (Fig. 11.38). Australian production has been characterized by significant annual variations due to changing weather conditions, particularly the occurrence of periodic droughts. The country is now the world's ninth largest producer and the fourth largest exporter of this commodity. Australian wheat farms are similar in size and mechanization levels to those in the United States and Canada. Sugar cane has been grown for over a century in coastal areas of Queensland, and it is one of the largest and most important farming sectors in the state. There are some 4,300 sugar cane farms today, and a typical farm is rather small by Australian standards (about 200 acres).

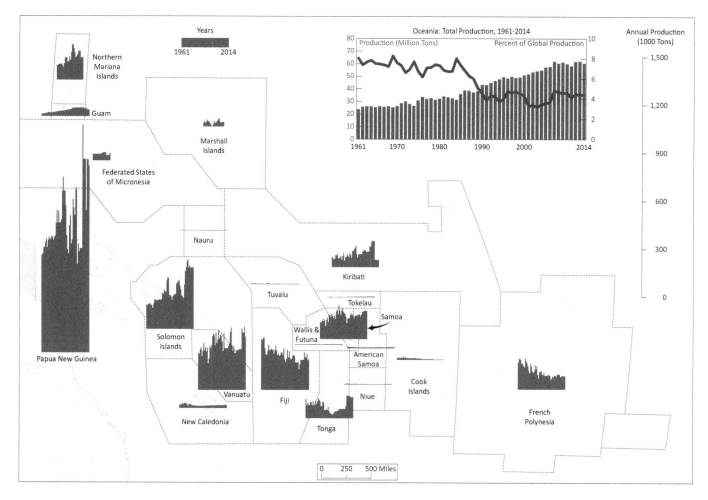

FIGURE 11.41 Production of coconuts in Oceania, 1961–2014—Despite a slow but steady increase in production totals, the region's global share of that production declined around the mid-1980s. *Source:* FAOSTAT.

Most of the raw sugar is exported, while refined sugar is consumed at home.

Horticulture has been growing in importance in both countries to meet the increasing demand for fruits and vegetables at home and abroad. Although Australia's warmer climate supports the cultivation of a greater variety of temperate and subtropical crops, New Zealand's horticulture is also well developed. Both countries produce large quantities of grapes, and their wines have been exported to many countries. Vineyards are found in several parts of Australia, but areas around Adelaide in South Australia produce almost half of the country's output (Fig. 11.39). New Zealand's wineries have put emphasis on the production of high quality wines for export and for the domestic market. Both countries are also major producers of apples and other deciduous fruits, and New Zealand is the world's third largest producer and top exporter of kiwi fruits. Interestingly, the kiwi fruit was commonly known as the Chinese gooseberry until a 1960s marketing campaign by New Zealand growers attached the name of the country's iconic bird to the fruit.

The coconut palm has been an important source of food and other materials for most residents of the Pacific islands. This tropical plant grows in coastal areas and can produce about fifty large nuts a year. The nuts contain milk and meat, which can be directly consumed or processed into coconut oil and copra (used in the production of soap and other cosmetics) (Fig. 11.40). Exports of coconuts and copra are major sources of revenue for Vanuatu (42 percent of all exports) and a few other countries. The palm is also a source of construction materials and porcupine wood used in furniture making (Fig. 11.41). The importance of coconut palms in the lives of many Pacific Islanders used to be summed up in what is now a politically incorrect phrase, the "coconut civilization."

Secondary Activities

Australia and New Zealand are highly industrialized countries and generate over 95 percent of the total manufacturing output in the region. However, their industrial base is not as strong as that of most other economically developed nations. Both countries faced several challenges to large-scale industrial development, including a small domestic market for manufactured goods, a distance barrier (high transportation costs) to foreign markets, and high labor costs. Today, the manufacturing sector accounts for about 15 percent of Australia's GDP, and the largest industries are (1) machinery and equipment manufacturing; (2) food, beverage, and tobacco processing; and (3) petrochemical, coal, and chemical industries. The small size of the market remains a key challenge. In 2017, the last of Australia's auto assembly plants (one owned by Toyota and another by General Motors) closed because they could not compete with lower-cost production elsewhere. New Zealand's even smaller secondary sector is best known for the food and beverage industries, mainly livestock and milk processing plants, as well as for furniture, electric fence, rock-crushing equipment, and household appliance industries. Most of the remaining countries of Oceania do not have well-developed industries except some food processing or metallic ore smelting plants, textile, and garment industries.

Transportation, Trade and Tourism

Great distances across Australia and Oceania, their peripheral location in relation to two of the three global economic hubs (Europe and the United States/Canada), and the limited or lack of economic self-sufficiency of most countries in this region increase the importance of their transportation and trading connections with each other and the rest of the world. Although these activities may not account for very high proportions of the gross domestic product, they are critical for economies in the region and, in some cases, national survival.

Because of the country's large size, low population density, and remote location of many economic activities, transportation plays a major role in Australia's economy. Road transportation is particularly important, and this country has more roads per capita than Europe and one of the highest fuel consumption rates per capita in the world. However, there are only two east-west road connections across the continent and two north-south links in the western half of the country. A large proportion of the country's network consists of unpaved roads. Passenger railroad transport is not well developed, but freight trains haul large amounts of minerals from several mining sites to seaports and processing plants. As mentioned earlier, there are three different rail-track gauge systems across the country which undoubtedly hamper the efficiency

of the national network that has only one east-west and two north-south lines across the country. Australia has a well-developed air transportation network. Its flag carrier Qantas flies to over fifty cities on every inhabited continent (Fig. 11.42).

Despite the high level of economic development in Australia and New Zealand, both countries have more similarities with developing than developed nations when the structure of their imports and exports is examined. While developed countries mainly import raw materials and export finished products, Australia and New Zealand strongly rely on the export of minerals and agricultural commodities and the import of manufactured goods. In fact, their economic prosperity has been based on the development of primary rather than secondary activities. About two-thirds of Australia's and New Zealand's exports consist of minerals and/or agricultural commodities. The United Kingdom used to be the main trading partner for both countries, but British membership in the European Union in 1973, as mentioned earlier, forced the Pacific nations to find other markets for their exports. Today, over half of Australian exports go to China, Japan, South Korea, and India. New Zealand sends most of its agricultural commodities and forest products (timber) to China, Australia, the United States, and Japan. Most imports to both countries come from China, the United States, and Japan. The rest of the region is also dependent on export of minerals, fish, agricultural, or forest products.

Australia and Oceania have a small share of the global tourist market (just over 1 percent) but tourism is one of the most viable industries in Oceania due to various barriers to other forms of economic development, including small populations, small land areas, remote location, and limited natural resource base. Unspoiled natural environments and great cultural diversity are major tourist attractions in many parts of the region. Tropical climates and surrounding waters attract several types of tourism, among them beach and adventure tourism, surfing, fishing, ecotourism, cultural tourism, and even romance tourism. This sector offers important development opportunities for many small countries as it accounts for large shares of their GDP. In Palau, for example, it is the most important economic sector, generating half of the GDP and employing over 40 percent of its labor force. However, tourism is also susceptible to natural disasters, political instability, and global economic conditions. Most tourists visiting Oceania are from Australia, New Zealand, and the United States, but the number of tourists from China, Japan, and South Korea has been growing in recent years. For example,

FIGURE 11.42 Qantas, Australia's largest airline—Qantas operates flights to cities around the world, reducing the "tyranny of distance" that historically acted as a constraint on Australia's development. *Source:* Pixabay.

about 90 to 95 percent of tourists visiting Guam and Northern Mariana Islands are from Asian countries. Most tourists visit Oceania during the winter season in their countries of origin.

Australia and New Zealand are also major tourist destinations for many Asian, American, and European tourists (Fig. 11.43). Tourism employs about 5 percent of their total labor force. Major tourist destinations are large cities, mainly Sydney, Melbourne, Brisbane, and Auckland, coastal beach areas (e.g. Gold Coast and Sunshine Coast in Queensland), the Great Barrier Reef, selected physical locations, some of which are considered sacred to the indigenous people (e.g. Uluru or Ayers Rock), and national parks and nature preserves. Australia is a popular destination for tourists from New Zealand and China while New Zealand is the same for Australian visitors.

New Zealand: A Welfare State?

Until recent years, New Zealand had been known as a "welfare state" because of the generous social and economic benefits available to its citizens. It had a long tradition of helping European (mainly British) settlers by promising them land, jobs, social security, and a cleaner environment than that in the United Kingdom. Since private companies were unable or unwilling to deliver these promises, the state took responsibility for providing them. New Zealand was the first country in the world to offer pensions to its residents, commencing in 1898. A series of other benefits was gradually introduced, including subsidies for housing (1905), pensions to widows (1911) and blind people (1924), and small family allowances (1926). The state added to its generosity by providing family benefits to mothers with children under sixteen years of age. The steady expansion of these benefits, based on progressive taxation and heavy borrowing, led to high government spending on these programs, amounting to 36 percent of all its revenues by the early 1960s. Some New Zealanders began questioning their welfare system as putting too much emphasis on the common good and a collective moral value system rather than on individual rights.

The welfare system has gone through a series of reforms, starting in the early 1970s, including greater decentralization (more power allocated to local governments), the removal of some moral criteria required for receiving certain benefits (e.g. making single mothers eligible for them), and greater individual responsibility (requiring individual contributions to the plan)[15]. Simultaneously, New Zealand has liberalized its economy by loosening many regulations and lowering tax rates.

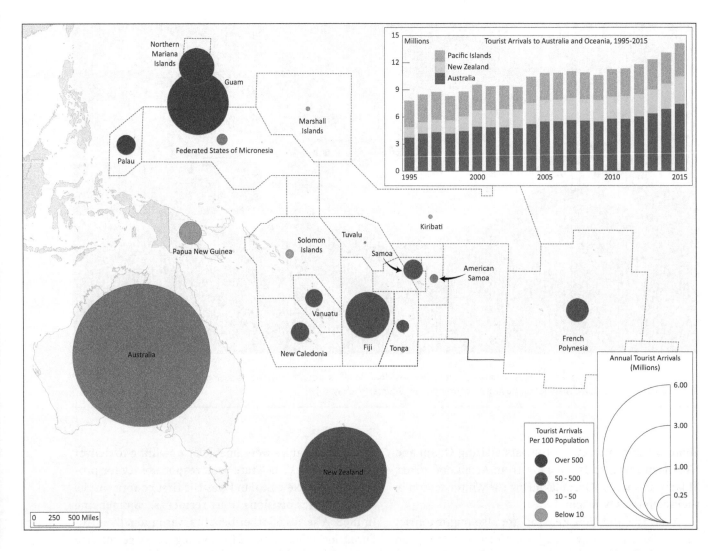

FIGURE 11.43 Tourist arrivals to Australia and Oceania—Over half of the tourists visiting this region go to Australia and New Zealand. Notice the popularity of Guam and the Northern Mariana Islands as tourist destinations (mainly for Asians). *Source:* World Bank.

FUTURE PROBLEMS AND PROSPECTS

This relatively remote and sparsely populated region, characterized by great cultural diversity and increasing global connections, faces several environmental, economic, and other challenges, often originating from outside the region. Global warming and rising sea levels are undoubtedly the most serious environmental concerns for many small Pacific islands. They may affect the quantity and quality of limited freshwater resources on coral atolls and other low islands, limit local food supplies due to their adverse impact on marine resources (fish stocks) and agricultural productivity (lower yields), and damage infrastructure (coastal erosion). Climate change may also lead to declining revenues from tourism and other economic activities and may lead to the relocation of some residents to safer places.

Several countries (e.g. Tuvalu and Kiribati) may be completely swallowed up by rising waters by the next century.

Very small national economies put many island countries at the mercy of wealthier donor states, like the United States or Australia, and impact their sovereignty. The dependence on a single export commodity makes these island countries vulnerable to shocks of global or regional economic cycles, reflected in the changing demand and price for that commodity. Limited supplies of some commodities may adversely impact countries' entire populations. Nauru is a prime example of such a country; although one the world's richest states in the 1970s, by 2016 it was poorer than countries like Botswana, the Dominican Republic, and Montenegro.

FIGURE 11.44 Overweight and obese people in Oceania, 1975–2014—Notice the steady increase in the proportion of obese people in all countries except Nauru (where it is already very high). Rates are lower in Melanesia, Australia, and New Zealand. *Source:* WHO Global Health Observatory.

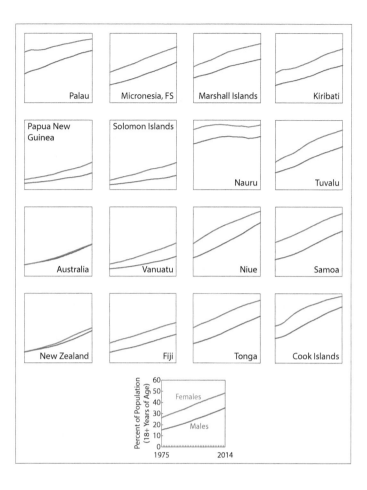

The great diversity of indigenous cultures, especially in Melanesia, may be at risk if globalization reaches many of its remote places. The loss of numerous cultural traditions (especially languages) and ecological adaptations would be a great setback for all humanity. Many cultural groups are very small, sometimes less than 1,000 members, and extremely vulnerable to outside pressures.

Health issues, particularly obesity and chronic diseases, have become major concerns in most small Pacific nations (Fig. 11.44). Out of the ten most obese nations in the world, nine are in this region, and the proportion of obese adults has been increasing in most of them. This very unhealthy trend may lead to increased mortality and put more pressure on the limited health care systems. However, the case of Nauru shows that this trend can be slowed down or even reversed if governments take proper action.

NOTES

1. Hobbs, J. J. (2009). *World regional geography* (6th ed.). Belmont, CA: Brooks/Cole.

2. McCoy, J. (Ed.). (2003). *Geo-data: The world geographical encyclopedia.* Farmington Hills, MI: Gale.

3. Parry, J. (2010). Pacific islanders pay heavy price for abandoning traditional diet. *Bulletin of the World Health Organization* 88(7), 485–5. Retrieved from http://www.who.int/bulletin/volumes/88/7/10-010710/en/

4. Rull, V., Cañellas-Boltà, N., Sáez, A., Giralt, S., Pla, S. & Margalef, O. (2010). Paleoecology of Easter Island: Evidence and uncertainties. *Earth Science Reviews*, 99(1–2), 50–60.

5. Kirkpatrick, J. B. (2011). The political ecology of soil and species conservation in a 'Big Australia'. *Geographical Research*, 49(3), 276–85.

6. Stokes, E. (1992). The Treaty of Waitangi and the Waitangi Tribunal: Maori claims in New Zealand. *Applied Geography*, 12(2), 176–91.

7. Jupp, J. (2002). *From White Australia to Woomera: The story of Australian migration.* New York, NY: Oxford University Press.

8. Dowling, R., & McGuirk, P. (2012). Cities of Australia and the Pacific Islands. In S. D. Brunn, M. Hays-Mitchell, & D. J. Ziegler (Eds.), *Cities of the World: World Regional Urban Development* (pp. 523–554). Lanham, MD: Rowman & Littlefield.

9. Simons, G.F. & Fennig, C.D. (Eds.). (2017). *Ethnologue: Languages of the world* (20th ed.). Dallas, TX: SIL International. Retrieved from http://www.ethnologue.com

10. Strathern, A. (2002). *Oceania: An introduction to the cultures and identities of Pacific Islanders.* Durham, NC: Carolina Academic Press.

11. McKenna, M., & Hudson, W. (2003). *Australian republicanism: A reader.* Carlton, Victoria, Australia: Melbourne University Press.

12. Fisher, D. (2013). *France in the South Pacific: Power and politics.* Canberra, Australia: ANU Press.

13. Geoscience Australia. (2007). History of Australia's minerals industry. Retrieved from http://www.australianminesatlas.gov.au/history/index.html

14. Charlton, A. (2014). Dragon's tail: The lucky country after the China boom. *Quarterly Essay*, 54. Retrieved from https://www.quarterlyessay.com.au/essays

15. Lewis, N., & Moran, W. (1998). Restructuring, democracy, and geography in New Zealand. *Environment and Planning C: Government and Policy*, 16(2), 127–53.

GLOSSARY

Aborigine A member of the indigenous population of an area; the term is typically used in Australia.

Absolute location The location of an object on the Earth's surface in terms of its latitude (angular distance to the north or south from the Equator) and longitude (angular distance to the east or west from the Prime Meridian).

Al-Shabaab An Islamic militant group originating in Somalia and operating in parts of East Africa since the early 2000s relying on terrorist methods in achieving its objectives of establishing an Islamic state and eliminating foreign (Western) influence from the region.

Andean Ridge One of the largest centers of illegal drug production (especially cocaine) in the world located in Bolivia, Colombia, and Peru.

Apartheid A policy of racial discrimination and segregation in the Republic of South Africa from 1948 until 1992 that classified its residents into four racial categories, denied basic civil rights to the non-white population, and established special residential areas (**bantustans**) for the African population.

Aquifer An underground layer of permeable and porous rocks saturated with large amounts of water.

Arab Spring A 2010–2011 series of popular uprisings in the form of demonstrations, civil disobedience, riots, internet activism, and urban warfare against governments of many Middle Eastern countries accused of authoritarian rule, corruption, violation of human rights, and inability to solve major economic problems.

Arithmetic density The number of people per unit of all land (productive and unproductive).

Association of Southeast Asian Nations (ASEAN) A ten-member regional grouping that promotes economic integration, free trade, and peace in Southeast Asia.

Atoll A ring-shaped island that remains after an ancient volcanic island subsides back into the ocean leaving the **coral reef** that once surrounded the island at the surface.

Bamboo Curtain Analogous to the **Iron Curtain** in Central Europe, an imaginary barrier formerly separating Communist China and its allies from capitalist democracies allied to the U.S.

Bantustan One of ten territories (also known as homelands) designated as place of residence for people of African origin during the **apartheid** era in the Republic of South Africa.

Berlin Conference A conference of thirteen European countries and the United States held in Berlin from 1884 until 1885 that led to the partition of Africa into colonial zones of seven European powers (Belgium, France, Germany, Great Britain, Italy, Portugal, and Spain); also known as the Scramble for Africa.

Bible Belt A region in the southeastern United States dominated by socially conservative evangelical Protestantism.

Black Death A devastating plague pandemic that resulted in the deaths of millions of people in Europe in the mid-14th century.

Black Triangle A triangle-shaped area in Germany, Poland, and the Czech Republic characterized by extreme levels of air and water pollution and acid rain.

Boko Haram An Islamic militant group originating in Nigeria and operating in parts of Western Africa since 2002 relying on terrorist methods in achieving its objectives of establishing an Islamic state and eliminating foreign (Western) influence from the region.

Bracero Program A program designed to bring cheap agricultural labor from Mexico to the United States between 1942 and 1964.

Brain drain The migration of talented and well-educated people from a country.

Brain exchange The flow of talented and well-educated people back and forth between different countries.

Brain gain The migration of talented and well-educated people to a country.

Burqa A loose-fitting head-to-toe garment fully covering a woman, commonly worn in certain conservative Muslim countries.

Bushfire A wildfire in scrubland or forest that spreads rapidly.

Caribbean Community (CARICOM) An organization of Caribbean nations founded in 1973 to promote economic integration and cooperation among its members.

Caste One of the many hierarchical categories into which Hindus are born.

Centrally planned economy An economic system based on the collective or government ownership of the means of production and an artificial state-controlled pricing system.

Char A low-lying area of land in Bangladesh that forms in the middle or along the shore of a river as sediments accumulate.

Chinese Communist Party The political organization which was victorious in the Chinese Civil War (1927–1950) and which has led the People's Republic of China since then.

Chinese Nationalist Party A political organization that controlled much of China in the early 20th century and which then fled to Taiwan after losing to the Communists in the Chinese Civil War (1927–1950) and has controlled the island almost ever since.

Chokepoint An internationally significant narrow waterway and transportation route; its closure would have enormous economic and strategic consequences for many countries, particularly developed ones.

Climate refugees The people who flee from areas, such as low-lying floodplains, adversely affected by climate change.

Climate The average weather conditions over an extended period of time (usually 30 years).

Closed city An urban settlement with restrictions on the temporary and permanent mobility of its residents and visitors and focused on military-related research and development activities in the former Soviet Union.

Collectivization The forced transfer of farmland from private to state (collective) ownership in the Soviet Union during the late 1920s and early 1930s and subsequently in some other Communist countries.

Coloureds The people of mixed European and African origin officially classified as a separate racial group during the apartheid era in the Republic of South Africa.

Columbian Exchange The exchange of plants and animals, but also of people, culture, and technology between the New World and the Old World in the 15th and 16th centuries after Columbus' discovery of the New World.

Commercial economy An economy based on the production of goods and services for the market; associated with large and modern production units characterized by high productivity.

Common Agricultural Policy (CAP) Created in 1962, the European Union's Common Agricultural Policy is aimed at providing stable affordable food supplies to Europeans while ensuring a decent standard of living for farmers through subsidies; it is highly controversial and has been modified multiple times.

Compromise capital A capital city whose location is chosen to balance competing regional forces in a country (e.g. Washington, DC's location between the north and south).

Confucianism A philosophy developed by the Chinese scholar Confucius (551–479 BCE) who emphasized ordered superior-inferior relationships, rituals, and ancestor worship as the keys to how people should behave in society.

Continental divide A line of mountain peaks and ridges that form a hydrological divide; the waters on one side flow into a different ocean than those on the other side.

Continental drift theory A theory stating that the position of continents on the surface of the Earth is dynamic and that the present-day configuration is the result of one huge landmass splitting into several parts which drifted away from each other over time.

Continental islands The parts of a continental shelf that are unsubmerged and surrounded by water such as New Guinea, Great Britain, and Newfoundland.

Coral reef A hard structure in the ocean formed from millions of skeletons of tiny marine animals that anchor themselves in shallow tropical and subtropical waters.

Coriolis Effect A deflection of a moving object in a rotating system; on the surface of the Earth, winds are deflected to the right in the northern hemisphere and to the left in the southern hemisphere.

Crude birth rate The number of births per 1000 population in one year.

Crude death rate The number of deaths per 1000 population in one year.

Culture A learned behavior or a certain way of life that is shared by a group of people.

Cyclone A large tropical storm in the Indian Ocean.

Daesh The Arabic name for the **Islamic State** (**IS**).

Dalit A member of the lowest or "untouchable" caste in the Indian **caste** system.

Daoism (also called **Taoism**) A philosophy that developed in China around the same time as **Confucianism** and which emphasized the importance of following a path or way (the meaning of *dao*) in accordance with nature.

Dark Ages A period of demographic, cultural, and economic decline in Western Europe after the fall of the Roman Empire; historians often prefer the term Early Middle Ages.

Debt bondage A kind of modern slavery in which one person is forced to work for another to pay off a debt.

Demilitarized Zone An area which by agreement between adversaries (e.g. North and South Korea) is free of military installations, operations, and forces.

Demographic transition A model explaining the relationship between fertility and mortality levels on the one hand and levels of socioeconomic development (or time) on the other.

Dependency ratio The ratio between the number of children (14 and younger) and older people (65 and older) combined and the number of working age adults (15–64).

Desertification The expansion of desert-like conditions to semi-dry areas through human activities (e.g. deforestation, overgrazing) or climate change.

Diaspora The dispersion of a population through migration, as in the dispersion of Jews from the Holy Land to places around the world.

Diffusion The spread of new things and ideas from the place of origin to other places over time.

Distributary A branch of a river that does not return to the main stem.

Domino Theory The idea that the fall of one state to Communism would lead to the fall of neighboring states to Communism, which would lead in turn to the fall of still other states.

Dowry A payment made by a bride or her family to the groom or his family on the occasion of their marriage.

Dust Bowl The drought-stricken southern plains in the United States which suffered severe dust storms in the 1930s.

Ebola A rare but often fatal viral disease spread through contact with infected animals or humans; periodic outbreaks of the disease have mainly affected Sub-Saharan Africa.

Edge city A cluster of office buildings and shopping malls on the outskirts of North American cities.

El Niño The climate phenomenon that occurs when water in the tropical Pacific Ocean becomes unusually warm; El Niño is felt across the globe in the form of drought or excessive rainfall.

Entrepôt A transshipment port to which goods are imported to be exported onward again.

Environmental determinism A belief in the strong environmental, particularly climatic, influence on human culture and character.

Environmental possibilism A belief in humans' ability to adapt to various environmental conditions depending on their culture and technology.

Ethnic cleansing The forced removal of an ethnic group from a territory to make the area ethnically homogenous; ethnic cleansing can occur in the context of **genocide**.

Ethnic religion Religion that is associated with a specific ethnic group; its followers do not engage in missionary activities among other people.

European Union (**EU**) A political and economic union of currently 28 member states in Europe.

Exclave A portion of a country's territory that is separated from the rest of that country by territory of another country.

Export-Promotion Manufacturing The industrial development based on exporting goods for which a country has a comparative advantage (often used in countries with low labor costs).

Fault (**geological fault**) A break or fracture in the Earth's crust; in active faults sections move in different directions, creating stresses that can cause earthquakes.

Favela The Portuguese term for a **squatter settlement** or shantytown, most often used for the settlements surrounding large Brazilian cities such as Rio de Janeiro.

Federal state A country in which political power and decision-making are dispersed to subnational units such as provinces in Canada.

Fertile Crescent A crescent-shaped area in parts of present-day Iraq, Iran, Syria, and Turkey considered to be the birthplace of agriculture, urban settlements, and civilization.

Fertile Triangle A part of the Russian Realm, extending across Ukraine, Belarus, southern Russia and northern Kazakhstan, with favorable natural conditions for agricultural development.

First Nations Canadian term for indigenous people in the country (excluding those in the Arctic which are known as Inuit).

Five Pillars of Islam A set of basic beliefs and practices required of all Muslims, including profession of faith, frequent prayer, charity, fasting, and pilgrimage to Mecca (the birthplace of Islam).

Fjord A long, narrow arm of the sea bordered by steep cliffs (U-shaped) formed through glacial erosion.

Forward capital A capital city located close to a country's border in order to project the country's political power into a disputed region.

Fossil fuels The energy sources formed from the remains of living organisms through pressure and heat over a long period of time; the three major types of fossil fuels are coal, oil, and natural gas.

Four Tigers The four small and medium-sized economies of Asia which followed Japan in experiencing very rapid economic development beginning in the 1960s: Hong Kong, Singapore, South Korea, and Taiwan.

Free market economy An economic system based on the private ownership of the means of production, profit motivation, and a supply-demand relationship in its pricing system.

Frozen conflict An unresolved conflict over a disputed territory (e.g. Transdniestra, Nagorno-Karabakh, South Ossetia, and Crimea) in the Russian Realm.

Genetically modified organism (**GMO**) A living organism whose genetic material has been altered through genetic engineering to improve positive characteristics such as high yield, size, resistance to diseases, tolerance of salt or drought, etc.

Genocide The systematic elimination of a national, ethnic, racial, or religious group.

Glasnost (openness) The policy of granting limited freedom of expression to Soviet citizens and news media introduced by Gorbachev in the second part of the 1980s.

Globalization The increased interaction and integration among people, businesses, and national governments through trade and investment facilitated by improved information, communication, and transportation technologies.

Golden Crescent A mountainous area along the borders of Iran, Afghanistan, and Pakistan that along with the **Golden Triangle** is one of the world's two principal areas of opioid production.

Golden Triangle A mountainous area along the borders of Laos, Myanmar, Thailand, and China that along with the **Golden Crescent** is one of the world's two principal areas of opioid production.

Grand Canal The world's oldest and longest artificial waterway, which links Hangzhou in eastern China with Beijing in the northern part of the country.

Great Rift Valley A distinctive landform and geologic feature (tectonic depression) running across eastern Africa and along the Red Sea with several elongated deep lakes and fertile soils of volcanic origin.

Green Belt An open area surrounding a city or town in which development is limited in order to provide better air and water quality, to protect habitat for plants and animals, and to provide people with easy access to outdoor recreation.

Green Revolution A period of sharp increases in the yields of major food crops, especially rice and wheat, in the 1950s-1980s achieved through cross-breeding to produce plant varieties capable of using higher applications of artificial fertilizer.

Gross domestic product (GDP) The total value of goods and services produced in a country (area) in a year.

Gross national happiness An alternative way of measuring development that prioritizes factors promoting human happiness such as clean air and water rather than just monetary wealth.

Gulag The system of forced labor for construction projects or extraction of natural resources in remote and/or environmentally harsh areas in the Soviet Union established by Stalin in the 1940s.

Harmattan A dry and dusty wind blowing from the Sahara to Western Africa during the winter season (December to March).

High island An island with high hills or mountains formed through volcanic activity.

Honor killing An act of homicide meant to avenge perceived dishonor the victim has brought to the perpetrator or the perpetrator's family.

Horticulture The commercial cultivation of fruits, vegetables, and flowers.

Human-environment interaction The relationship between people and their activities and the physical environment including positive and negative consequences of that relationship.

Ideographs A symbol that represents an idea or concept, such as the characters used to write Japanese and Chinese.

Import Substitution Industrialization A development strategy in which trade barriers are used to protect a national market for a country's own domestic manufacturers whose output replaces formerly imported goods.

Indentured laborer A person who works for another person for a fixed period of time (e.g. five to seven years) to pay off a debt—such as to pay back the cost of passage from one part of the world to another.

Indochina A traditional name for mainland Southeast Asia, especially the area colonized by the French and today comprising Vietnam, Cambodia, and Laos.

Industrial colonialism A late form of colonialism in which the colonial power profited by taking industrial raw materials (e.g. iron ore) from colonies and converting them to manufactured goods (e.g. locomotives) to be sold back to the colonies.

International Date Line A line that mainly follows the 180° meridian, with the date being one day later on the eastern side of the line.

Intifada A popular Palestinian uprising against the Israeli occupation of the West Bank and Gaza Strip.

Iron Curtain The largely impermeable border between Western and Eastern Europe during the Cold War (1945–1991).

Islamic State (IS) A terrorist organization formed in 2014 in opposition to the Shia-dominated Iraqi government and foreign influence in the country; known for its very brutal treatment (including beheadings) of its enemies and many innocent people. Also called **Islamic State of Iraq and Levant (ISIL)** or **Islamic State of Iraq and Syria (ISIS)**.

Islamism A political movement that seeks to reorder society in accordance with a strict and literal interpretation of Islam.

Jainism A religion found mainly in western India whose central principle is non-violence.

Janjaweed The Muslim militia groups of Arab pastoral nomads operating in western Sudan (especially in Darfur province) against sedentary farmers of African origin (also Muslims) accused of genocide and other atrocities by the international community.

Jewish Diaspora The forced removal of the Jewish people from their ancient homeland in the Middle East and their subsequent dispersal across Europe and later other parts of the world.

Jihad An Islamic concept of internal and external struggle or striving for perfection in religious beliefs and practices (internal) and defending Muslim communities against outside dangers (external).

Juche The political ideology of North Korea; it combines the idea of national self-reliance with other influences including Confucianism and Marxism.

Karst The landforms created by the dissolution of soluble rocks such as limestone, dolomite, or gypsum; characterized by barren ground, sinkholes, caves, underground rivers, and the absence of surface rivers and lakes.

Katorga The system of forced labor for construction projects or extraction of natural resources in remote and/or environmentally harsh areas in Tsarist Russia.

Khmer Rouge A brutal Communist regime that led Cambodia from 1975 to 1979.

Kibbutz (plural: Kibbutzim) A rural, mainly agriculture-based, settlement in Israel based on the principle of collective ownership of the means of production and social justice.

Knowledge economy An economy based on intellectual activities such as research; in developed countries the knowledge economy accounts for a large share of the entire economy.

Kolkhoz A large farm in the Soviet Union characterized by the collective ownership of land, machinery and buildings, and collective decision-making regarding its operation.

Koran (also Qur'an) The Islamic sacred scripture containing God's revelation to Mohammed that was written down by his followers.

Lama A spiritual leader in Tibetan Buddhism; the most significant is the Dalai Lama.

Land hemisphere The half of the globe that has seven-eighths of the world's landmass including all of Europe, Africa, and North America and most of Asia and South America centered in western France.

Latifundio (plural: Latrifundia) A large commercial estate in Latin America.

Lingua franca A language used by two people to communicate with one another when their native languages are mutually unintelligible.

Liquefaction The process where wet sediment behaves like a liquid; often caused by the severe shaking associated with earthquakes.

Localization The desire to preserve traditional culture and reluctance to accept new or foreign ideas and ways of life.

Location The position of an object on the Earth's surface in terms of its latitude and longitude or in relation to other objects.

Locust A grasshopper found in semi-dry regions; able to move great distances in large swarms and destroy crops and other vegetation.

Loess Fine, windblown sediments.

Low islands A low-lying island formed though the accumulation of sediments on a **coral reef** or through the uplifting of a coral reef.

Low-cost carrier An airline that uses all-economy-class seating, a single type of aircraft, high frequency operations, and other strategies to significantly lower airfares; also called a budget airline.

Maastricht Treaty One of the most important **European Union** treaties; signed in 1992, the treaty laid the foundations for a single currency, created a European Union citizenship, and increased cooperation of member states in regards to foreign policy and judiciary matters.

Machismo A strong sense of masculine pride and superiority associated with a man's responsibility to provide for and protect his family.

Madrassa An Islamic religious school.

Mahayana The form of Buddhism which is dominant in Japan, Korea, China, and Vietnam and which teaches that anyone can achieve enlightenment.

Malaria A mosquito-borne disease associated with fever, chills, and other flu-like symptoms found mainly in tropical regions of Africa.

Mangroves Shrubs or small trees growing in the brackish water of an intertidal coastal area.

Manufacturing Belt The core region of industrial activity in the Midwestern United States; the region is now characterized by deindustrialization.

Maori A member of the indigenous population in New Zealand.

Map The graphic representation of the Earth's surface (or a part of it) in which selected physical and/or human features are shown by symbols in their correct spatial location at a reduced scale.

Maquiladora (maquila) A manufacturing plant that imports components duty free to assemble them with low cost labor and export them duty free to other countries.

Marsupial A mammal, such as the kangaroo, whose incompletely developed young are carried in the mother's pouch.

Medical tourism Travel to another country with either better health care or less expensive health care for an operation or other medical service.

Megacity Now defined as a metropolitan area with over 10 million people; historically a city with a much larger population than most others.

Merchant colonialism An early form of colonialism in which the colonial power profited by taking valuable commodities (e.g. spices) from colonies and selling them in another part of the world.

Mercosur The large trade bloc created by Argentina, Brazil, Paraguay and Uruguay in 1991.

Mestizo A person of mixed Native American and European descent.

Minifundio (plural: Minifundia) A small subsistence landholding in Latin America; often farmed by indigenous people.

Monotreme A mammal, such as the platypus, whose young hatch from eggs.

Monroe Doctrine The United States policy from 1823 that warned European nations that the United States would not tolerate further colonization in the Western Hemisphere.

Monsoon A strong seasonally prevailing wind current bringing heavy precipitation in summer.

Mujahedeen A Muslim warrior for the faith, with the term used especially in reference to guerilla fighters in Afghanistan.

Natural increase The difference (positive or negative) between fertility (births) and mortality (deaths) for a certain area (or the whole world) in a given year.

Near Abroad The parts of the former Soviet Union outside of Russia considered of strategic and economic importance to the Russian government.

Net migration The difference between in-migration (immigration) and out-migration (emigration) for a certain area in a given year.

North American Free Trade Agreement (NAFTA) The agreement between Canada, the United States, and Mexico which created one of the largest free trade zones in the world; the agreement is controversial.

North Atlantic Treaty Organization (NATO) Founded in 1949, this organization of North American and European countries practices collective defense, meaning that an attack on one member is considered an attack on all members.

Official language The language used by the government of a given territory; a language with a special legal status.

Organization of Petroleum Exporting Countries (OPEC) An international organization of most major oil producing countries established in 1960 and designed to coordinate the policies of production and pricing of petroleum products.

Overseas Chinese The descendants of people who migrated from China.

Pacific Ring of Fire The horse-shoe shaped chain of volcanoes and earthquakes around the edges of the Pacific Ocean created by the subduction of tectonic plates.

Pastoral nomadism A type of livestock herding characterized by the perennial or periodic movement of animals in search of pastures and water in semi-dry and desert regions.

Pavement dwellers Urban squatters who live on sidewalks in South Asia.

People's communes The highest administrative level of collectivized agriculture in China, replaced by townships in 1983.

Perestroika (restructuring) The policy of economic modernization in the Soviet Union introduced by Gorbachev in the second part of the 1980s.

Permafrost The permanently frozen ground of varying thickness found in many cold regions; it presents serious obstacles to construction activities and transportation.

Personal plot A small collectively- or state-owned plot of land leased rent-free to a farming family for growing food crops and raising livestock for its needs.

Physiological density The number of people per unit of productive (agricultural) land.

Place A portion of the Earth's surface (e.g. city, county, state, country) that can be described by its physical and human characteristics.

Plantation A large farm specializing in the growing of cash crops such as cotton, coffee, tea, and sugar cane; in the past plantations were often dependent on slave labor.

Polder An area of land reclaimed from the sea through the construction of dikes and draining of the area.

Population density The number of people per unit of land, usually a square kilometer or a square mile.

Population growth rate The rate at which population is increasing or decreasing in a given year expressed as the percentage of the total population at the beginning on the year.

Population pyramid A graphical representation of the age and sex composition of a population.

Prairie A temperate grassland; a mostly flat grass-covered area in North America with few trees.

Precision farming A farming technique using global positioning system (GPS) technology that responds to variations in crop growth among or within fields.

Primary activities The economic activities associated with the extraction of natural resources (hunting and gathering, agriculture, fishing, forestry, and mining).

Primate city A city in a country or region that is disproportionally larger than other cities in the urban hierarchy.

Purchasing power parity (PPP) An exchange rate that equalizes the purchasing power of different currencies by eliminating price differences between countries.

Purdah The practice of female seclusion found in some Muslim and Hindu communities in South Asia.

Qanat A system of underground canals for collecting freshwater in dry, mainly hilly, regions.

Ramadan The ninth month of the lunar Muslim calendar during which Muslims must fast (no eating, drinking, sexual relations, smoking, etc.) from sunrise to sunset.

Reference map A map showing basic physical (e.g. landforms, water resources) and human (e.g. political boundaries, major settlements) features on the Earth's surface designed for a wide array of users.

Region An area defined by certain shared physical and/or human characteristics and different from the surrounding areas.

Relative location The location of an object on the Earth's surface in relation other objects on the Earth's surface.

Religious syncretism The mixing or blending of religions, for example of Catholicism with traditional African religions.

Reservation The legal designation for an area of land managed by a Native American tribe in the United States rather than the government of the state in which it is located.

Rift lake A lake, usually of elongated shape and very deep, created by tectonic movements along a **fault** or rift.

Russian demographic cross A demographic condition characterized by simultaneous fertility decline and mortality increase in Russia shortly after the collapse of communism in the early 1990s.

Russification The policy of encouraging or imposing various elements of Russian culture (mainly language) on non-Russian groups in the Soviet Union.

Rust Belt The region in the Midwestern United States affected by deindustrialization, economic decline, population loss and urban decay.

Sahel A transition zone between the Sahara and the savanna lands; prone to droughts and desertification.

Salinization The accumulation of water-soluble salts in the soil (mainly through improper irrigation methods) leading to its degradation and a subsequent decline in agricultural productivity.

Schengen Agreement An important **European Union** agreement signed in 1985 which abolished internal border checks among participating countries.

Schistosomiasis A tropical disease (also known as bilharzia) associated with headaches, fever, chills, and muscle pain spread through contact with freshwater contaminated with a parasite found in water snails.

Secondary activities The economic activities associated with processing natural resources (raw materials) into finished products; manufacturing and construction.

Sediment load The solid particles of various size carried along by a stream, with silt and other fine particles suspended in the water and larger particles rolling along the streambed with the current.

Sharia An Islamic legal system based on the teachings of the Koran and the prophet

Mohammed regulating human activities pertaining to worship, civil and criminal matters, and business transactions.

Shia Muslims One of two major Muslim groups that originated shortly after Mohammed's death due to differences of opinion regarding the religious leadership succession (which Shia believe should be limited to Mohammed's family and its descendants).

Shifting cultivation A type of farming mainly practiced in densely forested and sparsely populated tropical areas associated with temporary (one to a few years) cultivation of a previously cleared and burned area.

Shintoism A traditional religion in Japan whose hallmarks include the divinity of special peaks, rivers, trees, and other features of nature and ritual worship at thousands of local shrines spread across the country.

Sikhism A monotheistic religion found mainly in the northern border region of Pakistan and India and which stresses the importance of doing good in the world rather than observing rituals.

Silk Road An ancient trade route linking China and the Mediterranean via Central Asia.

Sovkhoz A large farm in the Soviet Union characterized by state ownership of land, machinery and buildings, and the state-controlled decision-making system regarding its operations.

Special economic zones Also called export processing zones, the areas designed to encourage export-oriented industrialization through low taxes and other favorable policies.

Spiritual tourism Travel to pilgrimage destinations and other sacred sites.

Squatter settlement Also called shantytown, an illegal settlement of improvised housing made of plywood, corrugated metal, and plastic sheets usually found on steep hillsides, in floodplains, near railroad tracks, or on dump sites.

State A political entity comprised of a certain territory, permanent population, and an established government exercising full control over that territory and its population and having sovereignty in international relations.

Steppe Areas of grassland located in the mid-latitude parts of Asia and Eastern Europe.

Storm surge The water pushed onto shore by a tropical storm or hurricane.

Subsistence economy An economy based on the production of goods and services for supporting a family's immediate needs; associated with small and traditional production units characterized by low productivity.

Sun Belt The region in the southern United States characterized by warm weather, growing economic opportunities, and population increase.

Sunni Muslims One of two major Muslim groups that originated shortly after Mohammed's death due to differences of opinion regarding the religious leadership succession (which Sunnis believe should be available to any qualified individual through consultation and election).

Taiga A boreal forest composed mainly of coniferous evergreen species (spruce, pine, and larch) located in the colder regions of the northern hemisphere.

Taoism See **Daoism**

Tariff A tax on the value of imported goods.

Tertiary sector The sector of the economy that provides services (e.g. financial, personal, educational) to its consumers; one of three sectors of the economy (the others are the **primary sector** focused on raw materials and the **secondary sector** focused on manufacturing) and an indicator of an advanced economy.

Thematic map A map showing the distribution of a selected phenomenon (topic) in terms of its qualitative or quantitative characteristics.

Theravada The form of Buddhism which is dominant in Sri Lanka and mainland Southeast Asia and which celebrates the monastic life and silent mediation as the means towards enlightenment.

Tornado Alley The area in the United States where tornadoes occur most frequently and are most destructive.

Total fertility rate The average number of children a woman has in her life time.

Trans-Atlantic Slave Trade The forced migration of millions of Africans to the New World between the 15th and 19th centuries.

Transmigration The organized movement of landless people from Indonesia's Inner Islands (especially Java) to the country's Outer Islands.

Treaty of Tordesillas The 1494 treaty between Spain and Portugal to divide the newly discovered lands in the New World between them.

Trypanosomiasis A tropical disease (also known as sleeping sickness) spread by **tse-tse fly** bites, found mainly in rural areas.

Tse-tse fly An insect found in hot and humid parts of Africa spreading a disease dangerous to cattle (nagana) and humans (sleeping sickness or **trypanosomiasis**).

Unitary state A country in which political power and decision-making is strongly concentrated in the national capital.

United Nations (UN) An international organization, established in 1945 and headquartered in New York City, committed to promoting peaceful coexistence among countries and maintaining international order.

Universalizing religion Religion that is considered proper for all humanity; some of its followers engage in missionary work to seek converts.

Urban primacy A measure of the degree to which a country's system of cities and towns is dominated by a single large city.

Virgin Lands Campaign Khrushchev's policy of converting large areas of grassland into farmland for growing mainly wheat and corn in the semi-dry parts of southern Russia and northern Kazakhstan during the 1950s.

Wat A Buddhist temple.

Water hemisphere The half of the globe that has only one-eighth of the world's landmass, centered on the Bounty Islands east of New Zealand.

White Australia Policy A legal prohibition on non-European immigration to Australia that was implemented in 1901 when the country gained its independence; it remained in place until the 1970s.

World culture realm A large region characterized by organized rule, a coherent system of environmental use, and a similar culture.

Zionism Religious and political movement originally aiming at re-establishing a Jewish state in the "Promised Land" (Palestine) and now at protecting and developing the state of Israel.

Zoroastrianism One of the world's oldest monotheistic religions, originating in present-day Iran 3,500 years ago and with small numbers of adherents today in Iran and India (where they are known as Parsis).

INDEX

Lightning Source UK Ltd.
Milton Keynes UK
UKHW050230010422
400921UK00003BA/59